SHARING
THE
DREAM

SHARING
THE
DREAM

WHITE MALES
IN MULTICULTURAL
AMERICA

DOMINIC J. PULERA

continuum
NEW YORK • LONDON

2004

The Continuum International Publishing Group Inc
15 East 26 Street, New York, NY 10017

The Continuum International Publishing Group Ltd
The Tower Building, 11 York Road, London SE1 7NX

Printed in the United States of America

Library of Congress Cataloging-in-Publication Data

Pulera, Dominic.
    Sharing the dream : white males in multicultural America / Dominic J. Pulera.
      p. cm.
    Includes bibliographical references and index.
    ISBN 0-8264-1643-8 (hardcover : alk. paper)
    1. United States – Race relations. 2. Pluralism (Social sciences) – United States. 3. Men, White – United States. I. Title.
    E184.A1P845 2004
    305.38′809073 – dc22

                                    2004019399

Grateful acknowledgment is made for permission to quote from:

"White Man" by Langston Hughes. From *The Collected Poems by Langston Hughes*. Copyright © 1994 by The Estate of Langston Hughes. Used by permission of Alfred A. Knopf, a division of Random House, Inc.

"Only a Pawn in Their Game," written by Bob Dylan. Copyright © 1963 by Warner Bros. Inc. Renewed 1991 Special Rider Music. International copyright secured. Reprinted by permission.

"Southern Man," written by Neil Young. © 1975 Broken Arrow Music (BMI). All Rights Reserved. Used by Permission. Warner Bros. Publications U.S. Inc., Miami, FL 33014.

"If the South Woulda Won," written by: Hank Williams Jr. Published: Bocephus Music, Inc. BMI. Copyright: 1988. Admin: Dave Burgess Enterprises. All Rights Reserved. Used by permission.

"Have You Forgotten?" written by Wynn Varble and Darryl Wade Worley. © 2003 Warner-Tamerlane Publishing Corp., EMI April Music Inc. and Pittsburgh Landing Songs. All Rights for Pittsburgh Landing Songs Administered by EMI April Music Inc. All Rights Reserved. Used by Permission. Warner Bros. Publications U.S. Inc., Miami, FL 33014.

To my lovely sister, Maria

Contents

Sharing the Dream

Brian Levin recalls with pride that his father, Howard Levin, was a medic in the U.S. Army in World War II.[1] Shortly after D-Day, the Germans captured the elder Levin and imprisoned him in a prison camp in Essen, Germany. One day they caught Howard Levin turning leaves in upside-down patterns to indicate where munitions were, so that Allied planes could bomb those targets. To punish him, the Germans were going to impale railroad spikes through his arms, legs, penis, and heart and put him on the outside of a train car that was visible to the other prisoners. But the Germans spared him because he was a medic. This traumatic experience profoundly influenced Howard Levin's outlook on life and always contributed to his belief in the importance of the medical profession. (The Germans recognized his medical abilities and let him live, because they needed someone with those skills in the prison camp.) The Russians, meanwhile, were treated worse than the Americans were. This is a story told by Roland Gant in his memoir, *How Like a Wilderness*; Gant was a friend of Howard Levin's in the prison camp.[2]

Brian Levin credits his father, a veterinarian, and his mother, an educator, for shaping his compassionate mindset. As a youngster growing up in Nassau County, New York, he often went to the South Bronx in the 1960s and 1970s with his father. Dr. Levin had a modest veterinary clinic there, where he enjoyed a well-deserved reputation as a fair and decent man who cared deeply about the pets in his care — and the people who owned them. Howard Levin, whose clients referred to him as "Doc," was well known in the South Bronx for his kindness, low prices, and neighborly attitude. Dr. Levin's multiethnic clientele included few Jews, but no clients ever made an issue out of his ethno-religious background. Brian Levin himself recalls that he confronted four instances of anti-Semitism as a youth, including one time when he was insulted for having a "hook nose." Another time, the father of a friend said to him, "The problem was that Hitler did not make enough lampshades."

1

And once Brian attended a party as a teenager, where one of his fellow partygoers ostentatiously discussed "lighting up" Jews. His worst experience with anti-Semitism occurred in the spring of 1973 or 1974, when young Brian was attacked by a gang of Italian-American youths in the Bronx who repeatedly referred to him as a "Christ-killer" as they pummeled him.

Levin has an eclectic background, one that suits him very well for his present work. This dynamic, open-minded man with brown hair and hazel eyes was born in December 1963, in Manhattan, and grew up in the Bronx, Roslyn Heights, New York, and New Hyde Park, New York. His father is of Russian-Jewish stock; his mother is of Austrian-Jewish extraction. He served as a New York City police officer from 1985 to 1989, fighting crime in Harlem and Washington Heights. In 1989, Levin received his bachelor's degree from the University of Pennsylvania *summa cum laude* and was elected to Phi Beta Kappa, among other honors. Then, in 1992, he graduated from Stanford Law School, where he had an A-average. (Levin was a co-recipient of the Law School's Civil Liberties Award.) Since graduating from Stanford, Levin has worked as a litigation attorney, at the Southern Poverty Law Center, and as an academic. In 1999, he accepted a position in the Department of Criminal Justice at California State University, San Bernardino, where he established the Center for the Study of Hate and Extremism.[3] Today Levin is the director of the fledgling Center and a tenured professor at CSU. He and his wife, Dr. Sara-Ellen Amster, have two sons; they live in Southern California.

Brian Levin is a globally recognized authority on extremism, hate crimes, and domestic and international terrorist activities. As one of the most quoted — and quotable — human rights figures in America, the 40-year-old social scientist frequently appears on national radio and television programs. He regularly attends government and academic conferences and speaks to university and community audiences. (Levin, as with many human rights figures, emphasizes the importance of community activism.) And he gives live testimony before legislative and congressional hearings and appears as an expert witness in trials. The native New Yorker also occasionally practices pro bono civil rights law. Levin himself defies categorization in an ideological sense. He dislikes ideological labels and encourages students who hold differing political perspectives to present their views in a respectful way in the classroom. For instance, this avatar of tolerance and inclusion regularly criticizes eco-terrorists, a position that does not endear him to everyone on the Left. Likewise, Levin generally opposes the death penalty and stresses the importance of protecting our civil liberties. He also supports certain provisions of the Patriot Act, backs the American involvement in Iraq, and "vigorously advocates greater inclusion of religious Christians in human relations dialogue."[4]

Indeed, Levin has a wide variety of interests in the field of human rights, even as he strives to be non-partisan in his work. A self-deprecating man who frequently publishes scholarly articles on such topics as extremism, terrorism, hate crimes, and civil liberties, Levin usually focuses on matters related to race, gender, sexual orientation, and terrorism monitoring in his academic research.[5] He also works closely with law enforcement. The former NYPD officer developed an extensive database on hate crimes (the Online Hate Crime Training Course) in conjunction with the Southern Poverty Law Center and the Federal Law Enforcement Training Center. Police officers from the United States and Canada utilize it. Levin sometimes goes to the FBI Academy Complex in Quantico, Virginia, to deliver lectures and conduct research. Moreover, he has taught hate-crime and terrorism classes at the FBI National Academy in Quantico. Today Brian Levin is in the prime of his career as a criminologist, commentator, and civil rights attorney. In his personal life and professional career, Levin consciously tries to promote and expand the opportunities available to all Americans, particularly members of traditionally disadvantaged groups. In doing so, he makes important contributions to intergroup harmony and cross-cultural understanding in our multiethnic society.

I

Images of white men in Cameroon — the phrase *whiteman* refers to Caucasians of both genders in Cameroonian English — come from many sources: movies, novels, magazines, postcards, advertisements, popular music, the Internet, fashion catalogs, and satellite and Cameroonian television. From the perspective of many Cameroonians, these media portrayals depict whites as affluent people who enjoy materialistic lives of ease and luxury. Cameroonians, to be sure, hold complex and nuanced opinions of white people and Western culture. Their views are shaped by many factors, including the history of European colonialism in West and Central Africa and the gap in wealth and power that exists between the West and sub-Saharan Africa. Indeed, many Cameroonians perceive that racial privilege benefits the Caucasians (primarily clergy, tourists, researchers, and volunteers) in this oil-producing and soccer-loving nation east and southeast of Nigeria. It is sometimes difficult for them to reconcile the humble economic circumstances of many whites in their country with the glamorous images of Western prosperity that saturate the Cameroonian media.[6]

Nationality, as it relates to Cameroon's colonial history, affects how Cameroonians evaluate white men and white women. In 1916, the French and British took control of Cameroon, which had been a German protectorate.[7] The European powers eventually created two colonies — French Cameroon and British Cameroon — out of Cameroon. Independence came for French Cameroon, now known as Cameroon, in 1960. The following year, northern British Cameroon opted to become part of Nigeria, whereas southern British Cameroon decided to join Cameroon. Today many Cameroonians have negative feelings about the French and the British that stem from the legacy of colonial rule.[8] A Frenchman may not win favor from Cameroonians, due to the French government's support of President Paul Biya, an unpopular figure among young people. Similarly, a visitor from the United Kingdom may be viewed negatively by some Cameroonians because they feel the British essentially ceded Anglophone Cameroon to the French.[9] Visitors from other Western nations are often warmly welcomed by Cameroonians. In particular, the people of Cameroon regard Holland, Germany, and the United States as desirable places to live.[10]

Positive images of Americans and American culture exist in Cameroon. Hip-hop music and the multiracial popular culture of the United States receive much attention there. Young Cameroonians speak with Americanisms, and those whose speech patterns resemble American English gain prestige from their manner of speaking. Cameroonians admire and emulate many aspects of American culture that derive from African-American actors, artists, performers, and fashion designers.[11] Young Cameroonians view speaking like an American rapper as a "symbol of sophistication," according to the sociologist Francis B. Nyamnjoh, a native of Cameroon who is the Head of Publications and Communications at the Council for the Development of Social Science Research in Africa (CODESRIA) in Senegal.[12] These positive perceptions of the United States undoubtedly affect the experiences of American visitors to Cameroon.[13] After all, language and nationality intersect with race and social class in determining how Cameroonians react to Western visitors.

The origins of these issues date back to the evolution of modern humans. At this point, we can reasonably assume that the visible differences — such as skin color, physiognomy, and body size and shape — between and among the human races evolved in response to the different environmental conditions the original humans encountered as they slowly spread out from the birthplace of modern humanity in eastern Africa 80,000 to 100,000 years ago. Reproductive isolation played a role in the evolution of modern humans as well. The people we know today as white males are the lineal descendants of the humans who migrated to Europe, North Africa, and the Middle East.[14] Perhaps 80 percent of white males are descended primarily or exclusively from the aboriginal Europeans. Throughout human history, there has been a considerable amount of intermixing between and among the peoples of the "white world." Many aboriginal Europeans have ancestors from multiple ethnic backgrounds.[15] Similarly, Middle Eastern farmers who migrated north-ward 9,000 to 10,000 years ago contributed significantly to the genes of the modern Europeans.[16]

The appearances of people in the Middle East and North Africa re-flect the tremendous amount of ethnic blending that has occurred there. The Berbers, a light-skinned ethnic group indigenous to North Africa, have contributed to the cultures of Morocco, Algeria, Libya, Tunisia, and Egypt. And the European and African slaves who lived in Arabia cen-turies ago intermingled with the natives of North Africa and the Middle East. Consequently, it is possible to see blond, blue-eyed Arabs as well as those whose appearances look similar to black Africans in Sudan, Ethiopia, and elsewhere. Egypt, for instance, has always been a mélange of white, brown, and black people. Indeed, the North Africans and the Middle Easterners (two of the three most populous Middle Eastern na-tions — Iran and Turkey — are not Arab countries) encompass as much diversity as their white counterparts in Europe. Even though Middle East-erners and North Africans make invidious distinctions based upon skin tone, facial features, and the other characteristics that we typically asso-ciate with race, there seems to be greater acceptance of human diversity in the Arab world than is the case in Europe or elsewhere in the West.[17]

Depending on how one defines whiteness, there are approximately 500 million to 700 million white males in the world. This number varies because societies differ in the ways that they classify people by race and ethnicity. The narrowest definitions of whiteness (and consequently white maleness) peg whiteness to Europeans and New World Europeans elsewhere. This strict definition of whiteness is used in many European nations. The more ecumenical definition of whiteness, like that in the

United States, limits membership in that racial group to people of European, Middle Eastern, and North African descent. The most expansive definition of whiteness, used most commonly in Latin America, may include people, based on socioeconomic status, who are not necessarily accepted as "white" by partisans of the other two definitions. Indeed, white maleness is a socially, culturally, legally, and politically constructed notion and phenomenon. The nations with the largest numbers of white males are the United States, Russia, Brazil, and Germany, in that order. Approximately 100 million white males live in the United States; they account for about 35 percent of the population.

White maleness usually does not exist as a social construct in racially homogeneous nations. The absence of race in monoracial countries leads people to focus on issues of equity in terms of gender, ethnicity, religion, language, and social class. While the people who share Y-chromosomes in those places certainly qualify as "white males," they identify themselves by their nationality — as Swedish, or Austrian, or Bulgarian, or Lebanese. Indeed, the social significance of white maleness in the United States is due to a complex set of racial, cultural, and economic factors. No other country boasts the amazing ethnic and racial diversity of America, or, for that matter, provides as many chances for people of all races and ethnic groups to prosper. The racial, cultural, and economic dynamics of the United States create dilemmas and conundrums — along with solutions and forms of advocacy — that exist nowhere else in the world.

Since about 1600, Caucasian males, particularly those of Northern European descent, have dominated commerce and diplomacy in the world. White maleness began to have social significance when European men — and their counterparts in the Middle East and North Africa — began to trade and interact with nonwhite peoples on a regular basis, beginning in the fifteenth century.[18] Over the centuries, the Western European powers, particularly Spain, Portugal, England, and France, established colonies in Asia, Africa, the Caribbean, the Americas, and the South Pacific. This colonial fervor reflected — and reinforced — the idea that the world was the white man's bailiwick and its people were his pawns, and that they would benefit from his supposedly superior knowledge and institutions. In any event, Caucasians have migrated to many parts of the globe during the last 500 years. Therefore, substantial white male populations exist outside their aboriginal homelands in Europe, the Middle East, and North Africa.

Social class has always been a factor that differentiates one white male from another. Before the Industrial Revolution most European, Middle

Eastern, and North African men were poor, functionally illiterate, and barely eked out a living. They died in plagues, starved in famines, and were crowded by overpopulation and primogeniture. At the same time, privileged white men accounted for the vast majority of the world's dominant figures. However, that does not mean that the vast majority of white men enjoyed significant privileges, except, perhaps, vis-à-vis members of other racial groups. If a white man was able to break out of poverty and shed the most conspicuous aspects of his socioeconomic background, he faced relatively few social or legal barriers as he ascended the occupational ladder. Throughout the years, the English-speaking white American male had plenty of role models in almost every profession, and he was very likely to see himself represented in the dominant pop-cultural images that bombard us.

White males in the United States are a tremendously diverse group. They differ in ideology, ethnicity, geography, nationality, language, religion, occupation, generation, education, accents, intelligence, motivation, skin color, socioeconomic status, sexual orientation, and physical appearance — weight, height, physiognomy, eye color, head shape. Overall, therefore, it is difficult to describe the contours of white male culture, at least in isolation from American culture, because white males play such an important role in shaping the norms, mores, and standards of the United States.[19] Certain cultural phenomena — golfing, ice hockey, deer hunting, country music, professional wrestling, and stock car racing — are favored disproportionately by white male Americans. Such a list would also include art collecting, nonfiction book purchases, and patronage of the opera and the symphony. But this is not to say that most white males are hockey fans, or that a majority of them indulge in any of the other aforementioned activities either.

Globally, fissures related to and stemming from ethnicity, nationality, language, religion, and social class beset the white male grouping. There is little transnational white male solidarity. White males in Europe, North Africa, Latin America, and the Middle East usually view their white American visitors solely as Americans. The white American male, after all, enjoys many privileges. Most of the world's leading centers of finance, education, entertainment, and technology are in the United States. The American citizenship and English-language facility that Americans acquire as their birthright give them a running head start over people who grew up in, say, Iran or Colombia. Likewise, Americans live in a free, stable, and democratic society, one with significant opportunities for social and economic mobility. These advantages notwithstanding, the average white male in the United States certainly does not consider himself to be especially affluent, powerful, or influential, although others, particularly people of color, may see him this way.

II

The poet Langston Hughes blended a potent mix of race and class in his poem, "White Man," that appeared in the December 1936, issue of *New Masses,* a magazine with a left-wing bent. In this poem, Hughes skewered elite white men around the world in general, and their counterparts in the United States in particular.[20] "White Man" clearly delineates the relationship between white male privilege and black disadvantage in Depression-era America.[21] The poem's opening lines are unambiguous:

> Sure I know you!
> You're a White Man.
> I'm a Negro.
> You take all the best jobs
> And leave us the garbage cans to empty
>   and
> The halls to clean.[22]

Throughout the 33-line poem, Hughes's references to the white man as a singular entity belie his focus on certain types of white men — namely, the affluent and wealthy members of the group.[23] Few white men, after all, are able to live the high life in Palm Beach (lines 8 and 9). Hughes's reference to white slumlords (lines 10 and 11) again describes a specific section of white male America. In lines 12 and 13, he includes a global reference: "You enjoy Rome — And *take* Ethiopia."[24] Then, in lines 15, 16, and 17, Hughes attacks elite white men for exploiting Louis Armstrong by allowing the jazz great to play the music, while white men "copyright it" and profit from doing so.[25] In lines 18 and 19, the 34-year-old poet cynically salutes Caucasian men: "You're the smart guy, White Man! You got everything!"[26] The implication, of course, is that elite white men enjoyed some, if not most, of their privileges because they excluded others from having a chance to do so.

But then Hughes shifts gears in lines 20 through 33, in which the budding Marxist privileges class over race and gender. Hughes weaves his theme of the evil white man into the context of Marx, capitalism, class privilege, and the *Communist Manifesto,* and concludes the poem by asking, "Are you always a White Man? Huh?"[27] By doing so, he seems to imply that, in some contexts, white maleness is not always the issue. These questions in the last two lines of the poem are more an indictment of capitalism than a matter of trying to exculpate whites for the myriad injustices visited upon African Americans. "White Man" is certainly not one of Hughes's best-known or frequently cited poems. However, it does reflect his politics and state of mind at this point in his career.[28] "White Man," moreover, represents an explicit attempt to delineate the interrelationships among race, class, and gender. Until the 1960s and 1970s, such narratives rarely appeared in mainstream poems, books, films, albums, and articles.

White males, to be sure, have been scorned as bad guys in some sectors of American society throughout U.S. history. From the beginning of Euro-American settlement in the New World, white exploitation of African Americans and Native Americans led to grumbling, dissent, and expressions of anger. In her study of blacks' views of whites during the period from 1830 to 1925, the historian Mia Bay found that African Americans at the elite and mass levels often referred to *white men* or *the white man* when they discussed the nation's dominant racial group at the time.[29] In fact, nineteenth-century African-American intellectuals frequently tried "to identify white men as the real brutes in the hierarchy of color and gender at the heart of American racial ideology," according to Bay.[30]

One must always parse the words of the black social critics carefully, to examine whether the speaker or writer clearly meant to single out white men *as white men,* or merely used the prevailing convention of the time, when s/he really referred to white people of both genders. The Black Muslims, led by Elijah Muhammad, caused no such confusion. They espoused the white-man-as-devil philosophy to win recruits and fire up the faithful.[31] Muhammad's disciple, Malcolm X, issued diatribes against Caucasian males that rank among the most vitriolic — and eloquent — criticisms of white male power and privilege during the twentieth century.[32] (To be sure, Malcolm X eventually rejected this tenet of Elijah Muhammad's dogma.)[33] But the unyielding white male control of American institutions limited the likelihood that such views would be widely disseminated in American society at large, or that they would take hold in any meaningful fashion.

The social movements of the 1960s led to critiques of the power structure of American society. These critiques challenged the fact that the United States could be accurately described as a "white man's country" or "a white man's land" (in those times, at least).[34] This happened in large part because Americans were more receptive to the claims and grievances of long-ignored minority groups than they had been in previous eras. These impetuses for change came in response to the activism of newly empowered groups such as white women and racial minorities, and their white male allies. In the 1960s, 1970s, and 1980s, many left-wing activists, academics, journalists, and politicians, who represented both genders and every imaginable racial and ethnic background, engaged in spirited discussions of the racial status quo and propounded critical reinterpretations of historical events and processes.

By doing so, the multiculturalists — feminists, ethnic advocates, white liberals, gay rights advocates, sympathetic white men, and others — laid the groundwork for an assault on the old boys' club. They questioned why white men dominated politics, Corporate America, Wall Street, Hollywood, and almost every other bastion of wealth and power in the United States. At the same time, the multiculturalists sought to diversify the curricula, the workplace, and the highest ranks of government and Corporate America. The old white-male order slowly began to crumble as a result of antidiscrimination laws and affirmative-action programs, the belief that expanding the opportunities available to women and minorities was simply the right thing to do, and the new social and cultural dynamics that accompanied the increasing heterogeneity of the American population.

American multiculturalists are united by their feelings of exclusion and belief that significant attention must be paid to previously excluded and marginalized groups. To be sure, the ranks of the multiculturalists include a sizable number of straight white males. Multiculturalists cite the historical record for many instances of racism, sexism, colonialism, imperialism, heterosexism, and other malefactions committed by individual white males, and point out how these historical events contribute to the inequities in contemporary America. There are many doctrinal differences separating the multiculturalists (it certainly is difficult to consider them a monolithic group), but they generally see eye to eye on one issue: the dominance of straight white men in American culture and society.[35]

The diversity imperative — particularly its enforcement mechanism, affirmative action — continues to be the most significant manifestation of multiculturalism in the United States. This term describes the vague but powerful notion that every sector of American society should reflect the demographic makeup of its service population, which is primarily defined in terms of race and gender. Sometimes coercive mechanisms speed the implementation of the diversity imperative, such as court orders to hire black police officers or the threat of a boycott unless a business spotlights Asian-American faces in its television ads. On other occasions, well-meaning decision-makers, including many affluent white men, adhere to the diversity imperative because they believe it is appropriate and necessary that *all* groups of Americans should be included in a visual sense, through the use of their coethnics as proxies.[36]

To many multiculturalists, the disproportionate representation of white males relative to their share of the population, workforce, or target group in a given context is prima facie evidence of racism or discrimination. Still, they tend to target specific instances of underrepresentation where they feel they can make a difference, rather than making blanket denunciations of white male influence across the board. As a rule, the multiculturalists focus on sharing power — more accurately, transferring power — from white, heterosexual, able-bodied males to all those who do not fit into this category. The villains in the multiculturalists' morality plays often are white males, particularly the white, affluent, heterosexual, able-bodied males who are well represented in the nation's social, cultural, political, and economic elites. Multiculturalists regularly place the burden of proof on the typical white guy to prove that he is one of the enlightened, sensitive members of his group, not one of those evil, venal, hateful bad guys who chomps cigars, ogles women in strip clubs, and plots to advance his own interests at the expense of everyone else.

Relatively few white males qualify as bad guys in the traditional sense — at least to the point that the legal system incarcerates them, they must pay restitution for their actions, or they are subject to social ostracism. The notion of the white male as a bad guy or villain often has a tongue-in-cheek aspect to it. In other words, it is acceptable to portray a bumbling father in a television commercial only if he is white. And the greeting cards that bash males in a lighthearted war-of-the-sexes fashion usually feature white guys. Other times the white male will not be seen as a bad guy, but rather as dorky, unhip, and clueless; the song, "Pretty Fly (For a White Guy)," epitomizes this stereotype. It would be totally unacceptable to mock or challenge any other group in this way, due to the unmistakable fact that white males as a group still outrank women and people of color in terms of their access to power, recognition, and resources. However, most Americans do not bear any animus toward the typical white male, so long as he pays his taxes, is a law-abiding citizen, and treats everyone fairly and respectfully.

III

The picture itself seemed innocuous enough. On April 6, 1995, a photograph of four white men — Naperville, Illinois, Mayor-elect George Pradel, his son, George Pradel, his campaign manager, Jim Stahel, and campaign committee member Dwight Hollonbeck — appeared in the *Chicago Tribune.* The four exuberant and bare-chested men were photographed in a hot tub as they toasted Mayor-elect Pradel's victory with champagne in Styrofoam cups.[37] The published photo (it was "on the front page of some Tribune editions, and on the local front in others") elicited dozens of reactions from readers. *Tribune* columnist Mary Schmich wrote an entire column about the topic. One woman described how the photo disgusted her because of what she saw as its unapologetic depiction of white male privilege. A male reader reacted by saying that the photo was printed only because it depicted white men.[38] John McCarron, a middle-aged white journalist at the *Tribune,* was surprised by the negative reaction of several of his female colleagues to the photo.[39]

The story lived on in the *Tribune* newsroom beyond the brouhaha in April 1995. Soon thereafter, one of McCarron's coworkers "clipped out a half dozen of the photos from surplus newspapers and Scotch-taped them to the backs of computer monitors that jut into the aisle leading to the men's room."[40] Initially, McCarron did not become too concerned about the photo montage because he thought it would only be posted for a short period of time. The story became more complicated — and irritating to him — when a colleague clipped a headline ("Chimps trade meat for power") from a newspaper story about the mating practices of male chimpanzees. She then pasted copies of the headline below the election-night photos of the four white men on the computer monitors. For five months, McCarron passed the visually arresting photo montage several times a day en route to the men's restroom. He was deeply offended by the insensitivity displayed by his colleague; after all, he resembled — and seemed to relate to — the men in the photo.[41]

In September 1995, McCarron wrote a column about this topic that was published on the *Tribune*'s op-ed page. The Irish-American journalist contended that the photo montage of four white men was an inexcusable example of a double standard, since the *Tribune* refused to tolerate any kind of harassment of women and minorities. He thought the photo montage contradicted the *Tribune*'s pro-diversity record, as evidenced by its extensive coverage of diversity issues and multicultural initiatives and its usage of appropriate gender-neutral and politically correct language (except for such terms as "bubba," "macho," and "good old boy"). McCarron proceeded to argue that the newspaper clippings represented a bigger trend: unflattering portrayals of white men in various parts of American culture.[42] Writing in September 1995, McCarron said, "White men, it turns out, are not yet covered with the same blanket of respect that now applies to the non-white and the non-male."[43] His column reflected the zeitgeist of the mid-1990s, when it became fashionable in certain circles to focus on situations in which white males were perceived to be treated unfairly.

The average white male may occasionally face opprobrium, vilification, and disparagement on the basis of his race and gender for three reasons. First, there are the undeniable misdeeds of some white males in the past and present. Secondly, white men continue to wield a disproportionate amount of power and influence in the present. Thirdly, some people perceive that the white male's trappings of material success may be somewhat illegitimate since they may have been achieved at the expense of women and minorities. Since these views permeate almost every aspect of mainstream thought and culture, the typical white male now must prove his sensitivity to the multicultural mores of twenty-first-century America. Still, women and people of color, particularly those individuals who hold positions of leadership, rarely disparage white males as a group. Most Americans would consider such rhetoric off-limits and inappropriate. Sometimes the most vociferous critics of white male privilege happen to be white males themselves.

Some conservative observers speak in apocalyptic tones about the position of white males in Multicultural America. For example, Paul Craig Roberts and Lawrence M. Stratton assert that "[t]he demonization of the white male delegitimizes him."[44] According to Roberts and Stratton, "The delegitimization, in turn, creates space for insensitivity and hatred. Academic life today is replete with ad hominem attacks on white heterosexual males that parallel those used by Nazis against Jews and by Marx and Lenin against class enemies."[45] Furthermore, Roberts and Stratton contend, "The attack on white males is generic and does not differentiate between Ku Klux Klan members and doctrinaire white liberals who have led the assault on whites for their alleged racist ways."[46] Notwithstanding the polemics of Roberts and Stratton, it seems that the typical white American male does not feel like a bad guy much, if any, of the time.

Race and gender are increasingly important factors in the socialization process for white males. The average white male learns that he is a male, distinct from females, and that he is white, distinct from people of color, in early childhood. However, it is usually much later, probably by his teens, that the typical white male learns he is a quote-unquote white male. But for many white guys, their status as white males may not register until college, when they encounter identity politics, diversity initiatives, and multiculturalism in its many varieties. And those white males who enter the workforce directly from high school usually encounter diversity or sensitivity training in some form or another. Until about 35 years ago, a white male in a racially homogeneous state like Maine might never have really thought about his race and gender. Even now, in many parts of America, the garden-variety white guy probably attaches more significance to his age, ethnicity, occupation, socioeconomic status, and religious beliefs than he does to his race and gender.

White males remain a decidedly individualistic group, one with significant ethnic, religious, cultural, and socioeconomic differences that contribute to their reluctance to embrace a group identity. Nonetheless, some white males consider themselves to be a victimized group in Multicultural America. According to the aggrieved white guys, affirmative-action dictates and what they see as the general climate of hostility toward members of their group have made them the most recent group of victims. This type of reasoning manifests itself in their grumbling that women and minorities get all the breaks, and results in their cries of "reverse discrimination" and court cases alleging favoritism for female and non-white students, contractors, and employees. Due to the predominance of white men in positions of influence, many Americans are understandably skeptical about such claims, which proliferated in the 1990s, and even view them as chimerical distractions from the pressing problems of sexism and racism.[47]

The "Angry White Male" was an adjunct of the white male-as-victim school of thought. This phrase was popular in 1995 due to the central role of white males in the then-raging debates over affirmative action and the burgeoning Patriot movement. At the time, social observers and commentators pointed out that the notion of "Angry White Males" was not only inaccurate but counterproductive in terms of fostering meaningful dialogue about issues related to race and gender.[48] The usage of the phrase "Angry White Male" declined precipitously during the late 1990s. It is rarely used today. As Billie Wright Dziech writes: "Despite the malcontents and misfits who capture headlines, the vast majority of white men do not claim racial or gender superiority. Poll after poll confirms that they are bothered not by the goals of affirmative action and multiculturalism, but by being disparaged and ignored in pursuit of those goals, a dilemma with which women and minorities easily can identify."[49]

During the last 20 years, many white conservatives have attempted to defend and preserve aspects of traditional white American male culture. Conservative foundations fund many of the lawyers, academics, and journalists who fight the leftists in the culture wars. Some conservatives have founded public-interest law firms that litigate reverse-discrimination claims. Academics, especially members of the National Academy of Scholars, support the teaching of classics and promote Western civilization in American universities. And right-wing journalists and media figures constantly harp on the excesses of identity politics in newspapers and magazines, and on talk radio and cable television. At the same time, there is little empirical evidence to suggest that most white males feel they face diminished opportunities and limited life chances due to their race and gender. Most white males recognize, though, that people from their racial and gender group will never again dominate virtually every sector of American society (as they once did).

My thesis in this book is a simple one. As the title suggests, virtually all white males in Multicultural America are sharing the fruits of the American Dream (in some way) with women and people of color. Some white males do so voluntarily; others do not. Moreover, I posit that *white males are so heterogeneous that it is difficult to generalize about them as a monolithic group, and to consider them as such in many contexts.* The oppressor/victim dichotomy is far too simplistic — and, in many cases, it is wholly inadequate — for us to understand the contemporary situation of white males. White males are clearly more powerful and privileged than any other group in America, but many white males wield little power and enjoy few privileges because of their race and gender. In addition, I argue that the overwhelmingly white male character of such highly visible venues as the U.S. Senate and executive suites of Fortune 500 companies will gradually diminish as evolving societal attitudes and the institutional changes since the passage of the Civil Rights Act of 1964 expand the opportunities open to women and people of color.

Until three to four decades ago, white men enjoyed the lion's share of opportunities throughout the United States. After all, the noble ideals embodied in the Declaration of Independence and the U.S. Constitution often did not get put into practice for women, people of color, persons with disabilities, and others.[50] Members of specific groups, white men chief among them, realized the American Dream more often than others. So the idea that a person could achieve significant upward mobility by dint of her or his ingenuity, initiative, and determination rang false for large sectors of the U.S. population, particularly African Americans, who faced substantial legal and social barriers to their success.[51] In his famous "I Have a Dream" speech in 1963, Dr. Martin Luther King Jr. eloquently expressed his vision for racial amity, unity, and brotherhood based on equal opportunities for all.[52] This year, on the occasion of the fiftieth anniversary of the Supreme Court's *Brown* decision, a number of observers have written pessimistically about how much progress still needs to be made before people of color, especially African Americans, enjoy the same opportunities as whites to realize their American Dreams.[53]

This book encompasses many issues that are profoundly important to us Americans, due to the number of white male Americans and the power that white men wield in our lives. These issues, moreover, are becoming ever more timely due to the fact that white males are slowly decreasing as a percentage of the American population. The increasingly multiethnic nature of the United States is reshaping American business, politics, entertainment, and so many other sectors of our society. Indeed, the United States is shifting from being a country where the power structure is predominantly white and male to one where females and minorities are major players too. During this transition period, it is still difficult for some Americans to talk about white males in mainstream American thought and culture. Any mention of such phrases as "white males," "white men," and "white guys" makes some people nervous. In fact, I had some white men candidly tell me they were wary of the topic when I submitted interview requests to them.

∽

Throughout this book I examine the "white maleness" of the American experience, including some aspects that we notice as having racial significance, but rarely discuss in detail. To do so, I rely on a wide range of sources, including interviews, census data, site visits, scholarly articles, and newspaper reports. I hope the vignettes that open each chapter and subheading convey the different facets of the white male experience in America. Due to the growing significance of globalism in the lives of most Americans, I periodically touch upon events in other parts of the world. This treatment is very broad in scope, so it is impossible to go into detail on every subject. For instance, most long-haul truckers and commercial airline pilots are white men, but the underlying reasons for the relatively homogeneous composition of these two occupational subgroups rarely receive any attention.

In *Sharing the Dream* I try to cast light on two important — and interrelated — topics: the heterogeneity of white male America, and the evolving role of white males in Multicultural America. I also discuss the future of white males and white maleness in the United States. I seek to be rigorously objective; therefore, the sources cited in this book take into account our nation's ideological heterogeneity. To this end, I interviewed dozens of men and women, who hold diverse ideological perspectives and come from a wide variety of ethnic and racial groups. This work is analytical, not prescriptive, although I believe that most white males in America (like any other group of people) are decent, hardworking individuals, who nurture their children, contribute to their communities, and improve the quality of life on our planet.

As a straight white man myself, I have had many experiences in different parts of America that inform my understanding of what it is like to be a white guy in our country. I live near some predominantly white communities, so I am quite familiar with many aspects of white male culture. Moreover, I visited many sites in America that venerate specific white men, such as Graceland, Monticello, Stone Mountain Park, the John Deere Commons, the Mount Rushmore National Memorial, and the Norman Rockwell Museum at Stockbridge. I went to every state in our nation in search of insights into white maleness, and I also visited many European countries to learn more about the antecedents of white American males. In addition, this book draws upon my experiences in parts of the United States and the world where white males make up a small percentage of the population.

This is the broadest treatment, to date, of the white male experience in America. It includes historical coverage, consideration of the present-day situation, and a fair amount of analysis regarding the future of white males. This treatment includes significant discussion of a myriad variety of issues, topics, and controversies that relate to white males and white maleness. In Part One I trace the contours of white maleness in America. In Part Two I focus on various aspects of the diversity imperative. And in Part Three I examine white male identity politics — the reactions of white males to various aspects of the new multicultural order. Finally, in the Epilogue, I look at the future of white males and white maleness around the globe, considered in the context of events in the United States.

PART ONE

A Nation of 100 Million

~ **chapter one** ~

White and Male

Joe Speranza fit the profile of the murderer the citizens of Johnston City, Illinois, were looking for on the morning of Thursday, June 10, 1915.[1] The previous evening, W. E. "Ed" Chapman, a 49-year-old farmer who lived one mile north of Johnston City, had been shot to death in his home at 8:30 p.m. News of the murder quickly spread around town. Although there were no obvious culprits, the townspeople quickly conjectured that some Italians had killed Chapman. After all, Ed Chapman's son-in-law, 26-year-old Ben Schull, the pit boss at the East Side Mine (McClintock Mine), had incurred the wrath of some Italian immigrants when he had let them go a few days earlier. Some of these individuals reportedly vowed to exact revenge against Ben Schull. By noon on Thursday, the local authorities had arrested three men of Italian extraction in connection with the slaying of Chapman; the accused men were initially incarcerated in the local jail. However, seeing that perhaps 1,000 people were milling around on the streets of this coal-mining town of 5,230 residents, the authorities decided to transport the Italians to Marion, a larger city six miles south of Johnston City.[2]

The people of Johnston City were angry about the murder of Ed Chapman, and they wanted justice — "hanging justice." Then the incipient lynch mob heard that Joseph Speranza, a coal miner and Italian national, had supposedly indicated his intention to cause trouble for Ben Schull. Speranza was a 30-year-old immigrant from Sicily; he may have been in the United States for three years.[3] The Johnston City police quickly arrested Speranza (whose surname meant "hope" *in italiano*) and placed him in the local jail. Due to the size of the crowd in Johnston City, the police were unable to take Speranza to Marion, where he might have been safe from vigilante justice. Sensing that a lynching was about to take place, the mayor of Johnston City and the town's police chief spoke to the crowd and tried to persuade them not to settle their grievances through extralegal means. Their appeals to reason were ignored by the mob, which broke down the doors of the jail at around 3:00 p.m.[4]

21

At this point Speranza was probably mute with fear, especially after the lynch mob put a rope around his neck. The mob took him two blocks southwest of the jail to a coal shed south of the Chicago & Eastern Illinois railroad depot. There members of the mob asked Speranza if he had anything to say for himself. The doomed man initially did not reply. After the lynch mob attached the rope to a rafter and Speranza "was jerked from the ground," he asserted his innocence in broken English and blamed another man, Joe Bingo, whereupon he was "strung up until dead." At this point, some members of the lynch mob began searching for the elusive Joe Bingo, who was already on his way out of town. The police eventually apprehended Bingo and placed him in the heavily guarded Williamson County jail in Marion, to prevent some enraged Johnston City residents from taking the law into their own hands a second time.[5]

There were several immediate repercussions from the Speranza lynching. By Thursday evening, the mood in Marion was such that a delegation of Johnston City's vigilantes might have lynched Bingo and the three other Italians from Johnston City. So all four men were taken into protective custody at a hidden location. Meanwhile, the governor of Illinois dispatched state militiamen to Johnston City to restore order. The coroner did an inquest on Friday, June 11, 1915, but none of the 25 witnesses he questioned claimed to be able to identify anyone who had participated in the lynching of Joe Speranza. Therefore, the coroner's jury decided that Speranza had been murdered by unknown parties, although the hanging occurred in broad daylight and no one wore any kind of mask or disguise. On the same day as the coroner's inquest, Ed Chapman was laid to rest in a funeral that boasted a record-setting attendance. The town fathers also held a conference to discuss the killing of Joseph Speranza (this was the first lynching in Williamson County's history).[6]

In any event, life had returned to normal in Johnston City by Saturday, June 12, 1915. There were false reports of fights between the Sicilians and the native-born Americans, but the state troops who stayed in Johnston City for several days kept the peace.[7] It soon became public knowledge that none of the four men detained for the murder of Ed Chapman had anything to do with his slaying. Nonetheless, some of the Sicilians concluded that Johnston City was no longer a hospitable place for them — 14 Sicilians left the city to join the Italian army a few days after Speranza's lynching.[8] Joe Speranza, meanwhile, did not get any peace even in death. On Saturday night, June 12, 1915, his murder became a form of entertainment: Twenty-four views of the lynching and associated events were shown at the Old Reliable Opera House in Marion. The "show" included pictures of Speranza's body in the morgue as well as shots of the prison cell where he spent the last few terrified hours of his life.[9]

Joe Speranza died at least in part because he was visibly different from the native-born white majority in Johnston City. In the 1910s and 1920s ethnic tensions often influenced the labor disputes and cultural conflicts in the mining country of southern Illinois. At the time of Speranza's lynching, the citizenry of Johnston City included 2,983 Americans, 817 Italians, 413 Lithuanians, 292 Austrians, 266 English, and 168 French.[10] Everyone, of course, knew the Italians were Caucasian — or they would not have been allowed to become naturalized Americans — but the Italians with dark complexions were probably viewed as alien by many native-born white Americans in southern Illinois. Speranza himself had olive skin, Mediterranean facial features, and an accent that reflected the fact that Italian was his native tongue. The lynch mob almost certainly did not see him as a "white" man, at least in the same way that the men of English, Irish, and German ancestry were considered white.

No one ever found out, with certitude, who murdered Ed Chapman; Speranza was not, in all likelihood, the slayer of Chapman.[11] Speranza's murder marked the tenth — and last — instance of a lynching of a person (or people) of Italian descent on American soil between 1886 and 1915.[12] It was the only lynching of an Italian to occur in a Midwestern state. In Johnston City and elsewhere in the coalfields of southern Illinois, the Italian immigrants eventually assimilated into American society and lost the most conspicuous aspects of their foreignness. Today 6.2 percent of the people in Johnston City claim Italian ancestry; they are culturally indistinguishable from the other residents of the city.[13] Nearly 90 years after Joe Speranza's death, the ethnic tensions of the coal-mining days that led to his lynching are only a fading memory in the minds of the oldest southern Illinoisans.

THE WHITE MAN COMETH

No one is more important to the history of St. Augustine, Florida, than Pedro Menéndez de Avilés. In 1565, the 46-year-old native of Avilés, Asturias, made his mark in American history due to his exploration of present-day northeastern Florida. A bearded man with reddish hair and fair skin, Menéndez was comfortable on the sea. The Spanish nobleman earned the respect of his peers — and a fair amount of money — by engaging in privateering, trading in the West Indies, and serving the Crown through his participation in its naval-defense initiatives. For these reasons, King Philip II turned to Menéndez when the Spanish monarch decided he wanted to colonize Florida. In March 1565, the two men signed a contract that made Menéndez the king's *adelantado,* or colonial official, in what the historian Eugene Lyon aptly described as "the enterprise of Florida."[14]

Philip II and Menéndez were partners in the colonizing expedition of 1565. The Crown provided Menéndez with partial funding for the *entrada.* Philip II hoped to establish agricultural settlements, convert the Florida Amerindians to Christianity, and thwart the expansion plans of the French Huguenots in the New World. The contract granted Menéndez titles, offices, benefits, and privileges if he established a permanent Spanish colony in Florida. In return, he had to expend a substantial amount of his capital (and that of his associates) to outfit and supply the expedition and develop the colony. The Menéndez expedition left Cádiz, Spain, on June 27, 1565; it included at least 1,000 soldiers, sailors, and colonists. After an arduous journey across the Atlantic Ocean, Menéndez reached the eastern coast of Florida. He formally claimed Florida for King Philip II on September 8, 1565. Menéndez also established a colony and named it San Agustín (St. Augustine). The colony was the first permanent European settlement in the United States.[15]

The first St. Augustinians faced many challenges. Food shortages bedeviled the colony, and there were several mutinies by Spanish soldiers. Moreover, the colonists coexisted uneasily with the Amerindian clans and bands in the area. And there was the omnipresent risk of an attack by the French Huguenots. Menéndez departed St. Augustine and the provinces of Florida in the fall of 1566. Thereafter, he periodically visited the New World; his proxies governed the provinces of Florida. Menéndez spent much of his time in the late 1560s and early 1570s raising the requisite funds to sustain the Spanish colony in Florida. The 55-year-old *adelantado* died on September 17, 1574, in Santander, Spain.[16] St. Augustine remained under Spanish control until 1821, except for the 21-year period from 1763 to 1784, when it was ruled by the English. In 1821 it came under U.S. control.[17]

During the 1880s, St. Augustine developed into a tourist destination. Throughout the years the town has relied on its historic past to attract visitors.[18] Therefore, St. Augustinians continue to celebrate Pedro Menéndez. They recognize Menéndez's birthday on February 15 with the Menendez Birthday Festival every year. St. Augustinians also hold a Menendez Landing celebration on the grounds of the Mission of Nombre de Dios every September. Moreover, a main thoroughfare on the

East Side of St. Augustine is named for Menéndez. The high school in this town of 11,592 bears his name as well, and a statue of Menéndez occupies a prominent place in the Front Gardens of City Hall.[19] One of St. Augustine's four sister cities is Avilés, a municipality of 84,835 in northwestern Spain. Menéndez's home in Avilés still stands today, and there is a monument that honors him in the city's Parque del Muelle.[20] Indeed, Menéndez continues to be venerated in Spain as well as the United States because of the important role he played in the Spanish colonization of the New World.

Beginning in 1492, when Christopher Columbus reached the New World for the first time, the European explorers flocked in droves to the Americas. Explorers from such nations as England, Spain, France, Holland, and Russia colonized and settled the lands of the present-day United States. In the course of their exploration and colonization efforts, the Europeans regularly came into contact with the Amerindians of the New World, trading with them, warring with them, and forming sexual unions with them. The English and the Spaniards covered the most ground when it came to exploring and colonizing the lands that make up the present-day United States. Although their tactics differed, the English and the Spaniards established numerous self-sustaining colonies in the New World. The imperial powers expected to benefit financially from their colonies; they also hoped to proselytize the Amerindians.

The European colonization of the land making up the original 13 colonies was spearheaded primarily by Protestants from the British Isles. Individuals of English, Scottish, Irish, and Scotch-Irish descent accounted for many of the new nation's leaders. The signers of the Declaration of Independence, for instance, included such men as John Adams, Samuel Chase, William Floyd, John Hancock, William Hooper, Francis Lightfoot Lee, Thomas McKean, Thomas Nelson Jr., James Smith, George Walton, and Oliver Wolcott. Besides the Brits in the New World, other European groups such as the Dutch, French, and Germans were well-represented among the white population during the colonial era.[21] When the United States and Great Britain buried the hatchet once and for all after the War of 1812, the Anglo-American relationship became an important one. Since then, the two nations have been bound together by culture, language, and ethnicity; Anglophiles have abounded in the American elites.[22]

Men of English ancestry play an especially important role in one highly visible realm of American life: the Presidency. Thirty-six of the 42 men who have served as U.S. Presidents (George W. Bush is classified as the

43rd President because Grover Cleveland served as the 22nd and 24th Presidents, respectively) have traced their ancestry to the British Isles. One president — Thomas Jefferson — was of Welsh extraction. Two presidents, James Monroe and Rutherford Hayes, were of Scottish descent. Seven occupants of the White House came from Scotch-Irish stock; Andrew Jackson and Woodrow Wilson were the most prominent members of this group. Twenty-six U.S. Presidents look to England as their ancestral homeland — at least six of these men are biethnic. The last eight Presidents, beginning with Lyndon Johnson, have come from English stock (Richard Nixon was part Scotch-Irish, while Ronald Reagan and Bill Clinton were part Irish).[23] In ethnic terms, the U.S. Presidency remains the most exclusive men's club in the world.[24]

To be sure, English Americans — more specifically, a group of them known as White Anglo-Saxon Protestants (WASPs) — played a very important role in the settling, establishment, and development of the American nation.[25] The historian David Hackett Fischer contends that the collective mindset and cultural attributes of the American people were largely determined by several groups of English-speaking immigrants who came to what is now the United States between 1629 and 1775. First, a number of Puritans left eastern England for Massachusetts beginning in 1629 and ending in 1640. Then there was the migration of people from southern England to Virginia — this group included many indentured servants — in the era from approximately 1642 to 1675. Thirdly, people left Wales and the North Midlands of England to go to the Delaware Valley during the period circa 1675 to 1725. Finally, migrants left North Britain and northern Ireland for Appalachia between 1718 and 1775.[26] These individuals accounted for much of the European immigration to the United States during this period.

Since the newcomers arrived in the present-day United States earlier than the other European immigrants, they played a disproportionate role in shaping the ethos, culture, and institutions of the new nation. Despite their linguistic, religious, and cultural similarities, substantial differences separated these groups of English-speaking Protestants with British mindsets. They differentiated themselves by their social ranks, historical generations, religious denominations, and regional origins in Britain. These differences — what Fischer describes as "four different sets of British folkways" — affected the development of regional cultures in America.[27] "Strong echoes of four British folkways," writes Fischer, "may still be heard in the major dialects of American speech, in the regional patterns of American life, in the complex dynamics of American politics, and in the continuing conflict between four different ideas of freedom in the United States."[28]

By the early part of the nineteenth century, the overwhelmingly British Protestant character of white America was already beginning to change. During the period from 1815 to 1860, Northern Europeans — particularly from Ireland and Germany — accounted for the vast majority of the 5,000,000 immigrants to the United States (2,000,000 came from Ireland, 1,500,000 from Germany, and 750,000 from England, Scotland, and Wales).[29] Irish Catholic immigrants, for instance, initially encountered a significant amount of nativism on religious and cultural grounds. However, as the Irish began to embrace the norms and mores — including white supremacy — of the native-born white majority, they were accepted as white Americans.[30] Likewise, the German immigrants precipitated a number of cultural clashes with native-born Americans, especially with regard to temperance, Catholicism, and the German language. Anti-German nativism would not completely subside until World Wars I and II sounded the death knell for large-scale public expressions of German ethnicity in the United States.[31]

My German-American ancestors experienced some nativism in the first decades of the twentieth century. When my German-speaking paternal grandfather and his older brother went to their rural one-room school in southeastern Wisconsin during World War I, some of the students would remark, "Here comes the little German army." Then a fight would break out. My maternal great-grandfather came to the United States from Germany in 1927. After several years, this reliable and industrious man found a job with the Santa Fe Railroad in Topeka, Kansas. During the Depression, the Santa Fe retained him over workers who had been employed by the railroad for many more years. (No union existed at the time.) Consequently, a number of disgruntled coworkers burned a cross on my great-grandfather's front lawn. Later, during World War II, my great-uncle Adolph, a sailor in the U.S. Navy, served on an American destroyer in the Pacific. One sailor repeatedly harassed Adolph by remarking upon the similarities between his forename and that of the German dictator. Adolph threw his harasser overboard one day in a fit of pique. Thereafter, no one questioned Adolph's patriotism.[32]

By World War II, the ethnic composition of white America had changed dramatically from what it had been in the 1880s and 1890s, due to large-scale immigration from Southern and Eastern European countries, particularly from Italy, Austria-Hungary, and the Russian Empire. Southern and Eastern European immigrants began to account for a majority of immigrants to the United States by 1896. This trend would continue until immigration-restriction legislation was enacted in 1924. The "new" immigrants, with their unfamiliar skin tones and physiognomies, qualified as white, of course. But many members of the native-born white majority often viewed the newcomers as different from the whites of the "old" immigration, particularly on cultural, religious, and linguistic grounds.[33] As the historian Matthew Frye Jacobson points out, "The contest over whiteness — its definition, its internal hierarchies, its proper boundaries, and its rightful claimants — has been critical to American culture throughout the nation's history, and it has been a fairly untidy affair."[34]

Whiteness in America had been a diverse phenomenon even before the mass arrivals of the Southern and Eastern European immigrants. The aboriginal peoples of the British Isles themselves encompass a fair amount of diversity when it comes to the color of their hair and eyes. Almost to a person, however, they usually have light skin. Moreover, most of them are Protestant. The Irish and Germans, while stigmatized by nativists, do not differ markedly in appearance from people of British ancestry. (The Germans, after all, are responsible for the Saxon in Anglo-Saxon.) Nor are Irish and German surnames substantially different from English surnames — again, this is not surprising because English is a Germanic language. Protestant nativists, moreover, were often hostile to Catholics and Jews in the period before the mass migration from Southern and Eastern Europe in the late 1890s and first decades of the twentieth century.

Eventually the influx of Southern and Eastern European immigrants worried members of the ethnic majority. They feared that the newcomers would tip the ethnic balance out of kilter and lead to the demise of the Northern European–derived civilization of the United States at the time. The restrictionists eventually gained the upper hand. In 1924 Congress enacted sharply restrictive immigration legislation — the National Origins Quota Act; it sharply curtailed migration from Southern and Eastern Europe. As a result of this legislation, quotas that favored immigrants from Northern and Western Europe were part of American immigration law for more than four decades. Thus there was a lengthy period to assimilate all the Southern and Eastern European immigrants, beginning in about 1925. It would become easier for Southern and Eastern Europeans to enter the United States due to the Immigration Reform Act of 1965, but by that time relatively few of them wanted — or, in the case of the Soviet people, were able — to come here anymore.[35]

In the 1930s, 1940s, 1950s, and 1960s, the United States continued to be a society dominated by Christian, particularly Protestant, men of Northern and Western European descent. Young men from the most recent immigrant groups — the Jews, Slavs, Greeks, Italians, and other white ethnics — were not readily accepted in the clubby bastions of exclusivity such as investment banking and white-shoe law firms. Protestant men of Northern and Western European descent carefully preserved and protected the ethnic and religious integrity of their turf. Initially, many descendants of the Southern and Eastern European immigrants lacked the requisite social and educational backgrounds to flourish at the elite levels of American society. Within a couple of generations, however, large numbers of these individuals had begun to pursue higher education as a means of breaking out of poverty or the working class forever. At the same time, the ethnic, cultural, linguistic, and religious differences that separated them from the native-born American majority began to fade as they assimilated completely into American society.[36]

Jews raced up the socioeconomic ladder faster than any of the "new" immigrant groups; they embraced higher education as their ticket to upward mobility. Jews proved to be so successful at obtaining admission to colleges, universities, and professional schools that many institutions of higher learning, especially in the East, established quotas that sharply restricted Jewish enrollments during the period from 1918 to 1947.[37] Over the years, anti-Semitism declined as a factor that limited Jewish advancement, as social attitudes evolved and Jews assimilated and began to shape and define American culture and society. Today anti-Semitism has declined to the point where it is no longer a significant obstacle to advancement by Jews in virtually any situation. By recognizing the importance of higher education and working very hard, Jewish Americans have come to be well represented in politics, the media, Hollywood, Wall Street, the professions, Corporate America, the entrepreneurial world, and almost every other sector of the American elite.[38]

The white ethnics of the Baby Boom generation are the ones who have enjoyed the upward mobility that their ancestors dreamed about when they first came to America. Many of them went to college and earned the requisite credentials to prosper in the mainstream world. They were American-born, for the most part, spoke English as their first (and often only) language. They were thoroughly American in every respect. After completing college and, frequently, graduate school, they went into the professions or the business world. As a result, the leadership of Corporate America now reflects the heterogeneity of the white male population.

Moreover, many Polish Americans, Jewish Americans, Italian Americans, and other "ethnics" are enjoying success as doctors, lawyers, educators, businesspeople, military leaders, college presidents, social figures, and more.[39]

The United States Commission on Civil Rights released a report in 1986 that delineated the socioeconomic advancement of Americans of Southern and Eastern European extraction. The commission's report noted:

> The results reveal that along virtually every dimension, Americans of southern and eastern European ancestry have generally succeeded as well or better than other Americans. This does not imply that many individuals of eastern or southern European heritage have not suffered from prejudice; it only suggests that for the groups as a whole, there is no overt indication of current and widespread discrimination against them in the labor market — that is, the [existence] of group-specific differences that cannot be explained by standard economic variables such as those accounted for in this report.[40]

Considering one important indicator, educational attainment, clearly men of Southern and Eastern ancestry have advanced dramatically in recent years. According to the 1990 census, 34.6% of white males born between 1916 and 1925 attended college and 16.2% of them completed bachelor's degrees. The disparity between the figures for men of solely British ancestry (46.6% and 23.5%, respectively) and Southern and Eastern European men (32.2% and 16.0%, respectively) in this cohort indicated that it can take a couple of generations before people from newer groups embrace education as their ticket to upward mobility. The Census Bureau found that 55.9% of white men born between 1956 and 1965 had attended college and 25.5% of them had completed bachelor's degrees. However, the percentages had virtually converged for two groups in this cohort: men of solely British ancestry (66.3% and 31.8%, respectively) and Southern and Eastern European men (64.4% and 33.8%, respectively). Interestingly, these trends were reflected in the data for women too.[41]

While the Southern and Eastern European Americans began to prosper in America, African Americans continued to suffer from discrimination and diminished life chances, due in large part to the fact that they differed visibly from the white majority. Black Americans, to be sure, encompass a tremendous amount of diversity in terms of their skin color, facial features, and hair types. The unequal power dynamic made it difficult for African women, especially during the antebellum years, to resist the sexual advances of white men. Whites favored the mulattoes over full-blooded Africans, and a color-based hierarchy that rewarded light-skinned blacks soon developed in the African-American community. At one point, there was a vigilance on the part of white supremacists that bordered on obsession in much of the country, particularly the South, when it came to defining who was — and was not — black.[42]

Even a man descended from the aboriginal people of Germany might be mistaken for an African American by an overzealous enforcer of racial boundaries. My great-uncle Adolph, who immigrated to the United States from Germany in 1927 at age 15, was once mistaken for a black man on a segregated bus in Topeka, Kansas. Adolph had wavy black hair, dark brown eyes, and light olive skin that turned brown in the hot Topeka summers. One summer day when Adolph boarded the bus, the bus driver assumed that he was an African American and told him that he had to sit in the "black" section, at the back of the bus. The driver must have been quite surprised when he heard Adolph's response — and how he spoke English with German inflections.[43] Such incidents occurred in different parts of America during the Jim Crow era, but they rarely involved people of Northern European ancestry. Usually the cases of racial ambiguity that challenged the system of racial classification in the segregation era involved Mediterranean Caucasians (Greeks, Syrians, Lebanese, Sephardic Jews, Southern Spaniards, and Southern Italians).

Many light-skinned African-American men chose to identify as black in the years before the civil rights era, despite the many social, legal, economic, and political disadvantages that accompanied doing so. The laws at the time defined people with even a smidgen of African blood as black, particularly in the South. If a person had visible sub-Saharan African ancestry, he had little choice but to identify as African American. Moreover, light-skinned African Americans had family ties in black America, and if they passed as white, they would have to give up those family relationships. Therefore, many mulattoes refused to pass as white or did so selectively, to improve their employment prospects or to avoid some of the indignities of segregation. As a result of these dynamics, African Americans became remarkably ecumenical in their acceptance of intraracial variations in coloration, hair types, and facial features.[44]

American Indians are similarly open to people with differing looks, due to the long history of intimate relations between white men and indigenous women. The European male settlers in the United States frequently formed sexual unions with the Amerindian women. Fur traders and mountain men often procreated with Native American women, the only group of ladies in the vicinity of their hunting, trading, trapping, and exploring. Such unions were generally regarded by Caucasians with less severity and disdain than the couplings of white men and black women. This was largely due to the fact that the white settlers generally had more respect for American Indians than they did for blacks. To be sure, not everyone was enthusiastic about the unions of whites and Native Americans: A white man with an Indian wife might face social disdain for his marital choice and be described by his fellow Caucasians as a "squawman."[45]

From the beginning of miscegenation between white men and Native American women, the Indian tribes integrated the mixed-blood offspring of their people. Some mixed bloods married full bloods, and embraced their Indian identity. Many mixed bloods married whites; then their children intermarried with other whites, until their proportion of Indian blood was minuscule. (African Americans and Native Americans also formed sexual unions as well.) Tribal rules regarding the acceptance of mixed bloods as tribal members have long varied from tribe to tribe. Male and female mixed bloods were accepted by white society based on how "Indian" they looked and whether they acted, dressed, spoke, and lived like white people. In any event, millions of white Americans and African Americans have some Native American ancestry. It is common for members of both racial groups to recount the Indian ancestor(s) in their family histories, without questioning their identities as whites or blacks.

The controversy surrounding racial miscegenation, particularly white-black unions, led to many state laws that prohibited interracial marriage.[46] No federal laws ever focused on the issue, but state laws often did so. "At one time or another," writes Rachel Moran, "thirty-eight states adopted laws regulating interracial sex and marriage. All of these laws banned black-white relationships, but fourteen states also prohibited Asian-white marriages and another seven barred Native American-white unions. No state ever officially banned Latino-white intermarriage, though, presumably because treaty protections formally accorded former Spanish and Mexican citizens the status of white persons."[47] (In some parts of the country, a dark-skinned Latino might have had difficulties obtaining a marriage license if s/he wanted to marry a fair-skinned

Anglo.) Antimiscegenation laws became quite common during the nine-teenth century, but no state or federal laws ever prohibited interethnic or interfaith marriages among whites. The U.S. Supreme Court nullified all antimiscegenation statutes with its decision in *Loving v. Virginia* in 1967.[48]

DEFINING AMERICA

"I want you to understand I'm a devout American," Victor G. Atiyeh re-calls that he told the heads of state he met with during his trip in 1984 to the Middle East, "so that our position, on whatever we talk about — it's not in terms of my having an Arabic background, but in terms of being an American."[49] During this trip, the 61-year-old governor of Syrian ances-try went to Syria, Egypt, Israel, and Saudi Arabia. Atiyeh met with Syrian President Hafez al-Assad, Egyptian President Hosni Mubarak, and Israeli Prime Minister Yitzhak Shamir. The lifelong Oregonian also made a visit to Amar el Husn, his father's native village in northern Syria (Atiyeh had been there in 1929 as well). Atiyeh's father, George Atiyeh, and un-cle, Aziz Atiyeh, had left Amar el Husn sometime before 1900 to go to Allentown, Pennsylvania. In 1900 the Atiyehs learned about some op-portunities in Portland, Oregon, so they went West. Linda Asly, Victor Atiyeh's mother, immigrated to the United States from Beirut (which was then part of Syria) upon marrying his father in December 1920.

Victor George Atiyeh was born in Portland, Oregon, on February 20, 1923. When Atiyeh was growing up in Portland, his parents stressed as-similation, so he and his two brothers — who are twins — never learned to speak Arabic. He graduated from Portland's Washington High School in 1941. Next, Atiyeh attended the University of Oregon for two years, where he was a football star (the Green Bay Packers offered him a contract), and then joined Atiyeh Bros., Inc., the family business, as a full-time employee after his father died. He served as president of Atiyeh Bros. from 1943 to 1979. This genial, courtly man with gray hair, a wide face, and dark brown eyes was elected to the Oregon House of Representatives in 1958 from a district in Washington County, west of Portland. Then, in 1964, he successfully sought a seat in the Oregon Sen-ate. Atiyeh served there for 14 years, and he was the Republican leader in the Oregon Senate from 1971 to 1979. In 1974 the Oregon Repub-licans nominated him for governor. Four years later, in his second try, the 55-year-old legislator-businessman became the first Arab American elected governor of a U.S. state.

Atiyeh proved to be a very popular governor. His affable manner, tell-it-like-it-is accessibility, and political philosophy ("very conservative" on fiscal issues and "very liberal" on social issues) won him many fans in the Beaver State during his eight-year tenure.[50] Today Atiyeh cites five major accomplishments that make him proudest. Firstly, under his leadership, Oregon "got through the recession [of the early 1980s] in good shape." Secondly, Atiyeh helped Oregon diversify its economy, which now revolves around wood products, agriculture, tourism, high-tech, and international trade, so the state could weather economic downturns better. Thirdly, the governor points out that "Oregon became the first state that collected, stored, and distributed food to the hungry." Fourth, Atiyeh played an important role in spearheading the passage of Oregon's law making racial and religious harassment a felony. And fifth, he is rightfully proud of the efficiency of his administration.[51] In recognition of his myriad accomplishments, Atiyeh has received dozens of awards, degrees, citations, and commendations over the years.

Today Victor Atiyeh is the preeminent elder statesman of Oregon's political elite. He currently does consulting related to international trade and serves as Chairman of the Board of Atiyeh International, Ltd., a carpet wholesaler run by his son, Tom, and daughter-in-law, Leslie. Meanwhile, Arab-American ethnic advocates, who regularly cite him on their lists of Arab-American luminaries, have claimed Atiyeh. Indeed, he is always ready to lend a hand to back an Arab-American cause or organization. As a state legislator, and later as governor, Atiyeh's ethnic heritage was a nonissue. In fact, he reports that no one, to his knowledge, has ever discriminated against him because of his Arab ancestry (he belongs to the Episcopal Church). Atiyeh notes, however, that he has faced discrimination from liberal interest groups based on the fact that he is a Republican. Now in his ninth decade, Atiyeh continues to participate in the cultural and political affairs of Oregon, as befits a man whose résumé includes so many political successes and significant civic contributions.

The present racial and ethnic classification schema in the United States defines whites as those individuals who are descended from Europeans, North Africans, and Middle Easterners. This schema takes into account the general consensus that the vast majority of the people in these parts of the world are Caucasian. The number of white males in the aggregate is growing far more slowly in percentage terms than that of people of color. This is the case in part because the fertility rates of white women are significantly lower than those of black and Hispanic women. At the same time, most immigrants are people of color. Although thousands of white male immigrants come to the United States each year, there are not enough of them in the aggregate to contribute much to the growth of the white male population here.

Most white male Americans trace their roots to Europe, even though they typically do not have one single ethnic identity. The largest ethnic groups for white Americans are the Germans (46,488,992), Irish (33,067,131), and English (28,264,856), with significant numbers of people of United States or American (19,644,182), Italian (15,942,683), French (9,775,761), and Polish (9,053,660) heritage too. In addition, many white Americans claim Scottish (5,423,030), Scotch-Irish (5,226,402), Dutch (5,221,803), Norwegian (4,541,254), Swedish (4,339,357), Russian (2,980,776), French Canadian (2,208,729), Welsh (1,898,279), Hungarian (1,519,788), Danish (1,502,600), Czech (1,396,279), Portuguese (1,321,155), and Greek (1,179,064) ancestry.[52] As time goes by, these ethnic designations are becoming less precise, because many white Americans have multiple ethnic identifiers and may simply identify as American.

A growing number of whites boast mixed ethnic origins — interethnic marriages, after all, are quite prevalent among native-born white Americans.[53] In many cases, however, white American males resemble their distant cousins in Europe, even after generations of ethnic mixing. Ethnic endogamy is rare among assimilated, native-born white Americans. Most white males marry white females, though. With each succeeding generation, the ethnic mixtures of white Americans become ever more complex. Those white males who have four or five ethnic identifiers, or whose ancestors came here so long ago that the exact dates are a mystery, are truly white American males. The typical white person usually has some idea of his ethnic antecedents, but a growing number of white males do not identify with any specific ancestral group besides that of their fellow Americans.[54]

Perhaps two percent of white males in the United States are descended from the aboriginal peoples of North Africa and the Middle East. Although most Americans consider everyone who is descended from the aboriginal Europeans to be white, they do not always feel the same way about North Africans and Middle Easterners, some of whom resemble light-skinned black Africans or brown-skinned South Asians.[55] Still, the average Arab-American male is unambiguously Caucasian. The Census Bureau counted 1,248,551 Arab Americans in 2000, a number that ethnic advocates say is too low. In 2000 there were 420,144 Lebanese Americans, 135,850 Syrian Americans, and 122,821 Egyptian

Americans. Likewise, non-Arab Middle Eastern Americans are commonly described and accepted as whites; this group includes Armenian Americans (368,909), Iranian Americans (346,204), Turkish Americans (136,498), and Israeli Americans (105,412).[56] In any event, Arab Americans often marry European Americans; these unions contribute to the panethnic nature of whiteness in modern America.[57]

Many academics and journalistic observers of American life consider Arab Americans and Muslim Americans to be minorities, even marginalized groups, in American society.[58] Throughout American history, numerous negative stereotypes about Arabs and Arab Americans — and Muslims and Muslim Americans — have existed in mainstream American media and entertainment.[59] The most pernicious stereotype about Arab Americans and Muslim Americans is that they aid and abet anti-American terrorists. This stereotype developed over the years as a result of such events as the Iranian hostage crisis from 1979 to 1981 and the various terrorist acts perpetrated by Middle Eastern bad guys during the 1980s and 1990s.[60] Many Arab Americans and Muslim Americans contend that stereotyping adversely affects their life chances in various ways, including hate crimes, public harassment, employment discrimination, disparaging looks and remarks, and profiling by airlines and law-enforcement authorities.[61]

The terrorist attacks on September 11, 2001, undoubtedly reinforced the spurious association that some Americans make between foreign terrorists and Arab Americans, Muslim Americans, and people who are seen as members of those groups.[62] Since 9/11, anecdotal evidence suggests that many Americans from Arab, Middle Eastern, and Muslim backgrounds now feel less welcome here than they did before the terror attacks.[63] Still, the anthropologist Nabeel Abraham points out that significant progress has been made since the 1980s in terms of the American public's reaction to Arab Americans and Muslim Americans in the wake of a crisis involving Middle Eastern villains. Arab Americans and Muslim Americans, after all, have become an increasingly visible part of America's multiethnic culture during the last decade. In the aftermath of 9/11, the U.S. cultural and political elites pointedly encouraged Americans to be tolerant of their Arab-American and Muslim-American neighbors.[64]

Latinos are another highly diverse group that receives much attention from the media. The Spaniards, of course, played a significant role in defining the cultures, economies, and politics of Spanish-speaking Latin America. Spanish explorers regularly formed sexual unions with women of color, a phenomenon that gave rise to the mestizo — and more than a few mulattoes — as well. European immigrants, especially those from Spain, also contributed to the peopling of Spanish-speaking Latin America. With the conspicuous exceptions of immigrants from Cuba and, to a lesser extent, Colombia, most of whom are white, the migration flows from Latin America to the United States are largely made up of mestizos and mulattoes. Latinos mainly come from Mexico, northern Central America, northern South America, and the Spanish-speaking Caribbean. To avoid making invidious distinctions between and among the Spanish-speaking peoples in their anti-discrimination programs, U.S. government policymakers categorize all of them as Latinos, regardless of race.[65]

White Hispanic males who speak with no accents are white at every juncture, but they also have the ability to claim affirmative-action benefits and protected-class status in many cases. Prominent Cuban Americans such as Andy Garcia, Oscar Hijuelos, Alberto Vilar, Alex Penelas, Carlos Gutierrez, and others resemble full-blooded Spaniards, but they technically qualify as "racial" minorities in certain circumstances, just as if they were black Dominicans or Indian-appearing *mexicanos*. There is no substantial evidence to suggest that a white Spanish speaker faces any more discrimination than any other white person from a Mediterranean background does, whether he is Portuguese, French, Italian, Greek, Bulgarian, or Turkish. One might make the argument, however, that there may be discrimination against the mixed-race people of the New World that affects white people with Spanish surnames in the United States.[66] In sum, the white Hispanic male may not be a "white male" in the typical sense of the word, but he certainly is white and male.

Biracial and multiracial males account for an increasingly significant part of the American population. Multiple factors affect the identification patterns of those biracial and multiracial males with white ancestors. Considering the available evidence, it seems unlikely that the vast majority of biracial males with white progenitors will choose an explicitly multiracial identity. Half-white men with an African-American parent (think Lenny Kravitz) are most likely to identify as people of color, considering the U.S. history surrounding the "one drop" rule.[67] Likewise, males of part-white and part–American Indian descent often self-identify as Native Americans. Individuals of white/Latino and white/Asian extraction, however, vary dramatically in terms of their self-identification patterns. To be sure, their physiognomic characteristics and identification patterns often reflect their cultural and racial proximity to the majority group.

Males of white/Asian ancestry constitute an important part of multiracial America, due to the fact that many whites and Asian Americans form sexual unions. Traditionally, mixed-race people of white and Asian extraction, such as Dean Cain and Keanu Reeves, have been accepted as white. This type of racial acceptance depends, to some extent, on how a person self-identifies in a racial sense, a decision that may be influenced by such factors as how "white" or "Asian" s/he looks, whether s/he has an Asian surname, and the extent to which the Asian-American parent stresses that part of the family heritage. This type of self-identification even varies within individual families.[68] These issues usually are most salient for people with Far Eastern ancestry. Mixed-race people of white and Asian ancestry face little overt discrimination, largely because middle-class Asian Americans constitute a vital and growing part of the American mainstream.

Racial endogamy, meanwhile, continues to be the rule in Multicultural America. Ninety-seven percent of whites marry other whites.[69] They usually form endogamous unions in racially heterogeneous communities because their social interactions tend to be with other Caucasians. In racially homogeneous sections of America, it is unsurprising that intraracial marriages among whites are the norm; few, if any, options for interracial marriage exist in such places.[70] Ethnic endogamy occurs most frequently in areas like Cajun country in southern Louisiana, where residential concentration and especially low socioeconomic status are factors that lead the descendants of the eighteenth-century Acadian refugees to marry within their ethnic group.[71] In the coming decades, rates of ethnic endogamy will decline among native-born white Americans, even as most whites continue to choose white marital partners.

White men and black women rarely marry each other, although it is somewhat more common for white women to marry black men. In 2002, for instance, there were 279,000 black male/white female married couples and 116,000 white male/black female married couples.[72] To be sure, there continue to be substantial social sanctions and stigmas associated with white male/black female relationships — as well as white female/black male unions — due in part to social attitudes stemming from the ignominious legacy of slavery and segregation. Eventually, we may see more African-American women dating and marrying white men due to the number of black men who are dating and marrying nonblack women and consequently changing the dynamics of the marriage market for black women, particularly those who are affluent and well educated.

In any event, the prevalence of white male-black female dating seems to have increased in recent years.[73]

White-Latino intermarriage occurs regularly in America. Young, native-born Cuban Americans — the men in particular — frequently marry Anglos. Thirty-one percent of native-born Mexican-American men under the age of 40 marry white women, and 28 percent of Mexican-American women in this group marry white men.[74] In his study of Mexican-Anglo intermarriage, Michael J. Rosenfeld found that "the social distance between Mexican Americans and non-Hispanic Blacks is greater than the social distance between Mexican Americans and non-Hispanic Whites."[75] Therefore, it is unsurprising that Anglos and Mexican Americans intermarry far more frequently than do blacks and whites. Anglo/Mexican-American unions are especially common among native-born Anglos and native-born Mexican Americans, those who are not segregated or socially isolated from whites.[76] One factor that may contribute to the increasing prevalence of Anglo-Latino intermarriage is that Anglos and Latinos often do not look dramatically different from each other.

Whites and Asian Americans often form marital unions too. In 1990, 21.2% of Asian Americans were married exogamously, either interethnically or interracially. Three factors — gender, nativity, and ethnicity — affect the outmarriage rates of Asian Americans. Foreign-born Asian women are significantly more likely to marry exogamously than foreign-born Asian men. Native-born Asian-American women are slightly more likely than their male counterparts to marry exogamously, except for Asian Indians. Naturally, native-born Asian Americans marry exogamously in greater numbers than their foreign-born coethnics due to their greater familiarity with American culture and the declining significance of cultural prohibitions against intermarriage from the Old World. Two ethnic groups — Japanese Americans and Filipino Americans — dramatically exceed the average for Asian-American outmarriage. This type of racial intermarriage often occurs as a result of the overlapping social circles of native-born whites and native-born Asian Americans.[77]

On another front, one's perceived cultural characteristics can lead to external classifications that may conflict with one's self-definition. We often define our peers in an informal sense according to such factors as gait; attire; circle of friends; manner of speaking; and preferences in music, movies, and literature. Men of color might be denigrated by their coethnics for "acting white" if they appear to embrace wholeheartedly mainstream values and attitudes. Conversely, a ponytail-wearing white guy with an interest in Native America might be called a "wannabe" by an Indian friend.[78] The so-called "wiggers" (young white males who imitate black mannerisms, folkways, and so forth) forfeit some of their whiteness, at least temporarily, by selectively embracing aspects of African-American urban youth culture. Some white males, for instance, wear doo rags, a type of headgear traditionally favored by African-American men.[79] These white guys, who prefer FUBU to Abercrombie & Fitch and who choose Snoop over Beck, retain the trappings of whiteness, unless they are dark enough that they might be mistaken for a mixed-race Puerto Rican or a light-skinned African American.

Likewise, white males with disabilities often find themselves treated as members of a minority group, separate from other white males. People with disabilities experience many of the same feelings of exclusion as ethnic and racial minorities. They know what it is like to be outsiders in an able-bodied world, just as people of color sometimes feel unwelcome in predominantly white environments.[80] White males with disabilities find that their conditions influence how others define them. For example, most Americans will see a white guy with a red-tipped white cane as a visually impaired person first, and a white man second. The extent to which a white male with a disability is impaired by his disability depends on such factors as the severity of his condition and the amount of material resources at his disposal. Of course it matters, too, whether his disability is outwardly visible and significantly impairs mobility, factors that may affect a person's treatment by the dominant group.[81]

The age at which a white male becomes disabled affects his life chances and his outlook on, and levels of identification with, able-bodied Americans. It is, of course, different to grow up as a white male who was disabled from birth or early childhood, and quite another to become disabled as an adult. The difference is crucial, because it determines whether the white male ever felt as if he were part of the majority culture. By way of example, only 8.1 percent of Americans in the 5–20 age range have disabilities, while 41.9 percent of those 65 years and older have disabilities.[82] Regardless, white males with visible disabilities are a quasi-minority. There are frequent discussions in legal and political circles about what constitutes a disability that qualifies one for protected-class status, in addition to constant litigation regarding this matter.[83]

As with other minorities, it is common for people with disabilities to contend that they share a unique identity and culture.[84] According to Duane Stroman,

Persons with disabilities are a diverse group whose visibility, self-awareness of being in a minority group, involuntary status, and practice of endogamy is variable across and within various categories of disability. At the same time the critical distinguishing features of being a minority group is that there exist cultural stereotypes about their differentness or deviance from normality or wholeness and the consequent discrimination against them.

From this viewpoint, those with disabilities are a minority although those with less severe disabling conditions and less visible ones typically have a lower consciousness of being a minority and may experience less stereotyping and discrimination from the able dominant group than persons with more severe and/or more visible disabling conditions.[85]

One of the biggest issues for Americans with disabilities is their access to equal opportunities in the workplace, a matter that the Americans with Disabilities Act of 1990 (ADA) was meant to address. Employers face the challenge of giving Americans with disabilities chances to develop their human capital without incurring prohibitively high expenses as a result of accommodating the special needs of these individuals.[86] In assessing the liability of employers in court cases involving litigants with disabilities, Ruth O'Brien points out, "The federal courts have asked, first, whether the person has a disability and, second, whether he or she is qualified for a position. A majority of the courts have used these threshold questions to determine if a person warrants protection."[87] The third question — that of the employer's responsibility to provide accommodations for his or her employees with disabilities — rarely comes up in court cases because the courts often decide cases on matters related to a person's disability and qualifications without getting to the other issue.[88]

To be sure, it seems that discrimination against people with disabilities still exists. Americans with disabilities have significantly higher rates of poverty and lower rates of employment compared to those who do not have disabilities. Certain factors, such as race, gender, and the type of disability, help determine how disadvantaged a person with a disability may be.[89] Drawing upon the Disability Supplement to the 1994 and 1995 National Health Interview Surveys, Jae Kennedy and Marjorie Olney report that "almost 10% of adults with disabilities who were in the workforce in the period immediately following passage of the ADA believed they had experienced some form of discrimination."[90] Within the disability community, younger workers and people of color are most likely to perceive discrimination on the basis of disability status.[91]

Although hearing Americans might think of deaf people as part of the disability community, many members of the deaf community do not consider themselves to be disabled because of their auditory condition. Many deaf Americans define deafness as a culture. According to this line of reasoning, "deaf" refers to one's hearing impairment, whereas "Deaf" describes the culture of deaf people. Deaf people, after all, have a common language — American Sign Language — as well as institutions, cultural characteristics, and historical similarities that bind them together in contradistinction to the hearing world. Many of the arguments about cultural distinctiveness offered by Deaf culturists resemble those made by members of ethnic minority groups. Perhaps the biggest debate in deaf America occurs over cochlear implants, which improve the hearing of many deaf people. A number of deaf Americans vehemently reject cochlear implants. They prefer to be deaf, and fear that having the ability to hear would destroy the uniqueness of Deaf culture and the cohesiveness of the deaf community.[92]

IN AND OUT

Tens of millions of Americans came to know Richard Hatch during the summer of 2000. Americans were riveted by the activities of Hatch and the 15 other contestants on the popular CBS reality show, *Survivor.* We watched the brazen Rhode Islander and his compatriots participate in such activities as larvae eating and jungle obstacles on Pulau Tiga, an island in the South Pacific. We also saw the American visitors to Pulau Tiga vote to send one of their fellow contestants back to the United States at the conclusion of each episode. The last person remaining on the island (the Survivor) at the end of the 39-day contest was to win the $1 million grand prize. From May 31, 2000, to August 23, 2000, television viewers watched Hatch and his three partners in a voting alliance (Rudy Boesch, Susan Hawk, and Kelly Wiglesworth) outlast the other contestants. In the end, Hatch won the $1 million prize as a result of his machinations.[93]

During this period, the details of Hatch's biography became widely known to the American public. Hatch was born on April 8, 1961, and grew up in Middletown, Rhode Island, a predominantly white community of 17,334 in the southeastern part of the Ocean State. He now lives in nearby Newport. A tall, stocky man with an English surname and a receding hairline, Hatch spent five years in the Army (he even attended

West Point for a time). Then he started his own corporate-training firm in 1986. Hatch enjoys camping and outdoor-adventure programs, hobbies that undoubtedly prepared him for *Survivor.* The Rhode Island native is also the adoptive father of Chris, an adolescent boy. Hatch, like many Americans, has battled weight problems over the years — at one point, he weighed 360 pounds. This intriguing biography helped Hatch establish a reputation as a likable rogue.[94]

Hatch happens to be openly gay. This fact certainly made his profile seem more exotic. He writes that his background as a gay man as well as his openness about his sexuality have enabled him to "live a much happier life" and win *Survivor*:

> Not only has it made me more successful, but being part of a minority community, subject to scrutiny by others, has inspired me to be more introspective and forced me to do whatever it takes to understand better who I am. It's also helped me learn what is meaningful about who I am and what matters to me in my life. But being gay has not always been easy.[95]

Hatch seems to be very comfortable with his sexual identity, even as he acknowledges that openly gay people encounter discrimination due to their sexual orientation.

To the general population, Hatch was known as much for being naked on *Survivor,* or for being heavy, or for being ruthless, as he was for being gay. Since Americans are accustomed to portrayals of openly gay people in the mass media, particularly on television and in the movies, there was no shock value associated with Hatch's presence on *Survivor.* To heterosexual Americans, he may have been "the gay guy" more so than someone who happened to be gay, but that was only because he was open about his sexuality on camera. Hatch earned $1.2 million in 2000 — and a spot on *Forbes*' "Celebrity 100" List in 2001, but he has now lapsed back into obscurity.[96] Nonetheless, Hatch's presence on *Survivor* was yet one more sign that sexual minorities were receiving recognition in the mainstream media as "regular" Americans.

No one knows how many gays and lesbians live in the United States. The estimates of the gay and lesbian population vary in response to the types of questions asked in addition to how the respondents define being gay and lesbian.[97] According to the authors of *Sex in America,* a landmark study published in 1994, "About 6 percent of the men in our study said they were attracted to other men. About 2 percent of the men in our study said they had sex with a man in the past year, a little more than 5 percent said they had homosexual sex at least once since they turned eighteen, and 9 percent said they had had sex with a man at least once since puberty."[98] But only 2.8 percent of the men in the aforementioned study classified themselves as homosexual or bisexual, as opposed to 1.4 percent of the women.[99] To be sure, there is considerable controversy over this topic; gay activists often contend that lesbians and gays constitute four to eight percent of the U.S. population.[100]

The visible communities of openly gay Americans tend to be in urban areas. Many gay guys leave their hometowns and migrate to large cities, so the population of a given place may have a substantially higher-than-average percentage of gay men than the general population at large. As the authors of *Sex in America* put it, "More than 9 percent of men in the nation's twelve largest cities identify themselves as gay. But just 3 or 4 percent of men living in the suburbs of these cities or in most of the larger cities of the nation say they are gay and about 1 percent of men in rural areas identify themselves as gay."[101] In large urban areas, gays patronize gay bars, gyms, clubs, bookstores, coffeehouses, and community centers. Many of them live in gay-friendly or predominantly gay neighborhoods. Every big city has at least one "gay" community, e.g., Chelsea (New York), Dupont Circle (District of Columbia), West Hollywood (metro Los Angeles), and the Castro district (San Francisco).

Nonetheless, gays and lesbians continue to be regarded dimly in many parts of straight America, three decades after homosexuality came out of the shadows with the gay liberation movement of the 1970s.[102] Opponents of gay rights in the United States frequently characterize protections for homosexuals as "special rights" and use intemperate language regarding "the homosexual lifestyle" that would be deemed unacceptable if it were used in reference to any ethnic minority group. Corporations and governmental entities often encounter controversy when they establish same-sex partnership benefits for their employees. The critics of such initiatives predicate their opposition to them on religious and cultural grounds; they believe that homosexuality is something that should not be legitimized in any way by institutions in the public and private sectors. While implicit attacks on gays and lesbians have slowly lost favor with mainstream political and cultural figures, someone who makes antigay remarks will not experience the same kind of ostracism that an antiblack or anti-Semitic person would face.

There are subtle social stigmas that continue to attach to homosexuality in the United States. Many Americans may support gay rights in the abstract, but they would be somewhat uncomfortable (initially, at least) with the idea of having a gay child. For example, a middle-aged mother might mention to a friend that her single son lives in San Francisco — and then she quickly adds that he has a girlfriend. In large urban areas, people may think that a single man over a certain age might be gay, particularly if he does not seem to date women on a regular basis. In addition, colloquial terms commonly used in American English indicate that bias against homosexuality continues to exist in our culture. Many young people, for instance, use the term "gay" to describe things they dislike. And it is still common for straight American males in particular to use the epithets *fag* and *queer* to denigrate their peers.[103] The aforementioned antigay epithets do not yet earn their users the same opprobrium that accompanies usage of the N-word, but it is less and less common to hear such terms used in polite society.

After all, Americans are demonstrating ever-greater tolerance with regard to gays and lesbians. "Public opinion polls over the last twenty years," write Clyde Wilcox and Robin Wolpert, "yield two important conclusions about citizens' attitudes toward gays and lesbians. First, a substantial minority of Americans holds very negative views of gays and lesbians. Second, these attitudes have recently begun to change, and this change has been surprisingly rapid."[104] The evolution of progressive attitudes on gay and lesbian rights can be attributed to several factors, including the visibility of gays and lesbians in the mainstream media, particularly popular culture; the gradual inclusion of lesbians and gays in the multicultural ethos that influences the attitudes of many younger, college-educated straight Americans; and the increasing number of openly gay Americans, a factor that leads more and more straight Americans to have personal contact with gays and lesbians.[105]

In any event, the gay and lesbian community is largely stratified by race. Some progressive activists, particularly in the lesbian community, see gay white males (GWMs) as hegemons who are less oppressed than other gays and lesbians.[106] They contend that for gay white males, the benefits of white privilege and male privilege compensate for the loss of heterosexual privilege, at least more so than is the case for women and people of color. As whites, GWMs can ignore race as a factor in their lives; gay blacks, Latinos, and Asian Americans do not have this luxury. This is why many African Americans reject the notion of parallels between the civil rights movement and the gay rights movement. Racism exists in the gay community, which manifests itself in a reluctance by white gays to fraternize with men of color.[107] Due to the nature of this subject, of course, there is no definitive quantitative evidence that

measures the interactions — in terms of dating and long-term relationships — of gay white men with men of color. Michelangelo Signorile, for
one, chides his fellow gay white men for their tendency to favor white
male lovers and partners.[108]

Stratification by gender is another point of division in the gay and
lesbian community. Gay men, naturally, fraternize mainly with other gay
men on their free time. Likewise, lesbians prefer the company of their
own gender when they socialize with each other. There are certain situations, though, in which gays and lesbians might unite — on campuses,
in the political arena, and in the corporate environment. Even though
lesbians and gay men may prioritize certain issues (such as breast cancer
research for women and anti-sodomy laws for men), they confront similar
challenges with regard to adoption and parental rights, domestic partner
benefits, and same-sex civil unions. So there are grounds on which they
will form political coalitions to work together. However, such coalitions
may exist only temporarily because many lesbians remain vigilant for
any assertions of male privilege on the part of gay men.[109]

Social class is yet another stratifying feature of life in the gay community. Gay white males — and lesbians and gays as a whole — are
widely separated by their socioeconomic differences. Advertisers assidu-
ously court gays and lesbians in general and gay white males in particular
because they are perceived to have significant amounts of disposable
income.[110] "In the world of the market," contends Suzanna Danuta Walters, "all the gays are men, all the men are white, and all the whites
are rich."[111] According to Walters, "The inevitable focus on the niche
most likely to consume freely relegates other gays (women, the poor,
minorities, the 'excessively' butch or feminine) even further into the shadows."[112] Other gays downplay the specious notion of gay affluence, in
large part because many sexual minorities are not prosperous by any
means. Moreover, lesbian and gay activists do not want straight people
to get the mistaken impression that gays do not need any legal protections
on the basis of sexual orientation.[113]

In addition, there is considerable ideological diversity within the gay
and lesbian community. Lesbians and gays continually debate the virtues
of assimilation versus separatism. They vary in terms of how important
their sexual orientation is with regard to matters of self-identification. In
other words, does a GWM see himself as *a gay person* or a *person who
happens to be gay*? Many people in the latter group would never march in
a gay-pride parade or openly display the rainbow flag, perhaps the best-
known symbol of gay and lesbian community. Similarly, gays and lesbians

differ as to whether they appropriate the epithet *queer*. Many gays and lesbians have reclaimed the Q-word, in much the same way that members of racial groups appropriate slurs directed against themselves. However, some sexual minorities prefer *gay* to *queer*, and they look skeptically on the reclamation of the Q-word by the younger generation.[114]

The term *queer* signifies a certain type of gay sensibility, one that is used by gays in the academy and elsewhere to reflect a particular ideology — namely, one of separation from straight society, or at least proud, even militant advocacy, of gay and lesbian rights.[115] "Since the late 1980s," writes Joshua Gamson, " 'queer' has served to mark first a loose but distinguishable set of political movements and mobilizations, and second a somewhat parallel set of academy-bound intellectual endeavors (now calling itself 'queer theory')."[116] Bruce Bawer, a critic of queer politics and queer theory, contends that such activities give sustenance to antigay Americans, who point to the ideological extremes in the gay community to support their attempts to marginalize gay and lesbian Americans.[117] It is difficult, of course, to determine how many gays and lesbians identify with queer politics and queer theory.

Gay white men often view *themselves* as markedly different from their heterosexual counterparts, based on their exclusion from straight society. GWMs, after all, are frequently defined by their sexual orientation more so than their race, ethnicity, occupation, geographical background, or any of the other social distinctions that traditionally distinguish Americans from each other. Take, for instance, the lesbian and gay studies programs at many colleges and universities. These programs focus a fair amount of attention on the characteristics and accomplishments of GWMs. The development of lesbian and gay studies courses parallels the explosion of scholarship on, and academic interest in, the lives of people from other historically disadvantaged groups such as women, Latinos, African Americans, and Native Americans.[118] In any event, many issues affect GWMs as gay people, not as GWMs or white males.

Their homosexuality gives GWMs a certain outsider's credibility and bestows upon them a form of minority status. Overnight, if a gay white man comes out as openly gay, he gives up his membership in the straight-white-male majority. Such GWMs are no longer garden-variety white guys; being open about their sexual orientation automatically distances them from the bastions of straight-white-male power and grants them membership in a minority group. GWMs qualify as minorities for the purposes of the diversity imperative, whereby gay firsts, pioneers, and trailblazers are celebrated by gays, regardless of their race or gender. Although gay white men are usually regarded as a de facto minority by multiculturalists, the federal government does not recognize homosexuality as grounds for protected-class status and, consequently, affirmative-action benefits.

The AIDS epidemic, which has decimated the gay community for the last 23 years, is perhaps the most visible issue that marks gay men as a minority in the United States. AIDS traditionally has been regarded by the American public as a disease that primarily affects gay white males, and much of the activism on the issue has been spearheaded by GWMs.[119] Nowadays, AIDS disproportionately affects people of color, particularly blacks and Latinos. In 2000, African Americans accounted for 47.1% of the AIDS cases affecting adults and adolescents, and Hispanics made up 19.4% of the AIDS cases. Whites, by contrast, accounted for 31.8%. Three-quarters of people with AIDS (PWAs) in 2000 were male: black males (31.5% of PWAs), white males (27.3% of PWAs), and Hispanic males (15.0% of PWAs).[120] The African-American community has been slow to respond to this public-health threat, in part because of lingering stigmas surrounding homosexuality in black America.[121]

Hate crime is another highly visible issue that affects GWMs. Straight white males are usually the perpetrators of hate crimes against gay white males; this is a powerful indicator that GWMs are not viewed by members of the straight-white-male majority as "white males" per se. In 1998 the murder of Matthew Shepard, an openly gay student at the University of Wyoming, received national media attention.[122] In 1999 the murders of two gay white men (Billy Jack Gaither and Barry Winchell) also made headlines. Because all three men were attacked and murdered by Euro-American guys, the press reports always referred to these victims of antigay bias as "gay," to distinguish them from the straight white men who killed them. Due to the racially homogeneous nature of numerous communities — and many peoples' social circles — straight white males seem to be responsible for most incidents of gay bashing against gay white males.

Every American is automatically granted the presumption of heterosexuality, in the absence of substantial evidence to the contrary. This is the case unless one signals otherwise through his attire, hangouts, jewelry, mannerisms, slang words, dating habits, movie rentals, self-description, reading materials, and tonal inflections. Most gay white males can pass as straight — that is, when they want to do so, or need to do so. Some of them even marry women and have families, or at least date unwitting females. One guy might be "out" of the figurative closet in all circumstances, while another may only be "out" to his family and close friends. The proliferation of gay-themed Web sites, such as Gay.com and PlanetOut, has made it even easier for gays to form a sense of community without incurring the social costs that sometimes accompany being openly gay.[123] Even so, many GWMs prefer partners who look and act straight, often with hypermasculine mannerisms and a pumped-up musculature.[124]

Openly gay Americans are now present in all walks of life, and thus there are many role models for gay and lesbian Americans — more so than ever before. The mainstream media now cover gay issues more comprehensively than in the past. Openly gay journalists and media personalities are also becoming more common.[125] In certain occupational niches like the arts and fashion design, being openly gay matters little or not at all. Openly gay men occupy prominent and influential posts in these occupations, so there is no social stigma associated with being "out." Likewise, the level of tolerance that openly gay and lesbian executives encounter in Corporate America seems to be increasing.[126] However, the dynamics regarding open homosexuality vary dramatically by occupation and geography. Openly gay men are seldom found in such "macho" occupations as construction and heavy manufacturing. Similarly, there are few support systems for gays in the rural, socially conservative sections of America.

Many Americans continue to impute negative associations to homosexuality. Therefore, the possibility of being outed as a homosexual is an omnipresent threat for many successful but closeted gays and lesbians. This is particularly true for people in the public eye, such as actors or politicians, whose appeal is dependent, to some extent, on being perceived as part of the mainstream. In the workplace, a person who comes out as gay may be regarded as the resident gay guy or lesbian by his coworkers. It is possible that an openly gay person may experience some harassment or coolness from his coworkers if he is open about his sexuality. However, sexual orientation is increasingly included as part of workplace sensitivity training, making it clear even to unreconstructed homophobes that overtly antigay behavior is inappropriate.

As the gay rights movement of the last 30 years has created a potent sense of gay pride, gays and lesbians are coming out at younger and younger ages. More than 1,700 gay-straight alliances (GSAs) exist in the nation's high schools. These clubs foster a nurturing environment for sexual minorities, who are more likely than heterosexuals to commit suicide, skip school, or do poorly on their studies because they often face taunting and harassment — and sometimes even assaults — from straight classmates. Lesbian and gay advocates often contend that many teachers and administrators are insufficiently knowledgeable or concerned about the tribulations of their gay, lesbian, bisexual, and transgender students. In any event, the matter of educating young people about homosexuality in the public schools, by including sexual orientation in antibullying programs and violence-prevention initiatives, continues to divide parents and communities, educators and administrators.[127]

Meanwhile, it has become very common for gay characters to appear in mainstream entertainment, particularly as supporting actors. The gay male characters in films and on television are usually chaste and often played by straight actors; they rely on verbal and nonverbal cues to signal their sexual proclivities. Straight Americans have contributed heavily to the popularity of *Will & Grace,* a popular sitcom that began airing on NBC in 1998. It presents a commodified, sanitized form of homosexuality, one that appeals to straight as well as gay audiences. Showtime's *Queer as Folk,* an edgy sitcom about young gays, has won over gay viewers — and a fair number of straight ones too — with its explicit portrayal of gay urban life. Moreover, HBO & Bravo's *Queer Eye for the Straight Guy,* a program that features gay men who give fashion and home-decorating advice to straight men, is quite popular. As a rule, the face of homosexuality in mainstream American entertainment is that of the gay white male, particularly one who happens to be hip, young, urban, and affluent.[128]

Gay white males seem likely to become an ever more prominent part of the American landscape, as the stigma associated with homosexuality becomes less significant and more people come out of the closet. Indeed, straight Americans are more accepting of gay people than ever before. Homophobia and heterosexism are slowly becoming verboten in polite society. Homophobic and heterosexist behavior does not yet merit the same kind of opprobrium as racism and sexism, but attitudes are changing in this regard. An increasing number of straight Americans back laws that ban discrimination based on sexual orientation and support their openly gay friends, coworkers, and family members. At least 125 newspapers — most notably, the *New York Times* — now print notices of same-sex union announcements in their pages.[129] Some straight men, meanwhile, describe themselves as "metrosexual," meaning that they focus much attention on such matters as grooming and lifestyle issues (that were traditionally and stereotypically regarded as the bailiwick of gay men).[130]

Yet it seems unlikely that gays and lesbians will ever become a protected class, as in blacks and Hispanics. The political will does not exist at present to extend affirmative-action benefits to gays and lesbians. Due to the nature of the American public's feelings about gays and lesbians, there has been no serious discussion of such initiatives. Nor does it appear very likely that the racial, socioeconomic, and gender divides that exist in the gay and lesbian community will disappear anytime soon. At the same time, coalition politics among sexual minorities (gays, lesbians, bisexuals, transgenders) is the name of the game on the campuses and in a growing number of other sectors of American society. Such individuals are often referred to by the acronym GLBT or LGBT (in many cases, lesbians are listed first), even though they are an extremely heterogeneous group of people, many of whom do not necessarily see eye to eye on many issues.

✍

The claiming of white maleness in the United States has been affected by social, legal, economic, cultural, and political factors throughout the years. During the period from 1878 to 1944 there were 52 federal court cases that sought to answer the question: Who is white? The question took on considerable significance because members of various ethnic groups needed to prove themselves to be white in order to be eligible for naturalized U.S. citizenship at the time. (Anyone born in the United States is automatically a U.S. citizen; birthright citizenship came into effect with the enactment of the Fourteenth Amendment in 1868.) The courts varied when it came to one group in particular — Asian Indians — in terms of whether they judged them to be white. In all of these "racial prerequisite cases," mixed-race people with some white ancestry were never judged to be white. These cases, along with the general evolution of the assimilation process, did much to shape how we view whiteness today.[131]

Americans self-identify themselves in a racial sense, but they often rely on the U.S. government's classification schema to guide their decisions. Many immigrants in particular come from countries where conceptions of "whiteness" and "people of color" do not exist. In any event, the U.S. racial classification schema today does not completely take into account the heterogeneity of the American population. There are some Indians and Pakistanis, for instance, who are unambiguously white in a Western sense, but they would be classified by the government as "people of color." Conversely, there are people in the Arab world whose features and skin tones indicate they have a substantial amount of black African ancestry; yet they are classified as "white" in the United States. No classification schema, of course, can take into account every nuance and idiosyncrasy associated with social constructions of race and ethnicity.

Today, affirmative-action programs encourage nonwhites (and many phenotypically white people from Latin America) to claim a minority identity. In sum, as the multiculturalists slowly broaden the frontiers of minority identity and status ever further, groups of white males outside the mainstream may win informal recognition and even formal protections as minorities. So we may see more and more cases in which people who are white and male qualify as minorities of some kind or another. Some white males will be de facto nonwhites by reason of their Hispanic ethnicity. Others will be minorities in certain contexts based on their disabilities or even their whiteness or white maleness. As America becomes more and more heterogeneous in an ethnic and racial sense, the list of people who qualify as members of the protected classes is growing each year. Multiculturalists defend diversity initiatives, chief among them affirmative action, by pointing out that people of color do not always have access to the same opportunities enjoyed by many white Americans.

White males sometimes leave the white male grouping, temporarily or permanently, and categorize themselves as members of another race.[132] Some white males do so for political or economic reasons, like the benefits they may gain from affirmative-action programs. Others do so because they identify strongly with another group, whether it is Latinos or American Indians. There are reports of white males who self-identify as Native Americans — and win recognition racially as such — based on the following blood-quantum levels: one-eighth, one-sixteenth, one-thirty-second, and one-sixty-fourth.[133] Many white males, to be sure, are enrolled members of the Cherokee Nation, but they identify as white in a racial sense. The Cherokee in particular have a long tradition of embracing members who are part white.

Dick Mayo, a resident of Sallisaw, Oklahoma, identifies as American Indian — he is one-sixteenth Cherokee and fifteen-sixteenths white. Mayo, a 74-year-old man with white hair and blue eyes, takes after his Norwegian-American mother in terms of his physical characteristics. He is English, Scottish, Irish, and Cherokee on his father's side. The life-long Oklahoman points out that how you classify yourself is a matter of culture, and he sees himself as a Native American.[134] During the 1970s, Mayo had a septic tank manufacturing business in the Southwest. In that capacity, he benefited from contracting rules that helped minorities make successful bids.[135] Today Mayo serves as Secretary/Treasurer and a member of the Board of Directors of the Port Authority of the Cherokee Nation. He reports that no Native Americans or whites, for that matter, have ever questioned his Indianness.[136]

Whiteness as a social construct is becoming increasingly amorphous, due to the migration of Latin Americans to the United States and the increasing prevalence of interethnic and interracial marriages. Latin Americans come from a wide range of ethnic and racial backgrounds; many of them appear to be Caucasian even if they have some Amerindian or sub-Saharan African ancestry. What we are seeing, to some extent, is the development of a Latino identity that seems to include whiteness and the mestizo culture without excluding either concept of race.[137] Similarly, mixed-race people, particularly those individuals of white and Latino origins and white and Asian descent, will often identify as white — and be considered white by other Americans. The blurring of racial and ethnic boundaries, particularly when one embraces the culture, language, and attire of the white mainstream, may point the way to a broadening of our present conceptions of whiteness and, consequently, white maleness.[138]

The actor Vin Diesel illustrates one interesting variation of this phenomenon. The 37-year-old native of New York's Greenwich Village embodies the inclusive look of twenty-first-century America and describes himself as "multicultural." Diesel does not discuss his ethnic background, but it seems that his ancestors came from Italy and sub-Saharan Africa. Diesel's popularity epitomizes the increasing visibility of omniracial stars in American popular culture — this group of multiethnic individuals includes Mariah Carey, The Rock, and Jessica Alba.[139] In fact, his difficult-to-classify appearance may give him appeal and credibility among at least one critical group of movie-goers: teenagers.[140] Multiracials such as Diesel epitomize the blending of races and the blurring of racial boundaries, developments that might eventually reconfigure our conceptions of whiteness and race itself.

~ chapter two ~

Rebirth and Regeneration

Allison Jones, an inventor and lawyer who lives in Americana, Brazil, looks, acts, and speaks as if he had been born in Georgia, Alabama, or Texas. This is not surprising, considering that Jones's ancestors left those states to go to Brazil in the last decades of the nineteenth century.[1] These *confederados* (Confederates) were part of the migration of 10,000 to 20,000 white Southerners to Brazil during the period from 1865 to 1885.[2] Allison Jones's great-great-grandfather, Colonel William H. Norris, and great-grandfather, Dr. Robert C. Norris, went to southern Brazil in December 1865. The elder Norris, a 65-year-old state senator from Alabama, established the American settlement in Santa Bárbara D'Oeste. Soon thereafter, Calvin MacKnight and his family came to Americana from Texas. (Santa Bárbara D'Oeste and Americana are two neighboring cities about 80 miles northwest of São Paulo.) Jones's mother, Judith MacKnight Jones, is the great-granddaughter of Calvin MacKnight. Then, in the 1890s, Cicero Jones immigrated to Brazil; his son, Dr. James Jones, was Allison Jones's father.[3] Over the years, Judith MacKnight Jones and James Jones both played important roles in preserving the history of the *confederados* in Brazil.

Allison Jones was born in Americana in 1943. He spoke only English, with Southern inflections, until he entered the Brazilian schools as a youngster. Jones, of course, is a patriotic Brazilian, who takes pride in his nation's polyglot heritage, its admixture of races, regions, and religions, and its fabled acceptance of racial, cultural, and socioeconomic differences. Allison Jones himself pronounces his surname in the polysyllabic Brazilian fashion — JO-nays — as opposed to the monosyllabic locution favored by Americans and the British. Throughout his life, Jones has maintained many of the customs that were observed by his American ancestors. He, his wife, Eloisa Jones, and their three daughters eat such foods as biscuits, cornbread, watermelon, and fried chicken. The Joneses often speak English at home; Allison Jones instructs his daughters in the important points of U.S. history. Jones also venerates the Confederate battle flag, which occupies a prominent place in his living room.[4] "That flag to me," he asserts, "means the good memories and good habits cultivated and inherited from my ancestors. It's got nothing to do with racism and outlawness."[5]

A genial man with an ironic sense of humor, Jones spends much of his free time disseminating knowledge about the American immigrants who went to Brazil. He speaks about the *confederados* to groups of Brazilian schoolchildren. He faithfully attends the *confederado* reunions four times a year at the Cemitério do Campo (Campo Cemetery), which is located between Santa Bárbara D'Oeste and Americana. And he participates as an active member in the Fraternidade Descendência Americana (Fraternity of American Descendants), an organization devoted to preserving the heritage of the *confederados*. Jones himself has visited — and worked in — the United States on two occasions. Each time, he was frequently mistaken for an American.[6] This is not surprising, considering Jones's Northern European appearance, fluency in American English, and familiarity with U.S. customs and history. Today Allison Jones is well known in Brazil, the United States, and elsewhere as an invaluable source of information on the *confederados*; scholars, journalists, and Civil War enthusiasts from around the world seek his knowledge, insights, and anecdotes.

ALL AMERICAN

Jim Kurtti's name increasingly comes to mind when people think about the Finnish Americans of Upper Michigan's Copper Country. During the last decade, Kurtti, a gracious and unfailingly cheerful man of average height with light brown hair and luminescent blue eyes, has become a pivotal figure in the movement to preserve and perpetuate the Finnish part of the Finnish-American identity and experience. The youngest of four children to a Finnish father and French Canadian/German/Irish mother (he is one-half Finnish, one-quarter French Canadian, one-eighth German, and one-eighth Irish), Kurtti grew up in the predominantly Finnish town of Bruce Crossing, Michigan, in the 1960s and 1970s. By 1975, when he entered Suomi College, the heavily Finnish two-year institution of higher learning in Hancock, Michigan, Kurtti had wholeheartedly embraced his Finnish heritage. He learned to speak Finnish fluently during his junior year of college, which he spent at Helsinki University. In 1980 he graduated from the University of Minnesota with double majors in Finnish and social work.[7]

Kurtti worked for 18 years in the juvenile court system in northwestern Michigan before he retired several years ago, as he gradually became ever more involved in Finnish-American cultural activities. In 1995 this grandson of Finnish immigrants started the first Finnish-language program for credit in a secondary school anywhere in the United States — at Hancock Central High School in Hancock, Michigan. Through his participation in the Finnish Theme Committee of Hancock, Kurtti also played an integral role in creating and organizing Heikinpäivä, the wildly successful winter celebration that now takes place in the town every January. Kurtti's activism, to be sure, extends beyond Hancock — he serves, for example, as a board member of Salolampi, the Finnish-language summer camp in northern Minnesota. And his involvement in Project 34, the organization devoted to the preservation of Finnish culture among third- and fourth-generation Americans, enables him to network with like-minded preservationists across the nation.

What had been an avocation for Kurtti — translating Finnish documents into English for Americans, tracing genealogies (his own and those of other Finnish Americans), substituting for an instructor of Finnish at Suomi College, writing articles about obscure aspects of Finnish-American history, teaching first-year Finnish to high school students on his lunch hour — became a full-time occupation in 2000. That is when Kurtti went to work at Suomi College, which had recently become a four-year institution and, in midyear, was renamed Finlandia University. After serving briefly as the college's special events coordinator, the fortysomething Michiganite became director of Finlandia's Finnish-American Heritage Center in August 2000.[8] At the same time, he began to edit *The Finnish American Reporter.*[9]

Kurtti's work is truly a labor of love: Finland and things Finnish permeate almost every aspect of this engaging man's life, from his habit of taking a sauna to the delectable Finnish foods he enjoys so much. His wife, Debbie, may be only one-quarter Finnish, but she grew up in a solidly Finnish community and strongly supports his endeavors, as do their two teenage sons, Christian and Anders. Indeed, the spacious, well-appointed Kurtti home near Hancock is a veritable showcase of Finnish curios, mementos, artifacts, and collectibles. The man of the house, after all, clearly ranks among the nation's preeminent Finnish-American cultural preservationists. Every day this proud son of Suomi works indefatigably to preserve the Finnish culture, language, and traditions in northwestern Michigan. His efforts resonate throughout the precincts of

Finnish America, including many places far beyond the borders of his isolated idyll.

Americans — and American ethnic groups — vary tremendously in terms of how important their ethnic heritage and ethnic identity are to them. Two of the largest ethnic groups in the country (the Germans and the English) have no ethnic identity to speak of, the English much less so than the Germans. Irish Americans and Italian Americans, on the other hand, have well-defined ethnic identities. Polish Americans are another well-known ethnic group, with fraternal groups, cultural organizations, ethnic celebrations, and ethnic advocacy groups. The continuing immigration from Poland reinforces the "ethnic" nature of Polish America.[10] Likewise, Americans of Scottish ancestry continue to celebrate their ancestry, with clans, tartans, bagpipes, Highland Games, tours of Scotland, and the like.[11] But other European ethnic groups — the Franco Americans come to mind — rarely highlight their heritage in an explicit sense.

German Americans exist as an ethnic group, but there is little German-American identity per se. Although there are German ethnic festivals and Oktoberfest celebrations, there seems to be little sense of an overarching German-American identity. No one thinks of the actor Rick Schroder or Senate Minority Leader Tom Daschle as "German," but they look it and have German surnames. Germans, after all, do not deviate markedly in appearance from Americans of British and Irish descent, who constitute a large part of white America. As with the British and the Irish, Germans generally have light skin, blond or brown and, on occasion, black hair, and blue, green, or brown eyes. Some German surnames, particularly the shorter ones, differ little from English names. No one thinks of Hamm, Boss, Lott, or Roth as foreign-sounding names. Finally, because of their high numbers, German Americans seem to feel little need to organize on the basis of ethnicity.

Likewise, Americans of English ancestry are not usually seen as having any sort of ethnic identity. There is little, if any, discussion of English Americans. (No one thinks of WASP men like Tom Hanks, Bill Gates, and George W. Bush as being "ethnic" in any sense of the word.) English imports, including the English language and English naming practices, serve as the benchmark for the quintessential American identity. Many white Americans look as if they are of unmixed English ancestry, as in Utah, where 29.0% of the residents are of English descent.[12] English Americans are especially common in the American South. In 2002, I saw a young man in northwestern Alabama who looked just like Britain's Prince Harry. Someone with a name like John Hunt is seen by many

Americans as having the most "American" name possible, even though that is an excellent English name as well. For Americans, there is no conflict between an English background and an American identity.

Descendants of the earliest English immigrants to the United States often take considerable pride in their ancestry. Today many Americans celebrate their descent from 26 Englishmen who traveled across the Atlantic Ocean on the *Mayflower* and landed at Plymouth Rock in 1620.[13] At least 35 million people around the globe are descendants of one or more of the 26 Mayflower progenitors.[14] Many *Mayflower* descendants know little about their ancestral ties to these intrepid Englishmen. Others, however, are very aware of their heritage. They honor it in various ways, such as by participating in the General Society of Mayflower Descendants.[15] (A white woman once told me that she named her son Bradford because he is a descendant of William Bradford. I mentioned to her that he had an "ethnic" forename, of the English variety.) Although Americans frown upon any kind of elitism, some people seem to feel that Mayflower descent carries with it hints of class privilege and social snobbery.

Another large ancestry group that probably includes many Americans who are of English extraction is that of individuals who select "United States or American" as their ancestry. There were 20.6 million of such individuals in 2000, compared to 13 million in 1990. The "American Americans" typically have ancestors who came to the United States so long ago that they have no meaningful ties of any kind to the Old World, so they identify themselves simply as "American." Their forefathers, of course, came from elsewhere, but one can assume two things, in most cases — that the migration occurred many years ago and the migration probably occurred from the British Isles, the most culturally congenial part of the world for Americans throughout the centuries. The number of American Americans surged dramatically between 1990 and 2000, suggesting that white Americans, particularly members of such groups as German Americans, Irish Americans, and English Americans, increasingly identify solely as American. Unhyphenated Americans are now America's fourth-largest ancestry group.[16]

Many of the smaller white ethnic groups receive little attention in American culture. Greek Americans are one such group, even though there are celebrated Greek ethnic enclaves (Chicago's Greektown and Astoria, Queens) and Greek Americans such as Jennifer Aniston and Pete Sampras are well-known celebrities.[17] Conversely, the Arab ethnic groups are likely to be more prominent than, say, Welsh, Dutch, or Croatian

Americans, due to the significance of current events. Welsh, Dutch, and Croatian Americans blend in well, in part because they have completely assimilated, there are not many of them, few significant concentrations of them exist on these shores, there are few recent immigrants from their native lands to reinforce their "foreignness," and they differ little from expected conceptions of how Americans are supposed to look. Few European-American subgroups, after all, differ markedly from the white mainstream.

Portuguese Americans are a small but growing part of European America. They are descended from the Azoreans, continental Portuguese, and Madeira Islanders who arrived on these shores in two main periods.[18] During the first period of Portuguese immigration, from 1870 to 1921, the Portuguese immigrants "embarked in American whaling ships on their regular stops in the Azores (Western Isles, as they were often called) and Cape Verde Isles," notes Professor Frank F. Sousa.[19] During the second period of Portuguese immigration, from 1958 to the present, natural disasters in the Azores led the U.S. Government to accord special immigration status to Portuguese immigrants.[20] There were 1,321,155 Portuguese Americans in 2000 — this group includes a fair number of recent immigrants. To be sure, Portuguese "immigration slowed down considerably in part as a result of restrictive laws enacted during the Reagan Administration," writes Frank Sousa.[21] Still, 65,900 Portuguese immigrated to the United States from 1981 to 2001.[22] Rhode Island is the nation's most "Portuguese" state (8.7% of Rhode Islanders claim Portuguese ancestry).

Nearly one-half (46.2%) of Portuguese Americans live in just two states: California (330,974) and Massachusetts (279,722). Professor Frank F. Sousa has a unique perspective on the two centers of Portuguese America. A native of the Azores who immigrated to California's Central Valley at age nine, he serves as the director of the Center for Portuguese Studies and Culture and General Editor of the Portuguese in the Americas Book Series.[23] "The Portuguese Americans of California," writes Sousa, "tend to be more dedicated to farming and are often more affluent than their counterparts on the East Coast, who traditionally have been city dwellers and factory workers."[24] The ranks of Portuguese Americans include three Members of Congress from California: Democrat Dennis Cardoza, Republican Devin Nunes, and Republican Richard Pombo.[25] A number of cities in southeastern Massachusetts (Taunton, Fall River, and New Bedford) continue to be heavily Portuguese, as are several neighboring communities in Rhode Island.[26]

As with Portuguese Americans, Norwegian Americans continue to be one of America's least well-known European ethnic groups. The majority of them came to the United States between 1865 and 1915, mainly in search of greater economic opportunities.[27] Today there are 4,541,254 Norwegian Americans. More than 46% of them reside in just four states: Minnesota (850,742), Wisconsin (454,831), California (436,128), and Washington (367,508). To be sure, there are specific communities in which the majority — or plurality — of the residents are of Norwegian descent. Decorah, Iowa, is one town where Norwegian Americans constitute a significant percentage of the population. In the 2000 census, 34.4% of Decorah's residents reported that they had Norwegian ancestry. Decorah, a town of 8,172 in the northeastern part of the Hawkeye State, is home to Luther College and the Vesterheim Norwegian-American Museum. Tova Brandt, a curator at Vesterheim, points out that it is "very easy" to be Norwegian in Decorah because the cultural heritage of the area reinforces the Norwegian-American identity there.[28]

Outside of the rural Midwestern bastions of Norwegian Americana, few people of Norwegian extraction, at least those under age 50, maintain more than a passing interest in the cultural and linguistic traditions of their ancestors.[29] The Norwegian influence is perhaps most evident in the surnames, appearances, and religious affiliations of Midwesterners. North Dakota is the most "Norwegian" state in America, as 30.1% of North Dakotans trace all or part of their ancestry to Norway. And Minnesota continues to be the largest state where Norwegian Americans wield significant influence in political and cultural affairs. In the states with sizable Norwegian-American populations — Minnesota, the Dakotas, Wisconsin, Iowa, Washington, and elsewhere — lighthearted ethnic jokes and stereotypes about Norwegian Americans remain popular. But there is no well-defined Norwegian-American image in American popular culture, along the lines of, say, Italian Americans.

It is common for Americans to embrace specific cultural products that draw upon particular ethnic traditions. The Cajun-cooking craze that took off in the 1980s is one such example; until recently, the Cajuns of southern Louisiana had been one of the most insular and least well-known ethnic groups in America. But in the last two decades, celebrity chefs like Paul Prudhomme have helped to popularize the cuisine of southern Louisiana throughout the United States.[30] At the same time, the Scottish-surnamed Garrison Keillor has become an American icon with *A Prairie Home Companion,* his show on Minnesota Public Radio. Keillor's radio show and books focus on the fictional town of Lake

Wobegon, a rural community of German Catholics and Norwegian Lutherans in his native Minnesota.[31] Sometimes, of course, the portrayal of a specific ethnic group in popular culture — *The Sopranos, The Beverly Hillbillies* — deliberately distorts real-life conditions for comedic or dramatic effect.

Irish Americans continue to play an important role in American culture. Many Americans proudly claim to be Irish and celebrate their identities as Irish Americans. Saint Patrick's Day is an important American holiday, and the annual parades in such cities as Chicago and New York are important political and cultural events. Irish Americans often patronize the Irish pubs and Irish import shops that flourish in much of America. Likewise, an Irish American might use the shamrock and green coloration to advertise his Irishness and car dealership or political candidacy at the same time. An Irish American may even allude to his ancestry — and the supposed Irish propensity to drink alcohol — as a means of justifying his habit of imbibing too much of "the drink." And as Stanley Lieberson points out, "Irish-American parents are far more likely to give their children names with an Irish connection than other parents."[32] As a rule, Irish Americans experience few conflicts with mainstream American culture when they celebrate their ethnicity.

Many American men (and women) focus on parts of their ethnic heritage — e.g., eating certain foods and attending ethnic festivals — but they do so without imperiling their sometimes hard-won acceptance by mainstream America. The typical white male American, after all, is native-born. Yet we Americans often like to preserve some semblance of a connection to the Old World, even if it is only in a rhetorical sense. So an American guy whose ancestors left Slovakia in 1900 might refer to himself as "Slovakian." Some Americans, moreover, participate in fraternal organizations such as the Sons of Norway and Sons of Italy. Still, very few native-born Americans feel any significant conflicts between their American identity and their ethnic heritage.[33]

Even though they make up a relatively small percentage of the overall white population, there are 4,842,000 foreign-born European Americans, many of whom came here in the last two decades.[34] All told, we received 2,324,900 immigrants from Europe between 1981 and 2001, with Poland and the United Kingdom being the largest sending countries. During this period, 288,900 Poles immigrated to the United States. The United Kingdom sent 309,700 immigrants to America from 1981 to 2001; some of these British newcomers to our shores may have been people of color. With the breakup of the Soviet Union, immigrants from the post-Soviet states — particularly Ukraine (178,100 immigrants from 1992 to 2001) and Russia (165,500 immigrants from 1992 to 2001) — have been arriving in the United States in large numbers.[35] In various parts of America, there are smaller white immigrant groups as well, such as Bosnians and Kosovars, who came here as refugees from the war-torn Balkans.

While people of Middle Eastern ancestry account for a small percentage of the white population as a whole, they make up a disproportionate number of the white immigrants to the United States. Iranians constitute the largest Middle Eastern immigrant group — nearly 300,000 of them came to the United States between 1981 and 2001. Southern California and metropolitan Washington are the centers of Iranian America. Lebanon, meanwhile, sent more people to the United States (93,400) during the period from 1981 to 2001 than Italy (61,100). Likewise, Iraq dispatched more of its people (70,400) to America than France (58,700) did, and more Jordanians (80,800) than Greeks (44,900) immigrated here during that period.[36] Although there are significant ethnic enclaves of recent Arab and Middle Eastern immigrants, many of them live inconspicuously throughout America; they often work as professionals and small businesspeople.

Age is a big factor in determining how quickly immigrants will adapt to the rhythms of American life. A white male immigrant who came to the United States at age five is going to have a completely different mindset (and accent) than one who arrives here at age 25, or especially at age 50 or age 55. The minute most males from Europe, the Middle East, and North Africa enter the United States, they immediately become "white males"; never mind that they may have little proficiency with the English language, or little wealth from their native lands. The life chances of white male immigrants, of course, are different if the newcomers arrive here as children, rather than as adults. Those who come to the United States as grown men may have to take jobs beneath their station in the Old World. These fellows will always speak with an accent, and probably never completely disengage from events in their original country.

Immigrants learn that America has more progressive standards with regard to race and gender than is the case in many countries. Nor does one's ethnicity or religion necessarily determine his choices and alignments in social and political matters here. A young white man of immigrant parentage who grows up in America — and sees himself as an American — will be exposed to minority youths and multicultural teachings in the public schools. Thus he is probably more likely to accept ethnic and cultural differences (or at least he will have more nuanced views of such matters) than his older compatriots. It can also be difficult for an immigrant from a patriarchal society to accept the equality between the sexes in the United States. As a consequence, some white male immigrants experience culture shock when they first come to America.

Immigrants may alter or modify their attire, customs, gestures, tonal inflections, and other characteristics in order to assimilate into American society. The adult immigrants maintain ties to their homelands through foreign-language media, the camaraderie of ethnic shops, clubs, churches, and social events, and through transatlantic phone calls and flights to the Old World. But the assimilation process kicks in almost immediately, for children and adults alike. Youths enroll in the American public schools where their fertile minds pick up the English language the way a sponge soaks up water. Some adults live in an ethnic enclave and find employment serving their ethnic community, or work for a coethnic who speaks their native tongue, so they never have to learn much English. Others quickly realize that English-language proficiency enables them to earn bigger paychecks, so they learn to speak passable English within a year or two.

Except for certain insular communities, like the Amish and the Old Believers, whose members willingly choose to isolate themselves from mainstream American society in order to preserve their culture, most immigrants and their descendants assimilate completely into American society within a couple of generations. The young people marry exogamously, and they often do not learn to speak their ancestral language. They select generic American forenames, rarely read the ethnic newspapers, and are less faithful in following the venerable cultural traditions of their parents and grandparents. Within 70 or 80 years, all that is often left of their original ethnic heritage is a surname and their grandparents' stories of life in the Old World. The acceptance of white male immigrants by the native-born majority depends, of course, on how well they do economically and the extent to which they speak with an accent and retain outward manifestations of foreignness.

Perhaps the subtlest indicator that an immigrant or man of immigrant stock is becoming fully American is that of his expectations. Most adult immigrants who come to the United States without many marketable skills or material possessions realize they themselves will probably never become rich or famous. Yet they know that their children, who will grow up speaking and understanding English as well as any other native-born Americans, may enjoy multitudinous opportunities. These second-generation Americans have good chances to obtain baccalaureate and advanced degrees, pursue intellectually stimulating and financially rewarding careers, and live in stable, prosperous communities with decent schools, excellent amenities, and good weather. No other country in the history of the world has afforded more opportunities to so many different people from so many different backgrounds. As a result, such factors as skin color and religious affiliation matter less to Americans than to people in most multiethnic, multiracial nations in the world.

LIVING IN AMERICA

On Friday, March 1, 2002, Dr. Erlend D. Peterson, the Associate International Vice President at Brigham Young University, received an urgent telephone call from the Ukrainian Embassy in Washington, D.C. The caller was Ann Santini, Director of International and Government Affairs for The Church of Jesus Christ of Latter-day Saints (LDS). Santini was with the Ukrainian Ambassador to the United States, Kostyantyn Gryshchenko. The ambassador requested Santini's help on short notice: Lyudmyla Kuchma, the First Lady of Ukraine, was coming to Utah on the following Tuesday to attend the Paralympic games. So Santini asked Peterson to make all the arrangements for Mrs. Kuchma's visit; he happily acceded to her request. By Monday, March 4, 2002, Peterson had planned an extensive itinerary for the first two days of Mrs. Kuchma's five-day visit to Utah. During her stay in the Beehive State, Mrs. Kuchma particularly enjoyed seeing BYU's International Folk Dance Ensemble perform "Hopak," the Ukrainian folk dance. After the dance performance, the First Lady went to a reception attended by BYU's Ukrainian students and American students who spoke Ukrainian and/or Russian as a result of their LDS missions in Ukraine.[37] All in all, Mrs. Kuchma enjoyed her experiences in Utah; Erlend Peterson's excellent planning and organizational skills helped make her trip a successful one.

Peterson typifies the leadership of The Church of Jesus Christ of Latter-day Saints, a multiethnic, multinational church with nearly 12 million members, in that he has a global worldview and reputation.[38] Erlend Dean Peterson was born on November 24, 1940, in St. George, Utah. This genial and gracious man traces his ancestry mainly to England; he also is of Welsh, Danish, and Norwegian descent. Peterson, or "Pete" to his many friends, grew up in an international household. His father,

Dean Andrew Peterson, loved Norway. The elder Peterson served as an LDS missionary in Norway from 1933 to 1936, and his experiences there profoundly affected him. Erlend Peterson and his sisters heard their father rhapsodize about Norway every day. They learned Norwegian folk songs and customs, and blessed their meals using a traditional Norwegian prayer. Young Erlend — his parents named him after a protagonist in the Nobel Prize–winning Norwegian author Sigrid Undset's trilogy, *Kristin Lavransdatter* — went to Norway for the first time in 1954, after having lived in Iran for three years. He returned to Norway in 1963 and 1964 for a stint as an LDS missionary. By his mid-twenties, Peterson was well prepared for a career that would include many international activities.

Since he received his bachelor's degree in Business Management from Brigham Young University in 1967, Erlend Peterson has served in positions of ever-increasing influence and authority at BYU, the predominantly Mormon institution of higher education in Provo, Utah. He and his wife, Colleen, live in nearby Orem. They have six children (five daughters and one son). Peterson has spent most of his career working in Admissions and Records at BYU, including 11 years as the Dean of Admissions and Records. The Utah native began to work on global outreach at BYU in 1973, when he assumed responsibility for the university's international admissions and scholarship programs. He is perhaps best known on campus for initiating the BYU Ambassadorial Lecture Series; this program brings as many as ten foreign ambassadors to Provo each year.[39] Peterson, who speaks fluent Norwegian and holds a doctorate in Higher Education Administration, was appointed Associate International Vice President at BYU in 2001. In this capacity, he is responsible for international issues on BYU's campus, and he hosts — and plans the schedules of — the VIP guests (noted cultural figures, high-ranking diplomats, current and former heads of state, and other dignitaries) who visit BYU. This internationalist regularly travels to Washington, Asia, Europe, and the Middle East; he meets with educators, administrators, diplomats, government officials, and heads of state.

Through his work, Peterson contributes to cross-cultural understanding and develops relationships between Americans and people in other countries. He is particularly familiar with Norway, a place where he has many personal and professional connections.[40] From 1988 to 1990 the Petersons lived in Oslo while Dr. Peterson served as president of the Norway Oslo LDS Mission.[41] Erlend Peterson is the Utah representative for Nordmanns-Forbundet (The Norse Federation), an organization for friends of Norway who reside outside of Norge, and he often invites

Norwegian dignitaries and students to come to BYU.[42] Consequently, the Secretary-General of Nordmanns-Forbundet nominated him for a Norwegian knighthood (Knight First Class, Royal Norwegian Order of Merit), an honor that he received in 1997. Moreover, "Sir Pete," as his friends now affectionately refer to him, received the distinction of being named a Pioneer of Progress for 2001 (only five Utahans are honored in this way each year).[43] These accolades recognize Peterson's integral role in promoting peace, tolerance, and good will in our interconnected, globalized world, due to his open-minded attitude, international orientation, and extensive interactions with prominent figures in many nations.

Most middle-aged and elderly white American men have experienced tremendous change during their lives: These changes include the emergence of the United States as the world's sole superpower and shifting power dynamics with regard to race and gender on the home front. During World War II and its aftermath, the United States became the most powerful nation on Earth. The men and women who survived the Great Depression and fought for America during World War II then helped America enjoy a period of unprecedented material prosperity in the postwar years. In the post–World War II era, the United States and the Soviet Union were the world's two superpowers. At the same time, we, as a society, began to confront the legacy of unequal treatment that had limited the rights, recognition, and opportunities afforded to women and people of color, particularly African Americans, in the world's most powerful democracy. The United States, of course, emerged as the world's only superpower after the dissolution of the Soviet Union in the early 1990s, at a time when pluralism and multiculturalism were more important to Americans than ever before.

White men — particularly white, able-bodied men — dominated the affairs of the nation at almost every level until about 1965. For most of American history, there was relatively little discussion among the elites that this situation should change. However, a consensus regarding the necessity of creating more opportunities for women and minorities developed in elite society during the 1960s and 1970s in response to the various forms of activism by blacks, women, and others. These ideas took shape in the form of various multicultural initiatives, including affirmative action, during the 1970s and 1980s. A sizable number of white male policymakers concluded that the exclusion of women and minorities from the power structure was not only morally reprehensible, but bad in a pragmatic sense as well. Consequently, white men helped design, promote, and implement diversity initiatives in politics, business, academia, and elsewhere. The leaders of the country at the time largely accepted the necessity of such programs.

During the period from 1945 to about 1970, the United States enjoyed unparalleled affluence, and white men and their families benefited from the lion's share of the prosperity. The economic conditions were such that a white man with a decent blue-collar or white-collar job could support his family at the middle-class level, and his wife did not have to work outside the home. Since the 1970s, changes in the U.S. economy have made it more difficult for white men to enjoy unparalleled access to the types of middle-management positions and manufacturing jobs that guaranteed so many white men middle-class lifestyles in the 1950s, 1960s, and 1970s. Likewise, aggressive affirmative-action programs began to open up positions in universities, professional schools, and the employment market to women and minorities. Virtually no one, of course, says a group (white men) that makes up less than one-half of the workforce should have a near-monopoly on most of the high-paying and prestigious positions. Nonetheless, some white males came to perceive that the drive for a level playing field disadvantaged them, due to the increased competition they faced in the workplace and in higher education.

Such factors as age, occupation, and geography affect the extent to which a white male is exposed to diversity issues and multicultural initiatives. Age is an especially important factor in this regard. Young white males are more affected by multiculturalism than any other group of white males. Women, for instance, outnumber them in the undergraduate programs at many colleges and universities. Occupation matters, too, in determining one's level of exposure to issues stemming from America's ethnic and racial diversity. White male academics, firefighters, police officers, public employees, and corporate figures in heterogeneous urban areas have significant exposure to diversity issues and multicultural initiatives. And we must consider the importance of geography in the context of this topic. As a rule, multiculturalism is less significant in the whitest parts of America, even though affirmative action based on gender may be the rule there. White men, for instance, rarely think about diversity issues and multicultural initiatives if they live in Idaho, Montana, or Wyoming. However, such issues may be important to them if they live in Hawaii, Delaware, or New Mexico, states with considerable racial and ethnic heterogeneity.

Socioeconomic status is perhaps the most significant factor that affects the extent to which the white male will feel discombobulated by multiculturalism. This is the case because competition for employment, admission to educational institutions, and other zero-sum situations can often devolve into ethnically charged contests. Working class white males probably feel most threatened by an influx of immigrants into the labor market. Immigrants often compete with working class Americans for good wages, and they sometimes lower the wage scales in a given sector of the economy. The controversies over affirmative action and multi-culturalism often affect middle-class and upper-middle-class white males, particularly in the academy, Corporate America, and the public sector. Wealthy white males, of course, encounter few limitations of any kind with regard to such matters.

Young white males are very accustomed to seeing females and minorities in positions of power. They encounter people of color in the media, as authority figures, and as playmates and friends. This phenomenon began with the Baby Boom generation, those white males (and others) born between 1946 and 1964. White males vary, of course, in terms of whether they accept the increased role of women and minorities in business, education, the media, and other venues; such variables as education, income, and region affect their attitudes on these issues. They are more likely than men two generations ago to accept a female boss, to take an active role in childrearing, and to be supportive of women working outside the home. Similarly, they strongly support equal rights for all Americans, regardless of their race, color, or national origin. Many white males, however, question the necessity of affirmative action as a means of promoting equal rights for people of color; they feel that strict enforcement of antidiscrimination laws is sufficient to protect minority interests.

Due to the increasing significance of multiculturalism in our lives, white males are learning about race and gender at younger and younger ages. White males can no longer go throughout life without thinking of themselves as white males. White males learn about the importance of race and gender from the media, in the schools, and in the workplace. Not realizing one's white maleness until, perhaps, age 12 or so, is a luxury afforded to few other groups in American society. (I myself do not remember the first time I realized that I was a white male, or, for that matter, what it meant to be one.) Many young white males puzzle over the fact that some people may see them as victimizers, oppressors, and patriarchs, when they themselves do not hold any questionable beliefs about race or gender or, for that matter, exhibit any reprehensible behaviors.[44]

As a rule, the cultural geography of white maleness varies by race, socioeconomic class, and other factors. There are at least six different types of situations for white males — in terms of cultural geography:

- those in which they make up an absolute or nearly total majority of the people in a given context;

- those in which white males account for a simple majority;

- those in which they are part of a predominantly white group;

- those in which white males are part of a simple white majority;

- those in which they are part of a white plurality;

- those in which whites constitute a minority, especially in an area or context that is dominated by a specific group of nonwhites.

There are few geographical areas in the United States where white males constitute a majority of the residents. For one, white females outnumber them in almost every community. And there are few areas where whites predominate — and where a massive gender imbalance tilts to males. Nonetheless, white males are used to being part of the American majority, racially and otherwise. To some extent, white males can largely dominate a venue, category, or geographical area even if their numerical presence is quite small, at least in percentage terms. They may enjoy majority status in a direct sense, as in the case of a corporate board where white males account for two-thirds of its membership. Moreover, they may enjoy majority status in an indirect sense, as in the case of white males who are part of the white majority in such states as Oregon and Wisconsin. White males also can create their own illusion of majority status by congregating in spaces — certain bars, private clubs, sporting events, gatherings in someone's living room — where they will account for nearly all of the people there.

White males and their white female counterparts constitute a majority in every U.S. region. Some regions are whiter than others: the West (58.4% white) and the South (65.8% white) are more racially heterogeneous than the Northeast (73.4% white) and the Midwest (81.4% white). The United States, by the way, is 69.1% white.[45] California, an Anglo-plurality behemoth, accounts for more than one-half of the West's population, so it is not surprising that the percentage of Anglos is lowest in that region. Racial experiences differ by region for white males, due to the differing demographics. A white Northeasterner will, in all likelihood, know more about Puerto Rican culture than his counterpart in the

South — outside of Florida. Moreover, these regional categories obscure the ethnic dynamics in specific parts of each region. The Southwest, for example, has ethnic and racial dynamics very different from those in the Deep South.[46] Thus white males who live in the same region may have qualitatively different experiences with regard to racial matters.

Whites constitute a majority of the population in 47 of the 50 U.S. states. Hawaii, of course, is a white-minority state, while California and New Mexico are Anglo-plurality states. And the District of Columbia has a black majority. Some white-majority states (e.g., Maine, Vermont, and New Hampshire) are predominantly white, while others — Texas, Florida, and New Jersey — are quite heterogeneous. But the demographics within white-majority states can differ dramatically. Many white South Dakotans interact with Native Americans on a day-to-day basis, but few of them regularly encounter large numbers of African Americans. Likewise, people in eastern Rhode Island often come into contact with Italian Americans and Portuguese Americans, two groups that are not especially numerous in eastern Kentucky. Generally the areas in which white males are the strongest numerically are those places where there is little in-migration by domestic migrants or international immigrants.

Pennsylvania is one such place. Few domestic migrants go to Pennsylvania, and the Keystone State has a low percentage of foreign-born residents (4.1%). Whites account for 84.1% of Pennsylvania's 12,281,054 residents; the state is 9.8% black, 3.2% Latino, and 1.8% Asian. Many Pennsylvanians have German (25.4%), Irish (16.1%), Italian (11.6%), English (7.9%), and Polish (6.7%) forebears. Our sixth most-populous state encompasses a significant amount of ethnic, cultural, and racial heterogeneity. Blacks narrowly outnumber whites in Philadelphia, while whites account for 85.6% of the Pennsylvanians who live in and around Philadelphia, in west-suburban Delaware County and in Chester, Montgomery, and Buck counties north and east of the city. As with Philadelphia, Pittsburgh has a sizable African-American population (the city is 27.0% black and 66.9% white); the Pittsburgh metro area is mainly white. And the state's capital, Harrisburg, has a black-majority population. Apart from Pittsburgh, Harrisburg, and Philadelphia, much of Pennsylvania is virtually all white and heavily rural, particularly the Appalachian portions of the state.

In Pennsylvania and elsewhere, white males continue to account for a fair number of the residents of urban America, although the foreign-born members of the group are disproportionately represented in such neighborhoods. Today many of the white males who live in our nation's largest, most ethnically diverse cities fall into one of four categories: (1) young single men; (2) affluent movers and shakers; (3) recent immigrants and their progeny; and (4) older people who lack the resources or desire to move elsewhere. This is particularly true of such cities as Chicago and New York. But this is not the case in a white-majority city like Phoenix. One can find plenty of white males, many of them foreign-born individuals who speak English with a slight accent, in such enclaves as the Westwood section of Los Angeles and the Brighton Beach neighborhood of Brooklyn. As a result of white flight, relatively few native-born white males attend the public schools in many of our large cities.

White males continue to make up a large percentage of the residents of suburban America. Typically, many Americans regard the suburbs as cleaner, safer, and more stable than the central cities. Whites often commute from the suburbs into the central cities to go to work. The suburbs, though, increasingly have self-sustaining cultural attractions and economic opportunities that rarely require people to enter the central cities. Members of certain ethnic groups cluster in specific suburbs. Glendale, California, for instance, is well known for its sizable Armenian-American community. Broward County, Florida, includes many Jewish Americans. Deer Park, New York, a city on Long Island, has a large number of Italian Americans. Many suburbs are racially heterogeneous, but some upper-end suburbs continue to be predominantly white. To be sure, many whites live in communities and metropolitan areas that are characterized by significant residential segregation.

Whites loom large in the demographics of rural America. Substantial ethnic, religious, and cultural differences separate rural whites from each other. For starters, the ethnic demographics and religious composition of rural communities differ by the place. In the American South, rural whites are very likely to trace their ancestry to the British Isles and/or Germany and to worship in a Protestant church. In the Northeast, particularly those areas settled by French Canadians, British ancestry and German ancestry are less common than in the South, and the Catholic Church reigns supreme. Likewise, a rural town or county may be almost completely white, like Derby, Vermont, where one can listen to French-language radio from neighboring Quebec, or majority black, like Chadbourn, North Carolina, an economically depressed community near the South Carolina state line. In rural America, people may have a different mindset about crime and security than their urban counterparts, because they often do not have "big-city" problems there, although methamphetamines and prescription-drug abuse are eroding this sense of security in sections of rural America.

Until the twentieth century, instances of ethnic displacement in American neighborhoods occurred mainly among different groups of white people. The related factors of migration and displacement often involved ethno-religious considerations as well as socioeconomic dimensions. During the nineteenth century, the ethnic composition of certain neighborhoods in New York City changed dramatically in response to the new waves of immigrants. When people moved to different neighborhoods, part of their reason for relocating undoubtedly had to do with their reluctance to be around people whom they considered to be ethnically and culturally alien. At the same time, many of them simply wanted to move to less-crowded, more affluent neighborhoods elsewhere. Similar issues also affected residential living patterns in some sections of rural America. In any event, the vastness of America — and the fact that nativists frequently moved away from immigrants instead of fighting with them — has helped to maintain social peace over the years.

The second stage of white flight began to occur in large part after World War II, in response to the mass migration of black Southerners to the large urban areas of the Northeast, Midwest, and West. Cities such as Chicago, Detroit, Milwaukee, and Los Angeles saw their black populations swell in number. White racial fears in urban America began to intensify during the 1960s, when African Americans started to make aggressive claims for power, recognition, and resources in the nation's most populous cities. At the same time, the quality of life in urban America began to decline in response to numerous factors, including the deterioration of the manufacturing economy. By the 1960s white people were fleeing the central cities of America in response to the urban ills that became common during that period. The departing whites usually went to the suburbs, where the schools were better, the crime rates were lower, and the cost of living was often less expensive than in the cities. Race, of course, played a role in these migration patterns.

There is a regional component to migration patterns as well. Georgia, Florida, North Carolina, Arizona, Texas, Colorado, Nevada, and Tennessee all gained more than 400,000 native-born residents during the 1990s. Domestic migrants were particularly attracted to the Atlanta (+530,137), Las Vegas (+392,606), Phoenix (+363,225), and Denver (+223,475) metropolitan areas.[47] As the demographer William H. Frey points out, native-born domestic migrants go to the aforementioned places "because of their growing economies, relatively low cost of living, and their climatic or environmental amenities."[48] Thus they eschew living in such states as Ohio, Michigan, Illinois, California, Connecticut,

New York, and New Jersey.[49] In the 1990s, several metropolitan areas lost large numbers of native-born domestic migrants, including Los Angeles (-888,603), New York (-279,521), San Francisco (-266,844), San Diego (-128,762), and Miami (-114,259).[50]

Foreign-born immigrants still cluster in six states (California, Texas, New York, Florida, Illinois, and New Jersey), but increasingly they are dispersing throughout the country. During the 1990s, 65% of foreign-born immigrants went to California, Texas, New York, Florida, Illinois, and New Jersey, compared to 71% of their counterparts who arrived before 1990 (William H. Frey describes members of the latter group as "secondary foreign-born migrants"). Some secondary foreign-born migrants have left California, Texas, New York, Florida, Illinois, and New Jersey for the fast-growing Sunbelt states, namely Nevada, Arizona, Georgia, and North Carolina. The booming job market attracts them to the Las Vegas, Phoenix, and Atlanta metropolitan areas. As a result of these migration patterns, new immigrants contribute more and more to the population growth of California, New York, New Jersey, and Illinois — states that registered losses of native-born domestic migrants and secondary foreign-born migrants in the 1990s.[51]

At this point, it seems very likely that regional migration will continue to transform the demographics of many American communities. William H. Frey writes:

> The new high immigration zones will be distinct and constitute the twenty-first century version of America's melting pots — ensconced largely in California, Texas, and the southwest; southern Florida; the upper eastern seaboard; and Chicago. The cultural and demographic tapestry evolving in this America will differ sharply from the older, more middle-class, and whiter — indeed, more suburban — America that exists elsewhere.[52]

It is uncertain at this point how these living patterns will affect race relations in Multicultural America 20 or 30 years from now.[53]

WORDS MATTER

"Yo. Scuse me, sir. Yo!" shouts Walter Wade Jr. when he sees Trey Howard enter Metronome, a hip Manhattan nightspot, with three white friends, in John Singleton's *Shaft*. Wade, a rich young WASP played with murderous aplomb by Christian Bale, takes it upon himself to make Howard feel unwelcome in the predominantly white venue. Wade presumes that the young, well-dressed African-American man does not belong at Metronome, and he speaks to him in an exaggerated urban vernacular. "They don't serve no malt liquor here," the postmodern bigot informs Howard. "No malt liquor. All right? No, aiight. Aiiight?" Howard, to his credit, does his best to ignore Wade. A few seconds later, however, the young white man continues with his vituperative monologue: "No forties, no, uh, chronic, no, uh, indo. Aiight? Hey, dawg. Is you deaf? Holler back." Finally, the slightly inebriated Wade says, "You got that, Tupac," a reference to the slain rap star, and he flashes him a hip-hop hand sign. By this point, Howard has had enough. He takes a white cloth napkin, cuts two slits for eyes, and drops the Klan hood over Wade's head.[54]

In doing so, Howard humiliates Wade — the nightclub's patrons laugh at this tall, slim man with a light complexion, brown hair, and an omnipresent smirk. When Howard leaves the club for a moment to smoke a cigarette and calm his nerves, Wade rushes outside and grabs the first available weapon, a silver pole from the street, and bludgeons him with it. The only witness to this brutal assault is a young waitress, Diane Palmieri. Wade threatens her so that she will not tell the police what he did to Howard. Later that evening Howard dies outside Metronome, after Detective John Shaft, played with streetwise dignity by Samuel L. Jackson, arrives to investigate the crime. Wade sees Howard convulsing on the stretcher, and he says to Shaft, "Homeboy's got rhythm, huh." This remark elicits a swift reaction from Shaft, who punches Wade in the nose (and then, a moment later, does so again for emphasis). The unrepentant Wade is soon released on $200,000 bail — his father is a supremely wealthy real estate developer. Then Wade departs for Switzerland. Shaft, meanwhile, makes it his mission to bring Wade to justice.[55] This part of the film takes place in 1998.

Two years later, in 2000, Wade returns to the United States. Acting on a tip from a source, Shaft learns that Wade is flying into the Westchester County Airport, and he arrests him on the limousine ride into Manhattan. The police take Wade to a holding cell in the 15th Precinct. Peoples Hernandez, a Dominican-American drug lord played brilliantly by Jeffrey Wright, is the only other prisoner there. (Hernandez had been apprehended earlier that day for threatening Detective Shaft.) Then the police take both men to Central Processing in downtown Manhattan, where Hernandez watches with interest as Wade successfully fights a young black man who wants his designer shoes. Shortly thereafter, Hernandez introduces himself to Wade, and the two men have a brief conversation.

Later, Wade is released on bail, this time for $1 million. He has to surrender his passport, though. Shaft quits the New York Police Department in anger; he vows to find the only witness — Diane Palmieri — who can place Wade at the crime scene. After doing some sleuthing, Shaft locates Palmieri and persuades her to cooperate with the prosecution.

In the meantime Wade decides to pawn the jewels his late mother bequeathed to him to pay for a hit on Palmieri. To this end, he goes to Peoples Hernandez's lavish apartment in the Washington Heights section of Manhattan. Hernandez wants Wade to deal drugs for him in upper crust Manhattan. Wade rebuffs the job offer, and says, "I mean, if it is really important to you, you can tell everybody you got a rich white boy on a rope. I really don't care."[56] Hernandez then agrees to eliminate Palmieri in exchange for $40,000; he admires Wade's wealth, infamy, and life of privilege.[57] After Hernandez's attempts to murder Palmieri prove to be unsuccessful, Wade and the Dominican-American drug dealer come to blows with each other. Hernandez eventually dies at the hands of Detective Shaft. And Trey Howard's mother shoots and kills Wade outside the courthouse on the day his trial for murder is about to begin. This event concludes the fictional saga of Walter Wade Jr., a story that unfolded because of the arrogant racist's willingness to make invidious distinctions between whites and blacks.

Indeed, American English includes many slurs and epithets, a number of which refer to white males. Every time an American ethnic group has arrived in the United States, various colloquial terms and neologisms have entered the lexicon. There are generic terms that refer to ethnic or racial groups that encompass certain types of white males: *micks* (the Irish), *wops* (Italians), and *Polacks* (Poles). English-speaking anti-Semites are fond of the epithet *Jew-boy* when referring to Jewish males. (Some Jews, to be sure, use the Yiddish term *shegetz* as a disparaging reference to non-Jewish males.)[58] Americans may use epithets to describe white males that encompass whites in general: *redneck, cracker,* and *hillbilly.* Each of these slurs has a slightly different meaning, but the racist and classist phrase *white trash* is probably used most often to refer to white males and white females. Another disparaging slang term, *Mister Charlie,* which traditionally referred to "a white man" or "white men collectively," seems to have fallen into disuse.[59]

Americans use a number of slurs and epithets to describe white Southerners; with few exceptions, these references are commonly understood throughout the United States. By definition, the term *redneck* traditionally has been used as a reference to "an uneducated white farm laborer, [especially] from the South" and "a bigot or reactionary, [especially] from the rural working class."[60] Likewise, the word *cracker* is a "disparaging and offensive" reference to "a poor white person living in some rural parts of the southeastern U.S."[61] *Hillbilly* tends to be applied to people "from a backwoods or other remote area, [especially] from the mountains of the southern U.S."[62] Finally, the vulgarity *peckerwood* is a term for poor whites, particularly white males, in the American South.[63] All of these terms, with the possible exception of *peckerwood,* are used regularly by people inside and outside the South. Conversely, "Bubba" continues to be a common men's nickname that is often adopted by white men and some African Americans (remember Forrest Gump's friend), particularly in the South. Few people attach any derogatory connotations to the name "Bubba," which can also be used as a synonym for white, working class Southern men, particularly those from rural areas.

The "white" slurs and epithets that remain popular, such as *redneck* and *hillbilly,* tend to be those that refer to socioeconomic class and a generic white identity. At one time, whites of different European ethnic origins regularly used ethnic slurs such as *limey* and *dago* with abandon. However, the popularity of such terms has declined in conjunction with the assimilation of the various European-American ethnic groups. Neither whites nor people of color use epithets like *kraut* or *bohunk* anymore, because there are few unassimilated "German" or "Czech" and "Hungarian" people left in the United States. As Arabs become an ever greater part of the U.S. population, derogatory terms to describe them are receiving greater usage — *raghead, sand nigger, camel jockey,* and the like. Moreover, newer American immigrant groups, such as Russians and Iranians, coin descriptive terms and phrases that express interethnic differences, but these have yet to penetrate the mass consciousness.

White boy is one phrase that receives considerable usage in contemporary America. During the last 20 years, it has become common for people of color to use the phrase *white boy* to refer to men who are well past boyhood. *White boy* is not quite a slur or an epithet, although it is mildly derisive and, to be sure, controversial among white males.[64] This perverse inversion of the power dynamics, of describing white men as *white boys,* would be denounced, quite properly, as racist if it were turned upon members of a minority group. (In the pre–civil rights era South, a white man would often refer to a black man as "boy" and the African American had to address him as "Mister," "Sir," or by using some other honorific.) Today white women and people of color may use the term *white boy* to describe their white male competitors in the workplace, and to characterize their isolation from the locus of power. And it is hip for self-aware white guys to refer to themselves (or embrace references to themselves) as *white boys*; they often do so in a tongue-in-cheek fashion.[65]

Decades ago, Americans discussed white males and white maleness in less explicit terms than they do today. Feminists spoke about *men* when they really meant *white men*. Likewise, when minorities described the power wielded by *whites*, they usually meant *white men*. White guys made overt references to themselves and their fellows as *white men* when they came into contact and conflict with blacks, American Indians, and other people of color. During the era of colonialism, when people of color referred to whites, they tended to call them *white men,* or use the singular reference — *the white man*. Native Americans also spoke of the "Great Father" or "Great White Father" in Washington, a description that neatly encapsulated the race of the U.S. president and the paternalism that underlay the U.S.-Indian relationship at the time. Today the term "the white man" has almost entirely disappeared from modern usage.

As Americans become ever more conscious of race and gender, it is unsurprising that explicit terms — *white men, white males* — for Caucasian guys are used with increasing frequency. There have been shifting references over the years to *the white man* and *white men*. And there are now specific references to *white men* and *white males*. The latter phrase was not used much before the 1970s and 1980s. In the United States, "the man" was understood by African Americans to refer to the white male–dominated power structure. (Whites use "the man" as a phrase that signals their nonconformism and disdain for a bourgeois lifestyle.) Some Latinos, meanwhile, refer to white men using the term *güero*, a word that literally means "blond man." When a Latino uses the term *güero* in relation to a white man, he often does so in a mildly disparaging fashion. White males, meanwhile, are still largely unaccustomed to thinking about themselves in terms of their race and gender.

Depending on the circumstances, the mention of such phrases as "white man," "white guys," and "white males" can make people reluctant to talk about race-and-gender issues. Those phrases clearly elicit different meanings from different people. The strategic consultant Harris Sussman says, " 'White male' is what I call the newest swear word in America."[66] To be sure, the phrase *white male* is sometimes used almost as an imprecation, with considerable baggage and hints of illegitimacy. Some phrases — "old boy," "good old boy," "good ol' boy," "good ole boy" — regularly appear in American conversations to denote white men who exclude women and people of color from their hiring and social networks.[67] The mere mention of white males and white maleness conjures up visions of affirmative action, controversies over diversity initiatives, and so many other explosive topics. Consequently, many whites simply avoid the topics of whiteness and white maleness whenever possible, just as they would be reluctant to engage in a discussion of politics and religion with strangers.

White males are often considered as members of a discrete group, distinct from white females, in analyses of racial and gender privilege in our society. However, people of color regularly look at whites as a singular entity. Many scholars, commentators, and ethnic advocates see race, rather than the combination of race and gender, as the most significant social category. White women and people of color inside white male–dominated institutions are more likely to focus on white males than whites, and to describe them as such. Educated people, those with the greatest exposure to theories of group disadvantage, are most likely to differentiate between white males and whites as a group. Multiculturalists periodically use the generic term "white male" — or a variant like "white men" — as a rhetorical call to arms to mobilize their imagined coalitions of white females and people of color. However, whiteness remains a more powerful unifying force than the uncertain coalition politics of multiculturalism, so these efforts usually prove to be successful only in elite circles.

Americans now use the adjectival phrase "white male" more so than in the past: The notions of race unconsciousness and gender unconsciousness for whites and males, respectively, have become increasingly anachronistic. In other words, it is no longer uncommon to make white maleness explicit as a variable to be studied, or to mention it in a book title, course title, or academic treatment. At least four recent novels highlight this trend: Gerald W. Haslam's *Straight White Male* (2000), Brock Clarke's *The Ordinary White Boy* (2001), Barbara D'Amato's *White Male Infant* (2002), and Ruaridh Nicoll's *White Male Heart* (2003).[68] Likewise, the satirist Michael Moore used the phrase in the title of his best-selling book, *Stupid White Men . . . and Other Sorry Excuses for the State of the Nation!*[69] Mark D. Naison's memoir, *White Boy,* is yet another recent example of this phenomenon.[70] Some day, perhaps, the term for men of white complexion and male gender might even become a single word — as in *whitemale* or *whitemales,* spellings used by Houston Baker.[71]

Eliminating sexism in the idiom is one of the hallmarks of feminism and multiculturalism. Language in the West has traditionally favored males. Until about two decades ago, we used the word "man" as a noun and a verb to signify males and females. In the past, *he, him,* and *his* often served as the common-sex pronouns in American English.[72] Enlightened Americans, however, no longer refer to the human race as *man,* or to humankind as *mankind.* Several years ago, *Time* magazine changed its "Man of the Year" to "Person of the Year." And the traditional notion of God as a male deity — and the reference to God using the male pronoun — has come under fire by some feminists.[73] Today one can purchase guides that advise writers on how to avoid sexist language. Grammar checkers on computers often flag terms as "gender-specific" and recommend alternatives that do not focus on one particular gender.

Enlightened Americans prefer gender-neutral words and phrases. A list of such words and phrases includes spouse, clergy, fisher, homemaker, layperson, kinsperson, news anchor, mail carrier, police officer, weather forecaster, and even snow person. Many gender-specific terms are still used by Americans, but such references are slowly falling out of favor. Few people use words that end with -enne, -ess, -ette, and -trix anymore, and we increasingly say the word *staff* instead of *man* in the verb tense. Likewise, the actor/actress and waiter/waitress dichotomies have been replaced by the gender-neutral actor and server, respectively. And "Men Working" or "Men at Work" signs are no longer so common on highway projects. Many Americans now refer to our national progenitors as the Founding Fathers and Founding Mothers — or just the Founders. Certain feminists even speak of "womyn" instead of women and describe history as "herstory." Nonetheless, the word chairman is often used in reference to female heads of boards and committees, and it is still legitimate to say that *she* is carrying *his* baby.

Gender-neutral language can complicate the writing process. (This is a complication that an increasing number of Americans welcome in the interest of being inclusive.) The *Chicago Manual of Style* describes the difficulties of writing in an inclusive fashion:

> On the one hand, it is unacceptable to a great many reasonable readers to use the generic masculine pronoun (he in reference to no one in particular). On the other hand, it is unacceptable to a great many readers either to resort to nontraditional gimmicks to avoid the generic masculine (by using *he/she* or *s/he,* for example) or to use *they* as a kind of singular pronoun. Either way, credibility is lost

with some readers. What is wanted, in short, is a kind of invisible gender neutrality. There are many ways to achieve such language, but it takes thought and often some hard work.[74]

Meanwhile, the custom of women automatically assuming their husbands' surnames remains resilient, even though it has come under fire from feminists for at least three decades. Beginning in the 1960s and 1970s, millions of American women decided to keep their birth names, as a result of the women's liberation movement and the inflow of American women into professional fields in sizable numbers. At least four factors — high levels of education, a significant career orientation, marriage at an older-than-average age, and left-of-center views on gender roles — increase the likelihood that a woman will choose not to follow conventional standards with regard to her marital name. Educated women seem to be more inclined than others to keep their birth names due in part to the fact that they often launch their careers under that name. In any event, nonconventional marital names are widely accepted, especially among younger women, even though such names are not particularly common among American women as a group.[75]

Traditionalism in the realm of marriage and surnames continues to reign supreme. "The practice of women taking their husband's surname as their own last name is the predominant naming choice for American married couples," according to David R. Johnson and Laurie K. Scheuble.[76] In the United States there are four different variations on how married women deal with the name game: they keep their birth name (Marie Smith); they use their birth name as their middle name (Marie Smith Johnson); they hyphenate their birth name and husband's name (Marie Smith-Johnson); or, most commonly, they take their husband's name (Marie Johnson). Some women, moreover, use their birth name professionally, but their husband's surname in social settings. Usually children get their father's surname or, in some cases, a hyphenated surname that includes their mother's birth name.[77] Even though the typical young woman takes her husband's surname, it seems to be less common for a lady to refer to herself as Mrs. [insert husband's name here] than it used to be, say, 40 years ago.[78]

Patronyms are the one aspect of our naming practices that is never mentioned by those who seek to rid the English language of sexist and gender-specific terms. There are two fronts on which this issue might come to the fore: race and gender. Those patronyms that originate in Europe, the Middle East, or North Africa come from "white" countries, but the connection between race and patronyms is made only by some African Americans who decide to change their names. The name changers select new appellations on the grounds that their European/American names do not reflect their heritage. Some of the name changers, of course, had "white" patronyms as their original names. Feminists have not raised the issue of patronyms in America in a systematic fashion; they focus far more on a woman's ability to keep her birth name. If that birth name is a patronym, so be it. In sum, these connections to race and gender are so tenuous that few people think or care about them.

There are many American patronyms that can be traced to Europe, the Middle East, or North Africa. Numerous affixes — *Di* (Italian for "son of"), *Fitz* (Irish for "son of"), *Mc* and *Mac* (Irish and Scottish, respectively, for "son of"), *O'* (Irish for "grandson of") — are clearly white (and male) in origin. To be sure, several prefixes that mean "son of," such as the Welsh *ap,* Arabic *Ibn,* and Hebrew *Ben,* are rarely used in the United States. Similarly, surnames that end in suffixes that mean "son of" reflect the white male influence on our naming practices. A list of such names would include the following affixes: *-enko* (Ukrainian), *-es* (Portuguese), *-ez* (Spanish), *-sen* (Danish or Norwegian), and *-son* (English, Swedish, or Norwegian). In the contemporary United States, Americans with such names as Di Franco, Fitzgerald, McIntyre, MacGregor, O'Brien, Lucenko, Rodrigues, Martinez, Bernsen, and Anderson all bear the names of their white male ancestors.[79]

Traditionally, newcomers to the United States focused on Americanizing — read anglicizing — the spellings and pronunciations of their forenames and surnames in order to fit into American society. Years ago many Jewish Americans, Polish Americans, Italian Americans, and others anglicized their names to sound more "American."[80] Americans seem to prefer shorter, even monosyllabic appellations. Actors, authors, political candidates, and others whose success depends on their mass appeal have long taken this preference into account.[81] Henry John Deutschendorf Jr., for example, was better known as John Denver. (Arnold Schwarzenegger never modified his name, however.) "As a country," notes the psychologist John Bargh, "we tend to distrust foreign names. There's something more 'American' about shorter names...."[82] Experts point out that Americans sometimes regard longer names as stiff sounding and presumptuous. Anyway, our brains process shorter words faster than longer ones.[83]

In Multicultural America, the disadvantages that once accrued to those who had identifiably "foreign" forenames and surnames have declined dramatically compared to, say, 70 or 80 years ago. More than a few Baby Boomers, in fact, gave their children flamboyantly ethnic forenames — in a desire to recapture the ethnicity that their ancestors may have relinquished in order to assimilate into American society. Of course, it is difficult to measure what, exactly, most Americans consider to be prototypically "American" names, and, what, if any, social costs affect those who do not have such names. Those whites with exotic Slavic appellations, Romance-language names, or polysyllabic Arabic or Middle Eastern forenames and surnames may find that their names distance them, to some extent, from the white mainstream in the United States. This is the case even if they are visibly similar to other whites, and speak with no noticeable accent.

Since 9/11, some Arab Americans and Muslim Americans have adopted American-sounding nicknames, while others have formally changed their names, so they win social acceptance from other Americans.[84] After the attacks, one Bosnian Muslim in North Dakota reportedly considered changing his forename from Hussein to the more Middle American–sounding Harry.[85] There are accounts of men and boys of South Asian and Middle Eastern ancestry from such places as Southern California and the New York metropolitan area who changed their forenames in the aftermath of 9/11. Some men formally petitioned the courts for name changes. Bedir became Mark. Tariq became Terry. Muhammad became Michael. Many more adopted American-sounding nicknames: Ali (Al), Samir (Sam), Achmed (Al), Jamaal (Jimmy), Yussef (Joe), Ibrahim (Abe), Muhammad/Mohammed (Mo or Mike).[86] These name changes indicate that some Arab Americans and Muslim Americans think they may face discrimination on the basis of ethnicity, religion, or national origin. The forename Muhammad illustrates how one's name can affect his life chances differently in different places. Muhammad is "the world's most common name," points out Asma Gull Hasan.[87] A man named after the Muslim prophet is part of the mainstream in Tunis and Karachi, but his forename may negatively affect his life chances in Tacoma and Kansas City.

These issues apply to common American forenames and surnames as well, due to the racial patterns in naming practices. Certain forenames (Leroy, Tyrone, Cedric, and Clarence) are commonly assumed to be "black" names, for instance. African Americans may be able to determine whether a person is black or white by seeing if he goes by a nickname (e.g., Dave instead of David), a practice that whites seem to engage in more so than blacks.[88] Due to the confluence of these factors, it is possible that many Americans can determine the race of an individual based solely on his or her forename. Some people may discriminate against — or in favor of — an individual on that basis.[89] The researchers Marianne Bertrand and Sendhil Mullainathan recently conducted a study in which they found that equally qualified job applicants with "white" forenames had a significantly better chance of getting jobs than applicants with "black" forenames.[90]

Male forenames, of course, vary by generation and are affected by such factors as ethnicity and socioeconomic class. Trends and tastes change over the decades, and names are no exception. Some male forenames like John and Michael have stood the test of time. But everyone knows that Dennis is a Baby Boomer — and that Jason is probably a Gen Xer. Likewise, a fellow with a forename like Carter or Huntington is going to be perceived differently than a gentleman named Earl or Elmer. The former names are perceived, rightly or wrongly, to be the preserve of blue bloods, whereas the latter names are thought by some people to be more prevalent among rural, less-affluent Americans. Various male forenames reflect white ethnic traditions. A list of such names would include Patrick (the patron saint of Ireland), Stanley (the anglicized version of Stanislaus, the patron saint of Poland), and Anthony (the anglicized version of Antonio, a common Italian first name). Few native-born white males have foreign-sounding forenames — and those who have such names often anglicize them to sound more American.[91]

∽

White male retirees enter a whole new dimension of their lives after they leave the workforce. "Many Americans," writes Dora L. Costa, "now look forward to retirement. Most enjoy the health and the income needed to pursue the good life."[92] One hundred years ago, retirement was simply not a viable option for the average American man. Men often retired only because their health was too poor for them to work, or they could not find jobs anymore. Now men can retire at their leisure, due to the economic advances of the last six decades.[93] On a personal level, many retirees enjoy considerable autonomy and financial security in their lives, as a result of Social Security and their pensions and savings. Lastly, retirement gives some white men a different political orientation, as they may be more interested than other white guys in age-related issues such as Medicare and Social Security.

The traditional notion of retirement kicks in at age 65, but the whole idea of "seniors," with the ubiquitous benefits and discounts, now encompasses 55-year-olds and 60-year-olds in many instances. (The American Association of Retired Persons allows people to become members once they turn 50.) Military personnel can retire with a decent pension after 20 years; if they entered the service at 18, this means they can retire at 38. Autoworkers, educators, and police officers usually are able to retire with good benefits and pensions after 30 years of work. Thus it is not unusual to see white male retirees in their fifties. Many retirees abandon their cold-weather homes for the sunnier climes of such places as Florida, Arizona, Nevada, and California, where they often congregate in areas with large numbers of people who share their generational outlook. As life expectancy rates increase, many people may collect pensions for more years than they worked to put money into the system.

In any event, the number of white males who remember life before Multicultural America is declining every year. One sees the pictures of these men virtually every day on the obituary page of every daily newspaper. The obituaries of most elderly white men are relatively similar, with important exceptions related to occupation, geography, socioeconomic status, and, to a lesser extent, perhaps, ethnicity and religion. The obituaries usually include coverage of the deceased's work, family, friends, hobbies, and military service. Formal education does not usually figure very prominently in these accounts. Many of the old-timers were married to the same woman for 50, 55, or 60 years. Frequently, their widows, along with many children, grandchildren, and even great-grandchildren, survive them. Often their obituaries mention parents of immigrant ancestry, whose names clearly indicate their country of origin, while the deceased's youngest descendants bear names like Tyler and Brianna.

Indeed, the deaths of these gentlemen signify the passing of the old order, one the likes of which will never be seen again in the United States. These men grew up in a world dominated by white men, where conflicts like labor versus management were fought between and among white men, primarily for the benefit of white men, and no one really questioned this arrangement or thought it would change. An energetic, hard-working man could support his wife and a family of three or four children with his salary — and that was without having a college education. Elderly men remember when divorce was far less common than it is today, and two-parent working families were not the norm in white America. They remember a time when women were regularly called "girls," and sexual harassment was tolerated, condoned, and even encouraged by some white guys in positions of authority. These men may use terms for ethnic minorities — I still hear elderly white Americans refer to African Americans as "Negroes" or "colored folk" — that were once considered polite but are now hopelessly out-of-date.

Today's young white males take things for granted that would have surprised their grandfathers to hear about 50 years ago. These young men often sport funky haircuts, cargo pants, and body piercings. They might self-identify in a way that puzzles the older generation. (In the summer of 2002, I saw a decal/bumper sticker on the back window of a Chevy truck in Harrison, Arkansas, which referred to the driver as a "Southern White Boy.") The typical 20-year-old white male today will probably spend more time on childrearing than his grandfathers did. He will rarely, if ever, refer to grown women as "girls." He will, in all likelihood, incorporate some knowledge of nutrition and healthful eating into his diet at some point. He will probably have more interactions with people of color than his progenitors. And he almost certainly will travel more and have a more diverse set of experiences than his father's father.

Several years ago, some of the men from the older generation were undoubtedly nonplused to see fashionable young ladies purchasing and wearing T-shirts emblazoned with such antiboy slogans as "Boys Lie," "I Make Boys Cry," "Boys Make Good Pets," and "Boys Are Great. Every Girl Should Own One." A number of retailers — including Hot Topic — created a fashion craze with the antiboy theme, despite their concerns about a backlash by mothers of sons and boys themselves. Most wearers of the T-shirts probably were not antiboy. Rather, they embraced the slogans as a means of displaying a proud, in-your-face expression of teenage feminism.[94] "Antiboy shirts elicit a fun response," contends Cindy Levitt, an executive at Hot Topic, "but antigirl shirts could be cruel. There's too much of a stigma. Our men's buyer keeps trying to come up with them, and I keep saying no."[95] Similarly, the "Boys Are Stupid" line of products (such items as T-shirts, boxer shorts, and baseball caps) wins favor with adolescent hipsters, even as it inspires controversy and discussions of gender roles in our society.[96] The popularity of these unconventional T-shirts reflected the lighthearted "battle of the sexes" so familiar to people who regularly browse for greeting cards.

The young women who defiantly sport these antiboy T-shirts are part of the movement that coined such phrases as "Girl Power" and "You Go, Girl." Contemporary young American women face fewer obstacles on the basis of gender than has been the case for any other generation in our nation's history. The attitude of many young Americans — male and female alike — is that women can do whatever they want, whenever they want, and they intend to do so. In other words, young women today seem to be saying, "If I want to be a Wall Street broker — that's fine, and if I want to be a full-time mother, that's fine, too. And maybe I want to do both things at different times in my life — and that's fine as well." The young men of today are pretty comfortable with the assertiveness of their female peers, in terms of their desire for genuine equality and freedom of choice. Perhaps the United States is becoming more like Sweden, where twentysomething, thirtysomething, and fortysomething men unquestioningly accept female authority figures and the prospect of sharing equally housework and childrearing responsibilities with their spouses.

chapter three

Heterogeneous Hegemons

Tom Joad received a most unwelcome surprise upon his release from the McAlester Penitentiary during the Depression. Tom had served four years of a seven-year sentence for murdering a man in a bar fight. After he was paroled for good behavior, Joad thought he would return to the family homestead near Sallisaw, Oklahoma. When he arrived in the Sallisaw area, however, he learned that his parents, five siblings, and two grandparents were preparing to leave their home in east central Oklahoma to go to the Central Valley of California in an attempt to find work. (Uncle John, Preacher Jim Casy, and Connie Rivers, Joad's brother-in-law, also accompanied the Joads on their trip to the West.) The economic hard times had led the Shawnee Land and Cattle Company to force them off company land (they were sharecroppers). Tom Joad went with his family on their westward journey, even though leaving the Sooner State meant that he violated the conditions of his parole.[1]

John Steinbeck told the story of the Joads in his epic novel, *The Grapes of Wrath,* which was published in 1939. Joad, who was about 30 years old, reached wider audiences in the 1940 cinematic version of *Grapes* — Henry Fonda played Joad superbly in the film.[2] Tom Joad (his formal name was Thomas Joad Jr.) had a garden-variety English name, and he may have had some Irish, Scottish, or German ancestry as well. His great-great-grandfather fought in the Revolutionary War. Although the Joads were old-stock Americans, native Californians considered Tom Joad and his family to be "Okies," a derogatory term that referred to the poor Southwestern whites who migrated to the Central Valley. The Depression years of the 1930s depopulated parts of Texas, Missouri, Arkansas, and, most famously, Oklahoma, as 315,000 to 400,000 Southwesterners (most of whom were white) made the trek westward to California in search of jobs.[3]

Race never played a role in either the literary or cinematic versions of *The Grapes of Wrath*. Social class was the main cleavage in the book and the movie. Joad himself differentiated between various groups of

whites — he did so on the basis of socioeconomic status, because virtually everyone he dealt with came from a Northern European background.
Tom Joad's spoken English, with its many solecisms and rural collo-
quialisms, reflected his modest socioeconomic background and limited
exposure to formal education. Joad developed a growing sense of class
consciousness as he came into contact with other poor, jobless migrants
from the Southwest, who, like himself, had taken to Highway 66 and
gone to California. But even as the Joads and their real-life counterparts
were harassed by the authorities in California and reviled by the residents
of the Central Valley, similarly situated people of color were doing even
worse in Depression-era America.

Steinbeck's novel is largely about white people. White men account for
almost all of the villains — and many of the heroes — in the book. The
list of white male villains in *Grapes* includes the person who issued the
orders to evict the Joads from company land, most of the men who hired
them and owned the farms in California, and the deputies and vigilantes
who enforced the existing social order throughout the Central Valley.
Conversely, there were many decent white men in *Grapes,* such as the
tenants and sharecroppers who were evicted from the land they farmed in
Oklahoma, the hardworking Southwesterners who toiled alongside Tom
and his family in the fields of Kern and Tulare counties, and the men who
conspired with Tom to advocate for better pay and working conditions.[4]
Indeed, Steinbeck nicely delineated some of the significant differences in
ideology and socioeconomic status that then separated white men in the
United States.

Tom Joad soon got into trouble in California when he killed a deputy
sheriff who had clubbed Preacher Casy to death. He eventually left his
family to go into hiding after he committed murder, but not before vow-
ing to his mother that he would work to effect societal change. Steinbeck
cast Joad as an Everyman who became infuriated by the injustices of
the world, a crusader who intended to try to remedy the inequities he
saw around him. (Steinbeck never specified, exactly, what actions Joad
would take in his quest for social and economic justice.) "Tom Joad,"
writes Robert Lee Maril, " . . . is both a reminder to many of the status
of the poor in contemporary society as well as the embodiment of the
potential for social change. He is a vital cultural symbol, an icon that
has weathered the years and continues to dog society's conscience by
reaffirming the moral legitimacy and political rights of all impoverished
Americans."[5]

Tom Joad proved to be the most memorable character in John Steinbeck's best-known work. A literary legend of the twentieth century, the Irish-German Steinbeck was born in 1902 in Salinas, California. He wrote *The Grapes of Wrath* in a five-month period between May 1938 and October 1938, after having done extensive field research in the Central Valley of California. Moreover, Steinbeck and his wife, Carol, had driven long stretches of Route 66 in 1937. Steinbeck's fieldwork led him to be sympathetic to the plight of the Southwestern migrants. His book became a massive best-seller after its publication in April 1939, even as it aroused controversy among the agribusinessmen of the Central Valley (who felt *Grapes* did not accurately depict the farmworkers' living conditions) and even among some white Southwesterners (who thought it portrayed them too simplistically). Steinbeck won the Pulitzer Prize in 1940 as a result of *The Grapes of Wrath,* and he was awarded the Nobel Prize in Literature in 1962, in part because he authored the novel.[6]

Even though we do not know what happened to Tom Joad — Steinbeck did not write a sequel to his literary masterpiece — the vast majority of the white Southwesterners who migrated to California eventually achieved success as they defined it.[7] Today the Southwesterners and their descendants have firsthand experience with ethnic diversity — Latinos constitute a significant (and growing) proportion of the residents of the Central Valley. Meanwhile, such artists as Woody Guthrie and, more recently, Bruce Springsteen and Rage Against the Machine have celebrated Tom Joad in their music.[8] Every year, many American high school students learn about Tom and his family when they read *The Grapes of Wrath* as part of their English curriculum.[9] Joad continues to be one of the most enduring fictional characters in American literature.[10] Writers and commentators periodically invoke his name in their attempts to focus attention on the less fortunate members of our society.

THE PRIVILEGED FEW?

As a youngster in rural west central Georgia in the 1940s and the 1950s, Dorothy Pitman Hughes grew up in a white man's world.[11] Stewart County, Georgia, was then a bastion of segregation; it may have had a substantial black population, but the local power structure — the elected officials, the large landowners, the prominent businesspeople, the law enforcement authorities — were, to a person, white and male. There simply were not many opportunities for black females such as Hughes to succeed in a world where racism and sexism limited their life chances. After

Hughes attended the segregated public schools in Stewart County, she left rural Georgia for good and went to New York City in 1957. Over the years, the redoubtable Hughes was active in the feminist and civil rights movements, as she tried to increase the opportunities open to women and African Americans. At the same time, she sought to raise awareness about what the multiculturalists now refer to as "male privilege" and "white privilege." Hughes eventually became an entrepreneur.

Dorothy Pitman Hughes has had numerous experiences that confirm the existence of "white male privilege."[12] For example, in 1983, a group of three black doctors sought to purchase the building that housed the West 80th Street Day Care Center, a nonprofit entity that Hughes had opened in Manhattan in 1971. The doctors were initially unable to obtain bank funding to finance their real-estate investment. Finally, Hughes persuaded them to come with her to a bank on New York's Fifth Avenue the next day. Hughes also brought along six white men of her acquaintance (all of whom wore suits). Two of the white men were supposed to be lawyers. Another represented himself as an accountant. The other three were reportedly media types. Hughes and her entourage went to the Manhattan bank without an appointment and requested a meeting with the bankers. After overcoming the bankers' initial reluctance to meet with them, the African-American doctors made their case for a loan and left at 4:00 p.m. with the requisite funds to purchase the building. Hughes says she does not believe they would have been heard — let alone received the loan — had the six white men not been part of their group that day.[13]

Later, Hughes retained the services of white men in her various business dealings, as she sought to integrate the white male world of the office-supply business in New York City. In 1985, she opened an office-supply store in Harlem. When Hughes visited an office-supply distributorship on 18th Street in Manhattan, the white salesman quoted her a price of nearly $10,000 for the list of supplies she needed for her shop. She was also supposed to use a cashier's check to pay for her items. In response, Hughes visited the distributorship again the next week with Keith, a young white man in his early twenties who was a friend of her daughter, Patrice Pitman. Hughes recalls that the white salesman charged Keith only $2,800 for the same items that Hughes had wanted the previous week, and he accepted a personal check from him. Keith served as a front man for Hughes for a number of years, until she became a member of the Stationer's Association of New York (SANY) in the early 1990s. Hughes also retained Keith and other white men to represent her interests with regard to banking issues and tax matters.[14] According to Hughes,

"They just don't take you seriously if you're a black woman trying to do business. Bring in a white male, and suddenly the doors swing open."[15]

Hughes's often lonely struggle to succeed as a black female entrepreneur received some airplay when the movie *The Associate* was released in 1996. This film is the fictional account of a Wall Street entrepreneur (Laurel Ayres, played by Whoopi Goldberg), who masquerades as a WASP man named Robert Cutty in order to be taken seriously by white males who would not think of doing business with a black woman. At the time, there were several news accounts that compared Hughes's real-life experiences to the story line of *The Associate*.[16] Today Hughes continues to work for black economic empowerment; this tall, dignified woman in her mid-sixties owns and operates the bookstore at Edward Waters College in Jacksonville, Florida. Hughes focuses her considerable energy these days on the issue of improving the living standard of African Americans through the creation and expansion of black-owned businesses. This devout Baptist has observed tremendous change in American society, but she contends that racism and sexism continue to be significant impediments for many Americans. While Hughes acknowledges that some progress has occurred for women and blacks during the last 40 years, she argues that white men as a group still enjoy many advantages in American society.[17]

Many multiculturalists contend that white males benefit from "white male privilege." The notion of white male privilege encompasses many different factors, but whiteness and maleness are its most prominent components. Whites, for starters, continue to enjoy a wide array of social and economic advantages in the United States, as measured by socioeconomic indicators such as income and infant mortality. Likewise, males are still ahead of females on a number of different fronts, again measured by many of the standard socioeconomic indicators, but younger women in particular have narrowed the gap considerably. The extent to which institutional racism and institutional sexism — those instances in which societal institutions act to limit the advancement of women and people of color, even in the absence of overt discrimination — affect the life chances of females and minorities is a matter of conjecture.[18] (There are, of course, many "isms." These include racism, sexism, classism, ageism, ableism, sizeism, lookism, heterosexism, religionism, and ethnocentrism.) Thus we need to explore the matter of whether white males enjoy advantages through their race and gender vis-à-vis similarly situated women and minorities.

One factor that seems to confirm existing discrimination in favor of white males — and against women and people of color — is the wage gap. White men, as a group, continue to have significantly higher incomes than women and blacks and Latinos. According to the National Committee on Pay Equity, in 2000 the "median annual earnings of year-round, full-time workers" were as follows: white men ($38,869), black men ($30,409), white women ($28,080), black women ($25,117), Hispanic males ($24,638), and Hispanic females ($20,527).[19] Asian Americans have higher median incomes than whites.[20] (To be sure, certain Asian-American subgroups dramatically trail the Asian-American median, and some Asian Americans contend that they are often unfairly passed over for high-ranking managerial and executive positions in Corporate America.)[21] Whether the wage gap between white males and women and non-Asian people of color can be explained by factors unrelated to contemporary discrimination, such as the fact that many women leave the labor force to care for their children, remains a matter of hot debate.

Besides income, health is an important indicator of well being in the United States. Whites enjoy good but not necessarily the best health of any ethno-racial group in America.[22] In fact, African Americans are the only racial group that is, in many cases, consistently and significantly worse off than whites when it comes to health. Take low-birthweight live births, for example; the national average (for the years 1995–1997) was 7.41%. By race, the percentages for low-birthweight live births were as follows: blacks (13.15%), Asians (7.07%), American Indians (6.62%), whites (6.34%), and Latinos (6.33%).[23] Similarly, race and social class intersect with regard to health insurance coverage. Non-coverage breaks down along racial lines: In 2001, the population of uninsured persons was 47.1% white, 30.1% Latino, 16.6% black, and 5.5% Asian and Pacific Islander.[24] Life expectancy rates continue to be an important indicator of a racial group's position in America. Measured at birth, white females enjoy the highest life expectancy rates in America (80.2), followed by black females (75.5), white males (75.0), and black males (68.6).[25]

Likewise, when it comes to rates of educational attainment, there are disparities between and among racial groups. These disparities matter because educational attainment usually translates into significant financial rewards. When it comes to high school dropouts, the group in American society that faces the bleakest economic prospects, the following are the dropout rates: white females (11.5%), white males (14.9%), black females (11.0%), black males (17.1%), Hispanic females (23.1%), and Hispanic males (35.9%).[26] Now let us examine the rates of achievement in higher education by ethnic group. In 2002, 26.7% of American adults

25 years old and over were college graduates, with the following rates by race/ethnicity: Asian and Pacific Islander (47.2%), white (27.2%), black (17.0%), and Latino (11.1%).[27] Black and Latino students are disproportionately concentrated in schools in poor neighborhoods and communities, where they often do not have access to the upper-level courses and extracurricular opportunities that are readily available to their peers in more-affluent school districts.

Multiculturalists, in addition, frequently discuss the dramatic overrepresentation of men of color, particularly African Americans, in the U.S. criminal justice system.[28] Overall, the male jail and prison population is 41.9% white, 41.2% black, 15.1% Hispanic, and 1.6% Other.[29] Likewise, nearly one-half, or 48.9%, of the male prisoners in state or federal correctional facilities are African American. White males constitute one-third of the state and federal prison population. Hispanic males account for 17.8% of this group, while American Indian men make up 1.8%.[30] Young black, Latino, and American Indian males sometimes encounter other Americans who regard them as automatic suspects, as putative criminals. Thirteen percent of black men cannot vote due to state felon disenfranchisement laws, which prohibit felons from casting ballots; two percent of American adults are disenfranchised in this fashion.[31]

The economic disparities between whites and people of color (namely, blacks, Latinos, and American Indians) structure the life chances of Americans — and lead to the aforementioned disparities related to health, education, and criminal justice. To a large extent, our explanations for these disparities are determined by our ideological predilections. Americans interpret data about race and ethnicity differently. To some Americans, any instance of disproportionality related to socioeconomic indicators that affects and involves people of color is prima facie evidence of racism and discrimination. Other Americans take an equally strong viewpoint, but they argue that there are legitimate reasons for the disproportionality, which have little or nothing to do with racism and discrimination. Most Americans probably hold beliefs on these issues that are somewhere in the middle between the two ideological poles.

White males themselves continue to be represented as the face of mainstream America in many contexts. As with so many aspects of American society, white maleness was once the "default," the invisible norm in most situations. Even today, such white actors as Matt Damon and Edward Norton almost certainly benefit from their "All-American" looks. Some observers contend that white rock, R&B, and hip-hop artists benefit from being white, in that record companies perceive them to be more "marketable" than similarly situated artists of color.[32] An example of this seeming privileging of white maleness occurred in the case of an entrepreneurial duo of two Internet businessmen — a black man (Timothy Cobb) and a white man (Jeff Levy). Cobb and Levy collaborated equally on an Internet research company, but the aspiring moguls designated Levy the CEO despite the fact that Cobb had originally conceived of the idea and had more business experience than Levy. Both men felt a white man would be taken more seriously by venture capitalists.[33] These putative perceptions of white male competence and mainstream status continue to exist, but are slowly fading away in response to the increasing visibility of powerful and successful women and people of color.

To the typical American, white males, particularly those who happen to be wealthy, would seem to be the most privileged group of people in the country. The intergenerational transmission of power, wealth, and privilege benefits more than a few white males — and white females. (One can be privileged without being wealthy, of course.) Being familiar with the norms, mores, and traditions of elite institutional cultures can enable a person to earn large amounts of money and gain power and influence in his or her occupational field. Affluent and wealthy Americans enjoy many advantages: They rarely, if ever, have to worry about being able to afford food, shelter, clothing, health care, and other basic human needs. In addition, the affluent or wealthy youth is socialized to have a significant amount of self-confidence — he may be raised to believe that he can accomplish virtually anything. Those individuals (the Kennedys, the Rockefellers) who come from prominent families benefit from the glamour and celebrity associated with a famous surname. Indeed, the Kennedy males continue to be perhaps the best-known dynastic exemplars of white male privilege in the American context.[34]

As a rule, white males are more likely than members of other groups to feel as if they are part of the mainstream culture, because it reflects their experiences more so than it does for members of other groups, save white females.[35] White males may be quite self-confident in certain contexts because they have never personally experienced the debilitating effects of racism and sexism. For instance, the economist Ian Ayres found that white male customers are charged less for new cars in Chicagoland than is the case for women and African Americans.[36] (Some white males, to be sure, have been victims of classism; this "ism" takes an even worse toll when it occurs in conjunction with, say, racial discrimination.) Many not-so-affluent Americans of all colors feel they face limited opportunities to succeed in this country. As a result, some of them do not try as hard as they could to develop their human capital, while others may engage in dysfunctional behavior. Some successful people of color are periodically described by their coethnics as "sell-outs" or "tools" of the white male–dominated establishment.

In a recent book, the sociologists Joe R. Feagin and Eileen O'Brien take up the issue of how white men — in their case, 100 elite white men — look at such issues as power and privilege. As a result of their interviews with academics, attorneys, businessmen, government officials, and others, Feagin and O'Brien delineate how these men feel about hot-button issues, e.g., interracial marriage and affirmative action. The two scholars also describe these men's contacts with and feelings about people of color, particularly African Americans. Feagin and O'Brien found that these elite white men held subtle biases and stereotypes about people of color, views that the two sociologists describe in terms of a "group ideology" and a "collective white consciousness." Their respondents reject discrimination as a major factor in explaining the disadvantages experienced by people of color; consequently, these white men may be skeptical of affirmative action as a means of creating equal opportunities for minorities. Elite white men hold these opinions, posit Feagin and O'Brien, as a result of the fact that most affluent and powerful Caucasians reside in predominantly white residential areas and inhabit mainly white social and professional settings. The coverage of racial issues in the media also influences the views of white men.[37]

Regardless of how one thinks about contemporary social and economic dynamics, it is indisputable that white males once enjoyed many advantages in American society. The historical underpinnings of "white male privilege" date back to slavery and the transfer of a patriarchal social structure from Western Europe. Richard F. America writes, "Past interracial relations in labor and capital markets, and in education and training, have continuing effects. Through intergenerational transfers and carryovers, they significantly influence current shares of income and wealth by class and race."[38] White women do not face the issue of compensatory damages in the same way as blacks or Native Americans, due to the fact that most multiculturalists would contend that they have benefited over the years from "white privilege." Debates over these issues extend to how the United States should deal with its history of discrimination against people of color, particularly blacks and Native Americans.

When we, as a society, outlawed discrimination based on race, we did not make wholesale provisions for remedying the injustices of the past.

This development leads to a legitimate question: Is it fair to allow certain groups of Americans to benefit from practices and institutions that were at least partially shaped by the racism, sexism, and discrimination of yesteryear? Nor is it necessarily fair, argue many Americans, to blame someone for something his ancestor may have done, particularly when it is difficult, if not impossible, to quantify the extent to which people in the present benefit from events in the past. Many white Americans, after all, trace their ancestry to people who arrived on these shores after slavery ended, and who lived in areas where racial segregation did not exist. Thus we have affirmative-action programs that define protected classes in terms of groups (e.g., women, African Americans, people with disabilities). Such considerations influence the tenor of policy debates, as well as discussions of white males as a group.

Analysts and scholars, especially on the Left, argue in favor of expanding our conceptions of what constitutes "affirmative action." This idea proceeds on the premise that whites, particularly white males, benefited in the past from a type of "affirmative action," one that was predicated upon the exclusion of women and minorities from jobs and programs that primarily benefited white males.[39] In her analysis of the effects of such exclusion, Judy Scales-Trent writes:

> In this country there has been affirmative action for white men for more than three hundred years. All we are trying to do now is balance things out by changing the beneficiaries of affirmative action for a while. Thus, when we talk about affirmative action, we are not talking about special treatment for people of color or for white women. We are talking about equal treatment — three hundred years for them, three hundred years for us. White men got good jobs and good pay for three hundred years because of their race and sex. Now it is our turn to get access to those same benefits, also because of our race and sex.[40]

To be sure, women and minorities have unquestionably made substantial gains, as measured by major socioeconomic indicators, during the last 30 years. There are several points that need to be raised here. Firstly, one might quibble about the amount of success enjoyed by women and people of color, and how it pales in comparison to what needs to be done to promote equal opportunity in our nation. Secondly, one could discuss how we define equity, fairness, and equal opportunity in America. Do these factors *really* exist in the absence of proportional representation in every major realm of American society? Thirdly, we need to try to determine the extent to which the advances made by women and people of color are attributable to affirmative action and diversity initiatives. These are important questions, because the answers determine whether Americans feel affirmative action and related programs are essential to promote opportunities for women and minorities.

The pay gap between men and women, meanwhile, continues to narrow. Full-time female workers made only 62.5% of the wages of full-time male workers as recently as 1979. During the 1980s the wage gap narrowed significantly, and by 1993, it stood at 77.1%. For the next nine years, it hovered in this range (it was 76% in 2001). Then, in 2002, the wage gap decreased to 77.5%. In 2002 the median full-time male worker saw his pay lag behind the rate of inflation (1.3 percent versus 2 percent), while his female counterpart saw her weekly pay increase by 5 percent. Part of the explanation for the declining gender gap in wages is tied to occupational segregation. There have been many layoffs and pay cuts in such male-dominated industries as technology and manufacturing. Women, though, are more likely to be found in the growing sections of the economy (such as government and health care). Women are also becoming more unionized than in the past, a development that generally results in increased wages.[41]

To be sure, women have not reached parity with men in terms of pay. The search for explanations for this disparity inevitably involves the possibility of discrimination, although it is sometimes difficult to ferret out explicit instances of structural bias or specific examples of unfair treatment. Women also have lower wages because they still do most of the housework and childrearing in American households. As a result, they have less experience in the paid labor force, and they frequently work in positions with flexible hours, which pay less than those with demanding schedules.[42] Childless women are more likely than women with children to experience parity — or near-parity — with men in wages. When women leave the workforce on a full-time or part-time basis, they often forfeit work experience, years of seniority, equity in pension programs, and possible earning power to raise their children. Ann Crittenden describes the effects of these hiatuses on women's wages as "the mommy tax."[43]

Nonetheless, many American women now outearn their male peers, a phenomenon that dates back to the expansion of opportunities for women that began in the 1960s. Indeed, a solid majority of married

American women now works outside the home. The increase in labor-force participation rates by married women has been a gradual phenomenon over the years. In 2002, the civilian labor force participation rate for females aged 16 years old and over was 59.6%, compared to 74.1% for males 16 years old and over. These figures are slowly converging: The projections for 2010 are 62.2% for females and 73.2% for males. White males had a labor force participation rate of 74.8% in 2002; the figure for white females in that year was 59.3%.[44] Due to these economic changes, American men, particularly younger men, are generally receptive to sharing the responsibilities of the provider role with their spouses. However, a *Newsweek* poll in 2003 found that 41% of Americans concurred with the following statement: "it is much better for everyone involved if the man is the achiever outside the home and the woman takes care of the home and family."[45]

Today more than three out of ten (30.7% in 2001) married American women who work outside the home make more money than their husbands. This phenomenon is increasing in significance as a result of the gender imbalance in college-graduation rates, in addition to the influx of women into important managerial and executive positions in Corporate America. Already, observers speculate that "the mommy tax" will decline in importance as a result of the greater earning opportunities available to women. Female poverty among the elderly may also become less of a problem. Not surprisingly, there is a positive correlation between the amount of domestic duties performed by men and the earning capacity of their spouses.[46] An increasing number of men serve as "enablers," in that they devote much of their time to advancing their wives' careers. Indeed, there are many high-powered female corporate executives whose husbands are full-time parents.[47]

The success of marriages where the woman is the main breadwinner depends on the expectations and agreements the two partners made when they were first married, as well as the extent to which they successfully share domestic duties. A woman may become resentful if she is suddenly required to be the sole breadwinner because her spouse loses his job, or otherwise experiences some kind of setback in the labor market. Some men dislike the fact that they do not contribute as much as their spouse to the family's bottom line, due to the loss of control and respect they perceive is an outgrowth of this reversal of traditional gender dynamics. Many men, of course, enjoy having a wife who outearns them, because they value the freedom to nurture their children and engage in rewarding but not very remunerative passions and professions. A man's reaction to this type of situation depends on his self-image, his attitudes regarding gender roles, and the reactions of those around him, in his family and elsewhere.[48]

ONWARD AND UPWARD

Virtually every American has heard a "Polish joke" at some point in his life. Indeed, Polish Americans have been the subjects of derogatory humor for approximately a century. As Polish immigrants flooded into the United States during the period from 1880 to 1920, they came to be seen by many Americans as physical laborers who were complacent, provincial, and unintelligent. This malicious stereotype probably developed because Poles took the only jobs available to them (usually requiring physical labor) and initially (as with most immigrants) did not speak English. This stereotype persisted even as Polish Americans joined the Great American Middle Class in the 1950s, 1960s, and 1970s. During these years, some urban and suburban Polish Americans became stereotyped as "ethnics," "hard hats," and others who were resistant to black progress. Polish jokes, meanwhile, persisted in popularity throughout this era of resurgent ethnicity. The typical "Polish joke" characterized the sons and daughters of Polonia as bigoted, guileless, obstinate, or ignorant, or some combination of these characteristics.[49]

"These degrading stereotypes were far from harmless," points out James S. Pula. "The constant derision, often publicly disseminated through the mass media, caused serious identity crises, feelings of inadequacy, and low self-esteem for many Polish Americans."[50] The public mockery of Polish Americans artificially devalued their status in American society, negating in a sense the significant social and economic advances they had made over several generations. Since the late 1960s, Polish-American groups and organizations have successfully challenged the stereotyping of Polish Americans that was once common in the media and our popular culture. Americans have developed a more positive image of Polish Americans for a variety of reasons, including the heroic fight of Solidarity against Communism in Poland, the 25-year-long tenure of Pope John Paul II (né Karol Wojtyla), and the emergence of many Polish-American celebrities and prominent figures.[51] Still, negative stereotypes about Polish Americans endure, at least on the World Wide Web, where one can find 334,000 hits on Yahoo when s/he types in the keywords "Polish jokes."[52]

In any event, millions of white male Americans — most of them native-born, an increasing number of them foreign-born — energetically seek to improve themselves through higher education and the energetic pursuit of socioeconomic mobility. In many cases, these ambitious white males come from poor or modest backgrounds. In other cases, they seek to maintain or slightly improve their socioeconomic status. Some white males, to be sure, do little to enhance their earning abilities — they either cannot or will not seek the additional training required beyond a high school diploma that is now necessary to earn a decent living. And it should be noted that the typical middle-class or upper-middle-class white male certainly does not view himself as privileged, not when he faces concerns about layoffs and unemployment, spiraling health-care costs, shrinking retirement portfolios, and soaring college tuitions looming ahead of him.

White male America continues to be divided by significant socio-economic disparities, which make it difficult for us to generalize about the life chances of this "nation" of approximately 100 million Americans. Yet the perception that white males enjoy many privileges can lead a person to ask the following question: "Why does a white male need help?" Eight years ago, the *New York Times* reported that a female student at Sweet Briar College in Virginia asked this rhetorical question during a discussion of why black colleges and women's colleges were acceptable, but men's colleges were inappropriate.[53] The philosophy underlying this question holds that the white male is unilaterally privileged, at least in contrast to similarly situated women and people of color. According to this type of reasoning, he should expect no special consideration in any kind of social and economic initiatives designed to improve the conditions of our nation's citizens.

White males, of course, do not benefit equally from "white male privilege." As Richard Bernstein points out, "Some white males have had it easy; they were practically born into their privileged positions. Others, many others, are just emerging from centuries of penury and discrimination themselves."[54] Some issues related to race, gender, and privilege implicate a specific ethnic group, and others apply to white males across the board. However, social class continues to be an important factor that distinguishes white males from one another. Although most white males are not poor, millions of them languish in poverty and near-poverty. Approximately nine percent (9.1%, to be exact) of white Americans live below the poverty level, compared to 12.6% of Asian Americans, 22.6%

of Hispanics, 24.9% of African Americans, and 25.7% of American Indians and Alaskan Natives.[55] There are significant concentrations of poor whites in the United States, including some who might be described as members of the "white underclass."[56]

In any event, considerations of race and class also implicate questions of whether race is, in fact, far more important than gender in structuring how white females identify their life chances. White women continue to bond with white men, as measured by the present rates of intermarriage. White females, after all, have white male sons, uncles, fathers, nephews, brothers, grandsons, sons-in-law, fathers-in-law, and brothers-in-law. They usually benefit from the social and economic successes of their white fathers and husbands.[57] Affirmative action and diversity issues often affect white females as whites, not as women. And some white females dislike what they see as preferential treatment for women and minorities at the expense of their white male relatives.[58] Not every white woman looks at the world this way, of course. Likewise, many white males directly benefit — through marriage or their mothers — from the advances made by white females in the workplace. Some of these advances may be attributable to affirmative action; so it could be said that many white males may profit, at least to some extent, from affirmative action for women.

Progressive white parents react differently to multicultural conundrums that result when their principles may conflict with their self-interest. One white woman told me that she chastised her son for complaining about "reverse discrimination" as the reason why he did not get into the University of Michigan Law School. He was admitted to Columbia, though. "You will land on your feet," she told him. Last year I asked a progressive white man a difficult question: How would he, an advocate of expanding opportunities for women and people of color, reconcile that belief with his aspirations for his son, a white male, to attend one of the nation's best colleges. To his credit, this man responded honestly by saying that being a parent trumps all other factors. In other words, he frankly acknowledged the reality of life in Multicultural America: few people, even professed liberals, want to give anything up to advance their ideological beliefs.

Likewise, working-class white males experience many problems these days due to sluggish wage growth, changing gender roles in the family, the decline of unions and the industrial economy, and the perception in some corners that women and minorities are making progress at their expense.[59] Lois Weis, Amira Proweller, and Craig Centrie write:

While white working-class men are privileged via their color, they are relatively less privileged than their economically advantaged white male counterparts. Too, they are currently losing the edge they had in the economy over men of color. White working-class men represent a position of privilege at the same time they represent the loss of such privilege. It is this simultaneous moment of privilege and loss that we excavate when we turn our attention to the production of white masculinity. It is their whiteness and maleness which privileges them. But it is also in this space of historical privilege that they begin to confront the realities of loss.[60]

In terms of socioeconomic achievement, whites are by no means a monolith. The tremendous intermixing that has occurred in white America makes it difficult, to some extent, to analyze precisely how well specific white ethnic groups are doing today. Still, the best data we have are those that come from self-identification in response to the ancestry question on the census form. Dante Ramos found that a number of white ethnic groups (Finns, Cajuns, Croats, Slovenes, Bulgarians, the Dutch, the French, the Scotch-Irish, and the Pennsylvania Germans) have lower median incomes than a number of ethnic groups (the Chinese, the Burmese, the Japanese, Pakistanis, Argentines, Sri Lankans, and Asian Indians) traditionally classified as minorities. Ramos noted that, strictly in terms of socioeconomic status, a number of white ethnic groups could make a case for being the recipients of government help. But socioeconomic status is not the sole criterion for definitions of advantage and disadvantage. Skin color is another important criterion in this regard, since many people of color feel they experience differential treatment on that basis.[61]

White Appalachian men — and women — are another American group that faces persistent stereotypes and discrimination. The people of Appalachia do not constitute a distinct ethnic group per se, even though many of them trace their heritage to the British Isles and Germany. However, the region's rural isolation, racial homogeneity, and tightly knit communities all contribute to a sense of Appalachian identity. Yet many Appalachians find relatively few employment opportunities in their region, and a significant percentage of them languish in poverty. Appalachia, after all, does not have a tremendous amount of economic diversification (coal employs few Appalachians these days). Over the decades, Appalachians have migrated to such cities as Akron, Dayton, Chicago, Detroit, Atlanta, Columbus, Cleveland, Cincinnati,

Pittsburgh, Indianapolis, and the District of Columbia in search of economic opportunities.[62]

When whites of Appalachian origin leave their mountain communities, they might confront subtle bias and pernicious stereotypes based on regional origin. "At once quintessential American insiders and archetypal Others," writes Dwight B. Billings, "mountain people, it seems, are acceptable targets for hostility, projection, disparagement, scapegoating, and contempt."[63] The national images of Appalachians date back to the 1870s, as educators, missionaries, industrialists, local colorists, and social reformers disseminated accounts about Appalachia that described its inhabitants as uniformly poor, backward, and uninterested in the outside world. Over the years, producers of American popular culture (think *Li'l Abner* and *Deliverance*) and our political figures (e.g., Robert Kennedy and Lyndon Johnson in the 1960s and Bill Clinton in the 1990s) have spotlighted the region's poverty.[64] In fact, white Appalachians are mentioned frequently in discussions of racial privilege and affirmative action, to illustrate the complexity of these issues.

Besides social class, physical appearance is an important factor that affects our life chances. Physical attractiveness, of course, is inherently subjective; it varies from culture to culture, and person to person. Beauty, however it is defined, gives physically attractive people social currency and economic benefits, according to the scholarly studies that examine the correlation between physical appearance and one's life chances. In the United States, the notion of physical attractiveness includes multiple components, such as height, weight, and facial features. People deemed to be physical attractive usually have more social opportunities than their "plain" peers. Likewise, studies of workplaces in the United States show that good-looking people benefit from their looks in an economic sense; factors such as height and weight are particularly important in this regard.[65] Today Americans pay increasing attention to such phenomena as "lookism" and "sizeism." Four jurisdictions — Michigan, Washington, D.C., Santa Cruz, California, and San Francisco — ban discrimination based on appearance (including height and weight).[66]

Cranial hair loss or androgenetic alopecia (AGA) certainly affects the appearance of many men, and it may have some detrimental effects on their life chances. According to the psychologist Thomas F. Cash, "Most men with AGA suffer at least moderate stress, and for a predisposed subgroup this may result in some unwanted reduction in the quality of life. For a minority, hair loss may become a major focus of body dysmorphic concern. Women clearly respond to the condition with greater distress and impairment than do men."[67] Studies show that cranial hair loss makes men seem older, less assertive, and less attractive, qualities that affect the number of opportunities available to bald and balding men in the social and economic spheres. Cranial hair loss may be especially difficult for men who are single, self-conscious, not very self-confident, 25 years of age or younger, and those who are very focused on their appearance.[68] Regardless of whether there is actual discrimination against bald and balding men, the widespread perception that such bias exists certainly affects the mindsets and outlooks of many American men. American and European men often shave their heads; this fashionable hairstyle (if one can call it that) may negate or decrease the social and economic significance of cranial hair loss — to some extent, at least.

Height is another factor that affects our life chances, particularly if one is considerably shorter than the U.S. average. A significant number of American men fall into the range of heights between 5′8″ and 6′. More than 20 percent of American men (20.8%, to be exact) are under 5′7″, 32.0% are under 5′8″, 46.3% are under 5′9″, 58.7% are under 5′10″, 70.1% are under 5′11″, and 81.2% are under 6′.[69] There is an ethnic component to height as well. A number of white males come from ethnic groups, such as the Greeks, Italians, Spaniards, Lebanese, and Syrians, whose members are generally not considered tall by American standards. It is difficult to quantify the extent to which an American man who is shorter than the national average will be socially and economically disadvantaged by his height.[70] Studies often show that shorter-than-average men (but not necessarily men of average height) may experience adverse treatment that affects their prospects in terms of income and occupational status, as well as whether women find them attractive. Likewise, they have more difficulty receiving the same kind of respect and career opportunities that automatically accrue to taller men — think "stature" in a literal and figurative sense.[71]

Weight is another factor that affects the social and economic life chances of males and females alike in the United States, particularly for those who are obese and overweight.[72] All told, 22.6% of U.S. adult males are obese and 66.5% are overweight (this figure includes the obese). Likewise, 22.3% of American female adults are obese and 49.9% are overweight. The figures for males by race/ethnicity are as follows: white males (22.4% obese and 66.7% overweight); black males (28.0% obese and 66.6% overweight); Hispanic males (21.9% obese and 71.5% overweight); and Asian and Pacific males (6.6% obese and

38.9% overweight).[73] There is a persistent stigma in American society that accompanies obesity, particularly if a person is quite large.[74] "Obese people," writes Gerhard Falk, "cope with job discrimination, social exclusion, public ridicule, trouble finding clothing, mistreatment by doctors, and even denial of health benefits."[75] The size acceptance movement seeks to advance the interests of large people through political activism as well as to provide social support for those who define themselves as "people of size" (or "fat" in the argot of some activists).[76]

Advocates and policymakers have begun to discuss the issue of whether big people should receive civil rights protections on the basis of body weight. The issue of size discrimination now merits increasing attention in the workplace and other sectors of American society. Any consideration of whether big people should receive protected class status on the basis of body weight depends on the issue of whether weight is an inherently changeable condition or a genetically predisposed condition.[77] Likewise, businesses and institutions such as airlines and hospitals face issues regarding whether they have obligations to accommodate the needs of people of size without charging them more for services.[78] The discussion of matters related to body weight is yet another indication that we, as a nation, are becoming ever-more sensitive to the needs, feelings, and rights of people who traditionally have felt like outsiders.

Few Americans stop to think that white males (including native-born white males) may ever experience accent discrimination in Multicultural America. Accent discrimination, after all, usually comes up as a topic that relates to foreign-born people who do not speak English as their first language.[79] "It is crucial to remember," writes the linguist Rosina Lippi-Green, "that it is not *all* foreign accents, but only accent linked to skin that isn't white, or which signals a third-world homeland, that evokes such negative reactions."[80] An immigrant from England or Scotland may be less likely than his counterpart from China or Iran to face accent discrimination based on national origin.[81] Indeed, Englishmen and Englishwomen who live in the United States report that they often receive compliments and preferential treatment in social circumstances due to their accents.[82] (Interestingly, the American accent can be an advantage in Britain, where people often associate it with competence in business.)[83]

The way that native-born white males speak English also affects — and reflects — their life chances. Take stuttering, for example. Those individuals who stutter as adults may face subtle discrimination in the social and economic spheres, because of their inability to communicate as fluently as those who speak without a stutter. Likewise, if a person persists in using improper grammar and nonstandard English, he is very likely to face limited opportunities in a number of different realms, particularly those that require a college education for entry. People who speak with marked accents report that they sometimes incur "accent penalties," in the form of social discrimination and lost employment opportunities, as a result of how they speak American English.[84] Accent penalties certainly affect the life chances of foreign-born Americans and, intriguingly, may affect the life chances of native speakers of American English as well.

While there was considerable anecdotal evidence that suggested some white males benefited from how they spoke American English, this thesis was not tested until 2000. That year, Dianne Markley, the director of co-operative education at the University of North Texas in Denton, Texas, wrote her master's thesis on the topic of American regional accents. Hers is the best existing study that specifically quantifies how Americans judge white men based on how they speak, and it has received widespread attention in the media. Markley used ten white male "voices" (the men were highly educated — seven held doctorates) from ten different states in her study. She asked 56 people from Corporate America and the public sector to rate the voices based on whether they would want to hire the person in question. Each of the ten white male "voices" read a 45-second passage that was carefully designed not to advantage any speaker of American English. Markley found that her respondents rated the California and Minnesota speakers highest, while they ranked the New Jersey and Georgia speakers lowest.[85] The main finding of her study, according to Markley, is an "overarching preference for a lack of a regional accent."[86]

Markley aptly notes that any value judgments related to regional accents depend on the "linguistic security and linguistic preferences" of one's interlocutor. These factors determine whether "your accent — or perceived lack of one — may be a hindrance or a help in accomplishing your goal with that person."[87] Markley, a native of East Texas, points out that the preference for a certain type of accent often varies by region. In other words, a person with a pronounced Southern accent might be rated poorly by many Northeasterners, but s/he would be judged highly by her or his fellow Southerners. This dictum applies across the board to everyone, even to speakers of accentless American English. Having spent the last 24 years working with corporations to place students in jobs and internships, Markley has observed that corporate recruiters are reluctant to hire people who speak with pronounced regional accents.[88]

FAMILY LIFE

Douglas E. Wilson is the Director of Adolescent Development (D.A.D.) for the Wilson 5 in Byers, Texas, a rural community in north central Texas. During the late 1990s he coined the acronym to describe his duties as the father of one daughter (Bailey) and two sons (Garrett and Cooper). Douglas Wilson was a full-time parent from 1999 through 2002; the Wilsons lived in north suburban Dallas at the time. A muscular white man with brown hair, brown eyes, and a goatee, Wilson is engaging, reflective, and insightful. He was born in April 1966, and grew up in the Casa View section of Dallas. Douglas Wilson and Lisa Shelton were married in 1990. Bailey was born in June 1992, followed by Garrett in September 1995, and Cooper in October 1996. For most of the 1990s, the Wilsons were both employed outside the home, and their children went to day care.[89]

Douglas Wilson had an epiphany in April 1999, when he was going to college at night, working 50 to 60 hours a week, and trying to be a good father and husband. Not surprisingly, he found this hectic schedule "nightmarish." So he and Mrs. Wilson, who was then a full-time parent, decided to shift roles. Douglas Wilson became the primary caregiver of their children, and Lisa Wilson reentered the paid workforce. She worked as the telecommunications coordinator for Rent-A-Centers Inc. in Plano, Texas. On nights and weekends, the Wilsons jointly cared for their children, who enjoyed helping Mrs. Wilson in the kitchen. Being an at-home dad enabled Douglas Wilson to do a number of things, such as complete his college degree. He graduated *cum laude* from Dallas Christian College in 2001 and is now an ordained minister. This lifelong Texan, of course, became a full-time parent to look after his children, not to focus on his studies.

Wilson always enjoyed his job as a parent, even though some people had difficulty accepting a man as the primary caregiver for the three Wilson children. At times, he felt the brute force of gender stereotypes. An older female journalist once referred to his occupation as "the mother's job." And one of Lisa Wilson's coworkers told Mrs. Wilson that her "lazy" husband should get a job. When Wilson and his children went to stores during the workday, they regularly encountered people who asked them if their father had "the day off," or if he worked swing shifts. To be sure, many mothers admired and praised Douglas Wilson for being an at-home dad. But, when he went to the park with Bailey, Garrett, and Cooper, some ladies feared that he was a kidnapper, and others ignored him completely or answered his questions with monosyllabic responses. His male friends, however, might have ribbed him about his occupation in a good-natured way, but they respected his choice and readily admitted that they probably could not handle domestic duties with the same aplomb.

Douglas Wilson reentered the paid labor force in 2002, when he accepted a position as the Youth Pastor of Byers Assembly of God Church in Byers, Texas, a rural community not far from Wichita Falls. The Wilsons swapped roles once again, and Mrs. Wilson is now a full-time mother. Due to the flexible hours of his schedule as a pastor, Wilson is able to spend a considerable amount of time with his children. The Wilsons' neighbors in rural northern Texas initially found it hard to believe that their pastor had been the full-time caregiver for Bailey, Garrett, and Cooper for three years. Stay-at-home dads, after all, continue to be virtually nonexistent in this part of America. A charismatic and forthright man, Wilson once edited a monthly newsletter, *The Slowlane Express,* for Slowlane.com, the top Web site for primary care-giving fathers. He also served as the director of At-Home Dads of Greater Dallas from 2000 to 2001. And he was regularly featured in print and electronic media accounts about full-time parents.[90] Today Douglas Wilson is one of the few men in America who has had significant experience as both a full-time caregiver and a full-time provider.

Contemporary American family life is more varied, diverse, and complicated than ever before. A series of social, cultural, economic, and demographic changes have done much to remake our conceptions of family. At one point, the domestic "ideal" of American family life was closely associated with a male breadwinner, a female stay-at-home mother, and obedient children (think: the Cleavers on *Leave It to Beaver*). The reality, of course, was far more complicated than this for immigrants, people of color, and the poor. The 1950s were the last decade in which a white, middle-class version of American family life was presented to the nation in our popular culture as the sole model to which everyone should aspire. There have been remarkable changes in American family life as a consequence of the greater acceptance of nontraditional family arrangements, the focus in recent decades on the equitable division of domestic labor, and the transformations in the U.S. economy that have made it more difficult for a single male breadwinner to support an entire family on his income.[91]

These social, cultural, and demographic shifts in American family life affect members of every racial and ethnic group. Perhaps most significantly, few Americans subscribe anymore to the idea that the father is the unquestioned patriarch of the family. This idea certainly does not resonate with young and middle-aged women in the Baby Boom generation. Many women in the 20–60 age bracket earn as much as, if not more than, their spouses, a fact that contributes mightily to democratic decision-making within the family. On a variety of topics, including blended families and the cohabitation of unmarried people of opposite sexes, our cultural attitudes have become more accepting of differing conceptions of family life. There is little stigma attached to divorce or single parenthood in mainstream society anymore. Americans, moreover, are less likely to marry than in the past, and when they do form unions, they do so at older ages.[92]

The approaches and practices of the millions of immigrants and their children who live in the United States are also changing American attitudes toward family types. Likewise, these immigrants may find the American emphasis on gender equality in the family unit to be a different type of practice. In much of the world, after all, the father is the undeniable head of the household, a position that derives as much from patriarchal traditions as it does from the fact that he is very likely to be the main breadwinner. The freedom and autonomy (relatively speaking, of course) enjoyed by young American adults would be unheard of in many cultures, particularly for female youths. Such traditions as no-fault divorce and female-headed single-parent families are highly unusual in many developing nations. The American divorce rate of approximately 50 percent is also remarkably high from the perspective of the typical Asian, African, Middle Eastern, Latin American, and Eastern European immigrant to the United States.

Immigrants are playing an important role in sustaining the "traditional family," that of two married parents with children at home. The percentages, by racial/ethnic group, for married-with-children households are as follows: Hispanics (35.8%), Asians (33.4%), whites (22.8%), and blacks (16.0%). Traditional families are common among Latino and Asian immigrants and among Generation Xers, regardless of their racial or ethnic background. There was only a slight decline in the percentage of American households that consist of this family type between 1990 and 2000; all told, 23.5 percent of American households fall into this category. Nonetheless, this image of hearth and home retains much of its outsized significance in American culture. It is very likely that the cultural attitudes of immigrants and their descendants will contribute mightily to the perpetuation of this family type.[93]

There are significant disparities between the rates of marriage of whites and Latinos and African Americans. This disparity was bequeathed to us by the ignominious legacy of slavery and segregation, in addition to the discrimination that African Americans experienced over the years in the labor market.[94] To be sure, it is becoming more common for Americans to be divorced or never married. In 2002, 58.9% of American adults were married, 24.4% had never married, 10.0% were divorced, and 6.7% were widowed. White and Hispanic adults had roughly similar marriage rates (61.1% and 57.6%, respectively), compared to African Americans (42.8%). Blacks had far higher percentages of adults who had never married (39.2%) within their ranks as opposed to whites (22.1%) and Latinos (31.8%). Divorce rates also differed by race in 2002: Black and white adults were more likely to be divorced (11.2% and 10.0%, respectively) than their Hispanic counterparts (7.0%).[95] These issues matter from an economic perspective (and, many would argue, a social viewpoint as well) because adults and children alike generally fare better in an economic sense in a household headed by a married couple.[96]

The single-parent family is the subject of much scholarly and journalistic attention. In 2000, 73.0% of the nation's 34,605,000 family households were made up of two-parent family groups. Mothers maintained 80.9% of the one-family groups. For whites, two-parent family groups accounted for 77.6% of family households. More than three-quarters (77.3%) of the one-parent family groups in white America were maintained by the mother. In black America, one-parent family groups accounted for 56.2% of the family households; women maintained 89.6% of the one-parent family groups. Two-parent family groups made up 71.1% of the family households among Latinos. And women maintained 82.3% of the one-parent family groups.[97] The typical example of this family type is generally not as financially prosperous as its two-parent counterpart. Scholars and policymakers regularly discuss the social issues related to single-parent families, such as the importance of paternal role models and the significance of parental involvement in a child's schooling.[98]

In any event, we have seen an evolution of gender roles on the home front with regard to housework over the years. A study released in 2002 by the Institute for Social Research (ISR) at the University of Michigan found that there has been an overall decline in the amount of housework performed by Americans. Back in 1965, Americans averaged 52 hours of housework per week (12 for men, 40 for women); today Americans do an average of 43 hours of housework per week (16 for men, 27 for women). According to the ISR study, women do a total of 51 hours of un-paid housework and paid labor outside the home each week, compared to 53 hours for men. Less housework is being done than ever before due to the increasing number of two-parent working families. Clearly, Americans of both genders are prioritizing other tasks, such as childrearing, over housework.[99] Men almost certainly will continue to increase the amount of housework they perform, as a result of evolving societal attitudes on gender relations and the increasingly significant role women play in earning family income.

Substantial numbers of American women are stay-at-home mothers (SAHMs). In March 2002, approximately one out of four "children under 15 living with two married parents" were in households with full-time mothers.[100] And many working mothers with children at home take part-time, not full-time, jobs. To be sure, there are lifestyle changes and economic consequences for women who take time out from their careers to have children. (It is often common for full-time parents to reenter the workplace once their children go to school.) Yet many American women continue to select this lifestyle choice. They do so for many reasons, including the expensive nature of child care, the experiences of Gen Xers who grew up in the 1970s and 1980s as "latchkey kids" in two-parent working families, and the traditional cultural mores prevalent in many of the rapidly expanding precincts of Latino America. Another factor that drove the phenomenon in the 1990s was the booming economy.[101]

Likewise, the contentiousness of the "Mommy Wars" (between full-time mothers and mothers who work outside the home) seems to have subsided a bit. During the 1970s, the whole idea of at-home motherhood became rather unfashionable in many corners, as feminists popularized the idea of women having careers and paid labor by women outside the home became necessary to sustain a decent standard of living for many American families. By the early 1990s, some observers detected a "new traditionalist" outlook with regard to stay-at-home motherhood. This lifestyle choice seems to be hip, fashionable, and even a status symbol for affluent families in much of America. Nowadays, it has become more difficult to demarcate the boundary between "working mothers" and "at-home mothers," due to such developments as telecommuting and flexible work schedules.[102] In any event, full-time mothers play an important role in enabling their husbands to focus fully on their careers, thus boosting their professional prospects.[103] Yet some observers — Ann Crittenden chief among them — contend that the social and economic contributions of homemakers and full-time caregivers do not receive the same kind of respect and value as those of men and women who work outside the home.[104]

There are numerous support groups and advocacy organizations for full-time mothers. Some of these organizations serve both functions, as in the Elmhurst, Illinois–based Mothers and More and the Fairfax, Virginia, organization, Family and Home Network. Mothers and More is a national advocacy organization, in addition to a support group with at least 175 local chapters, which organize events and activities for mothers.[105] The Family and Home Network, meanwhile, publishes *Welcome Home*, a monthly magazine, and focuses on education, support, and advocacy.[106] Cathy Myers, the executive director of the Family and Home Network, contends that full-time mothers experience "isolation" and "invisibility" in American culture.[107] The leaders and members of such organizations as Mothers and More and the Family and Home Network attempt to raise the profile of mothers (and full-time parents) in America, so that the social and economic contributions of these individuals receive greater recognition in our culture. Moreover, one-income families with a male breadwinner now merit media attention related to the economic and emotional challenges facing the men in such roles.[108]

Measured by almost any standard, there has been tremendous progress in terms of gender equity within the American family during the last three to four decades. Compared to, say, 1963 or even 1973, family decision-making is now more democratic and parenting responsibilities are shared more frequently (along with household chores). These developments are being driven, in part, by changing gender attitudes and the advent of the two-parent working family. Women still perform the solid majority of the labor associated with housework and childrearing in most households. But in an increasing number of American families, there is a clear emphasis on having both parents share these responsibilities equally.[109] As a rule, most Americans consider contemporary fathers to be competent parents; this opinion is especially common among younger Americans.[110]

Survey data show that there are differences between white fathers and fathers of color in terms of how involved they are as parents in two-parent families. Using data from the 1997 Child Development Supplement to the Panel Study of Income Dynamics, the sociologist Sandra Hofferth found that cultural factors, economic circumstances, and neighborhood factors shape the respective approaches of white, black, and Latino fathers.[111] Race, of course, affects how fathers approach parenting: An African-American dad would probably be more likely than a white father to warn his sons to be careful around the police, due to his concerns about racial profiling. In the main, though, economic circumstances prove to be quite significant in terms of structuring the opportunities available to fathers — and, of course, their spouses and children.

No development better reflects the changing nature of gender relations than the emergence of the stay-at-home dad (SAHD).[112] One hundred five thousand married fathers live in SAHD/working mother families with children under 15 (a universe of 189,000 children altogether). This type of family arrangement involves approximately one out of every 200 children under 15 who live in two-parent families.[113] According to Jason Fields of the U.S. Census Bureau, " ... children under age 15 living with both parents were 56 times as likely [in March 2002] to live with a stay-at-home mother while their father was in the labor force than they were to live with a stay-at-home father while their mother was in the labor force."[114] At the same time, there are two million preschoolers whose fathers spend the most time with them out of all their child-care providers "while their mothers are at work." Approximately 20 percent of preschoolers with employed mothers fit into this category.[115]

There are numerous reasons why stay-at-home dad/working mother families develop. Some fathers become SAHDs when they join the ranks of the unemployed. Others choose to be full-time fathers because their wife's job, not theirs, has health benefits (and they want to have one parent at home with their child or children). And still others prefer to spend their time as a parent, rather than as an employee.[116] In addition, millions of American men discharge many of the duties of a SAHD, even though they do not do so on a full-time basis. Some American men develop a flexible schedule at work so that they can contribute significantly to their family's child-care needs during the week. Indeed, many American fathers are alternating-shift workers; they play a role like that of a full-time father in their children's lives.[117] Thus we can reasonably conclude that the number of men involved as full-time parents dramatically exceeds, in all likelihood, the figures cited by the Census Bureau.

American culture includes numerous stereotypes about stay-at-home dads and the working mothers who serve as the primary breadwinners of their families. One such stereotype is that the SAHD is inept and bumbling at discharging his domestic duties. Another stereotype is that the SAHD is "a loser" because he somehow cannot seem to find a well-paying job (neglecting the possibility that he chose to be a full-time father, in many cases). And some Americans erroneously believe that the SAHD is some kind of "wimp," whose spouse calls all the shots in the family. Similarly, a woman married to a full-time father may confront stereotypes as well, e.g., people who think that a working mother cannot be a good parent.[118] Many SAHDs complain that the popular image of men in their line of work does not accurately reflect the nature of full-time fatherhood. Portrayals of these gender pioneers still include half-truths, antiquated stereotypes, and even subtle mockery.[119]

Stay-at-home dads often report that they have special needs that are different from those fathers who work outside the home. Full-time dads often experience feelings of isolation, and they may feel slightly uncomfortable about their status as gender pioneers. They also frequently find it difficult — initially, at least — to relinquish the provider role. (Some SAHDs have home businesses.)[120] SAHDs write newsletters, form playgroups, operate Web sites, and network in other ways with their peers. Every year, there is an increase in the number of social outlets for at-home dads, particularly in and around the nation's large cities. These efforts, which usually involve middle- and upper-middle class white men, create a sense of community for full-time fathers. There even is an annual conference of full-time fathers (the At-Home Dads Convention) at Oakton Community College in Des Plaines, Illinois; this gathering was first held in 1996. Similarly, there is the At-Home Dad Network, an organization that promotes networking among SAHDs. Peter Baylies, a 47-year-old SAHD from North Andover, Massachusetts, founded — and serves as the director of — the At-Home Dad Network.[121]

Baylies's colleague, Jay Massey, owns and operates Slowlane.com, the premier Web site for full-time fathers. Massey, the 46-year-old executive director of Slowlane.com, lives in Pensacola, Florida, with his wife, Dr. Joann Massey, and their son, Tucker. After Tucker was born in 1994, the Masseys did not want to put him in day care. For logistical and economic reasons, they decided that Mr. Massey would be Tucker's primary caregiver. In addition, Jay Massey runs a national Web-development firm from his home office. The biggest challenges for full-time fathers, according to Massey, are the isolation, especially for new dads, and the gender stereotyping.[122] In any event, he says the "stay-at-home dad is the ultimate feminist" because his focus on the domestic sphere allows his wife to concentrate on her responsibilities in the workplace.[123]

Massey's work on Slowlane.com was an outgrowth of his networking with other dads on-line after Tucker's birth in 1994. He became the owner and operator of Slowlane.com in the fall of 1997. (Chris Stafford founded Slowlane.com in March 1997.) Using his technological expertise and connections among SAHDs around the world, Massey built Slowlane.com into the best-known and most-visited site for full-time fathers and their loved ones. With his Web site, he hopes to diminish the feelings of isolation that bedevil many full-time fathers as well as to give them a "sense of community." Slowlane.com provides SAHDs with myriad on-line resources, reference materials, and networking opportunities. His Web site receives 4,500,000 hits each year, according to Massey. Massey, who is white, tries to make Slowlane.com reflective of the racial and ethnic diversity of American SAHDs, even though there is little information on primary caregiving fathers in minority communities.[124]

Indeed, full-time dads of color are virtually invisible in American society. One exception is Hogan Hilling, a 49-year-old SAHD of Asian ancestry who lives in Irvine, California, with his wife, Tina Hilling, and their three sons. Hilling, an author and inspirational speaker, conducts seminars on parenting issues through his organization, Proud Dads. In his work, he focuses on issues of importance to full-time dads and working fathers. Hilling is skeptical about fathers' groups that segment men by race and ethnicity. The Californian notes that whenever he assembles a racially diverse group of fathers, they discuss fatherhood in race-neutral terms.[125] Likewise, race never arose as an issue or theme in either *Mr. Mom* (1983) or *Daddy Day Care* (2003). Both films trace the odysseys of temporarily unemployed fathers (characters played by Michael Keaton and Eddie Murphy, respectively) who become full-time parents.[126] The national media have begun to focus some attention on full-time dads of color: The 2003 *Newsweek* cover story about SAHDs included photos of a Latino family and an African-American family.[127]

In any event, SAHDs are becoming increasingly common — and socially acceptable. According to Peter Baylies, full-time fathers are now regarded as "a little bit unusual, but not bizarre."[128] Baylies cites three factors to explain this attitudinal change: widespread dissatisfaction with day care, the growing realization that many women now outearn men, and the generally positive portrait of SAHDs in the media.[129] For example, all three of *Time*'s Persons of the Year in 2002 — Coleen Rowley, Cynthia Cooper, and Sherron Watkins — have husbands who are full-time fathers.[130] Likewise, Daniel Mulhern, the spouse of Michigan Governor Jennifer Granholm, serves as the primary caregiver of their three children.[131] SAHDs are no longer a novelty anymore, particularly in many middle-class and affluent families, where the lady of the house earns excellent wages and benefits that enable her husband to be the full-time caregiver of their children.

Gender roles and family arrangements will almost certainly become more fluid, variegated, and egalitarian in the future. American men and women will have more options than ever before, in terms of how they want to structure their family lives. It may become commonplace for young couples, particularly those with significant economic prospects, to decide before marriage which partner will be the primary caregiver of the children. Anecdotal evidence suggests that twentysomething males readily accept a situation in which their spouse is the main breadwinner.[132] Younger American men increasingly take it for granted that they will (and should) do 50 percent of the domestic labor. Still, it remains to be seen whether young American men will develop a more "European" attitude toward family and work that leads to a restructuring of corporate attitudes on success in the workplace and corporate policies for working parents.

◠

Hundreds of thousands, perhaps even millions, of American men have participated in "the men's movement" since its origins in the 1970s. The activism on these issues includes men's rights, fathers' rights, men's liberation, the Promise Keepers, and the mythopoetic men's movement. Although most of the individuals involved in these groups happen to be white men, they rarely, if ever, mention their *white* maleness in the context of these activities.[133] Indeed, it seems very unlikely at this point that millions of white males would ever organize themselves in advocacy groups to try to gain power on the basis of their white maleness. For at least a decade there have been sporadic efforts by specific white men to organize other white men *as white men* in the police, firefighting, and correctional worlds.[134] Many white men refuse to associate themselves with such organizations because they do not want to be seen as racist or sexist. This is why we are unlikely to see mainstream, general-interest magazines that invoke the white maleness of their staff and readership — in other words, a white male *Essence* or *Latina*.

To be sure, various aspects of white maleness are already being studied in the academy, particularly in the fields of men's studies and whiteness studies (but not as white male studies). The discipline of men's studies emerged on college campuses during the 1980s, as the progressive analogue to the development of women's studies in the preceding decade.[135] By the mid-1990s, men's studies was flourishing on campuses around the nation.[136] Around this time a new discipline — whiteness studies — began to draw attention; as with men's studies, the academics in this field were usually leftists or even radicals who wanted to analyze the bases of white privilege, not to valorize or celebrate whiteness in any way.[137] Both men's studies and whiteness studies have encountered their fair share of skeptics: The doubters wonder why groups (men and whites) that seem to dominate American society need to be studied in an explicit sense. This type of reasoning matters on the global front as well, where the annual International Women's Day (March 8) is an accepted and celebrated symbolic instance of inclusion. However, the efforts to establish and celebrate an official International Men's Day have thus far proved to be unsuccessful, on the grounds that men wield tremendous power and, consequently, there is no need to focus on them as a specific group.[138]

Back in the United States, there are numerous progressive white males, including writers, academics, educators, activists, intellectuals, and antiracist trainers and organizers, who promote awareness of "white privilege" and "male privilege." They frequently write about what they see as the inability of many white Americans to come to grips with the benefits they enjoy as a result of their race. Antiracist white activists also contend that whites should "free" themselves from the psychologically troubling position of being complicit in white racism.[139] Similarly, some men (no one knows how many) actively identify as feminists, and work to help end what many activists see as patriarchal practices in our society. They work on feminist issues, either as part of feminist organizations or in male-run profeminist groups.[140] Usually white males who work in the fields of antiracism or antisexism focus on one or the other "ism" — they typically discuss their activism in terms of race *or* gender, not race *and* gender.[141]

Race and gender, to be sure, affect the life chances of many Americans when it comes to the matter of golf — and private clubs where golf is a means of conducting business. The United States still has all-white country clubs, including places where Jews are rarely, if ever, admitted to membership.[142] No one, of course, wants to be excluded from a social venue. "It's bigger than a social issue," contends Ron Jackson, an African-American activist in Alabama. "It's an economic issue. Many deals and business relationships are built in social settings, and if blacks are excluded, then the playing field is not level."[143] Likewise, an informal requirement that golf be part of corporate sales constitutes an exclusionary matter for women and people of color on two fronts: if they do not play golf, traditionally the bailiwick of white men; and if they are unable to gain access to the best private clubs and golf courses (or the best days and tee times) to entertain their clients and clinch deals.[144]

It is difficult to determine how many private golf courses and country clubs have men-only membership policies or all-white membership rosters. The latter type seems to be less common than the former. Organizations with exclusionary membership policies usually try to keep a low profile, so as to avoid controversy. Augusta National Golf Club, for instance, still does not admit women as members.[145] The survey data show that Americans are closely divided on Augusta's men-only membership policy, and that women, young people, and African Americans oppose it.[146] Overall, the increasing acceptance of women and minorities at elite clubs reflects the increasing affluence of these individuals, as well as the widely held view that clubs should not exclude people based on such factors as race, gender, or religion. It is now embarrassing for a public figure to be revealed as a member of an exclusionary club. Still, this issue does not seem to resonate with the typical woman or person of color, because it affects only the most affluent people, those who can afford to pay the initiation fees and membership dues of the elite clubs.

The discussion over dismantling the invisible barriers to advancement by disadvantaged Americans extends to the college admissions process. Take the much-maligned practice of legacy preference, or preferential treatment for the children (or relatives) of alumni, who are regularly admitted to institutions of higher learning with lower grades and test scores than the average applicant because their parents (or some other relative) went to the institution. Likewise, elite colleges and universities often grant admission to the children of wealthy parents, even if those young people have less-than-stellar grades and test scores, on the grounds that their parents will probably make sizable financial contributions to the educational institution. According to many multiculturalists, these interrelated practices (some legacies come from families that donate large amounts of money to their alma maters) amount to affirmative action for the white and well connected. So the multiculturalists contend that affirmative action as it is traditionally defined is simply a counterpart to existing practices that benefit affluent and wealthy whites.[147]

The typical American spends little time reflecting on the interrelationships between and among race, class, gender, and other factors that affect our life chances. Scholars, researchers, and journalists usually propound the most compelling, controversial, and thought-provoking ideas regarding different types of privilege. Julian Bond once published an opinion piece in which he posited that the passage of the Civil Rights Act of 1990 would finally relieve white males of the "burden" of having women and minorities always questioning their success, since they once only competed against other white men in so many sectors of our society.[148] As the historian Eric Foner, himself a white male, points out: "I have yet to meet the white male in whom special favoritism (getting a job, for example, through relatives or an old boys' network, or because of racial discrimination by a union or employer) fostered doubt about his own abilities."[149] White males, of course, do not usually look at matters in this way — and many of them would say there is no compelling reason for them to do so.

PART TWO

The Diversity Imperative

∽ chapter four ∽

Fair Play

Phil Nadeau thoroughly enjoyed Somali Culture Night, an event held at the Franco-American Heritage Center in Lewiston, Maine, one evening in April 2002.[1] Nadeau (NAH-doh), the assistant city administrator of Lewiston, joined the 500 "curious" and "excited" people who watched Somali dances, ate Somali foods, chatted with Somalis, and listened to Somali music and Somali speakers discuss Somali culture. As Nadeau tells it, he was "proud," "elated," "surprised," and "encouraged" by the turnout on Somali Culture Night. This event to promote better community relations was, in Nadeau's words, the "first public embrace" of the Somali newcomers to Lewiston, whose presence there would soon bring national and international media attention to this predominantly white community on the banks of the Androscoggin River.[2] Somali Culture Night had been organized as a way to bridge the cultural gaps that separated the newcomers from the longtime residents of Lewiston. There was a certain symbolic significance associated with having this event at the Franco-American Heritage Center, which honors a group of people who were once outsiders in Lewiston, but now dominate the politics and culture of the city.[3] On that April evening more than two years ago, Nadeau, a proud Franco American, represented the local establishment as he welcomed the latest group of immigrants to Lewiston.

The Somali refugees began to arrive in Lewiston in February 2001; they were secondary migrants from such places as Greater Atlanta and the Twin Cities. The previous year, Somali community leaders in various parts of the United States started to encourage their coethnics to consider Maine a possible home. However, there was an acute shortage of housing in Portland, Maine, the traditional destination for immigrants and refugees in the Pine Tree State. So Lewiston, a population-losing town once known for its textile mills and shoe manufacturers, became a hot destination for the Somali secondary migrants, once they learned that Lewiston had plenty of available (and inexpensive) housing. In addition, the Somalis were attracted to Lewiston by the prospect of living in a safe community with good schools, a nice pace of life, and a generous social-welfare system that would aid their integration into the local economy. The first Somalis moved to Lewiston in February 2001; by September 2002, there were 1,100 of them there. Now the Somali population numbers approximately 1,200.[4] The Somalis stand out in Lewiston due to their attire, language, religion, and skin color: They are black Africans and Sunni Muslims in a predominantly white and Catholic town where people speak English and/or French.[5]

From February 2001 to December 2002 Nadeau focused on community relations with regard to the Somali migrants in his capacity as assistant city administrator.[6] During the first two years of the new millennium, this compassionate man was the person in the city most responsible for fostering intercultural dialogue and good community relations. He did so through his talks about tolerance and inclusion to civic groups and his one-on-one conversations with city residents. Due to his straightforward discussions of the challenges facing Lewiston, Nadeau dispelled many of the inevitable misconceptions that accompanied the influx of Somali refugees. Despite the depopulation afflicting Lewiston — the city had 39,757 residents in 1990, a number that dropped to 35,690 in 2000 — many Lewistonians adopted a wait-and-see attitude toward the newcomers, because of the limited number of jobs available to people with few skills. Moreover, a significant number of Somalis are relying on this cash-strapped city's social-service bureaucracy (and its General Assistance Program) to survive.[7] Many white Lewistonians initially worried about what they saw as the possible social and economic costs associated with the migrants, in the form of depressed wages, crowded schools, and increased property taxes.[8]

Throughout 2001 and 2002, Nadeau skillfully managed community relations at the local level and presented an accurate and optimistic view of the Somalis-in-Lewiston story to the local and, later, the national and international media. During these years, he fielded press inquiries about the Somalis, oversaw the training of those city employees responsible for hiring Somali staffers, worked with public-safety professionals to ensure that they were responsive to the Somali population, and fulfilled data-reporting requirements in accordance with local, state, and federal dictates. Today Nadeau is no longer involved in day-to-day matters regarding the Somalis. Due to the increasing demands of the Somali portfolio, the City of Lewiston created a new position, that of the Immigrant and Refugee Programs Manager, which was funded by a two-year grant of $100,000 from the Maine Department of Labor. In December 2002,

Victoria Scott, a naturalized American of Slovak ancestry who grew up in Windsor, Ontario, was hired to fill this position. Scott works closely with members of the Somali community to ensure that they receive access to the programs and services necessary for them to thrive in Lewiston.[9]

By virtue of his ethnic background, his pro-diversity attitude, and his longtime roots in Lewiston, Nadeau was well positioned to embrace the Somalis who migrated to his hometown. Nadeau, who is three-quarters French Canadian and one-quarter Irish, was born in downtown Lewiston in January 1955. He grew up in Lewiston and graduated from Saint Dominic Regional High School in nearly Auburn, Maine, in 1972. Then Nadeau joined the Air Force; he worked at the Pentagon from 1972 to 1976. Nadeau eventually returned to Lewiston, where he and his wife, Marcia, raised their family. This voluble man with brown eyes, graying hair, and a mustache worked as a small businessman for a number of years. In September 1993, he received his B.S. in Public Administration through the University of Maine at Augusta. From May 1994 to May 1999, Nadeau served as Town Manager of Richmond, Maine. Then, in May 1999, he became Assistant City Administrator of Lewiston.

Nadeau is sympathetic to the Somalis in part because he recalls when the Francos, as he calls them, had limited opportunities to succeed in Lewiston. The early-twentieth-century immigrants from Quebec — a group that included Nadeau's forebears — encountered discrimination from the city's English-speaking Protestants. People once regularly referred to the Franco-American residents of Lewiston as "frogs," an epithet that reflected the then-widespread belief that people of French extraction were preordained to do manual labor and manufacturing work. (These attitudes no longer exist now that Franco Americans in Maine's second most-populous city have fully assimilated into the mainstream.) Some Franco Americans resent the fact that the Somalis, unlike the French-Canadian immigrants of a century ago, have access to such benefits as job training, educational opportunities, and translating services. Nadeau, though, believes that the community will benefit by facilitating the upward mobility of the Somalis as quickly as possible.

Today the Somalis are slowly becoming integrated into the mainstream of Lewiston. The overall picture looks good, even though the city's Somali unemployment rate is 50 percent and some white Lewistonians remain suspicious of the East Africans in their midst. Indeed, the periodic national news accounts about Lewiston now emphasize the relative peace in the city.[10] A journalist recently described Lewiston as "...one example of how a community can work through immigrant tensions and become a more vibrant place to live."[11] This judgment is warranted because volunteers, social workers, and city administrators promoted intercultural understanding and dispelled stereotypes and misconceptions through public forums and educational campaigns. There also have been cultural exchanges between the Somalis and the native-born majority, as well as English classes, social programs, and job-skills workshops for the newcomers.[12] Throughout the last three and one-half years, Phil Nadeau has emphasized the importance of diversity, inclusion, and equal opportunities for immigrants in Lewiston, thus providing us with an inspiring and workable case study for other predominantly white communities that confront rapid demographic changes.

EQUALITY FOR ALL

Fred Lynch knows what it is like to be controversial.[13] The 58-year-old sociologist received national recognition in the early and mid-1990s, as a result of his research on affirmative action and diversity initiatives. In late 1989, Lynch published his first book, *Invisible Victims: White Males and the Crisis of Affirmative Action,* a study of how white males are affected by affirmative action, particularly reverse discrimination.[14] Then, in early 1997, Lynch put out *The Diversity Machine: The Drive to Change the "White Male Workplace,"* a book that traces the history, evolution, and significance of the diversity movement in American life.[15] All through these scholarly works, he expresses his ample skepticism about what he sees as the shortfalls of politically correct thinking and decision-making with regard to multicultural topics.

Lynch's ground-breaking works, not surprisingly, have attracted a fair amount of media attention over the years.[16] During the mid-1990s he appeared on perhaps 150 radio and television programs to talk about white males, affirmative action, and diversity initiatives. Lynch stays in the public eye through his frequent book reviews, opinion pieces, and periodical articles. In his writings, he often describes the generational, occupational, and socioeconomic differences that separate white males. Lynch notes that elite white men support, develop, implement, and defend affirmative action programs. Today he continues to be a commentator on multicultural issues, but his work now focuses mainly on Baby Boomers and health care. The gregarious professor enjoys teaching and exchanging ideas with his colleagues around the country. His views on affirmative action and related topics resonate with many racial conservatives and, likewise, meet with disapproval from many multiculturalists.

Throughout his life, Lynch has spent much of his time in multiethnic communities and workplaces, experiences that have given him considerable insights into our nation's racial dynamics. This inquisitive iconoclast was born on August 27, 1945. During his childhood, he lived in Grosse Pointe, Michigan, a predominantly white community near Detroit. Lynch spent his adolescent years in another mainly white suburb — Richland Hills, Texas, in suburban Fort Worth. A tall, stocky man with dark blond hair and deep blue eyes, Lynch traces his ancestry to England and Ireland. After he earned his doctorate in sociology at the University of California-Riverside in 1973, the native Midwesterner taught sociology at Pitzer College in California for four years. Subsequently Lynch taught sociology in the California State University system from 1977 to 1991, at Cal State-Los Angeles and, later, Cal State-San Bernardino. He joined the Government Department at Claremont McKenna College in 1991 and has taught there ever since. A resident of California for more than three decades, Lynch closely observes the demographic changes that are remaking the Golden State. He presently resides in Upland, a characteristically multiethnic California city near the Claremont campus.[17]

Despite the fact that many conservatives have embraced his work on affirmative action and diversity initiatives, Frederick Lynch is definitely a moderate in ideological terms, one who voted for Green Party presidential candidate Ralph Nader in 2000. He takes decidedly liberal stances on a number of issues, particularly with regard to the root causes of crime. Professor Lynch readily concedes that institutional sexism and racism continue to affect adversely the life chances of women and minorities. However, he believes that affirmative action on the basis of race and gender is not the right way to counteract racism and sexism. Lynch would prefer instead to see our policymakers focus on programs that improve the life chances of economically disadvantaged people from all racial backgrounds. As a respected academic at one of the nation's best-ranked liberal arts colleges, Lynch's distinctive voice continues to be part of the national dialogue on race, ethnicity, and gender. He has been a pioneer in describing and analyzing the impact of affirmative action and diversity initiatives on white males, and his ideas will undoubtedly be part of our national discussions of these issues for years to come.

The ongoing efforts to promote equal opportunities for women and people of color usually cover most members of these historically disadvantaged groups, although white women and Asian Americans do not always qualify for inclusion in this context. Multiculturalists contend that affirmative action and diversity initiatives are justified in virtually any case in which white males are overrepresented relative to their percentage of the population, electorate, or labor force. Affirmative action and diversity initiatives remain quite popular with women and people of color (and a fair number of white males), who contend that such programs expand the range and quality of the opportunities available to members of underrepresented groups. In many cases, affirmative action leads to descriptive — and substantive — representation for women and people of color; other times, it results in what many multiculturalists would describe as tokenism.[18]

At one time, white males held what amounted to monopolies in many institutions of American society, even though they constituted perhaps 45 percent of the adult population. Daniel C. Maguire, for one, contends that such monopolies are bad for our country. He writes:

> The challenge to white male monopoly has taken the initial specific form of preferential affirmative action. This means that, as a monopoly-breaking measure, members of disempowered and excluded groups will be given preference over white males in sufficient numbers to change the social patterns of distribution. This policy is not voluntary but enforced and it is based upon the philosophical assumption that individual rights and career opportunities may at times be sacrificed for necessary and significant social goals.[19]

There are many instances, as in the print media, where practical needs require adherence to the diversity imperative. Many newspaper editors believe that journalists of color improve the quality of coverage of minority communities. Thus the American Society of Newspaper Editors initially set a goal for 2000 of having the newsrooms of America reflect the racial demographics of the communities they serve. This goal has now been extended to 2025, because it was not met in 2000. At present, 12.53% of the staffers working at American newspapers are minorities — people of color account for more than 30 percent of the U.S. population.[20] In any event, news organizations have worked very hard to be inclusive in their media coverage. Some news organizations consciously try to make sure that the experts quoted in their stories reflect the demographic makeup of the community. These efforts do not meet with approval from everyone — William McGowan, for instance, contends that the mainstream press demonstrates bias in favor of liberal positions on such topics as race, immigration, affirmative action, gay rights, and feminism.[21]

In the post-9/11 era, the issue of diversity matters very much to the nation's intelligence community. Much of the work in intelligence gathering involves sending people into foreign locales, where their ability to gain the trust of others and learn about critical matters often depends on their cultural and phenotypic compatibility with the target population. There are many places worldwide where an Anglo male does not fit in well, even if he speaks the local language flawlessly and is very familiar with local customs. This task is especially difficult for white men with fair skin and light-colored hair. Native speakers of such tongues as Urdu, Arabic, and Farsi are needed for covert operations, and many speakers of these tongues look different than the typical American "spy." So the Central Intelligence Agency (CIA) is trying to diversify its ranks, largely for pragmatic, not symbolic, reasons.[22]

Whites, meanwhile, continue to dominate America's large corporations. Today whites in Corporate America have lower rates of attrition than their minority colleagues, who are not particularly common in the ranks of senior management. And employees of color remain concentrated disproportionately in lower-ranking staff positions. The typical affirmative-action plan for a big company focuses mainly on sweeping goals over the long term as opposed to specifics.[23] At the same time, white women and people of color regularly appear in the pages of the business press, an occurrence that is more common today than it was even five years ago. Race and gender rarely come up as issues in these articles about high-powered decision-makers, even though some observers of Corporate America lament the fact that white men still dominate the top ranks of the business world.

Women and minorities face special challenges when they seek to integrate the power structure. Chief among these is the existence of white male norms, mores, and standards that may disadvantage females and people of color who differ in some way from those aspects of what may be described as "white male culture." Proponents of this type of thinking contend that there is a certain demeanor, a way of acting, and a way of speaking that is preferred by members of the "dominant culture," who are thus partial, if only unconsciously, to particular narratives and specific types of people. In their study of the power elite, Richard Zweigenhaft and William Domhoff isolate three factors that determine whether women and minorities will replicate the successes of straight white Christian males: class (the higher one's social class, the more likely s/he will succeed), education (there is a positive correlation between educational credentials, particularly from elite institutions, and success), and color (the lighter a minority person is, the more likely s/he will have a chance to join the power elite).[24] In any event, Zweigenhaft and Domhoff contend " ... that newcomers who seek to join the power elite have to find ways to demonstrate their loyalty to those who dominate American institutions — straight white Christian males."[25]

An important issue, of course, revolves around the extent to which racial discrimination injures the life chances of job seekers of color, and thus necessitates affirmative action to remedy these disadvantages.[26] Due to the existence of de facto segregation in large parts of our nation, one factor that negatively affects workers of color is the location of an employer's business. In this era of affirmative action, an employer can subvert affirmative-action goals by locating his or her operations in an area where the workforce is predominantly white. An employer, to be sure, may go to a community with an inexpensive labor force — and that place turns out to be mainly white (by happenstance). Regardless of whether one intentionally sites his or her business in a racially homo-geneous place, the employer can legitimately say in such circumstances that the company is meeting affirmative-action requirements in hiring, retention, and promotion. Such issues will be minimal, in fact, due to the demographic composition of the labor force in that context. It is difficult for low-income residents of central cities to commute long dis-tances to suburban jobs, particularly if there are no inexpensive bus or train connections to those locales. This is an excellent example of a seem-ingly race-neutral issue that may limit the opportunities available to some workers of color.[27]

The ongoing demographic transformation of America, coupled with new ideas about affirmative action and diversity initiatives, led to the rise of the diversity movement during the first part of the 1990s. Such proponents of diversity as Price Cobbs, Lewis Griggs, and R. Roosevelt Thomas Jr. either organized or played prominent roles in the national conferences of the early 1990s that established the diversity movement. The audiences at the aforementioned gatherings included CEOs, con-sultants, policymakers, and human resource officers. Cobbs, Griggs, Thomas, and their compatriots advocated an approach to affirmative action and diversity initiatives that focused on the financial benefits and demographic imperatives associated with diversity. To support their case, these proponents of diversity cited two influential reports: *Workforce 2000* (Hudson Institute, 1987) and *Report on the Glass Ceiling* (U.S. Department of Labor, 1991). Both reports pointed out that the work-force and markets of the United States were increasingly dominated in numerical terms by women and people of color; hence, the efforts to hire, retain, promote, and appeal to members of these groups assumed greater importance with each passing year.[28]

As part of their work, the leaders of the diversity movement sought to change the existing "white male" cultures in organizations, so as to include the legions of females and minorities flooding into the workplace. Seminars, lectures, and workshops on these issues soon became an integral part of academic, corporate, and governmental training programs, in addition to the curricula and textbooks of business schools. The diversity professionals promoted themselves as being able to train employees, managers, and executives to deal with the challenges of managing diversity. At the same time, they sought to create organizational cultures that were comfortable for women and people of color, by ensuring that the norms, standards, and requirements of the organizations did not favor white males and privilege their social and cultural characteristics. The diversity professionals argue that increased creativity and productivity result from their diversity initiatives and training sessions. In addition, these programs may make it less likely that a corporation or institution might be vulnerable to discrimination lawsuits or expensive problems related to regulatory issues. During the 1990s, this type of thinking won favor with the elites of American society.[29]

Today large American corporations, foundations, think tanks, educational institutions, and government agencies routinely have diversity training sessions and incorporate significant rhetorical commitments to diversity into their hiring efforts, marketing initiatives, and public-relations blitzes. It is typical for an institution to want to win high marks for the ethnic and racial heterogeneity of its employees, in addition to good ratings as to how well people of color do in that particular institutional setting.[30] White men, of course, continue to be an important part of the U.S. workplace: White males made up 45.4% of the civilian labor force in 2000. This percentage is projected to drop to 43.8% by 2008.[31] At the same time, institutions, particularly corporations, are beginning to take into account the feelings of their rank-and-file white male employees when it comes to mentoring programs, employee groups, and other aspects of their diversity initiatives. Still, it is not uncommon for white men to walk away from a diversity training session and ask, "What about me?"[32]

In any event, how a white male feels about affirmative action and diversity initiatives depends on how he defines his self-interest. Many

white men, it should be noted, vigorously support such efforts to promote inclusion. This seems to be particularly true in politics, academia,
the media, the military, and Corporate America, institutions where white
men often enthusiastically endorse the diversity imperative. An increasing number of companies have modified their diversity initiatives and
affirmative-action programs to incorporate the concerns of their white
male employees. In particular, they try to address the widespread belief in white male America that such efforts could make it more difficult
for white men to be hired and earn promotions. More and more, corporations seek to create diversity programs that fully include white male
employees, so that they accept the legitimacy of, and enthusiastically participate in, such initiatives.[33] In any event, young white males realize the
job market is far more competitive than it was for men in the generations
that preceded them. For instance, white male candidates may say something along the lines of "they were looking for a woman or minority"
(and not necessarily with any rancor, either) to explain their inability to
get a job at a certain university during a hiring search.[34]

For about three decades, some whites, particularly white males, have
grumbled about "reverse discrimination," the idea that affirmative action and diversity initiatives have created new forms of discrimination,
by purportedly favoring women and people of color over similarly situated white males. Many white males feel ambivalent about, or hostile
toward, the aforementioned efforts to promote equal opportunities. They
sometimes believe that such programs disadvantage them as individuals,
by treating them as faceless members of an unquestionably powerful and
privileged group.[35] Here is how one white male responded to a 1993
survey about the topic:

> I am a white male. I am discriminated against because I'm not gay,
> I'm not a minority, I'm not a woman, I'm not handicapped and
> I'm white; therefore I get no favoritism, only the opposite. Our
> company is so busy trying to be fair to those who say, "You are ne-
> glecting me because I have this particular (whatever)" that they hold
> off the average white male, which is discrimination in reverse.[36]

It is very difficult to determine the extent to which reverse discrimination exists in American society. For starters, definitions of reverse
discrimination depend on the person, and where s/he stands ideologically. Some multiculturalists would argue that reverse discrimination (as
it is defined in the above quotation) is virtually nonexistent, while some

racial conservatives would contend that it is rampant throughout American society. No one knows how many white men consider themselves to be victims of reverse discrimination, although white men regularly make such claims in journalism, the academy, the military, and Corporate America. In an opinion piece published in 1991, Frederick R. Lynch wrote, "General population polls conducted by Gordon Black Associates in 1984 and by the National Opinion Research Center in 1990 suggest that 1-in-10 white men has been injured by affirmative action. This figure alone adds up to millions. Circumstantial evidence suggests even larger numbers."[37] However, the sociologist Fred L. Pincus contends that reverse discrimination is a myth — this is the subject of his book, *Reverse Discrimination.*[38]

One of the most interesting developments on the race-and-gender front has to do with the fact that women presently constitute a solid majority of the undergraduates on the nation's campuses. This development can be traced back, in part, to Title IX of the Education Amendments of 1972. As a result of Title IX, federally funded institutions cannot discriminate on the basis of gender in educational activities or programs. Observers credit Title IX with many benefits. For one, it led to more women completing undergraduate, graduate, and professional programs of study. Title IX also improved the options available to female students in the traditionally male bastions of math and science, which are critical for an increasing number of high-paying jobs. In addition, it expanded the range of possibilities for females in the workforce, particularly in terms of the professions (including law, medicine, and dentistry), that were once largely male. And perhaps most significantly, Title IX played an important role in altering and shaping the expectations many Americans have about the abilities and academic potential of females.[39]

For more than two decades now, women have been the stars on our college campuses. Women earned more undergraduate degrees than men for the first time during the 1981–1982 school year.[40] "Since 1984," notes one source, "the number of women in graduate schools has exceeded the number of men."[41] In the 2003–2004 school year, women were projected to earn 58.2% of all bachelor's degrees, 57.8% of the master's degrees, and 44.0% of the doctorates.[42] White middle- and upper-middle-class males are less affected by the gender disparity on undergraduate campuses than black and Latino men or, for that matter, white males from modest socioeconomic backgrounds.[43] This is an important point, because the discussions of males in the educational system, at least in the popular press, rarely involve much consideration of the unique issues that come into play when race intersects with gender. The experiences of white males at female-dominated undergraduate institutions differ, depending on the school, their discipline, and, perhaps, most importantly, their ability to work, compete, and interact with women on an equal basis.

Scholars and policymakers seek to understand why women now pursue higher education in greater numbers than men do. There are nuanced discussions of why this disparity between the sexes exists at the level of postsecondary education in our society. Some observers, for example, speculate that the learning styles of women allow them to connect better in the classroom. Others say that men, more so than women, embrace the images of short-term gratification in our popular culture, a factor that may lead them to be less likely to pursue higher education. One of the most interesting possibilities, which highlights the intersection of race, gender, and social class, is that men face more social pressure than women, particularly in black and Latino families, to hold jobs at the same time that they attend a college or university.[44] In any event, the male/female gap among undergraduates on campuses is actually growing: Women will make up 59% of those people earning bachelor's degrees during the 2010–2011 school year.[45]

As part of the increasingly broad conceptions of disadvantage in American society, some experts now predict dire consequences for us as a nation if young males of all colors do not receive more attention in the realm of public policy. In May 2003, *BusinessWeek* devoted an entire cover story (written by Michelle Conlin) to what it described as "the new gender gap."[46] Conlin speculated that the developing economic and educational imbalances between the sexes might result in "societal upheavals," which could have the effect of changing social policies, family finances, and work-family practices.[47] Michelle Conlin contends that " . . . attaining a decisive educational edge may finally enable females to narrow the earnings gap, punch through more of the glass ceiling, and gain an equal hand in rewriting the rules of corporations, government, and society."[48]

Nonetheless, many experts say that lingering instances of sexism continue to bedevil women of all races (as evidenced by the glass ceiling and the pay gap between the genders).[49] As recently as 2002, 28.5% of U.S. men were college graduates, compared to 25.1% of U.S. women. A slight gender gap existed in white America with regard to college-graduation rates: 29.1% of white males and 25.4% of white females have earned bachelor's degrees.[50] And for every educational category, the mean annual earnings of white males are significantly greater than those for white females. In 2001, the mean earnings per year for white males with bachelor's degrees were $65,046 versus $36,698 for white females with the same level of education. Similarly, the mean annual earnings for white males with doctorates were $98,158 — and $63,787 for white females. The gender gap in pay was even greater for whites who hold professional degrees: $122,560 for white males and $64,668 for white females.[51] These data seem to explain why some young women feel they have to work harder than their male peers in order to advance in American society.[52]

THE VALUE OF DIVERSITY

As an undergraduate, Derek Korbe attended every home football and basketball game at Alabama State University, the predominantly black institution of higher learning in Montgomery, Alabama.[53] Only one characteristic distinguished him from the vast majority of the ASU fans: his race.[54] Korbe is white, with red hair, blue eyes, freckles, a bushy red goatee, and very fair skin that burns easily in the hot Alabama sun. At six foot one and 260 pounds, the Irish-German Korbe resembles an Olympic powerlifter. The 29-year-old native of the Mobile area entered Alabama State University in January 1998. His mother was completing her master's degree there at the time. Korbe is considered a "minority" at ASU: White students qualify for minority scholarships at such Historically Black Colleges and Universities (HBCUs) as Alabama State University, Jackson State University, and Tennessee State University.[55]

When Korbe entered ASU, the university awarded him an Incentive Scholarship that covered the cost of his tuition and books for four years. This scholarship, among others, resulted from a court order that set aside $1 million in federal funds each year from 1995 to 2005 to finance the educational expenses of whites who attend ASU. Qualified white students at Alabama State University receive free tuition and books. In fact, the vast majority of ASU's 467 white students get scholarships.[56] Korbe, of course, liked the minority scholarship, but he never discussed the issue much with his African-American peers. It was a touchy subject with some of them. In any event, Korbe's status as one of ASU's "minority" students never bothered him. One semester he was the only white student in any of his classes — and all of his professors were white men. Indeed, Korbe offers only positive reflections on every aspect of student life at

ASU, including the professors, the coursework, the dorm life, and the social scene.

Korbe has lived, played, studied, and worked with African Americans for much of his life. His secondary school in Baldwin County, Alabama, was roughly 50 percent black and 50 percent white. Korbe's social circle included mostly whites throughout his high school years. After graduating from high school in 1993, Korbe spent several years working and traveling before he matriculated at ASU. He had an African-American roommate for a couple of years in the mid-1990s. During his four years as an undergraduate, this likable, easygoing man was a popular figure on campus, where students knew him as "D" or "Big D." His best friend in college was white, but virtually all of his other friends were African Americans. Every one of his college roommates happened to be black. As an undergraduate, young African-American women at ASU regularly asked this physically imposing ex-football player to escort them to their cars at night. Korbe enjoyed such rapport with his black peers that they sometimes joked, in a lighthearted fashion, about race.

By all accounts, Korbe is an ASU success story. This physical education major received his bachelor's degree in May 2002 (he earned a 3.2 G.P.A. during his undergraduate years). In recognition of his academic achievements, he made the 2002 edition of *Who's Who Among Students in American Universities and Colleges*. As a graduate student, Korbe once again benefited from ASU's minority scholarship. He earned a master's degree in counseling education from his alma mater in May 2004. Korbe, after all, wants to be an educator and coach. He intends to work in Alabama, Florida, or Georgia, so it is highly likely that he will teach and coach sizable numbers of black — and white — students. During his 13 semesters at ASU, Korbe was a pioneer and a trailblazer. His positive experiences there provide an excellent example of a white man who flourishes in a primarily black environment.

The multicultural mindset now takes into account an ever-broadening array of issues, models, and groups. Academics, journalists, and policymakers regularly discover unfolding social, cultural, economic, and political trends that relate to race, ethnicity, and gender. These trends often involve white males, who count toward diversity goals in a small but increasing number of cases, and not just as the default group against which "diversity" is traditionally measured. Indeed, white males occasionally qualify for affirmative action based on their maleness, whiteness, or even white maleness. Such instances, though rare today, are going to occur more frequently in the future, particularly in multiethnic areas where white males may be underrepresented in certain sectors of the labor force. For the time being, white males, as a rule, usually do not find themselves in the spotlight simply for being white males.

White males typically receive attention for the purposes of diversity based on other characteristics, such as their ethnicity, religion, social class, national origin, (dis)abilities, or even their race or gender. (One exception to this unwritten rule would be the periodic news stories about white athletes in primarily black contexts.) The media also focus on specific white males because of their activism, their idiosyncrasies, their acts of heroism, or their triumphs against adversity. *People* magazine, for example, alternates its coverage of celebrities with heartwarming stories of ordinary people who have done remarkable deeds, triumphed over great odds, courageously battled a disease, or who are quirky and not quite part of the mainstream. Similarly, *Reader's Digest* frequently publishes human-interest stories, which focus on everyday acts of love, faith, heroism, and commitment; such stories often feature white males whose appeal transcends race.

To be sure, white males periodically receive benefits and/or attention based on characteristics that do not explicitly take their whiteness or maleness into account. Ethnicity and national origin are two such factors. For example, Armenian Americans in the Los Angeles suburbs contend that Burbank has too few Armenians in city government, and that Glendale needs more Armenians on the police force.[57] Likewise, Arab Americans receive affirmative action in public contracting in San Francisco. And Italian Americans qualify as members of an affirmative-action category at the City University of New York (CUNY).[58] Meanwhile, white Hispanics are considered to be Latino, not Anglo, even if they are unmistakably Caucasian. Intriguingly, some localities and institutions, primarily in Ohio, recognize white Appalachians as members of a minority group eligible for participation in affirmative-action programs and other initiatives to increase the opportunities available to traditionally disadvantaged groups.[59]

The issues involving disadvantage and the Appalachian people are particularly salient in Cincinnati, Ohio, a city with a sizable Appalachian-origin population and a network of activists and policymakers who work on behalf of Appalachians. "Urban Appalachians," note two observers, "have gained recognition by city government, the school board, and community social agencies as Cincinnati's second largest minority group after blacks."[60] This designation takes into account the fact that many Appalachian migrants to Cincinnati have encountered prejudice and limited opportunities there. It is common to speak of Appalachians as one of Cincinnati's minority groups, due to the fact that the city's less-affluent Appalachians and African Americans are affected by similar issues, including few marketable skills, negative cultural stereotypes, residence in poor communities, and low levels of educational attainment.[61] As with African Americans, Appalachians in Cincinnati benefit from organizations that provide them with valuable assistance, e.g., the Urban Appalachian Council of Greater Cincinnati.[62]

Unless a person of Appalachian regional origin speaks with a pronounced regional accent — or highlights her or his origins in, say, Kentucky, Tennessee, or West Virginia — s/he is unlikely to face any social discrimination in most of the United States. Appalachians tend to be white and trace their ancestry to such places as the British Isles and Germany, so their names, physiognomies, and cultural heritage do not distance them from the American mainstream, unless they are poor. The difference between a white Appalachian and a person of color is that socioeconomic mobility will erase virtually all of the distinguishing features that stigmatize Appalachians in our society. In other words, a white school principal who grew up poor in rural Kentucky will not, in all likelihood, have any trouble hailing a taxi in Washington, D.C. His African-American counterpart from the Mississippi Delta might have some entirely different experiences in this regard. Thus the conceptions of diversity and minority status for Appalachians proceed on the premise that many members of this group need assistance on the basis of social class.

Jews, though, periodically find themselves included in the multicultural mosaic on the basis of ethno-religious considerations. Thus in 1992 Bill Clinton made a campaign issue out of what he saw as Jewish underrepresentation in the high ranks of the Bush administration.[63] In 1995 John Deutch became the first Jewish-American director of the CIA, but little attention was paid to this milestone.[64] During the 2000 election season, Democratic vice-presidential nominee Joseph Lieberman, an Orthodox Jew, made history as the first Jew on a major-party ticket in a presidential election. The Jewish faith of Virginia Republican Eric Cantor, the chief deputy whip of the U.S. House, has been duly noted by the media, in part because he is the only Jewish Republican in the lower chamber of Congress.[65] Since Jews are well-represented in numerical terms in most American institutions, they usually are lumped together with white Christians for diversity purposes.

Arab-American men, Christians and Muslims alike, sometimes qualify as "minorities" when it comes to certain considerations of diversity. The practice of describing Arab Americans as a minority group à la the protected classes seems to depend on the characteristics of the person in question, and the context in which the discussion occurs. Few Americans think of Ralph Nader (a Lebanese American), Ray Irani (a Lebanese American), or Mitch Daniels (a Syrian American) as minorities. Energy Secretary Spencer Abraham is occasionally referred to as a minority in media accounts, perhaps in part because of his "ethnic" appearance. In any event, there has been a flurry of news attention paid to Arab Americans in the last three years. These news stories about Arab-American soldiers, comedians, politicians, businesspeople, and others focus on the ordinariness of such individuals, as well as the challenges they face due to their ethnicity, national origin, and, in the case of Muslims, religious affiliation.

Portuguese Americans continue to be one white ethnic subgroup whose members are classified as minorities in certain contexts. During the 1970s the Office of Management and Budget (OMB) decided that the Hispanic category did not include people with Portuguese antecedents, as in those who came from Brazil or Portugal. Since 1981, however, Portuguese Americans have enjoyed various degrees of eligibility in terms of minority-contracting opportunities.[66] To be sure, Portuguese Americans are garden-variety non-Hispanic whites — the terms Latino and Hispanic in the present context usually refer to people who trace their ancestry to Spanish-speaking countries. But the three Portuguese-American members of the U.S. House of Representatives — California Democrat Dennis Cardoza, California Republican Devin Nunes, and California Republican Richard Pombo — are seen as Latino or Hispanic on occasion.[67] As with other Mediterranean Caucasians, e.g., the Greeks, the Italians, the Spaniards, and the Lebanese, the Portuguese encompass a significant amount of diversity in terms of their coloration and physical appearance. However, only the Spanish and Portuguese qualify for inclusion in some affirmative-action programs. The Iberian connection, it seems, is enough to allow Portuguese Americans periodic entry into the "Latino" camp.

Openly gay white males are another group of Americans who regularly find themselves described as minorities; indeed, the media often focus on them as a group separate from straight white males. Accomplishments by these individuals result in coverage similar to that of female and minority pioneers, role models, and trailblazers. James Hormel, a Clinton appointee, was the first openly gay U.S. ambassador. In 2000,

Vermont Democrat Ed Flanagan made history as "the first openly gay Senate candidate ever nominated by a major party."[68] And last year, Rev. Canon V. Gene Robinson became the Anglican Communion's first openly gay bishop (he was elected to head the Diocese of New Hampshire); this development inspired bitter controversy within the Episcopal Church and among Anglicans around the world. These milestones involving GWMs continue to occur in politics, religion, and other sectors of our society, as the stigma attached to open homosexuality fades.

Similarly, white males with disabilities of various types merit attention in the diversity arena based on their disabilities, not their whiteness or maleness. Such figures as Jim Brady, Mattie Stepanek, John Hockenberry, and Erik Weihenmayer have received considerable recognition, in large part because their personal stories about overcoming adversity resonate with Americans. In particular, the actor Christopher Reeve garners a significant amount of public attention due to his advocacy of research on spinal cord injuries.[69] As a group, politicians have become quite open and forthright about their physical infirmities. "Analysts," writes Dale Russakoff, "say the frankness mirrors changes in society, from growing acceptance of people with disabilities to an aging electorate facing its own health issues to a full-disclosure media culture in which the privacy of public figures has become an oxymoron."[70] White men with disabilities are often eligible for affirmative action and inclusion in discussions of multiculturalism, on the grounds that people with disabilities constitute a minority group.

Gender, at least in the realm of undergraduate admissions, is now a factor that allows males (many of whom are white) to qualify for informal affirmative action. Due to the decreasing percentage of men earning undergraduate degrees, some institutions, particularly liberal-arts colleges that lack large sports programs, practice affirmative action for male undergraduates. The purpose of these gender preferences is to keep some semblance of gender proportionality in the college population, even as female students have better academic records, on average, than their male counterparts. Male students may have a slight edge over similarly situated female applicants at many private, four-year colleges due to the idea that gender balance matters very much with regard to social life, class dynamics, and academic quality. Therefore, admissions officers and college administrators are reexamining, in many cases, their methods of evaluating applicants. Thus some admissions officials want to give SAT scores more significance in the admissions process (men tend to do well on the SAT).[71]

Many students, admissions officers, and college officials favor affirmative action for male applicants to undergraduate programs because they believe that some semblance of parity between the genders enhances students' academic and social experiences on campus. More so than ever before, schools face tremendous competitive pressures to be attractive to prospective applicants — gender balance is important to many undergraduates these days. This is a nonissue for the most elite universities; such institutions receive an abundance of applications. However, those schools with less elite reputations could find that gender proportionality is necessary to recruit and retain top-notch students. Therefore, some officials try to appeal to male students by producing brochures in more "masculine" colors and by adding more male faces to their marketing materials. Admissions officials also seek to attract male applicants — and students — by highlighting male-friendly topics such as their institution's sports teams and the male-dominated disciplines on campus (e.g., math, physics, and computer science).[72]

Americans on and off campus debate how to go about enticing more men to pursue higher education, in addition to the merits of gender preferences for men in the admissions process. There are those on the Multicultural Left, particularly women's rights advocates who remember when women faced outright discrimination as they attempted to integrate once all-male institutions, who see the gender-balance topic as a nonissue. They feel that men do not need gender preferences and that women — and men — should be admitted solely on the basis of their academic records, regardless of how this criterion will affect the gender balance in American higher education. Many admissions officers pay little attention to this argument. At the same time, there are questions about the legality of affirmative action for male undergraduates. It is possible that such gender-balancing programs will come under fire in the near future. Legal suits against this type of initiative might influence the methods used by colleges to recruit male students, and further skew the demographics on campus in favor of females.[73]

Regardless, occupational segregation continues to be an important part of the American workplace, from nursing to infotech. Each occupation has an "occupational culture," which is, of course, affected by the racial and gender composition of the labor force. Much of the American labor force continues to be affected by race and sex employment segregation.[74] There are few female car salespeople, for example; women account for eight percent of car sales agents in the United States. This statistic affects the environment in which female car sales agents work, and the likelihood that a woman will stick with what is, after all, a business with high turnover.[75] In the academy, observers regularly discuss the effects of the "feminization" of certain academic disciplines — namely, sociology, psychology, and anthropology — that were once primarily dominated by men. Part of this discussion involves considerations of whether the pay and prestige of these professions have declined as a result of the increasingly substantial female presence there.[76]

White males also face complex and interesting issues (as males) if they work in predominantly female occupations. For the record, women dominate the following occupations: hotel clerks (73% female), waiters (76% female), underwriters (76% female), cashiers (77% female), apparel-sales workers (78% female), file clerks (82% female), telephone operators (83% female), legal assistants (84% female), librarians (86% female), special-education teachers (86% female), dietitians (86% female), bank tellers (87% female), hairdressers and cosmetologists (90% female), dressmakers (92% female), teachers' aides (92% female), speech therapists (92% female), occupational therapists (93% female), registered nurses (93% female), typists (95% female), stenographers (95% female), cleaners and servants (96% female), child-care workers (97% female), secretaries (98% female), dental hygienists (98% female), and preschool/kindergarten teachers (98% female).[77] Men are making tentative steps into certain traditionally "female" occupations and professions, due to slowly changing male and societal attitudes on such matters.

There are important issues about gender privilege that arise when one considers the experiences of men in female-dominated occupations.[78] The sociologist Christine L. Williams has found that men are reluctant to enter predominantly female occupations such as nursing, social work, librarianship, and elementary school teaching, in part because the pay and prestige of such jobs are lower than those with a largely male workforce. To be sure, Williams found that men in traditionally female fields sometimes benefit from what she describes as the "glass escalator," in that they may be encouraged to go into higher-paying subfields within the profession and to try for administrative and supervisory positions.[79] Referring to the financial compensation of males in mainly female workplaces, Williams writes, "These salary figures indicate that the men who do 'women's work' fare as well as, and often better than, the women who work in these fields."[80]

It is becoming increasingly common for men to seek work in female-dominated occupations, including nursing, teaching, housekeeping, and child care. Some men do so because they want greater job satisfaction (and more flexible hours), while others hope to find employment in fields with plenty of openings and prospects for steady work. Women are watching this trend carefully. Some observers believe that the pay and prestige associated with such occupations as teaching and child care will not improve until the percentage of men increases in those fields. Other women, though, remain concerned that they will face increased competition from men for entry-level positions and management jobs in what continue to be female bastions.[81] There have been no concerted efforts to encourage men to enter these female-friendly occupations; rather, a combination of economic conditions and lifestyle choices have increased male participation in this realm of American life.

Stereotypes remain an issue that bedevils men in predominantly female occupations. "Younger men," writes Lisa Takeuchi Cullen, "seem less concerned about gender stereotypes than do their elders, perhaps because many grew up with working mothers, with girls as equals in the classroom or with female bosses. If women can be police officers or CEOs, they reason, why can't men be kindergarten teachers or librarians?"[82] That said, men who enter mainly female fields might be disparaged, joked about, or simply misunderstood for their career choices. Very few men work in child care, so some child-care agencies are reluctant to hire men, due to concerns about pedophilia and parental discomfort with male child-care workers. However, some busy urban parents of boys actually request male nannies. Perhaps most troubling to students of gender issues is the fact that many female-dominated occupations do not have much social prestige or many economic rewards, and men who enter such fields sometimes find themselves regarded by people as insufficiently ambitious.[83]

KEEPING THE FAITH

Sundays are very busy days for Father Bernard E. Weir of the Diocese of Davenport in southeastern Iowa. He begins each Sunday with an English-language Mass at 8:00 a.m. — and a Spanish-language Mass two hours later — at St. Mary's Church in Muscatine, Iowa. Then he drives 25 miles southwest of Muscatine to Columbus Junction, Iowa, to conduct a Spanish Mass at noon at St. Joseph's Church. And on the second and fourth Sundays of each month, Father Weir celebrates a Mass at 3:00 p.m., also in Spanish, at St. Mary's Church in West Burlington, Iowa, 35 miles southeast of Columbus Junction. Father Weir has been involved with the Latino community since July 4, 1991, when he was assigned by the Diocese of Davenport to be the pastor of St. Joseph the Worker Roman Catholic Church in Columbus Junction.[84] In 1991 Father Weir eagerly volunteered to minister to the Spanish-speaking immigrants in the Diocese of Davenport, as the Church leaders sought to integrate the Latino Catholics who migrated to southeastern Iowa to work in the meat-packing industry and other businesses.[85]

After all, Weir had always wanted to work with the disadvantaged and "the marginalized" ever since his boyhood in Albia, a small, predominantly white community in the south-central part of Iowa.[86] Bernard E. Weir was born on July 11, 1955, and he "grew up very white," as he puts it, in a working-class family.[87] The son of a Scottish-American father and an Irish-American mother, this kindly and talkative man has brown eyes, a neatly trimmed goatee, a full head of gray hair, and spectacles that give him a scholarly air. Weir, who came to the priesthood with a background in religious education, was ordained on June 21, 1986; he graduated from the University of Saint Mary of the Lake, the seminary in Mundelein, Illinois.[88] The newly ordained priest spent the first five years of his career working with Euro-American parishioners in such communities as Bettendorf, Iowa, and Burlington, Iowa. From July 1991 to June 1999 he conducted the English and Spanish Masses at St. Joseph's.[89] Then, in 1998, Weir became head of Our Lady of Guadalupe Mission in Muscatine, Iowa; in this capacity, he ministers to the Spanish-speaking immigrants of Muscatine. His pastoral responsibilities also include the Latinos of Columbus Junction and, since 2001, their coethnics in West Burlington. And he still ministers to Anglos, mainly in Muscatine.[90]

Weir strives mightily to embrace his Latino — and Anglo — parishioners. From the beginning of his career, he has voiced a pro-immigration, pro-diversity perspective from the pulpit, a stance that does not always endear him to his Anglo parishioners.[91] Father Weir empathizes with the Latinos, in part because of the eye-opening experiences he had when he spent six weeks at a language school in Guadalajara in 1992. For the first time, he "learned what it is like to be a minority."[92] Initially he spoke no Spanish, and no one mistook this fair-skinned *norteamericano* for a Mexican. Although many Mexicans treated him kindly, he also had the bus pass him by, at least one shopkeeper refuse to help him, and a man swear at him for no apparent reason. Weir eventually learned to speak the Spanish language, with the inflections of his native Iowa, during a couple of stints in 1994 and 1995 at a language school in Michoacán State. Today he calls himself "Padre Bernie Weir," a title that symbolizes his bifurcated Anglo/Hispanic identity and his inclusive perspective on matters related to culture, ethnicity, and nationality.[93]

As a rule, Father Weir ministers to his parishioners wherever they are, even if they do not attend church regularly. During the week Weir spends much of his time talking to Hispanics who do not come to church often. Some Latinos have schedules that require them to work on weekends. Others avoid going to church for personal reasons, but they remain devout Catholics. To reach these individuals, Weir attends as many social events as his schedule allows, including dances, weddings, soccer games, and *quinceañera* celebrations. He even reaches out to drug dealers and gang members. Padre Weir has become such a familiar figure in the Hispanic communities of southeastern Iowa, particularly in Columbus Junction, that no one looks twice if a person speaks to him about marital problems or goes to confession at a community event. The Catholic Church continues to prosper in Latino America due to the presence of enthusiastic, dedicated priests like Padre Bernie Weir, who reach out to their parishioners in a culturally sensitive fashion, and who involve the laypeople in their parish to the extent that the parishioners feel a close connection to the Church.

Roman Catholicism and Sunni Islam are the world's most racially and ethnically diverse religious denominations.[94] There are an estimated 1,067,053,000 Catholics in the world. Of these the largest share, 466,226,000, reside in Latin America, followed by Europe (285,554,000), Africa (123,467,000), Asia (112,086,000), North America (71,391,000), and Oceania (8,327,000).[95] The United States is home to the fourth-largest Catholic population in the world (after Brazil, Mexico, and the Philippines).[96] In 2002, for instance, 25 percent of American adults identified as Catholic.[97] American Catholics constitute a minority in what continues to be a majority-Protestant country, but they face little discrimination on the basis of religion anymore.[98] The U.S. Catholic population is presently 64% white, 29% Latino, 3% black, 3% Asian, and 2% Other.[99] Issues related to integration and assimilation have always been part of the dialogue in Catholic America — a century ago, Poles, Germans, Italians, and others criticized the Church for being insufficiently responsive to their needs.[100]

Every year, Catholic America becomes more ethnically and racially heterogeneous, due in large part to the continuing influxes of Catholic immigrants from such places as Latin America and the Philippines. At the same time, the ranks of the diocesan priests and Church hierarchy remain primarily white. The Catholic leadership in the United States, which is heavily Irish, consistently offers rhetorical support for the needs of immigrants and ethnic minorities, and it espouses positions on social-welfare issues that resonate with these individuals.[101] The United States Conference of Catholic Bishops (USCCB), for instance, has a Secretariat for Hispanic Affairs and a Secretariat for African American Catholics. Moreover, the organizational structures of many dioceses and archdioceses include offices for specific ethnic and racial groups. And U.S. Church leaders often speak at least two languages, including English and Spanish. The ecclesiastics, lay leaders, and hierarchy of the Church, as a rule, embrace the ethnic and racial diversity of Catholic America, particularly in a rhetorical sense.

Issues related to ethnic outreach, of course, differ from parish to parish, and from diocese to diocese. Some Anglo priests minister to homogeneous all-minority parishes with few, if any, ethnic tensions. Other white ecclesiastics minister to congregations where one panethnic group, such as Latinos, predominates, but where there are ethnic frictions within the parish. Then there are Anglo priests who minister to fractious multiethnic and multilingual congregations. Of course, white ecclesiastics differ dramatically in terms of how they react to demographic changes. Some white men in the Church actively seek multiethnic parishes; others enthusiastically embrace a changing parish or a new assignment to such a parish. Some white pastors, though, do not want to conduct pastoral outreach to immigrants and people of color, but are forced to do so because of demographic change. Still others are receptive to doing ethnic outreach, but fear they do not have the requisite cultural and linguistic skills to be effective in this type of ministry. In any event, there is probably no other institution in American society where so many white men spend so much of their time working with, and on behalf of, immigrants and people of color.

Father Edward Poettgen, the 50-year-old pastor of St. Polycarp Catholic Church in Stanton, California, offers many insights regarding the complexities of ministering to diverse groups of Catholics. St. Polycarp, after all, is 60% Latino, 20% Anglo, 10% to 15% Vietnamese, and 5% Filipino. There are three main language groups in this parish: Spanish, Vietnamese, and English (the Filipinos speak English). Father Poettgen goes by multiple names: "Cha Ed" (Vietnamese), "Father Ed" (English), and "Padre Eduardo" (Spanish). He notes that white ecclesiastics such as himself use signs, words, and symbols to convey their feelings of love and support for parishioners of color. Poettgen, a Spanish speaker, also describes the ethnic divisions that can develop in demographically changing parishes. For instance, "us-against-them" dichotomies are more likely to exist in parishes where there are two distinct ethnic/linguistic groups, as opposed to three or four mutually exclusive groups. Anglo parishioners, moreover, typically react to an influx of minority Catholics in one of three ways: by leaving the parish, by complaining about the newcomers but remaining in the parish, or by adapting to the new cultural and linguistic dynamics that come to the fore.[102]

The shortage of priests further complicates considerations of ethnic outreach and demographic change within the U.S. Catholic Church.[103] "Catholic priests," notes one observer, "are in short supply around the country, especially those with specialized language skills or certain ethnic backgrounds."[104] The Church presently has specific needs for particular types of ecclesiastics, as in Polish-speaking clergy in Chicago and Portuguese-speaking clergy in northern New Jersey. Spanish-speaking priests — and Latino priests in particular — are especially needed throughout the United States.[105] It is a matter of debate within the Church as to whether a white ecclesiastic can be completely effective in his ministry if he does not share the ethnic background (or speak the ancestral language) of a particular ethnic group.[106] Vietnamese-American Catholics stand out among the many communities of color in Catholic America because the supply of Vietnamese-American clergy is such that they are usually ministered to by their coethnics, not by white ecclesiastics.[107]

As in California and other multiethnic states, Anglo priests in New York often engage in pastoral outreach to Catholics of color. Hispanics now make up a majority of the Catholics in the Archdiocese of New York (Manhattan, the Bronx, Staten Island, and seven counties north of New York City). There are 2.4 million Catholics in the Archdiocese of New York, and 51 percent of them are Hispanic or of Hispanic origin.[108] Bishop Josu Iriondo, the Vicar for Hispanic Affairs for the Archdiocese of New York, points out that the priests of the Archdiocese must show "openness and receptiveness to discover the new spirit if we are to be successful in ministering to the vibrant Hispanic community."[109] Iriondo, who hails from Spain's Basque Country, says, "It is crucial for the Archdiocesan priests and others to value the varied ways of celebrating the Eucharistic liturgy and other personal and national devotions."[110] These issues matter very much in Greater New York, where multiethnic parishes are now the norm, particularly in Manhattan, the Bronx, and Staten Island. Church leaders celebrate the role of immigration in swelling the ranks of New York's Catholics, but they remain concerned about having a sufficient number of priests to minister to them.[111]

Issues related to ethnic outreach are quite important to parishioners and ecclesiastics alike in the Archdiocese of Chicago, which consists of Cook and Lake Counties. The population of this archdiocese of 2.4 million Catholics is 54% Anglo, 37% Latino, 4.2% Asian, 3.8% black, and 1% multiracial. Whites account for 93.3% of active diocesan priests there.[112] Father Esequiel Sanchez, the Director of the Office of Hispanic Catholics in the Archdiocese of Chicago, laments the paucity of Hispanics in the archdiocesan hierarchy. Even so, Sanchez emphatically rejects the notion that Latinos must be served by Latino priests, or that Anglo pastors must be fluent in Spanish to be effective in their ministry to Spanish-speaking Catholics.[113] Meanwhile, Cardinal Francis George, the Archbishop of Chicago, seeks more Spanish-speaking, Latino priests for Chicagoland's rapidly growing Hispanic communities.[114] Some Chicago priests who minister to multiethnic parishes face the difficult challenge of deferring to the religious sensibilities of Latino immigrants, who favor expressive forms of worship, while not antagonizing the native-born white parishioners who prefer to express their faith differently.[115]

Bishop John R. Manz, a native of Chicago, has been involved in Latino-outreach efforts in the Windy City and environs for four decades. Manz, a German American "with a little English" ancestry, began to develop his interest in the Latino community in 1963, when he was assigned to the dining hall at Niles Seminary. There, Manz interacted with the Mexican nuns who staffed the kitchen. From them, he learned to speak Spanish, and he developed a lifelong love for Latin American culture. He later worked with Mexican migrant workers in northeastern Illinois, as well as Catholics in a Panamanian parish. After his ordination in 1971, Manz ministered to Chicago Catholics in three "predominantly Hispanic" parishes over the next quarter century. He lived in the heavily Mexican Little Village section of Chicago for 18 years. Then, in 1996, Pope John Paul II named him an auxiliary bishop of the Archdiocese of Chicago. Manz heads Vicariate III, which is mainly Latino. Among his many duties, he handles issues related to media outreach and communications. Manz also focuses on international migration issues. He is a member of the USCCB's Committee for Migrants and Refugees and the Chairman of the USCCB's Committee on Latin America. From 1996 to 2003, he served as the Episcopal Liaison for Hispanic Affairs in the Archdiocese of Chicago.[116]

Manz readily comments on the rewards and challenges facing the Anglo ecclesiastics who minister to Latino Catholics. The 58-year-old bishop concedes that it "is a little harder at the beginning" for an Anglo priest in a Hispanic parish. However, a white priest can overcome any cultural and linguistic obstacles if he genuinely listens to, and cares for, his parishioners. Manz reports that Latinos are "accepting and supportive" of white pastors who learn the Spanish language and the nuances of their culture. At the same time, he knows of warm, generous Anglo priests who speak heavily accented or broken Spanish, but whose Hispanic parishioners relate to them very well on a personal level. Interestingly, Manz notes that Latinos may view a white ecclesiastic as a neutral figure who brings together the different Hispanic subgroups in a parish. Manz, to be sure, believes that descriptive representation in the Church hierarchy — and at the parish level — is necessary for Latinos and the other ethnic groups that comprise Catholic America. Therefore, he advocated for the appointment of a Mexican bishop in Chicago; Gustavo Garcia-Siller, a Mexican-born priest, is the newest auxiliary bishop there.[117]

Another Chicagoan, Father Michael L. Pfleger, is perhaps the nation's best-known white Catholic advocate of racial equality and social justice. A tall, slim man whose blond hair, blue eyes, and fair complexion reflect his German and Irish/French background, Pfleger is the pastor of St. Sabina Catholic Church in the Auburn-Gresham neighborhood of Chicago.[118] Pfleger regularly makes news in the Windy City. He often denounces racism ("America's addiction," according to Pfleger) and is active in many social causes and movements, on such issues as the war in Iraq, fair housing, racial profiling, affirmative action, and tobacco and alcohol advertising in the inner city. A native of the Southwest Side of Chicago, Pfleger was born on May 22, 1949. He has spent his entire adult life working in the African-American communities of Chicago. In 1981 the charismatic priest became pastor of St. Sabina, where he soon earned a reputation for being responsive to the spiritual needs and cultural preferences of his parishioners.[119]

Father Pfleger offers many insights about race in America that stem from his experiences as a white man who is closely associated with African Americans and their concerns. He entered the ministry because of the teachings of, and example set by, Dr. Martin Luther King. Pfleger reports that he has encountered considerable criticism from whites over the years, including a steady stream of hate mail, as a result of his efforts to promote racial justice. The 55-year-old priest says white racists have spat on him, verbally abused him, and even physically attacked him. Such expressions of bigotry do not daunt Pfleger, and he continues to fight what he sees as pervasive racism in the Catholic Church and American society.[120] Indeed, Pastor Pfleger enjoys a growing national reputation as a leading white voice against racism; he frequently speaks at churches and in other venues around the United States.[121] St. Sabina, likewise, often hosts leading African-American entertainers, intellectuals, political figures, and religious leaders.

Parishioners of color account for the vast majority of the 4,000,000-plus Catholics who live in Los Angeles, Ventura, and Santa Barbara Counties — the areas that comprise the Archdiocese of Los Angeles. The Catholic population of Greater Los Angeles is 70% Latino (mainly Mexicans and Mexican Americans), 15% Asian (primarily Filipinos, Vietnamese, and Koreans), 13% Anglo, and 2% African American.[122] The Archdiocese of Los Angeles has a long tradition of ethnic outreach.[123] All told, 300 Anglo priests minister to the Spanish-speaking population there. It is common for white pastors in many parishes to celebrate far more Spanish Masses than English Masses each week.[124] Humberto Ramos, the Associate Director of Religious Education for the Archdiocese of Los Angeles, notes that Anglo priests often "have adapted very well" to the demographic changes transforming the Los Angeles metropolitan area.[125] Many white ecclesiastics serve parishes with sizable Latino populations and "feel right at home," according to Ramos.[126] A priest's cultural sensitivity and linguistic adeptness matter far more than his ethnic or racial background to Catholic Angelenos.

This is certainly true of Father Colm Rafferty, the pastor of St. Columban Filipino Church in the Historic Filipinotown section of Los Angeles. Rafferty grew up in County Derry in Northern Ireland, and he was ordained in 1953. He has spent virtually all of his time as a priest in either the United States or the Philippines. The seventysomething pastor began to minister to the Filipinos of St. Columban in Los Angeles upon his return to the United States in 1996 after a ten-year stint on Luzon Island, where he learned to speak fluent Tagalog. Rafferty's detailed knowledge of the nuances of Filipino culture and the Tagalog language endear him to the 800 parishioners (all but one of whom is Filipino) at St. Columban. In addition, Rafferty often speaks at Filipino parishes in and around Los Angeles. Filipino Americans are initially surprised to see — and hear — an Irishman speaking Tagalog with ease. In response, Rafferty asks them in Tagalog, "Why are you surprised?"[127] Through his ministry to Filipinos and Filipino Americans, Father Rafferty breaks down barriers, shattering ethnic and cultural stereotypes in Greater Los Angeles.

Cardinal Roger Mahony, the Archbishop of Los Angeles, leads what is arguably the most ethnically and racially diverse group of Catholics in the Americas. A native of North Hollywood, California, Mahony spent his summers as a youth working with — and learning Spanish from — the Latinos employed in his father's poultry-processing business. The prelate, who was born on February 27, 1936, became a priest in 1962. He ministered to parishioners in the Diocese of Fresno for 13 years. Mahony then served as Auxiliary Bishop of Fresno from 1975 to 1980 and later as Bishop of Stockton from 1980 to 1985. A tall, slim man of German and Italian ancestry, Mahony became the Archbishop of Los Angeles in 1985. He was elevated to the College of Cardinals in 1991. Mahony's policy positions and public pronouncements are informed by his belief in social justice and feelings of affinity with the "poorest," the "powerless," and the "voiceless."[128]

The Cardinal has an enormously challenging and rewarding job as the leader of the nation's largest archdiocese, one in which parishioners of color account for 87 percent of the Catholics. Many Catholic Angelenos worship in predominantly Latino parishes; even in such churches, though, there may be ethnic and cultural differences between and among Mexicans and the various Central American subgroups. In addition, Cardinal Mahony notes that multiethnic, multilingual parishes are often divided by language into informal sub-parishes. Thus he says it is important to integrate the parish choirs and parish councils. Mahony himself regularly celebrates English and Spanish Masses, and he often emphasizes the richness of the cultural tapestry of Catholicism in Southern California. As a well-known and well-regarded prelate, the Cardinal regularly visits Rome and travels around the world. For instance, Mahony recently went to Vietnam; he met with government officials and conducted a Mass there.[129]

Mahony continually wins plaudits from Latinos and others in Southern California.[130] (One newsweekly recently described him as a "beloved" figure in Latino Los Angeles.)[131] The Cardinal enjoys significant popular appeal for a number of reasons, including his warm and gracious personality, his rhetorical emphasis on inclusion, his support for initiatives that benefit working-class Latinos, and his role as a leader of an institution revered by most Spanish-surnamed Americans. Mahony, to be sure, frequently speaks out on issues of importance to Hispanics, including immigration, affirmative action, and the "living wage."[132] Likewise, he is proud that the Catholic Educational Foundation disburses $4.5 million to $5 million annually in scholarships so that needy Los Angeles–area students are able to attend parochial schools.[133] Cardinal Mahony is perhaps best known for building the Cathedral of Our Lady of the Angels, which opened in Los Angeles in 2002.[134] The magnificent new cathedral complex, with its culturally and linguistically inclusive atmosphere, honors the faith traditions and ethnic diversity of Southern California's burgeoning Catholic population.[135]

The American Church, of course, will become increasingly multiethnic and multiracial in the coming decades.[136] Immigrants, particularly those from Latin America, are driving this phenomenon. Experts do not expect the growth of the Catholic population to abate, in part because the number of Catholic immigrants will outpace the number of native-born Catholics who leave the Church. Catholicism in the United States will become ever-more vibrant and complex as a result of the religious traditions and forms of cultural expression that the newcomers bring with them.[137] Despite myriad initiatives to recruit more minority priests, though, the demographics of the Catholic clergy are such that many ethnic parishioners will be ministered to by white priests in the foreseeable future. The cross-cultural outreach by Anglo priests to parishioners of color, coupled with the fallout from the sex-abuse scandals that rocked Catholic America in 2002, will play an important role in determining the future of the U.S. Church.

The Church hierarchy clearly recognizes the new demographics of Catholic America: Pope John Paul II regularly names men of color to be U.S. bishops. In December 2002, for example, the Pope appointed Monsignor Ignatius Wang to be an auxiliary bishop in the Archdiocese of San Francisco. Wang, a Chinese-born priest with a distinguished record of pastoral outreach, became the first Asian-American bishop in U.S. history. Although there are few Chinese Catholics in the three counties (San Francisco, Marin, and San Mateo) that make up the Archdiocese of San Francisco, Chinese Americans constitute an important — and growing — percentage (11.8 percent in 2000) of the population there. Bishop Wang notes that his appointment has symbolic significance in the Bay Area as well as throughout Asian America.[138] Similarly, U.S. cities with large black populations sometimes have African-American bishops, even though most blacks are not Catholics. And there is a demographic impetus for Latino bishops, due to the fast-growing population of Hispanic Americans. This development reflects the importance of immigration in shaping the contours of Catholic America.

The Catholic Church, meanwhile, occupies a significant role on the global scene. When the Pope makes a public pronouncement, whether it is on the war in Iraq or the sanctity of marriage, his remarks are widely noted and reported around the globe. Indeed, the pontiff is one of the world's most visible and recognized public figures. He has long earned the respect and admiration of many people because of his conspicuous inclusiveness. Pope John Paul II speaks several languages, travels frequently to different countries, and exhibits a clear compassion for people of all faiths. In his leadership role, the Pope "employs the various departments of the Roman Curia, which act in his name and by his authority for the good of the churches and in the service of the sacred pastors."[139] These include the 11 Pontifical Councils, which, along with other activities, follow some of the great concerns of Vatican II; they help shape and reinforce the message that the Holy See transmits to the world.[140]

The Church certainly takes into account the pastoral needs of marginalized and dispossessed people, as evidenced by the activities of the Pontifical Council for the Pastoral Care of Migrants and Itinerant People. Three of its nine sectors — migrants, refugees, and nomads — cannot help but touch issues related to race, ethnicity, and nationality. Father Michael Blume, a Divine Word Missionary, serves as its undersecretary. A courtly man who speaks five languages, Blume grew up in South Bend, Indiana. As a multicultural American he went to work in the Vatican after several years as a missionary in Africa — Blume lived in Ghana from 1974 to 1990. He headed the refugee desk at the Pontifical Council from 1995 before becoming the undersecretary in 2000. Blume has traveled frequently throughout the world as part of his duties. He and his colleagues, under the leadership of the Council's president, work primarily with conferences of bishops and also have contacts with ecumenical and humanitarian organizations, as they toggle between global and local issues in their pastoral outreach.[141]

Meanwhile, the officials at the Pontifical Council for Justice and Peace focus on three fields: justice, peace, and human rights. Monsignor Frank J. Dewane serves as the undersecretary of the Pontifical Council for Justice and Peace. Dewane, a native of rural northeastern Wisconsin, was ordained at age 38 in 1988 after a lengthy career in international business (which included a five-year stint in the Soviet Union). Dewane holds several advanced degrees and has worked as a canon lawyer and a diplomat for the Holy See at the United Nations. He became undersecretary of the Pontifical Council for Justice and Peace in 2001.[142] That year, Dewane was the deputy head of the Holy See's delegation to the World Conference against Racism, Racial Discrimination, Xenophobia, and Related Intolerance in Durban, South Africa.[143] Today Dewane and his associates emphasize such topics as poverty, corruption, climate change, safe drinking water, and war and armaments.[144] Their work exemplifies the Church's increasing focus on matters of importance to people in the developing world.

The changing face of American Catholicism reflects, and contributes to, the changing demographics of the Catholic Church worldwide. Europeans and European descendants in the New World make up a steadily decreasing percentage of the global Catholic community. By 2025, 44.5% of Catholics will be found in Latin America, compared to 20.3% in Europe, 16.7% in Africa, and 11.7% in Asia. (Catholics in the affluent Western countries contribute a significant amount of money to the Church, well in excess of their percentage of the total Catholic population.) Some observers are already speculating that Roman Catholicism may take on an increasingly conservative tone, due to the theological beliefs and ideological predilections of African and Latin American Catholics.[145] Likewise, there has been serious discussion throughout the world that Pope John Paul II's successor may be a prelate from Africa or Latin America.[146] White men, to be sure, will continue to play an important role in the affairs of the Catholic Church, as pastors, parishioners, and members of the Church hierarchy.

∽

The most prominent symbol of the United States — Uncle Sam — typically is represented as a white man: Samuel Wilson (1766–1854), was the real-life basis for the symbolic character "Uncle Sam." The term originated during the War of 1812. Wilson, then a resident of Troy, New York, was a meat-packer that the Army hired to supply American troops in the North with pork and beef. The soldiers referred to Wilson as "Uncle Sam." Initially they thought the heads of barrels bearing his products were branded with Wilson's initials; they mistakenly believed that the "U.S." brand on each barrel stood for "Uncle Sam" rather than "the United States." Soon this notion spread beyond Upstate New York to soldiers in other parts of the country, and it eventually took root outside the Army as well. Artists and cartoonists then developed pictorial representations of the new national symbol, beginning in the 1830s. Uncle Sam displaced earlier depictions of America, which had included Columbia, Yankee Doodle, and Brother Jonathan. The most enduring portrayal of Uncle Sam was created in 1917 by James Montgomery Flagg; his depiction of Uncle Sam adorned recruiting posters during World War I with the following message: "I Want You for the U.S. Army."[147]

Over the years, Uncle Sam has become the most common colloquial reference to the United States, in addition to being the pictorial symbol of the world's wealthiest nation as well.[148] Uncle Sam, notes one source, is "a personification of the government or people of the U.S.: represented as a tall, lean [Caucasian] man with white chin whiskers, wearing a blue tailcoat, red-and-white-striped trousers, and a top hat with a band of stars."[149] The rhetorical and pictorial representations of Uncle Sam continue to play an important role in American life. For instance, we often describe our taxpaying responsibilities as having "to pay Uncle Sam." This reference usually occurs in an essentially race-neutral context. Despite the movement toward diversity in American life, many traditional icons, such as Uncle Sam, have not come under fire yet. To my knowledge, no one has ever seriously questioned the depiction of Uncle Sam as a white male. Unlike, say, the Confederate battle flag, no one associates Uncle Sam with racial tensions or hostility.

On a related note, Santa Claus continues to be portrayed as a white man in the United States. The term Santa Claus (or, less commonly, Klaus) dates back to the period from 1765 to 1775. It originates from the Dutch *Sinterklaas,* alternative of *Sint Nikolaas,* or Saint Nicholas, who has evolved into the "white-bearded, plump, red-suited, grandfatherly man of folklore who brings gifts to well-behaved children at Christmas."[150] Santa Claus traditionally has been depicted as a white man in American society, due to the predominance of whites in the U.S. population. Although American artistic portrayals of Santa Claus usually feature white men, the ubiquitous shopping-mall Santas come in all ages, every color, and both genders. Depending on the context, Santa may be depicted as a man of color, particularly if the image is intended to reach a minority audience. The issue of inclusive portrayals of Santa, though, rarely receives much attention from whites or people of color alike. They simply do not consider it to be very important.

American corporate symbols and advertising mascots, meanwhile, often feature white males. These symbols come in three types. Firstly, there are products that bear the names, but not the pictures, of specific white men (e.g., Louis Kemp, Oscar Mayer, and Duncan Hines). Secondly, there are named and depicted symbols (Mr. Clean, Jack Daniels, Rusty Jones, Chef Boyardee, and Ol' Lonely, the Maytag Repairman come to mind) who happen to be white and male. Thirdly, there are unnamed and depicted mascots (the Marlboro Man, the Quaker Oats Man, the Brawny Paper Towel guy) that are well known but do not have formal names. These names and symbols stand for quality and continuity. There is little about the aforementioned products that overtly invokes anything having to do with white males. Perhaps this is why few Americans ever contend that such mascots and symbols should be retired.

Corporations rarely change their advertising mascots and corporate symbols, although it is common for them to update the mascot or symbol to keep up with new trends in attire and hairstyles. Consumers and corporations alike value the continuity offered by a recognized mascot or symbol. Likewise, it is difficult for a corporation to offer a racially representative mascot or symbol that appeals to everyone when a single "person" symbolizes the brand. Certainly it is conceivable that the marketing personnel who oversee the leading mascots and symbols might take into account the idea that an updated, multicultural pitchperson might represent the nation better than a traditional, white, male consumer icon. In any event, civil rights advocates focus little of their attention on this issue. The impetus for change in this regard comes from the nation's changing demographics, as well as proactive managers and executives who decided to update their mascots and symbols. General Mills, for instance, created an inclusive, multiethnic version of Betty Crocker in 1996.[151]

It is possible for a multiethnic nation like ours to rally around a contemporary symbol that features white men, as evidenced by the popularity of Thomas Franklin's famous photograph on 9/11. In late afternoon on September 11, 2001, three white firefighters raised the American flag at Ground Zero in Manhattan. Franklin, a photographer for *The Record* in Bergen County, New Jersey, captured the impromptu flag raising on film, unbeknownst to the firefighters — George Johnson, Dan McWilliams, and Bill Eisengrein. The inspiring and patriotic photograph, which showcased American resolve and tenacity, received worldwide attention, making it one of the defining images of 9/11.[152] As one writer notes, "The picture immediately evoked memories of the famous Associated Press photograph of U.S. servicemen raising the American flag on Iwo Jima during World War II."[153] In the past three years, there have been innumerable reproductions of Franklin's indelible image, on items as diverse as T-shirts, coffee mugs, parade floats, memorial snow globes, and magazine and newspaper covers. The three men in the photo, however, maintain a low profile; they make infrequent public appearances and rarely comment on 9/11 in media accounts.[154]

In January 2002 Thomas Franklin's seemingly innocuous photo became the subject of significant debate in New York. The controversy arose over a proposed memorial (in the form of a 19-foot bronze statue of three firefighters at the Brooklyn headquarters of the New York Fire

Department) to the 343 firefighters who died on September 11. In the process of developing plans for the memorial, the planners decided to make a statue of three men, but to represent them as white, black, and Latino. When this plan became public knowledge in January 2002, it came under fire from conservative commentators and the predominantly white rank-and-file of the New York Fire Department. The critics challenged the planned statue as an inaccurate rendering of the flag raising. Once the multiethnic-statue idea met with vigorous opposition — the critics included the three men depicted in the iconic photo — the plan to have a memorial of this type quietly came to an end.[155] Nonetheless, Thomas Franklin's photograph continues to receive attention: Johnson, McWilliams, and Eisengrein are portrayed on the Heroes of 2001 semipostal stamp released by the United States Postal Service in June 2002. This stamp will be on sale through the end of 2004.[156]

∾ chapter five ∾

The Power of Numbers

Gary, Indiana, Mayor Scott L. King entered electoral politics because of garbage. His political career dates back to the summer of 1990, when the Gary sanitation workers did not collect the city's garbage for three consecutive weeks, ostensibly because the local landfill had been temporarily closed due to environmental problems. To King, the city's inability to handle its trash symbolized the decrepitude that bedeviled Gary, a city founded in 1906 by U.S. Steel and dominated for decades by the industrial behemoth. King therefore decided to run for mayor to remedy the situation.[1] A native of the Northwest Side of Chicago, King was born in 1951. He graduated from Concordia College (now Concordia University) in 1973 and Valparaiso Law School in 1976. King had moved to Gary in 1980 because of the city's proximity to Lake Michigan, the low real-estate prices there, and his job at the time as a county prosecutor in Lake County, Indiana. He also served as an assistant U.S. attorney and later became a defense attorney, with an office in downtown Gary not far from City Hall.[2]

During his 1991 campaign in this city where eight out of 10 voters are black, King, who is white, portrayed himself as a political newcomer and promised to improve city services and promote economic development. In the end, the lawyer with the monosyllabic Anglo-Saxon name won support from white Garyites, firefighters and police officers, and young African Americans who disliked the city's political establishment. However, the incumbent, Thomas V. Barnes, outpaced the field in the May 1991 primary. Barnes defeated former Mayor Richard G. Hatcher by a 45%-to-25% margin; King placed a strong third, with 23%.[3] At this point, it seemed likely that King's candidacy was less a harbinger of a new era in American urban politics — whereby white candidates periodically won in black-majority jurisdictions — but more an anachronism, a candidacy by a smart, well-connected attorney who could be expected to return to his thriving criminal-law practice.

Indeed, no one was surprised when King lost his 1991 mayoral bid: City Hall had been run by African Americans since Hatcher was elected mayor in a racially acrimonious contest in 1967, when Gary was about one-half white and one-half black. Soon after Hatcher became mayor, the Rust Belt economy went into a tailspin; many of the factors that contributed to Gary's economic decline were beyond the mayor's control. By the 1970s, Gary had developed a serious crime problem, which worsened in the 1980s and 1990s largely because of gang warfare related to drug trafficking. During this period Gary grew progressively smaller, poorer, and blacker as whites, jobs, and businesses exited the city.[4] Northwest Indiana's largest city received unwelcome national attention in 1993 as the "Murder Capital of America," a dubious designation that the media bestowed upon it again in 1995 and 1996. It was in this climate that King decided to run for mayor a second time. His campaign theme, "Plans not Promises," resonated with Garyites who were tired of living in an urban dystopia, and he triumphed in the Democratic primary in May 1995 with 44.1% of the vote. The general-election result was never in doubt in this bedrock Democratic constituency. King won the mayoralty by a 78%-18% margin in the November 1995 balloting.[5]

The King era in Gary politics began when the new mayor was inaugurated on January 1, 1996; its protagonist quickly established his bona fides as a competent administrator and enthusiastic civic booster. Throughout his tenure, race has never been a major issue for Mayor King, in part because the fiftysomething chief executive maintains very close ties to the black community.[6] (His wife, Irene Smith-King, is African American, and they have two daughters and one son.) Since taking office, the mayor has improved the delivery and quality of city services and presided over a dramatic reduction in the city's sky-high crime rate. He visits the homes of Garyites after the workday ends, to investigate their complaints about potholes, broken sidewalks, and the like. Mayor King has also built a strong network of support in the city's black churches.[7]

During the period from 1996 to 2000, King solidified his hold on City Hall. In his first term as mayor, King used the expansive powers of his office to work around a city council that was hostile to much of his agenda, and he appointed department heads without the council's approval. Voters overwhelmingly approved of the mayor's job performance: King won the Democratic primary in May 1999 with nearly 70% of the vote. He was unopposed in the general election. The nine-member Gary Common Council now has a pro-King majority; the 1999 elections brought in six new members, including four who beat incumbents, giving Mayor King a majority for the first time.[8] Garyites clearly admire the leadership of this serious man of average height with a self-confident manner and full head of gray hair. Mayor King's race seems to be of little significance to most Garyites, who focus instead on the mayor's proven leadership and commitment to Gary.

King's electoral record reflects the substantial progress his administration, which includes many African Americans in the top posts, has made in improving the quality of life for Garyites. Gary's war on crime is King's biggest success so far — the number of murders dropped from 132 in 1995 to 62 in 2002 and 68 in 2003. (For nine consecutive years, Gary has had "the nation's highest per capita homicide rate.")[9] Mayor King cites a complicated series of factors to explain the city's success in reducing violent crime, such as the practice of having drug dealers tried in federal court rather than state court, the sting operations to curtail illegal gun sales at gun stores in the area, and the undercover busts of would-be drug buyers whose names, addresses, and occupations were listed in full-page Sunday advertisements in the local newspapers. Perhaps most importantly, the mayor dramatically increased the size — and salaries — of the police force.[10] The people of Gary have benefited significantly from the sharp decrease in crime there; by reducing crime, King also hopes to make Gary more attractive to tourists, shoppers, and businesspeople.[11]

Scott King demonstrated his political resilience in 2003 by winning reelection handily. The Steel Yard, a $45 million minor-league baseball stadium that opened in 2003, is King's most enduring urban-renewal project. The stadium hosts concerts, festivals, youth athletics, and minor-league sports. King and other civic boosters hope these sports and entertainment options will attract people and private investment to downtown Gary.[12] During the campaign leading up to the May 2003 Democratic mayoral primary, King's challengers criticized his leadership on a number of fronts, but the recurring issue was the costly baseball stadium — whether the money spent on it should have been used in other ways, and whether the lease was overly generous to the stadium tenants. King took 59.4% of the primary vote, a solid victory that confirmed his popularity in the city. The mayor easily defeated his Republican opponent in November 2003, and the pro-King majority on the Gary Common Council grew from five to seven (out of nine).[13]

Meanwhile, King remains undaunted by the many challenges facing his city, as he tirelessly advocates on behalf of Gary. The 2000 census found only 102,746 residents, a population loss of more than 12% from 1990. (Gary is now 83.4% African American, 10.1% white, and 4.9% Hispanic.) Gary's public schools continue to be troubled; the city's unemployment rate remains high despite the presence of two riverboat casinos; and economic development is a pressing issue because few employers wish to relocate there. King has ambitious plans for urban renewal, as he seeks to reduce the tax burden and attract employers to Gary through his efforts to promote economic development.[14] And the city intends to use casino revenues to construct a new elementary school with an adjacent Boys & Girls Club.[15] Due to such accomplishments, and his energetic leadership, King is one of the most popular and effective mayors in the Steel City's 98-year history.

CALLING THE SHOTS

"I don't care if you're black, white, green, or pink," Michael Butkovich frequently tells the students of Gallup High School in Gallup, New Mexico. This is a characteristically forthright expression of colorblindness from Butkovich, the principal of Gallup High. And it rings true in his school, where 75 to 80 percent of the 1,600 students are Native American, 15 percent identify as Hispanic, and only five percent are white. Overall, there is hardly any overt ethnic conflict at Gallup High School or in the Gallup area. Most whites, Latinos, and Native Americans get along with each other, even though some people of color complain about discrimination and social segregation. Race matters little, if at all, to Butkovich, a tall, muscular man with wire rim spectacles, whose brown eyes and brown hair reflect his Italian and Croatian heritage. He grew up in this multiethnic community of 20,209 (it is 33.9% American Indian, 33.1% Hispanic, and 26.9% Anglo) 20 miles east of the Arizona state line.[16]

Throughout his life, Butkovich has lived, worked, and shopped in multiethnic environments. Therefore, he is quite comfortable with the multiracial, multicultural nature of Gallup High School. At work and in the community, Butkovich moves easily among people from different ethnic and racial groups. He mixes the can-do attitude of an executive with the passion of an educator. An alumnus of Brigham Young University and New Mexico State University, Butkovich began his career as an educator in 1980. He initially worked as a special-education teacher and then taught regular education classes, including American history — his specialty was Southwestern history — and honors courses in the subject. Along the way he also coached football, basketball, and baseball. Eventually, Butkovich was selected to be an assistant principal at Gallup High

School. He raised his local profile in 1998 because of his highly successful one-semester tenure as the interim principal of a junior high school that had been plagued by disciplinary problems. Shortly thereafter, in August 1999, the lifelong area resident and father of two became principal of Gallup High.

The Gallup-McKinley County School Board, then a body of one white, one Hispanic, and three Native Americans, unanimously chose Butkovich to run Gallup High School. It is unusual for a white man to be selected by people of color for such a position. After all, white male principals in white-minority or white-plurality communities usually can explain their tenure for one of three reasons. First, the white man may have been selected for the job when whites were a majority in the town, and he kept it through his competence and/or seniority. Secondly, in a rapidly growing area, even one with significant diversity dictates, a white male may become principal of a multiethnic school by happenstance, simply because there are several positions open and not enough qualified people of color to fill them. Finally, some white-minority and white-plurality communities are led by whites for whom diversity is not a top priority, or, in the case of Gallup, minorities who hire whites to hold positions of authority. In selecting Butkovich as principal of a school with few Anglo students, the people of color on the Gallup-McKinley County School Board made it clear that substantive representation trumps descriptive representation for them.

Butkovich's job requires him to be a disciplinarian, a politician, an executive, and a long-range planner. The principal strives to be accessible: He regularly talks to his students about their lives and periodically engages them in frank discussions of racial issues. Butkovich urges the young people not to use racism as a "crutch" or a catchall excuse in their lives. But he also empathizes with the Hispanic and Native American youths when they complain about racism and discrimination, in part because he knows what it feels like to be an outsider, due to his experiences as a Catholic at predominantly Mormon BYU. Indeed, one quickly senses that this dynamic educator is an inherently fair person, who treats all kids equally and who sincerely believes that there are few genuinely "bad" youths. The Butkovich example reminds us that a white educator can successfully lead a school where most students are minorities, so long as he is rigorously honest and firmly committed to the values of fairness and equal opportunity.

White males may deal with multicultural issues in terms of three stages: awareness, acceptance (and, perhaps, anxiety), and adjustment.

The consultant Mark Yeoell, a naturalized American of English ancestry in his early fifties who grew up in Malaysia, Nigeria, Morocco, and the United Kingdom, describes this process in detail.[17] The first stage, of course, is Awareness. This stage is the awareness that other people besides white males need to have their beliefs, feelings, and issues taken into account just like white males. This is the easiest stage because one can be aware without having to accept responsibility in any way.[18] The second stage, Yeoell writes, involves accepting the "full ramifications of the status quo and our particular relation to it. This might mean accepting our heretofore conscious or unconscious complicity with the status quo or our antagonism toward it. In either case such acceptance means coming to terms with the necessary changes that such a bare-faced confrontation with reality implies."[19] This stage, not surprisingly, is typically accompanied by anxiety. The third stage relates to an adjustment in one's outlook on the world and one's behavior. This last stage, of course, is the most difficult, due to the changes that may be necessary to distribute social and economic capital more equitably.[20]

Yeoell also sees issues related to ethnic change in the context of whether these changes constitute a reformation or a transformation. When a person or an entity (a community, an institution, or even an entire society) undergoes a reformation, certain aspects of his behavior or the distribution of resources may change, but the fundamental nature of the person, community, institution, or society stays the same. Conversely, a transformation involves a significant amount of change that usually occurs quickly, dramatically, and irrevocably. Yeoell describes the American civil rights movement as an example of a reformation, while the Civil War marked a transformation — "albeit incomplete," contends this global thinker — in U.S. history.[21] "While the Civil War ended slavery as a 'legitimate' form of life in the USA," writes Yeoell, "racism is still alive and well in America. It has largely gone covert rather than continuing in its former egregious and overt manifestations."[22] America's ongoing discussion over how to embrace its multicultural present and future presently marks a reformation, not a transformation, according to Yeoell's schema.[23]

Yeoell sees three elements (Bonding, Order, and Balance) as critical to ensure that a multicultural, transgenerational "redefinition of relationship" occurs and endures over time.[24] Bonding is a matter of finding common meeting ground, a place in which we recognize and embrace "not only our differences but also" our sameness.[25] Then there is the issue of Order, as in "Who takes precedence and under what circumstances?"[26]

Yeoell points out that we can understand the concept of Order through our use of "the term 'deference scale,' which is an important tool for understanding the nature of power dynamics in human interactions."[27] He posits, "It seems to be a fact of life that all social interactions involve an often but not always fluid pecking order of hierarchy and deference. Respect for our elders is (or at least used to be) an example of a societal Order or Deference scale."[28]

"Sometimes," continues Yeoell, "these hierarchies of order become fixed around criteria that diminish and demean those who are lower in the deference scale."[29] "Often," notes Yeoell, "this sense of social order is, or has been, used to legitimize violence and brutality against those deemed 'lower' in the order. Whether socially sanctioned or not, the power differentials associated with our sense of Order in society continue to structure how we relate to each other."[30] Finally, the matter of balance revolves around our willingness to give and receive "parity of value" in our social and economic dealings with each other.[31] These issues are especially critical to the contemporary white male experience, due to the fact that white males now regularly face calls to share power, recognition, and resources with females and people of color.

White males can be — and often are — an integral part of virtually any discussion of diversity issues. But some Americans assume that those individuals who have the greatest interest in such matters stand to benefit the most (in a material sense) from diversity initiatives and other efforts to improve the life chances of women and people of color in our society. I myself am often asked about how I became interested in race, ethnicity, and gender, considering that I am part of advantaged groups (whites, males, heterosexuals, the able-bodied, and so forth) on virtually every front. On occasion, people are genuinely surprised to find out that someone with my research interests is, in fact, white.[32] The subtitle of a 2003 newspaper article about a public lecture of mine in Idaho said the following: "Lessons on difference taught by unlikeliest of teachers."[33] Some white men, of course, enjoy excellent reputations in communities of color due to their work for social justice and equal opportunity.[34]

In any event, there are multiple issues we need to look at when considering the effects of a white male's minority status on him personally. Firstly, how permanent is his status as a minority? In what context(s) does his minority status occur — at work, in school, in his social life? Does one minority group dominate things in a particular context, or is it instead a situation in which whites are a plurality or a minority, but no ethnic or racial group predominates? Secondly, how was the person socialized? Indeed, how a white male reacts to minority status depends on his personality, his upbringing, and even his self-esteem. Thirdly, what resources does the person have to overcome the inevitable discomfort that he may feel as a result of his minority status? Does he come into competition with minorities in the workplace, in the classroom, or in the social arena? Or does he continue to benefit from his whiteness in the minority-dominated context, perhaps because of the attitudes of white authority figures?[35]

Most white males in such situations do not feel like minorities in a true sense, in that they are genuinely poor, powerless, and disenfranchised. For starters, there is a difference between a white-plurality and a white-minority situation. In the former context, whites are one ethnic group among many. In the latter context, whites find themselves outnumbered and perhaps outmaneuvered by a discrete ethnic/racial group. And it is qualitatively different to be part of a white minority in a black-majority or an Indian-majority environment versus being one in a Latino-majority or an Asian-majority environment. In the case of blacks and Native Americans, especially in less-affluent areas, there is often a history of discrimination by whites that makes minorities suspicious of Caucasians. Ethnic differences tend to be softer and less pronounced in Anglo/Latino and white/Asian interactions and relations. These dynamics reflect the legacy of historical events and contemporary developments.

Social class is an especially important dynamic that determines feelings of minority status for white males. Minority status is probably felt most acutely by white males only if their socioeconomic status is such that they come into direct contact or competition with people of color on a regular basis. If a white guy attends a public school with a minority majority (especially one in which a single ethnic group predominates), or he is employed by a company where most of his coworkers are minorities, he may feel beleaguered and adopt a zero-sum mentality about the allocation of power, recognition, and resources. Such experiences can be difficult for white males, who, after all, are accustomed to majority status. Even the poorest white men are aware that members of their racial/gender group predominate in the leadership positions of American society.

Not all white men, of course, identify with the white male elites on any level, but the white maleness of our leadership class may lead some white men to have a false sense of entitlement that validates their notions of white male privilege. So it can be especially unsettling for them to deal with the specter of minorities competing successfully with them for jobs.

Some white men may fall back on misplaced notions of race and gender superiority to console themselves in the wake of their imagined defeats at the hands of those whom they may not consider to be their social equals. Psychologically, affluent white males, or those who find themselves in the power structure of a community even if they are not affluent, never truly experience what it is like to be a member of a minority group. White Americans can always move to a different white-majority area and start anew, so the notion of minority status is highly mutable for the typical white person.

White males might learn about the color line when they find themselves in a minority-dominated context for the first time in their lives. Being a pioneer is different for white males than it is for white females and, particularly, people of color, because they have been socialized as members of the nation's majority group. Still, such a position can be economically difficult and psychologically troubling for them, especially if they lack the requisite financial assets and educational credentials to compensate for any dislocation they feel. A poor white male, for instance, cannot move to another community as readily as his more-affluent white male counterpart. Still, it is important to distinguish between "genuine" minority status (as in the type experienced by Detroit's poor whites) and numerical-minority status (e.g., the type often experienced by colonials). By way of example, an upper-middle-class white Arkansan who goes to work for a multinational company in Lagos shifts from being part of the omnipotent majority in his native land to a privileged representative of Western culture in Nigeria. Our Arkansan, in other words, is not a genuine minority in Africa.

The Belgian researcher Eric Florence, who regularly visits China as part of his work, offers insights in this regard that apply to Americans as well. Florence, of course, has had the experience of being the first white man to visit certain Chinese villages. He says that no one pays any attention to him in the big Chinese cities; foreigners are common there. However, people often stare at him in Chinese villages, where visits from Westerners are rare. So I asked Florence if his experiences as an "outsider" in China have given him any insights into what life might be like for, say, an African who lives in Belgium. In response, Florence said that when he visits China, he always benefits from being a privileged Westerner. The Chinese automatically assume that his blond, Northern European appearance means he comes from a rich nation, and they react to him on that basis. Our hypothetical African in Belgium will probably have brown or black skin; many Belgians may readily assume that he hails from a poor nation.[36] Indeed, race and color (along with language, religion, and nationality) often structure Western perceptions of majority and minority status.

White males face equally rich and potentially vexing experiences as students, educators, principals, and administrators in America's multiethnic public schools. How well individual white males fit into our system of public education depends on the particular person, the attitude of the school administration, and the general ethnic climate in the community. Anglo students who attend public schools in heterogeneous school districts, particularly in large cities, certainly receive significant exposure to ethnic, racial, and cultural diversity. Some of them enjoy their experiences; others do not. White male teachers at the middle school and secondary school levels in diverse communities usually have numerous minority colleagues. However, there is typically only one principal or superintendent, so people of color may make him the target of their ethnic grievances. The role-model issue in particular can influence the selection of a principal or administrator and, to a lesser extent, teachers as well. To be sure, white male teachers, principals, and administrators sometimes gain reputations for being unusually sensitive to the needs of their minority students.

White men run the public school systems in many large U.S. cities, including Chicago, Los Angeles, Philadelphia, and New York City. During the 1980s and 1990s there was a significant focus in New York City on having a chancellor of the city's schools, most of whose students are black or Latino, who reflected the demographics of the student population. In recent years, though, the issue of a chancellor's race/ethnicity has been virtually irrelevant to the search for a leader in this realm. Instead, New Yorkers focus most of their attention on who is best qualified to make improvements in the city's system of public education. By 2000, New York's minority decision-makers mostly emphasized the prospective chancellor's leadership capabilities and occupational characteristics, not his or her ethnic or racial background.[37] It seems that people of color in many other urban school districts share the views of their New York counterparts on this matter.

Politics, especially in executive positions and single-member electoral districts, is an area where white men often govern majority-minority constituencies. To be sure, some of these constituencies have white pluralities and white-majority electorates. But white males frequently represent single-member electoral districts (as U.S. House members, state legislators, and city council-members) where minorities predominate among the population, if not the voters. Few white men win election from majority-black constituencies, particularly in the South. Many communities, after all, have complicated black-white racial politics that lead African Americans to prefer descriptive — as well as substantive — representation of their interests. Most African Americans are native-born citizens; they vote in numbers roughly equivalent to their percentage of the U.S. population. Therefore, white candidates can rarely win these days in black-majority constituencies without earning appreciable African-American support. The white men who represent multiethnic constituencies often win because they court different groups and form coalitions across ethnic lines.

The electoral dynamics differ, to some extent, for white men who represent or seek to represent majority-black and majority-Indian constituencies versus majority-minority, majority-Latino, and majority-Asian constituencies. Blacks and American Indians often have had more difficult and troubling relations vis-à-vis whites than has been the case for Latinos and Asians. This dynamic makes it difficult for white candidates (especially Republicans) to win in black-majority or Indian-majority precincts, unless whites outvote minorities in such contexts. In addition, immigrants account for a much larger percentage of the Latino and Asian populations than is the case for African Americans and Native Americans. For Hispanics and Asians, their numbers significantly outpace their percentage of the electorate, so an Anglo candidate in a Latino-majority or an Asian-majority constituency may win elections solely because there are not enough eligible Latino or Asian voters to defeat him.

Law enforcement is perhaps the touchiest arena of all when it comes to white men who serve as authority figures when people of color account for the majority of those in the population served by a particular institution. After all, blacks, Hispanics, and Native Americans tend to have dealings with the law (in percentage terms) more often than whites and Asian Americans. And many people of color feel uncomfortable if the faces of authority in law enforcement and the criminal justice system are all white. Whenever there is a highly publicized allegation of police brutality, minorities understandably become angry if the police officers in question are white and the victim is a person of color. This is why people of color often argue in favor of community policing, on the grounds that police officers will be sensitive to the neighborhoods that they patrol and also build rapport with the residents. Cities often have residency requirements for police officers so as to strengthen police-community relations and enable cities to retain tax revenues.[38]

White men, it seems, are rarely chosen anymore to head big-city police departments, which is not surprising considering that many of the nation's largest cities no longer have white majorities.[39] Such cities as Dallas, Phoenix, Detroit, and Philadelphia have African-American police chiefs or police commissioners (the term varies by the city). Interestingly, New York City is the place where white men routinely serve as police commissioner. Every New York police commissioner since 1992 has been white. Los Angeles now has a white police chief: William Bratton, a veteran of policing who has headed the police departments in Boston and New York, respectively. And the Chicago Police Superintendent, Philip J. Cline, is white; he succeeded an African American in a black-plurality city. Superintendent Cline demonstrated his sensitivity to Chicago's racial politics by immediately naming Dana Starks, who is African American, as first deputy superintendent.[40] So it seems that white men can be acceptable choices to head police departments in cities where whites constitute a plurality or even a minority of the population.

Unlike the police chief or police commissioner, the voters elect the sheriff, a fact that generally requires him to be responsive to the diverse population groups of the area he serves. Whites often outvote blacks in those counties where voting cleaves along racial lines. Due to the disproportionate number of African Americans in the criminal justice system, some white sheriffs and district attorneys may remain in office in majority-black counties due to the punitive effects of felony disenfranchisement. Racial controversies periodically flare up in small counties, particularly in the American South, where African Americans may grumble about "plantation politics" and complain about subtle racism in the local power structure. The same might be true in an Indian-majority county, as in Bennett County, South Dakota.[41] Sometimes a historically disadvantaged minority group asserts its power at the ballot box and effects change in this way.

THE VANGUARD

Sherman Patrick credits his second-grade teacher for spurring his interest in the Arab world.[42] Patrick's teacher had a son in Operation Desert Storm, and she brought pictures of the Middle East to show to her class. The scenery of the desert and the pictures of a different culture were "exciting and interesting," remembers Patrick. This experience piqued his interest in the Middle East; in the sixth grade, he wrote a paper about Iran in which he discussed the Shi'a/Sunni distinction in Islam. Moreover,

Patrick's ninth-grade history teacher taught him and his classmates about Arab history and Arab customs. At Bishop Ireton High School, the small Catholic secondary school he attended in Alexandria, Virginia, he learned about Islam as one of the world's great monotheistic religions. And in the tenth and eleventh grades he continued to be captivated by Arab-related topics. Patrick, for instance, watched *Lawrence of Arabia* for extra credit as part of the coursework in his American history class. His interest in Arabia developed further in subsequent years until Patrick decided that he might want to make it his life's work to improve relations between Arabs and Westerners.

This aspiring Arabist is a Euro-American Christian native of Northern Virginia. He was born in 1983 in Manassas, Virginia, on the outer edge of the metropolitan sprawl that characterizes the D.C. area. Patrick grew up in the Washington suburbs, in such predominantly white places as Woodbridge, Virginia, and Lake Ridge, Virginia. His father is descended from Irish immigrants, while his mother's family traces their ancestry to the Pennsylvania Dutch. Patrick's parents divorced when he was a child; once they remarried, his multiethnic, multicultural experiences became ever more compelling and interesting. His stepfather's mother is an ethnic Frenchwoman from Morocco who grew up in France. And his stepfather's father is a Ukrainian who immigrated to the United States after World War II. Patrick's father, meanwhile, married a Mexican-American Virginian whose parents grew up in San Antonio; their children, Patrick's half siblings, have Irish names and an appreciation of their Irish as well as Mexican heritage. Patrick himself is 5'11", with light skin, blondish-brown (dirty blond) hair, and light blue eyes. In August 2001 he entered the College of William and Mary in Williamsburg, Virginia.

Throughout his undergraduate career, Patrick has been systematically preparing for his intended career as an U.S. diplomat in Arabia. He wants to devote his professional life to international relations, specifically diplomacy in the Arab world or, possibly, some kind of journalistic endeavor. At William and Mary, this proud progressive takes many classes in sociology, government, and Middle Eastern studies. (He is a government major.) Patrick rhapsodizes about the Arab "zeal for life" and revels in the subtleties of the Arab language. Due to the topicality of Arab-Western relations, he regularly discusses foreign-policy issues with his fellow Americans. In doing so, he uses the language and vocabulary of the middle to reach Euro-American Christians. Patrick is very, very careful to contribute to intercultural understanding without being pigeonholed as an apologist for extremist elements in the Arab world. And he emphasizes that Americans need more exposure to the Arab people, as well as Arab culture and Arab history.

Soon Sherman Patrick will be making his first visit to the Arab world, to improve his spoken Arabic and learn more about the culture he admires and respects so much. When I asked this well-spoken future diplomat how he felt his appearance might affect his reception by Arabs, Patrick said he thought that his ethnic characteristics would lead people to ask him questions. Rather than be concerned that his Northern European looks could make him a target of anti-American vitriol, Patrick relishes the fact that he will continually surprise Arabs by speaking fluent Arabic and conversing intelligently with them about events in the Middle East. These moments of surprise, he notes, will give him many opportunities to engage Arabs in dialogue; such encounters will foster intercultural understanding. And Patrick intends to do just that, after he completes his degree at the College of William and Mary in May 2005.

In our time, white men develop their sensitivity to ethnic and racial issues as a result of many different influences, including community organizing, political activism, scholarly research, personal experiences, and family relationships.[43] Some white males acquire a passion for social justice after they live in a developing nation and/or learn to speak a language spoken by people in a Third World country. Indeed, white male internationalists regularly specialize in a specific continent and/or nation, as in Latin America in general and Brazil in particular. Some white males, to be sure, actively seek out experiences that bring them into sustained contact with people of color, e.g., by serving as a Peace Corps volunteer in a Third World country, or by teaching students of color and studying issues of interest to minorities. Yet the white person who presumes to focus on, or specialize in, a "nonwhite" topic may face constant scrutiny and criticism for being a cultural imperialist.

White males exhibit their multicultural sensitivities in different ways. Many whites know what race means in our society — and they certainly may be critical of the privileges that accrue to them as white people. Consequently, many white males avoid paternalistic kinds of actions that might be well meaning (in a naïve kind of way) but are nonetheless offensive to women and people of color. They also realize that there are certain situations in which the police and others in positions of authority or business — clerks, teachers, taxi drivers, et cetera — may treat them differently than a similarly situated male of color, particularly an African American. Due to the rhetorical, if not substantive, emphasis on celebrating diversity in our culture (as well as the pro-diversity message one receives in our schools and workplaces), the younger generations of white males have been sensitized to the new dynamics regarding diversity, inclusion, and multiculturalism.

Perhaps the best way a white male gains insights into minority experiences comes through friendships with people of color, the dating of minority women, and particularly, marriage to a woman of color. The white man who dates or marries a woman of color may encounter stares from strangers, untoward comments from his family and friends, and other verbal and visual cues that signal his relationship is somehow not a good idea. Moreover, he may hear stories of racism from his Significant Other and her family. And when he and his wife have children, he will observe how other white people treat his mixed-race children, particularly if they appear to be nonwhite.[44] Similar dynamics occur in the lives of transracial adoptive parents and the transracial adoptees themselves, who may face searching questions about racial identity.[45] All told, interracial social and family relationships are becoming more common: At least 15 percent of whites are now part of transracial kinship networks.[46]

Those white males who appear omniracial often experience life differently depending on how they are perceived by people from different ethnic and racial groups. Any white American with dark brown hair and dark brown eyes inhabits the fuzzy border line between white and nonwhite in certain contexts, including the ubiquitous white/Latino dichotomy and even the white/black or white/Asian Indian boundaries. (A young Indian-American woman once remarked to me, "Your hair is so black." I think she meant that it surprised her to see someone with fair skin and dark hair — she herself had black hair.) It is, of course, impossible to determine the extent to which being mistaken for a member of a minority group affects the outlook and identification of a white American. At the very least, whites who have faced discrimination on the basis of being perceived as a person of color will probably have greater sensitivity toward the indignities that minorities, particularly African Americans, periodically experience in their lives.

Aside from physical appearance, there are numerous situations in which a white male's personal characteristics may distance him from the majority group, and in doing so, give him some unique opportunities to understand another culture or otherwise have empathy for people. Surnames are one such instance. A white man with a Spanish, Italian, or Portuguese surname may be viewed differently by Latinos than an Anglo with an English, German, or French surname. Linguistic dexterity is yet another example. The white man who speaks Spanish or Mandarin is likely to be received better by Hispanics and Chinese Americans, respectively, than if he were a monolingual English speaker. Language also becomes a critical reference point, in that Americans and others ask a person whether he speaks Spanish, or they speak to him *en español*, to ascertain whether he is Latino. In these ways, naming practices and linguistic similarities highlight perceptions of commonalties that lead (inadvertently, in many cases) to cross-cultural understanding.

The political sociologist Christopher Hewitt, who teaches at the University of Maryland-Baltimore County (UMBC), relates a fascinating example as to how one's foreign accent can exempt him from responsibility for past misdeeds by white Americans. Hewitt, a naturalized American who grew up in England's North Midlands, says that his English accent gives him some leeway with his African-American students, who feel that it distances him from what they may see as a racist power structure that was established, developed, and perpetuated by native-born white Americans.[47] Due to the racial polarization that exists in metropolitan Baltimore, some African-American students at UMBC might regard a white professor suspiciously. Their reaction to Hewitt resembles closely the differential treatment that black immigrants sometimes receive from whites as a result of their foreign accents. Whites often regard black immigrants more positively than native-born African Americans. Some of Hewitt's black students replicate this behavior by viewing him more positively than his native-born white peers.

Matt Streadbeck, likewise, was able to reach people — Brazilians, in his case — due to his appearance. Streadbeck, a tall, fair-skinned man with blond hair and blue eyes in his late twenties, served for two years as a missionary for the Church of Jesus Christ of Latter-day Saints in the Brazilian state of Minas Gerais. Relatively few people in Minas Gerais share Streadbeck's coloration or physical features. (To be sure, millions of Brazilians resemble Streadbeck, particularly in the southern states of Paraná, Santa Catarina, and Rio Grande do Sul.) The Orange County, California, native says his ethnic characteristics helped him to get "a foot in the door" (literally and figuratively). Brazilians were curious about him, and their inquisitiveness enabled him to reach people who otherwise might not have opened their doors to hear his religious message. Streadbeck, a resident of suburban Los Angeles, speaks Spanish and Brazilian Portuguese; two of his brothers were missionaries in the Philippines, and one spread the gospel to South Africans. He himself may draw upon his international experiences and work overseas someday.[48]

Similarly, Scott VanLoo spends his time promoting intergroup harmony and cross-cultural awareness. VanLoo, who was born in August
1970, grew up in Greeley, Colorado. A well-built man with brown eyes,
neatly trimmed sideburns, and brown hair that he wears in a ponytail,
VanLoo resembles a Nordic Spaniard or an Argentine footballer. Indeed,
VanLoo is often mistaken for Argentine, Puerto Rican, and Native American. The longtime Coloradan is one-half Lebanese and one-half European
American (mainly Dutch). VanLoo, though not Latino, identifies strongly
with the Spanish-speaking culture. He grew up in a bilingual household. His Lebanese-American mother teaches Spanish to public school
students — she comes from Brawley, California, a heavily Latino town in
the U.S.-Mexico border region. VanLoo himself is the father of two sons;
their mother is a Mexican national. He presently serves as director of the
César Chávez Cultural Center at the University of Northern Colorado in
Greeley, Colorado. VanLoo also does diversity consulting and conducts
training sessions for educational institutions. In his personal life and professional activities, he regularly interacts with people of color; they often
account for the majority of his peers, associates, and colleagues.[49]

VanLoo identifies strongly with his Arab-American roots, and he
empathizes with Arab Americans who feel they face discrimination in
contemporary American society. This proud Lebanese American, who
criticizes U.S. foreign policy toward such Arab nations as Lebanon,
distinguishes between the European-American and the Arab-American
experiences in white America. Due to his Arab-American ancestry, Van-
Loo posits that he lives life as a minority and a member of the dominant
culture at the same time. (His European surname enables him to pass
for Anglo.) When VanLoo traveled with his Lebanese-American aunt —
her surname is Abdelnour — with a reservation in her name in the immediate post-9/11 era, he says they were stopped at every airport. As a
VanLoo, however, he never encountered any suspicious airport personnel. Such experiences contribute to his humane outlook and empathy for
the disenfranchised. Sometimes people of color view VanLoo with suspicion because they mistakenly consider him to be a garden-variety white
person. He has encountered hostility from minorities on five or six occasions, because they do not initially understand his interest in, or fully
recognize his expertise on, multicultural issues.[50]

Josh Buehner is another young white man who focuses on many types
of diversity: He does so in his human rights activism and budding business career. Buehner, an earnest man of European ancestry who was
born on Christmas Day in 1977, says his compassionate views in favor

of social justice and sympathy for the disadvantaged were shaped by his childhood years in Oregon. For a time, he, his brother, and his mother received public assistance. (Buehner's brother had health problems, which required his mother to stay home with him.) Buehner remembers how people looked at him when his mother used food stamps at the supermarket. He recalls feeling a sense of difference because they were poor. Buehner and his family moved from multiethnic northern California — the Santa Rosa area — to predominantly white North Idaho in 1991. They now enjoyed a measure of prosperity and Buehner had a comfortable upbringing in North Idaho. After he graduated from Lakeland High School in Rathdrum, Idaho, in 1996, Buehner matriculated at North Idaho College (NIC) in nearby Coeur d'Alene. He served as president of NIC's Human Equality Club. Buehner later studied at Eastern Washington University before he went to work for Safeco Insurance Companies' Spokane office.[51]

Buehner first emerged as a human rights activist in the mid-1990s. While he lived in Idaho, he was deeply involved in the Kootenai County Task Force on Human Relations, a local human rights group. (Buehner served as vice-president of the Task Force from December 2001 to September 2002.) During the late 1990s, he spoke about human rights issues at numerous meetings, gatherings, and conferences in the Inland Northwest.[52] Buehner, who embraces the nonviolent, pacifistic approach of Gandhi and Dr. King, has a wealth of stories related to his personal activism.[53] He fervently believes in social-justice issues, including gay and lesbian rights. Buehner and his wife, Jamie, are considering adopting a sibling for their young daughter, Kylie. An employee of Safeco in Seattle, he spends a considerable amount of time on diversity issues in his capacity as a specialist on corporate culture at the insurance behemoth. Buehner reports to two white men: Mike McGavick, the CEO of Safeco, and Allie Mysliwy, Safeco's senior vice president of Human Resources.[54]

Mike McGavick is one of the most passionate advocates of diversity in Corporate America. A dynamic man of Irish and Norwegian ancestry, McGavick was born in February 1958 and grew up in Seattle. As a youngster from a middle-class household, he learned early about justice, fairness, and the value of public service from his parents. They taught him to treat everyone equally and instilled in him a desire to make a difference. Young McGavick heard stories about how his Irish-American grandfather had been narrowly defeated in his campaign for local office in Tacoma, Washington, due to a whispering campaign that he was "a papist," who would put his fidelity to the Pope ahead of American values.

McGavick's father, Joe McGavick, served a term in the Washington leg-islature. Longtime Washington Republican politician Slade Gorton was (and is) a family friend. Politics was a constant topic of discussion at the McGavick family dinner table. Joe McGavick broke ranks with his party to support integration.[55] Not surprisingly, his son is quite comfortable with racial diversity and multicultural issues.

Mike McGavick's remarkable career has taken him from prominent roles in Washington politics to the helm of a profitable Fortune 500 com-pany.[56] At 22, he played an important role in Slade Gorton's winning U.S. Senate campaign in 1980. McGavick then worked on Gorton's staff on Capitol Hill for a time before earning his bachelor's degree in political science from the University of Washington in 1983. He managed Slade Gorton's successful comeback campaign for the U.S. Senate in 1988, and then served as his chief of staff from 1989 to 1991. After a stint in pub-lic relations, McGavick directed the American Insurance Association's Superfund Improvement Project from 1992 to 1995. Then, in 1995, he joined Chicago's CNA Financial Corporation. By 2000, he ran the com-pany's largest division, the $3.5 billion-a-year commercial-insurance unit. Due to the progress made in his unit at CNA, McGavick was chosen to be the president and chief executive officer of the Seattle-based Safeco, a company facing financial problems. (He is now the chairman of Safeco as well.) After beginning work in January 2001, this decisive and vision-ary leader cut costs, streamlined operations, and hired new management. Soon Safeco was profitable again.[57]

Literally from the beginning of his tenure at Safeco (starting with the company-wide satellite talk the day after he was hired), McGavick made it clear through his actions and public pronouncements that diversity was very important to him.[58] He took the title of Chief Diversity Officer in addition to Chief Executive Officer. By doing so, McGavick emphasized that diversity mattered to him — and indicated that he wanted to be held accountable for the success (or failure) of the company's diversity initia-tives.[59] Kevin Carter, an assistant vice president in his early forties who hails from Cleveland, is Safeco's Leader of Corporate Diversity Initia-tives.[60] "The leader," notes Carter, is "responsible for coordinating and monitoring the corporate diversity strategy; leveraging the office of the CEO and collaborating with Safeco's Senior Leadership Team for organi-zational ownership of the diversity strategy."[61] Carter, who is black, reports directly to Mike McGavick and Allie Mysliwy.[62]

McGavick evinces significant enthusiasm about the social and eco-nomic benefits of diversity. He posits that the integrated military led to better race relations, as veterans returned home after their military service with enlightened views about racial issues, and in turn supported integration in their communities. Now he envisions Corporate America playing the same role in a different epoch, by giving Americans a model of how we can accept, embrace, and profit from our ethnic and racial diversity, a paradigm that we can use in our lives beyond the workplace. Moreover, McGavick says that Safeco has to move aggressively into underserved markets and diverse ZIP codes if it is to maintain its profitability over the long term.[63] "If you study demographics," McGavick contends, "the buying power of America is shifting hands very, very rapidly. If you want to be in the kinds of businesses we're in, if you are not able to sell to a diverse America, if you don't reflect that America and understand its needs, you cannot compete. Ten years from now, companies that didn't pay attention to this today, in my opinion, will be at a significant competitive disadvantage or will fail."[64]

Safeco is enjoying considerable success with its various diversity initiatives.[65] The company recruits, hires, retains, and promotes sizable numbers of women and minorities. People of color account for 20.4% of Safeco's workforce. They made up 35.7% of new hires in 2003. Likewise, 13.4% of Safeco managers are people of color and 44.6% are women. White males still make up a majority of those who are part of the Leadership Performance Plan (the top 700 to 750 positions at Safeco), as opposed to 11.7% for people of color and 38.0% for women.[66] And white males account for nine of the ten members of Executive Management — the Senior Leadership Team — at Safeco. Each SLT member is the chief diversity officer for his or her organizational unit. Kevin Carter, meanwhile, reports that on two separate measurements of diversity (the Diversity Scorecard and the Corporate Diversity Strategy), there has been significant progress in the last year — for vendors, employees, and agents alike.[67] The same is true in the marketplace, where Safeco enjoys "double-digit growth in diverse ZIP codes with lower-loss ratios."[68] "Diversity," says Carter, "is driving profitability at Safeco."[69]

Safeco has clearly made steady progress during the last decade in terms of creating a workplace that reflects and values the contributions of both whites and people of color. Josh Buehner is part of the Corporate Diversity Advisory Group, the 17-member committee that Mike McGavick convened in 2001.[70] Buehner is the youngest member of the group, which reports directly to McGavick, and one of four white men in it.[71] As one of the group's four project managers, he played an integral role in developing Safeco's Corporate Diversity Strategy, a document that guides and outlines the company's plans to diversify its workforce and marketing efforts.[72] Indeed, Mike McGavick argues that white males are absolutely essential to making diversity work — that women and people of color need white males to work with them on diversity issues.[73] It remains to be seen what the environment will be like for people of color at Safeco in the future. However, 2002 was the first year that Safeco retained more workers of color than it lost. This milestone, coupled with the favorable hiring data for minorities, signals that Safeco's workforce may soon mirror the demographics of the United States.[74]

Raphael Madison, who worked at Safeco for a quarter century, offers a valuable perspective on multicultural issues there and elsewhere.[75] A native of Houston, Madison joined Safeco in Texas in 1978.[76] He soon became Safeco's first black marketing representative and eventually held an executive position in the firm's Seattle headquarters. (When he retired from the company in 2004, Madison was an assistant vice president of Safeco and the company's director of Diversity Marketing.) This tall, slim man in his early fifties mentors youths in his free time. Madison has a very inclusive perspective: In 1994, he told his colleagues in Human Resources that the company's diversity initiatives would not be completely successful until they had white males conducting diversity workshops. He says that white men who conduct diversity workshops "know what buttons to push" [when they try to reach other white men].[77] The down side for white males who specialize in diversity issues, according to Madison, is the attacks by other white guys — "that they've sold out," in his words.[78] Recently, he backed a white male candidate for a job as a Diversity Marketing Specialist. Some of his colleagues did not think a white man was appropriate for this position, but the person in question had grown up in a white-minority environment and Madison knew he could reach customers of color.[79]

The work environment at Safeco provides us with some fascinating insights into how white males react to multicultural issues in a company that is transforming itself.[80] To include everyone in the company's diversity initiatives, Kevin Carter defines diversity and inclusion "in three stages: (1) building knowledge and respect, (2) developing effective communication and interaction and (3) collaborating toward a common goal."[81] White males regularly tell Carter that they see themselves in inclusion, as he defines it.[82] The company also takes diversity far beyond the traditional categories of race and gender to include such characteristics as parental status, age and generation, and sexual orientation.[83] Some white men at Safeco remain concerned that the company's diversity initiatives will result in fewer opportunities for them. Josh Buehner has had at least one white man approach him to complain that things were, in his opinion, moving too rapidly on the diversity front.[84] In any event, both Buehner and McGavick say that one cannot simply quantify the point at which Safeco becomes a company in which all groups are well represented and feel valued there — rather, one will feel it, by observing how the Safeco employees react to their coworkers and workplace conditions.[85]

PLAYING THE GAME

Very few players in the National Basketball Association (NBA) look like Dirk Nowitzki. The 7–0 tall, 240-pound German has shaggy blond hair and blue eyes and, as with many of his countrymen, a light complexion. Nowitzki was born on June 19, 1978. A native of Würzberg, a city of 128,000 in northwestern Bavaria, young Dirk developed a fondness for basketball before his teen years. As he grew taller and taller, he became more interested in the sport. Throughout his teen years, Nowitzki played basketball and followed the NBA in America with great interest. He reportedly idolized Scottie Pippen and avidly watched the NBA playoff games, which aired in the early morning hours in Germany. At age 15, Nowitzki met Holger Geschwinder, a onetime basketball star who became his mentor. Geschwinder refined and expanded Nowitzki's talent. He used such tools as chess, music, ballet, and fencing to make Nowitzki a better basketball player. Nowitzki gained the attention of NBA talent scouts with his stellar performance in 1998's Nike Hoop Summit.[86]

The German phenom entered the NBA draft in 1998; the Milwaukee Bucks chose Nowitzki and then traded him to the Dallas Mavericks. At the beginning of his NBA career, he encountered some minor adjustment difficulties, as he acclimated himself to the English-language culture in general and the NBA in particular. It was initially difficult for him to be so far away from his native land. After an unimpressive first season (1998–1999), Nowitzki progressively improved during his second season (1999–2000) and third season (2000–2001). By Nowitzki's fourth season (2001–2002), he had become a recognized star in the NBA, when he was eighth overall in the league in terms of points and rebounds per game. A center-forward for the Mavericks who wears No. 41 on his jersey, Nowitzki became prominent in 2001 when the Mavs, as fans refer to them, made the NBA playoffs for the first time since 1990.[87]

Indeed, Nowitzki has really blossomed in the last couple of years. He is winning recognition as one of the most promising players in the NBA. A two-time NBA All-Star (2002, 2003), Nowitzki was part of the 2002 All-NBA Second Team and the 2003 All-NBA Second Team. He was MVP of the 2002 World Basketball Championships.[88] As Olivier Pheulpin writes:

> Nowitzki is unique. There's no way to describe his ability to fight for a rebound with some of the NBA's best athletes, grab the ball with no obvious difficulty, run the floor like a point guard, and then stop suddenly at the three-point line, unconcerned by the presence of a defender, and find nothing but the net — you have to see it to believe it. You have to see Nowitzki to understand the amazing superiority of this young German over almost all his peers, to fully understand the impossible matchup he offers opponents.[89]

Nowitzki, of course, experiences life as a white player in what continues to be a predominantly black league. But racial issues have become more complicated in the NBA due to the increasing number of foreign players, many of whom are white.[90] During the 2002–2003 season, foreign hoopsters accounted for nearly 19 percent, or 65, of the NBA's players. In fact, the growing ethnic and geographical diversity of the sport may be increasing basketball's popularity, domestically and throughout the world.[91] *Time* reports that Nowitzki "belongs to a swelling corps of international players who are winning hearts, minds and dollars, both in the U.S. and abroad. While helping make basketball arguably the world's fastest-growing sport, he and the other sharpshooting globetrotters have managed to captivate hard-to-please hoops fans in the U.S."[92] Several of Nowitzki's teammates are foreign, including Eduardo Najera (a Mexican), Steve Nash (a Canadian), Jon Stefansson (an Icelander), and Tariq Abdul-Wahad (a Frenchman).[93] Nowitzki and his teammates symbolize the multiethnic, multinational, and multicultural future of the NBA — and of American professional sports — as they strive to win an NBA Championship someday.

Race has always been a touchy subject in the sports world. Black athletes in particular were frequently prohibited from participating in major-league and college team sports in the first half of the twentieth century. There were once all-white teams in a number of different collegiate and professional sports. Things slowly began to open up for African-American athletes, such as when Jackie Robinson became the first black Major League Baseball player in 1947. Only in the post–World War II era, especially since about 1960, have African Americans been fully able to explore their options in the athletic arena. As a result, blacks now dominate the ranks of professional basketball and football, and they also rank highly in amateur sports such as long-distance running.[94] It is clear that cultural and environmental influences, not genetic or biological factors, explain the predominance of people from particular ethnic and racial groups in different athletic pursuits. Indeed, there are myriad cultural and environmental reasons that account for the prevalence of Dominican *béisbolistas*, Kenyan long-distance runners, and French-Canadian hockey players.[95]

Race continues to matter significantly in college and professional sports, as measured by the *2003 Racial and Gender Report Card.*[96] Here are the figures for male college student-athletes in NCAA Division I for the 2000–2001 academic year:

- basketball (57.1% black, 32.5% white, 5.1% non-resident aliens);
- football (49.4% white, 42.1% black);
- baseball (81.3% white, 6.7% black, 5.6% Latino).

Overall, whites accounted for 61.6% of athletes in NCAA Division I men's sports, compared to 24.3% for blacks, 4.7% for non-resident aliens, 4.4% for those who selected Other, and 3.3% for Latinos.[97]

Here are the demographics of the major men's professional leagues for the 2001–2002 season:

- National Basketball Association (78% black, 20% white);
- National Football League (65% black, 33% white);
- Major League Baseball (60% white, 28% Latino, 10% black, 2% Asian);
- National Hockey League (98% white, 1% black);
- Major League Soccer (60% white, 22% Latino, 16% black).[98]

Due to the demographics of the nation and the demographics of professional athletics, race is almost always a relevant aspect of any discussion of U.S. college and professional team sports.

Indeed, *Sports Illustrated* asked a very interesting — and controversial — question in a 1997 cover story, "What Ever Happened to the White Athlete?" The article examined the matter of why young white males seemed less interested than their black peers in team sports in general and football and basketball in particular. There are two overlapping reasons for this development: the seeming predominance of black athletes in American sport and the lack of intense interest in team sports as a means of upward mobility in white precincts. The young white male athlete increasingly focuses on white-dominated team sports or mainly white athletic activities such as snowboarding, rock climbing, and mountain biking. *Sports Illustrated* conducted a six-month study of this issue. The publication commissioned a national poll of 1,835 youths at the middle school and high school levels. The journalists also interviewed athletes, academics, executives, and coaching personnel. They drew the conclusion that young white males were going to be less and less likely in the future to participate in team athletics, even as young people of all races worship black athletic heroes.[99]

The *Sports Illustrated* study found that young white male athletes were often affected by racial stereotypes regarding their athletic abilities. These self-defeating stereotypes often came from whites themselves, and stemmed from the high-profile success of African-American athletes in such sports as college and professional football and basketball. Consequently, whites increasingly compete in sports like baseball or ice hockey that seem hospitable to them. They are less likely to play football or basketball, either because they are outplayed by black athletes or intimidated by the competition. These developments perpetuate a cycle in which whites are reluctant to participate in certain sports, leading to fewer role models for white athletes, and so forth. Some white youths even feel as if they cannot play certain positions (e.g., cornerback, wide receiver, defensive back) since African Americans predominate in them.[100] This is a form of "positional segregation," a phenomenon typically experienced by athletes of color.[101] Sport is unquestionably the most racially and ethnically heterogeneous American institution, a dynamic felt most acutely by the current generation of young white males.

According to the findings in the 1997 *Sports Illustrated* poll, young whites and young blacks frequently diverge on the issue of whether they are able to succeed in U.S. team sports. The young blacks polled generally were quite confident about their athletic abilities and the possibilities available to them in that realm. Young whites, on the other hand, were more likely to be uncertain as to whether there was a place for them anymore in particular American team sports. One reason for this dynamic, according to *Sports Illustrated,* is that there are fewer highly successful white athletes in college and professional sports to serve as role models for subsequent generations of white youths.[102] For instance, white male pugilists rarely figure into current discussions of championship boxing.

To be sure, as Jon Entine notes, " . . . whites still dominate the 'country-club' sports of tennis, golf, and swimming, sports that require expensive equipment or facilities such as hockey, skiing, bicycling, and gymnastics, Olympic-type sports such as fencing, polo, archery, and rowing which attract only a limited number of competitors. Whites also do relatively well in certain field events, most notably the discus, shot-put, javelin, and pole vault."[103]

Hockey continues to be far and away the whitest of America's major professional sports. White men account for the overwhelming majority of hockey players — and they constitute much of the fan base as well. The NHL is a transnational league, with an especially enthusiastic fan base in Canada. There are 30 teams in the National Hockey League (NHL): six in Canada and 24 in the United States.[104] As recently as 1999, 60 percent of NHL players came from Canada.[105] French-Canadian men in particular have a long and venerable tradition of contributing to the NHL. The same is true of white Americans and players from such Northern European countries as Russia and Finland. It is fair to say that the players and fan base of professional hockey are ethnically, but not racially, diverse. Michael Farber describes "the NHL's image as a white sport, a niche sport, the NASCAR of the north."[106]

As is the case throughout North America, any situation in which people of color are underrepresented receives attention, and hockey is no exception. To be sure, there are highly successful black hockey players: As of November 2003, NHL team rosters included 14 black players — most prominently, Jarome Iginla, the captain of the Calgary Flames. Iginla made history as the first black to captain an NHL team. Some black players in the NHL have complained about racism on the part of specific white players, and the NHL has taken an increasingly tough stance on discrimination of any kind. If there were more NHL players of color, it is possible that more minorities would go to NHL games; professional hockey, after all, currently does not have enough fans to sustain all the teams.[107] The NHL, meanwhile, attempts to promote greater participation by youths of color in the sport through NHL Diversity, a program that supports and provides programming to at least 30 youth hockey organizations in the United States and Canada.[108]

Auto racing, or stock car racing, is one of the last redoubts of white maleness in sports. Auto racing has become progressively more popular due to savvy marketing and fortuitous trends in the postwar years, beginning with the formation of the National Association for Stock Car Auto Racing (NASCAR) in 1947, an organization controlled by the France family.[109] With such series as the NASCAR Nextel Cup Series, NASCAR Busch Series, and NASCAR Craftsman Truck Series, NASCAR is the center of auto racing in the United States.[110] NASCAR was once a Southern sport — it originated in Dixie decades ago — and white Southern men spearheaded its development. In recent years, NASCAR has become more mainstream, more respectable, more popular, and more national than ever before. Sponsors seek marketable drivers, especially those who are youthful, handsome, clean-cut, and media-savvy.[111] Whites currently account for the vast majority of NASCAR fans, drivers, crewmembers, and at-track officials.

NASCAR is growing in leaps and bounds. The NFL and NASCAR are the two top draws in television sports ratings. Atlanta is the largest TV market for NASCAR, followed by New York and Los Angeles, which tie for second-place. Sixty percent of NASCAR's fans are men, 40 percent are women. Fans of NASCAR report average family incomes ($50,000-plus per year) that accord with those of other major sports. Analysts expect NASCAR to have even greater growth now that NASCAR's top race series is called the Nextel Cup. Many mainstream corporations may regard telecommunications sponsorship as more family-friendly than the cigarette sponsorship of the Winston Cup (the former name of the Nextel Cup).[112] In any event, the commercial sponsors of NASCAR racing teams — and the politicians who court NASCAR fans — essentially appeal to whites, particularly white males.

"As NASCAR tries to break out of its Southern roots and become a mainstream sport," writes Chris Jenkins, "officials have become more sensitive about racing's lack of racial diversity."[113] As with country music, the racial exclusivity of stock car racing tends to reinforce itself. If African Americans and other minorities do not see themselves represented in the sport, and they feel unwelcome as a result, the dynamics will continue as they are. There is a perception in communities of color that they may not be welcome in auto racing, which is reinforced — for African Americans, at least — by the Rebel flags that frequently fly at NASCAR races. At this point, NASCAR marketing does not specifically target any racial or ethnic group. But it is possible that more drivers of color might lead to more fans of color.[114] "Without diversity," writes the journalist Robert Lipsyte, a NASCAR fan, "the sport won't (and doesn't deserve to) remain the new pastime."[115]

White men run the lion's share of the major men's professional teams — baseball, football, basketball, hockey, and soccer. They own most major men's professional teams and are disproportionately represented in the ranks of the teams' front-office personnel.[116] This state of affairs does not meet with approval from everyone, due to the large number of nonwhite professional athletes. That is why Major League Baseball, for instance, has "a minority-hiring program that requires clubs to interview minority candidates for any meaningful positions in the front office or dugout that become available."[117] In addition, the leading sports agents continue to be a disproportionately white (and male) group, although it seems that an increasing number of athletes of color are selecting nonwhite agents.[118] These demographics suggest that men of color do not yet enjoy equal opportunities to succeed in all aspects of American sports.

White males continue to be well represented in the ranks of sportswriters and sportscasters, particularly at the elite levels. White male journalists often analyze, interpret, and pontificate about events that largely involve African-American men, particularly in professional football and basketball. "Radio and television announcers," writes Richard Lapchick, "have the enormous ability to influence the way the public perceives athletes. Thus, it is important that the people in the media be as diverse as the players on the courts and the playing fields."[119] As of the 2001–2002 season, here are the percentages (in terms of race) for the sports' radio and television announcers: NBA (77% white), MLB (83% white), NFL (87% white), and the NHL (100% white).[120] It remains to be seen how, if at all, the coverage of athletes of color would change if minorities were better represented among America's sports journalists.

Perhaps the greatest pressure regarding diversity issues accompanies the hiring and firing of head coaches, the most powerful and visible figures in the coaching hierarchy. As of the 2000–2001 academic year, white men held 87.4% of the head-coaching positions in the NCAA's Division I Men's Sports.[121] To be sure, the major men's professional leagues differ dramatically in their openness to minority candidates. When it comes to the racial backgrounds of head coaches and managers in the five major men's professional leagues, the NBA offers the most opportunities for African Americans, followed by Major League Baseball and the NFL.[122] Due to criticisms regarding the paucity of black NFL head coaches (there were five, as of January 2004), the NFL established a Workplace Diversity Committee, and an NFL team must interview at least one candidate of color for every head-coaching vacancy, or be fined by the league.[123] The dramatic underrepresentation of African Americans in the head-coaching ranks of the NFL, as well as in college football, will continue to be an issue of concern for years to come.

Regardless, the white male public avidly follows the exploits of black hoopsters, ballplayers, and gridiron heroes. White men demonstrate their interest in sports in many ways. They frequent sports bars. They attend athletic events. They watch the games (and the commentary) on television. They wear caps, T-shirts, jackets, and sweatshirts that signal their team loyalties. And they endlessly dissect the teams' tactics, strategies, and performances on talk radio. This arena is one in American society where white fans, especially white men, play a substantial role in making up the audiences at games and at home that help fund the huge salaries earned by the most highly talented African-American athletes. These legions of white men emphatically support their favorite sports teams. White fans, who are mainly men, account for 85 percent of the people who attend college and professional basketball games.[124] White male sports fans, for the most part, do not concern themselves with racial dynamics when they cheer for their favorite football, baseball, or basketball teams. They evaluate matters in terms of their regional loyalties and the strength of the team's players and coaching staff, to determine whether they support a team.

Still, an inevitable question arises: Does the white male athlete assume special significance in a majority-black realm? In other words, does a talented (or not-so-talented) white player benefit from an inversion of affirmative action? Some African Americans allege that whites will often get greater airplay and more lucrative endorsements than their skills would merit, because they are a relative rarity in certain sports. There is no question that many white men would not complain if they saw more white faces and bodies on the basketball court and on the football field. Yet most white fans seem to accept unconditionally that black males have a very important role to play in American college and professional sports. Some observers speculate, though, that the increasingly "urban" image of the NBA is costing it fans in rural and suburban areas.[125] No one can say with certainty that Americans, particularly white Americans, would respond differently to professional basketball or any other sport, for that matter, with a prominent African-American presence, if the vast majority of the players were white men.

Scholars regularly focus on these issues with regard to the NBA. Numerous studies demonstrate that the racial composition of an NBA team is likely to be affected by the demographics of the area in which the team plays. According to such studies, team owners and others may change the team's composition in response to customer discrimination.[126] Another study found that the more white players there are on a team, the better the local TV ratings for the televised NBA games.[127] In terms of NBA salaries, a comprehensive study of the topic concluded that white and African-American players with equal skills and productivity receive similar compensation.[128] Periodically, there is talk of a Great White Hope in the NBA (e.g., Larry Bird or Keith Van Horn), a native-born white player who is presumed by some observers to have an outsized appeal on and off the court that owes more to his race than to his athletic talents.

Two social scientists, Robert W. Brown and R. Todd Jewell, tested this proposition in terms of white male college basketball players.[129] Brown and Jewell write:

> ...[W]e estimate the effect of team racial composition on yearly gate revenues using a data set on NCAA Division I men's college basketball teams. The empirical results suggest that fans are willing to pay a premium of over $100,000 in annual home gate revenues to have an additional white player on their team's roster. Therefore, basketball programs are faced with a sizable economic incentive to discriminate against recruiting black players, even though the programs themselves may have no discriminatory preferences. If college basketball programs do respond to customer discrimination, then the incentives against recruiting black players counteract the apparent educational opportunities provided by college athletics. Customer discrimination, therefore, has important ramifications for the future earnings of prospective black student-athletes.[130]

Due to the demographic transformation of the American population, white males almost certainly will decline as a percentage of those who participate in amateur and professional athletics. This development will likely be common in most (but not necessarily all) sports. White males, to be sure, are going to account for the vast majority of the players on boys' baseball, football, and basketball teams in such places as North Idaho, Upper Michigan, eastern Kentucky, and small-town New England. Likewise, young men in Mexico and the Caribbean will seek to emulate their heroes and become American baseball stars. And there are many young African Americans in urban America who will aspire to success in professional athletics.[131] In any event, the native-born white American male will probably become even more of a fan than a player in traditional team sports. We can almost certainly expect there to be more and more controversy over the relatively small number of minority owners, coaches, managers, and executives of major men's professional sports teams.

Men of color seem likely to play a major role in professional sports for years to come, as those sports become more global in their appeal. Meanwhile, the global nature and multiethnic makeup of Major League Baseball is helping to attract American viewers (including people of color) and international fans to America's pastime.[132] Major League Baseball, long popular in Japan, is in vogue there mainly because of such Japanese superstars as Hideki Matsui and Ichiro Suzuki who play professional baseball in America.[133] Basketball, meanwhile, is a sport that appears to be stagnating in terms of its U.S. attendance figures and television ratings. However, the growing global nature of the game is attracting new fans in many countries, including China, where Yao Ming of the Houston Rockets is a major star.[134] But soccer has yet to take off here, although the rapidly increasing number of Latino immigrants and their descendants may eventually fuel its rise as a popular U.S. sport.[135]

&

There are going to be many situations in America's future where white males — as whites and white males — will be a plurality or a minority of the population. The most interesting racial and ethnic dynamics will occur in those contexts where white males compete with women and minorities on an even footing, as ordinary guys, without enjoying privileged positions. As our big — and small — cities become ever more diverse, there will be few places where a white male can live in a city of at least 100,000 people (excepting such communities as Livonia, Michigan, and Sioux Falls, South Dakota) and not experience ethnic and racial diversity on a regular basis, at least if he is young. But it is possible that middle- and upper-middle-class whites may segregate themselves (informally, of course) in the racially polarized parts of America. For example, many upper-income white males attend predominantly white private schools.[136]

Some interesting dynamics might result as white males account for an increasingly smaller percentage of the U.S. population. Once it becomes clear that whites — and white males — are not as dominant as they once were, perhaps the whole notion of minority status might become more associated with mutable characteristics like one's socioeconomic status, especially if white males explicitly organize themselves as an ethnic interest group. In a psychological sense, it is difficult to avoid the conclusion that the typical white male will probably not enjoy being part of a minority group. Since whites and people of color alike often exaggerate the number of minorities in a given context, many white males may feel like minorities even when a community has a white plurality or a white majority.[137] Likewise, it seems to be common for whites and people of color alike to think that the United States is soon going to become a white-plurality country, even though this demographic milestone may not occur for another 40 or 50 years.[138]

It can be jarring for whites when they realize that the demographic shift that is occurring on a national basis may permanently erode their previously unchallenged sense of majority status. However, as America's demographics change, the outlook of each succeeding generation of white males evolves in response. So the average white male who is born in 2025 will be far more comfortable with multicultural issues than his grandfather who was born in 1965. In the future, white males will routinely experience minority status — or at least the feeling of being part of the white plurality or a multiethnic mix where no group predominates. But we are still far away from the day when a white male is going to know what it is like to be the only white male in his workplace, or the only white student in his class.

Eric Newhall, Associate Dean of the College and Director of the Core Program at Occidental College, offers many insights on such multicultural matters.[139] A native of Portland, Oregon, who teaches courses in American literature and American studies, Newhall graduated from Oxy in 1967, when the student body was virtually all-white and the faculty was mainly white and male. Occidental hired Newhall, who is white, to teach for one year in 1975. He soon established a reputation as a progressive, fair-minded professor. As Newhall's year at Occidental came to an end in the spring of 1976, Oxy students launched a petition drive to retain him. Two student groups that strongly supported Newhall were Ujima, an African-American association, and MEChA (Movimiento Estudiantil Chicano de Aztlán), a Chicano organization. Occidental's administration was surprised to see members of these groups backing Newhall, because they had been advocating for more faculty of color. Eventually, the administration extended six adjunct courses to Newhall, and he remained on campus and ultimately gained a tenure-track position. Today Newhall looks back on the aforementioned experience with profound gratitude, because the backing of the students clearly helped him to retain his position at Occidental.[140]

Over the decades, Newhall and his pro-diversity colleagues have transformed Oxy — this elite liberal arts college boasts one of the nation's most ethnically and racially diverse undergraduate student populations.

During the 1980s and 1990s the institution evolved from being a school with a predominantly white student body and faculty to an institution whose undergraduates and professors more accurately reflect the demographics of Southern California (and the nation). Indeed, Occidental is presently undergoing a cultural and demographic transformation into a quintessentially multicultural institution of higher learning. Today young people from diverse ethnic and racial backgrounds apply in record numbers to this hip, inclusive, and academically rigorous school.[141] White male students at Oxy certainly receive excellent preparation for life in Multicultural America. For instance, the Intercultural Community Center (ICC) on campus sponsors events, lectures, programs, and workshops that give students and faculty greater awareness of social-justice issues. Alice Y. Hom, the ICC's Director, and Sriyanthi Gunewardena, the ICC's Program Coordinator, work with students from a wide range of ethnic and racial backgrounds.[142]

Members of the Occidental College community appear to get along pretty well. To learn more about this topic, I spoke to the two individuals at Occidental (Dr. Frank Ayala, the Dean of Students, and Rameen Talesh, the Associate Dean of Students) who focus much of their attention on intergroup relations among Oxy's students.[143] Everything, of course, is not "perfect" at Occidental; informal self-segregation that cleaves along ethnic, racial, and social lines exists on campus, but it seems to be less prevalent than at many of the college's peer institutions. To promote interaction across ethnic and racial lines, Newhall advocates learning and living communities (LLCs), by which students pick a first-year seminar (there are 15 to 16 students in each of Oxy's 30 seminars) and then they live in a residence hall with the other students in that seminar and three other seminars. As the Director of the Core Program, Newhall oversees the first-year seminars at Occidental. Students in most seminars edit each other's papers; this practice enables young people from different backgrounds to learn how to write better and, at the same time, learn more about each other.[144]

Eric Newhall regularly discusses multicultural issues with his students, including the white men. He reports that white male students periodically ask him for help in reconciling what they see as a multicultural conundrum. They want to be very successful in their careers, but they are uncertain as to whether such aspirations are appropriate or even possible these days, considering what they see as the emphasis in American society on improving the life chances of women and minorities. Newhall tells the young white men that they must recognize the value of diversity and, accordingly, treat everyone fairly and respectfully. At the same time, Newhall emphasizes his belief that workplace diversity is not a zero-sum issue: White males can — and will — prosper in a multiracial environment where affirmative action and diversity initiatives actively promote the hiring, retention, and promotion of women and people of color. Newhall notes that white male students and, for that matter, all students at Occidental will emerge from their experiences there (in the LLCs and beyond) with better critical-thinking skills and what he describes as "intercultural competence."[145]

Newhall says that white males have an important role to play in "the emerging pluralistic society."[146] He posits:

> I find it helpful to use the metaphor of a circle, or in Native American culture — the Sacred Hoop. I think white men need to see that they are (should be) part of a circle rather than at the privileged center of a circle. That's the key shift that needs to take place in our culture. To move from the CENTER to being a PART of the circle is, in fact, to SHARE. What needs to be shared? Power, voice, resources would be a good start.[147]

Moreover, Newhall believes that it is in white males' best interests to share the dream with women and people of color. "Everyone," says this exemplar of multicultural thinking, "benefits when society becomes more just. Conversely, everyone is at risk when large numbers of citizens are marginalized and treated unfairly."[148]

chapter six

The American Pantheon

On November 25, 1991, Sheldon Hall appeared before an assemblage of Plymouth, Massachusetts, residents dressed as the Spanish conquistador Juan de Oñate.[1] Hall, or Oñate, told the Plymouthites that Oñate and his band of Spanish colonists had held a thanksgiving celebration on April 30, 1598, on the south bank of the Rio Grande near present-day San Elizario, Texas. (The Rio Grande changed course during the 1830s, so the area in which the feast occurred is now U.S. soil.) The outdoor banquet celebrated the survival of Oñate and his followers after an arduous three-month trek through the Chihuahuan desert — they were en route to northern New Mexico. Hall's challenge to the chronological primacy of the New England narrative of Thanksgiving resulted in his arrest by the Plymouthites, along with his wife, Jane, and the dozen other El Pasoans who accompanied them to Plymouth. The Pilgrims charged them with "blasphemy and spreading false rumors." Then there was a mock trial at Plymouth's Courthouse, after which the judge set them free.[2] In April 1992, a delegation of Pilgrims journeyed to El Paso to defend their claim to Thanksgiving; the New England tourists were arrested in San Elizario and they, too, were tried by a judge and eventually released.[3] These good-natured publicity stunts — both parties dressed in period attire for their respective visits to each other's turf — received media attention around the globe.

Sheldon Hall has been the driving force behind the efforts to inform Americans about the First Thanksgiving and the importance of Oñate's expedition to our nation's history. One day in 1986, while he was working on a project to preserve the historic Spanish presidio and two historic Spanish missions in Greater El Paso, Hall came across a book, *History of New Mexico,* at the University of Texas-El Paso Library. Captain Gaspar Pérez de Villagrá's epic poem, published in 1610, is a first-person tale of Oñate's colonizing expedition to New Mexico — its antecedents, the expedition itself, and the early years of the colony. Hall read the book and began to think about how the story outlined in its pages was over-looked in the traditional accounts of early American history.[4] His perusal of this book spurred him to set into motion the events that led to the First Thanksgiving. The El Pasoans began to rewrite an important chapter of American history with the First Thanksgiving Celebration in April 1989. The festivities included the reenactment of the events of April 1598 on the grounds of the Chamizal National Memorial in El Paso, along with related activities in San Elizario, a small, historically significant town on the outskirts of Greater El Paso.

Oñate, though, is controversial in El Paso, as in New Mexico, particularly because of an incident in 1599 in which he ordered that 24 adult Acoma Indian men should have their right feet amputated in response to an Acoma ambush that killed a number of Spaniards, including Oñate's nephew.[5] Hall acknowledges the controversy over Oñate's edict, but he says the punishment, though severe, was necessary to prevent future Indian uprisings.[6] Furthermore, he points out that several historians question the veracity of various aspects of the foot-chopping narrative.[7] To be sure, Hall notes that he "does not admire Oñate the man but [he] tremendously admire[s] the accomplishments" of the Spanish explorer. Oñate, after all, founded the first permanent European settlement west of the Mississippi and left an indelible imprint on the Southwest due to his exploratory efforts throughout the region and his pivotal role in the establishment of the livestock industry and the beginning of the Franciscan missionary program there.[8] Don Juan de Oñate is the Christopher Columbus of El Paso, which is why the city chose him to be part of its 12 Travelers series of statues honoring important figures in El Paso's history; Hall advocated on behalf of the Oñate statue.[9]

Sheldon Hall comes from a family with a venerable tradition of civic involvement and great accomplishments. A native of Columbus, Ohio, Arthur Sheldon Hall was born in Cleveland on September 10, 1917. Hall's heritage is predominantly English, with significant amounts of French and Dutch ancestry as well. He is a lineal descendant of Charlemagne, Alfred the Great, William the Conqueror, several Magna Carta barons, Edward I, Roger Williams, nine colonial governors, seven colonial clergy, and a host of other luminaries. Hall graduated from Miami University with a degree in industrial management in 1939; he captained the Cross-Country State Championship team there. Then he served in the Army Air Corps — the precursor to the Air Force — during World War II. After the war, Hall moved to Texas, and he eventually settled in El Paso in 1960. For many years this courtly man with white hair, brown eyes, English features, and a trim figure was the president and owner of the Blair-Hall Company, a general-contracting firm that constructs commercial buildings in El Paso. Hall is a lifelong history buff. He and his youngest son, Frank, the family genealogist, are members of the Society of the Cincinnati, whose membership is limited to direct descendants of officers in the Continental Army.[10]

Over the years, Hall's civic leadership and advocacy for historical preservation have brought him considerable recognition in El Paso, the state of Texas, and beyond. Around 1980 he became a leader in the *Granaderos de Gálvez,* an organization that honors the memory of Bernardo de Gálvez, the governor of Spanish Louisiana during the Revolutionary War, who aided the American cause immeasurably at critical junctures. Since 1985 he has been the honorary consul for Spain in West Texas and southern New Mexico, a position that requires him to look out for the interests of Spanish citizens in these areas. Hall also served on the Texas Historical Commission from 1989 to 1995. Moreover, he was the chair of the Christopher Columbus Quincentenary Texas Jubilee Commission between 1990 and 1992. From 1995 to 1998 Hall served as chair of the El Paso Quadricentennial Commission, which planned and coordinated the three-day celebration that marked El Paso's four-hundredth birthday in 1998. In addition, he was knighted by the Spanish government — they awarded him the Cross of Isabel La Católica. Hall himself is a lineal descendant of El Cid (Rodrigo Díaz de Bivar), the eleventh-century Spanish hero who fought the Moors, and a distant relative of King Juan Carlos I of Spain. Not surprisingly, the Halls regularly visit España — they have covered more of the country than most Spaniards.

Due to the hard work of Sheldon Hall and others, El Paso's First Thanksgiving has become the most credible alternative claimant to Plymouth's title as the preeminent Thanksgiving narrative in the country.[11] To promote the story of El Paso's First Thanksgiving, the Halls and a friend from the El Paso Convention and Visitors Bureau attended two state conventions of social-studies educators and three of the National Social Studies conventions. At each convention, the three El Pasoans set up a booth with a banner that read, "Are You Teaching the Correct First Thanksgiving?" They also dressed in period costumes — the men as conquistadors, complete with armor, and Mrs. Hall as a Spanish lady. Naturally, the costumed preservationists received considerable attention from the educators as they strolled around the convention floor (one member of the party staffed the booth, while the others mingled with the educators). Likewise, Hall founded the Mission Trail Association, an organization that promoted the First Thanksgiving, and he served as its president for nine years. The Mission Trail Association prepared individual kits, which included a children's book and an educational video, about the First Thanksgiving, that it sold to educators around the country.

For the last 18 years, Sheldon Hall has been the unquestioned leader of the quest to broaden Americans' perspectives on the Thanksgiving holiday.[12] Today many of the fourth-grade history teachers in the El Paso public schools teach the First Thanksgiving to their students. Furthermore, the elementary-school textbooks and social studies curricula in many states now include coverage of the alternative claimants to the title of the First Thanksgiving, without necessarily passing judgment on the validity of their claims. Hall usually plays a role in the planning of the annual First Thanksgiving celebration, which takes place in El Paso and in San Elizario. In 2001, this grandfather of eight was the grand marshal of the parade in San Elizario. His labors have not been in vain — millions of Americans now have some familiarity with the El Paso narrative regarding Thanksgiving because of Sheldon Hall's persistent pursuit of historical truth.

ALIVE AND WELL

In January 2001 the Franklin Delano Roosevelt Memorial in Washington, D.C., became more complex — and more accurate — when President Bill Clinton dedicated the life-size bronze statue of Roosevelt that portrays him using a wheelchair.[13] The statue greets visitors at the seven-acre Memorial's entrance; it depicts President Roosevelt sitting in the self-designed wheelchair that he used every day for more than 20 years. The addition to the Memorial includes a bas-relief quotation — it is 50 feet long — from Eleanor Roosevelt, FDR's First Lady. Eleanor Roosevelt's quotation indicates that her husband's polio endowed him with courage, strength, patience, and persistence. No world leader had been depicted using a wheelchair before. Clinton's dedication of the statue marked the end of a long and drawn-out battle on the part of disability advocates to have the FDR Memorial represent all aspects of America's thirty-second president.[14]

It took several years before disability advocates and their allies succeeded in their lobbying efforts in favor of a full portrayal of FDR's disability. The Franklin Delano Roosevelt Memorial included little mention or coverage of Roosevelt's disability when it first opened in May

1997. Disability advocates started lobbying in 1995 in favor of a depiction of Roosevelt in his wheelchair. In the mid-1990s, the Franklin Delano Roosevelt Memorial Commission rejected these advocacy efforts because they sought to portray him as he lived in public life, when he disguised his use of the wheelchair. But in 1997 both houses of Congress passed the resolution requiring the memorial to depict Roosevelt's disability, and President Clinton signed it into law. The law dictated that private donations were to pay for the statue. The Rendezvous with Destiny Campaign Committee, which was formed by the National Organization on Disability, raised $1.65 million for this purpose. In 1998, the National Park Service said it would add the statue after extensive advocacy by the disability community.[15]

Roosevelt, after all, had contracted polio in 1921 and he lost the use of his legs. The redoubtable Dutch American went through a period of rehabilitation and emerged as an important American political figure, first as governor of New York (1929–1933) and then as President of the United States (1933–1945). Throughout these years, Roosevelt downplayed his disability.[16] Hugh Gregory Gallagher writes:

> Although there are over thirty-five thousand still photographs of FDR at the Presidential Library, there are only two of the man seated in his wheelchair. No newsreels show him being lifted, carried, or pushed in his chair. Among the thousands of political cartoons and caricatures of FDR, not one shows the man as physically impaired. In fact, many of them have him as a man of action — running, jumping, doing things. Roosevelt dominated his times from a wheelchair; yet he was simply not perceived as being in any major sense disabled.
>
> This was not by accident. It was the result of a careful strategy of the President. The strategy served to minimize the extent of his handicap, to make it unnoticed when possible and palatable when it was noticed. The strategy was eminently successful, but it required substantial physical effort, ingenuity, and bravado.[17]

Today disability advocates embrace FDR as their icon because of his historical prominence and remarkable triumph over adversity. The addition of a statue depicting FDR in his wheelchair to the FDR Memorial resonated with people in the disability community. Franklin D. Roosevelt has long been venerated by millions of Americans for his shrewd political acumen and visionary leadership during the Depression and World

War II. Now he has become the top role model for America's disability community. The statue of a wheelchair-bound Roosevelt at the FDR Memorial is an important symbolic instance of inclusion for people with disabilities.[18] The debate over accurately portraying FDR in the FDR Memorial highlights his role as a traditional white male icon and his role as a hero on the basis of his disability, as a member of a minority group.

Icons and heroes are important to Americans and, indeed, to people in virtually every nation around the world. Each society develops narratives, a "usable past," to link its endeavors to those of preceding generations and, in doing so, give some degree of meaning to the present. This process occurs through the celebration of events and institutions that help the living generations understand where they came from, in addition to socializing them with the values and belief systems of the society and culture. Due to the important role white males have played in shaping and ruling America, white male leaders and achievers traditionally have received the lion's share of attention in our culture and textbooks. Of course, the multiculturalists have criticized this state of affairs for being unduly exclusionary. And there have been complex reinterpretations of various historical figures and events. Even today, though, white males receive a significant amount of coverage in American art, music, history, literature, philosophy, and other disciplines.

Americans recognize in many ways the contributions of those who are sometimes described as "dead white males." This phrase succinctly describes the American and European white men who have played such a significant role in our culture. Take Mozart. The eighteenth-century Austrian composer never visited the United States, but he remains an instantly recognizable symbol of high culture here. The phrase "dead white male" can be used in a derisive or tongue-in-cheek fashion, although I do not use it here in that way. For instance, I overheard a young white woman disdainfully telling another young white woman in the summer of 1994 on the campus of the University of Wisconsin-Parkside that she was going to write a paper about "dead white males." And last year John Updike penned a review of several books about Ralph Waldo Emerson that was entitled "Big Dead White Male"; the review appeared in the *New Yorker*.[19] Another way that observers sometimes refer to "dead white males" is as Dead White American Males (DWAMs) and Dead White European Males (DWEMs).[20]

Americans venerate DWAMs and DWEMs differently in different contexts. We celebrate certain icons and heroes on a national level, without regard to any regional distinctions. Then there are others whose regional antecedents take priority, either because they were particularly significant in one part of the country, or their actions were controversial outside of that region. At the local level, many towns, institutions, and corporations celebrate icons whose significance is linked to that community. This veneration may take the form of a statue, a holiday, the name of a school, or the portrait that hangs in the hallway of a library. Then there are other types of veneration, particularly in the form of consumer products that bear the name of the founder, that do not explicitly honor an individual in a specific sense but instead rely upon the positive connotations of his name to attract and reassure customers.

In fact, the extent to which the names of so many different products, institutions, and the like reflect the significance of "dead white males" is so dramatic that is impossible to delineate them in detail. DWAMs and DWEMs have plants (poinsettias), diseases (Alzheimer's disease), terms (sadism, Marxism), roadways (the Dan Ryan Expressway), airports (LaGuardia), museums (the Field Museum), universities (Harvard, Stanford), scientific principles (the Heisenberg uncertainty principle), and prestigious awards (the Nobel Prize, the Pulitzer Prize) named after them. The Dow Jones Industrial Average is named for two DWAMs: Charles Dow and Edward D. Jones. Similarly, few people stop to think that the Mason-Dixon line was named for Charles Mason and Jeremiah Dixon. And there are consumer icons such as Ford, Hilton, Dom Perignon, Duncan Hines, and Colonel Sanders. Educated American writers and speakers frequently cite DWAMs (Thomas Jefferson, Walt Whitman) and DWEMs (John Locke, Alexis de Tocqueville) in their writings and speeches. Still, most Americans pay relatively little attention to the implicit honoring of DWAMs and DWEMs that takes place when their names continue to have currency in our times.

Americans have traditionally venerated the Europeans who affected the development of the culture, institutions, and boundaries of the present-day United States. Christopher Columbus, the European "discoverer" of America, is our country's best-known DWEM icon. We honored the Italian mapmaker Amerigo Vespucci when the new nation called itself the United States of America. Spanish explorers entered the pantheon as well, due to their extensive travel through, and colonization of, California, much of the South, especially Texas, Florida, and the Deep South, the Southwest, and Midwestern states such as Kansas and Missouri. Thus Hernando de Soto is honored in parts of America, especially in Mississippi.[21] Revolutionary War heroes are another group that receives recognition — namely, the Marquis de Lafayette and, to a far lesser extent, Casimir Pulaski, Tadeusz Kosciuszko, and Bernardo de Gálvez. The critical role Lafayette played in the Revolutionary War led him to be honored by place-names in such places as Lafayette, Louisiana; Lafayette, Indiana; Fayetteville, Arkansas; and Fayetteville, North Carolina. These examples demonstrate how contemporary Americans venerate DWEMs, usually without any significant controversy.

Throughout the nineteenth century and much of the twentieth century, the immigrant youngsters accepted the icons and heroes of the American pantheon with little dissent. The older immigrants, of course, remained more aloof from these Americanizing influences. Youngsters from various immigrant backgrounds learned to respect and cherish George Washington, Thomas Jefferson, and Abraham Lincoln as their heroes. Over the years, as the composition of the white population began to change, men with non-British surnames began to show up in the history books as well. Many of the female icons, though, were old-stock Americans with Anglo-Saxon forebears. Up until the 1960s, American schoolchildren mainly learned about heroes who largely traced their heritage to the Protestant parts of the British Isles. Few whites made any fuss over this. The Catholic and Jewish immigrants were more interested in assimilating into their host society than in challenging its cherished icons. In any event, the cultural and political climate at the time was not receptive to such challenges.

Two federal holidays (Presidents' Day and Columbus Day) honor white men. Since the early 1800s, Washington's Birthday has been a legitimate national holiday. Washington's Birthday or, as it is more commonly known, Presidents' Day, is celebrated on the third Monday in February. This holiday honors the memory of George Washington and, indeed, all the other presidents, particularly Abraham Lincoln.[22] However, few people, except for retailers, celebrate Washington, Lincoln, or any other presidents during this period. This is not the case with Columbus Day, the federal holiday in October that commemorates Columbus's arrival in the New World in 1492. Columbus does double duty as an American icon and an Italian-American icon. Italian Americans proudly honor Columbus's memory with parades, dinners, and other festivities. The Martin Luther King federal holiday, which began in 1986, is the first national holiday to honor a person of color; no new federal holidays seem to be forthcoming at this point.

Certain state holidays have significant symbolic importance in the South. Debates over how to honor Confederate heroes in general and

Robert E. Lee in particular continue to affect the discourse there. Alabama, Arkansas, and Mississippi jointly honor Martin Luther King (who was born on January 15) and Robert E. Lee (who was born on January 19) with an annual holiday. Texas celebrates Confederate Heroes' Day on January 19 each year. Virginia celebrates Lee-Jackson Day (the holiday honors Robert E. Lee and Stonewall Jackson) on the Friday preceding the commemoration of King on the third Monday in January — the date of the federal holiday.[23] Virginia's King Day celebration takes priority over Lee-Jackson Day, however; the racial, cultural, and political dynamics of the state lead Virginians to focus on honoring Dr. King rather than Generals Lee and Jackson. Indeed, it will be difficult for Virginia's supporters of Confederate iconography to carry the day anymore. The Old Dominion State's sizable black population and its growing number of immigrants and domestic migrants favor diversity and feel no connection to the Confederate icons.

One way that the United States seeks to present itself is through its postage stamps, which are a powerful indicator of a nation's demographic composition and its receptiveness to inclusion. DWAMs (particularly American presidents) predominated on U.S. stamps through the 1960s. Over the years, there have been American stamps honoring such figures as Mothers of America (1934), Dr. G. W. Carver (1948), The American Woman (1960), Chief Joseph (1968), and Paul Laurence Dunbar (1975). Susan B. Anthony appeared on a 50-cent stamp in the 1950s. In keeping with the nation's demographic transformation and multicultural makeover, the United States Postal Service offers stamps that take into account America's ethnic, racial, gender, cultural, and religious diversity. White male figures from our nation's history continue, of course, to appear on U.S. postage stamps — they represent a wider variety of occupations and accomplishments (Roy Acuff, Andy Warhol, and Harry Houdini recently graced 37-cent stamps) than was previously the case.[24]

Americans regularly recognize and contribute to the influence of white males in other ways, such as when we invoke the names of DWAMs and DWEMs as a convenient shorthand for various qualities, attributes, and rhetorical points. American English includes such adjectives as Machiavellian (Niccolò Machiavelli) and Shakespearean (William Shakespeare). And there are nouns that draw upon white males' names: McCarthyism (Joseph McCarthy), Social Darwinism (Charles Darwin), Pavlovian response (Ivan Pavlov), Freudian slip (Sigmund Freud), and Rorschach test (Hermann Rorschach). These terms, of course, have meanings that relate to some aspect of their namesakes' fame. To say that somebody is an "Einstein," for instance, is to use this DWAM's reputation for genius as a touchstone, as a reference point, to describe a contemporary person who is smart. At the colloquial level, there might be someone who discusses his own economic situation and says, by way of comparison, that he is "no Rockefeller."

Virtually every native-born American adult understands certain references to white-male-related people, places, and products. A person might refer to an individual's surname, drawing upon the reputations of the DWAMs that give it currency, as in "He's a Kennedy" or "She's a Vanderbilt." Someone might speak about an item of clothing (It's Armani or Versace) or a piece of art (a Picasso or a de Kooning). There are words — eponyms — that originated with white men but are now such lower-case words as bowdlerize (Thomas Bowdler), boycott (Charles C. Boycott), diesel (Rudolf Diesel), gerrymander (Elbridge Gerry), guillotine (Joseph Guillotin), leotard (Julius Leotard), sandwich (John Montagu, 4th earl of Sandwich), and silhouette (Étienne de Silhouette).[25] Then there are fictional archetypes (Horatio Alger, Mr. Smith — Senator Jefferson Smith) who are commonly assumed to be, and are depicted as, white males. The ubiquity of these reference points indicates how pervasive the white male influence is in American culture.

Many of the top brand names in the world, according to *Business-Week,* are named for white males. Some examples include: Disney (Walt Disney); Hewlett-Packard (William Hewlett and David Packard); Gillette (King Camp Gillette); JPMorgan (John Pierpont Morgan), Louis Vuitton (Louis Vuitton), Adidas (Adi Dassler), Levi's (Levi Strauss), Polo Ralph Lauren (Ralph Lauren), Johnnie Walker (John Walker), and Jack Daniel's (Jack Daniel).[26] Few people care about these brands' historic and associational ties to white men. Anyway, the connection often is so removed or obscure as to make it almost meaningless, and many of these product lines rarely, if ever, depict the white male namesake. Some of these products and brand names, to be sure, explicitly emphasize the connection to the white male namesake. The visage of Colonel Sanders is a prominent part of KFC's marketing, for example. These examples indicate the continuing influence of living and deceased white males, from the U.S. and abroad, in our nation.

Corporations vary in terms of whether they emphasize or highlight the white male founder, namesake, or driving force behind the product or brand name. Many entrepreneurs (Bill Gates, Sam Walton, Ray Kroc) did not name their brands — Microsoft, Wal-Mart, and McDonald's, respectively — after themselves. Likewise, there are few overt connections between Disney the company and Walt Disney the man in Disney's marketing strategy. Nor do pictures of John Deere appear on any John Deere & Company products — but his name is important to the farm equipment maker. Some names decline in significance over time (Woolworth's), while others mature and become American institutions (the Mayo Clinic). Norman Rockwell exemplifies a ubiquitous "brand name" that is part of the popular consciousness; Rockwell's name signifies a style of painting, a type of Americana, and a certain chronological era. His paintings continue to be featured in calendars, date books, and other formats.

The veneration of deceased celebrities represents a relatively unexamined venue in which Americans celebrate DWAMs and the occasional DWEM. Elvis Presley is undoubtedly the most famous DWAM icon in American popular culture. Elvis fans venerate him through his music, the myriad products bearing his name and likeness, and by fueling the celebrity impersonators who perform as Elvis.[27] In 2001, 2002, and 2003 Elvis Presley was the top-earning deceased celebrity, according to Forbes.com's annual list.[28] America's icons change over time, of course, as a consequence of the normal changes in taste that occur with each generation. Moreover, one-third of American youths are minorities and they feel little connection to such DWAMs as Babe Ruth, Elvis Presley, or Charles Lindbergh, in part because the historical narrative they are taught in the schools does not emphasize the accomplishments of such men, as it once did.[29]

In any event, no icon receives more attention in Western society than Jesus Christ, the son of God in Christian theology; the depiction of Jesus in art remains an intriguing site of race, color, and representation. "No pictures were made of Jesus while He was alive," writes Megan Rosenfeld, "nor do any of the four Gospels describe Him, so no one really knows what He looked like."[30] Jesus has often been portrayed by white Westerners as a Northern European in the Christian religion, a point that has been the subject of criticism by people of color in recent decades.[31] The Christian immigrants from Europe brought "white" images of Christ with them when they came to the United States, and they further developed the Northern European portrayal of Christ in America. Today Jesus is customarily depicted as a white man in mainstream American (and Western) media, artistic, cinematic, and photographic portrayals of Him.[32]

The best-known portrait of Jesus in modern times is Warner Sallman's *Head of Christ* (1940). Sallman's most famous devotional portrait depicts Jesus in a head-and-shoulders pose with blue eyes, fair skin, and auburn hair. Due to excellent marketing by Sallman's distributors, the image has been reproduced more than 500 million times, on lamps, clocks, prints, plaques, buttons, stickers, bookmarks, calendars, billboards, key chains, coffee mugs, funeral cards, and church bulletins. In the postwar years of the 1940s and 1950s, Sallman's image of Jesus was the preeminent devotional picture in U.S. homes, churches, and workplaces. Beginning in the 1960s, though, its very ubiquity rendered it too common and, perhaps more importantly, the increasing ethnic and racial diversity of the American population made it less appealing to people of color. While Sallman's *Head of Christ* still represents Jesus to many older Americans, there are now innumerable Jesus images, symbolizing Christ with widely divergent skin tones, hair types, and facial features.[33]

African Americans regularly represent Jesus as a black man; this type of depiction has become more common in the last ten to 15 years, as an outgrowth of Afrocentrism. People of faith seek to represent Jesus in their image as a matter of pride and relating to Christ.[34] "It has long been tradition in churches throughout the world for images of Jesus to mirror the faces of the faithful," writes Laurie Goodstein. "Jesus is often depicted in Latin America as Hispanic, in Asia as Asian, and in Africa as black."[35] In the United States, meanwhile, Afrocentrism has affected Christian worship among black Americans in many ways. For years there have been vigorous debates among clergy, the laity, and theologians about the depiction of Jesus as a white man in African-American churches. One finds black images of Christ in murals, statues, paintings, and stained-glass windows in black churches around the country. Still other African-American congregations refuse to accept portrayals of Jesus as a man of color, especially those with large numbers of older people who grew up with white Jesus images in their homes, churches, Bibles, and Sunday school lesson books.[36]

Some observers have sought to approximate Jesus's appearance using the tools of modern science. The Discovery Channel documentary, "Jesus: The Complete Story," which aired in 2001, describes how Jesus may have looked based on the skull type, skin tone, and hair type of his 1st century contemporaries.[37] Referring to the documentary's speculation about Jesus's appearance in relation to traditional Northern European portrayals of Him, Megan Rosenfeld writes, "It's far more likely He had swarthy skin, a wide face with a prominent nose and short curly black hair and beard. His skin would have been wrinkled and tough from squinting into the Middle Eastern sun, and since He lived at a time when 33 was well into midlife, His face would have had the sags and creases of age."[38] The images of Jesus as a European remain symbolically significant in our culture, even as people such as the British medical artist Richard Neave conclude that Jesus, in all likelihood, may have had a Semitic appearance.[39]

CHANGING THE NARRATIVE

On June 25, 1876, George Armstrong Custer, his Indian scouts, and the men of the Seventh Cavalry Regiment were roundly defeated by their Native American foes in the Battle of the Little Bighorn.[40] Sioux, Arapaho, and Cheyenne warriors killed every last one of them (265 in total) during the legendary battle that became known as Custer's Last Stand. When he went to his death, Custer was fighting one of the battles in the intermittent Indian Wars between the U.S. government and the Native American nations during the 1870s and 1880s. The Indians won the battle but lost the war; soon thereafter, the United States began venerating Custer. In 1879 the U.S. government designated the Little Bighorn Battlefield as a National Cemetery. And in 1946 the federal government established a National Monument — the Custer Battlefield National Monument — in southeastern Montana. Americans focused their attention on DWAM heroes in the national narrative at the time; the Indians' perspective received little consideration.[41]

Naturally, many Native Americans disliked the name of the Custer Battlefield National Monument. By the early 1970s there were rumblings of discontent in Indian Country about the monument to Custer, which is located on the Crow Indian Reservation. After considerable work by Native Americans and their allies, in 1991, Congress changed the monument's name to the Little Bighorn Battlefield National Monument. (The monument is a division of the National Park Service.) The 1991 legislation mandated the building of a memorial to the Indians who fought in the Battle of the Little Bighorn; Congress came up with the $2.3 million in funding for the memorial ten years later.[42] Each June, two separate reenactments of the battle take place in southeastern Montana.[43] At the same time, the Little Bighorn Battlefield National Monument, which draws 500,000 visitors per year, has become Indian-friendly, with Indian superintendents and Native American interpretations of the events. In 2003 the National Park Service dedicated a monument that commemorates the Native Americans who died during the fabled battle.[44] Less and less attention, it seems, is paid to Custer with each passing year at the Little Bighorn Battlefield National Monument.

But Custer is not forgotten in this world. The blond Indian fighter who died at age 36 was venerated almost immediately upon his death, due to the Alamo-like scene where he met his Maker — and the fact that it connected to the American public's fascination with the West and white America's interest in all things Native American. Custer's widow, Elizabeth Bacon Custer, devoted the rest of her life (from 1876 to 1933) to ensuring that her husband would be remembered as a valorous hero. Custerphiles and Custerphobes have sparred over the meaning of the battle ever since. To be sure, Custer's Last Stand has received considerable attention in books, films, cartoons, paintings, advertisements, and television productions. Custer's critics castigate him for his role in oppressing Native Americans and furthering the westward expansion of white settlers. Some critics also question his military strategy at the Battle of the Little Bighorn. Clearly, Custer and his soldiers no longer are admired uncritically by white Americans, as they take into account the Native American perspective on the man his Indian contemporaries referred to as "Yellow Hair."[45]

Some Americans, to be sure, continue to honor Custer in a wide variety of ways. The 2,002-member Custer Battlefield Historical and Museum Association works to preserve Custer's memory, in the context of the Battle of Little Bighorn.[46] White settlers in the West honored Custer's memory through place-names. Numerous towns, counties, and businesses bear Custer's name in the Western states, particularly Montana and South Dakota. Montana is home to the Custer National Forest. South Dakota has a Custer State Park. Whites predominate in many of the communities named after Custer; they have little interest in changing the place-names to stop honoring him. In fact, such an idea would undoubtedly be met with hostility by many conservative whites. In any event, the changing role of George Armstrong Custer in America's national narrative symbolizes the evolving nature of historical memory and constructions of meaning and remembrance in a multiracial nation.

Since the 1960s, multiculturalists have sought to diversify America's narratives, celebratory efforts, and monuments to reflect the nation's multiethnic makeup. There is a finite amount of space and time that can be devoted to topics. So a more-inclusive narrative requires that some white males have to bite the dust. The literary canon, for instance, once featured such authors as Mark Twain, Geoffrey Chaucer, and William Shakespeare. Similarly, the hagiography and fileopietistic treatments of the past have been replaced by revisionist accounts that challenge the veracity of traditional narratives and expand the historical coverage to include people who were previously ignored, excluded, discounted, and downgraded due to their race, ethnicity, gender, social class, sexual orientation, and other characteristics. These symbolic instances of inclusion matter to people in Multicultural America: It is no longer possible to unite Americans around an all-white-male cast of heroes and leaders.

The changing of the guard takes different forms and shapes. There has been more of a focus on putting the white male aspect of our nation's heritage on the same footing, figuratively, as that of other groups, as evidenced by the course "White Male Writers" at Georgetown University, which made national headlines in 1991.[47] In other words, white male writers have moved from *constituting* the canon to *being part of* the canon. The multiculturalists seek to expand the number of texts considered "worthy" of inclusion in the literary canon. Throughout academia, their efforts take into account such factors as revisionist conceptions (and reinterpretations) of art, history, literature, philosophy, and other disciplines. Over the years, the evaluations and interpretations of various historic figures and phenomena have shifted in response to new scholarship and changing conditions in our society. These changes better inform Americans, correct omissions in the historical record, and provide members of underrepresented groups with role models.

Multiculturalists develop new interpretations of American history that change our understanding of the role white male figures played in our nation's history and publicize the role of women and minorities in the American narrative. Some white revisionists are motivated by a critical philosophy of history, literature, or some other discipline to question the traditional motives of a person or a group of people. Other revisionists have a multicultural bent, and they build up females, people of color, and other traditionally underrepresented groups such as the working class to be a more important part of the literary canon or the history textbooks. Students learn about multicultural perspectives in such disciplines as black studies, women's studies, Chicano/a studies, disability studies, and lesbian and gay studies.

The putative homogeneity of the white population in America discourages the insertion of ethnic-specific icons to diversify significantly the "white" portion of the canon and American history. During the 1960s and 1970s, there was considerable scholarly interest in the heritage, accomplishments, and cultural output of white ethnic groups. What had been a heavily Anglo-Saxon set of narratives and icons has diversified, in part because of the increasing heterogeneity of the white American population. Still, people from the British Isles dominated early American history, so any broad treatment of white America in that period will necessarily focus on those individuals. Conversely, we have not seen any dramatic ethnic-specific responses within the white population regarding DWAMs or DWEMs who were unsympathetic to their situation, as in Greek Americans who lobby against the recognition of figures who criticized Greek immigration.

Multiculturalists apply the diversity imperative to the past through books, films, scholarly articles, and other media. In doing so, they try to bring to light stories that have been neglected, forgotten, or ignored, because a particular person or group of people frequently belonged to a group outside the mainstream of American society at the time. Traditionally underrepresented groups receive their due now. To some extent, there is consideration of whether these efforts "distort" the narrative by bringing other people and groups to the fore. This very delicate issue involves questions of worth and importance. Since white men dominated politics, diplomacy, and commerce in the past, it is necessary to focus on other aspects of American life, history, and culture if we are to have a national narrative that broadly reflects the ethnic and racial diversity of our past, present, and future.

The historical narrative and the literary canon are constantly evolving in response to the nation's changing demographics and our new sensibilities regarding multicultural issues. Some multiculturalists contend that J. D. Salinger's *The Catcher in the Rye* is an outdated choice for high school syllabi in Multicultural America. The protagonist, Holden Caulfield, after all, is an affluent white male. Many teachers do not think that Holden Caulfield reflects the diversity of today's high school students.[48] Along these lines, in 1998 the San Francisco Board of Education unanimously voted in favor of a requirement that ninth, tenth, and eleventh graders must be taught texts by authors who represent America's diversity, in terms of race, ethnicity, and sexual orientation. The board members specified no quota, however.[49] Such changes will continue to occur as the nation adopts an inclusive, multicultural mindset regarding history, literature, philosophy, and other facets of America's heritage.

These multicultural initiatives lead us to acknowledge the overlooked achievements of women and people of color. Americans now recognize the role that non-Western cultures have played in developing scientific knowledge that we traditionally identified with Westerners.[50] Similarly, we acknowledge that the Founders may have been influenced by Native American principles and practices when they crafted the Constitution.[51] Indeed, specific individuals are receiving credit for events, accomplishments, and heroism that were ignored or discredited in the past. Some examples of once-overlooked achievers include the inventor Granville T. Woods, the explorer Matthew Henson, and the scientist Rosalind Franklin. Entire groups of people are now recognized for their important roles in particular periods of American history, such as black cowboys in the nineteenth-century American West and the invaluable contributions of the Native American Code Talkers during World War II.

U.S. military history is rife with examples of African Americans who have not received their due in the nation's history books. Paul (PJ) Matthews, a native of the Houston area in his late fifties, aims to remedy this lamentable omission. He spends much of his time disseminating the story of the Buffalo Soldiers, the nineteenth-century black soldiers in the 9th Cavalry and the 10th Cavalry who battled outlaws, Indians, gun smugglers, and Mexican bandits and revolutionaries in the American West. Matthews first became interested in the Buffalo Soldiers when he read a two-paragraph account about them in a military history textbook while he was an undergraduate student at Prairie View A & M University in 1964. Matthews, who is black, served with distinction in the Army during the Vietnam War; he earned a Bronze Star, a Combat Medical Badge, and an Army Commendation Medal. For decades he has worked to persuade his fellow Americans to pay more attention to the achievements and contributions of African-American soldiers in general and the Buffalo Soldiers in particular.[52]

In 2001, Matthews founded the Buffalo Soldiers National Museum in Houston, Texas. The museum, which focuses on the African-American military experience, hosts 25,000 visitors each year. Matthews is now retired after working for 30 years (most recently as an executive business manager) at Merck & Company. He serves as the museum's curator, a position that requires him to give frequent presentations about the Buffalo Soldiers to civic, educational, and community groups. Trooper Matthews wants young people, particularly African Americans, to learn about the illustrious achievements of their forebears, so as to give them a sense of purpose in their daily lives. To achieve this goal, he intends to expand the Buffalo Soldiers National Museum, make sure the story of the Buffalo Soldiers is part of the textbooks, push for posthumous recognition of African-American war heroes, record and preserve the oral histories of black veterans, and establish an on-line registry of all the African Americans who have served in the military throughout U.S. history.[53]

The Southwestern whites (the "Okies" in the vernacular) who migrated to California's Central Valley in the 1920s, 1930s, and 1940s are another group of Americans whose history is starting to receive an increasing amount of scholarly attention. After all, many academics in the fields of American history and American literature seek to broaden the existing narratives to include the stories of *all* Americans, including once-marginalized groups like the "Okies." The term "Okie," which used to be an epithet but is now a badge of honor for many Anglo Californians, lumped together hundreds of thousands of people from different states and different socioeconomic backgrounds. The typical representations of the Southwesterners in films, literature, and other media focus on the Dust Bowl period. This is the case even though large numbers of Southwesterners migrated to California in the 1920s and the 1940s as well.[54]

Doris Weddell plays an important role in the movement to preserve the culture and history of California's "Okies." Weddell, a 71-year-old Anglo native of Modesto, California, first grew interested in the history of the Southwestern whites in 1979, after she became the librarian of Lamont, California, a predominantly Latino town southeast of Bakersfield. As librarian, Weddell received calls from people from around the world with questions about the "Okies," because the government camp featured by John Steinbeck in *The Grapes of Wrath* is two miles south of Lamont. For two years, from 1990 to 1992, Weddell had a Dust Bowl Room at the Lamont library. She took the materials in it with her when she transferred to the Bakersfield library, and they formed the nucleus of the Dust Bowl Collection in her Bakersfield home. Since Weddell retired from the Kern County library system in 1995, she has worked full-time on Dust Bowl–related issues. This indefatigable historian catalogs historical artifacts and educates people of all ages through her public lectures, presentations, and tours of the famous government camp (the Arvin Farm Labor Center, or Weedpatch Camp, in the local vernacular) in Kern County, California.[55]

Earl Shelton, a native Oklahoman, works closely with Weddell on these efforts. A tireless square dancer and charming raconteur with a phenomenal memory, Shelton was born in December 1933 near Scipio, Oklahoma. The youngest of four sons born to Tom and Vergie Shelton, he lost his mother when he was only four. In 1941, Tom Shelton and his two youngest boys drove from Oklahoma to California to join the two oldest sons who had already gone out there to seek their fortunes. Upon their arrival in California, the Sheltons soon found lodging at Weedpatch Camp. Earl Shelton lived at the camp for 13 years. Now he is retired after working for four decades at an oil refinery.[56] Ray Rush is another alumnus of Weedpatch Camp; an Oklahoma native in his early seventies, Rush lived there from 1941 to 1945. The Bakersfield, California, entrepreneur writes country music. His song, "Leo B. Hart," honors the founder of the camp's Arvin Federal Emergency School, or Weedpatch School, as the locals referred to it.[57] Rush and Shelton regularly share their memories of the Dust Bowl migration and life at Weedpatch Camp with students, scholars, journalists, and others.

Shelton, Weddell, and their compatriots seek to preserve the culture and history of the Southwesterners who went to California's Central Valley. These historical preservationists regularly meet with the American journalists (the *New York Times* and the *Washington Post* have covered the story) and the foreign media figures (including those from Japan, Norway, South Korea, and Great Britain) who trek to Kern County, California, every year to learn more about the "Okies." They also have an award-winning exhibit at the annual Kern County Fair. Weddell gives at least 20 talks and 40 tours of Weedpatch Camp each year as well. Similarly, she serves as co-chair of the committee that puts on the annual Dust Bowl Days Festival in Lamont, which is sponsored by the Greater Lamont Chamber of Commerce. Weddell and Shelton work with others, including Ray Rush and Margaret Lutz, a Lamont journalist, in the Dust Bowl Historical Foundation.[58] The foundation has raised $350,000 to preserve Weedpatch Camp's three remaining 1930s buildings: the Library, the Post Office, and the Community Hall. Eventually there will be regular tours of the camp, in addition to a library and research center there.[59]

Expanding the narrative also involves rewriting it, as evidenced by the decline in significance of DWAMs in specific contexts over the years. Statues of controversial historical figures merit attention, as in those of Don Juan Oñate (Espanola, New Mexico), Robert E. Lee (Richmond, Virginia), and Nathan Bedford Forrest (Selma, Alabama). Moreover, many American buildings, particularly libraries and universities, are adorned with portraits of middle-aged or elderly, often WASP, men who are the namesakes of the buildings or important figures in the institution's development. Usually the pictures are not controversial, unless they portray slaveholders or Confederate heroes, but minorities may feel excluded by the iconography anyway. For example, Brooklyn Borough President Marty Markowitz created a brouhaha in January 2002 after he took office, when he decided to diversify the portraits on the walls of Brooklyn's capitol — Borough Hall. Markowitz said he felt the portraits should be representative of Brooklyn's multiracial, multicultural reality.[60]

There are many specific examples of recent efforts to reevaluate the legacy of many important DWAMs and DWEMs in American history. Americans no longer honor the discredited icons and heroes whose politics and actions have led them to fall out of favor in Multicultural America. Columbus Day, for instance, has been quite controversial for at least 15 years. Native Americans criticize Columbus for bringing the Europeans to the Western Hemisphere, a fact that decimated the Native population through war, disease, and overwork. There have been numerous instances in which the Columbus holiday is no longer celebrated, or has been downgraded in importance.[61] Likewise, the D. W. Griffith Award of the Directors Guild of America was renamed the Lifetime Achievement Award in 1999 due to Griffith's antediluvian views on race relations.[62] These changes reflect the conflicts and compromises that typify racial and ethnic dynamics in the United States.

There are many controversies over Confederate icons in the American South, particularly regarding the names of public schools. Numerous public schools in Southern states were named for Confederate luminaries (Robert E. Lee, Stonewall Jackson, and Jefferson Davis chief among them) when whites held the power — and there was a consensus among white Southerners at the time that such men deserved recognition. Now many of the aforementioned schools have black majorities; in some cases, the Confederate icons whose names grace the public schools received this honor during the period of white backlash after the Supreme Court's ruling in *Brown v. Board of Education*. Some schools that once honored Confederate leaders have been renamed for African Americans, particularly now that blacks have significant political clout in many contexts. The Orleans Parish School Board in Louisiana has a policy that bans school names that venerate any slave owners or racist individuals. Some African Americans prefer to focus on the social and economic inequities in American society, though, before dealing with the symbolism of Confederate names on schools.[63]

In the years preceding Multicultural America, white males competed against only 40 or 45 percent of the population, because women and minorities were almost entirely excluded from participation in many pursuits and occupations. Therefore, it is legitimate to raise the question about whether their accomplishments should be viewed through a different type of contextual lens — a perspective that takes into account the fact that they did not compete against everyone in society at the time. In other words, in a totally fair society, perhaps they would not have seemed as great as they do today, or would not have received the same kind of opportunities available to them at the time. To what extent, if any, should we reevaluate the accomplishments of white males in the past on this basis? Roger White, a character in Tom Wolfe's *A Man in Full*, even suggests that an asterisk should be placed next to segregation-era white athletes' names in the record books to indicate that they played in an atmosphere where many talented individuals were excluded from participation due to racial segregation.[64]

This notion of contextualism has (so far, at least) received little support from most Americans. Accepting it would require rewriting American history on a mass scale. Anyway, multiculturalists often focus on women and minority personages rather than denigrate openly the DWAMs and DWEMs of the past. In other words, a college student may be assigned to read Hurston rather than Hawthorne in his or her introductory English course, but no one in the class is going to disparage the author of *The Scarlet Letter*. Similarly, multiculturalism may mean focusing on social and cultural history rather than political and diplomatic history, or including much more information about Asian, African, Middle Eastern, and Latin American history. There is simply less of a focus on DWAMs and DWEMs today. The mainstream history textbooks may now allude to the bad things that happened to people of color — and mention sex discrimination — but the multiculturalists focus more on celebrating and uplifting traditionally neglected groups than on attacking DWAMs and DWEMs.

There have been counterattacks on the new multicultural program, with people saying that we should return to traditional studies of American and Western art, history, literature, and philosophy, lest we lose the fundamental core of our societal values. The columnist John Leo says, "Inclusiveness is good in general but wretched when it means altering historical reality to impose proper quotas on past events. Retro quotas are an old story in schools, textbooks, and the art world."[65] This kind of counterattack focuses on the situation of DWAMs and DWEMs as a group, and it tends not to be oriented toward any artist, author, or historical figure in particular. Such arguments against political correctness were made by a number of authors in the 1980s and 1990s, most prominently Allan Bloom in *The Closing of the American Mind* (1987).[66] The counterargument, of course, is that multiculturalism has given us a richer and more accurate view of our nation's artistic, literary, cultural, and historical heritage. This is the argument made by Lawrence W. Levine in *The Opening of the American Mind* (1996).[67]

In recent years, we have seen works of historical scholarship that explicitly focus on white males and conceptions of white maleness. Some of these treatments examine whites as a group, but involve discussion of white males. And in the past decade or so we have begun to see books that explicitly focus on the white male dimension of topics, as in Martin Green's *The Adventurous Male: Chapters in the History of the White Male Mind* (1993) and John F. Kasson's *Houdini, Tarzan, and the Perfect Man: The White Male Body and the Challenge of Modernity in America* (2001).[68] Other titles reference the white male aspects of specific historical events and developments.[69] And we may see more works that spotlight overlooked accomplishments by white males, as in Richard M. Sudhalter's *Lost Chords: White Musicians and Their Contribution to Jazz, 1915–1945*.[70] Due to the present emphasis on diversity in its myriad forms, we can expect such treatments to be more common in the coming years.

LEGAL TENDER

George Washington — or at least the U.S. dollar bills bearing his likeness — came through in a pinch for my family and me when we arrived in Montevideo, Uruguay, on November 30, 1999. We had taken the hydrofoil from Buenos Aires to Montevideo. However, we neglected to obtain Uruguayan pesos before disembarking from the hydrofoil. Therefore, I queried our taxi driver, a white man in his forties, beforehand about whether he would accept U.S. dollars for a fare. "*¿Acepta dólares?*" I asked him in accented Spanish. He looked at me blankly. I repeated my query. Again, he looked at me uncomprehendingly. I repeated myself another time. This time, he nodded, and we jumped into his taxi and went to our hotel. It was a short ride.

After we alighted from the taxi at the Holiday Inn in downtown Montevideo, I paid the driver three dollars. (The meter said 24 pesos — and the exchange rate at the time was roughly eleven-to-one.) He seemed satisfied with the fare. Shortly thereafter, we procured some Uruguayan pesos and George Washington did not factor again into our travel plans until we returned to the United States.[71] George Washington, of course, had little to do with the willingness of our Uruguayan taxi driver to accept American currency. The Uruguayan probably had no idea who Washington was and in all likelihood couldn't have cared less. However, he knew that U.S. currency was stable and easily convertible, even in Uruguay, where dollars were not then used as frequently as in neighboring Argentina.

This incident exemplified the global value of American currency. Had we gotten into the taxi in Montevideo and asked *el taxista* if he accepted Canadian dollars or British pounds or Japanese yen, I doubt he would have answered affirmatively. To be sure, our Uruguayan cabdriver's willingness to accept U.S. dollars was probably largely attributable to his frequent interactions with dollar-wielding Argentine visitors to his country. That George Washington was a Virginian, the Father of His Country, the general who defeated the British in the Revolutionary War, and the first U.S. President were matters of no consequence to him. Nor he did care about George Washington's race, gender, and ethnicity. Green was the only color that mattered to our Uruguayan taxi driver.

George Washington continues to be one of America's most revered heroes; therefore, it is fitting that the United States honors him by putting his likeness on one of its mass-circulation banknotes. Consequently, many people in the world, from Montevideo to Mogadishu, have some familiarity with George Washington's somber visage because U.S. currency is the de facto global currency. As with our cabdriver in Montevideo, they rely on the stability and convertibility of the green banknotes that bear the pictures of Washington, Jefferson, Lincoln, Hamilton, Jackson, Grant, and Franklin. However, their fondness for greenbacks does not mean that they respect, honor, and venerate George Washington or the other DWAMs on U.S. banknotes. Indeed, Americans and foreigners alike pay relatively little attention to the identities of the men whose likenesses adorn this nation's currency.

The United States is an economically and politically stable behemoth — thus most internationalists consider the American dollar to be one of the world's most important currencies. People around the globe receive goods and services in return for U.S. banknotes, each of which costs roughly 4.2 cents to print.[72] It is difficult to ascertain how important representations of the people, events, and places depicted on the nation's currency are; after all, most Americans probably could not name more than half the personages who appear on our coins and banknotes.[73] (Anyway, the increasing prevalence of digital money — credit cards, debit cards, and the like — is making this topic less significant than it was, say, 20 years ago.) Other issues, such as jobs, health care, education, and the war in Iraq, take priority for Americans, but this issue matters nonetheless in terms of how we perceive ourselves as a nation.

The depiction of historical figures and their likenesses on U.S. mass-circulation coins and banknotes is a twentieth-century phenomenon. Before then, there were often mythical figures or archetypes on coins and banknotes. We began putting likenesses of historical figures on our currency when white men accounted for most of the nation's "mainstream" icons and heroes. Thus it is unsurprising that white men have been the figures who typically appeared on U.S. currency. White men account for all but two of the depictions, likenesses, and portraits of specific people on mass-circulation banknotes and coins throughout American history.[74] In any event, no living person is depicted on the U.S. coins. George Washington started this tradition, namely because of his aversion to anything that seemed redolent of monarchy. Currency designs, after all, would become politicized if living figures were portrayed on coins or banknotes.[75]

Depictions of women and people of color — usually archetypes as opposed to real people — have periodically appeared on U.S. mass-circulation coins. The U.S. one-cent piece portrayed Native American imagery between 1859 and 1909. The "Indian Head" cent does not feature a genuine Native American; rather, it depicts "a representation of Liberty wearing an Indian headdress..."[76] Moreover, an unnamed Native American man appeared on the front of the U.S. five-cent piece (the Bison, Buffalo, or Indian Head nickel) between 1913 and 1938. A bison is depicted on the coin's reverse.[77] And the United States once had gold "Indian Head" coins in various denominations. These were mythic portrayals, not actual Indians, adorned with "Indian" accouterments, e.g., the obverse of the $10.00 gold coin depicts the Head of Liberty wearing a Native American war bonnet.[78] The first actual woman (Susan B. Anthony) appeared on a mass-circulation U.S. coin in 1979; similarly, the first person of color (Sacagawea) did so in 2000.[79]

The portrayal of women, blacks, and Native Americans who appeared on early U.S. private banknotes — the U.S. government did not begin issuing banknotes until 1862 — indicates how white males regarded members of those groups at that time.[80] According to Richard Doty, "We must always bear in mind that those who were ordering, creating, and using the notes were predominantly white males; the depiction of others would therefore be filtered through the dominant group's perception of the truth."[81] The people depicted on nineteenth-century private banknotes were mainly white. Depending on the decade, the portrayals of women on the notes included goddesses, ordinary people, tempters, and consumptives. The white male creators of the notes usually depicted African Americans in work-related contexts; sometimes the portrayals were realistic, other times they were romanticized. Similarly, the notes represented Native Americans as if they were "backward," at least those who eschewed involvement with the Euro-American way of life.[82] The depictions on the private bank notes, not surprisingly, reinforced as well as reflected the power dynamics of the time.

The Confederacy, to be sure, had black slaves on some of its banknotes during the Civil War in the 1860s. The slaves portrayed on the Confederate currency often performed some type of work, as in picking cotton. This issue came to light largely because of the artwork of John W. Jones, a South Carolinian of African ancestry who is well known for his allegorical paintings of Confederate currency in the context of the Confederacy's white oligarchy. Jones's artwork has received national attention for several years. Scholars and others infer that the white Confederates depicted black slaves on Confederate currency because of their essential nature to the Southern economy. These images, say some scholars, indicate that the Confederate stance on the Civil War was heavily influenced by the white oligarchs' desire to preserve the system of slavery that benefited them economically.[83]

In any event, five of the six U.S. mass-circulation coins depict white men who served as U.S. presidents. In 1909, the U.S. Mint began releasing pennies with a profile of Abraham Lincoln, to mark the hundredth anniversary of his birth. A new reverse to the coin, featuring the Lincoln Memorial, coincided with the 150th anniversary of Lincoln's birth in 1959.[84] The quarter began to bear George Washington's likeness in 1932, to commemorate the bicentennial of his birth.[85] The U.S. Mint introduced the nickel with Jefferson's portrait on the obverse and Monticello on the reverse in 1938. According to *A Guide Book of United States Coins,* the artist Felix Schlag's "design established the definite public approval of portrait and pictorial themes rather than symbolic devices on our coinage."[86] The Franklin Roosevelt dime was introduced in 1946, the year after FDR died.[87] And John F. Kennedy's likeness first appeared on the half dollar in 1964, just months after he was assassinated in Dallas.[88] During the last quarter century, two different women (Susan B. Anthony and Sacagawea) have been depicted on the underused dollar coin.

In 1979 the United States Mint began issuing a silver-colored, octagon-shaped dollar coin featuring Susan B. Anthony, the nineteenth-century advocate for women's rights. "Placement of Susan B. Anthony's likeness on the dollar," notes one numismatic guide, "represented the first time that a woman, other than a mythical figure, has appeared on a circulating U.S. coin."[89] The Susan B. Anthony dollars were not particularly distinguishable from quarters in size or color, so it was not surprising that many Americans confused them with quarters and half dollars. The coin never won the public's favor and it was only minted in 1979, 1980, 1981, and 1999.[90] In recent years I have used Susan B. Anthony dollars regularly — one obtains them as change from the Postal Service's vending machines — and, as a result, have observed the differing reactions Americans have to this coin. Upon receiving one or more dollar coins, clerks have squealed in delight, scrutinized the dollar carefully as if it were a quarter, or actually mistaken it for a quarter. Millions of Americans have had such experiences, which is why the U.S. Mint decided to issue a new dollar coin.

The United States Dollar Coin Act of 1997 mandated a new dollar coin, one that was different in appearance and composition from the coin that preceded it. The dollar coin, issued in 2000, portrays Sacagawea, the Shoshone guide and interpreter for the white explorers Meriwether Lewis and William Clark. She carries her infant son, Jean Baptiste, on her back. The current dollar coin has a plain edge and a golden color; unlike its predecessor, it does not resemble any other mass-circulation U.S. coins.[91] Most Americans do not seem to care that this was the only mass-circulation U.S. coin with a woman or person of color on it. For starters, most Americans do not focus much attention on the likenesses depicted on the nation's coins and banknotes. And most of us do not view the dollar coin as an integral part of our coinage — it is seen more as a novelty, unlike, say, the quarter. In the past, whites seemed more comfortable honoring Native Americans than was the case for African Americans, even if the valorizing was done in a symbolic and paternalistic fashion.

The Golden Dollar, launched in 2000 to great fanfare, has not caught on with the American public for a number of reasons. The principal barrier that prevents the dollar coin from being used more frequently is that Americans use the dollar bill commonly and are resistant to substituting the dollar coin for paper currency. Americans are also unaware of the money the government would save if the durable dollar coin replaced the easily worn-out dollar bill. Some of us feel that the dollar bill is easier to transport than the dollar coin. In addition, Americans may have adverse perceptions of the dollar coin considering that neither the Susan B. Anthony dollar nor the Sacagawea dollar proved to be a success. Thus it is going to be difficult to follow the lead of Canada, Australia, the United Kingdom, and the euro zone, all of which have the equivalent of $1 and $2 coins. The smallest note in the aforementioned places is a $5 bill.[92]

U.S. Mint officials have considered redesigning American coins in recent years — specifically, the people and pictures depicted on them. (They did not want to make any alterations to the coins' size, shape, or composition.) Some coin collectors advocate changes to the currency, so as to improve the coins' aesthetic appeal and popularity with the American public.[93] The Jefferson nickel is undergoing a temporary makeover as part of the "Westward Journey Nickel Series." The portrait of Thomas Jefferson still graces the nickel's obverse, but the reverse side of the coin is going to be modified on the 2003, 2004, and 2005 nickels to commemorate the Louisiana Purchase as well as Lewis and Clark's expedition 200 years ago. Beginning in 2006 the nickel's obverse will once again depict Monticello.[94] American coins rarely undergo any type of redesign, except for the Bicentennial designs for the quarter, half dollar, and dollar coin in 1976 and the Statehood Quarter program from 1999 to 2008.

Similarly, our banknotes have been largely the same since the first few decades of the twentieth century. At one time, U.S. banknotes were considerably larger, and the artwork on the bills was significantly more ornate, than is the case today. In 1929, with the release of the Series of 1928 notes, the Treasury Department standardized our paper currency, introducing banknotes similar in size and appearance to the ones that we use in the twenty-first century. At that time, Treasury Department decision-makers placed George Washington, Thomas Jefferson, Abraham Lincoln, Alexander Hamilton, Andrew Jackson, Ulysses Grant, and Benjamin Franklin on the mass-circulation notes. In those days, there also were $500 notes, $1,000 notes, $5,000 notes, and $10,000 notes. No new bills in the latter formats have been printed since 1946, although the existing large-denomination notes remain legal tender.[95] Indeed, the average American typically uses only four bills — the $1, the $5, the $10, and the $20.[96]

The U.S. Bureau of Printing and Engraving explains how the men on our paper currency were chosen for this honor:

> The portraits currently appearing on the various denominations of paper currency were adopted in 1929 when the size of the notes was reduced. Prior to the adoption of this smaller sized currency, a special committee was appointed by the Secretary of the Treasury to study this aspect of the design. It was determined that portraits of

Presidents of the United States have a more permanent familiarity in the minds of the public than any others. This decision was somewhat altered by the Secretary of the Treasury to include Alexander Hamilton, who was the first Secretary of the Treasury; Salmon P. Chase, who was Secretary of the Treasury during the Civil War and is credited with promoting our National Banking System; and Benjamin Franklin, who was one of the signers of the Declaration of Independence. All three of these statesmen were well known to the American public.[97]

In the 1990s the U.S. Treasury Department redesigned the nation's banknotes, largely to thwart counterfeiters. The updated banknotes were released in the following sequence: $100s (1996), $50s (1997), $20s (1998), and $10s and $5s (2000). Every bill received a facelift, except for the $1 and $2 notes. Indeed, U.S. banknotes will undergo regular updates every few years. Due to the scanners, color copiers, and ink jet printers at the disposal of aspiring counterfeiters, the Bureau of Engraving and Printing carefully tested and evaluated new features, including a watermark, color-shifting ink, fine-line printing patterns, and an enlarged off-center portrait.[98] However, the Bureau of Engraving and Printing reassures us: "The currency still has a familiar American look. The size of the notes, basic colors, historical figures and national symbols are not changing. New features were evaluated for their compatibility with the traditional design of U.S. currency."[99]

The U.S. Bureau of Engraving and Printing is once again updating the security features on our nation's banknotes, giving our paper currency a new look again, in order to thwart counterfeiters and protect the integrity of U.S. currency. This latest redesign began in 2003 with the release of the new blue, green, and peach $20 note. Andrew Jackson still graces the note's front and the White House appears on its reverse side, even though both are rendered differently than in the past. Despite these changes, the $20 note is recognizably similar to its predecessor, making it more difficult to counterfeit without dramatically changing the note's appearance. A global public-relations campaign accompanied the release of the redesigned $20 bill. The redesigned $50 note will appear in 2004; the new $100 note comes out in 2005. The $5 and $10 notes may be redesigned as well. There will be no redesign of the $1 and $2 notes, though. Different denominations will have different colors.[100]

Interestingly, the monochromatic whiteness of the faces on our currency has received little criticism or attention, for that matter. Perhaps leaders of ethnic-advocacy organizations have concluded that they do not want to spend precious time, political capital, and lobbying resources trying to change the portraits on the currency in exchange for what would be, at best, a symbolic payoff. Nonetheless, our nation's changing demographics suggest that we can expect ethnic advocates to push someday for more diversity on the nation's coins and banknotes. A catalyst is needed; it simply has not happened yet. Perhaps in an ever more diverse America we will move toward a euro-like acceptance of bland national symbols rather than specific historical personages on our currency. Many multiethnic societies — e.g., Guyana, South Africa, Northern Ireland, and Trinidad & Tobago — do not portray any specific icons or heroes on their banknotes, probably to avoid antagonizing any one group. The Scandinavian countries and especially Australia stand out in terms of their gender-inclusive depictions of national heroes on their currency. (Every Australian banknote features a man on one side and a woman on the other side.)

In any event, dollarization is common throughout the world.[101] "At the present time," notes one source, "the United States dollar remains the world's foremost reserve currency, primarily held in $100 denominations."[102] Several Latin American countries (Panama, Ecuador, and El Salvador) use the U.S. dollar as their only currency. A number of sovereign states in the Pacific — Palau, Micronesia, East Timor, the Marshall Islands — are dollarized as well.[103] The same is true of the Turks and Caicos Islands (a British colony) and the British Virgin Islands (a dependent territory of the United Kingdom). China, moreover, pegs the yuan to the dollar.[104] Many countries have their own monetary units, but U.S. dollars are popular there as in Russia. In late 2002 approximately 55 percent of U.S. circulating currency ($620 billion in total) circulated in countries besides the United States.[105] At any rate, dollarization spreads the visages of DWAMs around the world.

At the same time, the European common currency, the euro, is one of the world's most respected currencies, along with such monetary units as the Swiss franc, the U.S. dollar, the British pound, the Canadian dollar, the Japanese yen, and the Australian dollar. Twelve nations in the European Union have adopted the euro: Austria, Belgium, Finland, France, Germany, Greece, Ireland, Italy, Luxembourg, the Netherlands, Portugal, and Spain. Approximately 306 million people live in the euro zone, a number that slightly exceeds the U.S. population of 294 million. Moreover, the Gross Domestic Product of the 12 nations totals some $7.6 trillion, compared to $10.4 trillion for the United States.[106] The actual euro coins and notes began circulating during the first two months of 2002 in the euro zone. Each of the eight euro coins has a common side and a country-specific side. Euro banknotes do not feature personages or national identifying marks; they come in seven denominations: €5, €10, €20, €50, €100, €200, and €500.[107] At this point, it is uncertain as to what extent the euro will supplant the dollar as the world's global currency.

"Still," writes Robert Block, "the common European currency has presented the first real competitor to the dollar in world markets since the modern system of international exchange was adopted in 1944."[108] Since its introduction in January 1999, the euro has oscillated widely in its value vis-à-vis the dollar, from a low of 82.30 cents in October 2000 to a high of $1.2929 in February 2004. Two thousand three was a great year for the euro, as such factors as a weak U.S. economy and the uncertainties of U.S. foreign policy made the euro seem like a safe haven for investors. In fact, it became so strong in relation to the dollar, hurting European exports, that European policymakers began to speak out in favor of a weaker euro.[109] Thus far, it seems that the European monetary union has not yet contributed greatly to European integration, in part because the euro-zone nations have differing fiscal policies and priorities.[110]

∽

The demographic pressures to include women and minorities will increase dramatically in the coming years, as members of these groups become more numerous and more powerful. Most instances of historical celebration that involve the nation or multiethnic states, communities, or institutions will be scrutinized carefully for demographic balance, historical fairness, and multicultural inclusiveness. This is why the Confederate icons of the white South may not be celebrated in mainstream contexts in the future. Some native-born white Southerners do not care for such icons and many blacks dislike them, even if they sometimes feel there are far more important issues for them to focus on in their activism and political involvement. Similarly, the newcomers to the South — whites and people of color alike — generally do not feel any attachment to the nineteenth-century heroes.

One of the most interesting compromises on the naming front occurred soon after the June 2003 death of Atlanta's first black mayor, Maynard Jackson. Atlanta, of course, is a black-majority city and African Americans are well represented in Greater Atlanta. Jackson had been a three-term Atlanta mayor; as Atlanta's chief executive, he oversaw an extensive expansion of Atlanta's airport from 1977 to 1980. The airport expansion played a major role in making Atlanta's airport one of the busiest in the world and the basis for the city's global reputation. Jackson also made history during the airport expansion because he required that women- and minority-owned firms receive at least one-quarter of the contracts. By doing so, he helped diversify the clubby ranks of Atlanta's white male contractors. Jackson reportedly took great pride in his accomplishments regarding the world-class airport and wanted his name on it. For all these reasons, Jackson supporters said the city should honor him by naming the airport after him. However, the airport was already named for one of Jackson's predecessors, William B. Hartsfield, a white man who had been mayor of Atlanta for 23 years, during which he focused close attention on the development of the airport.[111]

The renaming controversy in Atlanta took place against the context of continuing social and economic differentials in the city and environs. White Atlantans still enjoy better life chances, on average, than do black Atlantans. Moreover, Atlanta is actually becoming whiter in percentage terms in response to white gentrification and black flight from the city. Atlanta, to be sure, is a city where blacks wield most of the political power. The city debated numerous solutions to the naming dispute. Eventually, Mayor Shirley Franklin, a former Jackson acolyte, asked the Atlanta City Council to vote in October 2003 in favor of a new name for the airport: Hartsfield-Jackson Atlanta International Airport. The mayor, who is black, carried the day with this compromise.[112] Today Georgia's world-class airport is known as Hartsfield-Jackson Atlanta International Airport (it was once named William B. Hartsfield Atlanta International Airport).[113] After some initial acrimony, the racially charged airport-renaming controversy was settled in the time-honored Atlanta tradition of racial compromises.

In the future we will almost certainly see more highlighting of white males for specific niches in identity politics: as gays, as persons with disabilities, as members of specific ethnic groups. Gay men venerate such icons as the Irish writer Oscar Wilde, the American poet Walt Whitman, and the martyred San Francisco Supervisor Harvey Milk, all of whom were white men. Gays increasingly name landmarks for Milk, particularly in San Francisco.[114] Milk is catching on as a place-name for gay-themed schools and institutions in other parts of America, too, as evidenced by such examples as New York City's Harvey Milk High School and the Harvey Milk Center in Charleston, West Virginia. Such honors are bestowed on gay-specific places; great controversy would ensue in many parts of America if people sought to name a "mainstream" road, library, building, or institution after an openly gay man. Less controversy is associated with naming landmarks after white men with disabilities or Spanish-surnamed white men.

Interestingly, Latinos regularly honor, venerate, and celebrate a specific group of DWEMs: Spaniards. As historians develop a usable past for U.S. Latinos, they focus, to some extent, on the Spaniards who came here in the sixteenth, seventeenth, and eighteenth centuries. Thus we have begun to see the reclamation of Spanish explorers as Hispanic heroes for veneration by the U.S. Latino population. This type of celebration occurs during Hispanic Heritage Month and in books for young people. One children's book about Hispanic American heroes includes many Spaniards, such as Juan Ponce de León, Hernando de Soto, Francisco Vásquez de Coronado, Pedro Menéndez de Avilés, Juan de Oñate, Gaspar Pérez de Villagrá, Father Junípero Serra, and Bernardo de Gálvez.[115] Many Latinos seem to view these white men of Spanish origin as Hispanic heroes, due to their Spanish surnames and Spanish history.

Today some Spanish-American icons do double duty as Hispanics and European-American men. These Spanish Americans qualify as Hispanic icons, not white male ones, even though they are of course DWAMs too. The distinguished philosopher George Santayana, a Spanish American, appears in a book of Hispanic heroes, for example.[116] And it has become commonplace in some circles to claim Supreme Court Justice Benjamin N. Cardozo, whose ancestors were Sephardic Jews, as the first Hispanic Supreme Court Justice.[117] This idea does not seem to have caught on with the general public, however, as speculation mounts as to when the "first" Latino will be appointed to the Supreme Court. It is difficult to determine when, exactly, a Spanish American receives credit as a Latino icon. The great admiral David Farragut, a Civil War hero of Spanish ancestry, is often characterized as a Hispanic role model. However, some Spanish Americans such as Jerry Garcia (who was one-half Galician) receive little recognition as Latino heroes.

White males, to be sure, continue to be honored for reasons other than their discrete ethnic, religious, or personal characteristics, as evidenced by the popularity of Ronald Reagan.[118] America's fortieth president, who inhabited the White House from 1981 to 1989, is a conservative icon.[119] Conservatives venerate Reagan, particularly through the Ronald Reagan Legacy Project. It was founded in 1997, under the aegis of Americans for Tax Reform, a conservative advocacy group. The Ronald Reagan

Legacy Project honors Reagan through its efforts to name important landmarks for him throughout America and in the world's formerly Communist nations. To date, Reagan admirers have won numerous victories in this regard, as in the *USS Ronald Reagan,* the Ronald Reagan Turnpike (Florida), the Ronald Reagan Washington National Airport (Arlington, Virginia), the Ronald Reagan Federal Building (Washington, D.C.), and the Ronald Reagan Federal Building & Courthouse (Santa Ana, California).[120]

There have been discussions of honoring Reagan on our nation's money, particularly the dime. The dime-redesign idea came about in November 2003, when the controversy over a made-for-television movie about Ronald and Nancy Reagan led Republican Representative Mark Souder of Indiana to advocate portraying Reagan on the dime. He introduced a resolution (the Ronald Reagan Dime Act) in Congress in November 2003, which eventually had 89 co-sponsors. Democrats, predictably, were not keen on this idea: Reagan may have been the twentieth century's great conservative president, but Franklin Roosevelt was its great liberal president. Massachusetts Democrat Jim McGovern responded with a bill that affirmed the importance of maintaining Roosevelt's likeness on the dime. This piece of legislation drew the support of 80 co-sponsors. The dime-renaming dispute died down at the end of 2003, but such discussions will undoubtedly recur in the coming years.[121] Now that Reagan is no longer alive, conservatives seem very likely to make a concerted effort to honor him on a coin or banknote.[122]

PART THREE

White Male Identity Politics

∼ chapter seven ∼

Big Mouths

"The First and Last Supper" was a 1971 episode of the enormously popular television sitcom, *All in the Family,* that dealt with racial stereotyping and residential integration. The episode begins with Archie Bunker's discussion of God and evolution, as the Bunker family patriarch reads aloud from the Holy Bible at the dinner table. His pert, twentysomething daughter, Gloria, and her husband, Mike Stivic (Meathead to Archie), are liberals and atheists. They live with Archie and his cheerful but naive wife, Edith. The dining-room table discussion turns to how people sometimes use God to justify their own ends, as was the case with the then-raging debate over the Vietnam War. Archie describes the Vietnamese Communists as "godless gooks." Mike, of course, disputes this point, but Archie tolerates no more discussion of the matter. Then Lionel Jefferson, a young black man who is part of the first African-American family on the block, comes over to visit the Bunkers. Archie greets Lionel and goes upstairs to shave. Once Archie is out of earshot, Lionel inquires as to whether the Bunkers would be joining his parents for dinner that evening. Edith, Archie's often-beleaguered wife, had accepted the Jeffersons' dinner invitation without telling Archie, whose antiblack prejudices were well known to his family — and viewers of the situation comedy. Gloria and Mike discuss this matter with Edith while Archie is upstairs shaving. (Mike and Archie had planned on going to the Mets game that evening.) When the head of the Bunker household comes downstairs again, he learns about the dinner invitation from Gloria.[1]

Archie is unhappy about the prospect of dining with an African-American couple and he immediately resolves to cancel the engagement. He is upset that Edith would have committed him to socializing with "colored people." After Gloria accuses him of being prejudiced, Archie responds by referring to blacks as "jungle bunnies" and claiming that African Americans want "to raise their station" by dining with white people. Mike mocks Archie for implying that African Americans seek to dine with him to improve their social status. Archie, for emphasis, then says that blacks are "inferior" to whites. Gloria asks her father how he reconciles his prejudice with his belief in God. Mike, in turn, accuses Archie of hate, to which Archie responds by characterizing his son-in-law, who is Polish American, as a "dumb Polack." Archie then says he does not want to dine with his "unequals." He instructs Edith to call the Jeffersons to cancel the dinner engagement, in part because he and a white neighbor, Jim McMahon, are circulating a petition to persuade the other white homeowners on the block not to sell their homes to black buyers. Edith does not want to telephone the Jeffersons out of respect for their feelings. So Archie himself calls Mrs. Jefferson to tell her that the Bunkers would not be joining them for dinner because his wife sprained her ankle. Thus Archie thinks he has solved the problem. His family, though, is unhappy with him.[2]

Eventually, the dinner proceeds as planned — at the Bunker home, of all places. Shortly after Archie's telephone call, Lionel Jefferson visits the Bunker residence again and says that his parents were coming over that evening with the dinner they had prepared for the Bunkers, so that Edith would not have to cook. Lionel sees that Mrs. Bunker has no problems whatsoever with her ankle. So he asks Archie if there is a problem regarding the dinner. Lionel pointedly notes that they are having trouble with his father — "Says he just doesn't want to sit down with Whitey." Later that evening, the Bunkers begin preparing for the dinner, as Mike and Gloria leave for the Mets game. Meanwhile, Jim McMahon shows up with a copy of the petition that he and Archie are circulating in an effort to persuade their fellow homeowners not to sell any more homes to African Americans. Archie rushes McMahon into the kitchen so that he will not see the Bunkers' black houseguests, who might arrive at any minute. McMahon, though, spies the Jeffersons entering the Bunker residence. He asks Archie if he is "some kind of double agent." Soon after Archie returns to the living room, Mr. Jefferson finds the petition and starts reading it aloud. An embarrassed Archie claims that it is a handbill and takes the petition from him.[3]

Archie, to be sure, meets his match in Henry Jefferson. Shortly after the petition incident, Mr. Jefferson begins speaking with Archie, using the white man's ashtray with the Apollo 14 insignia as a conversation starter. First, Queens' most famous armchair philosopher jousts with Henry Jefferson over the virtues of spending money on space exploration versus social programs. Then the two men spend several minutes debating the racial heritage of God and Jesus, with Archie insisting they were white — and Jefferson just as firmly describing them as black. They also discuss such matters as black athletic superiority and racial favoritism in the space program. As his coup de grâce, Jefferson says to Archie, "Like I already proved to you, we got God, who is black." This comment effectively ends their conversation. Soon thereafter, the Jeffersons discover that Edith really did not have a sprained ankle. Edith explains the deception to the Jeffersons. Then Louise confides that her husband, George, had not wanted to dine with a white family. So her brother-in-law, Henry, came in George's place. George Jefferson, it turns out, had gone to Shea Stadium to see the Mets. Soon the Bunkers and the Jeffersons sit down to enjoy the feast that Mrs. Jefferson had prepared for them. Archie had three servings of Mrs. Jefferson's scrumptious cuisine (it was not soul food, as he might have thought).[4]

The aforementioned episode illustrates why this son of Queens was one of twentieth-century America's best-known and debated cultural figures. The actor Carroll O'Connor brought Archie Bunker to life on CBS's situation comedy, *All in the Family,* from 1971 to 1979 and then on *Archie Bunker's Place* from 1979 to 1983. Archie holds very traditional — one might say antediluvian — views on gender roles and racial and ethnic issues. Bunker and his family reside in a comfortable home in a working class Queens neighborhood. Bunker grew up during the Depression. He left school to enter the workforce so that he could provide for his family. Archie also served his country during World War II. This White Anglo-Saxon Protestant (WASP) resident of Queens stands five feet eleven and weighs approximately 200 pounds. Archie has fair skin, blue eyes, and a less-than-full-head of gray hair. He speaks in a solecistic vernacular that he peppers with malapropisms and ethnic and racial slurs and epithets. A blue-collar American, Bunker works two jobs — on a loading dock and as a taxi driver. He prides himself on being hard working, patriotic, a believer in God, and a *real* American. Archie resists change and what he sees as radical, seditious, and anti-American liberal ideas and proposals.[5]

Archie Bunker is nostalgic for the social and political setting of yesteryear, the period of time in which he felt that he knew what was expected of him and other WASPs. The opening and closing songs on *All in the Family* — "Those Were the Days" and "Remembering You" — are unsubtle reminders of Archie's nostalgia. It is disconcerting for him to see those who, in his opinion, do not play by his rules advance because of their activism, political influence, and civil rights lobbying. In his rush to define himself as worthy, Archie consistently references the Other, usually employing slurs and epithets (*wop, coon, Hebe, spic, Polack,* and so forth) to describe white ethnics and people of color. Moreover, he believes the most retrograde ethnic, racial, religious, and national stereotypes imaginable. Many episodes of *All in the Family* revolve around Archie's attempts to apply his bigoted philosophy to real-life situations, but Mike and Gloria constantly thwart him from doing so. Edith, one suspects, largely agrees with her daughter and son-in-law, but she is bound by tradition and, yes, her love for Archie not to be too forthright about her feelings. Archie, of course, does not see himself as a bigot; he feels that his views stem from logically reasoned explanations for human nature.[6]

Archie Bunker was an important fictional character on American television from 1971 to 1983. He was conceived in a period of great social strife, as he spoke for many people in Middle America and the Silent Majority. Indeed, Archie and his clan tackled numerous controversial issues during *All in the Family*'s eight-year run. (*All in the Family* was the top television show in America from 1972 to 1976.) Norman Lear, who developed and produced the sitcom, espoused liberal political beliefs. Carroll O'Connor himself was a liberal, notwithstanding how convincingly and compellingly he created the character of Archie. During the last five years or so of his "life," Archie Bunker became more middle-class in his orientation, and his bigotry seemed more superficial and less meanspirited than it had been in the early years. Archie himself became a small business owner, beginning in the fall of 1978. He ran Archie's Place, a neighborhood bar. After *All in the Family*, Archie starred in its less-successful sequel, *Archie Bunker's Place*, from 1979 to 1983.[7] Today one can still catch *All in the Family* in reruns. The phrase "Archie Bunker" remains synonymous with unthinking, white, working-class bigotry. Indeed, Archie Bunker was the prototypical Angry White Man before the phrase entered the American lexicon in the 1990s.

PROTEAN POSES

The 1993 film *Falling Down* opens on a crowded freeway in Los Angeles.[8] A middle-aged white man in a small car (played superbly by Michael Douglas) becomes steadily more infuriated as a fly buzzes around him in his hot vehicle. Finally, the man has a crazed epiphany and abandons his vehicle — traffic is not moving, anyway, due to road construction. The buzzing fly is a metaphor for all the frustrations in his life. His abandonment of the vehicle signals that he is unwilling to deal with these frustrations in a conventional way anymore. An unemployed defense worker who goes bonkers, the man we later learn is named William

"Bill" Foster has been laid off for more than a month. Yet he still goes to work every day, albeit with an empty briefcase. His license plate reads D-FENS. Foster is wearing dark dress pants, a short-sleeved white shirt, and a nondescript tie. He sports an unfashionable haircut, a pocket protector, and 1950s spectacles. Foster lives with his mother. His ex-wife, Elizabeth, has a restraining order against him; he has a "horrendous temper," according to her. (Elizabeth and her daughter, Adele, live in the Venice section of Los Angeles.) *Falling Down* takes place on little Adele's birthday. Foster wants to be with his ex-wife and daughter on that day.

During the film, which begins in the morning and ends in early evening, Foster journeys progressively closer to Venice, as he punctuates his long walk with periodic telephone calls to his former spouse. This white-collar Rambo begins his trek with a briefcase — it symbolizes Foster's ties to the normal world. Later, he spends time walking with the briefcase in one hand and a gym bag full of automatic weapons in the other. Then Foster abandons the briefcase and carries only the gym bag. Finally, he wears a green Army surplus jacket as he carries the gym bag. These changes in attire and luggage symbolize Foster's gradual estrangement from the mainstream, even as he expresses discomfort when people think he is a nut and are scared of him. Foster becomes progressively crazier, particularly after he speaks to his wife and she lets him know that he is unwelcome at her home on his daughter's birthday. Foster, after all, had never accepted the divorce and never paid child support. John Q. Public becomes an urban renegade, as he acquires, uses, and then discards an assortment of weapons — a baseball bat, a switchblade, and an arsenal of guns and automatic weapons.

Foster is an equal-opportunity offender. In his first confrontation in the film, he clashes with a Korean storekeeper who overcharges him for a can of Coke. He exhorts the man to speak English and demolishes part of his store with the storekeeper's baseball bat as he announces that he is "rolling prices back to 1965." Foster believes the can of Coke should cost 50 cents — this was 1993, after all — not the 85 cents the storekeeper wanted for it. Later, he sits down to patch the hole in his black oxfords with newspaper from the Classifieds (complete with circled "Help Wanted" ads). Two young Latino thugs accost Foster. They want his briefcase. He responds to their attempt to take it from him — and one man's switchblade — by beating them with his baseball bat. Later, the gang members try to kill him in a drive-by shooting and crash their car in the process. Foster calmly strolls up to the car and picks up the gang members' gym bag full of automatic weapons. Now he is armed with some serious firepower. Foster, to be sure, is not an unreconstructed bigot. He interacts amiably with people of color in different contexts, although he makes nativist remarks on a couple of occasions about the need for his interlocutors to learn English. Indeed, many of Foster's gripes involve raceless issues that bemuse and irritate Americans of all colors, from unnecessary roadwork to brusque and officious service at a fast-food restaurant.

This all-American straight arrow frequently comes into conflict with other white men. Foster disdainfully encounters a white male bum who falsely claims to have been a veteran. Nor is he happy about the rich white male country-club golfer who treats him disrespectfully. And Foster shoots up a telephone booth after a white man harasses him for spending too much time on the phone. Similarly, he punches a cranky white male driver who is haranguing a white female driver. Foster also engages in conflict-filled dialogue with white construction workers on two separate occasions — one of which involves roadwork that he believes is unnecessary. And he is critical of the white male manager of a fast-food restaurant. At one point, an Army-Navy surplus store owner, played with racist, sexist, homophobic, and anti-Semitic gusto by Frederic Forrest, insists to Foster that the two of them — one a Nazi sympathizer and the other a deranged Organization Man — were one and the same. Foster vigorously disagrees with this assessment. Then he kills the Nazi wannabe, after the man attempts to handcuff him so that he could turn him into the police.

Falling Down concludes as Bill Foster attempts, unsuccessfully, to reconcile his idyllic vision of work, family, and country with the sad reality of his life. "I am obsolete," laments Foster at one point. He finally encounters Elizabeth and Adele, as they flee their home to avoid him. Foster meets his demise in a confrontation with the Los Angeles Police Department's Prendergast (Robert Duvall) at the end of the pier in Venice. During their standoff, Foster voices his incredulity that people see him as "the bad guy" when he had done "everything they told me to." "They lied to me," laments this self-identified paragon of fundamental American values. Soon Prendergast has to shoot Foster, after the younger man pulls a water pistol on him, and he dies. Michael Douglas's compelling performance in *Falling Down* earned him the cover of *Newsweek* in its March 29, 1993, issue, making the Hollywood star (in an extreme close-up) the poster guy for "White Male Paranoia: Are They the Newest Victims — or Just Bad Sports?"[9] He bolstered his reputation in this regard by starring in *Disclosure,* a 1994 film that explicitly invoked white male issues regarding affirmative action and sexual harassment.[10] These two films led J. Hoberman to describe Douglas as the standard-bearer for white male backlash in American popular film.[11]

Falling Down notwithstanding, there are relatively few instances of white male backlash bubbling up in American popular culture. This is the case because of the rhetorical emphasis on harmony or lack of dissension (at least that which breaks down along racial, ethnic, gender, religious, or socioeconomic lines) in U.S. society. Still, the cultural critic Richard Goldstein connects white male backlash against the advances of minorities and women to events in popular culture. According to Goldstein,

> All of these pop-cultural changes are very related to political issues. At the same time that the angry white male arose as an icon in politics, it arose in heavy metal, hip-hop, and comedy, too. It was a backlash against feminism and a male paranoia that was an issue in culture at the time. Sam Kinison and Andrew Dice Clay spewed the most violent misogyny on television, *Saturday Night Live* was another bastion of it — it was what you might call 'hip macho.' Shock-jocks did the same thing; Howard Stern did it with a more bohemian edge.[12]

Today many forms of cultural expression reflect white male sensibilities, but there are relatively few songs, sitcoms, and movies that explicitly take into account white males' reactions to life in Multicultural America. Indeed, much of the white male influence in American popular culture has little to do with race, ethnicity, or gender. The lighthearted "redneck" humorist Jeff Foxworthy, for instance, gently celebrates the lives of the working-class whites who are often ignored in America's multicultural pageant.[13] Some media figures, to be sure, regularly write in an explicit sense about white males and white male–related issues. Such columnists as the *Chicago Tribune*'s Mike Royko (who died in 1997), *U.S. News and World Report*'s John Leo, and Creators Syndicate's Paul Craig Roberts have long written about white males from a sympathetic standpoint.

In any event, American television rarely encompasses extended discussions of race, ethnicity, and gender, particularly relating to white males (at least in an overt sense). Since the 1970s there has never been another popular sitcom that even comes close to Archie Bunker and *All in the Family* in terms of dissecting multicultural issues. The white male icons on television during the last 15 years or so — the likes of Seinfeld, Ray Romano, Drew Carey, Ed Bundy, and Homer Simpson — focus on the vicissitudes of daily life (as did *All in the Family*), but without any significant social commentary. The typical white male character on network television rarely delves into "divisive" multicultural issues. Those viewers who want to explore diversity-related matters in popular entertainment are most likely to gravitate toward cable. Much of the controversy that arises on television today comes about as a consequence of the portrayal of gay and lesbian characters. And ethnic stereotypes periodically arise as issues on such programs as *The Sopranos*.

In modern American cinema, explicit considerations of white maleness are quite rare. To be sure, enduring white male cinematic icons (e.g., John Wayne, Clint Eastwood, Sylvester Stallone) occupy an important place in American popular culture. John Wayne, of course, always played himself in film after film; the Duke remains beloved by many Americans for his image as a God-and-country patriot. Clint Eastwood is an iconic figure in part because of his role as the tough-guy Inspector Harry "Dirty Harry" Callahan. Similarly, Sylvester Stallone made Rocky Balboa (the aspiring ethnic) and John Rambo (the disillusioned Vietnam veteran) household names. The aforementioned actors stood for certain values, all of which resonated with large numbers of white American men, but they rarely, if ever, explicitly mentioned race, ethnicity, gender, social class, or religion in any of their on-screen performances.

But there are plenty of films, such as *Shaft* (2000) and *Malibu's Most Wanted* (2003), in which white males and their interactions with women and people of color are an integral part of the plot and story line. Multiculturalism is a regular topic in American films, but usually in a humorous, lighthearted fashion. Popular films are rarely didactic. Typically, one finds that the casts of major Hollywood films usually reflect the ethnic and racial diversity of Multicultural America, even if white stars still account for most of Hollywood's A-list. Periodically, a mainstream American film with a white male protagonist — take *Malibu's Most Wanted* — will gently mock our nation's racial divisions and stereotypes. Yet it is rare for American movies to refer explicitly to white men in a title, as in *White Men Can't Jump* (1992) or *White Man's Burden* (1995).

Humorists and stand-up comedians regularly touch on multicultural issues — and no one has been more explicit in his focus on straight white males than the comedian Jeff Wayne. Indeed, Wayne unapologetically devotes his stand-up routine to the role of straight white males in Multicultural America. A native of Newport, Kentucky, who now resides in Los Angeles, Wayne had a one-man show, "Big Daddy's Barbecue (It's OK to

Be a White Male)," that received favorable attention in the mid-1990s. Ted Lange, who is black, directed it. In his 90-minute routine, which Wayne delivered many times, particularly in 1993, 1994, and 1995, this middle-aged, middle-class white man takes on many topics, including feminism, homosexuality, and political correctness.[14] "I believe we're all created equal," Wayne told audiences. "I tell all women and minorities, 'Don't blame me for the past. You want to dig up my grandpa and kick his (butt)? You go right ahead.' "[15]

Wayne's shtick proved to be very topical in the early 1990s and mid-1990s, when white male issues received considerable attention in American culture and politics. The politically incorrect comedian pleaded for tolerance: "People say the white male hates everyone. My show tries to convey that white males of my generation and the last generation were brought up to believe in live and let live."[16] Wayne himself also presented himself as an Everyman, the prototypical white American man, as he assumed the role of spokesman for America's 100 million white males. "We're not occupying our time trying to figure out how to oppress people," posited Wayne. "We're pretty oppressed ourselves. We have to work for what we get. Everyone says they're owed. When is the debt finally settled? Who owes me?"[17] As with many white males, Wayne focuses on individualism and rejects notions of group rights.

Wayne released an album, *It's O.K. to Be a White Male,* in 1995, at the height of the media furor over the so-called Angry White Men. The album, a live performance by Wayne, covers such topics as racism, sexism, homophobia, gender relations, capital punishment, and political correctness. Wayne has a bawdy, down-to-the-earth style (one that includes regular invocations of the F-word). Interestingly, the Bluegrass State native describes himself tongue-in-cheek as "white trash from Kentucky" and characterizes white Kentuckians as a minority. He contends that less-affluent whites, particularly those of Southern origin, constitute the last acceptable group that one can mock these days.[18] Wayne, to be sure, covers issues and questions that are on the minds of many middle-class white guys in America. Despite his topicality, however, Wayne has not — as of yet — reached a national audience through a film or television program.

Today the satirists, humorists, and comedians with the greatest popular appeal often come from the Left, not the Right, as evidenced by the tremendous success of Michael Moore. Indeed, Moore is perhaps America's best-known comedic populist. Born in 1954, the Irish-Catholic Moore hails from the Flint, Michigan, area. After working in alternative journalism and other pursuits, Moore first came to national attention in 1989 with his documentary, *Roger & Me,* about the economy of Flint, the quintessential Rust Belt city. The burly, baseball cap–wearing author, filmmaker, and satirist has risen to prominence by skewering powerful white men, including Roger Smith, Philip Knight, George W. Bush, Richard Cheney, and Donald Rumsfeld. Moore is a veritable multimedia celebrity. He regularly authors best-selling books, as in *Stupid White Men.* Most prominently, he directs films and documentaries, including *Bowling for Columbine* and *Fahrenheit 9/11.* (During the 1990s Moore had two television shows — *TV Nation* and *The Awful Truth* — and he directed a feature film, *Canadian Bacon.*) He is not oblivious to race in his work; Moore periodically (and explicitly) discusses race relations, racial privilege, and the status of white people in contemporary America.[19]

Moore became a major figure in American popular culture during the George W. Bush Administration; his palpable disdain for America's 43rd President resonates with disaffected leftists, here and abroad. "Comedy and populism combine in Moore to produce a political force of especial potency, ridicule knocking down what anger leaves upright," writes Larissa MacFarquhar.[20] Moore regularly mocks America's corporate and political elites; his ideas have found a receptive audience among many Americans in recent years. Sometimes he makes an explicit connection between his class-conscious, corporate-bashing politics and the white maleness of our economic and political elites. In any event, Moore continually generates controversy. The native Midwesterner continues to win plaudits from the Left as he challenges the Bush administration on Iraq, its ties to corporate interests, and other matters. Moore strongly opposed the Iraq War.[21] In 2004, controversy erupted over the Academy Award–winning director's *Fahrenheit 9/11,* which focuses on the September 11 terrorist attacks and the Iraq War from a left-wing perspective.[22]

Michael Moore notwithstanding, conservatives (particularly white male conservatives) seem to focus the most attention of any ideological group on white males and white male–related issues. This is in keeping with the general trend in American conservatism today; the American Right is usually skeptical of multiculturalism, diversity initiatives, and most, if not all, types of affirmative action. In accordance with this philosophy, conservatives often are quite critical of efforts they see as vilifying white males — either as a group or as individuals — on the basis of their race and/or gender. This is not to say that conservatives are celebrating white males per se; however, they will frequently stand up against what they view as politically correct attempts to diminish the importance of white males in American society and culture.

Ideology explains, to some extent, why white men predominate in the ranks of those journalists, talk radio hosts, and television talkers who defend white males from what they see as multicultural excesses. After all, white men are more likely to be conservative than any other group of Americans that is defined by race and gender, e.g., white women, black men, black women, Latino men, and so forth. While white men are certainly not monolithic in an ideological sense, the ranks of conservatives include high percentages of white males (relative to their share of the U.S. population). So those who are likely to be conservative and promoting white male issues, if one can call them that, are going to be disproportionately white and male.

Another reason the conservative advocates of right-wing positions on race-and-gender issues continue to be disproportionately white and male relates to the conservative movement's inclusiveness (or lack thereof). Conservatives are not famed for being the most inclusive group of people in the world. This is not to say that they are racist, sexist, or exclusionary, by any means. It is just that the conservative ideology (these days, at least) seems to be, "Anyone is welcome to join us, but we are not going to make any special efforts to recruit people outside our circles." Since conservatives and right-leaning individuals usually do not practice affirmative action, this reduces the likelihood of their ranks being diverse — as some people who may share their ideological predilections feel unwelcome in organized conservative circles.

An interesting issue arises regarding the race and gender of participants in explicit discussions of white males in U.S. popular culture and many other contexts. In other words, when a person is perceived to be acting in his self-interest, his actions do not have the same kind of resonance that they would if he were perceived to be a disinterested observer, who is acting in the best interests of a company, organization, community, or even nation. By way of example, white male exponents of a pro–white male perspective do not have the same amount of credibility as do females and people of color who express similar views. So if an African-American talk show host challenges affirmative action, a position that is perceived to benefit the interests of white men and not blacks, he is very likely to have more credibility on this issue in the self-interest department, at least, than his white male counterpart.

Likewise, the white male defender of multiculturalism enjoys a certain amount of currency. This is the case largely because of the perception that he is going against his putative self-interest by favoring diversity initiatives that may limit the life chances of individual white males, or so many conservatives would contend. Eric Newhall describes white male supporters of multiculturalism as people who have a sense of "enlightened self-interest."[23] Many, if not most, of the prominent white men in Hollywood and other sectors of the entertainment industry seem to agree with Newhall on this point. While they may not be especially active in advocating on behalf of specific multicultural initiatives, they generally endorse liberal causes and back the Democratic Party and its candidates. By doing so, they contribute significantly — at least in certain situations — to causes and candidates that seek to dismantle white male privilege in American society. This is the case even though such actions may ultimately disadvantage specific white males in particular contexts.

ALL TALK

Jim Hightower might be described as the peripatetic populist. This cowboy hat–wearing Texan routinely travels throughout America, as he walks picket lines, visits union halls, and draws appreciative crowds of left-wing activists and citizens. Hightower is known for his Rolling Thunder Chautauqua Tour, which involves periodic public festivals in different parts of the country. These festivals seek to promote coalition-building among local progressive activists.[24] Such activities are the brainchild of Hightower, whose Web site describes him as "America's #1 Populist." There are folksy "Hightowerisms," which one can find in Hightower's books, CDs, videos, cassettes, and newsletter.[25] Hightower has achieved a prominent reputation among American progressives largely because of his gift of gab, as he has gone from being a Texas politician to one of the nation's leading voices in the alternative media.

Jim Hightower espouses a racially neutral populism. Race rarely comes up in his speeches and writings.[26] Hightower appeals mainly to white progressives, although his philosophy accords with the political beliefs of many people of color as well. He eschews discussions of ideology in favor of a class-based politics that emphasizes the needs of the bottom 80 percent of American wage earners.[27] Hightower has demonstrated a consistent ability to make politics fun, to mock his political foes in a humorous fashion. He articulates the standpoint of the Little Guy (defined in raceless terms, but often seen informally as white) who fights the Monied Interests. This philosophy is interesting in and of itself, considering that the Left focuses much of its attention on race and gender — as well as social class — these days.

Hightower's philosophy, of course, stems from his biography. He was born in 1943. This English-surnamed man grew up in modest circumstances in Denison, Texas. Hightower graduated from the University of North Texas and was a legislative aide to Texas Senator Ralph Yarborough in Washington. The cofounder of the Agribusiness Accountability Project, he served as national coordinator for Oklahoma Senator Fred Harris's 1976 presidential campaign. Upon returning to Texas, Hightower edited *The Texas Observer,* a biweekly. Later, he was director of the Texas Consumer Association. Then he served as Texas Agriculture Commissioner from 1983 to 1991, losing his bid for a third term to a Republican in 1990. The 1990s was a busy decade for Hightower: He delivered speeches around America, hosted two radio shows, and began publishing his newsletter, among other activities. It was at this time that Hightower became a self-styled spokesman for what he views as the economically and politically disenfranchised American majority.[28]

Hightower disseminates his populist message through his books, writings, public speaking, and national radio commentaries. This progressive populist seeks to revitalize grass-roots politics.[29] His monthly newsletter, *The Hightower Lowdown,* offers a populist political fix to its 100,000-plus subscribers. Hightower makes in excess of 100 speeches each year, and at least 75 publications carry his newspaper column. Moreover, he regularly appears on radio and television programs throughout America. According to Hightower's Web site, "He broadcasts daily radio commentaries that are carried in more than 100 commercial and public stations, on the web, on Armed Forces Radio, Radio for Peace International, One World Radio and Sirius Satellite Radio."[30] In all of his work, Hightower distinguishes between "the Powers That Be" and "the Powers That Ought To Be." People in the latter camp include consumers, environmentalists, working families, and small businesspeople.[31] "There is no one like Jim Hightower on the American scene today," writes Matthew Rothschild of *The Progressive.* "Clever and impassioned, this folksy populist may be the best advocate for progressive politics in the country."[32] Hightower presents a credible alternative to what many progressives see as the centrist and corporate orientation of the mainstream media.

Similarly, many American conservatives propound the idea that right-wingers remain shut out of the mainstream media discourse in this country. Despite their significant political successes during the 1980s, conservatives felt the media did not treat conservatives fairly, or simply ignored their views entirely. This was a perception that conservative talk show hosts — Rush Limbaugh, chief among them — fostered in their diatribes against the mainstream media. Since conservatives largely distrusted the mainstream media, they fueled the rise of Limbaugh and other conservative talkers.[33] Indeed, Jason Zengerle credits "the perception of liberal media bias" as an important factor "in the success of conservative talk radio."[34] Now there is a thriving conservative media establishment — and the Right enjoys significant political power today — but conservatives still portray themselves as outsiders who are ignored or disparaged by the "liberal" magazines, newspapers, broadcast networks, and other media.[35]

Today many Americans perceive talk radio to be a bulwark of conservative media influence. Although talk radio dates back to the 1950s, it did not really take off until conservative talkers began assembling sizable audiences in the 1980s. The number of talk radio stations exceeds 1,200 today, a figure that has remained stable over the last five years.[36] Due to the dictates of political correctness, it seems that some hosts have seemingly tried to outdo one another in their attempts to flout — and challenge — the tenets of multiculturalism. "Talk radio's surge in popularity is one of diversity's most unintended consequences," writes William McGowan. "While it may not always have its facts nailed down, this populist, largely conservative medium does get out the news that mainstream journalists have long ignored or suppressed. It also gives voice to ideas and perspectives that have been shunned or derided by traditional news outlets where diversity-driven orthodoxy has crimped the parameters of acceptable discourse."[37]

Conservative white male hosts play a significant role in talk radio's popularity. The top hosts are as follows: Rush Limbaugh (14.5 million listeners); Sean Hannity (11.8 million listeners); Dr. Laura Schlessinger (8.5 million listeners); Howard Stern (8.5 million listeners); Michael Savage (7.0 million listeners); Jim Bohannon (4.0 million listeners); Don Imus (4.0 million listeners); and George Noory (4.0 million listeners).[38] Some of these individuals, like Dr. Laura, have little or no racial significance. Similarly, there are hundreds of conservative and right-of-center white male hosts in the local markets. Such white male hosts as Michael Savage, G. Gordon Liddy, and Oliver North offer viewers consistently conservative perspectives that one is not likely to find on National Public Radio (NPR), for example. To be sure, there are considerable stylistic and ideological differences among even the conservative hosts, who range from right-of-center to far right.

The popular stereotypes hold that the typical talk radio listener is white, male, and conservative. "Currently, talk radio listeners are mainly white men over the age of 35, many of whom consider themselves conservative — but not all," writes Mark de la Viña.[39] Fifty-three percent of talk radio listeners are Independents, 25% are Republicans, 12% are Democrats, 6% are Libertarians, and 4% Other. Talk radio, to be sure, encompasses urban talk radio, sports talk radio, and conservative talk radio.[40] Thus far, liberal hosts have proven unable to succeed, for the most part, in talk radio. The list of failed liberal talk show hosts includes Mario Cuomo, Jim Hightower, and Alan Dershowitz. Consequently, right-wing talkers dominate the medium. This is cause for consternation among liberals, who want to counteract the success of conservative radio talk show host Rush Limbaugh and his ideological peers.[41]

Indeed, Rush Limbaugh is the king of talk radio: The nation's preeminent "talker" is blunt, humorous, and political. The Cape Girardeau, Missouri, native was born in 1951, and he has hosted *The Rush Limbaugh Show* since 1988.[42] This heavyset white man is generally acknowledged to be the driving force behind the right-wing domination of talk radio. The Limbaugh story dates back to 1988. Ed McLaughlin, a top figure in the radio industry, sought to develop a nationally syndicated program with a central personality. He learned about Limbaugh from a friend. At the time, Limbaugh had a local show on a Sacramento station. Limbaugh was a pioneer even then because of his daytime broadcasts and emphasis on political issues, which were unusual for talk radio at the time. McLaughlin gave Limbaugh a national venue when he "offered AM stations Limbaugh's noon-to-three show for free," according to Jason Zengerle, as long as they would relinquish part of their advertising inventory. Initially, 56 stations accepted McLaughlin's offer.[43] Limbaugh is very talented and very entertaining — and he soon became a national figure.

Limbaugh's show changed the world of talk radio forever, as others sought to emulate his example. Today he is heard on 600 stations nationwide. Dozens of national and local hosts seek to imitate Limbaugh and his conservative brand of political talk radio.[44] Observers suggest that Limbaugh's tremendous success is attributable to a combination of politics and entertainment. Limbaugh has a gift for coining and/or popularizing expressions that resonate with conservatives, e.g., "feminazis" and "Billary" (a reference to Bill and Hillary Clinton). An unabashed conservative Republican, Limbaugh has been an icon of the Right for more than a decade now. Race periodically surfaces in Limbaugh's commentaries, usually in the context of multiculturalism and political correctness, two phenomena that Limbaugh regularly disparages on his radio show.

White men count prominently among Limbaugh's listeners (the Dittoheads, as they are known), who enjoy hearing their hero attack liberals, political correctness, Bill and Hillary Clinton, and other bêtes noires of the Right. Limbaugh's focus on conservative issues and his emphasis on self-reliance resonate with many white male Americans. He says, in essence, what they think. Consequently, a significant number of white male Americans enjoy Rush Limbaugh's radio commentaries and cheer him for standing up to what they see as the liberal propagandists. Limbaugh remains quite popular even though he spent more than a month off the air in 2003 in a rehabilitation program for his admitted drug addiction — and he faces an ongoing federal investigation regarding allegations of money laundering. Despite Limbaugh's personal problems and legal difficulties, his ideologically consistent message and skills as an entertainer help him maintain his tremendous popularity.[45]

Sean Hannity, the top-rated radio host and cable television talkmeister, has become one of the most significant conservative political voices on the American scene today. Hannity was born in 1961 and raised on Long Island, where he lives with his family today. A college dropout who is a former house painter and building contractor, Hannity has benefited from his ability to express conservative views in a feisty yet friendly manner. He was a radio talk show host in Huntsville, Alabama, and Atlanta, Georgia, when he came to the attention of Roger Ailes, who was developing the Fox News Channel. Ailes brought Hannity on board in 1996. Hannity rose to national prominence as the conservative star of Fox News Channel's *Hannity & Colmes,* a popular cable television show. (Hannity's cohost Alan Colmes espouses a left-of-center political perspective.) Then Hannity launched the nationally syndicated *Sean Hannity Show* on ABC Radio Networks in 2001. He has the second-highest ratings of any radio talk show host in the country.[46]

Indeed, Hannity's appeal owes much to his diligent preparation, passionate presentation, knowledgeable discourse, and willingness to share the microphone with guests who are his ideological opposites.[47] A bestselling author who is known for aggressively advocating his conservative views, Hannity explains what differentiates him from his conservative peers in broadcasting: "One of the things I think works for me is, I am passionate about my belief system but I try never to forget the human side of the debate. I don't take it personally, and I don't make it personal. You can play golf with liberals, be neighbors with them, go out to dinner. I just don't want them in power."[48] Hannity's approach to ideological debate resonates with right-of-center viewers and listeners, and he undoubtedly will shape conservative discourse in America for years to come.

Since the early 1980s television has been a forum in which conservative and liberal voices have battled for dominance on the airwaves, particularly now that cable news shows are popular with certain demographic groups. CNN's *Crossfire,* which began airing in 1982, was a pioneer in the food-fight approach to talk television, in which ideological antagonists clash with each other over policy issues. This show, which has spawned many imitators, seamlessly blends news and entertainment. With the increasing popularity of conservative shows (and the niche marketing typical of cable networks), conservative voices are regularly heard on CNN, MSNBC, and the Fox News Channel. Today conservatives have many news choices. They can watch the Tucker Carlson-Bob Novak duo on CNN's *Crossfire,* enjoy *Scarborough Country* with Joe Scarborough on MSNBC, view *From the Heartland with John Kasich* on the Fox News Channel, and cheer for their favorites on many other shows.

Since its founding in 1996, the Fox News Channel has provided a right-of-center perspective in cable news that has won it legions of viewers and made the network's name synonymous with conservative politics. In just eight years, Fox has become *the* cable news channel to watch, routinely outpacing its chief rival, CNN, as well as MSNBC. Fox says it offers a "fair and balanced" perspective on the news. However, many media mavens perceive the network to lean to the right-wing edge of the political spectrum. There are a number of right-of-center hosts on Fox, including Bill O'Reilly, Sean Hannity, and John Kasich. Fox News, to be sure, features a diverse group of experts. Fox itself is not uniformly conservative — but the channel emphasizes patriotism, features many conservative personalities, and generally offers a safe haven to people who feel their views are not represented by the "liberal media" of the three broadcast networks (ABC, CBS, NBC).[49]

Bill O'Reilly is Fox News's biggest name — and one of America's most important commentators.[50] An Irish American from Long Island who was born in 1949, O'Reilly is one of the nation's leading conservative opinion makers. The longtime television journalist joined the Fox News Channel at its inception in 1996. He has hosted *The O'Reilly Factor* on

Fox News for eight years. O'Reilly seems to balance a generally conservative perspective with a distrust of many elites and a fair amount of class-consciousness. He holds some unconventional views for a right-of-center talk show host; O'Reilly backs gay rights and does not support the death penalty, for instance. One leading brand consultant attributes O'Reilly's popularity to his image as a "rebel," a "renegade," someone who is unafraid to tilt at the windmills to challenge the elite consensus if it does not benefit the vast majority of the American people, in O'Reilly's opinion. Other adjectives used to describe him include "edgy" and "pushy" (and not necessarily in a bad way).[51]

O'Reilly has developed a multimedia brand that encompasses books, radio, television, newspapers, and the Internet. The popular commentator is viewed each weekday evening by 2.1 million people, on average, making *The O'Reilly Factor* one of the nation's most popular cable television shows. O'Reilly himself expects to remain on top of his game because his viewers thrill to his attacks on Hillary Clinton, undocumented immigrants, liberal multiculturalists, corrupt corporate chieftains, the left-wing media elite, and other targets. O'Reilly, who hastens to describe himself as politically independent, also writes a newspaper column, operates a thriving Internet site, and broadcasts a radio show (*The Radio Factor with Bill O'Reilly*) that is heard on 400 radio stations each weekday. He appears to see himself as a Man of the People. This is one reason why he eschews ghostwriters: The Fox News luminary says he writes his books, speeches, newspaper columns, and TV-show scripts.[52]

Despite the conservative shibboleth that the media are "liberal," there is substantial discontent among African Americans and white liberals regarding the content of the mainstream media. The thriving black talk radio scene in the U.S. takes into account the views of African Americans, which might otherwise be neglected by mainstream media outlets. Today many white liberals distrust much of the media establishment. This phenomenon stems in large part from what they see as the mainstream media's willingness to accept the results of the Florida recount and describe uncritically the Bush administration's rationale for war in Iraq. Their intense dislike for President Bush has led them to view the mainstream media as being complicit in Bush's program. American liberals increasingly complain about media bias. Left-wing authors, bloggers, and talk show hosts highlight this view. They often challenge what they see as the dominance of the conservative media in American society.[53]

At the end of March 2004, liberals counterattacked their conservative talk radio antagonists with Air America Radio, a left-wing radio network. Air America is presently airing on 15 stations throughout the United States. Its weekday lineup includes the following shows: *Morning Sedition*; *Unfiltered*; *The O'Franken Factor*; *The Randi Rhodes Show*; and *The Majority Report*. Air America's personalities encompass a fair amount of ideological diversity: Marc Maron, cohost of *Morning Sedition*, is on the far left while *The O'Franken Factor*'s Al Franken is merely left-of-center. Franken is Air America's biggest star, one whose popularity among Democrats led him to receive considerable attention in the days surrounding Air America's launch. In the main, Air America's hosts strongly support the Democratic Party and vehemently oppose President Bush. Air America Radio clearly tries to attack Republicans, conservatives, and the current administration. One motivation for Air America's founders was their desire to put a Democrat in the White House. They also hope to give liberal, left-of-center, and moderate Americans talking points to counter their more conservative peers.[54]

Al Franken, Air America's top on-air personality, has achieved significant success as a left-wing satirist during the George W. Bush years, as he attacks the current administration, the conservative powers-that-be, and the right-wing presence on talk radio. Franken, who is white, came to public attention during his years on *Saturday Night Live*. Such fellow humorists as Jon Stewart, Janeane Garofolo, and, of course, Michael Moore, share his disdain for President Bush. Franken is more of a comedian than Moore — his politics are left-of-center, to be sure, but he lacks the hard edge that sometimes characterizes Moore's work. In addition, Franken voices positive feelings about the military, a view that distinguishes him from many on the Left. He is passionately anti-Bush, to be sure, a stance that confirms his Democratic affiliation. Franken embodies the connections between and among media, politics, and entertainment. He himself may run for the U.S. Senate from Minnesota in 2008; few political observers doubt his ability to run a credible race.[55]

MAD AS HELL

W. Axl Rose probably did not encounter many people of color during his first 18 years of life. The lead singer of Guns n' Roses was born on February 6, 1962, in Lafayette, Indiana, a small city in the west-central part of the Hoosier State. During the 1960s and 1970s the vast majority of the people in Lafayette (like Rose and his family) were native-born whites of Northern European descent who spoke English as their native language. A slim man of average height with green eyes and long red hair, Rose fit in well, at least in an ethnic sense, in every part of Lafayette. But he did not enjoy life in west central Indiana, where the high school dropout earned a well-deserved reputation for nonconformity and juvenile delinquency. Still, race was simply a nonissue for Rose during his youth — almost everyone in Lafayette was Caucasian.[56]

In 1980 Rose decided to pursue his dreams of rock stardom, and he left behind the racial homogeneity of Lafayette for multiethnic Los Angeles. The 18-year-old heartlander arrived in a city that, at the time, had nearly three million residents. Los Angeles was then 48.0% Anglo, 28.0% Hispanic, 16.7% African American, 7.0% Asian American, and 0.5% Native American. As a result, Rose regularly encountered minorities, immigrants, and openly gay people — three groups that were virtually nonexistent in Lafayette. Rose was unsettled by the ethnic and cultural diversity of Los Angeles, and he mainly fraternized with young whites who shared his aspirations and socioeconomic background. He and four bandmates formed Guns n' Roses in 1985. The rock group's first album, *Appetite for Destruction* (1987), proved to be one of the most successful releases in the history of popular music.[57]

Rose's feelings of cultural dislocation in Los Angeles informed his most inflammatory song, "One in a Million," which was released in 1988 as part of Guns n' Roses' second album, *GN'R Lies*. He coauthored the intemperate lyrics to "One in a Million." This autobiographical song (which is six minutes and eight seconds in length) includes harsh social commentary as well as plaintive expressions of a young man's dreams of stardom. Rose bashes the police as well as *niggers* in the second stanza.[58] But he reserves his real venom for the first eight verses of the fourth stanza, as he attacks gays ("faggots" according to Rose) and immigrants. He seems to think that members of these groups should be less visible in American society. Ethnic enclaves and linguistic diversity meet with disapproval from Rose. Some critics, not surprisingly, assailed Rose as racist, anti-immigrant, and homophobic because of this song.[59]

The controversy generated by "One in a Million" perplexed Rose, who did not seem to consider himself to be any more racist, nativist, or homophobic than the typical white, working-class male of his generation. In the seventh stanza of "One in a Million," he distances himself from bigots and radicals. Indeed, Rose assured audiences that he was not a racist, while he asserted his right to artistic freedom. Even though Rose's musical commentary on cultural diversity probably had little to do with Guns n' Roses' popularity, "One in a Million" exemplified — and contributed to — the white male backlash against multiculturalism in U.S. popular culture during the late 1980s and early 1990s.[60]

Indeed, popular music often serves the role of communicating social messages in American society and culture. Over the years, musical artists have made significant contributions to our understanding of racial, social, and cultural dynamics. Such white male artists as Bob Dylan, Woody Guthrie, and Bruce Springsteen have communicated a social message through their music. To be sure, a song can be symbolically or metaphorically important but have no overt racial significance, as in Sergeant Barry Sadler's "The Ballad of the Green Berets" (1966). Similarly, a ballad may be socially and racially noteworthy: In 1969, for instance, James Brown released his immensely popular song ("Say It Loud: I'm Black and I'm Proud") about his pride in being black. An artist may record a single song that has racial significance — a.k.a., Elvis Presley's "In the Ghetto" (1969) — while others (e.g., Bruce Springsteen) do so as part of a deep and abiding concern for social justice.

The social impact of popular music depends on who the intended audience for the music is, and how the listeners interpret it. Sometimes a message will be heard loudly and clearly within a particular musical subculture, one that is not necessarily part of mainstream American culture. So some voices may not be heard in the mainstream very often, even if those voices are influential with people in specific contexts. Take the music of Charlie Daniels, for example. In the aftermath of 9/11, the veteran country musician recorded two bellicose songs — "This Ain't No Rag; It's a Flag" and "The Last Fallen Hero" — that received considerable attention in the country-music subculture. The songs largely penetrated the mainstream culture as a result of the controversy that attended them.[61] Our focus here is on white male artists with mass appeal who have recorded music in Multicultural America that deals with social, cultural, and racial issues that are either directly or indirectly related to the changing demographics of, and power dynamics in, Multicultural America.

After the death of the civil rights leader Medgar Evers in 1963, the folk singer Bob Dylan wrote and recorded a song ("Only a Pawn in Their Game") that celebrated Evers and also challenged the nexus of race and class that affected the lives of white Southerners. The song is about Evers — and the white man who murdered him. Dylan's ballad highlights the pernicious politics of race:

> A South politician preaches to the poor white man,
> "You got more than the blacks, don't complain.
> You're better than them, you been born with white skin," they
>   explain.
> And the Negro's name
> Is used it is plain
> For the politician's gain
> As he rises to fame
> And the poor white remains
> On the caboose of the train
> But it ain't him to blame
> He's only a pawn in their game.[62]

Dylan, interestingly, refuses to scapegoat the poor white man in the South, even as he emphatically criticizes the racist power structure of Mississippi in the early 1960s.

In "Only a Pawn in Their Game," Dylan argues that the poor white man is enmeshed, even trapped, in a racist game in which he is merely a bit player who is exploited by the white oligarchs. They use white supremacy as a chimerical distraction to keep poor white men from questioning the distribution of economic and political power in segregation-era Mississippi, or so Dylan contends. In the song's critical lines, the Minnesota-born balladeer sings:

> The deputy sheriffs, the soldiers, the governors get paid,
> And the marshals and cops get the same,
> But the poor white man's used in the hands of them all like a tool.
> He's taught in his school
> From the start by the rule
> That the laws are with him
> To protect his white skin
> To keep up his hate
> So he never thinks straight
> 'Bout the shape that he's in
> But it ain't him to blame
> He's only a pawn in their game.[63]

Then, in 1970, the Canadian-born singer Neil Young released a song, "Southern Man," that was considerably less sympathetic to the

Southern white man, as Young generalized about an entire group of people. "Southern Man" directly criticizes the Southern white man in the following lyrics:

> Southern man
> better keep your head
> Don't forget
> what your good book said
> Southern change
> gonna come at last
> Now your crosses
> are burning fast
> Southern man[64]

The rest of the song mentions, not so obliquely, white privilege and hints at the need for some kind of reparations for slavery. "Southern Man" also alludes to the bugaboo of interracial sexuality, a topic of concern to many Southern white men during the Jim Crow era.

The Southern rock group Lynyrd Skynyrd responded to "Southern Man" with their ballad, "Sweet Home Alabama" (1974). The song includes lines that dismiss Neil Young and his critique of white Southern men. "Sweet Home Alabama" became a hit single, a classic of American rock and one that inspires multiple interpretations about the band's ideological sympathies. Skynyrd's members may have been taken aback by the popularity of "Sweet Home Alabama" — and reluctant to engage in the racial and cultural politics that attended their lyrical musings. The Southern rockers found that their song was embraced by white Southerners of right-wing predilections who disliked Young's criticism of the South.[65] Interestingly, Neil Young seems to have enjoyed Skynyrd's ode to the Yellowhammer State: He praised "Sweet Home Alabama" in at least one interview.[66]

In any event, the white rapper has some interesting opportunities to present innovative messages — to white America — in his music. Most prominent rappers may be men and women of color, but the consumers of the music continue to be heavily white. Due to the nature of the art form — and the fact that most rap artists are black — there would be little, if any, tolerance for whites attempting to lecture to African Americans about racial matters. But white rappers, rap-rockers, and hip-hop artists have a rare opportunity to be positive role models for other whites, at least in terms of how they embrace another culture and show respect for it in their lyrics and public personas. However, few white artists in the hip-hop milieu ever earn the requisite credibility and prominence that would allow them to promote racial tolerance in a significant way.

The list of white rap-rockers and hip-hop artists includes several men who sing about racial issues. Everlast, for one, regularly records songs with explicitly racial titles. For instance, his 2000 album, *Eat at Whitey's,* includes tracks like "Whitey" and "Black Jesus."[67] Kid Rock's lyrics regularly emphasize his racial background, as evidenced by his references to trailers, *white boys,* and his Irish ancestry. Although he is not a rap-rocker so much as an old-school rapper, Eminem is the biggest solo artist of this pack of shouters. His critics regularly characterize him as homophobic and misogynistic, due to some of his lyrics and public pronouncements.[68] Eminem touches on race in his work, as in the song "White America" on *The Eminem Show* (2002).[69] To be sure, many white rap-rockers and hip-hop artists emulate their African-American peers in that they keep their music largely apolitical.

Country music, a medium dominated by white artists, is the most common forum in white America for musical ruminations on culture and politics. Country music continues to be popular in white America. And country songs are basically about white people, although race is never mentioned in the lyrics. Country music artists frequently invoke the theme of social class, to be sure. Granted, the ranks of country music fans have become much more heterogeneous in the last two decades, particularly as country went mainstream. Indeed, one often hears country music in the Mexican-American and Native American precincts of the United States. But African Americans continue to remain aloof from country music, which leads to a vicious circle: Many blacks do not listen to country because they perceive it to be "white" music, and therefore the record companies do not market the music to them.[70] Country music, likewise, has long had a reputation for social conservatism and expressions of patriotism, which is reinforced by the God-and-country themes of many artists — the Dixie Chicks notwithstanding.

In 1969, at the height of the nation's debate over the Vietnam War, country musician Merle Haggard released the song, "Okie from Muskogee." In his signature song, Haggard denigrates hippies, peaceniks, draft evaders, disobedient college students, and other left-leaning individuals. He informed audiences in his refrain that "I'm proud to be an Okie from Muskogee," referring to the multiracial town in northeastern Oklahoma. Merle Haggard and Roy Burris wrote the song.[71] The dateline for Muskogee was no accident. Oklahoma, then as now, was a bastion of social conservatism, in contradistinction to the liberal attitudes of the secular coastal elites. Haggard's song resonated on multiple counts. For one, it symbolized the acceptance of the white Southwesterners in the American pageant. Likewise, it celebrated the value system of "the Okies," a group of people who seldom were mentioned in the halls of power. The song received plaudits from leading conservative politicians, including Richard Nixon and George Wallace, who embraced its social significance as a ballad that appealed to the Silent Majority.[72] Another similarly important song that resonated with Middle Americans was Merle Haggard's "The Fightin' Side of Me" (1970), which excoriated those who did not take their patriotism seriously.

As Haggard faded from the country music scene, Hank Williams Jr. picked up his mantle as a socially conservative balladeer.[73] The son of country legend Hank Williams Sr., Hank Jr., as he is known to country fans, makes no mistake about his socially conservative, emphatically pro-American politics. The fiftysomething country music icon has sung such hard-edged cultural commentaries as "Don't Give Us a Reason," "I've Got Rights," "The Coalition to Ban Coalitions," and "A Country Boy Can Survive."[74] These songs highlight Williams's hyper-patriotic attitude, his staunchly anticrime perspective, and his emphasis on personal responsibility. The singer, who espouses unabashedly conservative politics, reflects a certain type of white, Southern, male sensibility. Williams, to be sure, recently released a lighthearted paean to tolerance: "Why Can't We All Just Get a Long Neck?"

Williams explicitly signals his sympathies on the racial/ethnic front in his controversial 1988 song, "If the South Woulda Won." Much of the tune is a lighthearted evocation of the white South, with its celebration of such white Southern icons as Elvis, Patsy Cline, and Hank Williams Sr. and its references to Cajun cooking, Arkansas wine, Virginia fiddles, Kentucky horses, Tennessee whisky, and Dixieland jazz. Williams's song also celebrates women who have the smile and accent typical of Georgians. However, "If the South Woulda Won" includes some political lines as well. Williams advocates for American automobiles to be built in factories in North and South Carolina, as well as a ban on Chinese-made cars. He also declaims, "We'd put Florida on the right track, 'cause we'd take Miami back and throw all them pushers in the slammer."[75]

The song is not as innocuous as it may seem to the casual listener. Its refrain makes it clear where the artist's sympathies lie. Throughout the song, we hear variations of "If the South woulda won, we woulda had it made." The *we* in this song undoubtedly refers to white Southerners, as evidenced by the cultural reference points that Williams mentions in his lyrics. The song advocates situating the national treasury in Tupelo, Mississippi, as well as returning the capital to Alabama, an unsubtle reference to the Confederate States of America. Due to such lines, most African Americans would not look kindly on this song, especially because it ends by saying "Might even be better off!" with regard to speculation about what life would be like in a Southern-dominated United States of America.[76] Today, "If the South Woulda Won" is a classic country tune, one that undoubtedly wins favor from many of country's white male listeners.

One of country's greatest paeans to working class whites, particularly males, came with Garth Brooks's 1993 song, "American Honky-Tonk Bar Association." This song celebrates hard-working Americans, denigrates welfare, invokes patriotism, condemns bureaucratic ineptitude, criticizes government spending, and mentions "your frustration." It mocks the American Bar Association, a favorite conservative target. Part of the song's chorus describes the membership of this fictional organization, whose ranks include working people, devotees of gunracks and flag waving, and fans of loud music. "American Honky-Tonk Bar Association" was well received by many Americans at the time. Brooks, by the way, also released a song about tolerance, "We Shall Be Free," in 1992. Most of his music, though, focuses on apolitical topics.

In the aftermath of 9/11, the country musician Toby Keith emerged as one of the entertainment world's most emphatic supporters of U.S. military action to combat terrorism. In 2002 Toby Keith scored a major hit with his single, "Courtesy of the Red, White and Blue (The Angry American)." In his song, Keith explicitly references 9/11 and he appears to delight in the U.S.-led bombing campaign in Afghanistan. The tune's aggressive lyrics thrill God-and-country patriots and repulse leftists. Keith's bellicose ballad warns the terrorists that they are going to incur America's wrath. This hit song was part of Keith's album, *Unleashed* (2002).[77] Moreover, the Oklahoman's most recent album, *Shock'N Y'all* (2003), includes the songs "American Soldier" and "The Taliban Song."[78] "Most people think I'm a redneck patriot," says Keith. "I'm O.K. with that."[79]

In 2003, no song was more prominent in expressing the pro-war view than the country artist Darryl Worley's "Have You Forgotten?" Worley and Wynn Varble wrote the hit song. "Have You Forgotten?" is also the title of Worley's 2003 album.[80] In the song, Worley mentions 9/11 and Osama bin Laden; he links Saddam Hussein and the 9/11 terrorists in his justification of the war:

I hear people saying we don't need this war
I say there's some things worth fighting for
What about our freedom and this piece of ground?
We didn't get to keep 'em by backing down
They say we don't realize the mess we're getting in
Before you start your preaching
Let me ask you this my friend

Have you forgotten how it felt that day
To see your homeland under fire
And her people blown away?
Have you forgotten when those towers fell?
We had neighbors still inside
Going through a living hell
And you say you shouldn't worry 'bout Bin Laden
Have you forgotten?[81]

Darryl Worley, Toby Keith, and Charlie Daniels sought to unite Americans around a specific message of patriotism, one that probably appealed most to white males. To be sure, there is nothing explicitly "white male" about these men's songs regarding 9/11 and the Iraq War. We know from country music's demographics and the nationalistic nature of these tunes, however, that they probably resonated most in white (male) America. Indeed, the lyrics of Keith, Worley, and Daniels echo, in a sense, the thoughts of the scholar Peggy McIntosh regarding white male reactions to 9/11 and the Iraq War. McIntosh posits that white males were significantly more likely than white women and people of color to favor military action in Afghanistan and the war in Iraq.[82] Similarly, Norman Mailer believes that many white males support the U.S.-led war in Iraq for reasons that directly relate to the reconfigured power dynamics in Multicultural America.[83] In any event, the pro-military tunes of the aforementioned country music artists unquestionably reflected the views of a substantial segment of white male America.

∽

During the 1990s and the early part of the twenty-first century, the actor Charlton Heston assumed a prominent role in speaking out on social and cultural issues. As Ed Leibowitz points out, "His career as a heroic leading man — as Moses, as Ben-Hur, as El Cid — has given him matchless reserves of political capital."[84] Heston, who was born in October 1924, was a major figure in twentieth-century Hollywood due to his roles in such films as *The Ten Commandments* (1956), *Ben-Hur* (1959), *El Cid* (1961), and *Planet of the Apes* (1968). The Academy Award–winning actor is descended from old-stock Americans: The branches of his family tree stretch back to England and Scotland. Heston has long been active in politics. He served as a six-term president of the Screen Actors Guild during the 1960s. The onetime liberal Democrat participated in the 1963 March on Washington and periodically dabbled in politics in the 1960s and 1970s. But Heston, who was a Democrat as a young man, began to move to the Right in the 1970s. He voted for Richard Nixon in 1972, the first time he backed a GOP presidential candidate. Heston became a National Rifle Association (NRA) member during the 1970s and actively supported Ronald Reagan's 1980 presidential campaign.[85]

Heston's political activism increased in frequency during the 1980s, and he was a prominent figure in the Culture Wars of the 1990s. The aging star vociferously supported Second Amendment rights and right-to-work laws, even as he staunchly opposed the nuclear freeze movement and rap music with explicit lyrics. A frequent campaigner for conservative causes and politicos, Heston had his own political action committee (Arena PAC). Upon becoming president of the National Rifle Association in 1998, Heston announced his intention to engage in cultural warfare over the core issues that define Americans. Once he was elected NRA president in 1998, it became common to see vehicles in the heavily Republican states bearing the bumper sticker "CHARLTON HESTON IS MY PRESIDENT." This popular bumper sticker simultaneously expressed conservative disdain for President Bill Clinton as well as the Right's admiration for Heston.[86]

As president of the National Rifle Association from 1998 to 2003, Heston occupied a position of considerable importance in the Culture Wars. He used his post as a bully pulpit to express his disdain for multiculturalism in general and to promote Second Amendment rights in particular. During his presidency of the NRA, Heston regularly campaigned on behalf of NRA-endorsed political candidates, most (but not all) of whom were Republicans. He also continued to speak out on a variety of issues related to affirmative action, diversity initiatives, and multicultural matters. During this period Heston energized conservative audiences with his red-meat rhetoric on such topics as feminism, homosexuality, and political correctness.[87] Heston made headlines again when the Hollywood giant announced in 2002 that he had Alzheimer's disease. He retired as NRA President in 2003 and has left public life since then.

In the 1990s, Heston regularly defended white males as a group, as he defiantly celebrated the white male influence in American history. Heston writes:

> The U.S. Constitution was handed down to guide us by a bunch of wise, old, dead, white guys who invented the country.
>
> Many people flinch when I make that remark in speeches. Why?
>
> The fact is, what I say is true. The framers of the Constitution *were* white guys, old and undeniably wise, and they sure Lord invented the country. Most of those boy-soldiers who died opposing slavery at Lincoln's invitation in the 1860s were white, too. Why should I be ashamed of them?[88]

Patrick Buchanan, an ideological compatriot of Heston's in many respects, continues to fight for the Right in the nation's Culture Wars. This outspoken cultural conservative was born in Washington, D.C., on November 2, 1938. Buchanan's world view is characterized by traditionally conservative views on social issues (e.g., strong opposition to abortion and gay rights), very right-wing positions on racially tinged issues (multiculturalism in general and affirmative action in particular), and an isolationist vision of American nationalism (protectionist views of trade policy and a limited U.S. role in global affairs). Buchanan worked for three Republican Presidents: Richard Nixon, Gerald Ford, and Ronald Reagan. A longtime commentator and syndicated newspaper columnist, Buchanan helped to found CNN's *Crossfire* and *The Capital Gang* and NBC's *The McLaughlin Group*.[89]

Buchanan enjoyed a role as one of America's most prominent cultural warriors in the 1990s. He ran for the Presidency in 1992 and 1996 as a Republican, when he was described by some observers as the candidate of the so-called Angry White Males.[90] The fiery conservative advocated hard-right stances on immigration, affirmative action, and international trade, in addition to an "America First" foreign policy and a ringing endorsement of the Euro-American influence on the American nation. He drew plaudits and criticism for his speech to the 1992 Republican National Convention:

> My friends, this election is about more than who gets what. It is about who we are. It is about what we believe, it is about what we stand for as Americans. There is a religious war going on in our country for the soul of America. It is a cultural war, as critical to the kind of nation we shall one day be as was the Cold War itself.

And in that struggle for the soul of America, Clinton and Clinton are on the other side, and George Bush is on our side. And, so, we have to come home — and stand beside him.[91]

Buchanan still tries to play an important role in America's social, cultural, and political debates, but he no longer does so as a candidate for electoral office. Buchanan left the Republican Party in 1999 and was the Reform Party presidential nominee in 2000; he received only 446,743 votes and retired from electoral politics thereafter. The three-time presidential aspirant now seeks to influence the national discourse as a commentator and professional polemicist, through his syndicated newspaper column, his television show (MSNBC's *Buchanan and Press*), his magazine (*The American Conservative*) and his books (*The Death of the West*).[92] Buchanan is also the chairman of The American Cause, a conservative advocacy organization.[93] He no longer enjoys any real significance in political terms, as he did in 1992, 1996, and 1999 (before his third-party candidacy went nowhere), but he remains a significant figure on the Right.

Buchanan often considers the experiences of white males in Multicultural America in the context of his discussions of race, nationalism, and economic policy. "White males," contends Buchanan, "are the victims of quotas, affirmative action, set-asides, and reverse discrimination. They are the preferred targets of abuse by academics, journalists, and feminists, as well as the Jacksons, Sharptons, and Bonds."[94] Buchanan often refers to whites and Christians as groups, without specifically breaking out white males as a subgroup. The conservative commentator's sympathies seem to lie with native-born, Euro-American Christian heterosexual Americans who share his culturally conservative political philosophy. Indeed, he focuses much of his attention on issues related to race, religion, and culture, considered domestically and internationally. Buchanan toggles between restrictive conceptions of race and nationality in the American context and broad conceptions of American identity vis-à-vis people in other countries.

~ **chapter eight** ~

Changing America

On October 19, 1960, Dr. Martin Luther King was one of the 52 civil rights activists who were arrested after they attempted to desegregate the Magnolia Room in Rich's in downtown Atlanta. King was then sentenced for six months (later reduced to four months) in prison for violating his probation for a minor traffic violation earlier in the year. The unduly harsh sentence came at a particularly inopportune time for King, whose wife was five months pregnant. Upon hearing about King's arrest, Harris Wofford and Louis Martin, both of whom were part of the Civil Rights Section of Democratic presidential candidate John F. Kennedy's campaign, decided it would be a good idea for the Massachusetts senator to call Dr. King's wife, Coretta Scott King, to express his sympathies as a means of reaching out to King and his supporters. On October 26, 1960, Wofford brought the idea to Sargent Shriver's attention; the Kennedy brother-in-law was responsible for the campaign's Civil Rights Section. Then Shriver made the case for the telephone call to Senator Kennedy, who called Mrs. King that morning and told her of his concern for her and her family. On the following day, Robert Kennedy telephoned the judge in De Kalb County, Georgia, and requested that he release King. Soon thereafter, the future Nobel laureate was allowed to make bail.[1]

Harris Wofford and Louis Martin decided to leverage the political capital that the Kennedys had earned with their telephone calls, particularly because the conventional wisdom was that those calls might have hurt the Democrats among white voters in certain precincts. So they produced a pamphlet — *The Case of Martin Luther King* — that cited numerous positive statements by members of the King family and others regarding the Kennedys' telephone calls. The pamphlet also juxtaposed JFK's pro-King actions with the silence of his Republican opponent, Vice President Richard Nixon, on the matter. In the ten days before the election, Wofford and his associates oversaw the reproduction and distribution of almost two million copies of the pro-Kennedy pamphlet. On Election

Day, November 8, 1960, the Kennedys' calls resonated in Black America, as 68 to 78 percent of African Americans voted for JFK over Nixon. Compared to 1956, the percentage of African-American voters increased, as did the percentage for the Democratic presidential candidate in Black America. There was no perceptible white Southern backlash against Kennedy on the issue because of his adroit handling of racial politics. Due to the significant pro-Kennedy vote by blacks in the critical states of Illinois and Michigan, the work of Wofford and his compatriots clearly made an important difference in John F. Kennedy's exceedingly narrow victory.[2]

Harris Wofford's background seamlessly blends significant involvement in domestic affairs with a deep and abiding interest in international affairs. Harris Llewellyn Wofford Jr. was born in New York City on April 9, 1926, and he grew up in Johnson City, Tennessee, and Scarsdale, New York. He traces his roots to England, Scotland, France, and Wales (Llewellyn is Welsh). From the beginning, this tall, dignified man with gray hair and blue eyes was an emphatic supporter of racial equality and the Democratic Party, views that did not always meet with approval from some of his family members.[3] In any event, Harris Wofford is a man of the world. His interest in global issues dates back to his childhood; this proud internationalist has always been aware that whites are a minority in the world.[4] As a teenager, Wofford founded the Student Federalist organization. His first book, *It's Up to Us*, published in 1946 when he was 19, takes up the story of the Student Federalists, who wanted "a World Federal Democracy, the United States of the World."[5] After serving in World War II, Wofford graduated from the University of Chicago in 1948. He and his wife, Claire Wofford, spent much of 1949 visiting India and Pakistan. They then published a book about their experiences, *India Afire*, that sold about 25,000 copies after it was published in 1951.[6]

By this time, Wofford had decided to devote much of his career to civil rights, in part because of his experiences in post-independence India. In 1950 Wofford matriculated at Howard University Law School: He sought to practice civil rights law and the school had a good program in that field.[7] Moreover, writes Wofford, " . . . I realized I had never lived and worked among Negroes in circumstances where we were on an equal footing."[8] He was the first white man ever to study at Howard University Law School. This racial pioneer received joint law degrees from Howard and Yale in 1954. Meanwhile, Wofford was deeply influenced by the Gandhian approach to nonviolent civil disobedience. He delivered a pivotal speech ("Gandhi – The Civil Rights Lawyer") at Hampton

Institute in November 1955; the theme of his lecture was the need to employ Gandhian ideas in the nascent civil rights movement. Wofford sent copies of his speech to people around the country, including Dr. Martin Luther King. In late 1956 he met King for the first time. Wofford served as a top advisor to the civil rights leader and collaborated with him on one of his books. During the late 1950s Wofford was also counsel to Father Theodore Hesburgh, an important member of the U.S. Commission on Civil Rights. And he worked on civil rights issues (as part of the integrated Civil Rights Section) during Kennedy's 1960 campaign.[9]

Then Wofford served as chairman of the White House Subcabinet Group on Civil Rights from 1961 to 1962. President John F. Kennedy's top advisers were cautious about moving too quickly on civil rights. At the same time, African-American activists were increasingly vocal about their interest in seeing far-reaching civil rights legislation enacted into law. Wofford spent much of his time mediating between the two camps. Today he argues that the Kennedys should receive more credit for their governmental action to promote civil rights. By the early 1960s, however, the time had come for an African American to occupy Wofford's role in the Kennedy administration.[10] "That didn't worry me personally," writes Wofford, "since there were other things I wanted to do in my life, but it was late for a white man to be a President's Special Assistant for Civil Rights."[11] Wofford soon left his post in the White House to work with Sargent Shriver in setting up the Peace Corps.

Wofford occupied important positions in law, academe, and the government during the period from 1962 to 1991. He became the director of the Peace Corps' Ethiopia program and the Peace Corps' Special Representative to Africa after he resigned from the White House staff. During the Johnson administration, Wofford served for a time as associate director of the Peace Corps. And Wofford participated in the historic Selma-to-Montgomery march for voting rights in 1965. He served as president of the State University of New York, College of Old Westbury from 1966 to 1970 and then served as president of Bryn Mawr College from 1970 to 1978.[12] Wofford was a lawyer in private practice from 1978 to 1986 and Pennsylvania Democratic Party Chairman in 1986. And he served as Pennsylvania Secretary of Labor and Industry from 1987 to 1991. During this period, Wofford continued to write and speak about civil rights and citizen service in different contexts; his magisterial book, *Of Kennedys and Kings,* published in 1980, delineated his perspective on the politics and social turmoil of the 1960s.[13]

In recent years Wofford has enjoyed a fair amount of national attention. Pennsylvania Governor Robert Casey appointed him to the U.S. Senate in May 1991 to fill the term of the late Republican Senator John Heinz. Wofford made national headlines when he defeated the heavily favored Republican, former Attorney General Richard Thornburgh, by a 10-point margin in the November 1991 special election to fill the rest of the term. He built a multiracial coalition around such bread-and-butter issues as universal health care and a middle-class tax cut; his campaign was a harbinger of Bill Clinton's victory in 1992.[14] Wofford himself was one of the five finalists on Clinton's shortlist for a running mate in 1992.[15] A proud liberal, Wofford narrowly lost his race for a full term in the Senate in the Republican landslide of 1994. He later served as CEO of the Corporation for National Service during the Clinton administration. Today this paragon of civic involvement is Co-Chair of America's Promise: The Alliance for Youth.[16] Now in his late seventies, Harris Wofford can take pride in a lengthy and distinguished career in public life in which he has made significant contributions to our understanding of civil rights, the importance of national service, and the significance of global affairs.

GOING TO COURT

Edward Hood and George Rudebusch were among the white male professors who did not receive pay increases at Northern Arizona University (NAU) in May 1993. That year, NAU President Eugene Hughes decided to increase the salaries of certain faculty members. However, he did so selectively, ostensibly to compensate for racial and gender inequities in faculty salaries. NAU only raised the salaries of faculty members below the mean in 1993. One-half of the faculty were affected — those below the mean.[17] According to Edward Hood, "Faculty below the mean at the three ranks were adjusted toward the mean for those ranks. Minority males were raised by $3,600. All females were raised by $2,400. White males below the mean were excluded from the raise. According to the NAU salary study, there was a $750 disparity for females, but there was a $2,400 adjustment. There was an $87 difference per year between majority and minority salaries, with a $3,600 average adjustment."[18] In 1994 white males below the mean with no female cohort received pay raises of $1,200, while those with female cohorts received pay raises of $2,400. But, says Hood, "[n]o white male below the mean who was excluded in 1993 was raised to his predicted salary to the faculty model for predicted salaries."[19]

Many NAU faculty members, therefore, felt that the raises were unfair and decided to challenge the pay action through the legal system. First, there was a class-action lawsuit comprising 240 NAU faculty members when it was filed in 1995.[20] In addition, there was a Title VII claim. There were 192 white males below the mean who were affected by the pay action, and 152 of them participated in the EEOC investigation of the pay raise. The EEOC discontinued the investigation in 1995. Seventy-five of the white males then wrote individual letters to the Justice Department for a notice of right to sue. Forty of the white males decided to participate in the Title VII suit, which was filed in 1995. (Their lawyers took the case on a contingency basis.) The white male plaintiffs lost the Title VII trial in U.S. District Court in Prescott, Arizona, in a jury trial in December 2000. Then, in 2002, the Ninth Circuit Court of Appeals ruled that a violation of the Equal Protection Clause had occurred, but they granted immunity to Eugene Hughes, who had been NAU President in 1993. The Ninth Circuit reversed, in part, the jury verdict. The class-action suit, meanwhile, came to an end in December 2002 when the Ninth Circuit granted Hughes immunity on the Equal Protection claim.

Edward Hood and George Rudebusch have long been the NAU faculty members who were most involved in the case. Their involvement dates back to the mid-1990s, when the EEOC ended its investigation. At the time, there were approximately 12 faculty members who convened an "equity planning committee" of sorts. Hood and Rudebusch soon became the most energetic advocates of resolving what they saw as an injustice (in terms of the pay action) through university channels. Then-NAU President Clara Lovett rebuffed their attempts at resolution. So Hood and Rudebusch found a lawyer who would take the case on a contingency-fee basis.[21] "The lawyer," writes George Rudebusch, "requested a representative for the class."[22] Rudebusch became the representative because he, not Hood, was tenured at the time. The men thought that Rudebusch's tenured status gave him "a bit more protection, as it seemed, from current university administration," recalls Rudebusch.[23] Consequently, Rudebusch has received a fair amount of media attention, particularly in Arizona, over the years. Both men report that they have encountered few people who consider them to be insensitive, intolerant, or racist for their involvement in this case.

Edward Hood and George Rudebusch are longtime faculty members at NAU. Born on April 10, 1954, Hood grew up in North Carolina, New Jersey, and one of the Marshall Islands in the Pacific. Hood, who bears a striking resemblance to Mexican President Vicente Fox, traces his ancestry to England, Germany, and Holland. This internationally recognized expert on Latin American — specifically, Central American — literature joined NAU's Department of Modern Languages in 1991. Hood and his wife, Jovita Hernandez, have an infant son, Camden Edward Hernandez Hood, whose name reflects his multiethnic heritage. Hood himself reports that he rarely finds himself in an all-Anglo environment. George Rudebusch, similarly, is a Baby Boomer whose forebears came to the United States from Northern Europe, mainly from Germany. A native of Wisconsin, he was born on August 2, 1957. This tall, charming man with light brown hair and blue eyes specializes in ancient philosophy. Rudebusch taught at the University of Hawaii at Manoa from January 1983 through May 1988 and came to NAU in the fall of 1988. He is the lead plaintiff in the Title VII case — the suit bears his name (*Rudebusch v. Hughes*).[24] He and his wife, Hope Rudebusch, have three children, two of whom are white and one of whom is black. Both men seem quite comfortable in multiethnic, multicultural environments.

The NAU pay case is coming to a close; there will be some kind of resolution soon. The 40 white male plaintiffs contend that they have missed out on $2 million in salary and retirement benefits because of the disparity that dates back to 1993. The issue, according to Edward Hood, is "whether using the predicted salary of similarly situated white male faculty for the minority and female adjustments somehow overcompensated these minority and white female members, i.e., whether the adjustments were more than remedial."[25] If these salary increases were not just remedial, the university is facing liability regarding the matter of the 40 white males. In July 2004, Judge Robert C. Broomfield found that a Title VII violation had occurred. Now he has to determine the university's liability. This case is already being cited in legal opinions and journal articles. In any event, Hood, Rudebusch, and their co-plaintiffs have spent much of their time in the last several years taking a stand on principle; their odyssey involves important questions related to race, gender, equity, and the allocation of resources.

Over the years, the courts in America have played an important role in mediating racial issues that explicitly (or implicitly) involved white males. Until about three decades ago, the legal system in the United States was almost completely dominated by whites and males. At one time white men accounted for virtually all of America's judges, juries, and attorneys. Today, though, we are seeing increasing racial and gender diversity in our legal system. Only white men sat on the Supreme Court until 1967, when

Thurgood Marshall became the first black member of the nation's highest judicial body. And Sandra Day O'Connor made history as the first female Supreme Court Justice in 1981. The makeup of America's federal, state, and local courts increasingly mirrors the diversity of the country, so a female judge or a black prosecutor rarely merits much attention anymore in many contexts.

White males have always maintained, challenged, and defended the racial status quo through the legal system. Before the advent of Multicultural America, white males had the most capital invested in maintaining the system of racial and gender privilege that benefited them. The law intersected with this racial hierarchy through such issues as the racial prerequisite cases and the legal proscriptions on interracial marriage in many states. For centuries, a white man could commit crimes against African Americans with virtual impunity in certain parts of America; few judges or juries would give him more than a token sentence for his malevolent actions. The actions and decisions of white male lawyers, judges, juries, and prosecutors affected the tenor and nature of race relations and racial dynamics in our nation for many years. The courts made decisions and handed down rulings that defined, expanded, and enforced the boundaries of racial and gender privilege in American society during those years. This was most evident in the South, but it took place in many other parts of the country as well.

Judges and judicial appointments became hotly debated political issues due to the importance of the judiciary in protecting and expanding the civil rights advances of the 1950s, 1960s, and 1970s. The politicization of judicial appointments in a racial sense occurred after judges regularly ruled on civil rights–related matters, particularly in the South. Indeed, judicial appointments were a significant political issue during the 1960s and 1970s, as they continue to be today. Conservative politicians railed against "activist judges" who allegedly "legislated from the bench." Interestingly, the courts contributed significantly during the 1950s, 1960s, and 1970s to plans to promote racial justice, because politicians were either unable or unwilling to take steps that would be unpopular with the voters. This was particularly true with regard to busing and desegregation issues. Today conservatives rely more and more on the courts for support on issues like affirmative action. Politicians, even those sympathetic to colorblind public policy, do not want to expend valuable political capital on issues that, in their opinion, can be dealt with by the courts. Nor do the courts generally get too far ahead of where the public is on most issues — witness the reluctance of the Supreme Court to curtail completely affirmative action or abortion rights, two hot-button issues for social conservatives.

Since the early 1970s, the courts have been dealing with issues regarding white maleness, but in a very different way than had been the case previously. For the first time in American history, individual white males confronted situations in which their whiteness or maleness might actually be a slight disadvantage in certain contexts. Until this point, the language of racism, civil rights, and discrimination in mainstream discourse had focused solely (and appropriately) on people of color. Some whites and men began to use this language to highlight what they saw as the new injustices that resulted from the efforts to remedy past injustices and current inequities. Since the early to mid-1970s, the white male plaintiffs of reverse-discrimination cases before the Supreme Court (such men as Marco DeFunis, Allan Bakke, Brian Weber, Paul Johnson, and Randy Pech) have received national media exposure.[26]

Reverse-discrimination cases can become giant morality plays, in that a specific white male plaintiff becomes a stand-in for all similarly situated individuals in the United States. Such cases simultaneously focus on individual rights and group rights. The individual, of course, is the white male plaintiff who insists that he should be treated as an individual, even as many multiculturalists say that he is the representative of a privileged group. Thus they contend that one cannot look at the individual without analyzing the advantages of the group — and the putative disadvantages of other groups, particularly women and minorities, who are supposed to be covered by affirmative action and diversity initiatives. White males can often be the staunchest proponents of individualism in American life. Those white males who feel victimized by affirmative action and diversity initiatives reject any characterizations of themselves as members of a group (as in whites, males, or white males).

In the courts and elsewhere, white males often do not experience life as white males per se, but rather as whites or males. Relatively few high-profile cases involve race and gender simultaneously. In many of the most prominent reverse-discrimination cases before the Supreme Court, race is the paramount concern. There has been one prominent reverse-discrimination case before the Supreme Court that involved gender, not race — that of Paul Johnson, a white male, who was passed over for a promotion in favor of a white female at the Santa Clara County, California, Transportation Agency.[27] Race remains a strong factor in our society, and it is altogether unsurprising that gender often takes a back seat to it in court battles. And it seems that there is less controversy — unless the issue is abortion — when a legal issue involves gender rather than race. In fact, many of the hottest issues before the Court in Multicultural America encompass largely raceless matters: abortion, gay rights, and the like.

Court cases that involve racial or gender issues often make the newspapers, particularly those suits that reach the federal courts. Such cases can seep into the popular consciousness, as a result of the momentous issues being covered in the lawsuit. An important case, such as *Bakke* or *Gratz,* can serve as a catalyst to examine the progress of specific initiatives and mechanisms designed to increase the opportunities available to people from historically disadvantaged groups in our society. Such cases result in the discussion of important societal dynamics that we live with every day, but rarely take the time to examine. Some lawsuits involve white males as males (Title IX cases, for instance), while other lawsuits frequently involve white male plaintiffs as whites (as in voting-rights cases) or older workers (age discrimination cases).

The sociologist Fred Pincus empirically tested the prevalence of white and male claims of reverse discrimination. He did so by examining "unpublished EEOC data for FY 1995–2000" and "appeals court decisions involving discrimination" in 1998, 1999, 2000, and 2001.[28] Pincus correctly hypothesized that "[r]ace discrimination allegations by whites and sex discrimination allegations by men are much less common than traditional allegations of discrimination by people of color and women."[29] One must adjust for population size when s/he considers the frequency of EEOC claims of race and sex discrimination. After doing so, Pincus found that blacks file race discrimination claims at a rate 55 times higher than that of whites. Similarly, women file sex discrimination claims with six times more frequency than men do. And from his analysis of the federal appeals court data, Pincus reports that the percentage of discrimination-related appeals filed by whites and men is even smaller than is the case for the EEOC claims.[30]

Pincus adds to our understanding of this topic by looking at the occupations of the plaintiffs in reverse-discrimination cases in the appeals courts. For his study period of 1998 to 2001, Pincus found that professionals and managers accounted for 43.8% of the plaintiffs in reverse discrimination cases in the federal appeals courts. More than one-quarter (27.1%, to be exact) of them were police and firefighters. The remaining occupational categories were blue collar (8.3%), white collar (6.3%), service (4.2%), and other, unknown (10.4%). The defendants in the appeals court cases studied by Pincus were state or local governments (52.1%), the federal government (16.7%), private corporations (27.1%), and other

(4.2%). Pincus speculates that the significant percentage of managers, professionals, police officers, and firefighters in reverse-discrimination appeals court cases might mean discrimination occurs more frequently in such occupations, affirmative action is implemented most aggressively in those contexts, or that individuals in those occupational categories have access to the requisite resources to file reverse-discrimination cases.[31]

Women and people of color have brought what Fred Pincus describes as "traditional discrimination" cases for decades; white males file these suits, too, which focus on cases that involve female or minority coworkers or supervisors who allegedly treated a male or white plaintiff unfairly.[32] Pincus writes:

> Regardless of the race or sex of the plaintiff, the court usually relies on the "McDonnell Douglass framework" to determine if discrimination has occurred. This framework has a three-step procedure. (1) The plaintiff must establish a prima facie case of discrimination. This means that the plaintiff has to present enough evidence that a reasonable jury could consider a guilty verdict. Part of a prima facie case is demonstrating that similarly situated employees who were not members of the protected class were treated differently. (2) If the plaintiffs establish a prima facie case, the burden then falls on the defendant (employer) to articulate some legitimate, nondiscriminatory reason for its actions. (3) If the defendant is successful in stating a nondiscriminatory reason, the plaintiff must prove that the stated reason was a pretext and that the real reason was discrimination.[33]

These criteria are difficult to prove in any case, and that includes white and male plaintiffs in reverse-discrimination cases. Pincus notes that we must make sure that a race discrimination claim by a white or a sex discrimination claim by a male actually involves affirmative action. He found, to be sure, several cases of whites who were injured by illegal interpretations of affirmative-action policies. Pincus describes such cases as "reverse discrimination."[34] As a strong supporter of affirmative action, Pincus notes that a legal affirmative action policy may result in some whites not being hired or promoted. He refers to this type of situation as "reduced opportunity." (Many Americans would consider that to be reverse discrimination.) Likewise, there are cases in which the job or promotion would not have gone to the whites even in the absence of an affirmative action policy. Sometimes, too, whites or males have claimed in cases that they faced race or sex discrimination but affirmative action is not a reason for the discrimination claim. Pincus describes it as "intentional discrimination" when the courts uphold such claims.[35] He concludes: "Those who argue that the legal system is stacked against white men are simply wrong."[36]

White males often do not file suits or claims when they believe they face reverse discrimination. There are a number of reasons — including the cost, controversy, and time-consuming nature of filing a case — why more white men (and women and people of color) do not pursue discrimination suits. Firstly, legal cases are expensive, unless one can find an attorney or a law firm who will take the case on a contingency basis. Many white male plaintiffs in high-profile reverse-discrimination lawsuits rely on the aid of conservative public-interest law firms. Secondly, legal cases involving reverse discrimination generate significant controversy. A white male plaintiff in such a suit might be seen as a racist and/or a sexist by the Left and "a whiner" or "sore loser" by many others. And he may fear that people will not believe his allegations. Many white males do not want this type of unflattering attention. Thirdly, the plaintiff in a reverse-discrimination case may wait years for what he hopes will be some kind of vindication. This type of experience can be emotionally trying as well as time-consuming.[37]

To be sure, there is a large difference between the situation of white male plaintiffs in a reverse-discrimination class action lawsuit and that of an individual plaintiff in a reverse-discrimination lawsuit. In a class action, a white male plaintiff finds himself as part of a group. He does not receive the same kind of publicity that he would if he were an individual plaintiff. Reverse-discrimination class-action lawsuits periodically receive attention, such as the class action by 99 white males against the Maryland State Police (settled in 1995) and the class action by 620 white males against Ford Motor Company (settled in 2001).[38] Individual plaintiffs, though, can sacrifice much of their privacy for a multiyear period as a case winds its way through the courts. Sometimes a white male plaintiff wins a large judgment in a reverse-discrimination case, as Howard McNier did in his suit against San Francisco State University in 1999. McNier received a judgment of $2.75 million after a jury trial regarding a hiring decision.[39] In addition, white male participants in a class-action suit may have the psychological boost of not feeling as if they are alone out there fighting the world on this issue.

Thomas Stewart, the president of Frank Gurney, Inc., a subcontractor in Spokane, Washington, feels he regularly faces reverse discrimination in his bids on numerous jobs, but he has thus far never filed a lawsuit on the issue.[40] Stewart, a civil engineer who graduated from Gonzaga

University in 1964, owns and operates the eponymous firm founded by his stepfather, Frank Gurney, in 1959. The contractor has a well-deserved reputation for integrity and quality workmanship. Stewart and his 40 employees install 20 to 25 miles of guardrails on highways in eastern Washington, northern Idaho, and western Montana each year. His two thirtysomething sons (Carl and Glen), both graduates of Washington State University, work with him at Frank Gurney. Stewart says that he and his colleagues began to lose work on the basis of race and gender in the early 1980s, as a result of the set-aside subcontracting requirements of the Surface Transportation Act (STA) of 1982. Stewart documented his experiences; today he has 25 to 30 letters that state he was the lowest bidder for a particular job, but the contractor had to subcontract to a women- or minority-owned business in order to comply with federal regulations.[41]

Stewart and his family have grappled with the issue of set-asides over the years — it has been a source of consternation to them.[42] "Like most other Americans," Stewart told members of Congress in 1995, "I want no more than the chance to succeed — or even fail — on my individual merits. It's really as simple as that. It's just not fair to punish my firm because neither minorities nor women own it."[43] Stewart points out that he supports affirmative action but not quotas. He has always faithfully followed affirmative-action requirements in hiring — for instance, hiring Native Americans when he does jobs in Montana. Stewart himself reports that he feels "frustration beyond belief" when he submits the lowest bid for a subcontracting job but it is rejected because the contractor must use a minority- or female-owned subcontractor due to set-asides. A serious man whose collection of antique cars includes his prize-winning 1959 Corvette, Stewart makes it clear that he is "refusing victimhood status."[44]

Indeed, Stewart regularly shares his story in the media and with governmental officials. Sometimes profiles of him appear in the print media, particularly in Spokane and environs. On July 19, 1995, for example, he was pictured on the front page of *USA Today,* as part of the newspaper's coverage of affirmative action in public contracting. The nation's largest-circulation newspaper also ran an article on him.[45] Stewart testified before the U.S. Equal Employment Opportunity Commission in 1986. And he testified before Congress in 1995.[46] In 2002 Senator Mitch McConnell read on the Senate floor some of Stewart's 25 to 30 rejection letters related to his low bids. Stewart has never filed a lawsuit on the issue, in part because the litigation process is slow and expensive. At least one conservative public-interest law firm has approached him about filing a reverse-discrimination case. While Stewart never closes the door on the possibility of filing a suit, he prefers at this point, at least, to publicize what he sees as the injustices of set-asides in public contracting without going to court.[47]

THE POLITICS OF RACE AND GENDER

No major-party presidential nominee in American history has been more conspicuously inclusive in his search for a running mate than Walter F. Mondale. The 1984 Democratic presidential nominee considered at least nine possible vice-presidential candidates. Mondale's list included one Latino, two African Americans, three white women, and three white men. Mondale wanted his list of potential running mates to reflect the diversity of the American people and the Democratic Party. Moreover, he sought a vice-presidential candidate who would energize the Democratic Party and provide his campaign with attention, momentum, and a bit of flair. Eventually, he chose Geraldine Ferraro to run with him, a selection that electrified the Democratic National Convention in San Francisco and spurred great excitement among feminists. The three-term congresswoman from Queens, after all, was the first woman and the first Italian American (and the only member of both groups, to date) ever to be nominated for a spot on a major-party national ticket.[48]

Inclusiveness has been a constant theme throughout Walter Mondale's distinguished career in politics. Walter Frederick Mondale was born on January 5, 1928, in Ceylon, Minnesota; he grew up in the virtually all-white precincts of small-town southern Minnesota. His father was a Methodist minister.[49] The Scottish-Norwegian Mondale cites several factors to explain his dedication to civil rights and racial equality. Firstly, his parents, who were devout Christians, taught him that "every person is a child of God" and that "denial of opportunity is a sin." Secondly, he entered public life at a time when segregation was beginning to crumble and liberal positions on civil rights enjoyed significant popular support in Minnesota. Thirdly, mid-twentieth-century Minnesota had a small but very active black population, whose presence raised the consciousness of white Minnesotans on matters related to racial equality.[50] Indeed, Mondale and his mentor, Hubert Humphrey, rank as two of the most significant white political advocates of civil rights in modern American political history. Both men hailed from what was then a predominantly white state.

"Few white men in American public life have advocated racial equality with greater consistency than Walter Mondale," writes Jeremy D. Mayer.[51] The future presidential candidate became Minnesota Attorney General in 1960, at age 32; he focused much of his attention on civil rights issues in that position. When Vice President–elect Hubert Humphrey vacated his Senate seat in November 1964, Minnesota Governor Karl Rolvaag appointed Mondale to succeed him. The young senator was elected to a full term in 1966 and reelected in 1972. Two of his most significant accomplishments in the Senate had racial significance — the Fair Housing Act of 1968 and the filibuster reform bill of 1975. Throughout these years, Mondale was one of the nation's most ardent proponents of busing to achieve desegregation (he was known for a time as "Mr. Busing").[52] In 1976 Democratic presidential nominee Jimmy Carter, a son of the white South who embraced equal rights for African Americans, selected Mondale as his running mate. After the Democrats won the Presidency, Mondale served with distinction as Carter's vice president from 1977 to 1981. He was the administration's point person with the civil rights community. The Carter-Mondale ticket lost in 1980 and Mondale soon began preparing for his own presidential race.[53]

As someone who was popular with the Democratic Party's many constituencies, Mondale entered the race for the Democratic presidential nomination in 1983 as the presumptive favorite. Two significant challengers emerged during the presidential primary campaign: Colorado Senator Gary Hart and civil rights leader Jesse Jackson. Hart, who is white, campaigned on a centrist platform that presaged the New Democratic appeal of Bill Clinton in the 1990s. As the first serious African-American presidential candidate, Jackson focused mainly on winning black votes in his 1984 campaign (his 1988 bid for the White House was conspicuously multiracial).[54] Many black civil rights leaders endorsed Mondale rather than Jackson — they respected the Minnesotan's admirable record on civil rights issues. Mondale, in fact, rejected the advice of some African-American Democrats to openly challenge Jackson; he recognized and appreciated the historic nature of Jackson's candidacy. In any event, the veteran Democrat wanted to emphasize party unity in his campaign.[55] Since Mondale enjoyed an excellent reputation in black America, he probably would have won an overwhelming majority of the black vote had Jackson not run. Thus Jackson's candidacy complicated Mondale's ultimately successful efforts to defeat Hart, his main challenger for the nomination.[56]

Race, to be sure, never played an overtly significant role in the 1984 general election. Mondale took a major political gamble when he told the Democratic National Convention in July 1984 that he would raise income taxes to tackle the nation's growing budget deficits if he were elected to the White House. Also, his liberal positions on such issues as national defense and social spending were anathema to many white Americans. At bottom, though, Mondale faced an impossible task: that of dislodging the enormously popular Republican incumbent, Ronald Reagan, who enjoyed high approval ratings in White America. The nation was at peace and most whites were satisfied with the Republican administration's stewardship of the economy.[57] Reagan defeated Mondale by 59% to 41% in the popular vote and 525 to 13 in the Electoral College. Nineteen eighty-four was an election that compellingly demonstrated the racial divide in the American electorate. Reagan won by overwhelming margins among white voters (64%-35%) and white male voters (67%-32%), particularly in the South. By contrast, Mondale took 90% of the black vote and 62% of the Latino vote.[58]

Mondale's 1984 presidential campaign marked the last time that the Democrats chose a presidential nominee who ran as an heir to the New Deal tradition in American politics.[59] Indeed, Mondale embraced organized labor, African Americans, and the Feminist Left, three groups of Americans whose ideological positions did not resonate with large numbers of white voters, who strongly supported Ronald Reagan. In retrospect, it is clear that an unreconstructed liberal candidate such as Mondale — even his foes acknowledge that Mondale has always been ideologically consistent — would have been hard-pressed to win the Presidency under any circumstances in 1984. Today Mondale is proud that he stood up for his principles during the 1984 presidential election season.[60] Moreover, this American liberal icon notes the significance of the 1984 campaign, particularly his choice of Ferraro as a running mate: "While we lost, what we did then, and the campaign we waged, still resonates today: in the number of women doctors, in the soaring numbers of lawyers, business executives, and ministers who are women, — everywhere barriers have weakened, as they have in politics."[61]

White males were the dominant group in U.S. politics until the advent of Multicultural America. Women first voted in national elections in 1920. Before the passage of the Nineteenth Amendment, which mandated women's suffrage, the only people who voted, for the most part, were white men. (African-American men were largely disenfranchised, at least in the South, after 1900.) Politicians aimed many of their appeals at white men, who were perceived to influence their wives' voting decisions, even after women began voting en masse. Of course, the interests of white men and white women are not necessarily mutually exclusive, by any means. There is a considerable overlap between the two groups in terms of their priorities and ideological beliefs. During the 1970s, 1980s, and 1990s, the identification of the Democrats with the Multicultural Left — and cultural liberalism — led white males in the South and other parts of America to desert the Democrats in droves, particularly in presidential elections.[62]

White males are the most Republican racial/gender group in American society. The support of white men for the GOP is evidenced by the vote totals in white male America in the last seven presidential elections:

   1976 (51% Republican; 47% Democratic)
   1980 (59% Republican; 32% Democratic; 7% Independent)
   1984 (67% Republican; 32% Democratic)
   1988 (63% Republican; 36% Democratic)
   1992 (40% Republican; 37% Democratic; 22% Independent)
   1996 (49% Republican; 38% Democratic; 11% Reform)
   2000 (60% Republican; 36% Democratic; 3% Green)[63]

The Republican percentage among white males declined dramatically in 1992 and 1996 because third-party candidate Ross Perot did well among this demographic group. In the 2000 presidential election, white males accounted for 39% of the national electorate and nearly one-half of the Republican presidential vote.[64]

White males often vote Republican, in part because of issues related to socioeconomic status. White men as a group do well economically, at least compared to similarly situated women and people of color, so they are less likely to feel they need a strong federal government to look out for their interests. As a group, white males typically support low taxes, fiscal frugality, and limited government, at least more so than any other group of Americans. Upper-income white Christian men must be counted among the most Republican group of voters in the country, particularly if they are involved in business or entrepreneurial ventures. Middle-class and upper-middle-class white men also vote heavily Republican, on average, particularly if they are native-born, able-bodied, Euro-American, Christian heterosexuals. White male union members are somewhat more Democratic than white males as a group, but they sometimes vote for the GOP based on social issues like gun control. Republicans even win large numbers of votes among working class and sometimes lower-income white men, who identify with the party and its candidates on certain social issues. In any event, white men typically vote Republican as they gain more education and income (although this correlation declines, to some extent, among those with postgraduate degrees).[65]

Ethnicity and religion are two factors that dramatically affect the political allegiances of white male voters. Northern European Americans typically are the most conservative and Republican group of Americans, particularly if they are Protestant. Indeed, white Protestant men are the most heavily Republican ethno-religious group in the country. This is particularly true in the American South. White Protestant men, after all, have long been the dominant group in America. Since Republicans typically have been associated with the "insiders," it is not surprising that white Protestant men would lean heavily to the GOP. White men of Southern and Eastern European origin once favored Democrats more than Republicans. This was a function of the overwhelming Democratic allegiance of Catholic and Jewish Americans. Members of these formerly excluded groups are now part of the American Establishment. Today white Catholic men lean Republican, although Jews maintain their traditional loyalty to the Democratic Party. Democrats continue to win large numbers of votes among specific groups of white men who may not feel as if they are part of the majority all the time, as in gays and immigrants.

Region is an important factor in determining how white males vote in elections. White men in the South and West tend to be more likely to vote Republican than their counterparts in the Midwest and Northeast. The South is more socially conservative than other parts of the country, and the West is similarly conservative, although the attitudes on social issues there are more libertarian than in Dixie. White males in the South are more Republican than their counterparts elsewhere in the country for a number of reasons, including the lack of unionization there, the South's traditional support for a strong national defense, and the substantial presence of blacks there (especially in the Deep South). White male voters in the Mountain West are much more heavily Republican than their coethnics in California and the Pacific Northwest. In any event, white male rural voters are strongly Republican. White male suburbanites lean toward the GOP, but they are not as heavily Republican as their rural counterparts. And the Democrats often receive the backing of white males in the central cities. Indeed, the political — and cultural — geography of America encompasses significant variations in regional attitudes and ideological beliefs.

Age and generational cohort are other important factors that structure the voting preferences of white male voters. White men under 40
(particularly those who are native-born, Euro-American, heterosexual,
Christian, and able-bodied) are perhaps the most heavily Republican cohort of white men. They back the Republicans because of the GOP's
stances on fiscal policy, national security, and social issues. "Only 16 percent of young white males are registering now as Democrats," notes the
political scientist Anna Greenberg. "Young white men are a real problem for the Democratic Party."[66] Their support for the GOP undoubtedly
correlates in some way to the Democrats' identification with the Multicultural Left. Many young white men may feel somewhat discombobulated
or at least disengaged by the general focus on inclusion and multiculturalism in the Democratic Party. It is nearly impossible to poll accurately on
this question in a macro sense, because whites sometimes obscure their
positions on multicultural issues to give pollsters what they see as "politically correct" responses. The ranks of the Republican Party, which
include few vocal multiculturalists, seem to be comfortable for many
younger white men.

The gender gap between men and women in the electoral process first
became evident in the presidential election of 1980. Since then, there
has been a marked difference between the voting preferences of men and
women. Men of all races are more likely than women of all races to support Republicans and conservative candidates, and to favor lower taxes,
limited government, and a less-active governmental role in terms of the
social safety net and related matters. There is a pronounced gender gap
in white America and, to some extent, among voters of color as well.[67]
The gender gap is perhaps most significant among voters with much
education. As Susan Page writes, "Highly educated men and women increasingly view the political world in dramatically different ways: Men
are mostly Republicans, women are predominantly Democrats."[68] In any
event, discussions of the gender gap in American politics often involve
catchy phrases to describe coveted demographic groups, e.g., the Angry
White Men of 1994, the soccer moms of 1996, and the security moms
and NASCAR dads of 2004.

White male voters received considerable attention in the immediate
aftermath of the 1994 elections, due to the role the white male vote
played in the Republican landslide that year. In 1994 the Republicans
regained control of the U.S. House for the first time in 40 years, and
the GOP also retook control of the U.S. Senate, which it had lost in

1986. Approximately one-half of white men backed Democratic congressional candidates during the 1980s and in 1992. In 1994, though, 63% of white males supported GOP House candidates, compared to 51% of all voters. (White men accounted for 42% of the national electorate that year.) Many white male voters backed GOP congressional candidates because of their dislike of President Bill Clinton's liberal policies during his first two years in office. They also tilted toward the Republicans because of their concerns about the economy and their future financial well being. Republican congressional candidates surged among white male high school graduates and those who had attended but not graduated from college. White Southern men backed the GOP with the largest percentages, even as the Republican shift occurred in every region. Republicans won a majority of white men in every age group, but they did best among young white men, those aged 18 to 29.[69]

After the 1994 elections, many media and political observers began to speak about the "Angry White Men" who supposedly banded together to put the Republicans in power that year. *Washington Post* columnist Charles Krauthammer, a conservative, challenged the Angry White Male view of the 1994 election. Krauthammer points to numerous polls that contradict the notion that white men turned out in droves to vote Republican in 1994 because they were "angry."[70] "In fact," writes Krauthammer, "the Angry White Male is a myth, an invention of political partisans who wish to rationalize and ultimately delegitimize the election of 1994. After all, neither anger, nor whiteness, nor maleness are coveted attributes these days. The invention of the Angry White Male pointedly ascribes the current Republican ascendancy to a toxic constituency, akin to the petty bourgeoisie that brought fascists to power in the Europe of the 1930s."[71] By the late 1990s, the idea of the Angry White Male, while still common in certain circles, began to lose efficacy as a viable political concept. The phrase no longer has any resonance in political terms — and it is now only rarely heard in American social and cultural discourse.

In any event, affluent white male donors enjoy significant influence in the American political process. "White males, particularly those involved in business, have more disposable income to invest in politics and are more likely to see returns from those investments," notes the political scientist Paul Herrnson.[72] Indeed, the ranks of political donors are heavily white and male. The new campaign-finance law increases the individual limit for campaign contributions per election from $1,000 to $2,000. Republicans may benefit from the new law since donors are, on average, more pro-business and conservative than the general population. Advocates of publicly financed campaigns contend that the present state of affairs advantages the affluent. Politicians, after all, pay much attention to the views and ideas of present and prospective donors. Less-affluent Americans, whose ranks are disproportionately nonwhite, wield little influence in the political process.[73]

Hot-button issues affect — but rarely determine, at least completely — the voting decisions of white men. White male politics often does not focus on such issues as affirmative action. The typical white male voter may dislike or feel ambivalent about affirmative action, but the issue does not significantly affect his voting decisions. However, multicultural issues may influence white males' conceptions of a political party's overall priorities and objectives. In other words, they may feel that the Democratic Party is too liberal on cultural issues. The Democrats' strong support of multicultural initiatives affects how many white male voters view the party and its candidates (considered, of course, in conjunction with many other issues). "Bubba," meanwhile, is one of the nation's hoariest political archetypes: He is the prototypical Southern white man, a Christian with socially conservative views who lives in a rural area and hails from a working- or middle-class background.[74] According to political legend, "Bubba" is perhaps most sensitive to hot-button social issues, such as gay marriage and the Confederate flag, in deciding whom to support in an election.

During the 2004 presidential campaign, Democratic presidential contender Howard Dean highlighted his willingness to speak about race. Dean, the former governor of Vermont, the nation's second-whitest state, refused to concede any votes in any community to his challengers. Indeed, he prided himself on being a candidate who discussed race before white audiences. And he often mentioned the need for Democrats to appeal to Southern white men by focusing on bridge issues — health care, the economy.[75] In the fall of 2003, Dean mentioned his interest in being "the candidate for guys with Confederate flags in their pickup trucks."[76] The former Vermont governor eventually apologized for this controversial remark after he was criticized for it by his Democratic rivals. However, Dean noted that the Democrats had to do better among male voters, particularly those from blue-collar backgrounds, if they were to be successful in future elections.[77]

One demographic that includes many white men in the South and elsewhere is NASCAR fans. Auto racing has long been a touchstone for Republican candidates and for those Democrats who seek to appeal to white social and cultural conservatives. Democratic presidential candidate Jimmy Carter appeared at the Firecracker 400 in 1976, an appearance that signaled the growing importance of the auto-racing demographic. Carter also invited NASCAR drivers to the White House. And over the years, high-ranking Republicans have regularly appeared at stock car races. President George W. Bush energetically courts NASCAR fans. The White House welcomes stock car champions such as Tony Stewart and Matt Kenseth. In February 2004 President Bush made a highly visible appearance at the Daytona 500. By appearing at the premier event of NASCAR's Nextel Cup Series, the president reinforced his connection to the values of family, country, and religion that resonate with the NASCAR fans.[78]

Last year some political strategists defined "NASCAR dads" as one of the key swing voter groups of 2004. These are Southern and Midwestern white men who hold socially conservative views and come from working- and middle-class backgrounds. They were once known as Reagan Democrats. Today they are mostly Republican. Democrats hold out hope that recent job losses might enable them to be competitive in certain parts of the South this year. But Republican consultants contend that NASCAR dads resemble the Reagan Democrats of years past in their cultural conservatism, backing of a strong national leader, and worries about maintaining their middle-class status. The NASCAR demographic appeals significantly to politicians, in part because it is so large and NASCAR fans are so brand-loyal. While NASCAR fans are mainly presumed to be Republicans and social conservatives, some observers posit that their ranks encompass more centrists, Democrats, and Independents than the stereotypes would have you believe. This is why some political strategists are skeptical that there is such a bloc of voters, one that is genuinely in play between the parties in the 2004 presidential election.[79]

One issue that affects the votes of white males — NASCAR dads and others — is guns. A significant number of white men, particularly in the South and the rural areas of such states as Missouri, Michigan, New York, and Pennsylvania, strongly support Second Amendment rights. Democrats (outside of the South and rural America) typically endorse gun control laws. Republicans (apart from the Northeast and some suburbs) regularly back expansive notions of gunowners' rights. In election after election, the gun issue has been a litmus test for some white male voters. I remember asking a white male classmate if his parents were going to vote for Democratic presidential candidate Michael Dukakis in 1988. He answered my question negatively, ostensibly on the grounds that "Dukakis wants to take away our guns." This attitude has frequently affected how white males voted in elections. The gun issue made it more difficult for Democrats to reach rural white men who might be willing to support the Democrats on economic issues. Polling data demonstrated that the gun issue significantly helped the Republicans take back the U.S. House in 1994. Nonetheless, gun control remained a hot issue for Democrats throughout the 1990s, particularly after the 1999 shootings at Columbine High School in suburban Denver.[80]

There has been a significant evolution in thinking on the gun issue among Democrats during the last four years, in large part due to the experiences of Democratic presidential candidate Albert Gore in 2000. During the 2000 Democratic presidential primary campaign, Gore and challenger Bill Bradley voiced very strong pro–gun control rhetoric. In the general election that fall, Gore attempted to advocate a more nuanced position on the gun issue, so as to avoid hemorrhaging support to Republican George W. Bush. The 2000 presidential election results ensured that the Democrats would reexamine their positions (and positioning) on the gun issue after Gore lost such states as Missouri, Arkansas, Tennessee, and West Virginia. So in the early years of this century, Democrats increasingly avoid discussing the gun issue (even as they usually support many gun control measures) or, in the case of Howard Dean, highlight their pro-gun positions. Indeed, during the 2004 presidential campaign, the leading Democratic presidential candidates largely skirted the topic of strong gun control laws. This paradigm shift came after the Democrats had spent a significant amount of time over the last decade calling for federal regulation of firearms.[81]

Every election cycle, the pundits, political professionals, and others always discuss the Democrats' chances among white male voters. In 1996 and 2000, for instance, there was a flurry of media attention paid to the white male vote in the presidential election. Republicans Robert Dole and George W. Bush were solidly favored by white male voters, and the media described the reasons why this was the case. Neither Bill Clinton nor Al Gore appealed to the majority of white male voters, particularly native-born, Euro-American, heterosexual, able-bodied Christian men. The numbers were especially bad for the Democrats among this demographic group in rural areas and in the South. It seems likely that the Democrats will focus much more attention on white male voters in the future. The white male percentage of the U.S. electorate hovers around 40 percent, which requires the Democrats to score solid margins among white women and voters of color to compensate for their likely inability to win more than 40 percent of the white male vote in many elections.

TAKING THE INITIATIVE

When Ohio Senator Eugene Watts introduced legislation to eliminate race-based affirmative action in Ohio's state contracting program in 1993, the issue barely registered on the political radar screen in Ohio.[82] A former Sixties liberal and a believer in a "big tent" Republican Party, Watts felt that minority preferences in public contracting contradicted the colorblind ideal he had worked for as a young man in the civil rights movement. But few of Watts's legislative colleagues saw any political advantage to be gained from trying to curtail affirmative-action programs. Moreover, Republican Governor George Voinovich asked him to lay off the issue, "partly because of principle and partly because of his unwillingness to antagonize black voters during his upcoming reelection campaign."[83] Watts, a tall man with gray hair, sky-blue eyes, and Celtic features, deferred to the governor's wishes because he did not have enough legislative support to override an expected gubernatorial veto of his bill.

Watts's biography is the story of a very bright young man who rose from what he describes as "exceedingly modest circumstances" to achieve success in the military, academy, and politics. The future legislative maestro was born on October 17, 1942, and grew up in Saint Louis, where his father served on the police force. A first-generation college student whose parents never went beyond the eighth grade, Watts was a National Merit Finalist who earned numerous college scholarships and fellowships for graduate school. He graduated with a bachelor's degree in history from Knox College in Galesburg, Illinois, in 1964. Watts participated in fair-housing demonstrations while he was a student at Knox. The young liberal went on to Emory University in Atlanta where he earned a master's degree and a doctorate in history, and continued his activism in the civil rights movement. After receiving his Ph.D. in 1969, Watts served in the U.S. Army in Vietnam for two years and was awarded the Bronze Star. He moved to Ohio in 1972 when Ohio State University in Columbus hired him. Professor Watts specialized in the history of crime and punishment until his retirement in 2000. Moreover, he was one of the most prominent figures in the Ohio legislature from 1985 to 2000.[84]

Watts entered electoral politics in the early 1980s because of his work on veterans' affairs and other issues. In 1984 the Democrat-turned-Republican won election to the Ohio Senate; he defeated a Democratic incumbent in the working-class and heavily Democratic 16th District.[85] During his 16-year political career, he earned a reputation as a productive lawmaker with a penchant for colorful one-liners and a willingness to take on controversial causes.[86] Watts served as Majority Whip of the Ohio Senate from 1989 to 1991. The Irish American became Assistant President Pro Tempore of the Ohio Senate in 1991, a position he held until 1999. Throughout, Watts compiled a consistently conservative record on issues ranging from taxes to crime to education. Today he is best known in Ohio for his attention to education. In fact, Watts was the driving force behind Ohio's tenth-grade proficiency test, a piece of legislation that many observers consider to be his most important legislative accomplishment.[87] Another related issue that made him popular in some corners — and vilified in others — was his successful advocacy of Ohio's "No Pass/No Play" law. "Watts' statewide law," points out the *Cleveland Plain Dealer,* "forced every school district to set a minimum grade-point average for students involved in interscholastic activities."[88]

In keeping with his conservative philosophy, Watts revisited the issue of affirmative action during the three legislative sessions of the mid- and late 1990s. In 1997, he joined forces with Representative Michael Wise to sponsor legislation to get an initiative repealing state affirmative action programs on the ballot without having to mount a costly signature-gathering campaign. When it became evident that this piece of legislation had no chance of passage, Watts and Wise did not bring it to a vote so their colleagues would not be forced to take a stand on a controversial initiative. And in 1996 and 1999, Watts introduced legislation that would have replaced minority preferences in state contracting with benefits for socially and economically disadvantaged contractors, regardless of race. Neither bill ever made it to the floor of the Ohio Senate. (Watts did not have sufficient votes to override gubernatorial vetoes of these pieces of legislation.)[89] Watts retired from the Ohio Senate in 2000 due to term limits. During the 1990s he was a pioneer in Ohio politics, one whose legislative activity regarding affirmative action and his attempt to authorize a ballot initiative on the topic paralleled — and, to some extent, foreshadowed — the burgeoning movement to curtail racial and gender preferences throughout the nation.

The efforts to repeal racial and gender preferences through ballot initiatives began to take off in earnest during the mid-1990s. Twenty-four states allow their residents to vote on ballot initiatives. The initiative process is often described by supporters as citizen democracy in action, while others decry the ability of interest groups to rally people through signature-collection campaigns and effective media advertising.[90] One matter that always comes up in the debate over an initiative on racial and gender preferences is the notion that such a discussion is "divisive" and will exacerbate ethnic and racial tensions in a multiethnic state or community. The anti-preferences forces always try to define the issue of affirmative action in terms of "quotas" and "preferences." The other side highlights affirmative action and tries to define the debate in terms of diversity and inclusion.[91] Americans, after all, are strongly opposed to quotas and preferences, but they are moderately supportive of "soft" forms of affirmative action and diversity initiatives.

Ward Connerly is the driving force behind the movement to repeal racial and gender preferences in public hiring, admissions, and contracting through the initiative process. Born into precarious economic circumstances in Leesville, Louisiana, on June 15, 1939, Connerly comes from a multiethnic background that includes African, Irish, French, and Choctaw ancestry. He moved to Sacramento, California, as a youngster. Connerly began his career in state government. Then, in 1973, he and his wife, Ilene, formed Connerly & Associates, Inc., a consulting firm in Sacramento, California, that focuses on association management and land development consulting. An expert on housing and development topics, Connerly serves as President and Chief Executive Officer of Connerly & Associates. This longtime Republican is a good friend to Pete Wilson, the GOP Governor of the Golden State from 1991 to 1999. Governor Wilson appointed Connerly to a 12-year term on the University of California Board of Regents in 1993.[92] In 1995 Connerly successfully introduced SP-1 — a resolution before the University of California Board of Regents to eliminate preferences in admissions throughout the University of California System.[93] This was a very controversial proposal, one that occasioned significant media coverage and made Connerly a national figure.

Ward Connerly regularly articulates his colorblind philosophy on race in America. His worldview emphasizes self-reliance. He strongly believes in antidiscrimination legislation. But he opposes government programs that give people advantages on the basis of their gender, race, ethnic origin, or any other characteristic.[94] Connerly singles out his Uncle James Louis for having influenced his philosophy, describing Louis as a hardworking, straight-shooting gentleman, someone who was never false with people in his dealings with them.[95] Connerly's biography could have been written by Horatio Alger — it is the odyssey of a very bright, determined young man who worked his way up to enjoy considerable material success and, in his later years, significant political influence on important policy issues. Connerly is fairly conservative in his political philosophy; he holds "right of center" views on most issues with libertarian leanings on certain social issues.[96] He is skeptical of racial classification in general and affirmative action in particular. These issues matter greatly to Connerly, who is a longtime resident of the nation's most ethnically and racially diverse state and one whose children and grandchildren are multiracial.[97]

Connerly inspires strong feelings on multicultural issues; indeed, he is one of the most prominent (and controversial) figures on racial matters in American society. The Sacramento businessman often encounters hostility from liberals of all colors in the Golden State and elsewhere.[98] Connerly does not mince his words. For instance, he says, "Civil rights are for everyone, including white males."[99] A genial, gracious, and charming man, Connerly often disarms his critics on a personal level. Connerly's accomplishments give him star power and substantial currency, in that the media and local political figures take notice when he speaks out on affirmative action in a specific city or forum. One conservative source describes him as "... America's most ardent proponent of colorblindness, a successful grassroots political leader, and a bold thinker on questions of race, education, and government policy."[100]

In 1997 Connerly founded two complementary but mutually exclusive organizations — the American Civil Rights Institute (ACRI) and the American Civil Rights Coalition (ACRC) — to promote his vision of the anti-preferences movement. Both organizations have their headquarters in Sacramento, California. The ACRI is a 501(c)(3) organization that describes itself as "a national civil rights organization created to educate the public about racial and gender preferences."[101] The ACRC is a 501(c)(4) organization that engages in lobbying and initiative campaigns as it "... works with grassroots supporters and leaders on the local, state, and federal level to end racial and gender preferences and classifications."[102] The names of these organizations as well as those of the various anti-preferences ballot proposals (the California Civil Rights Initiative, the Houston Civil Rights Initiative, the Washington State Civil Rights Initiative, the Florida Civil Rights Initiative, the Michigan Civil Rights Initiative) highlight Connerly's skepticism about the traditional civil rights community, which is composed of left-leaning organizations like the National Council of La Raza and the National Association for the Advancement of Colored People. These names mark an attempt to define a paradigmatic shift in how we Americans view "civil rights," extending the concept to encompass ideas that we typically think of as conservative.

Ward Connerly is the chairman of the ACRI; his two top aides there are Justin Jones, who is black, and Diane Schachterle, who is white. Justin Jones serves as the ACRI's Director of Policy and Planning. Jones grew up in Louisville, Kentucky: He is a Gen Xer whose mother hails from Jamaica and whose father comes from South Carolina. He first became involved in conservative activities while he was a college student.[103] Jones works with Diane Schachterle, the ACRI's Director of Public Affairs. Schachterle is a middle-aged woman of Northern European ancestry (she is three-quarters German and one-quarter Danish) who is a native of California's Central Valley. She emphasizes social class when she discusses the nature of disadvantage in our society. Schachterle herself comes from an agricultural family. She never received any encouragement from her high school counselors to attend college, even though she was salutatorian of her high school class.[104] Jones and Schachterle participate in forums, speak before groups, conduct media interviews, and otherwise disseminate the message of colorblind opportunity.

Strategic considerations matter very much to the anti-preferences forces. One must allocate the requisite money and develop the appropriate organization in states where one can gather enough signatures to put an initiative on the ballot that has a reasonable chance of winning and attracting national attention. Therefore, Connerly and his associates choose their targets carefully. They opted not to go into Nebraska, for instance, because it is a low-population state and there were no significant cases there that would seize the public's imagination.[105] Thus far, Connerly and company have had two high-profile victories — California's Proposition 209 (1996) and Washington's Initiative 200 (1998). They have experienced one high-profile loss: California's Proposition 54 (2003). The initiative on affirmative action failed in Houston in 1997, but Connerly was not deeply involved in that campaign. Florida, where an initiative has yet to qualify for the ballot, turned out to be a victory of sorts. Connerly's activism on the affirmative-action issue in 1999 is widely credited with spurring Florida Governor Jeb Bush to enact his "One Florida" plan in public education and contracting. Connerly, then, can serve as a catalyst to inspire political figures to effect change even in the absence of a ballot initiative.

Affirmative action is an issue that confounds both political parties, and neither Democrats nor Republicans generally want to see public referenda on affirmative action affect the tone, style, and issue agenda of national, state, and local elections. Democrats oppose such initiatives on philosophical grounds; nor do they want to antagonize their constituents in the Multicultural Left. And Republicans seem to have concluded that there is little political advantage to be gained from focusing on the affirmative-action issue, so they increasingly either oppose anti-preferences initiatives or are very quiet about them. Republicans seem happy to leave this issue to the courts, where judges appointed by GOP presidents often strike down affirmative-action programs. The Republicans' recalcitrance on this issue occurs even though the majority of whites will vote in favor of anti-preferences initiatives if they are given the chance. In any event, both sides try to frame the issue in different ways. The anti-preferences side stresses race, while the pro–affirmative action forces highlight gender. Proponents of affirmative action decry the ballot initiatives that mention "preferential treatment" instead of affirmative action as deceptive and misleading.

California's Proposition 209 (the California Civil Rights Initiative) was the first ballot measure to prohibit racial and gender preferences in public hiring, contracting, and university admissions at the state and local levels.[106] Two white academics, Glynn Custred and Tom Wood, languished in obscurity for years as they tried to get an initiative prohibiting public-sector affirmative action on the ballot. Their efforts went nowhere until after the 1994 elections. Suddenly, the prospect of an initiative on affirmative action in the nation's largest state — a must-win contest for President Bill Clinton in the 1996 election — became the subject of much media and political attention. In December 1995 Ward Connerly became chairman of what soon would be known as the Proposition 209 campaign. He took over the signature-gathering operation because he wanted to preserve SP-1, his resolution regarding admissions in the University of California system. Connerly ran the campaign well and the initiative eventually qualified for the November 1996 ballot.[107]

The campaign over Proposition 209 became quite heated during the fall of 1996. Liberals and Democrats mobilized to defeat the initiative. The pro-209 forces ran a nonpartisan campaign that helped the initiative maintain its lead in the polls. The anti-209 forces attempted to appeal to white women on the gender issue to defeat the ballot measure. And the California Republican Party may have cost the initiative some support by trying to tie Republican presidential candidate Robert Dole to it. Regardless, the initiative passed by a 54.6% to 45.4% margin in November 1996. Sixty-three percent of whites backed it, compared to 26% of African Americans, 24% of Latinos, and 39% of Asians. At this time, whites still accounted for most voters in California, so the initiative passed easily. Proposition 209 clearly became a racial issue, at least to some extent, as 66% of white men and 58% of white women voted in favor of it.[108] Affirmative action ultimately played virtually no role in California presidential politics, as Bill Clinton won the state easily and both major-party candidates rarely mentioned the issue.[109]

Affirmative action next faced an electoral test in Houston in November 1997. Edward Blum, a white investment broker, patterned Proposition A (the Houston Civil Rights Initiative) after Proposition 209 in California. Proposition A sought to end Houston's municipal contracting program for female- and minority-owned businesses (the Minority, Women and Disadvantaged Business Enterprise Program). The language of Proposition A initially characterized it as an anti-discrimination measure. As such, it received overwhelming support in the polls. However, Houston Mayor Bob Lanier, an Anglo man in his early seventies, worked indefatigably to defeat the measure. After lobbying by Lanier, the Houston City Council voted in October 1997 to alter the language of the initiative to refer to curtailing affirmative action. Then the measure suddenly became far less popular. Unlike California at the time, Houston had an Anglo plurality, not an Anglo majority (the city was then approximately 33% Latino, 26% black, and 6% Asian). While whites, as elsewhere, constituted a larger share of the Houston electorate than their share of the population, people of color, particularly African Americans, accounted for slightly less than one-half of the Houston electorate in November 1997.[110]

An unusual coalition of Houston's communities of color and its corporate and political elites banded together to defeat Proposition A by a ten-point margin. Mayor Lanier galvanized Houston's civic, business, and political elites in favor of affirmative action for a number of reasons, including the ethnic and racial diversity of contemporary Houston, the importance of having a diverse group of businesspeople in a global economy, and the racial harmony that many Houstonians felt the contracting program had fostered.[111] Lanier himself regularly delivered a potent message of inclusion that included this line: "Let's not turn back the clock to the days when guys like me got all the city's business."[112] The election results demonstrated a significantly polarized electorate on the affirmative-action issue. Approximately 55 percent of white women and

72 to 73 percent of white men voted for Proposition A. Voters of color overwhelmingly opposed it — 92 to 95 percent of African Americans voted against the ballot measure. Proposition A went down to a 55%-45% defeat, a result that many observers interpreted to mean that the momentum of the anti-preferences movement had slowed significantly.[113]

The initiative war on the issue of preferences took off next in Washington State. In March 1997 two white men (Tim Eyman and Scott Smith) filed a ballot proposal, "the Washington State Civil Rights Initiative." In the fall of 1997 Ward Connerly named conservative radio talk show host John Carlson the chairman of the campaign to pass the initiative. The American Civil Rights Coalition contributed money to cover the expenses of signature-gathers so that the measure would qualify for the ballot. Once this step occurred, the Washington Legislature decided to allow Washingtonians to vote on the initiative rather than enacting it into law by legislative fiat. Initiative 200 was very similar to Proposition 209, in that it did not mention affirmative action but rather sought to prohibit discrimination and "preferential treatment" in education, contracting, and employment at the state and local levels.[114] Initiative 200 merited substantial media attention, particularly in the aftermath of Proposition A's defeat in Houston. The media wanted to see if there was a bandwagon effect in the anti-preferences movement, or if California was solely an anomaly on this issue.

As in California, the debate over Washington's I-200 involved gender as well as race. Most Washington voters are white, so race was definitely a factor in the initiative campaign. There was a well funded $1.6 million NO!200 campaign, while Ward Connerly's ACRI and ACRC spent approximately $750,000 to promote I-200. Democratic Governor Gary Locke led the opposition campaign, which was assisted by Washington's corporate elite and a wide array of left-leaning advocacy groups. Due to the demographics of the Washington electorate, Locke and company sought to fight the battle on gender by appealing to white women. But in November 1998, Initiative 200 passed by a margin of 58.3% to 41.7%. The proposition succeeded because of its strong support from white voters, particularly white men. Voters of color opposed I-200. Whites supported I-200 because many of them felt that affirmative-action policies might "actually discriminate for minorities against whites, white men in particular."[115]

Following his success in Washington State, Connerly decided to make his next stand on the affirmative-action issue in Florida, a large, multi-ethnic state with tremendous importance in presidential politics. But the state's political leaders, both Democrats and Republicans, were immediately skeptical of Connerly's proposed Florida Civil Rights Initiative. Newly elected Republican Governor Jeb Bush was in no hurry to have an initiative on the ballot that could rally blacks and other people of color against his brother, George W. Bush, in the 2000 presidential election. Jeb Bush sought to take the wind out of Connerly's sails with the announcement of his One Florida Initiative in November 1999. It eliminated racial and gender preferences in state contracting decisions and admissions to Florida's public universities. Meanwhile, Connerly faced difficulties in terms of getting anti-preferences initiatives on the Florida ballot. In May 2000 the Florida Supreme Court had not yet ruled on the ballot proposals (as it must on all initiatives before they qualify for a statewide plebiscite). By this time, it was virtually impossible to collect the requisite signatures — 500,000 in total — to qualify the constitutional amendments for the November 2000 election. So, in May 2000, Connerly suspended the campaign for the Florida Civil Rights Initiative that year.[116]

Connerly's next high-profile initiative was Proposition 54, the Racial Privacy Initiative, which made it on to the October 2003 recall ballot in California. Diane Schachterle served as the initiative coordinator for Proposition 54.[117] Proposition 54 sought to limit the amount of information about race and ethnicity that could be collected by state and local public institutions, including schools, hospitals, and governments. The measure encountered significant opposition from doctors, teachers, civil rights groups, law enforcement organizations, and others, all of whom contended that it would be impossible to monitor and tackle ethnic and racial disparities if the initiative were enacted into law. Proposition 54 failed to pass by a 64%-36% margin, despite having led in the initial opinion polls. Forty-two percent of white voters backed the measure, compared to 30% of Latinos and 21% of African Americans. In any event, the anti–Proposition 54 forces ran a well-coordinated media campaign and dramatically outspent the advocates of colorblindness. The state's GOP leadership largely avoided discussing Proposition 54 or came out in opposition to it (as did successful Republican gubernatorial candidate Arnold Schwarzenegger). Moreover, the arguments in favor of the ballot measure were lost in the drama of the high-voltage recall campaign.[118]

The next ballot test of affirmative action is very likely to occur in Michigan. When the Supreme Court focused attention on Michigan with the two affirmative-action cases in June 2003, the Great Lakes State suddenly surged in the consciousness of the anti-preferences forces. In July 2003, Ward Connerly announced that he intended to give Michiganites an opportunity to vote on the issue of affirmative action in the November 2004 election.[119] The Michigan Republican hierarchy was unenthusiastic, to say the least, about Connerly's proposed Michigan Civil Rights Initiative (MCRI). Some Republicans, like Michigan GOP Chair Betsy DeVos, felt the initiative would be "divisive." The cynics said that the Republican Party leadership wishes to avoid energizing Democratic partisans who would come out and vote on this issue in November 2004. (Leading Republican opponents of the initiative disputed this view.)[120] The situation in Michigan illustrates how events related to ballot initiatives on affirmative action often implicate partisan politics in presidential-election years, just as they did in California in 1996 and Florida in 2000. Connerly points out that the reluctance of state and national Republicans to embrace the initiative helps his cause, by underscoring that this is not a partisan issue.[121]

The Michigan Civil Rights Initiative, should it qualify for the ballot and win passage by the Michigan electorate, will prohibit racial and gender preferences in state hiring, contracting, and university admissions. Jennifer Gratz is the director of the Michigan Civil Rights Initiative. The MCRI petition drive has been tied up in the courts over disputes regarding the language on the petition forms — supporters of the proposed initiative now hope to place it on the ballot in 2006. The MCRI faces opposition from a host of prominent Michigan politicians, including Democratic Governor Jennifer Granholm. These politicos contend that if the MCRI passes, there will be less diversity on Michigan's college campuses and that fewer women and people of color will work in state and local government. The opponents of the MCRI target Connerly and seek to discredit the ballot proposal by characterizing it as something foisted upon Michigan by outsiders from California and elsewhere. Connerly correctly points out that the MCRI will pass if it qualifies for the ballot. The polls show strong support for the initiative.[122]

During their more than nine years of activism, Connerly and the other proponents of colorblindness have contributed significantly to the dialogue on the role of race and gender in public policy. Many Americans, of course, disagree with Connerly's positions and dispute his vision for America's future. But the anti-preferences initiative campaigns have created much debate in California, Houston, Washington, Florida, Michigan, and elsewhere on the efficacy of the current efforts to expand the opportunities available to white women and members of minority groups. Proposition 209 and Initiative 200 continue to govern public policy in California and Washington, respectively. Connerly, meanwhile, regularly appears around the nation in his never-ending quest to promote what he sees as colorblind public policy. One accomplishment that Connerly points to is in the realm of nomenclature: the increasing use by journalists and others of the term "preferences" as opposed to "affirmative action." Interestingly, numerous supposedly "liberal" (according to conservatives) media outlets utilize the P-word in their coverage of affirmative action.[123]

◠

In the meantime, the types of litigation involving white males will be ever more complicated and involve newer and different types of issues. There will be more cases about who should be "counted" in terms of diversity, a term that has often been characterized in terms of race and ethnic origin. It certainly will be interesting to see how these types of cases will play out as white males predominate less and less in certain contexts. We can expect to see an upsurge of cases involving white males who may go to court on grounds other than their white maleness. Grievances based on race and/or gender might be the real source of their complaints, of course, but they may choose to focus on some other discrete characteristics, such as age or disability status, that might seem more "acceptable" and less inflammatory than white maleness in the public arena. By all accounts, legal cases involving white males and discrimination will encompass a broader set of actors and a broader set of circumstances than in the past.

Increasingly, reverse-discrimination cases involving whites focus on white females instead of white males. The growing significance of white female plaintiffs in reverse-discrimination cases is one of the most interesting developments in the realm of litigation surrounding affirmative action and related issues. There were three white male co-plaintiffs with Cheryl Hopwood in the landmark *Hopwood* decision (1996), but the media focused mainly on Hopwood.[124] Similarly, there was a white male co-plaintiff (Patrick Hamacher) with Jennifer Gratz in the Supreme Court case involving undergraduate admissions at the University of Michigan: *Gratz v. Bollinger* (2003). Gratz, though, received the lion's share of publicity in the case.[125] Barbara Grutter, a white woman, was the plaintiff of the other Michigan case (*Grutter v. Bollinger*) regarding admissions at the University of Michigan Law School.[126] White male plaintiffs lack the symbolic resonance of white female plaintiffs in such cases. White conservatives may feel that white female defendants are more attractive candidates for making their allegations of "reverse discrimination" to the American public. The inclusion of white females under the rubric of "reverse discrimination" makes the issue seem more mainstream, by expanding the constituency of potential "victims" from 35 percent to 70 percent of the U.S. population.

The results of the presidential election of 2004 will play an important role in determining the future of American jurisprudence regarding racial issues. During the last 28 years, after all, Democrats have held the presidency for 12 years and the Republicans for 16 years. The presence of Democratic appointees on the nation's courts generally leads to decisions that favor affirmative action. Republican judicial appointees, conversely, are more likely to be skeptical of affirmative action. So if President George W. Bush wins his reelection bid, the judiciary will continue the rightward tilt that it began to take during the Reagan-Bush years (1981 to 1993). The balance of power in Congress is such that it will be difficult for a president of either party to place many rigid ideologues on the federal bench. In any event, the country is closely divided on the affirmative-action issue, and the Court's decisions in *Gratz* and *Grutter* last year accurately reflected America's mood.

In the political arena, we will continue to see careful targeting of specific groups of white males, either as white males or on the basis of some other characteristic (e.g., their parental status, their sexual orientation, or their generational cohort). We can expect to see fewer explicit appeals to white male voters (à la Jesse Helms's "white hands" ad in 1990), as their percentage of the electorate becomes smaller. Interestingly, white males can become the invisible Other in a Democratic appeal, as they were in feminist criticisms of the white maleness of the U.S. Senate in general and the Senate Judiciary Committee in particular during the Thomas-Hill hearings in 1991; this issue resonated with some Democratic primary voters in 1992.[127] We are also going to see more situations in which white males are a coveted voter group, as in the historic 2003 Louisiana gubernatorial campaign between Democrat Kathleen Blanco and Republican Bobby Jindal.

The GOP in particular faces interesting constituency pressures in response to the changing demographics of the American population — and the American electorate. While whites still account for about 80 percent of the voters in most national elections, that percentage slowly decreases each year. In a closely contested national election, white males often account for about 50 percent of the Republican vote totals. However, as the percentage of white males decreases in the American population, the Republican Party faces the challenge of winning greater support from women and people of color.[128] "We've taken white guys about as far as that group can go," said former Republican National Committee Chairman Richard Bond in 2001. "We are in need of diversity, women, Latino, African American, Asian. The degree to which Bush and congressional Republicans can ground the notion of compassionate conservatism to appeal to women, Latinos, African Americans and Asians, that is where the future of the Republican Party is."[129] Republicans will not win a significant number of votes from African Americans anytime in the near future, so they focus much of their outreach on Latinos, who are growing rapidly in numbers and occupy a critical role in many key states, including Texas, Arizona, Florida, Illinois, Nevada, New York, California, and New Jersey.

Just when the Republicans thought they were locked out of contention in California politics for the foreseeable future, along came Arnold Schwarzenegger. The moderate Republican's star power and inclusive campaign, coupled with the unpopularity of the Democratic incumbent, Gray Davis, combined to make Schwarzenegger a runaway winner in the October 2003 recall election. The Austrian immigrant defeated Democrat Cruz Bustamante by a 49%-31% margin. Conservative Republican Tom McClintock received 13% of the vote. White male voters were a critical component of both the Schwarzenegger and McClintock coalitions.[130] Still, we should not assume that there will be a Republican resurgence in California just yet: Schwarzenegger is an unusually gifted politician and his election took place under unique circumstances.

~ chapter nine ~

The Perils of Prejudice

When Richard Butler left Southern California and moved to North Idaho in 1973, few of his new neighbors probably thought that the middle-aged aerospace engineer would bring international attention to their community. However, northern Idaho and the Inland Northwest began to receive unwanted news coverage in the early 1980s because Butler had established the Church of Jesus Christ – Christian and its political arm, Aryan Nations, on his 20-acre compound near Hayden Lake, Idaho. The compound became a gathering place for extremists throughout the Western world. Pastor Butler, as his followers call him, preaches a racist and anti-Semitic Christian Identity message, that Jews are "the spawn of Satan" and people of color are "mud people." Butler's presence contributed most to the caricatures of northern Idaho. During the last two decades, this area has been unfairly stereotyped as a national center of activity for white separatists, survivalists, and supremacists, due to the presence of a small number of such individuals there. They were attracted by the area's relative isolation, its natural beauty, its racial homogeneity, and its reputation in white-supremacist circles for being the future base of an all-white homeland.[1]

The global image of Idaho as a bastion of extremists, hatemongers, and malcontents dates back to the early 1980s, when Butler and his acolytes began to flex their muscles in the region. They disseminated their message to the world through such means as publishing, a prison ministry, and, later, the Web. Gatherings of the so-called Aryans at Butler's compound for the annual "Congresses" and their periodic marches in Coeur d'Alene, drew international attention to this beautiful part of America. But the vast majority of North Idahoans eschews racism and keeps its distance from the white supremacists. Anecdotal evidence suggests that North Idaho's undeserved reputation for hate has hurt efforts to attract tourists and businesses to the area. In fact, North Idahoans may be more sensitive to human rights issues than many other Americans due to the unfair stereotypes that exist about their region in the national consciousness.[2] The Aryans were consistently opposed by many people in North Idaho, particularly members of the Kootenai County Task Force on Human Relations. In 1981 concerned citizens formed the Task Force in response to instances of ethnic and religious harassment.[3] Kootenai County, Idaho, by the way, has 108,685 residents, 94.4% of whom are white.

A troika of three sixtysomething white men (attorney Norman Gissel, Realtor Marshall Mend, and academic Tony Stewart) has been the most consistently involved group of human rights activists in Kootenai County during the last two decades.[4] Gissel is the historian, Mend the salesman, and Stewart the strategist of the trio.[5] Marshall Mend and Tony Stewart were involved in the Task Force from its beginning in 1981. Mend, a gregarious salesman who owns a thriving real estate firm in Hayden, Idaho, is a Los Angeles native of Russian-Jewish descent. Likewise, Tony Stewart has taught political science at North Idaho College in Coeur d'Alene since 1970; the courtly raconteur grew up in Robbinsville, North Carolina, and moved to the Northwest for graduate school. Both Mend and Stewart became activists out of civic-mindedness and their desire to support neighbors who had been attacked by bigots. Norman Gissel came aboard in 1984. Gissel, a burly man with a Danish surname who hails from Sandpoint, Idaho, has long been active in civil rights causes and the Task Force was a logical fit for him. His wife, Diana, is the current president of the Task Force. Tony Stewart is the organization's secretary.

Few community human rights activists anywhere in the Western world have worked for so long, with as much success, and attracted so much attention as have Mend, Gissel, and Stewart. With the exception of their professional and family commitments over the years, these three men have spent all their free time in the last two decades working on human rights issues. In a live-and-let-live conservative atmosphere, Mend, Gissel, and Stewart rallied the community against Butler. By doing so, they made it clear to the world time and time again that Butler and his followers had very, very few adherents in the region. Still, the stereotypes remained. White supremacists in North Idaho consider Norman Gissel and Tony Stewart to be the ultimate race traitors. Gissel and Stewart, after all, are white Christian men who work for "the enemy," the most significant betrayal imaginable to white nationalists and separatists. All three men have routinely received death threats from their adversaries. They were undeterred by the challenges; a desire for justice and an effort to preserve the good name of their community seem to have inspired Mend, Gissel, and Stewart to work with so much dedication on these issues.

Gissel, Mend, Stewart, and their compatriots wisely never engaged the Aryans in public confrontations over the years lest they help the Aryans to free publicity. The human rights activists refused to give Butler's organization any exposure, something that undoubtedly occurred every time a crowd of angry, out-of-town counterdemonstrators confronted the Aryans. A series of creative strategies was employed to combat Aryan Nations; many of these were formulated by Tony Stewart in concert with Gissel, Mend, and others. In April 1989, while the Aryan Nations convened a meeting of neo-Nazis at the compound, the Task Force sponsored a weeklong series of events in Kootenai County to commemorate the twentieth anniversary of the Idaho Human Rights Commission. Similarly, in July 1998, the human rights activists responded to the Aryans' march through downtown Coeur d'Alene with "Lemons to Lemonade," a fund-raising campaign that sought pledges for every minute the Aryans marched; in doing so, they raised $35,000 for human rights work. The activists' unique approach and nonpartisan orientation enabled them to build significant good will in the community.

Aryan Nations no longer represents a threat to the good name of North Idaho, as the neo-Nazi organization is in decline. The beginning of the end for the Aryan Nations dates back to July 1998, when Butler's guards assaulted a mother and son (Victoria and Jason Keenan) whose car backfired outside the group's compound. Eventually, Victoria Keenan filed a civil suit against Richard Butler and the Aryan Nations in Kootenai County District Court because of the attack on her and her son. Norman Gissel represented the Keenans pro bono; he donated over 2,000 hours of his time to work on their case. The suit was prosecuted by Coeur d'Alene attorney Kenneth Howard and a team of lawyers from the Southern Poverty Law Center, led by the famed litigator Morris Dees. In September 2000 the jury of Kootenai County residents responded with a unanimous verdict against Butler and the Aryan Nations; the neo-Nazi leader and his organization faced a $6.3 million judgment that effectively put them out of business. The Keenans received Butler's main asset, the Aryan Nations compound. The philanthropist Greg Carr, a native of Idaho Falls, Idaho, purchased the 20-acre compound from the Keenans for $250,000 in 2001. Carr contributed another $25,000 for cleanup of the compound, as well as $1 million to the Human Rights Education Institute in Coeur d'Alene. Tony Stewart and Rob Bishop, a contractor who worked for Carr, spent many hours restoring this beautiful, pristine tract of land, which is now widely referred to as the Peace Park.

Gissel, Mend, Stewart, and their compatriots continue to work hard to promote tolerance, inclusion, and equal rights in the Northwest. Since the verdict against Aryan Nations, the three men have been in demand as speakers in different parts of America, particularly in the Inland Northwest and surrounding areas. Aryan Nations, meanwhile, is bedeviled by factional disputes, declining membership, and financial difficulties limiting its effectiveness among white supremacists. Butler, now in his mid-eighties, suffers from ill health.[6] Meanwhile, a human rights center will open in Coeur d'Alene in the near future. (The center will chronicle the history of North Idaho's human rights movement and, according to Marshall Mend, "will promote human rights in this country and around the world.")[7] Tony Stewart is president of the Human Rights Education Institute board, which oversees the Center. Indeed, Stewart, Gissel, Mend, and the other human rights activists in North Idaho seek to make Coeur d'Alene an internationally recognized center of human rights activity, a fitting capstone to their decades of dedicated and successful advocacy on behalf of equality and human dignity.[8]

ON THE FAR RIGHT

Between approximately 1:15 p.m. and 1:30 p.m. on the afternoon of October 23, 1984, three members of the Hall County, Nebraska, Sheriff's Department attempted unsuccessfully to serve replevin papers to Arthur Kirk at his 240-acre farm outside of Cairo (pronounced KEER-oh), a small town amid the wheat fields of central Nebraska 20 miles north of Interstate 80. Kirk's repeated refusals to come up with a sufficient payment for a note held by Norwest Bank Grand Island led to the replevin papers. The three law enforcement officers left the Kirk residence after their testy encounter with the belligerent farmer. They returned to Grand Island and eventually obtained an arrest warrant from Hall County Judge Weaver. At that time, Judge Weaver advised them to use the SWAT team to handle the Kirk matter; Kirk, after all, had threatened the law enforcement personnel. By 8:00 p.m., the SWAT team had arrived at the Kirk property. The SWAT team members began preparing for a siege. That evening, telephone negotiations occurred between Kirk and law enforcement. From 9:00 p.m. to 9:23 p.m., Kirk spoke to his wife, Deloris, by telephone (fearing for her safety, the police had not allowed her to return home). Kirk then left the house and charged the SWAT team, firing an automatic weapon. The SWAT team returned fire and Kirk was hit. With two bullet wounds, he soon bled to death. By 9:46 p.m., the standoff was over.[9]

During the telephone negotiations, the 49-year-old farmer of Irish and German ancestry offered his interlocutors a profane soliloquy in which he blamed Jews for his financial predicament, ostensibly because they ran the world and arranged the financial structures so that it was impossible for a white Christian man such as himself to make a living. Many American farmers faced hard times during the 1980s, but most of them did not blame their troubles on Jews and international conspiracies, as did Kirk. During his telephone exchange with a member of the Nebraska State Police in the minutes before he died during the evening standoff, Kirk's anti-Semitic invective and defiant resistance to the police amassed outside reflected the conspiratorial worldview he had developed as a result of his involvement in such organizations as the Posse Comitatus and the National Agricultural Press Association. Kirk frequently attacked Jews in his defiant exchanges with the law enforcement official. He apparently thought the Israeli Mossad was assembled against him and prepared to storm his home.

Over the years Kirk had seized upon the canards of the far right, which blamed Jews, bankers, and international conspiracies for many farmers' inability to stay afloat in the worst crisis to hit rural America since the 1930s. Once his financial situation had worsened, Kirk turned to the Posse Comitatus, an antitax, anti-Semitic, anti-government group popular in certain sections of rural America. When authorities searched the Kirk farm, they found 27 weapons. The Kirks' kitchen table was laden with mounds of literature, including a copy of the anti-Semitic *Protocols of the Elders of Zion,* antigovernment publications from the Posse Comitatus, and pamphlets outlining various types of conspiracy theories. Indeed, Kirk viewed banks, lawyers, the justice system, and the government through the prism of the antigovernment movement's conspiratorial mindset. Arthur Kirk felt much anger, hatred, and frustration that he turned on the authorities.[10] The Kirk shooting was another example of how extremist ideological beliefs could drive a farmer to the brink, as had been the case with Gordon Kahl, the anti-tax protester from North Dakota who had murdered two federal marshals and later died in a shootout with authorities in 1983.[11]

Kirk joined Kahl in the pantheon of far-right heroes when he charged the SWAT team and was mowed down by the assembled law enforcement officials. Deloris Kirk traveled throughout the Midwest, speaking to farmers and tax protesters about her take on the shooting. The evangelist Larry Jones and Rick Elliott of the National Agricultural Press Association were some of the individuals who assisted Mrs. Kirk as she disseminated her views and painted an image of her husband as a martyr. Kirk's death elicited controversy in Nebraska; therefore, Governor Bob Kerrey named Samuel Van Pelt, a retired judge with a stellar reputation, to review the matter. Judge Van Pelt assembled a meticulously prepared 607-page report on Arthur Kirk's death that exonerated the authorities of any wrongdoing.[12] Many people in the Farm Belt did not endorse Kirk's anti-Semitic views by any means, but they sympathized with his predicament. Kirk's death was one of the widely cited developments of the agricultural crisis of the 1980s, as it intersected with the largely unsuccessful efforts of extremist groups to win recruits among white farmers during that period.

Racism, extremism, and anti-Semitism continue to be important topics of discussion in our multicultural society. Today there is very little overt racism, extremism, or anti-Semitism in America. To be sure, racism takes many different shapes and forms, and one's perspective on its prevalence in American society depends, to a large extent, on the ideological predilections of the observer. Racial conservatives tend to see little racism and argue that a person, by virtue of his own efforts, can overcome any existing barriers. Racial liberals, though, posit that racism is a defining feature of American life and, accordingly, they believe that we must enact color-conscious public policies to overcome it. People in the middle often acknowledge the importance of race in determining one's life chances, but they also argue that such factors as social class assume great importance as well. Even as race seems to have joined politics and religion as topics that one dare not discuss with strangers, it is difficult to find anyone who holds or expresses overtly racist views in positions of authority at any high level of American society.

We cannot quantify with any precision the number of white males who endorse the ideas disseminated by white supremacists. It is safe to say from all existing empirical and anecdotal evidence that very few white males would ever engage in violence against someone based on that person's ethnicity, race, religion, national origin, or sexual orientation. Very few white Americans, as with members of any other group, could be considered overtly racist by almost any standard of objective opinion. (Of course, some leftists would say that anyone who holds conservative views on racially tinged issues, e.g., affirmative action and bilingual education, is an unreconstructed racist.) In any event, a white person who seeks to inoculate himself against charges of racism by mentioning that he has many friends of color may be seen by multiculturalists as insensitive, clumsy, and even racist.

The emphasis on tolerance and inclusion has become so pervasive in our society that many racists feel obligated to adopt the language of multiculturalism to defend their views. They contend that they do not "hate" anyone and use catchphrases like "cultural preservation" when they discuss their exclusionary agenda that favors European-American Christian heterosexuals. The haters often eschew using racial epithets and refrain from making crude racial jokes, at least in public forums. This "highbrow" approach distinguishes them, they say, from the stereotypical Klansman of yesteryear. Instead, they use code words and ambiguous expressions to communicate their bigotry. In any event, the charge of racism is a formidable one in Multicultural America. To be a racist is so uncool and unfashionable that many white supremacists insist they are "racialists," not racists — a distinction without a difference in the eyes of most Americans.[13]

It is a matter of controversy about what, exactly, leads white Americans to hold and espouse racist views these days. The debates over these issues involve political considerations, to some extent, because once we establish the baseline of what is considered racist, then there is the matter of what kinds of ideas and events contribute to racism. Virtually everyone in the American mainstream agrees that any figure (à la Trent Lott) that appears to evince nostalgia for the Jim Crow era should be censured for his beliefs. Not everyone in the American mainstream, though, concurs that the Confederate flag symbolizes racism in every context. Virtually everyone in the American mainstream agrees that there are no IQ differences between and among racial and ethnic groups. Not everyone in the American mainstream, however, concurs that a nonracial, principled advocacy of curbs on immigration is racist. These kinds of discussions often are affected by the context of, and parties involved in, the particular dialogue on the issue.

Mississippi Senator Trent Lott is typically regarded as a mainstream conservative Republican, although his seeming nostalgia for certain aspects of the Jim Crow South created such an uproar that Republicans compelled him to take a less-prominent role in the U.S. Senate. But Republicans did not make him into a complete political outcast. The late William Pierce, though, was clearly an extremist who made no pretension to aspiring to participate in the American mainstream. The former academic physicist and founder of the neo-Nazi National Alliance achieved great prominence in the white-supremacist underground because he authored the best-selling racist novel *The Turner Diaries* (1978) and its less popular sequel, *Hunter* (1989).[14] In sum, there is a general consensus that any figure who routinely — and explicitly — disparages people from other racial groups is ineligible for inclusion in our nation's cultural, ideological, and political mainstream.[15]

The news media regularly devote far more coverage to racists and racist rallies than their level of public support seems to justify. Likewise, these topics receive significant media interest since the racist rallies make for media spectacles. The antiracist counterdemonstrators often outnumber the racists ten to one at such rallies. The police who handle crowd control typically outnumber them as well. Antiracist organizations frequently ignore the racists, who thrive on media attention. The media cover the bigots and extremists because they are unusual; very few Americans, after all, agree with their hateful philosophy. This is not to say that racism is not a threat to people, by any means. But the typical American views bigots and extremists as oddities and ideological misfits. This makes them newsworthy and amplifies the volume by which we hear (and see) their views expressed in the media. As the sociologist Kathleen Blee writes, "While racist groups are becoming more visible, their messages of racial hatred and white supremacy find little support in the rest of society."[16]

In the late 1990s it was estimated that 100,000 to 200,000 Americans belonged to white supremacist groups, in that they were active supporters who attended meetings, made financial contributions, and purchased literature. When it comes to the number of people in specific types of racist groups, the estimates vary significantly.[17] According to the Southern Poverty Law Center (SPLC), there were "708 active hate groups in the United States in the year 2002." The SPLC only counted organizations that were active in 2002, with such efforts as rallies, marches, meetings, speeches, leafleting, criminal acts, or publishing literature. The SPLC's list includes Neo-Nazi, Ku Klux Klan, racist skinhead, Christian Identity, black separatist, and neo-Confederate groups.[18]

White supremacists thrive in the correctional system, in part because white men in our prisons feel minority status quite acutely. Correctional institutions, after all, are one part of America where white males often find themselves outnumbered. While most white male prisoners probably never affiliate with racist prison gangs or adopt the views of white supremacists, there seems to be a higher-than-average percentage of white male racists in the correctional system. Some white prisoners, to be sure, join gangs or ally themselves with white-supremacist prison gangs (e.g., the Aryan Brotherhood) for purposes of protection, not ideology. Others join religious sects, as in racist neopagan groups such as Odinism or Asatru, in order to have religious privileges inside prison. Observers remained concerned, with good reason, about what happens when racist prison gang members rejoin the general population after serving their time.[19]

Overall, the radical right is a complex aggregation of extremists who vary tremendously in their ideological predilections and the issues on which they focus. They generally share a few beliefs in common: suspicion of the federal government; concern about the changing demographic composition of the U.S. population; disdain for multiculturalism in general and diversity in particular; and feelings of antipathy toward Jews, gays and lesbians, and people of color.[20] Racist, nativist, and extremist social and political movements (perhaps most prominently, the Ku Klux Klan in the 1920s) have occupied positions of significance in American life at various times in the nineteenth and twentieth centuries.[21] There are significant personal, ideological, and factional rivalries, differences, and points of contention between and among the groups of the radical right. Groups constantly come and go, and rise and fall in response to such factors as government prosecutions of extremists, the peccadilloes of specific movement figures, changing aspects of the political and cultural landscape, and even the health of movement leaders.

White nationalists recruit young people through such methods as the Internet, white power music, white nationalist comic books, and face-to-face recruitment. It is possible that white youths may decide to join a hate group because they identify with the rebelliousness implicit in such a decision; by doing so, they may satisfy some psychological wants. If they are part of certain social milieus — namely, ones in which society is changing quickly and whites who feel disenfranchised — the white-supremacist message might appeal to them. White supremacists try to communicate their message to potential white recruits by seizing upon increases in minority populations, a rise in crime rates, and opposition to racial preferences. White-supremacist recruiters do best among young whites who feel angry, frustrated, and oppressed. The new breed of white supremacist often focuses at least some of his recruiting energy on young people as well as educated and affluent white adults.[22]

Those individuals who belong to white-supremacist organizations are not dramatically different from the American population as a whole when it comes to income, occupation, and education. Communities that suffer from economic problems are particularly fertile grounds for hate groups — still, white-supremacy groups recruit members from a wide variety of class backgrounds. But it is possible for Americans of all different socioeconomic backgrounds (excepting the wealthy) to see themselves as facing limited opportunities as a result of their perception that they have limited opportunities for socioeconomic mobility.[23] In any event, most white supremacists limit their activities to talk. There are those radical rightists, however, who practice "leaderless resistance" in their war on the system.[24] Acting by themselves or in concert with a few accomplices, lone wolves seek to kill people in many cases to make a specific "political" point. The list of lone wolves includes such individuals as Timothy McVeigh, Benjamin Smith, Buford Furrow, Eric Rudolph, and others. And there are white racist serial killers (Joseph Paul Franklin) and white racist rampage killers (Richard Baumhammers).[25] Few Americans agree with people who hold extreme views, a factor that contributes to the feelings of acute marginalization felt by many on the radical right.

Hate crimes are an important part of any discussion of bias in modern-day American society. White males commit 62 percent of domestic hate crimes, according to Brian Levin, a criminologist who is an expert on the topic.[26] In response to a question about hate-crime victimization by race, Levin has this to say:

> ... [A] guesstimate would be about half of hate crime victims are white, although most are attacked because of some other characteristic besides their race. The number of people attacked because they are white according to the latest FBI figures (2002) was 910 victims. There were 4,580 total victims attacked because of their race, and 9,222 total reported victims for all hate crime. However, there were 1,084 Jewish victims attacked because they were Jewish, 1,487 attacked because they were gay, lesbian, or bisexual, 1,409 victims attacked because of ethnicity (of which 639 were Hispanic), and 50 attacked because of disability. The FBI does not tell us what the race of these other victims are, but I think it is safe to presume nearly every anti-Jewish hate crime had a white victim, and the majority of the anti-Hispanic, anti-gay, lesbian, and anti-disability are white as well.[27]

The white right, basically, could be termed the white male right or, more specifically, the white male Christian heterosexual right. Most white-supremacist groups, after all, advocate patriarchal beliefs and structures. Men typically hold most or all of the leadership positions.

The typical white male supremacist feels entitled to social, economic, political, and military power. He feels this way for a variety of reasons,
including religious fiat, moral legitimacy, biological destiny, and historical legacy. However, there is a significant disconnect for white male
supremacists, since they believe they are powerless. Their fathers — white
men all — surrendered this power, according to their twisting thinking,
while the federal government working on behalf of women, immigrants,
and people of color stole it from them. The omnipresent villains in this
bigoted worldview are Jews who, the white supremacists allege, dominate
global economic and political affairs. Many racist groups seek to recruit
white women, who, after all, are important to their efforts to promote
white supremacy. Today women account for much of the membership of
organized white racist groups and, in some cases, hold leadership posts
as well.[28]

White male supremacists construct restrictive notions of "appropriate
gender and sexual behavior" in order to preserve their conceptions of
racial purity. They typically venerate white women as "procreators of
the race," view white men as destined to be "white saviors," and believe that non-Christians, people of color, and gays and lesbians threaten
their hegemony. Discussions of race, gender, and sexuality in white-
supremacist discourse reinforce white, male, heterosexual power, a factor
that structures discussions of such matters as abortion, homosexuality,
and racial miscegenation. Male white supremacists are obsessed with
maintaining what they see as the "purity" of the white race, so they seek
to control women and reproduction. They particularly despise interracial
dating and marriage. After all, interracial sexuality and racially mixed
children constitute threats to the racially restricted world desired by white
supremacists.[29] Abby L. Ferber writes, "Responding to what is perceived
as a threat to both racial and gendered certainties, the contemporary
white supremacist movement is primarily concerned with rearticulating
white, male identity and privilege."[30]

At the same time, a number of venues have proven to be hospitable
for the ideas of the radical right, even as white-supremacist groups have
fallen into decline in many respects. Leonard Zeskind, a leading expert
on the radical right, contends that mainstream politics and organizations are influenced by some white-supremacist ideas. He posits that
the blurring of boundaries between mainstream conservative ideas and
the discourses of white supremacists weakens racist organizations. This
happened before in American history, says Zeskind, when segregation
counteracted the advances of Reconstruction and led to the demise of

the nineteenth-century Ku Klux Klan. Sam Francis, an influential intellectual voice of the radical right, argues that the movement's future will be determined by such organizations as the Council of Conservative Citizens and American Renaissance, a pseudo-scholarly journal and associated foundation, which present a white-supremacist message in relatively mainstream terms, at least compared to the Aryan Nations and the National Alliance, for instance.[31] Similarly, the Southern Poverty Law Center's *Intelligence Report* recently criticized Peter Brimelow, the founder and president of the Center for American Unity and its influential Web page (VDARE) for being overly cozy with racial extremists.[32]

It is, of course, difficult to predict the future of the radical right in this country. Mark Potok writes:

> The fact is, the radical right seems to be here to stay. Even as some sectors of the movement founder, other areas — anti-immigrant groups, neo-Confederates, the more genteel "academic racists" and others — are expanding. The increasing hegemony of multicultural ideology, the political and economic effects of advancing globalization, and a host of other factors have fostered an angry backlash that is helping the movement to grow. In fact, what we are witnessing is the realignment of the radical right — a reshuffling of groups, leaders and causes.[33]

Approximately 40 years after the civil rights movement won some of its greatest victories, white supremacy continues to be with us, but it no longer commands the de facto support of large sections of the country, as it once did.

In any event, white males, even the most disgruntled ones, are not likely to ever turn to hate groups in large numbers. To be sure, there will always be some young white men who embrace white supremacism during their teenage years or college years. The fact that racism is so politically incorrect these days lends it credibility with some who wish to be different. Yet few white Americans would ever embrace hate and extremism as ideologies. Such ideas are considered to be so abhorrent by the vast majority of Americans that few people consider them seriously. Likewise, most of the messages in our society reinforce the ideas of tolerance, inclusion, and equality. The fact is, that most young people (and Americans of all ages) reject hate and haters for a variety of reasons, including the ultimate teenage put-down — that the bigots are "losers."

An anecdote from my days at a public high school in small-town Wisconsin comes to mind. It was a nice day in the spring of 1991, and a bunch of us (six or seven white male high school juniors and seniors) were waiting for the lunch period to begin, as we left physical education class. One of the young men in the group had swastikas painted on his combat boots. Another young white man, a devotee of hip-hop music, asked him with more than a hint of disgust in his voice, "Do you really believe in that stuff?" The young neo-Nazi wannabe quietly and somewhat sheepishly, it seemed, assented with a nod of his head. No one said anymore and the encounter was over. Both young men had the fair complexions and blond hair that white supremacists typically celebrate as the apotheosis of the "Aryan ideal." One had chosen to advocate tolerance, the other to support bigotry (although he never proselytized among his classmates, to my knowledge). But the hip-hop fan spoke with the confidence that his peers supported his position, as they all did, of course.

WHITE WRONGS

Don Black is a high-tech maven of white supremacy. A giant cross superimposed against a circle with the words "White Pride World Wide" greets visitors to Black's Stormfront.org – "White Nationalist Resource Page." "Stormfront," writes Black, "is a resource for those courageous men and women fighting to preserve their White Western culture, ideals and freedom of speech and association — a forum for planning strategies and forming political and social groups to ensure victory."[34] *Stormfront.org* is a detailed Web site, with such options for surfers as a Discussion Forum, Women's Page, Kids Page, Links Portal, and other pages. There are German-language and Spanish-language pages on the Web site. Black avoids using racial slurs in his writings and public pronouncements. He believes that white Americans, in all likelihood, need to form a separate, racially homogeneous state to preserve their culture and heritage. This view, not surprisingly, does not appear very often in the news media, and he thinks that *Stormfront.org* and its electronic peers provide an important pro-white counterpoint to the mainstream media.[35]

A native of Alabama in his early fifties, Black's involvement in white supremacy dates back to his high school years. As a University of Alabama student, he helped David Duke rejuvenate the Knights of the Ku Klux Klan. In 1981 Black and a number of associates from the world of hate plotted to invade Dominica, a sovereign nation in the Caribbean. They were arrested for this ploy. From 1982 to 1985 Black was incarcerated in a federal prison as a result of his role in the failed invasion attempt. During his time in the Texas prison, Black enrolled in a local college's course on computers and he learned computer-programming skills. Black was released from prison in 1985. Soon thereafter, he abandoned the Klan even as he remained involved in different white-supremacist groups and activities. In March 1995, he founded *Stormfront.org* — it is based out of his home in West Palm Beach, Florida. This tall, reserved man with a muscular build and graying dark brown hair is married to David Duke's ex-wife. Black owns and operates a consulting business. *Stormfront.org* receives approximately 20,000 hits each week. He does encounter some dissenters — the Black family periodically receives bomb threats and hackers have attempted to vandalize *Stormfront.org*.[36]

Black has a junior partner in his racist enterprise: his red-haired teenage son, Derek, who is the Webmaster of *Stormfront.org for Kids*.[37] White supremacists seek to use the Web to win converts among children and young adults, a coveted, important, and impressionable demographic group. In doing so, Derek Black works closely with his racist father. Don Black is proud of Derek, who parrots his father's white-pride message in teenage language on the Web site. Young Derek has been in home school since the third grade, with his mother, Chloe Black, teaching his lessons to him. Derek Black criticizes public schools for their supposed mediocrity, for exposing white students to nonwhite students who might physically attack them, and for not teaching them pride in their race and its accomplishments. Not surprisingly, the younger Black mentions that he receives hate mail as a result of his controversial beliefs. Derek Black says that American public school teachers do not focus enough, in his opinion, on the contributions made by whites to world history.[38]

As a result of *Stormfront.org,* Don Black has gained a reputation as one of the nation's most prominent white nationalists, particularly during the period from 1995 to the present. Indeed, Black regularly appears on U.S. television shows. Today the aging former Klansman enjoys tremendous reach in the radical right, here and abroad. Jeffrey Kaplan, for one, describes Black's Web site as "the cyberspace flagship of the racist right."[39] Indeed, *Stormfront.org* is the most popular racist site on the Internet.[40] Black pioneered global outreach among white supremacists. *Stormfront.org* was the first significant U.S. hate site on the Web. The history of racist Internet sites will undoubtedly mark the appearance of *Stormfront.org* as "the beginning of an era in which racist propaganda is easily available almost anywhere in the world, regardless of local laws," according to the *Intelligence Report*.[41] Black, not surprisingly, posits that the radical racist right has benefited tremendously from the Internet.[42]

Don Black's influence on, and significance in, the radical right shows no signs of abating, as he attempts to promote transnational white racial solidarity through the Web.

Indeed, there are increasing interconnections between and among white radical rightists across national boundaries, particularly since the end of the Cold War. Many white supremacists increasingly see race as more significant than nationality in their ideological worldview, a belief that naturally promotes international cooperation among the members of the radical right. Such ideas as Holocaust denial and pan-Aryanism, and such media as the Internet and white power music fuel this transnational cooperation. American racists, including David Duke, Gary "Gerhard" Lauck, Tom Metzger, and William Pierce, have worked to promote international ties between the U.S. radical right and its foreign counterparts.[43] There are significant symbolic and stylistic similarities between American racists and their European counterparts. Neo-Nazi youth in Germany adopted Confederate flag insignia and Ku Klux Klan imagery. German skinheads used such English-language phrases as "White Power" and "White Aryan Resistance." German white supremacists and U.S. neo-Nazis had face-to-face meetings to discuss strategy; they also maintained contact via fax, e-mail, and the telephone. White supremacists in Europe and the United States were excited by the end of the Cold War, because it reconfigured the Western issue agenda and led them to feel they might have more opportunities to reach people in the new geopolitical environment.[44]

Anti-Semitism is a constant among white supremacists. Most American and European supremacists intensely dislike Jews and the State of Israel. White supremacists, in fact, usually do not consider Jews to be "white." Holocaust denial is a staple of the radical right, here and abroad. American Holocaust deniers benefit from free-speech protections and the institutionalized nature of Holocaust denial in the United States, in contrast to their European sympathizers, who face far more restrictive laws regarding Holocaust denial and racially inflammatory statements.[45] Indeed, the Euro-American radical right is obsessed by anti-Semitic ideas and philosophies. The transatlantic racists often venerate Nazi Germany and fear that the "Aryan race" will soon become extinct.[46] Another familiar discourse within the Euro-American radical right (and in other parts of the world as well) is the *Protocols of the Elders of Zion,* an anti-Semitic screed that falsely purports to document the Jewish plan to take over the world. In the era of the Internet, anti-Semites and anti-Zionists frequently cite the *Protocols* in their attacks on Jews and the State of Israel.[47]

The First Amendment to the U.S. Constitution protects hate speech as a legal form of expression, unless the speaker or writer crosses the line and actually commits violence against another person. Such nations as France and Germany criminalize hate speech, making it far more difficult for European haters to voice their opinions in speeches and writings than is the case for their American counterparts.[48] The United States offers significant protections for hatemongers because our legal system generally does not censure hate speech. Due to the Internet, the U.S. and European legal systems have increasing opportunities to come into conflict. Any American can post bigoted content on Web pages and Web sites for access (provided that it meets with the approval of his or her Internet Service Provider's terms of access) by an international audience, one that includes people who live in European nations, where such material is largely prohibited by law.[49]

For more than two decades, American extremists have used computer technology to network with each other and their like-minded compatriots overseas.[50] The first communication advance used by white supremacists in the computer age occurred with computer bulletin board systems (BBSs) in the 1980s. Such groups as the Aryan Nations and the White Aryan Resistance used BBSs to disseminate their racist messages. Online discussion boards supplanted BBSs as the preferred means of communication for racists and extremists by the early 1990s. The public usually can participate in the discussion boards to rebut or respond to messages. During the mid-1990s, antigovernment groups began using discussion boards to complement other means of communication media, such as fax networks and short-wave radio transmissions.[51] The computer-savvy members of the radical right have enabled people with these political views to reach potentially millions of people who otherwise would not have had access to their message of hate and division.

The Internet is popular among extremists for numerous reasons. Firstly, it costs little and one can present and distribute information in a high-quality kind of way. Secondly, one can specifically target messages and information to self-selected audiences. Thirdly, the Internet allows extremists to develop the illusion of a community of extremist believers. Fourthly, the haters can distribute material globally without trifling with jurisdictional issues related to national boundaries. Fifthly, extremist activity on the Web reinforces the message of traditional media (radio, cable television) and offers a potentially larger audience. Consequently, the Internet is one of the most potent tools in the extremist arsenal, here and abroad.[52]

Contemporary extremists often network with each other, disseminating their ideological messages, and attempting to effect radical change through their usage of the Internet: e-mail, hacking, research, chat rooms, hidden instructions, private message boards, and listservs (closed e-mail networks). Online extremists enjoy important free-speech protections unless they advocate violence in concrete, as opposed to abstract, terms. The expert Mark Potok points out that the Internet has limitations as a recruitment tool — people are more likely to join hate groups as a result of interacting with racists, attending speeches by prominent extremists, and going to white power music concerts. The Internet, to be sure, is a powerful marketing tool for the multimedia offerings of hate groups, as in the National Alliance.[53]

U.S. hate sites certainly are accessed by racists throughout the world. The Southern Poverty Law Center counted 443 "active hate web sites in the United States in the year 2002." This list includes 64 Neo-Nazi sites, 120 Ku Klux Klan sites, 32 Christian Identity sites, 28 Neo-Confederate sites, 16 Racist Skinhead sites, and 13 Black Separatist sites.[54] Many countries have laws that ban or severely restrict hate sites on the Web, so operators of such sites tend to set up shop in the places that allow them. The United States hosts many foreign-language hate sites, due to First Amendment protections of free speech. No one knows how many foreign sites exist on American servers. However, there are 500 or more German-language hate sites housed on U.S. servers. The legal implications of these issues prove to be complicated, particularly when one type of message is banned in, say, France, but is legal in the United States.[55] Hate-group activity will be increasingly electronic in nature, due to the stigma attached to membership in such organizations and the ease and anonymity of communication via the Internet.

Short-wave radio plays a little-known role in disseminating the extremists' message of hate and division. Extremists began using short-wave radio in the early 1990s to promote far-right programs. Every month the radical right purchases approximately 1,100 hours of short-wave time. The medium has extraordinary reach — there are in excess of 200 million listeners to short-wave radio at any hour of the day. All told, there are 1 billion receivers with 2.5 billion people who listen to short-wave radio worldwide. Short wave is far more accessible than the Internet, because the set-up costs continue to be far lower. One does not need a computer or an Internet Service Provider (ISP); rather, it is possible to access short wave virtually anywhere in the world. All one needs is a $50 receiver. Millions of people throughout the world listen to U.S.-based short-wave broadcasts as a means of learning the English language. American extremists, therefore, find short-wave radio to be a significant means of communication.[56]

Similarly, white power music plays an important role in reaching young people throughout the Western world. The racist Skinhead music scene dates back to the late 1970s in Britain. However, white power music only began to flourish on the international scene after the end of the Cold War. Then distributors in the U.S. and Europe really began to increase their sales volume and international scope. Similarly, numerous neo-Nazi groups began to rely on white power music as an important source of funding for their operations. British neofascist groups started to recruit Skinheads in the 1970s — that is when the significant dichotomy between racist and anti-racist Skins first developed. The racist Skins soon developed a white power music that reflected their beliefs and sensibilities, as evidenced by the popularity of Skrewdriver, a neo-Nazi music group. The racist (and anti-racist) Skinhead movements spread throughout Europe and to North America during the 1980s. Such hate groups as the White Aryan Resistance (WAR) and the Church of the Creator sought to recruit Skinheads soon after Skin groups hit these shores more than two decades ago. U.S. Skinheads soon developed a reputation for violence.[57]

Racist music took off after the Berlin Wall came down in 1989. Western European extremists no longer had to worry about communism; instead, they began to focus on Jews, immigrants, black Africans, and their national governments. The end of communism in Eastern Europe made far-right politics attractive to many young people (and some older ones as well), due to such factors as social instability, economic uncertainty, and questions of identity. The white power music industry then blossomed between 1992 and 1997, as many racist labels opened for business in Europe. Despite some violent conflicts between white power groups in the 1990s, the increasing popularity of racist music led to greater transatlantic cooperation between and among white-supremacist individuals and organizations. Neo-Nazis increasingly view the radical right from a global perspective, one in which the cause of white supremacy transcends national boundaries — in essence, the whole idea that race trumps nation. This ideological standpoint took on greater significance as the white power music scene led to more and more trans-Atlantic contacts.[58]

The multimillion-dollar white power music industry continues to grow, as it produces funds and recruits for hate groups in the Western world. In recent years, the Internet and inexpensive airfares have contributed significantly to the internationalization of white power music. The music, which often celebrates and promotes violence, provides many young extremists throughout the West with a shared language and a common ideology ("pan-Aryanism"). White power music is a larger business in Europe than in the United States, despite the fact that many European countries ban it or make it very difficult to distribute. The racist tunes particularly win fans in Eastern Europe. One can find white power music in every European country; it is popular in such places as Serbia, Poland, Germany, Hungary, Slovakia, and the Czech Republic. European governments regularly deport extremist aliens, prohibit white power music groups, and raid racist organizations that may sell or distribute the music. Racist music, therefore, is largely an underground phenomenon in much of Europe, a fact that heightens the profit margins for distributors. The United States, a haven of free speech, has become, in essence, the global headquarters of the white power music business. One can hear racist music anywhere in the world any time of the day, due to radio shows on the Internet.[59]

As of the fall of 2001, there were more than 40 online distributors offering white power music for sale to American consumers. The domestic distributors offered albums from 123 U.S. bands and 229 foreign bands. The smorgasbord of choices encompasses numerous music genres: white power rock, fascist experimental music, National Socialist Black Metal, and racist country and folk music. White power rock is the most commonly represented type of band, followed by National Socialist Black Metal. Racist country music, not surprisingly, is mainly an American phenomenon. Germany, Great Britain, and Sweden in particular are home to many white power bands.[60] Panzerfaust Records, Micetrap Records, and, to a far lesser extent, Resistance Records continue to be the leading purveyors of white-supremacist music (domestic and foreign bands alike) in America.[61]

The electoral sphere, though, is one realm of the radical right where American extremists have had far less luck than is the case for their European counterparts. Far-right political parties have won in excess of 15% of the nationwide vote in Italy, France, Norway, Turkey, Belgium, Austria, and Switzerland during the post–Cold War era. These parties capitalized on the complex economic and demographic factors that suffused Europe in recent years, by attacking economic globalization, bashing refugees and immigrants, and denigrating the out-of-touch governing elites, among other issues.[62] But far-right candidates have had very little luck in American electoral politics, in part because there is no proportional representation in the electoral sphere. Consequently, it is virtually impossible for someone espousing wildly unpopular political ideas to ever win office from a single-member legislative or congressional district, or in a citywide or statewide election.

The extent to which one believes that mainstream politicians and political ideas are affected by the radical right depends, in large part, on her or his ideological perspective. This is particularly true when it comes to analyzing the importance of the Religious Right in American politics and culture. Cultural observers and commentators typically consider such doyens of religious conservatism as Dr. James Dobson, the Reverend Jerry Falwell, and televangelist Pat Robertson to be part of the American mainstream, at the right-wing edge of it. Many of the left-wing watchdog groups and cultural commentators, though, consider those individuals to be "extreme" and not part of the mainstream at all. Another figure who inspires debates about his presence in the mainstream is Patrick Buchanan. The conservative commentator certainly espouses views on race and culture that inhabit the fringe of mainstream beliefs. And he has won support from some white nationalists and self-styled "racialists." At the same time, Buchanan never overtly embraced the radical right. No American figure of any standing in the political mainstream advocates for the radical right's favorite political issues — there is insufficient support for such ideas to win widespread public approval and, consequently, the backing of a major politician or political movement.

David Duke is the only radical-right figure in recent times to win significant support from an electorate anywhere in America. The white Louisianan began his involvement in hate groups as a teenager during the 1960s. In the 1970s he became prominent on the radical right as a clean-cut, smooth-talking Ku Klux Klan leader. Duke, who was born in 1950, eventually left the Klan and formed the National Association for the Advancement of White People (NAAWP). Duke rarely received any attention in the mainstream media until 1989, when he was elected a state representative (as a Republican) in a special election from a legislative district in suburban New Orleans. Suddenly, Duke became the subject of international media coverage. The former Ku Klux Klan leader, who also had repeatedly demonstrated neo-Nazi sympathies, purported to have left behind his more extreme political views as he tried to adopt the language and demeanor of a mainstream conservative politician.[63]

David Duke enjoyed significant political attention in Louisiana, the nation, and the Western world during his numerous campaigns for state and federal office in the 1990s. Throughout the 1990s Duke, a nominal member of the GOP, made Republicans distinctly uncomfortable because he tarred their party with a racist, intolerant image nationally. Running on a platform that focused mainly on conventional right-wing themes, Duke won 60 percent of the white vote in his 1990 U.S. Senate race and 55 percent of the white vote in his 1991 gubernatorial candidacy. Duke sought the 1992 Republican presidential nomination, but Pat Buchanan eclipsed him in that contest. And in 1996 he placed fourth in a multicandidate field for Louisiana's open U.S. Senate seat, with 12% of the vote. During the late 1990s, Duke explicitly embraced more and more extreme racial and anti-Semitic views. The publication of his autobiography, *My Awakening,* in 1998 made this clear. Duke still placed a respectable third (with 19% of the vote) after running an explicitly racial campaign for a predominantly white congressional district in suburban New Orleans in 1999.[64] In 2000 he formed the organization that was the precursor of the hate group, the European-American Unity and Rights Organization, or EURO, that he currently operates as its national president.[65]

During the 1990s Duke burnished his international reputation through several trips he made to Europe. Duke in particular visited Russia a number of times between 1995 and 2002; he regularly peddled an anti-Semitic message to people there, whom he thought would be receptive to it. The Russian edition of Duke's book, *The Jewish Question through the Eyes of an American,* sold thousands of copies in Russia. He spent much of his time in Russia meeting with far-right politicians and select groups of extremists. The American bigot tried to advise his Russian compatriots on matters associated with public relations, but his tips had little salience in the Russian context. Duke decided to continue his expatriate lifestyle after federal agents raided his Louisiana home in November 2000; the U.S. government suspected Duke of tax and mail fraud.[66]

From late 2000 until December 2002, Duke traveled to Europe, the former Soviet Union, and other parts of the world. He attempted to present himself as a highly regarded American writer, politician, and commentator. Duke mainly gave lectures, sold his books, and met privately with important extremist figures in the countries he visited. His autobiography appeared in Russian and Ukrainian, and he addressed audiences in such places as Russia, the Ukraine, and Bahrain. Duke resided part-time in northern Italy. He went to such European countries as Austria, Romania, Germany, and Switzerland. In the aftermath of 9/11, Duke enhanced his anti-Semitic reputation by propounding the noxious theory that Israel was somehow involved in the worst terrorist attack in American history. He found some support for this view in Russia and segments of the Islamic world; the onetime neo-Nazi attempted to cast himself as an authority on issues related to the Middle East. At the end of 2002, though, Duke returned to the United States, where he pled guilty to two counts of tax and mail fraud. Then Duke served a brief prison term; while it seems likely that his political career is over, it remains to be seen what role he will play in the radical right.[67]

DOING THE RIGHT THING

Chip Berlet had an eye-opening experience one day in 1970 when he and his college roommate Walter Gill stopped at a small store in Denver — "a convenience store, a little store," as he remembers it — to purchase some sundries. Berlet and Gill were similar in virtually every respect. Both of them were very polite. Both of them were bookworms. Both of them enjoyed classical music. Both of them were preppy dressers. Both of them came from educated, upper-middle-class backgrounds. Both of them were leaders of the student newspaper at their university — the *University of Denver Clarion*. And both men, of course, behaved appropriately while they were in the store. But the shop's white personnel followed Gill, not Berlet, through the aisles. There was only one conceivable reason that the white salespeople treated Gill differently than Berlet: His race. Gill is black and Berlet is white. After leaving the store, the two men discussed what had happened. It surprised Berlet that such racial profiling occurred; Gill, in turn, found it difficult to believe that Berlet did not know that such events happened regularly to African-American men.[68] This experience strengthened Berlet's already strong commitment to civil rights.[69]

Since his teen years, Berlet, who grew up in an upper-middle-class household in northern New Jersey, has worked for social justice. John Foster "Chip" Berlet was born in Paterson, New Jersey, on November 22, 1949. A tall, burly man with a mustache, glasses, and white hair (it was blond when he was younger) and blue eyes, Berlet's appearance reflects his Northern European heritage — his father was of French and French-Swiss descent and his mother traced her ancestry to England and Scandinavia. This longtime community activist and antiracist figure is white, Christian, heterosexual, and able-bodied. He has spent much of his professional life trying to expand the opportunities available to women, minorities, the poor, gays and lesbians, people with disabilities, and others who traditionally have experienced disadvantage in our society.

Today Berlet enjoys an international reputation as one of America's best-known experts on hate and supremacy. Since 1982 he has worked at Political Research Associates and its precursor, Midwest Research, a progressive think tank.[70] The political scientist Jean Hardisty is the founder and president of PRA, which has its offices in the Boston suburb of Somerville. Berlet is Senior Analyst at PRA. His colleagues include Dr. Nikhil Aziz, Pam Chamberlain, and Palak Shah. Berlet regularly authors articles in magazines, newspapers, and scholarly journals. And he frequently appears on radio and television programs throughout America, including *Nightline* and National Public Radio. Berlet studies various topics, including prejudice, scapegoating, demonization, conspiracism, demagoguery, and authoritarianism. Over the years, he has conducted investigations on hate groups, police misconduct, theocratic fundamentalism, right-wing backlash movements, violations of civil liberties, and related matters. This genial bear of a man is editor of *Eyes Right!: Challenging the Right Wing Backlash* (1995) and co-author of *Right-Wing Populism in America* (2000).[71]

Berlet tries consciously to share the dream with women, people of color, and the disadvantaged in every context of American society. This is true on multiple fronts, personally as well as professionally. Berlet and his wife, Karen, share domestic responsibilities (he is the family cook, for instance). In doing so, they have created a model of gender equality on the home front for their son, Robert. Back at the office, Berlet regularly fields requests for speaking engagements and media appearances around the nation. Sometimes he deliberately turns down media appearances so that bookers and producers pay more attention to lesser-known experts. And he regularly co-authors articles in popular publications (Berlet usually is the single author of his scholarly work). In addition, he teaches young journalists at Z-magazine's periodic ten-day Media Training Workshop in Woods Hole, Massachusetts. A good-natured and open-minded person, Berlet wins plaudits for his sincerity and knowledge; he enjoys a well-deserved reputation as a prominent progressive voice in the world of human rights.

Thousands of Americans spend much or all of their professional time working on issues related to human rights, as well as monitoring, studying, and counteracting extremists, hate groups, and white supremacists. There are many ongoing efforts in different disciplines and occupational categories to fight hate and promote tolerance. These efforts involve journalists, academics, researchers, activists, lawyers, government officials, and professionals who work at organizations that specifically tackle such issues on a day-to-day basis. Indeed, human rights activists, leaders, and professionals play an important role in the fight against hate and extremism by gathering knowledge about hate groups and extremist activities and sharing it with the public, policymakers, and law enforcement authorities.

Likewise, academic scholars do much to educate us about such topics as bigotry, intolerance, and far-right politics. These scholars are found in law, history, sociology, criminology, anthropology, political science, and other disciplines. Jeffrey Kaplan points out that the academic literature often informs the perspective of the watchdog groups and, sometimes, the journalists who report on these issues.[72] Just as the extremists have formed transatlantic alliances to promote white supremacy, so too have the academics who study them and seek to blunt the force of their pernicious influence. Kaplan, an American historian of culture, enjoys an international reputation, as do a number of his U.S. colleagues. Similarly, the British scholar Roger Eatwell is one of the European academic experts who is well known and regarded highly on both sides of the Atlantic.[73] It seems likely that there will be even more transnational cooperation between and among scholars of hate, extremism, and white supremacy in the coming years.

There are numerous community, government, and national organizations that monitor hate groups and advocate for civil rights and human rights.[74] Many organizations focus on specific topics related to a particular group (e.g., gays, blacks, Muslims) or follow the developments in a given area (e.g., the Reading-Berks Human Relations Council in Pennsylvania). The watchdog groups and anti-racist monitoring groups may differ ideologically and in terms of their foci and strategies and tactics. Of the small watchdog groups, perhaps the best known ones are the Center for New Community in Chicago, the Center for Democratic Renewal in Atlanta, and Political Research Associates in suburban Boston.[75] The biggest and best-known watchdog groups are the American Jewish Committee, the Anti-Defamation League, the Southern Poverty Law Center, and the Simon Wiesenthal Center (listed in the order of their founding), all of which provide much information about hate groups and extremist activities to educators, law enforcement personnel, and others.

The American Jewish Committee (AJC) is an important Jewish human rights organization and a significant force in combating bigotry against various groups of people, based on race, color, creed, and other factors.[76] This interrelated mission is reflected in the AJC's mission statement:

- to safeguard the welfare and security of Jews in the United States, in Israel, and throughout the world;

- to strengthen the basic principles of pluralism around the world, as the best defense against anti-Semitism and other forms of bigotry;

- to enhance the quality of American Jewish life by helping to ensure Jewish continuity and deepen ties between American and Israeli Jews.[77]

The AJC dates back to 1906, making it the oldest human relations organization in the country. David A. Harris serves as the AJC's executive director. A Non-Government Organization, the AJC has 33 regional offices, many national office departments, several overseas offices, and numerous international partners.

Kenneth Stern is the American Jewish Committee's expert on anti-Semitism and extremism, here and abroad. Stern, a lawyer, author, and longtime human rights advocate, has worked at the American Jewish Committee since 1989. The fiftysomething Stern is known for his prescience — he authored a report issued by the AJC that warned of the dangers of militia groups just days before the Oklahoma City bombing in April 1995. Lately, he has focused mainly on monitoring anti-Semitism in domestic and international contexts, in addition to being a leading figure in the movement to establish the academic discipline of hate studies. As a result of the international nature of anti-Semitism, Stern's work is very global in scope and brings him into contact with the established Jewish communities in various European countries. He regularly travels to Europe for his work. Stern deals with short-term issues every day. Also, he is looking toward the future to confront potential problems before they arise. Stern asks, "What is likely to happen in the future?" as the demographic composition of America changes.[78] Due in part to Stern's expertise, the AJC continues to be on the forefront of domestic policy issues related to hate, extremism, and tolerance.

The Anti-Defamation League of B'nai B'rith (ADL) is another important Jewish human rights organization that pays much attention to these issues. Founded in 1913, the Anti-Defamation League conducts an extensive series of efforts to counteract hate and encourage tolerance.[79] Abraham H. Foxman is the National Director of the Anti-Defamation League; he is assisted by a top-notch staff that enjoys access to an impressive amount of financial and intelligence resources. The ADL gathers information on many topics, including anti-Semitism, civil rights, extremism, the Holocaust, interfaith issues, international affairs, Israel, religious freedom, security awareness, and terrorism. The ADL focuses many of its considerable resources on research and education. This information is shared with educators, the public, and law enforcement (through the ADL's Law Enforcement Agency Resource Network). Similarly, the ADL has an extensive series of 30 U.S. regional offices. It also has international offices in Russia and Israel. Due to its prominence, the ADL is one of the most respected watchdog groups, as well as perhaps the antiracist-monitoring group most vilified — and feared — by bigots, racists, and extremists.

The ADL's Brian Marcus focuses on the domestic and international aspects of hate groups in the electronic sphere. Marcus, who once worked with David Goldman at Hatewatch.org, a now-defunct Web site that monitored hate on the Internet, and for Brian Levin at the Center for the Study of Hate and Extremism, is the Director of the Internet Monitoring Unit in the Civil Rights Division of the ADL. He went to work for the ADL in 2001.[80] A native of Westchester County, New York, Marcus is a white man in his early thirties. His work on monitoring hate groups and extremist activity grew out of his interest in conspiracies, a topic that has intrigued him since high school. Marcus conducts research and disseminates information to people in education, law enforcement, and other institutions. In 2002, Marcus authored an ADL study on racist video games, a new twist on hate, as the extremists attempt to appeal to young people and make money at the same time.[81] Marcus's work requires him to have a global focus, due to the international reach of the Internet. International terrorism is a big area of interest for Marcus, as is Christian Identity, the subject of his ongoing doctoral dissertation.[82]

The Southern Poverty Law Center, meanwhile, is one of the leading antiracist monitoring groups in the Western world. Morris Dees and Joseph Levin Jr. cofounded the SPLC in 1971 as a public interest law firm. Richard Cohen serves as president of the Southern Poverty Law Center, an organization with numerous components, including the Intelligence Project, Teaching Tolerance, Tolerance.org, and the Civil Rights Memorial Center.[83] The Intelligence Project, which was originally known as Klanwatch when it starting tracking the activities of the U.S. radical right in 1981, publishes the *Intelligence Report,* a quarterly, and offers training to assist human rights groups and law enforcement officials in their efforts to combat hate.[84] Similarly, Teaching Tolerance is a program that the SPLC started in 1991 to promote anti-bias education among educators (particularly K–12 teachers).[85] Tolerance.org, another program of the SPLC, dates back to 2001. It seeks to encourage acceptance and understanding through anti-bias activism in such realms as our homes, our schools, our workplaces, and our communities.[86] The SPLC is also home to the Civil Rights Memorial, a monument to the civil rights pioneers who died in the fight for racial equality.[87]

The SPLC's Morris Dees is a larger-than-life figure. He is the most prominent antihate litigator in America. A native of rural central Alabama, Dees was born in 1936. He became a multimillionaire in the late 1960s after his entrepreneurial skills in direct-mail marketing paid off substantially for him. Once he secured his financial future, the charming Alabamian decided to devote his career to public interest law. With the founding of the SPLC, Dees has been involved in human rights work for more than three decades. As the chief trial counsel for the SPLC, Dees has made headlines with his strategy of filing civil suits against hate groups, bankrupting them in the process, and effectively ending their ability to organize, harass their targets, and disseminate their hate-filled message. Dees, the SPLC legal team, and their local co-counsels have had numerous high-profile victories — against the United Klans of America in 1987, the White Aryan Resistance in 1990, the Christian Knights of the Ku Klux Klan in 1998, and the Aryan Nations in 2000.[88] As a result of the SPLC's civil suits, there have been "judgments against 46 individuals and nine major white supremacist organizations for their roles in hate crimes," according to the *Intelligence Report.*[89] The author of numerous books and the subject of a made-for-television movie, Dees has received many honors and much recognition for his work.

The Southern Poverty Law Center publishes *Intelligence Report* — the leading American quarterly that covers racism, hate, and extremism. Each quarter, the glossy periodical breaks important stories related to these topics. Mark Potok edits the *Intelligence Report.* Dr. Heidi Beirich and Bob Moser collaborate with him on *Intelligence Report,* which also includes the work of freelance journalists and experts from other watchdog groups. The intrepid journalistic investigators spend their time tracking extremist activity wherever it occurs, and then they write about it. Potok, who was born in 1955 in Paris, is the son of a Polish-born

Jewish father and an Episcopalian mother who hailed from Tulsa. Potok has a thoroughly international background (he spent his youth and adolescence in Greece and Vermont). Later, the honors graduate of the University of Chicago worked for a number of newspapers, including the *Miami Herald* and as the Southwest bureau chief for *USA Today*. Potok became editor of the *Intelligence Report* in 1997.[90] Soon he transformed the publication into America's definitive periodical on hate and extremism.

Potok has dual duties — his official job title is "Director of Publications and Information" — at the SPLC: He edits the *Intelligence Report* and provides expert analysis to the media. Potok selects the story ideas for the *Intelligence Report*; under his leadership, the publication has broken news stories about many racist and extremist subjects, e.g., the white-supremacist nature of the Council of Conservative Citizens and the surprising number of mainstream politicians with ties to the organization. He regularly appears on radio and television programs around the country to discuss hate and extremism. Potok is frequently quoted in magazines and newspapers as well, and he has testified before Congress. This free-speech proponent often attends conferences in Europe, where he sometimes comes under attack for defending America's First Amendment protections for haters and extremists.[91] These activities enhance his reputation as the preeminent editorial commentator who follows the American radical right.

The Simon Wiesenthal Center, meanwhile, is the most recent addition to the ranks of the nation's major watchdog groups, and it is an internationally recognized resource for tolerance education. The Center, which is named for Simon Wiesenthal, the famed Nazi hunter, was founded in 1977 by Rabbi Marvin Heir.[92] The SWC defines its mission thus: "The Simon Wiesenthal Center carries out its mission of preserving the memory of the Holocaust by fostering tolerance and understanding through community involvement, educational outreach, and social action through its national and international offices."[93] Under the leadership of Rabbi Hier (the dean of the Center), Rabbi Abraham Cooper (the associate dean), and Rabbi Meyer May (the executive director), the Wiesenthal Center is an institution with a presence on four continents.

The SWC offers numerous programs to promote tolerance, including its extensive work on digital hate, the media offerings of its Moriah Films Division, and the Museum of Tolerance's Tools for Tolerance program for law enforcement. Led by Mark Weitzman, its Task Force Against Hate and Terrorism targets extremism in a variety of contexts,

including foreign countries, local communities, and educational and governmental institutions. The Task Force sponsors conferences, training,
and publications for the media, the military, academic scholars, and
law enforcement.[94] Richard Eaton is a researcher for the Task Force;
he focuses on hate groups and extremist activity throughout the world.[95]
Gloria McMillan, a consultant to the Task Force, works with Eaton and
Weitzman.[96] The Simon Wiesenthal Center is well known for its Museum
of Tolerance, which opened in Los Angeles in 1993. The SWC also has
opened the New York Tolerance Center, the East Coast counterpart of
the MOT, a development that emphasizes the organization's commitment
to education.[97]

Due to the importance of the Simon Weisenthal Center and the stature
of its leaders, the SWC enjoys significant influence as a human rights
organization. Indeed, the Center has a well-developed global operation.[98]
It is an official Non-Government Organization at such international
agencies as the United Nations, the Council of Europe, the Organiza-
tion for Security and Co-operation in Europe (OSCE), and the United
Nations Educational, Scientific and Cultural Organization (UNESCO).
The SWC's main office is in Los Angeles. There are also offices in New
York, Miami, Paris, Toronto, Jerusalem, and Buenos Aires. Dr. Shimon
Samuels serves as the Director for International Liaison for the Simon
Wiesenthal Center. Dr. Samuels, Rabbi Hier, Rabbi Cooper, and Rabbi
May frequently meet with heads of state and heads of government, in
addition to leading cultural, corporate, political, and religious figures.[99]

The Wiesenthal Center's Rabbi Abraham Cooper is one of the best-
known human rights advocates in the Western world. Cooper was born
in 1950. This native of the Flatbush section of Brooklyn has advocated on behalf of Jewish and human rights issues throughout the world
for the last three decades. Rabbi Cooper is responsible for the Wiesenthal Center's global social action agenda, which includes such items as
tolerance education, monitoring extremist groups, counteracting anti-
Semitism worldwide, and Nazi war crimes and restitution. Cooper, who
is a globally recognized expert on matters regarding the Internet and digital hate, often testifies before international governmental bodies. He also
coordinates international conferences on such topics as anti-Semitism,
restitution to Holocaust survivors, and digital hate. In Asia, particularly Japan, South Korea, and the People's Republic of China, Rabbi
Cooper has worked to combat negative anti-Jewish stereotypes in part
through the creation of venues to promote dialogue and better intergroup relations. And in 2001 he served as an important spokesperson

who advocated on behalf of Jews worldwide and the State of Israel at the World Conference against Racism, Racial Discrimination, Xenophobia, and Related Intolerance, in Durban, South Africa.[100]

Cooper blends the global and local seamlessly in his professional life. He regularly has audiences with heads of state and heads of government, including Pope John Paul II, Argentine President Néstor Kirchner, and Sudanese President Omar al-Bashir. Moreover, he supervises the SWC's Task Force Against Hate and has overseen the CD-ROM reports on digital hate that the Center issues each year. Cooper is the editor-in-chief of the Wiesenthal Center's *Response* magazine. His column frequently appears in newspapers in the United States, Western Europe, and elsewhere. At the same time, Cooper emphasizes the importance of grass-roots activism in human-rights advocacy, a point highlighted by people in different parts of the movement. Rabbi Cooper himself is involved in civic and political activities in California.[101] He was one of the 15 people on the Blue Ribbon Committee to help develop the selection criteria for the next Los Angeles Police Chief. And Cooper was part of Governor-elect Arnold Schwarzenegger's transition team in 2003. Likewise, he oversaw the creation of the Museum of Tolerance's Interactive Learning Center on the Holocaust and World War II.[102]

On another front, Kenneth Stern of the American Jewish Committee hopes to test the effectiveness of anti-bias education programs, in order to emphasize the components of the most successful programs and incorporate those aspects into curricula. Tolerance programs and Holocaust programs, Stern notes, are offered as antidotes to hate and extremism. Stern asks several questions. Firstly, do the programs work? To make this determination requires spending a considerable amount of time and money evaluating a specific cohort of people to judge whether the programs are, in fact, successful in terms of decreasing bias and increasing tolerance. Secondly, if the programs work, how and when do they work best? Does the gender of the participants (boys versus girls) play a role? Does the urban/rural distinction make a difference? Stern says there have been no long-term evaluations of the effectiveness of different types of anti-bias education programs.[103]

In the academy, there is growing interest in studying hate as an academic discipline. Since the mid-1990s Kenneth Stern has been writing and speaking about the need for hate studies. His advocacy and the efforts of like-minded individuals culminated in the formation of the Gonzaga University Institute for Action Against Hate. The Institute was founded in 1997 after a series of harassing incidents affected minority students on Gonzaga's campus in Spokane, Washington. Gonzaga University Law School Professor George Critchlow cofounded the Institute and has long been an enthusiastic proponent of the Institute's three-pronged approach to fighting hate (research, advocacy, and education). A sometime Fulbright Scholar to Romania, Critchlow works closely with Professor Jerri Shepard, the Institute's present director. The Board of the Institute for Action Against Hate includes such well-known experts on hate and extremism as Professor Brian Levin, the American Jewish Committee's Kenneth Stern, and Simon Wiesenthal Center consultant Gloria McMillan.[104]

Gonzaga University, then, is on the cutting edge of a new academic discipline: hate studies. The Institute for Action Against Hate publishes the *Journal of Hate Studies* every year. Gonzaga University hosted the International Conference to Establish the Field of Hate Studies in March 2004; Kenneth Stern presented the keynote address. Sometime in the near future, Gonzaga University will offer a baccalaureate program in hate studies. This is a beginning step in terms of creating hate studies as a viable academic discipline. Stern says that he eventually hopes to see other institutes at other universities, as people from different institutions flesh out the idea of hate studies.[105] The disciplines that contribute to this emerging academic field include law, media, history, sociology, education, political science, religious studies, and social psychology.[106]

As Kenneth Stern writes:

> This launching of the field of hate studies will be the first step toward pulling the various disciplines together so that they can cross-pollinate each other, and give special focus to how they intersect with the outside world. Then we can create a generation of scholars who will look with a wide gaze, keeping in mind all the interrelated aspects: how hate impacts the individual alone, the individual inside the group, the group, the community, the nation, the world.[107]

Eventually there will be what Stern describes as "testable models" for such institutions as NGOs, education, government, and law enforcement in their anti-bias efforts, as they address hate and try to reduce, if not eliminate, its pernicious effects on our lives.[108]

～

James Cameron is someone who is eminently qualified to expound on matters related to racism, human rights, and the progress of American history. Cameron occupies a unique role in U.S. history: He is "America's only living survivor of a lynching."[109] Cameron, an African American, was born in February 1914, in Wisconsin. On August 6, 1930, he was living in Marion, Indiana, when he was involved in a robbery attempt that resulted in the death of Claude Deeter, a white man, and involved the alleged assault of Mary Ball, a white woman. Cameron, it should be noted, killed no one and assaulted no one. On the evening of August 7, 1930, a mob of whites stormed the Grant County, Indiana, jail and lynched 19-year-old Tom Shipp and 18-year-old Abe Smith, the other two young men involved in the robbery and alleged assault. Cameron was beaten severely by the mob but he was rescued from being lynched at the last minute. Certain lynchers concluded that Cameron was not a guilty party and therefore did not deserved to be lynched. Still, the young man received a four-year sentence in state prison for his role in the aforementioned episode.[110] (In 1993, Indiana Governor Evan Bayh issued a pardon to Cameron.)[111] "Because of this personal experience," notes one source, "Cameron dedicated his life to promoting civil rights, racial peace, unity and equality."[112]

Beginning in the 1980s James Cameron developed a national profile on racial issues. In 1982 the autodidact and longtime civil rights activist self-published his autobiography, *A Time of Terror,* which details the lynchings and his prison experiences. Then, in 1988, he founded America's Black Holocaust Museum in Milwaukee, Wisconsin. The Museum offers a comprehensive overview of the African experience in the United States, from the Middle Passage to the present. It regularly receives visitors from around the world. The Museum often hosts cultural, political, and civil rights luminaries. Indeed, Cameron has become the foremost keeper of the story of the Marion lynching; the Lawrence Beitler photograph that chronicled it forever is part of America's collective consciousness. This story really took off in 1994 when Black Classic Press reissued *A Time of Terror.* Cameron was the subject of substantial interest in the American and, to some extent, European media. Several documentaries have been made about the Marion lynching, and Cameron has told his story hundreds of times for journalists and lecture audiences.[113]

During the last two decades, Cameron's patient and detailed recollections of a once-forgotten story have provided Americans with an instructive look at the powerful force of racism in American history, as he reflects on how things have — and have not — changed since his youth. The 90-year-old civil rights advocate notes that there has been considerable progress in race relations, e.g., the increased number of positive portrayals of African Americans in U.S. popular culture. Cameron cites his Catholic parish, All Saints Catholic Church in Milwaukee, as an example of interracial amity. All Saints was once a mainly white parish. Now it is about 50 percent white and 50 percent black. Still, Cameron says there is tokenism at the highest levels of American business and politics, and far too few blacks in the halls of power. Cameron celebrates the greatness of America and the possibilities for upward mobility available to those individuals who pursue educational opportunities. At the same time, he is troubled by the fact that Americans have yet, in his opinion, to unite and become "a single and sacred nationality."[114]

Now we turn to Stetson Kennedy, who is one of America's most enduring champions of human rights.[115] A spry, blue-eyed white man who grew up in a relatively affluent family in Jacksonville, Florida, Stetson Kennedy was born on October 5, 1916. From the beginning, Kennedy recalls that he had a social conscience. "I like to think that every child is born with an innate sense of what's fair and unfair," says the veteran human rights advocate. "There was very much that was unfair in the world I was born into (as there still is), and I was dead-set against it — all of it. Jim Crow was simply the most unjustified, wanton, gross, cruel, all-pervasive persecution of fellow human beings in sight, so I concentrated my fire on it."[116] Many of Kennedy's friends and family members disavowed him after he began, as a teenager, to write and speak on behalf of disadvantaged Americans, chief among them blacks and poor people of all races.

Throughout his long life, Kennedy has had many occupational titles, including author, lecturer, historian, folklorist, union organizer, political activist, investigative journalist, human rights advocate, and infiltrator of domestic and international terrorist groups.[117] He rose to national prominence in the 1940s when he went undercover and joined the Ku Klux Klan in Georgia. The redoubtable Kennedy revealed the Klan's secrets to the media and law enforcement, "exposing its leaders and financial backers, and putting a damper on attendance, recruitment, and acts of terrorism."[118] In his career, he worked with such twentieth-century cultural luminaries as Woody Guthrie, Richard Wright, Jean-Paul Sartre, and Zora Neale Hurston. Over the years Kennedy has lived in such places as Paris, Miami, and Manhattan. His primary residence since 1960 has been a two-story cedar cottage on the banks of Lake Beluthahatchee in rural St. Johns County, Florida. From 1952 to 1960 he lived abroad, spending his time in Europe, Asia, and North Africa, as he wrote, lectured, and participated in pivotal events, such as the Hungarian Revolution of 1956.

Kennedy has often been a lonely voice for racial justice. He was harassed, threatened, verbally abused, and attacked on numerous occasions by white supremacists after his identity as a Klan infiltrator became public knowledge. In 1950 Kennedy sought to promote equal rights with an independent write-in candidacy for the U.S. Senate in his native Florida. This "colorblind candidate running on a platform of total equality" won the backing of the Florida Progressive Voters League, a black group. Throughout the 1940s, 1950s, and 1960s, Kennedy aroused the antipathy of white Southern racists because he proudly identified with the cause of African Americans. He was the only white resident of Jacksonville to sit-in during the 1960s, for instance. In that decade Kennedy was a correspondent for, and Florida editor of, the *Pittsburgh Courier,* a nationwide newspaper with considerable influence in black America. And from 1965 to 1979, he served as director of planning for an antipoverty program, the Northeast Florida Community Action Agency. In this capacity, he assisted clients from poor backgrounds of all races, in keeping with his lifelong focus on helping the disadvantaged.

Today Kennedy regularly receives honors and recognition for his work as one of the leading white pioneers of the fight against white supremacy in the Jim Crow era. All told, his seminal books (*Palmetto Country, Southern Exposure, The Klan Unmasked, Jim Crow Guide,* and *After Appomattox*) have been translated into at least 20 languages over the years, and are currently in print at the University Press of Florida.[119] Kennedy reports that universities in such places as Japan, France, Australia, and the United States use his books to teach what he describes as "Alternative American Studies."[120] Though heartened by the "appreciable progress" we have made fighting discrimination, Stetson Kennedy posits that "America went very far out of her way to discriminate, and will have to go much farther yet to purge herself of discrimination."[121] At age 87, this courtly and compassionate man continues to write and speak about the environment, human rights, and preserving traditional folk culture, the three main foci of the Stetson Kennedy Foundation.[122] Throughout his life, Stetson Kennedy has fought valiantly ("full-time and over-time," according to him) for civil rights, social justice, and equal opportunities for all people.[123]

⟪ epilogue ⟫

Promises to Keep

Many Mexican newcomers to De Queen, Arkansas, purchase their automobiles at Gentry's Trading Post, a thriving establishment on the East Side of town that sells a wide variety of pre-owned vehicles. There, they are very likely to come into contact with the proprietor, Dink Gentry, who has been selling automobiles for more than 40 years. Gentry, a mild-mannered man in his early sixties with light brown hair that is speckled with gray, is the antithesis of the stereotypical used-car dealer. He gives his customers a detailed history of each car's previous owner(s) and allows them plenty of time to test-drive the vehicles. As a result, most of his business comes from repeat customers; some locals have been part of his clientele for nearly four decades. The Latinos are learning what the Anglos in Sevier County, Arkansas, have known for a long time: that this folksy, kind-hearted man who greets them at the door of Gentry's with a friendly "hey, amigo" can be trusted to keep his word. People with Spanish surnames now fill the ample ranks of his satisfied customers — they constitute 50 to 55 percent of Gentry's clientele.[1]

Moreover, Gentry and his wife of 38 years, DeLois, own dozens of rental properties around town, and many of their tenants are Mexican immigrants. (Mrs. Gentry manages the rental properties, while Mr. Gentry focuses on the cars.) The Gentrys establish rapport with their tenants, 80 percent of whom are Hispanic, by using Spanish-language rental forms and by giving them some leeway with regard to tardy rental payments. A number of the Mexicans who once rented homes from the Gentrys have bought these homes from them. As the Latino presence has soared in southwestern Arkansas — there are three poultry-processing plants within 35 miles of De Queen — the Gentrys have embraced their new neighbors, doing business with them, treating them fairly, and prospering in return.[2]

Through their hard work, shrewd business decisions, and equitable treatment of their renters and customers, the Gentrys have realized the American Dream. Kenneth W. Gentry was born in July 1942, in De

Queen, a small town in the southwestern corner of the Natural State about an hour northwest of Texarkana. Early in life, his Uncle Pete gave him the nickname Dink. He got his start in business trading horses and mules as a youth. Dink and DeLois Gentry were married in 1966. They have two sons: Kenneth "Bud" Gentry Jr., and Jimmy Ray Gentry. Bud Gentry works with his father in the family corporation (the Gentrys own five businesses). Jimmy Ray Gentry is an expert auctioneer.[3] Over the years, the Gentrys built their businesses the old-fashioned way: They worked long hours, treated their customers well, and established an enduring reputation for honesty and fairness.

Today the predominantly Anglo De Queen of Bud and Jimmy Ray Gentry's youth no longer exists. In 2000 the Census Bureau counted 2,225 Latinos out of a rapidly growing population of 5,765. De Queen is now 52.4% Anglo, 38.6% Hispanic (almost all of them Mexicans and Mexican Americans), 6.0% black, and 1.9% American Indian. In contrast to some longtime residents of De Queen, who dislike the Latino influx and the subsequent increase in population of nearly 25 percent during the 1990s, the Gentrys welcome the new ethnic dynamics.[4] Alejandro Camarillo, a loan officer at First State Bank who socializes with Bud Gentry, often does translating for Dink Gentry. Camarillo describes him as "a people's person" who "makes you feel equal."[5] Indeed, Gentry is far more than a businessman. He serves, in effect, as an agent of the assimilation process, someone whose affordable cars and rentals enable the Mexican immigrants to establish their lives in De Queen. Similarly, Gentry's scrupulous business practices give them confidence that their host society values their presence and rewards their diligence.

I

The idea of The Fighting Whites first came to Scott VanLoo during the winter of 2001–2002. For months, he listened to his Native American friends voice their concerns about the Indian symbols — specifically, the Indian mascot and the team name "Redskins" — at Eaton High School in Eaton, Colorado. For months, he watched his friends unsuccessfully attempt to persuade the all white and all male Eaton School Board to change the mascot and team name. Finally, VanLoo, who describes himself as a liberal Democrat, decided to take action. In February 2002, he conceived of The Fighting Whites as the name of an intramural basketball team at UNC. VanLoo wanted to focus attention on non-Indians who adopt Native American mascots for their schools and sports teams.

By doing so, he hoped to effect change in Eaton, a predominantly white town six miles north of Greeley, where he works at the University of Northern Colorado.[6]

At about the same time, Charles Cuny, a Lakota Indian from South Dakota, organized the intramural basketball team of three Latinos, three Native Americans, and six Caucasians. The basketball players adopted a mascot — a smiling, middle-aged white man in a suit who appears to be from the 1950s — and the motto, "Every thang's gonna be all white." VanLoo designed the mascot, which appeared on the team's jerseys. During this period, VanLoo regularly consulted with Solomon Little Owl, the director of Native American Student Services at UNC. Then the UNC campus newspaper, *The Mirror,* published a story on The Fighting Whites in early March 2002, which soon led to local, national, and international media coverage of the team. VanLoo did not want attention focused on him, so he encouraged Little Owl and the other team members to speak to the media. Little Owl, a Crow Indian from Montana who was captain of The Fighting Whites, became the team's de facto spokesperson. Charles Cuny and Jeff Van Iwarden, a white team member from Colorado, also did many media interviews during this period.[7]

In the last two and one-half years, The Fighting Whites have received considerable recognition and developed an impressive fundraising operation. The trailblazing basketball players regularly get accolades and media coverage.[8] In May 2003, for instance, etown, the nationally syndicated radio show, recognized The Fighting Whites with its "achievement award." VanLoo accepted the award on behalf of his teammates.[9] The team raises money through the sales of caps, T-shirts, mugs, bumper stickers, and other memorabilia. In January 2003, The Fighting Whites donated $100,000 to the UNC Foundation. This gift established The Fighting Whites Minority Endowment Scholarship Fund.[10] Although the Redskins and Indian mascot continue to exist at Eaton High School, VanLoo, Little Owl, and their teammates have focused much attention on the issue of Indian iconography in sports and, at the same time, created educational opportunities for students of color due to their successful fundraising efforts.

The typical white male baby born in Colorado (and every other state in the Union) this year will undoubtedly have many multicultural experiences during his life. He will be expected to embrace the diversity imperative, as women and minorities assume ever-greater positions of importance in the halls of power. The diversity imperative, moreover, may come to include traditional affirmative-action efforts less and less.

Softer forms of inclusion will probably be the order of the day, as the courts continue to be skeptical of explicit race-and-gender-based remedies to compensate for the underrepresentation of women and minorities. In other words, movie producers will think twice before they cast two white men in the lead roles for an action film. They may give serious thought to having a man of color in a lead role. The white male viewing audience will think nothing of this, and, if anything, might enjoy the movie even more as a result of the diverse casting. In any event, white males are progressively becoming a smaller percentage of the U.S. population, a fact that seems unlikely to change anytime soon.

The day is coming in the not-so-distant future when white, heterosexual, able-bodied, native-born American males will account for no more than 25 percent of the U.S. population. People from this group have traditionally held the most important leadership posts in American society, and they have wielded most of the power in this country. There are many important consequences of this aspect of America's demographic transformation. As the percentage of white males decreases, there has been an increase in the percentage of people eligible for inclusion in many affirmative-action programs. It will be interesting to see what will happen in those cases where white males are underrepresented in proportional terms. There almost certainly will be more examples in which white males receive affirmative action on the basis of gender (as they do today at some universities), on the basis of a specific ethnic or cultural background, or even on the basis of whiteness or white maleness.

We can expect specific groups of white males to focus more and more on characteristics that distinguish them in some way from the majority group in American society. Gay white males are making significant progress in terms of receiving recognition as members of a minority group on the basis of their sexual orientation. Alderman Tom Tunney, the first openly gay city council member in Chicago history, has proposed set-asides in city contracting for businesses owned by gays and lesbians.[11] The mere discussion of affirmative action for sexual minorities reflects the evolving attitudes of the American people with regard to gay and lesbian rights. Likewise, people in the disability community have an increasingly prominent public profile, as the able-bodied American public becomes ever more sensitive to the issues that affect Americans with disabilities. There is greater knowledge of, and interest in, the complex issue of what, exactly, constitutes a "disability." After decades of activism, people of size are now being included in such discussions; their issues and concerns were rarely, if ever, mentioned in mainstream discourse even ten years ago.

Certain parts of American society still remain relatively unaffected by the diversity imperative. Few Fortune 500 companies appear ready to go outside the stable of seasoned white male executives for their CEOs. But the largest companies are all making concerted efforts to diversify their executive ranks. For example, General Electric, one of the world's most valuable companies, makes diversity a top priority — even though white men account for most of the top executives at the Fairfield, Connecticut, company.[12] White men, meanwhile, continue to dominate late night, the evening news, and the Sunday political shows on television.[13] Already we know that Brian Williams will succeed Tom Brokaw as NBC's nightly news anchor after the 2004 elections.[14] Yet the entrenchment of the diversity imperative is assured forever, due to America's changing demographics and the predominance of multiculturalism in our nation.

The White House continues to be one of the most exclusive bastions of white male privilege, a fact that is related to pipeline issues. Few women or people of color typically hold the positions — namely, governorships and seats in the U.S. Senate — needed to establish the credibility and fundraising prowess to compete successfully at the highest levels of the American political system. To be sure, the Democratic presidential field in 2004 included two African Americans: Al Sharpton and Carol Moseley-Braun. But neither Sharpton nor Moseley-Braun won much popular support. Already, two Democrats who would break the mold of white male presidential candidates — New York Senator Hillary Rodham Clinton (a white woman) and New Mexico Governor Bill Richardson (a Latino man) — are reportedly testing the waters for 2008.[15] It now seems likely to be only a matter of time before a woman or person of color makes a serious bid for the Presidency, or is the vice-presidential candidate on a winning ticket.

One cannot easily quantify the symbolic and substantive importance of having a female and/or minority president or vice-president. Take Secretary of State Colin Powell, who is often cited as an example of an individual who symbolizes America's openness to people of color. Most Americans seem to embrace this view. However, there appear to be few diplomatic issues where Powell has offered a "black" perspective that differs dramatically from the "white male" perspectives at the State Department. It is not uncommon for people in the African-American community to say that they believe that Powell is not really "black," due to his closeness to the white male–dominated leadership of the nation (and the Republican Party). Few blacks, though, would say something like that about Vernon Jordan, a close confidant of President Bill Clinton, whose political beliefs cleave closely to mainstream opinion in black America.[16] These matters of descriptive representation continue to be quite important in the United States and, it seems, to people in other countries as well.[17]

At the same time, explicit considerations of white males and white maleness are becoming more common in American society and culture, particularly academia and journalism. Many such considerations continue to be couched in terms of maleness and whiteness. But identity politics exert considerable influence over how we Americans see ourselves. As white males become an ever-smaller percentage of the U.S. population, it is perhaps inevitable that they will be removed from their present position as the "default" group when we talk about race and gender, and be considered as just another race-and-gender combination, such as Latinas or African-American men. With the increasing focus on race and gender in our schools and our workplaces, we can expect the typical white male to become more cognizant of race and gender, including his own.

This heightened interest in white males might lead to an upsurge in the number of specialists in the helping professions who focus mainly on white males. Indeed, it is not difficult to imagine that certain psychologists could begin to work mainly with white male teenagers or middle-aged white professional men. Other specialists might concentrate on the issue of suicide as it relates to white males, who are disproportionately likely to commit suicide. Diversity trainers who specialize in meeting the needs of young white male workers could become an occupational subgroup. These types of helping professionals would be most in demand in highly diverse areas, where ethnic minority groups have their own liaisons and professional support organizations. In fact, it is possible to foresee the day when large colleges and universities, even some big high schools, might employ liaisons that will work with the white male students. These professionals would help white males adjust to the realities of life in a multiracial society.

II

Very few Icelandic men ever think of themselves as "white," at least while they live in their beautiful Nordic homeland. Iceland, after all, is one of the world's most homogeneous countries. The vast majority of residents of this island nation of 294,000 trace their ancestry to the Celts and Norwegians who first settled it in the ninth and tenth centuries. (People of foreign origin constitute six percent of the Icelandic population.) Most Icelanders are Evangelical Lutherans.[18] And the Icelandic language remains, well, completely Icelandic. A committee creates new Icelandic words for recent additions to the global lexicon. As a group, the Icelanders look relatively similar: Generally they have blond or brown hair, light-colored eyes, and very fair skin. Gender comes up as an equity issue in Iceland, considering that race is largely a nonissue there. Social class, too, matters in Iceland, as it does everywhere. In the main, though, Iceland enjoys a significant amount of social cohesion, which stems from the island's small population, the absence of major ethnic, religious, and cultural differences there, and a strong sense of national pride that stems, in part, from a lengthy history of domination by other Scandinavian nations.

Icelanders, it should be noted, are a very international and globally aware population. Icelandic students regularly learn about the world's ethnic, cultural, and religious diversity. In March 2003, for instance, I presented an English-language public lecture on race in the United States at the University of Iceland. I confronted no language barrier during my talk; the typical Icelander speaks and understands English quite well. Indeed, Icelanders often study and travel abroad. After my public lecture, one Icelandic man told me about how he had studied at the University of Chicago — and lived in an area with a substantial number of African Americans. The Icelanders experience ethnic and racial diversity, even in Iceland, to be sure. They regularly see African Americans in Reykjavík: These individuals usually work at the U.S. Naval Air Station Keflavik in southwestern Iceland. And Reykjavík has Chinese restaurants, whose ethnic Chinese owners sometimes hire Icelandic staffers. The typical Icelander's experiences with ethnic and racial diversity, of course, differ greatly from those of her or his American counterpart.

Relatively few predominantly white countries approach race and gender in quite the same way as does the United States. American-style diversity initiatives and multicultural policies exist in Canada, Australia, and New Zealand. Affirmative action for women, but not for immigrants and ethnic minorities, is common in some Western European countries and elsewhere in the world. Many societies around the world, including Morocco, have quotas for women for seats in national legislatures.[19] No broad affirmative-action programs that define people of color as beneficiaries exist in the multiracial nations of Spanish-speaking Latin America.

Whites constitute a minority in a number of Latin American nations, but the boundary between white and nonwhite is blurry in Spanish-speaking Latin America. Explicit racial conflict and political appeals based on race are relatively rare there. To be sure, discussions of racial discrimination and quotas for blacks are rapidly becoming part of the discourse in Brazil, the Portuguese-speaking behemoth where the boundary between black and white is far less rigidly defined than in North America. Despite Portuguese-speaking Brazil's intriguing racial and ethnic dynamics, the notion of white maleness does not exist there — at least in a form recognizable to students of race and gender in the United States.

For at least 15 years, though, racial issues have been matters of significant concern to the cultural, economic, and political elites of Canada, where white males are a distinct and often-discussed group. According to the federal census in 2001, whites make up 83.7% of Canada's 29,639,035 residents, compared to a visible minority population of 13.1%, and an aboriginal population of 3.2%.[20] Canada is very immigrant-friendly: It admitted 228,575 new immigrants in 2002.[21] Most immigrants to Canada are visible minorities, and the national ethos encourages them to maintain their cultural and linguistic traditions. The 1995 Employment Equity Act benefits members of the "designated groups," the Canadian equivalent of protected classes: "women, aboriginal peoples, persons with disabilities and members of visible minorities."[22] White maleness as a topic frequently comes up in Canada, with attendant discussions of racism, sexism, white male privilege, and reverse discrimination. These issues will be matters of interest for years to come: Canada is undergoing a demographic transformation similar to the one presently unfolding in the United States.[23]

Likewise, the two predominantly white nations of Oceania (Australia and New Zealand) are confronting significant ethnic and racial changes. Whites constitute 92% of the Australian population; Australia is also 7% Asian and 1% Aborigine and other.[24] Australia has significant affirmative-action programs — for women and members of "designated groups."[25] As a result of the Equal Opportunity for Women in the Workplace Act 1999, Australia's Equal Opportunity for Women in the Workplace Agency (EOWA) issues guidelines and monitors reporting so that women Down Under experience equitable treatment in the workplace.[26] Likewise, people of color account for 20.9% of New Zealanders: New Zealand is 79.1% European, 9.7% Maori, 7.4% Asian and other, and 3.8% Pacific Islander.[27] Affirmative action is part of public policy in

New Zealand, just as it is in Australia.[28] Much of the discourse regarding race relations in New Zealand focuses on the efforts to remedy the disadvantages faced by many Maoris, the nation's indigenous residents. Issues related to diversity and multiculturalism spark contentious debates about fairness and opportunity in both New Zealand and Australia.

Many nations in Western Europe now have considerable ethnic and racial diversity. Since many, if not most, of the immigrants to Western Europe come from poor countries, it is not surprising that they often lag behind the majority groups in the West on a wide variety of socioeconomic indicators. Few Western European nations, though, seem inclined to establish U.S.-style affirmative-action programs for immigrants and people of color. This is the case for several reasons. Ethnic minorities make up a smaller percentage of the population in Western Europe than in the United States. The immigration of Arabs, Middle Easterners, and people of color (these categories, of course, are not always mutually exclusive) to Western Europe has largely occurred in the last four to five decades. And the Western European nations do not have lengthy histories of racial discrimination against people of color on the home front, as does the United States.[29] Thus males in Western Europe encounter different issues and dynamics related to race and gender, compared to their American counterparts.

To be sure, European scholars study life in Multicultural America. The Belgian political scientist Marco Martiniello, who serves as the director of the Centre d'études de l'ethnicité et des migrations (CEDEM) at the University of Liège, specializes in issues related to race, ethnicity, and migration.[30] A frequent visitor to the United States, Martiniello regularly publishes work on topics related to affirmative action and diversity issues in America.[31] Similarly, the French scholar Daniel Sabbagh is a political scientist who teaches at La Sorbonne in Paris. His academic interests include multiculturalism in France and the United States.[32] He is the author of a lengthy French-language book on U.S. affirmative-action policy.[33] (The English-language translation of Sabbagh's treatise will be published in 2005 or 2006.)[34] Indeed, European academics systematically analyze racially and ethnically diverse societies worldwide " ... to understand how they deal with the multicultural situation and possibly to learn from them," as Marco Martiniello puts it.[35]

France is one society where debates over American-style multicultural issues are starting to enter the public discourse. Ethnic minorities (North Africans and black Africans, chief among them), constitute perhaps ten percent of the French population of 60 million residents. Approximately eight percent of the French are Muslim, primarily of Moroccan, Algerian, and Tunisian descent. These Arabs and Berbers are, on average, darker and poorer than the aboriginal French. Their cultural, linguistic, and religious characteristics distance them from the French mainstream. Black Africans, meanwhile, are closer than North Africans in many respects to the aboriginal French. The French welcome newcomers, provided that they intend to become completely assimilated French people. Affirmative action for ethnic and racial minorities would contradict this model; therefore, it does not exist in France. However, discussions of public policy are beginning to include the possibility of affirmative action for ethnic minorities in employment and higher education, in order to facilitate the assimilation of people of North African extraction into French culture.[36] Hence it is possible, though unlikely, that the concept of "white maleness" may develop in France.

The United Kingdom is another society where people regard race and gender differently than in the United States.[37] Whites account for 92.1% of the population of the United Kingdom; ethnic minorities constitute 7.9% of the 58,789,194 people there.[38] The United Kingdom does not have affirmative action; rather, it has "positive action" — various projects, programs, initiatives, and enterprises that grew out of the 1976 Race Relations Act. Positive action is voluntary, and it is similar to "soft" forms of affirmative action in the United States, e.g., grants, training, and outreach for ethnic minorities. (Anything that resembles preferences is illegal in the United Kingdom.)[39] Several factors in the U.K. limit discussion of race and consequently affirmative action. The country is predominantly white, and there are a large number of different ethnic minority groups, whose issue agendas differ from each other. In addition, immigrants of color have mostly arrived in the U.K. since the 1950s; there is no national history of state-sanctioned discrimination against ethnic minorities.[40] Thus the British are less likely than the Americans to look at issues through the prism of race and gender.

The five Scandinavian nations are known worldwide for their energetic efforts, which include affirmative action, to promote opportunities for women. Gender equality is a regular part of the discourse in Scandinavia. Each Scandinavian nation has a Ministry of Gender Equality (Sweden, Denmark) or a Ministry that has responsibility for issues related to gender equality (Iceland, Norway, Finland).[41] In addition, numerous statutes in Scandinavia promote equal rights for women: the Gender Equality Act (Norway), the New Equal Status Act (Denmark), the Act on Equality between Women and Men (Finland), and the Act on the Equal

Status and Equal Rights of Women and Men (Iceland). These laws reflect Scandinavia's progressive traditions, which include family-friendly public policies and generous social-welfare programs. Despite lingering disparities between the sexes, complete gender equality is closer to being realized in Scandinavia than in any other place in the world.[42] As a result of immigration, the Scandinavians (particularly the Danes and Swedes) are beginning to confront the social and racial issues that bedevil such countries as France, Germany, Belgium, the Netherlands, and the United Kingdom.

Immigrants, after all, have played an important role in post–World War II Sweden; they and their descendants may account for eight to ten percent of the Swedish population. The Swedish scholar Dag Blanck, who teaches at Uppsala University, points out that there have been two waves of immigration to Sweden since the end of World War II: the period from 1950 to 1970, and the period from 1970 to the present. The first wave of immigrants came to Sweden as workers, and they have largely assimilated well into Swedish society. The recent immigrants are more likely to be refugees; their assimilation has been less successful. Consequently, some Swedish academics and policymakers now discuss the possibility of affirmative action as a means of creating educational and employment opportunities for the newcomers. However, the universality of the Swedish welfare system — and the corresponding focus on programs that benefit *all* people in Sweden — would, in all likelihood, lead most Swedes to oppose the idea of affirmative-action programs for ethnic minorities, according to Blanck.[43]

III

Dirk Hermann is one of the public faces of Solidarity (Solidariteit in Afrikaans), an important trade union in South Africa. A white man with brown hair, blue eyes, and a round face, the 32-year-old Hermann handles information and strategy for Solidarity.[44] This predominantly white, 128,000-member union represents workers in such industries as motor, steel, mining, telecom, aviation, engineering, and chemical manufacturing.[45] Hermann regularly appears on South African radio and television programs, and South African journalists frequently quote him in newspaper articles. An Afrikaans-speaking former union organizer who works out of Solidarity's headquarters in suburban Pretoria, he voices the views of the trade union's heavily Afrikaner male rank-and-file on numerous issues, particularly employment equity.[46] Hermann cautions that affirmative-action dictates that promote the hiring, promotion, and retention of people of color make many white South Africans feel isolated, alienated, resentful, estranged, and powerless.[47]

The issue of affirmative action keeps Hermann very busy — it continues to be a matter of great concern to Solidarity's members, particularly because of the vagaries of the New Economy. In December 2002, the Department of Public Enterprises indicated that poor Africans were the only group eligible to purchase discounted shares in the parastatal (state-owned enterprise) Telkom as part of the Khulisa share offer. Solidarity initiated legal action to ensure that income, not race, would be the deciding factor in this case. In January 2003, the trade union dropped its legal action after it reached an agreement with the Department of Public Enterprises that opened up participation in the share offer to all poor people in South Africa.[48] Solidarity, meanwhile, has allocated funds to finance reverse-discrimination suits against large corporations in South Africa, at least until the nation's government takes a different approach to affirmative action.[49] "A balance," says Hermann, "must be found between the preferential treatment of the designated group (blacks, women, and the disabled) and the rights of the non-designated group (white men)."[50]

Hermann is trying, with some success, to reshape South African public policy on the issue of employment equity. Through his advocacy efforts and academic research (he is pursuing a doctorate in industrial sociology), Hermann seeks to provide policymakers with models that allow them to enhance employment opportunities for the African majority without injuring the life chances of the minority groups in this developing nation.[51] Hermann also wants to halt the emigration of skilled workers from South Africa. Thus he participates in the Come Home Campaign, to convince South African expatriates to return home and would-be emigrants to stay in the land of their birth.[52] In sum, Hermann plays an important — and increasingly influential — role in the policy debates over affirmative action, an issue that figures prominently in current discussions of race and equity in South Africa's multiracial democracy.

Today the notions of inclusion and redress take on special significance in South Africa, a country where the African majority was once relegated to a second-class status.[53] Africans make up 75.2% of South Africa's residents, while whites account for 13.6% of the population and Coloureds are 8.6% and Indians 2.6%.[54] Africans have dominated South Africa's political life since the end of white-minority rule and the advent of multiracial democracy in 1994. They seek to increase their share of power, recognition, and resources in South Africa. To this end, the Employment Equity Act of 1998 mandates affirmative action for the "designated groups": blacks, women, and people with disabilities.[55] Another piece of legislation, the Promotion of Equality and Prevention of Unfair Discrimination Act (2000), will tackle direct and indirect discrimination in many areas of South African life now that it is largely operational.[56] Race is the main focus of affirmative-action programs. Yet employment equity has not palliated the discontent of many Africans, due to the disproportionate power of whites in every sector of South African society (except for the political arena).[57]

Africans usually contend that the discriminatory policies of the apartheid era (1948 to 1994) necessitate compensatory policies to enable people of color to enjoy the First World living standards of South Africa's white minority. They assert that white South Africans, particularly white males, benefited significantly from the monopoly they once held in the labor market and power structure in South Africa, so employment equity is a needed corrective to remedy the racial imbalance in the distribution of power and resources in South Africa. (As a legacy of apartheid, many Africans have low skills and limited capital.) Whites, to be sure, wield a significant amount of economic power in South Africa, particularly in the banking, mining, farming, manufacturing, and tourism sectors.[58] Even today, white males are disproportionately represented in the ranks of South Africa's magistrates, prosecutors, and higher courts.[59] Similarly, rugby and cricket were traditionally white male bastions, and there has been significant pressure on the rugby and cricket establishments to open their arms to African players.[60]

A sizable number of white South Africans perceive that the standard of living for the nation's largest minority group has dropped in the last decade. This is certainly the case for less-affluent white South Africans. In any event, these perceptions stem from such factors as a lengthy economic recession and uncertainty about the future of the country.[61] And for the first time in recent South African history, tens of thousands of whites are experiencing poverty and privation — the rate of black poverty is still much, much higher than that of whites — in South Africa's weak economy.[62] The white working class and lower middle class have been hit the hardest by recent economic changes, including the advent of employment equity. However, it is middle-class and upper-middle-class whites, those with marketable skills, who are leaving the country. Approximately 400,000 South Africans live abroad, particularly in the United Kingdom, Australia, the United States, New Zealand, and Canada (in that order).[63]

No one knows the precise demographics of the South African expatriate population, but the anecdotal evidence suggests that English-speaking whites make up a large component of it.

Indeed, it is important to look at the white population in South Africa in terms of Afrikaners (60% of Caucasians) and the English-speakers (40% of Caucasians). Afrikaners are whites of Dutch, French, and German origins who speak Afrikaans as their native tongue. They once faced discrimination at the hands of the British; English-speaking whites, most of whose ancestors came from the British Isles, have always exercised great influence in the economic affairs of South Africa. These divisions date back more than 100 years, to the time when English-speaking whites ruled over the Afrikaners. After the National Party won control of the South African government in 1948 and instituted the policy of apartheid, Afrikaners predominated in the public service and among the employees at the parastatals. The English-speaking whites, though, focused on commerce and industry; they were more affluent as a group than the Afrikaners. During the apartheid era, Afrikaners enjoyed tremendous influence in South African politics and culture. Today, though, Afrikaners have far less influence than they had, say, 15 years ago.[64]

In many respects, the transition to multiracial democracy has been more difficult for Afrikaners than English-speaking whites. Afrikaner music, heroes, and culture are now relegated to a peripheral place in a country where Afrikaners, after all, make up about eight percent of the population. Many Afrikaners relied on the public sector for jobs during the apartheid era. Therefore, the expansion of opportunities for Africans in this realm has caused some Afrikaners to suffer a decline in their standard of living.[65] Afrikaners, moreover, often do not have the financial resources to emigrate, or the fluent command of English necessary to assimilate quickly in Canada, Australia, New Zealand, the United States, or the United Kingdom.[66] English has now become the "bridge" language of South Africa (as in India and Nigeria). Afrikaans is merely one of 11 official languages in the country. Many Coloureds, to be sure, speak Afrikaans as their native tongue; they frequently identify with the Afrikaners on cultural grounds. Looking toward the future, the political scientist Robert Mattes, who is an expert on South African public opinion, says there is a "prospect of a nonracial coalition of Afrikaans speakers."[67]

Opinion polls give us some insights into the contemporary views of white South Africans with regard to racial issues. Robert Mattes regularly conducts surveys in South Africa and elsewhere on the Continent.

His polls "consistently demonstrate that white South Africans are most likely to feel that they are doing worse than South Africans of other races, and that they have little optimism for the future of the economy and the country as a whole."[68] Likewise, the South African Institute of Race Relations commissioned a national survey on racial issues in 2001. This opinion poll found that Afrikaans-speaking whites are more likely than the English-speaking whites to be negative about the direction of race relations in South Africa on virtually every indicator. Afrikaans-speaking whites are also far less likely than English-speaking whites to believe that contemporary racism is an impediment for Africans.[69] In sum, white South Africans often experience discontent for a variety of reasons, including the nation's high crime rates, the reduced purchasing power of the rand, and the inevitable dislocation that some of them feel as the government proceeds with its plans to expand the opportunities available to Africans.[70]

White South Africans hold conflicted but not entirely negative views about life in the new South Africa.[71] In 2002, the Afrobarometer, an opinion survey, found that 46% of white South Africans had positive feelings about their nation's system of government. Likewise, 44% of whites polled by the Afrobarometer in 2002 had positive expectations for South Africa's political system in the immediate future. Both of these findings represented dramatic upticks in optimism about the future among white South Africans.[72] Yet in 2002, 65% of whites polled by the Afrobarometer were positive in how they rated "the way the country was governed under apartheid." Interestingly, 20% of Africans, 33% of Coloureds, and 59% of Indians also responded in this way. The respondents focused on ostensibly nonracial issues, e.g., corruption, trustworthiness, law enforcement, and effectiveness in delivering services, as they compared the apartheid-era government to that of the multiracial democracy. Most South African nostalgists do not support apartheid per se; rather, they believe that South Africa was more orderly, prosperous, and efficient in the old days. At the same time, the nostalgists forget or downplay the negative aspects of the apartheid era.[73]

Reconciliation continues to be a main theme of life in South Africa, as schools, businesses, the media, and government agencies try to realize the vision of a "rainbow nation," the phrase popularized by Archbishop Desmond Tutu.[74] South Africa's African majority desires greater redistribution and transformation, according to one national survey on race relations. However, Africans are willing to support gradual changes to avoid social upheavals.[75] South African President Thabo Mbeki has begun to focus on the complex and troubled relationship between whites and Africans. He contends that whites are prospering economically and, at the same time, are no longer isolated internationally, as they were during the last years of the apartheid era.[76] Regardless, whites are significantly more skeptical than Africans, Coloureds, and Indians regarding the possibility of creating "one united South African nation." The survey data, though, show that steadily increasing percentages of white South Africans believe that such a scenario is possible.[77]

∽

Globalism and multiculturalism virtually ensure that white males will be increasingly international and multicultural in their viewpoints. There is no end in sight to the ethnic, cultural, religious, linguistic, and economic differences that separate residents of the world's predominantly white and white-majority nations. White American males will almost certainly continue to be the most affluent group (defined by race, gender, and nationality) of people in the world. At any rate, significant differences separate the whites of the affluent Western countries. The people of these countries certainly do not always see eye to eye with each other. Some of the most vigorous opposition to the U.S.-led war in Iraq came from the French and Germans. Regardless, people of color constitute an ever-increasing percentage of the human race: As the years go by, whites — and white males — will account for a smaller and smaller percentage of the world population.

Meanwhile, many young white males in the United States casually accept the multiculturalists' central points, and acknowledge that the old way — that of unquestioned white male dominance — simply did not work, was inequitable, and so forth. Others remain positive about multiculturalism in general, but are concerned about where they fit into the new multicultural order. At the same time, pockets of disadvantaged white males exist throughout much of the country, from the underclass precincts of Portland, Oregon, to the rural poverty of central Appalachia. Unfortunately, millions of Americans, including a substantial number of white males, do not have the requisite skills to achieve success in any of the high-growth occupations that point the way to a solid, middle-class existence in the coming decades. Perhaps, then, we could see certain groups of white males become resentful of the advances made by women and people of color. This resentment might manifest itself in a smirky or even bitter kind of skepticism about multiculturalism and diversity initiatives.

By 2020 we can expect the vast majority of white males to live in white-plurality places or those where the percentage of whites is much less overwhelming than it is today. But white males will probably never be a minority in the United States, at least in a figurative or cultural sense. Besides his socioeconomic class, the white male's place of residence may be the most important factor that determines his outlook on multiculturalism. Some white males will live in isolated, racially homogeneous areas, where they will never fully encounter multiculturalism in its myriad varieties. Regardless, few white males will ever permanently leave the United States. If a white guy dislikes the complexion of his neighborhood, he usually moves to one with demographics that are more amenable to his ethnic and cultural dictates. Still, it would be difficult for the typical white American male — or any other American, for that matter — to imagine what it would be like to live in a racially homogeneous nation.

Many people of color define their status as minorities in comparison to the putatively advantaged, a group that includes white, heterosexual, able-bodied males. Similarly, Ralph Ellison once posited that white Americans see themselves as members of the majority group in relation to African Americans. He mused about how the United States might be different if there were no blacks here.[78] Ellison's speculations are thought-provoking, and ones that we might raise about white males as well, although few people have ever done so. Indeed, it is almost impossible to conjure up an America without white males. They are a very important part of our culture, society, economy, and political system. Furthermore, white males account for much of America's heterogeneity, and their talents and perspectives enrich us as a nation. Americans now face the challenge of creating the conditions and institutions that allow white males to continue to participate fully in every realm of our society — and achieve success as they define it — while ensuring that females and people of color have equal opportunities to do the same. It remains to be seen what the contours of this new, equitable, multicultural society will look like, but every American should (and will) have a place in it.[79]

Notes

Prologue: Sharing the Dream

1. Most of the biographical information in these paragraphs about Professor Brian Levin comes from my lengthy interviews with Mr. Levin (Professor Brian Levin, interview by author, San Bernardino, California, January 7, 2003; Professor Brian Levin, interviews by author, Southern California, November 27–28, 2003 and April 1, 2004; Professor Brian Levin, telephone conversations with author, October 28, 2003, November 22, 2003, January 21, 2004, and March 21–22, 2004). For an excellent profile of Mr. Levin, see Alan Llavore, "A Most Civil War Against the Most Uncivil Acts," *Cal State San Bernardino Magazine* 12 (Fall/Winter 2003): 18–20, 32.

2. Roland Gant, *How Like a Wilderness* (London: Victor Gollancz, 1946).

3. To learn more about the Center for the Study of Hate and Extremism, go to http://hatemonitor.csusb.edu.

4. Professor Brian Levin, e-mail to author, April 14, 2004.

5. Levin coauthored a book on civilian militias in 1996. See Thomas Halpern and Brian Levin, *The Limits of Dissent: The Constitutional Status of Armed Civilian Militias* (Amherst, Mass.: Aletheia Press, 1996).

6. Francis B. Nyamnjoh and Ben Page, "*Whiteman Kontri* and the Enduring Allure of Modernity among Cameroonian Youth," *African Affairs* 101 (October 2002): 607–634.

7. Cameroon was a German protectorate from 1884 to 1916.

8. French and English are the official languages of Cameroon; many Cameroonians, of course, speak African languages. For a discussion of the language issue in Cameroon, see Piet Konings and Francis B. Nyamnjoh, *Negotiating an Anglophone Identity: A Study of the Politics of Recognition and Representation in Cameroon* (Leiden, Netherlands: Brill, 2003).

9. Professor Francis B. Nyamnjoh, interview by author, Gaborone, Botswana, February 13, 2003.

10. Nyamnjoh and Page, "*Whiteman Kontri* and the Enduring Allure of Modernity among Cameroonian Youth," 611, 628.

11. Nyamnjoh, interview.

12. Ibid.

13. Ibid.

14. Steve Olson, *Mapping Human History: Discovering the Past Through Our Genes* (Boston: Houghton Mifflin Company, 2002). For a different perspective, see Vincent Sarich and Frank Miele, *Race: The Reality of Human Differences* (Boulder, Colo.: Westview Press, 2004).

15. As Ann Gibbons points out, "More than 80% of European men have inherited their Y chromosomes — which are transmitted only from father to son — from Paleolithic ancestors who lived 25,000 to 40,000 years ago. Only 20% of Europeans trace their Y chromosome ancestry to Neolithic farmers. Thus, the genetic template for European men was set as early as 40,000 years ago, then modified — but not recast — by the Neolithic farmers about 10,000 years ago." Ann Gibbons, "Europeans Trace Ancestry to Paleolithic People," *Science* 290 (November 10, 2000): 1080.

16. Olson, *Mapping Human History,* 166–167, 171–174.

17. See, e.g., Bernard Lewis, *Race and Slavery in the Middle East: An Historical Enquiry* (New York: Oxford University Press, 1990); Ronald Segal, *Islam's Black Slaves: The Other Black Diaspora* (New York: Farrar, Straus, and Giroux, 2001).

18. Alan Heston, "Crusades and Jihads: A Long-Run Economic Perspective," *Annals of the American Academy of Political and Social Science* 588 (July 2003): 112–135.

19. For reflections on this topic, see Aly Colon, "Is There a White Male Culture?" *Seattle Times,* August 20, 1995, at L1. See, too, Richard Sherman, "The Subjective Experience of Race and Gender in Qualitative Research," *American Behavioral Scientist* 45 (April 2002): 1247–1253; Michael Welp, "Vanilla Voices: Researching White Men's Diversity Learning Journeys," *American Behavioral Scientist* 45 (April 2002): 1288–1296; Christina G. S. Palmer, "Risk Perception: Another Look at the 'White Male' Effect," *Health, Risk, and Society* 5 (March 2003): at p. 71 (via EBSCO*host*).

20. Langston Hughes, "White Man," in David R. Roediger, ed., *Black on White: Black Writers on What It Means to Be White* (New York: Schocken Books, 1998), 124–125.

21. Hans Ostrom describes "White Man" as follows: "It [the poem] is spoken by a collective persona representing 'Negroes' and is addressed to a collective 'listener' within the poem, the 'White Man.' " Hans Ostrom, *A Langston Hughes Encyclopedia* (Westport, Conn.: Greenwood Press, 2002), 422–423.

22. Hughes, "White Man," 124.

23. Ibid., 124–125.

24. Ibid., 124.

25. Ibid.

26. Ibid., 125.

27. Ibid.

28. For an overview of Hughes's extensive writings, see Ostrom, *A Langston Hughes Encyclopedia.*

29. Mia Bay, *The White Image in the Black Mind: African-American Ideas about White People, 1830–1925* (New York: Oxford University Press, 2000).

30. Ibid., 110.

31. Claude Andrew Clegg III, *An Original Man: The Life and Times of Elijah Muhammad* (New York: St. Martin's Press, 1997), passim; Karl Evanzz, *The*

Messenger: The Rise and Fall of Elijah Muhammad (New York: Pantheon Books, 1999), passim.

32. Malcolm X with the assistance of Alex Haley, *The Autobiography of Malcolm X* (New York: Grove Press, 1965); Malcolm X, *The End of White World Supremacy: Four Speeches,* edited and with an introduction by Imam Benjamin Karim (1971; reprint, New York: Arcade Publishing, n.d.).

33. In his *Autobiography,* Malcolm X describes how an event during his trip to Saudi Arabia in 1964 caused him to have an epiphany that gradually led him to soften his views on white men. (A wealthy Arab diplomat — a Caucasian man — gave up his luxurious hotel suite so that Malcolm X could use it.) "That morning," writes Malcolm X, "was when I first began to reappraise the 'white man.' It was when I first began to perceive that 'white man,' as commonly used, means complexion only secondarily; primarily it described attitudes and actions. In America, 'white man' meant specific attitudes and actions toward the black man, and toward all other nonwhite men. But in the Muslim world, I had seen that men with white complexions were more genuinely brotherly than anyone else had ever been." Malcolm X, *The Autobiography of Malcolm X,* 338–339.

34. Stetson Kennedy, *Southern Exposure* (1946; reprint, Boca Raton: Florida Atlantic University Press, 1991), 78–91; Stetson Kennedy, *Jim Crow Guide: The Way It Was* (1955; reprint, Boca Raton: Florida Atlantic University Press, 1990), 26–36; Francis D. Adams and Barry Sanders, *Alienable Rights: The Exclusion of African Americans in a White Man's Land, 1619–2000* (New York: HarperCollins, 2003).

35. For an informed discussion of multiculturalists and multiculturalism, see Nathan Glazer, *We Are All Multiculturalists Now* (Cambridge, Mass.: Harvard University Press, 1997).

36. Dominic Pulera, *Visible Differences: Why Race Will Matter to Americans in the Twenty-First Century* (New York: Continuum, 2002), 6–7. For right-of-center perspectives on the history of "diversity" in the United States, see Peter H. Schuck, *Diversity in America: Keeping Government at a Safe Distance* (Cambridge, Mass.: Belknap Press of Harvard University Press, 2003); Peter Wood, *Diversity: The Invention of a Concept* (San Francisco: Encounter Books, 2003).

37. The photo appears in the April 6, 1995, issue of the *Chicago Tribune,* Sec. 1, p. 1.

38. Mary Schmich, "Naked Truth Floats to Surface in Photo of 4 Men in a Tub," *Chicago Tribune,* April 9, 1995, Sec. 2, p. 1.

39. John McCarron, "In Defense of White Men," *Chicago Tribune,* September 11, 1995, Sec. 1, p. 13.

40. Ibid.

41. Ibid.

42. Ibid.

43. Ibid.

44. Paul Craig Roberts and Lawrence M. Stratton, *The New Color Line: How Quotas and Privilege Destroy Democracy* (Washington, D.C.: Regnery Publishing, 1995), 153.

45. Ibid.

46. Ibid.

47. Lynn Duke, "Cultural Shifts Bring Anxiety for White Men; Growing Diversity Imposing New Dynamic in Workplace," *Washington Post,* January 1, 1991, at A1; Robert Blau and Kerry Luft, "White Men Find Rules Aren't Same," *Chicago Tribune,* October 20, 1991, Sec. 1, at p. 1; David Gates, "White Male Paranoia," *Newsweek* 121 (March 29, 1993): 48–53; John R. Graham, "The End of the Great White Male," *USA Today* 122 (November 1993): 26–27; Michele Galen et al., "White, Male, and Worried," *BusinessWeek* (January 31, 1994): 50–55; Lance Morrow, "Men: Are They Really That Bad?" *Time* 143 (February 14, 1994): 52–59; Herbert Stein, "White Male Rage Sweeps America," *Wall Street Journal,* February 9, 1995, A14; "Are White Men *Really* Oppressed?" *Glamour* 93 (May 1995): 114.

48. Thomas B. Edsall, "Masculinity on the Run; From Workplace to Bedroom — to Timothy McVeigh," *Washington Post,* April 30, 1995, at C1; E. J. Dionne Jr., "Slandered White Men," *Washington Post,* May 2, 1995, A19; Charles Krauthammer, "Myth of the Angry White Male," *Washington Post,* May 26, 1995, A27.

49. Billie Wright Dziech, "Defusing Racial and Gender Conflicts," *USA Today* 125 (September 1996): 30.

50. Kennedy, *Jim Crow Guide,* 229.

51. Jim Cullen, *The American Dream: A Short History of an Idea that Shaped a Nation* (New York: Oxford University Press, 2003).

52. Drew D. Hansen, *The Dream: Martin Luther King Jr., and the Speech That Inspired a Nation* (New York: Ecco, 2003).

53. Derrick Bell, *Silent Covenants: Brown v. Board of Education and the Unfulfilled Hopes for Racial Reform* (New York: Oxford University Press, 2004); Sheryll Cashin, *The Failures of Integration: How Race and Class Are Undermining the American Dream* (New York: PublicAffairs, 2004).

Chapter 1: White and Male

1. I visited Johnston City, Illinois, on March 26, 2002 and March 27, 2002, and I spoke to the two experts on Johnston City history: Helen Lind (interview by author, Williamson County, Illinois, March 26, 2002) and William N. Macfarlane (interview by author, Williamson County, Illinois, March 27, 2002). Mr. Macfarlane's history of his hometown is the best treatment available on this topic. See William N. Macfarlane, *The Magic City of Egypt* (Johnston City, Ill.: William N. Macfarlane, 1991).

2. "First Public Lynching in History of County Took Place Thursday," *Marion (Ill.) Daily Republican,* June 11, 1915; "Four Italians to Be Returned to Marion at Once," *Marion (Ill.) Daily Republican,* June 15, 1915.

3. We do not know with certainty when Speranza arrived in the United States. We know from the Williamson County (Illinois) Death Records that Speranza was born in 1885.

4. "First Public Lynching in History of County Took Place Thursday."

5. Ibid.

6. Ibid.

7. "Johnston City Is Quiet and Orderly After Lynching," *Marion (Ill.) Daily Republican,* June 12, 1915; "Martial Law Not Declared over Johnston City," *Marion (Ill.) Daily Republican,* June 12, 1915; "No Outbreaks at Johnston City," *Marion (Ill.) Daily Republican,* June 14, 1915.

8. "Four Italians to Be Returned to Marion at Once"; "14 Sicilians Leave Johnston City for Italian Army," *Marion (Ill.) Daily Republican,* June 17, 1915.

9. "Lynching Views," *Marion (Ill.) Daily Republican,* June 12, 1915.

10. *Dunn and Kirkpatrick's Johnston City Directory* (Johnston City, Ill.: Dunn and Kirkpatrick, 1915), 5.

11. In 1920, Frank Bianco, a man who had been arrested for the murders of two teenagers in West Frankfort, Illinois, five miles north of Johnston City, volunteered that his accomplice, Settimi DeSantis, had murdered Ed Chapman. DeSantis, however, never confessed to the murder. Lind, interview.

Speranza's two siblings (Michaele and Gracona Speranza) sued the city of Johnston City in April 1916 by way of the Italian Consul of Chicago to gain compensation for his death. They asked for $5,000 in damages in what amounted to a wrongful-death suit. Seven months later, a federal court in East St. Louis, Illinois, gave the estate of Joseph Speranza a settlement of $900. This settlement tacitly acknowledged Speranza's innocence. "Johnston City Sued for $5,000," *Marion (Ill.) Daily Republican,* April 21, 1916; "Johnston City Must Pay $900," *Marion (Ill.) Daily Republican,* November 16, 1916.

12. The other lynchings of Italians occurred in the following places: Vicksburg, Mississippi (1886); New Orleans, Louisiana (1891); Kings County, Washington (1892); Guthrie, Oklahoma (1892); Denver, Colorado (1893); Hahnville, Louisiana (1896); Tallulah, Louisiana (1899); Erwin, Mississippi (1901); and Tampa, Florida (1910).

13. Johnston City is 98.1% white; the city's largest white ethnic subgroups are German Americans (17.5%), Irish Americans (14.9%), and people who choose United States or American (11.7%) when asked about their ancestry.

14. Eugene Lyon, *The Enterprise of Florida: Pedro Menéndez de Avilés and the Spanish Conquest of 1565–1568* (Gainesville: University Presses of Florida, 1976), 1–46. For an overview of Menéndez's life, see Eugene Lyon, ed., *Pedro Menéndez de Avilés* (New York: Garland Publishing, 1995).

15. Lyon, *The Enterprise of Florida,* 46–119.

16. Ibid., 119–210.

17. Kathleen A. Deagan, ed., *America's Ancient City: Spanish St. Augustine, 1565–1763* (New York: Garland Publishing, 1991).

18. In the past century, black-white relations have been an important issue to St. Augustinians. St. Augustine is a white-majority community — its Caucasian population includes a fair number of Minorcans — and African Americans presently constitute 15 percent of the population. The town received national attention in 1964 due to the civil rights protests and demonstrations there.

David R. Colburn, *Racial Change and Community Crisis: St. Augustine, Florida, 1877–1980* (New York: Columbia University Press, 1985).

19. I went to St. Augustine, Florida, on September 2, 2001 and January 14, 2004. For information about St. Augustine, see the City of St. Augustine's Web site: www.ci.st-augustine.fl.us.

20. I visited Avilés, Oviedo, Spain, on May 20, 2002. To learn more about Avilés, go to the City of Avilés's Web site: www.ayto-aviles.es.

21. Maldwyn Allen Jones, *American Immigration*, 2d ed. (Chicago: University of Chicago Press, 1992), 1–77.

22. For qualitative accounts of contemporary American Anglophilia, see Katharine W. Jones, *Accent on Privilege: English Identities and Anglophilia in the U.S.* (Philadelphia: Temple University Press, 2001), 13–14, 61–107.

23. Lu Ann Paletta and Fred L. Worth, *The World Almanac of Presidential Facts*, 2d ed. (New York: World Almanac, 1988).

24. Michael Dukakis, a Greek American, was the Democratic presidential nominee in 1988.

25. The term WASP can be used to describe Americans besides those descended from the English, but this is the narrowest — and most commonly accepted — definition of this ethno-religious group. For an excellent overview of WASPs, see Robert C. Christopher, *Crashing the Gates: The De-WASPing of America's Power Elite* (New York: Simon and Schuster, 1989).

26. David Hackett Fischer, *Albion's Seed: Four British Folkways in America* (New York: Oxford University Press, 1989), 6.

27. Ibid.

28. Ibid., 6–7.

29. Jones, *American Immigration*, 78–151.

30. Noel Ignatiev, *How the Irish Became White* (New York: Routledge, 1995).

31. David H. Bennett, *The Party of Fear: From Nativist Movements to the New Right in American History*, 2d ed. (New York: Vintage Books, 1995), 41, 53, 60, 72, 79, 108, 122, 127, 131–132, 135–136, 138, 140–144, 146–147, 149–150, 160, 183–187, 189, 215.

32. Hans Weiter, interview by author, Topeka, Kansas, August 13, 2001.

33. Jones, *American Immigration*, 152–211; Matthew Frye Jacobson, *Whiteness of a Different Color: European Immigrants and the Alchemy of Race* (Cambridge, Mass.: Harvard University Press, 1998); Desmond King, *Making Americans: Immigration, Race, and the Origins of the Diverse Democracy* (Cambridge, Mass.: Harvard University Press, 2000); Cheryl Shanks, *Immigration and the Politics of American Sovereignty, 1890–1990* (Ann Arbor: University of Michigan Press, 2001), 55–95; David R. Roediger, *Colored White: Transcending the Racial Past* (Berkeley: University of California Press, 2003), passim.

34. Jacobson, *Whiteness of a Different Color*, 5.

35. King, *Making Americans*, 11–253; Jones, *American Immigration*, 212–290; Jacobson, *Whiteness of a Different Color*, passim.

36. Christopher, *Crashing the Gates*, passim.

37. Marcia Graham Synnott, "Anti-Semitism and American Universities: Did Quotas Follow the Jews?" in David A. Gerber, ed., *Anti-Semitism in American History* (Urbana: University of Illinois Press, 1986), 233–271.

38. Richard L. Zweigenhaft and G. William Domhoff, *Jews in the Protestant Establishment* (New York: Praeger, 1982); Leonard Dinnerstein, *Antisemitism in America* (New York: Oxford University Press, 1994), passim.

39. Christopher, *Crashing the Gates,* passim.

40. Leonard Dinnerstein and David M. Reimers, *Ethnic Americans: A History of Immigration,* 4th ed. (New York: Columbia University Press, 1999), 171–172.

41. Richard D. Alba, "The Melting Pot: Myth or Reality?" in Stephen Steinberg, ed., *Race and Ethnicity in the United States: Issues and Debates* (Malden, Mass.: Blackwell Publishers, 2000), 212–215.

42. Joel Williamson, *New People: Miscegenation and Mulattoes in the United States* (New York: Free Press, 1980), 1–139; F. James Davis, *Who Is Black? One Nation's Definition* (University Park: Pennsylvania State University Press, 1991), 31–50; Kathy Russell, Midge Wilson, and Ronald Hall, *The Color Complex: The Politics of Skin Color among African Americans* (New York: Harcourt Brace Jovanovich, 1992), 9–40; Randall Kennedy, *Interracial Intimacies: Sex, Marriage, Identity, and Adoption* (New York: Pantheon Books, 2003), 42–213, 281–366.

43. I thank my great-uncle, Hans, for sharing this story with me: Hans Weiter, interview by author, Topeka, Kansas, August 13, 2001.

44. Williamson, *New People,* 111–139; Davis, *Who Is Black?* 51–80.

45. Brian W. Dippie, *The Vanishing American: White Attitudes and U.S. Indian Policy* (Lawrence: University Press of Kansas, 1982), 247–262.

46. Kennedy, *Interracial Intimacies,* 214–280; Rachel F. Moran, *Interracial Intimacy: The Regulation of Race and Romance* (Chicago: University of Chicago Press, 2001), 17–100.

47. Moran, *Interracial Intimacy,* 17.

48. Ibid., 17–100; Kennedy, *Interracial Intimacies,* 214–280. For the Supreme Court's landmark decision on interracial marriage, see *Loving v. Virginia,* 388 U.S. 1 (1967).

49. Doug Bates, "An American, an Arab," *(Portland, Or.) Oregonian,* November 18, 2001, F2. Unless otherwise noted, all the information in these paragraphs comes from my interview with Governor Victor G. Atiyeh in Portland, Oregon, on June 13, 2002. Governor Atiyeh kindly shared with me many documents related to his distinguished career in public life.

50. Atiyeh, interview. Atiyeh stepped down from the governorship in January 1987. Oregon limits its governors to two terms in office.

51. All of the quotations regarding Governor Atiyeh's accomplishments come from my interview with him.

52. www.hhrf.org/natoexpansion/ancestry.htm.

53. Alba, "The Melting Pot: Myth or Reality?" 218–220.

54. Laurent Belsie, "A New Nationalism on the Rise," *Christian Science Monitor,* June 11, 2002, 2–3.

55. Americans often conflate "white" and "European American," ignoring the Arab and Middle Eastern component of whiteness in the United States. Most white Americans, to be sure, trace their ancestry to Europe, but not all whites are European Americans.

56. www.hhrf.org/natoexpansion/ancestry.htm.

57. Andrzej Kulczycki and Arun Peter Lobo, "Patterns, Determinants, and Implications of Intermarriage among Arab Americans," *Journal of Marriage and Family* 64 (February 2002): 202–210.

58. David Attyah, who is Arab American, writes, " . . . I identify both as white and nonwhite." He goes on to say, "I'm the beneficiary of white privilege based on the way I look." At the same time, he notes, "I'm an Arab American. Culturally and ethnically and personally, I feel very alienated from white culture. Arab Americans are simultaneously raced and not raced. We're invisible and present in this culture at the same time. So in most contexts, I would not identify as white." For these quotations, see "David Attyah," in Cooper Thompson, Emmett Schaefer, and Harry Brod, *White Men Challenging Racism: 35 Personal Stories* (Durham, N.C.: Duke University Press, 2003), 129.

59. Jack G. Shaheen, *The TV Arab* (Bowling Green, Ohio: Bowling Green State University Popular Press, 1984); Jack G. Shaheen, *Reel Bad Arabs: How Hollywood Vilifies a People* (New York: Olive Branch Press, 2001).

60. Nabeel Abraham, "The Gulf Crisis and Anti-Arab Racism in America," in Cynthia Peters, ed., *Collateral Damage: The New World Order at Home and Abroad* (Boston: South End Press, 1992), 255–278; Nabeel Abraham, "Anti-Arab Racism and Violence in the United States," in Ernest McCarus, ed., *The Development of Arab-American Identity* (Ann Arbor: University of Michigan Press, 1994), 155–214.

61. Human Rights Watch, *"We Are Not the Enemy": Hate Crimes Against Arabs, Muslims, and Those Perceived to be Arab or Muslim after September 11* (New York: Human Rights Watch, November 2002).

62. Ibid.

63. Robert E. Pierre, "Fear and Anxiety Permeate Arab Enclave Near Detroit; Muslim Americans Feel They Are Targets in War on Terror," *Washington Post,* August 4, 2002, A3; Jodi Wilgoren, "Going by 'Joe,' Not 'Yussef,' but Still Feeling Like an Outcast," *New York Times,* September 11, 2002, G15; Bay Fang, "Under Scrutiny, Always," *U.S. News and World Report* 133 (December 30, 2002/January 6, 2003): 26, 28, 30–31.

64. Professor Nabeel Abraham, interview by author, Dearborn, Michigan, September 12, 2002.

65. Dominic Pulera, *Visible Differences: Why Race Will Matter to Americans in the Twenty-First Century* (New York: Continuum, 2002), 85–87.

66. Ibid., 87.

67. "Lenny Kravitz," in Judith Graham, ed., *Current Biography Yearbook, 1996* (New York: H. W. Wilson Company, 1996), 275–278.

68. Yu Xie and Kimberly Goyette, "The Racial Identification of Biracial Children with One Asian Parent: Evidence from the 1990 Census," *Social Forces* 76

(December 1997): 547–570; Maria P. P. Root, "Multiracial Americans: Changing the Face of Asian America," in Lee C. Lee and Nolan W. S. Zane, eds., *Handbook of Asian American Psychology* (Thousand Oaks, Calif.: Sage Publications, 1998), 261–287; Maria P. P. Root, "Factors Influencing the Variation in Racial and Ethnic Identity of Mixed-Heritage Persons of Asian Ancestry," in Teresa Williams-León and Cynthia L. Nakashima, eds., *The Sum of Our Parts: Mixed-Heritage Asian Americans* (Philadelphia: Temple University Press, 2001), 61–70.

69. Roberto Suro, "Mixed Doubles," *American Demographics* 21 (November 1999): 59.

70. Maria P. P. Root, *Love's Revolution: Interracial Marriage* (Philadelphia: Temple University Press, 2001).

71. Carl L. Bankston III and Jacques Henry, "Endogamy among Louisiana Cajuns: A Social Class Explanation," *Social Forces* 77 (June 1999): 1317–1338.

72. U.S. Census Bureau, *Statistical Abstract of the United States: 2003* (123rd ed.) (Washington, D.C.: U.S. Government Printing Office, 2003), Table 62.

73. Root, *Love's Revolution,* passim; Renee C. Romano, *Race Mixing: Black-White Marriage in Postwar America* (Cambridge, Mass.: Harvard University Press, 2003). See, too, "Why More Black Women Are Dating White Men," *Jet* 102 (August 26, 2002): at p. 12 (via EBSCO*host*); Zondra Hughes, "Why Some Sisters Date Whites and 'Others,' " *Ebony* 58 (May 2003): 55–56, 58.

74. John D. Skrentny, "Introduction," in John David Skrentny, ed., *Color Lines: Affirmative Action, Immigration, and Civil Rights Options for America* (Chicago: University of Chicago Press, 2001), 12.

75. Michael J. Rosenfeld, "Measures of Assimilation in the Marriage Market: Mexican Americans 1970–1990," *Journal of Marriage and Family* 64 (February 2002): 161.

76. Ibid., 152–162.

77. Sharon M. Lee and Marilyn Fernandez, "Trends in Asian American Racial/Ethnic Intermarriage: A Comparison of 1980 and 1990 Census Data," *Sociological Perspectives* 41 (Summer 1998): 323–342.

78. Ian Frazier writes that his Indian friend, Floyd John, jokingly refers to him in this way. See Ian Frazier, *On the Rez* (New York: Farrar, Straus, and Giroux, 2000), 3–4.

79. Shelly Branch, "If You Don't Have a 'Do,' Why Wear a Doo Rag?" *Wall Street Journal,* September 12, 2003, at A1.

80. John D. Skrentny, *The Minority Rights Revolution* (Cambridge, Mass.: Belknap Press of Harvard University Press, 2002), 263–275; Duane F. Stroman, *The Disability Rights Movement: From Deinstitutionalization to Self-Determination* (Lanham, Md.: University Press of America, 2003), 83–117.

81. Michelle R. Hebl and Robert E. Kleck, "The Social Consequences of Physical Disability," in Todd F. Heatherton et al., eds., *The Social Psychology of Stigma* (New York: Guilford Press, 2000), 419–439.

82. U.S. Census Bureau, *Statistical Abstract of the United States: 2003,* Table 197.

83. Linda Hamilton Krieger, ed., *Backlash Against the ADA: Reinterpreting Disability Rights* (Ann Arbor: University of Michigan Press, 2003).

84. Doris Zames Fleischer and Frieda Zames, *The Disability Rights Movement: From Charity to Confrontation* (Philadelphia: Temple University Press, 2001), 200–215.

85. Stroman, *The Disability Rights Movement,* 116.

86. Ruth O'Brien, *Crippled Justice: The History of Modern Disability Policy in the Workplace* (Chicago: University of Chicago Press, 2001). For an excellent account of the activism that has led to so many advances for people with disabilities, see Fleischer and Zames, *The Disability Rights Movement.*

87. O'Brien, *Crippled Justice,* 203–204.

88. Ibid., 204.

89. Jae Kennedy and Marjorie Olney, "Job Discrimination in the Post-ADA Era: Estimates from the 1994 and 1995 National Health Interview Surveys," *Rehabilitation Counseling Bulletin* 45 (Fall 2001): 24–30.

90. Ibid., 27.

91. Ibid., 24–30.

92. Carol Padden and Tom Humphries, *Deaf in America: Voices from a Culture* (Cambridge, Mass.: Harvard University Press, 1988); Joseph P. Shapiro, *No Pity: People with Disabilities Forging a New Civil Rights Movement* (New York: TimesBooks/Random House, 1993), 74–104; Katherine A. Jankowski, *Deaf Empowerment: Emergence, Struggle, and Rhetoric* (Washington, D.C.: Gallaudet University Press, 1997). See, too, Edward Dolnick, "Deafness as Culture," *Atlantic Monthly* 272 (September 1993): 37–40, 43, 46–48, 50–53; Andrew Solomon, "Defiantly Deaf," *New York Times Magazine* (August 28, 1994): 38–45, 62, 65–68; Bonnie Poitras Tucker, "The ADA and Deaf Culture: Contrasting Precepts, Conflicting Results," *Annals of the American Academy of Political and Social Science* 549 (January 1997): 24–36; Bonnie Poitras Tucker, "Deaf Culture, Cochlear Implants, and Elective Disability," *Hastings Center Report* 28 (July–August 1998): 6–14.

93. Marc Peyser, " 'Survivor' Tsunami," *Newsweek* 136 (August 28, 2000): 52–59; Ben Pappas, "The Survivor," *US Weekly* (September 18, 2000): 54–57.

94. Rich Hatch, *101 Survival Secrets: How to Make $1,000,000, Lose 100 Pounds, and Just Plain Live Happily* (New York: Lyons Press, 2000), 13–29, 31–36.

95. Ibid., 34.

96. "The Power List," *Forbes* 167 (March 19, 2001): 145.

97. Robert T. Michael et al., *Sex in America: A Definitive Survey* (Boston: Little, Brown, and Company, 1994), 169–183.

98. Ibid., 175.

99. Ibid., 176.

100. Dan Black et al., "Demographics of the Gay and Lesbian Population in the United States: Evidence from Available Systematic Data Sources," *Demography* 37 (May 2000): 139–154; Rebecca Gardyn, "A Market Kept in the Closet,"

American Demographics 23 (November 2001): 36–40, 42–43; David Whelan, "Do Ask, Do Tell," *American Demographics* 23 (November 2001): 41.

101. Michael et al., *Sex in America,* 177.

102. For a definitive history of the gay rights movement, see Dudley Clendinen and Adam Nagourney, *Out for Good: The Struggle to Build a Gay Rights Movement in America* (New York: Simon and Schuster, 1999).

103. Shawn Meghan Burn, "Heterosexuals' Use of 'Fag' and 'Queer' to Deride One Another: A Contributor to Heterosexism and Stigma," *Journal of Homosexuality* 40:2 (2000): 1–11.

104. Clyde Wilcox and Robin Wolpert, "Gay Rights in the Public Sphere: Public Opinion on Gay and Lesbian Equality," in Craig A. Rimmerman, Kenneth D. Wald, and Clyde Wilcox, eds., *The Politics of Gay Rights* (Chicago: University of Chicago Press, 2000), 412.

105. Ibid., 409–432. For information about how race affects attitudes in this regard, see Gregory B. Lewis, "Black-White Differences in Attitudes toward Homosexuality and Gay Rights," *Public Opinion Quarterly* 67 (Spring 2003): 59–78.

106. Stephen H. Miller, "Gay White Males: PC's Unseen Target," in Bruce Bawer, ed., *Beyond Queer: Challenging Gay Left Orthodoxy* (New York: Free Press, 1996), 24–37.

107. Keith Boykin, *One More River to Cross: Black and Gay in America* (New York: Anchor Books/Doubleday, 1996), particularly 30–84, 212–235; Allan Bérubé, "How Gay Stays White and What Kind of White It Stays," in Birgit Brander Rasmussen et al., eds., *The Making and Unmaking of Whiteness* (Durham, N.C.: Duke University Press, 2001), 234–265.

108. Michelangelo Signorile, *Life Outside: The Signorile Report on Gay Men: Sex, Drugs, Muscles, and the Passages of Life* (New York: HarperCollins Publishers, 1997), 99–100.

109. Jean Reith Schroedel and Pamela Fiber, "Lesbian and Gay Policy Priorities: Commonality and Difference," in Craig A. Rimmerman, Kenneth D. Wald, and Clyde Wilcox, eds., *The Politics of Gay Rights* (Chicago: University of Chicago Press, 2000), 97–118.

110. Alexandra Chasin, *Selling Out: The Gay and Lesbian Movement Goes to Market* (New York: St. Martin's Press, 2000); M. V. Lee Badgett, *Money, Myths, and Change: The Economic Lives of Lesbians and Gay Men* (Chicago: University of Chicago Press, 2001), 102–132; Suzanna Danuta Walters, *All the Rage: The Story of Gay Visibility in America* (Chicago: University of Chicago Press, 2001), 235–289.

111. Walters, *All the Rage,* 285.

112. Ibid.

113. For background on this topic, see Badgett, *Money, Myths, and Change,* passim.

114. Alessandra Stanley, "Militants Back 'Queer,' Shoving 'Gay' the Way of 'Negro,' " *New York Times,* April 6, 1991, Sec. 1, pp. 23, 24; Craig Wilson, "There's Little Queer about the Word Anymore," *USA Today,* August 5, 2003,

D2. See, too, Joshua Gamson, "Must Identity Movements Self-Destruct? A Queer Dilemma," *Social Problems* 42 (August 1995): 390–407.

115. Ibid.

116. Gamson, "Must Identity Movements Self-Destruct?" 393.

117. Bruce Bawer, "Introduction," in Bruce Bawer, ed., *Beyond Queer: Challenging Gay Left Orthodoxy* (New York: Free Press, 1996), ix–xiv.

118. Robert J. Corber, "Lesbian and Gay Studies in Today's Academy," *Academe* 84 (September–October 1998): 46–49.

119. Mark Carl Rom, "Gays and AIDS: Democratizing Disease?" in Craig A. Rimmerman, Kenneth D. Wald, and Clyde Wilcox, eds., *The Politics of Gay Rights* (Chicago: University of Chicago Press, 2000), 217–248.

120. These data come from the Centers for Disease Control and Prevention Web site (www.cdc.gov).

121. Cathy J. Cohen, "Contested Membership: Black Gay Identities and the Politics of AIDS," in John D'Emilio, William B. Turner, and Urvashi Vaid, *Creating Change: Sexuality, Public Policy, and Civil Rights* (New York: St. Martin's Press, 2000), 382–406.

122. Beth Loffreda, *Losing Matt Shepard: Life and Politics in the Aftermath of Anti-Gay Murder* (New York: Columbia University Press, 2000).

123. Walters, *All the Rage*, 280–285.

124. Signorile, *Life Outside*, especially 3–74.

125. Larry Gross, *Up from Invisibility: Lesbians, Gay Men, and the Media in America* (New York: Columbia University Press, 2001).

126. Cliff Edwards, "Coming Out in Corporate America," *BusinessWeek* (December 15, 2003): 64–65, 68, 70.

127. Michael Bochenek and A. Widney Brown, *Hatred in the Hallways: Violence and Discrimination Against Lesbian, Gay, Bisexual, and Transgender Students in U.S. Schools* (New York: Human Rights Watch, 2001); Robert Tomsho, "Schools' Efforts to Protect Gays Face Opposition," *Wall Street Journal,* February 20, 2003, at B1; Amanda Paulson, "Debate on Gay Unions Splits along Generations," *Christian Science Monitor,* July 7, 2003, at p. 1.

128. Walters, *All the Rage,* 59–176.

129. Patricia Callahan, "How a Gay Union Led to Paper's Soul-Search," *Wall Street Journal,* July 26, 2002, at B1; New York Times, "Times Will Begin Reporting Gay Couples' Ceremonies," *New York Times,* August 18, 2002, Sec. 1, p. 30; Holly J. Morris and Vicky Hallett, "Public Displays of Affection," *U.S. News and World Report* 133 (September 9, 2002): 42–43; Greg Jonsson, "Paper Will Run Announcement of Gay Couple's Anniversary; Post-Dispatch Joins Others Nationwide in Accepting Ads," *St. Louis Post-Dispatch*, September 13, 2002, C4.

130. Olivia Barker, "Regular Guys Cast a Jaded Eye at 'Metrosexual' Trend; Web Logs, Comedy Spoofs Feeding on a Backlash," *USA Today,* January 22, 2004, at D1.

131. Ian F. Haney López, *White by Law: The Legal Construction of Race* (New York: New York University Press, 1996), passim.

132. Some white guys leave the white male grouping temporarily or even permanently by engaging in transvestitism or other transgender activities. This kind of transgender switch is largely devoid of political significance, and it usually occurs for deeply personal and idiosyncratic reasons.

133. Carol Morello, "Native American Roots, Once Hidden, Now Embraced," *Washington Post,* April 7, 2001, at A1; Sara Steindorf, "American Indians on the Rise," *Christian Science Monitor,* December 6, 2001, 11, 13.

134. Dick Mayo, interview by author, Sallisaw, Oklahoma, July 26, 2002.

135. Mayo points out that he knew of one septic tank installer who had a Certificate of Degree of Indian Blood (CDIB) of 1/1250th Indian ancestry. Dick Mayo, letter to author, September 23, 2002.

136. Mayo, interview.

137. Solomon Moore and Robin Fields, "The Great 'White' Influx," *Los Angeles Times,* July 31, 2002, at A1.

138. Ibid.

139. Jess Cagle, "The Next Action Hero," *Time* 160 (August 5, 2002): 61–62.

140. Lorenza Munoz, "In Today's Spy Games, Worldliness Is Not Enough," *Los Angeles Times,* July 29, 2002, at F1; John Horn, " 'XXX' Threat," *Newsweek* 140 (August 5, 2002): 57.

Chapter 2: Rebirth and Regeneration

1. Allison Jones, interview by author, Americana, São Paulo, Brazil, December 1, 2002. I thank Allison and Eloisa Jones for their graciousness and hospitality during my visit to Americana and its environs. Mr. Jones took my family and me to see many places of interest in and around Americana.

2. There were many reasons why American emigrants chose to go to Brazil after the Civil War. For one, Emperor Dom Pedro II extended a warm welcome to the *confederados,* in part because of their expertise in the textile industry. And Brazil supported the Confederate States of America (CSA) during the Civil War. The *confederados* were also attracted to Brazil by the temperate climate, the legality of slavery there, the availability of inexpensive land, and many other factors. The *confederados* formed several colonies in Brazil, most famously in Santa Bárbara D'Oeste (pop. 169,735) and Americana (pop. 182,084). Today at least 100,000 Brazilians trace some or all of their ancestry to the American immigrants.

For background on the *confederados,* see Eugene C. Harter, *The Lost Colony of the Confederacy* (Jackson: University Press of Mississippi, 1985); William Clark Griggs, *The Elusive Eden: Frank McMullan's Confederate Colony in Brazil* (Austin: University of Texas Press, 1987); Cyrus B. Dawsey and James M. Dawsey, eds., *The Confederados: Old South Immigrants in Brazil* (Tuscaloosa: University of Alabama Press, 1995). I interviewed Eugene and Dorothy Harter, who know much about the history and culture of the *confederados,* in Chestertown, Maryland, on September 25, 2002.

3. Jones, interview.

4. Ibid.

5. Stephen Buckley, "A Taste of Dixie in Brazil; In Americana, They Wave the Confederate Flag — With Some Reservations," *Washington Post,* August 22, 1999, A23.

6. Jones, interview.

7. This vignette draws upon my extensive conversations with Jim Kurtti, both on the telephone and in person. Mr. Kurtti spent an entire day (May 17, 2000) showing me around the Keweenaw Peninsula. I also went to northwestern Michigan on March 25, 2000.

8. To learn more about the Finnish-American Heritage Center, go to www.finlandia.edu/fahc.html.

9. *The Finnish American Reporter* Web site (www.finnishamericanreporter .com) is a good source of information about this publication.

10. James S. Pula, *Polish Americans: An Ethnic Community* (New York: Twayne Publishers, 1995).

11. Celeste Ray, *Highland Heritage: Scottish Americans in the American South* (Chapel Hill: University of North Carolina Press, 2001).

12. Highland, Utah, has the highest percentage of English Americans — 43.1% — of any U.S. community with 5,000 or more residents. And Provo, Utah, qualifies as the U.S. city of 100,000 or more people with the highest percentage of English Americans: Fully 30.4% percent of its residents have English roots. G. Scott Thomas, "Census: Americans Moving Away from Ancestry," *Business Journal of Tampa Bay,* October 7, 2002.

13. The list of the 26 Mayflower progenitors includes the following men: John Alden, Isaac Allerton, John Billington, William Bradford, William Brewster, Peter Browne, James Chilton, Francis Cooke, Edward Doty, Francis Eaton, Moses Fletcher, Edward Fuller, Samuel Fuller, Stephen Hopkins, John Howland, Richard More, William Mullins, Degory Priest, Thomas Rogers, Henry Samson, George Soule, Myles Standish, John Tilley, Richard Warren, William White, and Edward Winslow.

14. Jim Faber, "Pilgrim Pride," *Family Tree Magazine* (June 2000). Online at www.familytreemagazine.com/articles/june00/pilgrims.html.

15. To learn more about the General Society of Mayflower Descendants, go to www.mayflower.org.

16. Thomas, "Census: Americans Moving Away from Ancestry"; Michael Powell, "Rethinking Who They Are; Census Shows People Are Declining to Report Their Heritage," *Washington Post,* May 25, 2002, A10; Laurent Belsie, "A New Nationalism on the Rise," *Christian Science Monitor,* June 11, 2002, 2–3; John Frank, "One Nation, Indescribable; More People Describe Their Ancestry as 'American,' Census Finds," *Roanoke (Va.) Times and World News,* July 4, 2002, at A1.

17. For an informative article about Greek America, see Stavros T. Constantinou, "Profiles of Greek Americans," in Kate A. Berry and Martha L. Henderson, eds., *Geographical Identities of Ethnic America: Race, Space, and Place* (Reno: University of Nevada Press, 2002), 92–115.

18. Leo Pap, *The Portuguese-Americans* (Boston: Twayne Publishers, 1981), 18–53, 79–102.

19. Professor Frank F. Sousa, e-mail to author, April 21, 2004.

20. Ibid.

21. Ibid.

22. U.S. Census Bureau, *Statistical Abstract of the United States: 2003* (123rd ed.) (Washington, D.C.: U.S. Government Printing Office, 2003), Table 8.

23. Sousa, e-mail; Professor Frank F. Sousa, telephone conversation with author, September 17, 2002.

24. Sousa, e-mail.

25. Michael Barone and Richard E. Cohen, *The Almanac of American Politics 2004* (Washington, D.C.: National Journal, 2003), 194–196, 211–213, 218–219; David Hawkings and Brian Nutting, eds., *CQ's Politics in America 2004, The 108th Congress* (Washington, D.C.: CQ Press, 2003), 88–89, 102, 107.

26. For background on the attitudes of Portuguese Americans in Massachusetts, see Clyde W. Barrow, ed., *Portuguese-Americans and Contemporary Civic Culture in Massachusetts* (North Dartmouth: University of Massachusetts Dartmouth, Center for Portuguese Studies and Culture and the Center for Policy Analysis, 2002).

27. Odd S. Lovoll, *The Promise of America: A History of the Norwegian-American People,* 2d ed. (Minneapolis: University of Minnesota Press, 1999), 7–40.

28. Tova Brandt, interview by author, Decorah, Iowa, June 24, 2002.

29. Odd S. Lovoll, *The Promise Fulfilled: A Portrait of Norwegian Americans Today* (Minneapolis: University of Minnesota Press, 1998).

30. C. Paige Gutierrez, *Cajun Foodways* (Jackson: University Press of Mississippi, 1992).

31. For the Web site of *A Prairie Home Companion,* see www.phc.mpr.org. Keillor has published four books about Lake Wobegon: Garrison Keillor, *Lake Wobegon Days* (New York: Viking, 1985); Garrison Keillor, *Leaving Home* (New York: Viking, 1987); Garrison Keillor, *Wobegon Boy* (New York: Viking, 1997); Garrison Keillor, *Lake Wobegon Summer 1956* (New York: Viking, 2001).

32. Stanley Lieberson, *A Matter of Taste: How Names, Fashions, and Culture Change* (New Haven, Conn.: Yale University Press, 2000), 178.

33. Herbert J. Gans, "Symbolic Ethnicity: The Future of Ethnic Groups and Cultures in America," *Ethnic and Racial Studies* 2 (January 1979): 1–20.

34. U.S. Census Bureau, *Statistical Abstract of the United States: 2003,* Table 52.

35. Ibid., Table 8.

36. Ibid.

37. The information about Mrs. Kuchma's visit to Utah comes from the following source: Dr. Erlend D. Peterson, e-mail to author, February 15, 2003. This vignette draws upon my interview with Dr. Erlend D. Peterson in Provo, Utah,

on April 10, 2003, as well as my telephone conversation with Dr. Peterson on January 23, 2003, multiple e-mail communications with him, and many materials related to his remarkable career that he kindly shared with me. I also interviewed his son, Andrew Erlend Peterson (Andrew E. Peterson, telephone conversation with author, March 20, 2003).

38. For a balanced overview of The Church of Jesus Christ of Latter-day Saints, see Richard N. Ostling and Joan K. Ostling, *Mormon America: The Power and the Promise* (New York: HarperSanFrancisco, 1999).

39. In 1996, Peterson was responsible for the Statehood Centennial Ambassador Visits Program, in which 42 foreign ambassadors visited Utah. The following year, Peterson began the BYU Ambassador Visits Program.

40. Erlend Peterson is a great-great-great-grandson of Svend Larsen, an important figure in the Scandinavian history of The Church of Jesus Christ of Latter-day Saints. "Svend Larsen," notes Erlend Peterson, "was the first resident Norwegian to join the Church of Jesus Christ of Latter-day Saints in 1851 and transport the first Mormon missionaries from Denmark to Norway." Peterson, e-mail, February 15, 2003.

41. Erlend Peterson's father, Dean Peterson, had been a mission president in Norway during the 1960s. His son, Andrew Peterson, is presently serving as an LDS missionary in Norway.

42. For more information about Nordmanns-Forbundet, visit the organization's Web site: www.norseman.no.

43. The license plates on Peterson's Ford Mustang read "Sir Pete."

44. Billie Wright Dziech, "Coping with the Alienation of White Male Students," in Barbara A. Arrighi, ed., *Understanding Inequality: The Intersection of Race/Ethnicity, Class, and Gender* (Lanham, Md.: Rowman and Littlefield Publishers, 2001), 51–55.

45. U.S. Census Bureau, *Statistical Abstract of the United States: 2003,* Table 23.

46. Latinos make up a sizable percentage of the residents of Arizona, New Mexico, and West Texas, but there are relatively few Hispanics in Louisiana, Mississippi, Alabama, Georgia, and South Carolina.

47. William H. Frey, "Census 2000 Reveals New Native-Born and Foreign-Born Shifts Across U.S." PSC Research Report No. 02–520 (Ann Arbor: Population Studies Center, University of Michigan, August 2002), 19, 20.

48. Ibid., 6.

49. Ibid.

50. Ibid., 20.

51. Ibid., passim.

52. William H. Frey, "Immigration and Demographic Balkanization: Toward One America or Two?" in James W. Hughes and Joseph J. Seneca, eds., *America's Demographic Tapestry: Baseline for the New Millennium* (New Brunswick, N.J.: Rutgers University Press, 1999), 92–93.

53. For perspectives on recent developments on regional migration, see William H. Frey, "Escaping the City — And the Suburbs," *American Demographics* 24 (June 2002): 21–23; Roderick J. Harrison, "Moving Out When Minorities Move In," *American Demographics* 24 (June 2002): 23–24.

54. *Shaft*, VHS, directed by John Singleton (2000; Hollywood, Calif.: Paramount Pictures, 2000).

55. Wade addresses Shaft as "Slick" in one exchange, and as "Bro" in another. Shaft has a variety of names for his nemesis, including "Richie Rich," "Running Man, "white boy," and "silver-spoon motherf----r."

56. Throughout the film, Hernandez and his crew refer to Wade as *blanquito*, or white boy.

57. Two cops (Shaft and a white coworker named Luger), masquerade as muggers and rob Wade of the $40,000 that he was supposed to give to Hernandez. Hernandez then makes Wade one of his "boys," or drug couriers, to pay for the hit on Palmieri.

58. Robert B. Costello, ed., *Random House Webster's College Dictionary* (New York: Random House, 1992), 1234.

59. Ibid., 868.

60. Ibid., 1129.

61. Ibid., 316.

62. Ibid., 633. See, too, Anthony Harkins, *Hillbilly: A Cultural History of an American Icon* (New York: Oxford University Press, 2004).

63. Costello, ed., *Random House Webster's College Dictionary,* 994.

64. Eric Zorn, "Boy Oh Boy, Burris Gaffe Sheds Light on Racial Shadings," *Chicago Tribune,* March 2, 1998, Sec. 2, at p. 1; Rick Reilly, "White like Me," *Sports Illustrated* 96 (February 4, 2002): 152.

65. Paul Cameron, a twentysomething native of the Chattanooga, Tennessee, area, is one white male who reports that his black friends refer to him as a "white boy." He enjoys their good-natured ribbing. When he was a student at Tennessee State University, a predominantly black institution in Nashville, Cameron earned the sobriquets "Crazy White Boy" and "Cool White Boy Who Drives a Truck" from his African-American peers. Paul Cameron, telephone conversation with author, March 30, 2001.

66. Michele Galen et al., "White, Male, and Worried," *BusinessWeek* (January 31, 1994): 52.

67. Costello, ed., *Random House Webster's College Dictionary,* 575, 942.

68. Gerald W. Haslam, *Straight White Male* (Reno: University of Nevada Press, 2000); Brock Clarke, *The Ordinary White Boy* (New York: Harcourt, 2001); Barbara D'Amato, *White Male Infant* (New York: Forge/Tom Doherty Associates, 2002); Ruaridh Nicoll, *White Male Heart* (Boston: Justin, Charles, and Company, 2003).

69. Michael Moore, *Stupid White Men ... and Other Sorry Excuses for the State of the Nation!* (New York: ReganBooks, 2001).

70. Mark D. Naison, *White Boy: A Memoir* (Philadelphia: Temple University Press, 2002).

71. See Houston A. Baker Jr., "Caliban's Triple Play," in Henry Louis Gates Jr., ed., *"Race," Writing, and Difference* (Chicago: University of Chicago Press, 1986), 381–395; Richard Bernstein, *Dictatorship of Virtue: How the Battle Over Multiculturalism Is Reshaping Our Schools, Our Country, and Our Lives* (New York: Vintage Books/Random House, 1995), 131.

72. *The Chicago Manual of Style,* 15th ed. (Chicago: University of Chicago Press, 2003), 157, 160.

73. For an interesting historical explanation of how God came to be viewed as a male by many humans, see Robert S. McElvaine, *Eve's Seed: Biology, the Sexes, and the Course of History* (New York: McGraw-Hill, 2001), 135–150.

74. *The Chicago Manual of Style,* 15th ed., 233.

75. David R. Johnson and Laurie K. Scheuble, "Women's Marital Naming in Two Generations: A National Study," *Journal of Marriage and the Family* 57 (August 1995): 724–732.

76. Ibid., 731.

77. Laura Stafford and Susan L. Kline, "Married Women's Name Choices and Sense of Self," *Communication Reports* 9 (Winter 1996): 85–92; Jean M. Twenge, "Mrs. His Name": Women's Preferences for Married Names," *Psychology of Women Quarterly* 21 (September 1997): 417–429; Claire E. Etaugh et al., " 'Names Can Never Hurt Me?' The Effects of Surname Use on Perceptions of Married Women," *Psychology of Women Quarterly* 23 (December 1999): 819–823.

78. Numerous American women 50 and older still refer to themselves as Mrs. John Doe. And in some small-town newspapers, it is still the practice to refer to newlyweds as Mr. and Mrs. John Doe.

79. For background on these issues, see Elsdon C. Smith, *American Surnames* (Philadelphia: Chilton Book Company, 1969); Elsdon C. Smith, *New Dictionary of American Family Names* (New York: Harper and Row, 1973); J. N. Hook, *Family Names: How Our Surnames Came to America* (New York: Macmillan Publishing Company, 1982); H. Amanda Robb and Andrew Chesler, *Encyclopedia of American Family Names* (New York: HarperCollins, 1995).

80. Hook, *Family Names,* 321–344.

81. Julia Keller, "Mono a Mono: Election Is Battle of the One-Syllable Names," *Chicago Tribune,* March 21, 2000, Sec. 5, at p. 1.

82. Ibid.

83. Ibid.

84. Wayne Parry, "U.S. Arabs Changing Names," *Tulsa (Okla.) World,* March 21, 2002, 2.

85. Donna Magnuson, telephone conversation with author, January 10, 2002.

86. Parry, "U.S. Arabs Changing Names"; Brian Donohue, "Their Own Names Are What They Fear," *Newhouse News Service,* March 6, 2002, at p. 1; Jodi Wilgoren, "Going by 'Joe,' Not 'Yussef,' but Still Feeling Like an Outcast," *New York Times,* September 11, 2002, G15; Marjorie Valbrun and Ann Davis, "Less Welcome: In Pakistani Areas of New York City, A Lingering

Fear," *Wall Street Journal,* November 13, 2002, at A1; Tanya Schevitz, "FBI Sees Leap in Anti-Muslim Hate Crimes; 9/11 Attacks Blamed for Bias," *San Francisco Chronicle,* November 26, 2002, at A1.

87. Asma Gull Hasan, *American Muslims: The New Generation,* 2d ed. (New York: Continuum, 2002), 9.

88. Lena Williams, *It's the Little Things: The Everyday Interactions that Get Under the Skin of Blacks and Whites* (New York: Harcourt, 2000), 154–158.

89. According to Lena Williams, "Many blacks worry that as names become readily identifiable by race, black children will be stigmatized or subjected to other people's prejudices." Williams, *It's the Little Things,* 158.

90. Marianne Bertrand and Sendhil Mullainathan, "Are Emily and Brendan More Employable than Lakisha and Jamal? A Field Experiment on Labor Market Discrimination," November 18, 2002. www.econ.yale.edu/seminars/strategy/st02/bertrand-021204.pdf.

91. Lieberson, *A Matter of Taste,* passim.

92. Dora L. Costa, *The Evolution of Retirement: An American Economic History, 1880–1990* (Chicago: University of Chicago Press, 1998), 188.

93. Ibid.

94. Ann Zimmerman, "If Boys Just Want to Have Fun, This May Bring Them Down," *Wall Street Journal,* November 10, 2000, at A1.

95. Ibid.

96. David Crary, " 'Boys Are Stupid' Shirts Bring Protest; Some Stores Are Pulling the Clothing Line from Their Shelves," *Associated Press,* January 29, 2004.

Chapter 3: Heterogeneous Hegemons

1. In this account, I rely on the following edition of the novel: John Steinbeck, *The Grapes of Wrath* (1939; reprint with an introduction by Robert DeMott, New York: Penguin Books, 1992). I went to Sequoyah County, Oklahoma, on July 26, 2002. Moreover, I regularly visit the Central Valley, the agricultural heartland of California that stretches from Kern County to Sacramento County. Dick Mayo published an illuminating four-part series, "Sequoyah County and the Depression's Great Migration," in the *Sequoyah County (Okla.) Times* (November 17, 2002, November 24, 2002, December 1, 2002, and December 8, 2002).

2. Charles J. Shindo, *Dust Bowl Migrants in the American Imagination* (Lawrence: University Press of Kansas, 1997), 147–165.

3. For the definitive study on this topic, see James N. Gregory, *American Exodus: The Dust Bowl Migration and Okie Culture in California* (New York: Oxford University Press, 1989).

4. Dr. Guy Logsdon, the Oklahoma state folklorist, points out that many people were cotton farmers in southern and eastern Oklahoma in the 1920s and 1930s. Cotton prices started falling in 1925. By the early 1930s, cotton prices had hit rock bottom. When the Agricultural Adjustment Act was enacted

in 1933, it gave landowners subsidies for letting their land lie fallow. So in many cases tenants and sharecroppers were booted off the land they had farmed for years, because the landowners wanted to collect subsidies for those plots of land. Displaced white tenants and sharecroppers generally went west, while their African-American counterparts headed north. Dr. Guy Logsdon, telephone conversations with author, October 3, 2002 and January 6, 2003. See, too, Guy Logsdon, "Okie," in *Encyclopedia of Oklahoma History and Culture* (this book will be released in 2007). www.ok-history.mus.ok.us/enc/okie.htm.

5. Robert Lee Maril, *Waltzing with the Ghost of Tom Joad: Poverty, Myth, and Low-Wage Labor in Oklahoma* (Norman: University of Oklahoma Press, 2000), 3.

6. Shindo, *Dust Bowl Migrants in the American Imagination,* 55–74; John Steinbeck, *Working Days: The Journals of The Grapes of Wrath, 1938–1941,* ed. Robert DeMott (New York: Viking, 1989); Robert DeMott, " 'A Truly American Book': Pressing The Grapes of Wrath," in James Barbour and Tom Quirk, eds., *Biographies of Books: The Compositional Histories of Notable American Writings* (Columbia: University of Missouri Press, 1996), 187–225; Robert DeMott, *Steinbeck's Typewriter: Essays on His Art* (Troy, N.Y.: Whitston Publishing Company, 1996), 146–205.

7. Gregory, *American Exodus,* 245–246; Dan Morgan, *Rising in the West: The True Story of an "Okie" Family from the Great Depression Through the Reagan Years* (New York: Alfred A. Knopf, 1992).

8. Woody Guthrie, "Tom Joad — Part 1," *Dust Bowl Ballads* (1940; reissue, New York: Buddha Records/BMG Distribution, 2000); Woody Guthrie, "Tom Joad — Part 2," *Dust Bowl Ballads* (1940; reissue, New York: Buddha Records/BMG Distribution, 2000); Bruce Springsteen, "The Ghost of Tom Joad," *The Ghost of Tom Joad* (New York: Columbia Records, 1995); Rage Against the Machine, "The Ghost of Tom Joad," *Renegades* (New York: Sony Music Entertainment, 2000).

9. Penguin sells approximately 150,000 copies of *The Grapes of Wrath* every year. Daisy Maryles, "Behind the Bestsellers: 'East' Heads North," *Publishers Weekly* 250 (June 30, 2003): 15.

10. *The Grapes of Wrath* was, after all, the tenth-best novel of the twentieth century, according to the Board of the Modern Library.

11. For biographical information, see Dorothy Pitman Hughes, *Wake Up and Smell the Dollars! Whose Inner-City is This Anyway! One Woman's Struggle Against Sexism, Classism, Racism, Gentrification and the Empowerment Zone* (Phoenix: Amber Books, 2000).

12. Dorothy Pitman Hughes, telephone conversations with author, March 4–5, 2003 and February 1, 2004.

13. Ibid.

14. Ibid.

15. Tony Allen-Mills, "Whoopi Film Unlocks Tale of White Mischief," *Sunday Times,* October 27, 1996, 24.

16. Ibid.; Betsy Streisand, "A Hollywood Story Harlem Had First," *U.S. News and World Report* 121 (October 28, 1996): 16; Denene Millner, "Risky Business; Unlike Whoopi Goldberg's 'The Associate,' This Entrepreneur Finds Happy Endings Scarce," *(New York) Daily News,* November 4, 1996, 35.

17. Hughes, telephone conversations.

18. Joe R. Feagin and Clairece Booher Feagin, *Discrimination American Style: Institutional Racism and Sexism* (Englewood Cliffs, N.J.: Prentice-Hall, 1978).

19. For these data, see the Web site of the National Committee on Pay Equity at http://feminist.com/fairpay/f_qape.htm.

20. U.S. Census Bureau, *Statistical Abstract of the United States: 2003* (123rd ed.) (Washington, D.C.: U.S. Government Printing Office, 2003), Tables 680, 684, and 687.

21. For reflections on Asian-American success in the United States, see Frank H. Wu, *Yellow: Race in America Beyond Black and White* (New York: Basic Books, 2002), 39–77.

22. For a wealth of statistics on this topic, see Ellen A. Kramarow et al., *Health and Aging Chartbook. Health, United States, 1999* (Hyattsville, Md.: National Center for Health Statistics, 1999).

23. The data for Asians and American Indians include Hispanics. Kramarow et al., *Health and Aging Chartbook,* Table 13.

24. U.S. Census Bureau, *Statistical Abstract of the United States: 2003,* Table 154.

25. These data are from 2001. U.S. Census Bureau, *Statistical Abstract of the United States: 2003,* Table 105.

26. U.S. Census Bureau, *Statistical Abstract of the United States: 2003,* Table 272.

27. Ibid., Table 227.

28. For much useful information on racial disparities in the criminal justice system, see Marc Mauer and The Sentencing Project, *Race to Incarcerate* (New York: New Press, 1999).

29. These data are from 2000. Men account for 87.4% of the inmates in U.S. jails and prisons. U.S. Census Bureau, *Statistical Abstract of the United States: 2001* (121st ed.) (Washington, D.C.: U.S. Government Printing Office, 2001), Table 330.

30. These data are from 1997. Men account for 93.8% of the prisoners in state and federal correctional institutions. Bureau of Justice Statistics, *Correctional Populations in the United States, 1998* (Washington, D.C.: U.S. Department of Justice, Office of Justice Programs, n.d.), ch. 5.

31. Robert R. Preuhs, "State Felon Disenfranchisement Policy," *Social Science Quarterly* 82 (December 2001): 733–748. See, too, Jeff Manza, Clem Brooks, and Christopher Uggen, "Public Attitudes toward Felon Disenfranchisement in the United States," *Public Opinion Quarterly* 68 (Summer 2004): 275–286.

32. Anthony DeCurtis, "Is Rock 'n' Roll a White Man's Game?" *Time* 147 (April 29, 1996): 78–79; Neil Strauss, "Blue-Eyed Rhythm and Blues: Does Race Matter?" *New York Times,* November 3, 2002, Sec. 2, at p. 1; Kelefa Sanneh, "Unguarded Lyrics Embarrass Eminem," *New York Times,* November 20, 2003, at E1.

33. Amy Harmon, "A Limited Partnership," in Correspondents of the New York Times, *How Race Is Lived in America: Pulling Together, Pulling Apart* (New York: Times Books/Henry Holt and Company, 2001), 79–95.

34. Laurence Leamer, *The Kennedy Men: 1901–1963: The Laws of the Father* (New York: William Morrow, 2001); Laurence Leamer, *Sons of Camelot: The Fate of an American Dynasty* (New York: William Morrow, 2004).

35. For a book about African Americans that relates to this topic, see Deborah Mathis, *Yet a Stranger: Why Black Americans Still Don't Feel at Home* (New York: Warner Books, 2002).

36. Ian Ayres, "Fair Driving: Gender and Race Discrimination in Retail Car Negotiations," *Harvard Law Review* 104 (February 1991): 817–872; Ian Ayres and Peter Siegelman, "Race and Gender Discrimination in Bargaining for a New Car," *American Economic Review* 85 (June 1995): 304–321; Ian Ayres, "Further Evidence of Discrimination in New Car Negotiations and Estimates of Its Cause," *Michigan Law Review* 94 (October 1995): 109–147; Ian Ayres, *Pervasive Prejudice? Unconventional Evidence of Race and Gender Discrimination* (Chicago: University of Chicago Press, 2001), 88–162.

37. Joe R. Feagin and Eileen O'Brien, *White Men on Race: Power, Privilege, and the Shaping of Cultural Consciousness* (Boston: Beacon Press, 2003).

38. Richard F. America, "Introduction," in Richard F. America, ed., *The Wealth of Races: The Present Value of Benefits from Past Injustices* (New York: Greenwood Press, 1990), xvii.

39. For arguments that whites, particularly white males, have long benefited from affirmative action, see Eric Foner, "Affirmative Action and History: Hiring Quotas for White Males Only," *Nation* 260 (June 26, 1995): 924, 926; Judy Scales-Trent, *Notes of a White Black Woman: Race, Color, Community* (University Park: Pennsylvania State University Press, 1995), 118; Karen Brodkin, *How Jews Became White Folks and What That Says about Race in America* (New Brunswick, N.J.: Rutgers University Press, 1998), 38–40, 42–44; Philip F. Rubio, *A History of Affirmative Action, 1619–2000* (Jackson: University Press of Mississippi, 2001), passim; Leonard Pitts, "Affirmative Action's Big Winners: White Males," *Chicago Tribune,* October 21, 2003, Sec. 1, p. 25.

40. Scales-Trent, *Notes of a White Black Woman: Race, Color, Community,* 118.

41. David Leonhardt, "Gap Between Pay of Men and Women Smallest on Record," *New York Times,* February 17, 2003, at A1.

42. Ibid.

43. Ann Crittenden, *The Price of Motherhood: Why the Most Important Job in the World Is Still the Least Valued* (New York: Metropolitan Books/Henry Holt and Company, 2001), 87–109.

44. U.S. Census Bureau, *Statistical Abstract of the United States: 2003,* Table 588.

45. Peg Tyre and Daniel McGinn, "She Works, He Doesn't," *Newsweek* 151 (May 12, 2003): 49. See, too, Pamela L. Taylor, M. Belinda Tucker, and Claudia Mitchell-Kernan, "Ethnic Variations in Perceptions of Men's Provider Role," *Psychology of Women Quarterly* 23 (December 1999): 741–761.

46. Tyre and McGinn, "She Works, He Doesn't," 44–52; Michelle Conlin, "Look Who's Bringing Home More Bacon," *BusinessWeek* (January 27, 2003): 85.

47. Betsy Morris, "Trophy Husbands," *Fortune* 146 (October 14, 2002): 78–82, 86, 90, 94, 98.

48. Ibid.; Conlin, "Look Who's Bringing Home More Bacon"; Tyre and McGinn, "She Works, He Doesn't," 44–52; Amy Goldstein, "Breadwinning Wives Alter Marriage Equation," *Washington Post,* February 27, 2000, at A1; Sue Shellenbarger, "As Moms Earn More, More Dads Stay Home: How to Make the Switch Work," *Wall Street Journal,* February 20, 2003, at D1.

49. James S. Pula, *Polish Americans: An Ethnic Community* (New York: Twayne Publishers, 1995), 132.

50. Ibid., 133.

51. Ibid.

52. On June 19, 2004, I conducted a search on Yahoo using the keywords "Polish jokes." There were 334,000 hits.

53. Mike Allen, "Separatism Is In, Except for White Men," *New York Times,* June 30, 1996, Sec. 4, p. 5.

54. Richard Bernstein, *Dictatorship of Virtue: How the Battle Over Multiculturalism Is Reshaping Our Schools, Our Country, and Our Lives* (New York: Vintage Books/Random House, 1995), 130.

55. U.S. Census Bureau, *Statistical Abstract of the United States: 2003,* Table 697.

56. For a description of the issues and debates surrounding white poverty, see John Hartigan Jr., "Green Ghettos and the White Underclass," *Social Research* 64 (Summer 1997): 339–365.

57. Feagin and Feagin, *Discrimination American Style,* 37–39.

58. On this point, see Ellen Ladowsky, "That's No White Male...," *Wall Street Journal,* March 27, 1995, A20; Sonya Jason, "...That's My Son," *Wall Street Journal,* March 27, 1995, A20.

59. Michelle Fine et al., "(In) Secure Times: Constructing White Working-Class Masculinities in the Late 20th Century," *Gender and Society* 11 (February 1997): 52–68; Lois Weis, Amira Proweller, and Craig Centrie, "Re-examining 'A Moment in History': Loss of Privilege Inside White Working-Class Masculinity in the 1990s," in Michelle Fine et al., eds., *Off White: Readings on Race, Power, and Society* (New York: Routledge, 1997), 210–226.

60. Weis, Proweller, and Centrie, "Re-examining 'A Moment in History,' " 211–212.

61. Dante Ramos, "Losers: White Minorities Get Shafted," *New Republic* 211 (October 17, 1994): 24–25.

62. Clyde B. McCoy and James S. Brown, "Appalachian Migration to Midwestern Cities," in William W. Philliber and Clyde B. McCoy, eds., with Harry C. Dillingham, *The Invisible Minority: Urban Appalachians* (Lexington: University Press of Kentucky, 1981), 35–78. For recent books about Appalachian experiences in urban America, see Kathryn M. Borman and Phillip J. Obermiller, eds., *From Mountain to Metropolis: Appalachian Migrants in American Cities* (Westport, Conn.: Bergin and Garvey, 1994); Phillip J. Obermiller, ed., *Down Home, Downtown: Urban Appalachians Today* (Dubuque, Iowa: Kendall/Hunt Publishing Company, 1996); Phillip J. Obermiller, Thomas E. Wagner, and E. Bruce Tucker, eds., *Appalachian Odyssey: Historical Perspectives on the Great Migration* (Westport, Conn.: Praeger, 2000).

63. Dwight B. Billings, "Introduction," in Dwight B. Billings, Gurney Norman, and Katherine Ledford, eds., *Confronting Appalachian Stereotypes: Back Talk from an American Region* (Lexington: University Press of Kentucky, 1999), 3.

64. For a collection of essays about these stereotypes, see Dwight B. Billings, Gurney Norman, and Katherine Ledford, eds., *Confronting Appalachian Stereotypes: Back Talk from an American Region* (Lexington: University Press of Kentucky, 1999). See, too, John O'Brien, *At Home in the Heart of Appalachia* (New York: Alfred A. Knopf, 2001), passim; Anthony Harkins, *Hillbilly: A Cultural History of an American Icon* (New York: Oxford University Press, 2004).

65. Elaine Hatfield and Susan Sprecher, *Mirror, Mirror . . . : The Importance of Looks in Everyday Life* (Albany: State University of New York Press, 1986); Linda A. Jackson, *Physical Appearance and Gender: Sociobiological and Sociocultural Perspectives* (Albany: State University of New York Press, 1992); Eng Seng Loh, "The Economic Effects of Physical Appearance," *Social Science Quarterly* 74 (June 1993): 420–438; Daniel S. Hamermesh and Jeff E. Biddle, "Beauty and the Labor Market," *American Economic Review* 84 (December 1994): 1174–1194; Jeff E. Biddle and Daniel S. Hamermesh, *Beauty, Productivity, and Discrimination: Lawyers' Looks and Lucre* (Cambridge, Mass.: National Bureau of Economic Research, 1995); Daniel Hamermesh and Amy M. Parker, *Beauty in the Classroom: Professors' Pulchritude and Putative Pedagogical Productivity,* NBER Working Paper No. w9853, July 2003.

66. Evelyn Nieves, "New San Francisco Ordinance Decrees That All Sizes Fit," *New York Times,* May 9, 2000, A20; Jim Herron Zamora, "New S.F. Law Bans Size Bias; Height and Weight Added to Codes on Nondiscrimination," *San Francisco Examiner,* May 9, 2000, at A1; John M. Glionna, "S.F. Again on Cutting Edge with Bid to Ban Weight Bias," *Los Angeles Times,* May 14, 2000, A32; Carey Goldberg, "Fat People Say an Intolerant World Condemns Them on First Sight," *New York Times,* November 5, 2000, Sec. 1, p. 36.

67. T. F. Cash, "The Psychosocial Consequences of Androgenetic Alopecia: A Review of the Research Literature," *British Journal of Dermatology* 141 (1999): 404.

68. Ibid., 398–405.

69. U.S. Census Bureau, *Statistical Abstract of the United States: 2001,* Table 196.

70. Some tall — and very tall — Americans believe that anti-height bias exists in American society. There is a height-consciousness movement that advocates for the interests of tall Americans, with regard to such issues as more legroom on airplanes and the removal of such phrases as "that's a tall tale" from our lexicon. John Leo, "The High and the Mighty," *U.S. News and World Report* 135 (August 18/August 25, 2003): 27.

71. Hatfield and Sprecher, *Mirror, Mirror...,* 198–204; Jackson, *Physical Appearance and Gender,* 172–176; Julian V. Roberts and C. Peter Herman, "The Psychology of Height: An Empirical Review," in C. Peter Herman, Mark P. Zanna, and E. Tory Higgins, eds., *Physical Appearance, Stigma, and Social Behavior: The Ontario Symposium, Volume 3* (Hillsdale, N.J.: Lawrence Erlbaum Associates, Publishers, 1986), 113–140; Leslie F. Martel and Henry B. Biller, *Stature and Stigma: The Biopsychosocial Development of Short Males* (Lexington, Mass.: Lexington Books/D.C. Heath and Company, 1987). See, too, "Workplace Rewards Tall People with Money, Respect, UF Study Shows," Press Release, October 16, 2003. www.napa.ufl.edu/2003news/heightsalary.htm.

72. As Rob Stein points out, "Obesity is defined as having a body mass index (BMI) of at least 30. Overweight is defined as having a BMI of 25. BMI is a formula in which a person's body weight in kilograms is divided by the square of his or her height in meters." Rob Stein, "San Antonio Has Highest Rate of Obesity," *Washington Post,* March 3, 2003, A3.

73. U.S. Census Bureau, *Statistical Abstract of the United States: 2003,* Table 209.

74. See, e.g., Jeffery Sobal, "Sociological Analysis of the Stigmatisation of Obesity," in John Germov and Lauren Williams, eds., *A Sociology of Food and Nutrition: The Social Appetite* (South Melbourne, Victoria, Australia: Oxford University Press, 1999), 187–204; Gerhard Falk, *Stigma: How We Treat Outsiders* (Amherst, N.Y.: Prometheus Books, 2001), 85–107; Rebecca Puhl and Kelly D. Brownell, "Stigma, Discrimination, and Obesity," in Christopher G. Fairburn and Kelly D. Brownell, eds., *Eating Disorders and Obesity: A Comprehensive Handbook,* 2d ed. (New York: Guilford Press, 2002), 108–112.

75. Falk, *Stigma,* 103. For studies that document discrimination against people of size, see Puhl and Brownell, "Stigma, Discrimination, and Obesity," 108–112; Mark V. Roehling, "Weight-Based Discrimination in Employment: Psychological and Legal Aspects," *Personnel Psychology* 52 (Winter 1999): 969–1016; Sondra Solovay, *Tipping the Scales of Justice: Fighting Weight-Based Discrimination* (Amherst, N.Y.: Prometheus Books, 2000), 25–127; Rebecca Puhl and Kelly D. Brownell, "Bias, Discrimination, and Obesity," *Obesity Research* 9 (December 2001): 788–805.

76. Douglas Degher and Gerald Hughes, "The Adoption and Management of a 'Fat' Identity," in Jeffery Sobal and Donna Maurer, eds., *Interpreting Weight: The Social Management of Fatness and Thinness* (New York: Aldine de Gruyter,

1999), 11–27; Jeffery Sobal, "The Size Acceptance Movement and the Social Construction of Body Weight," in Jeffery Sobal and Donna Maurer, eds., *Weighty Issues: Fatness and Thinness as Social Problems* (New York: Aldine de Gruyter, 1999), 231–249.

77. Solovay, *Tipping the Scales of Justice*, 27, 28–29, 128–170, 190–195.

78. Rhonda L. Rundle, "Obesity's Hidden Costs; Hospitals Are Forced to Add Bariatric Lifts, Sturdier Beds to Care for Heaviest Patients," *Wall Street Journal*, May 1, 2002, at B1; Martin Miller, "On Some Airlines, Size Does Matter," *Los Angeles Times*, June 21, 2002, at E1; Rose DeWolf, "Discrimination Increasingly Cropping Up against the Obese," *Knight Ridder Tribune News Service*, September 13, 2002, at p. 1.

79. On this issue, see Mari J. Matsuda, "Voices of America: Accent, Antidiscrimination Law, and a Jurisprudence for the Last Reconstruction," *Yale Law Journal* 100 (March 1991): 1329–1407.

80. Rosina Lippi-Green, *English with an Accent: Language, Ideology, and Discrimination in the United States* (London: Routledge, 1997), 238–239.

81. According to Rosina Lippi-Green, "Immigrants from the British Isles who speak varieties of English which cause significant communication problems are not stigmatized: the differences are noted with great interest, and sometimes with laughter." Lippi-Green, *English with an Accent*, 239.

82. Katharine W. Jones, *Accent on Privilege: English Identities and Anglophilia in the U.S.* (Philadelphia: Temple University Press, 2001), 108–140.

83. Steve Stecklow, "Bloody Sticky Wicket: Americans in Britain Often Blow the Accent," *Wall Street Journal*, September 30, 2003, at A1.

84. Lippi-Green, *English with an Accent*, 202–216; Walt Wolfram and Natalie Schilling-Estes, *American English: Dialects and Variation* (Malden, Mass.: Blackwell Publishers, 1998); Allan Metcalf, *How We Talk: American Regional English Today* (Boston: Houghton Mifflin Company, 2000).

85. E. Dianne Markley, "Regional Accent Discrimination in the Hiring Process: A Language Attitude Study" (M.A. thesis, University of North Texas, August 2000).

86. Dianne Markley, interview by author, Denton, Texas, January 29, 2002.

87. Ibid.

88. Markley, interview; Dianne Markley, telephone conversation with author, May 13, 2002.

89. All the material in this vignette comes from the following interviews with Reverend Wilson: Reverend Douglas Wilson, interview by author, The Colony, Texas, January 29, 2002; Reverend Douglas Wilson, telephone conversations with author, January 10, 2002 and October 31, 2003.

90. Wilson, for instance, was pictured in a *BusinessWeek* article about changing gender roles in the American family. See Michelle Conlin, "Look Who's Barefoot in the Kitchen," *BusinessWeek* (September 17, 2001): 76.

91. Stephanie Coontz, *The Way We Never Were: American Families and the Nostalgia Trap* (New York: BasicBooks, 1992); Stephanie Coontz, *The Way We*

Really Are: Coming to Terms with America's Changing Families (New York: BasicBooks, 1997).

92. Ibid.

93. William H. Frey, "Married with Children," *American Demographics* 25 (March 2003): 17–19.

94. M. Belinda Tucker and Claudia Mitchell-Kernan, eds., *The Decline in Marriage among African Americans: Causes, Consequences, and Policy Implications* (New York: Russell Sage Foundation, 1995).

95. U.S. Census Bureau, *Statistical Abstract of the United States: 2003,* Table 61.

96. Coontz, *The Way We Really Are,* 137–140, 162–167.

97. U.S. Census Bureau, *Statistical Abstract of the United States: 2003,* Table 70.

98. Coontz, *The Way We Really Are,* 97–108.

99. Dirk Johnson, "Until Dust Do Us Part," *Newsweek* 139 (March 25, 2002): 41.

100. Jason Fields, *Children's Living Arrangements and Characteristics: March 2002* (Washington, D.C.: U.S. Census Bureau, June 2003), 10. www.census.gov/prod/2003pubs/p20–547.pdf.

101. Marilyn Gardner, "Mothers Who Choose to Stay Home," *Christian Science Monitor,* November 14, 2001, 13–16; Rifka Rosenwein, "The Baby Sabbatical," *American Demographics* 24 (February 2002): 36–39; Kim Clark, "Mommy's Home," *U.S. News and World Report* 133 (November 25, 2002): 32–33, 36, 38; Michelle Conlin, Jennifer Merritt, and Linda Himelstein, "Mommy Is Really Home from Work," *BusinessWeek* (November 25, 2002): 101–102, 104; Genaro C. Armas, "Census: More Children Have Moms Who Stay at Home," *Seattle Times,* June 17, 2003, at A1; Claudia Wallis, "The Case for Staying Home," *Time* 163 (March 22, 2004): 50–56, 59.

102. Clark, "Mommy's Home," 32; Conlin, Merritt, and Himelstein, "Mommy Is Really Home from Work," 102; Alecia Swasy, "Status Symbols: Stay-at-Home Moms Are Fashionable Again in Many Communities," *Wall Street Journal,* July 23, 1993, at A1; Sue Shellenbarger, "Women's Groups Give Peace a Chance in War of At-Home and Working Moms," *Wall Street Journal,* December 12, 2002, at D1.

103. Crittenden, *The Price of Motherhood,* 131–148.

104. Ibid., passim.

105. For more information about this organization, see www.mothersandmore.org.

106. To learn more about the Family and Home Network, go online to www.familyandhome.org. This account draws upon my interview with Cathy Myers (Cathy Myers, telephone conversation with author, March 17, 2003).

107. Myers, telephone conversation.

108. Sue Shellenbarger, "The Sole Breadwinner's Lament: Having Mom at Home Isn't as Great as It Sounds," *Wall Street Journal,* October 16, 2003, at D1.

109. See, e.g., Scott Coltrane, *Family Man: Fatherhood, Housework, and Gender Equity* (New York: Oxford University Press, 1996); Anna Dienhart, *Reshaping Fatherhood: The Social Construction of Shared Parenting* (Thousand Oaks, Calif.: Sage Publications, 1998); Francine M. Deutsch, *Halving It All: How Equally Shared Parenting Works* (Cambridge, Mass.: Harvard University Press, 1999); Nancy E. Dowd, *Redefining Fatherhood* (New York: New York University Press, 2000).

110. John Fetto, "Does Father Really Know Best?" *American Demographics* 24 (June 2002): 10–11.

111. Sandra L. Hofferth, *Race/Ethnic Differences in Father Involvement in Two-Parent Families: Culture, Context, or Economy* (Ann Arbor, Mich.: Institute for Social Research/University of Michigan, February 24, 2001).

112. Stay-at-home dads reject the terms "Mr. Mom" or "househusband" (the analogue to "housewife"). They prefer such terms as Stay-at-Home Dad, full-time father, or primary care-giving father.

113. Fields, *Children's Living Arrangements and Characteristics: March 2002*, 10.

114. Ibid.

115. "Facts for Features: Father's Day: June 15," Press Release. www.census.gov/Press-Release/www/2003/cb03-ff08.html.

116. Libby Gill, *Stay-at-Home Dads: The Essential Guide to Creating the New Family* (New York: Plume, 2001), 21–32. For information about gay SAHDs, see Ginia Bellafante, "Two Fathers, with One Happy to Stay at Home," *New York Times,* January 12, 2004, at A1.

117. Deutsch, *Halving It All,* 169–194.

118. Gill, *Stay-at-Home Dads,* 73–82. See, too, Kemba J. Dunham, "Stay-at-Home Dads Fight Stigma," *Wall Street Journal,* August 26, 2003, at B1.

119. Marilyn Gardner, "Stay-at-Home Dads Want More Than Laughs," *Christian Science Monitor,* May 7, 2003, 17.

120. Gill, *Stay-at-Home Dads,* passim.

121. Peter Baylies, telephone conversation with author, April 30, 2002; Rebecca Griffin, "An At-Home Dad Who Started a Newsletter for Others Like Him Got a Whole Lot More Media Attention Than He Ever Dreamed," *Lawrence (Mass.) Eagle-Tribune,* March 24, 2002. See, too, Baylies's Web site (www.athomedad.com).

122. Gill, *Stay-at-Home Dads,* 30–31, 150; Jay Massey, telephone conversations with author, April 2, 2002 and September 15, 2003; Toddi Gutner, "When the Husband Stays at Home," *Business Week Online,* January 11, 2001. www.businessweek.com/bwdaily/dnflash/jan2001/nf20010111_073.htm.

123. Massey, telephone conversations.

124. Ibid. For more information about this Web site, go to www.slowlane.com.

125. Gill, *Stay-at-Home Dads,* 24–26, 149–150; Hogan Hilling, telephone conversation with author, August 8, 2002. Mr. Hilling is the author of *The Man Who Would Be Dad* (Sterling, Va.: Capital Books, 2002). He operates a Web site (www.prouddads.com).

126. Eddie Murphy has a white sidekick in *Daddy Day Care*.

127. Tyre and McGinn, "She Works, He Doesn't," 46, 47.

128. Baylies, telephone conversation.

129. Ibid.; D'Vera Cohn and Sarah Cohen, "Census Sees Vast Change in Language, Employment; More People Work at Home; More Speak Little English," *Washington Post*, August 6, 2001, at A1.

130. Amanda Ripley and Maggie Sieger, "The Special Agent," *Time* 160 (December 30, 2002–January 6, 2003): 34–40; Amanda Ripley, "The Night Detective," *Time* 160 (December 30, 2002–January 6, 2003): 44–47, 49–50; Jodie Morse and Amanda Bower, "The Party Crasher," *Time* 160 (December 30, 2002–January 6, 2003): 52–56.

131. Sara Scott, " 'First Man' Promotes Support Role," *Grand Rapids (Mich.) Press*, January 5, 2003, A19; Ashley Schinella, "Media Watch," *Welcome Home* 20 (May 2003): 22–23.

132. Sue Shellenbarger, "As Moms Earn More, More Dads Stay Home: How to Make the Switch Work," *Wall Street Journal*, February 20, 2003, at D1; Barbara Kantrowitz, "Hoping for the Best, Ready for the Worst," *Newsweek* 151 (May 12, 2003): 50–51.

133. Kenneth Clatterbaugh, *Contemporary Perspectives on Masculinity: Men, Women, and Politics in Modern Society*, 2d ed. (Boulder, Colo.: Westview Press, 1997), passim; Michael A. Messner, *Politics of Masculinities: Men in Movements* (Thousand Oaks, Calif.: Sage Publications, 1997).

134. Examples of such groups include the White Officers Association of the Houston Police Department and the European American Firefighters of San Jose.

135. For background on the origins and purpose of men's studies, see Harry Brod, "Introduction: Themes and Theses of Men's Studies," in Harry Brod, ed., *The Making of Masculinities: The New Men's Studies* (Boston: Allen and Unwin, 1987), 1–17; Harry Brod, "The Case for Men's Studies," in Harry Brod, ed., *The Making of Masculinities: The New Men's Studies* (Boston: Allen and Unwin, 1987), 39–62.

136. Rene Sanchez, "Men's Studies Coming of Age in New Campus Rite of Passage; Female Attendance Attests: It's Not Just a Guy Thing," *Washington Post*, November 17, 1996, at A1.

137. Darryl Fears, "Hue and Cry on 'Whiteness Studies'; An Academic Field's Take on Race Stirs Interest and Anger," *Washington Post*, June 20, 2003, at A1.

138. Eunice Smith, interview by author, Paris, France, February 24, 2004.

139. See, e.g., Christine Clark and James O'Donnell, eds., *Becoming and Unbecoming White: Owning and Disowning a Racial Identity* (Westport, Conn.: Bergin and Garvey, 1999); Eileen O'Brien, *Whites Confront Racism: Antiracists and Their Paths to Action* (Lanham, Md.: Rowman and Littlefield Publishers, 2001); Becky Thompson, *A Promise and a Way of Life: White Antiracist Activism* (Minneapolis: University of Minnesota Press, 2001); Bernestine Singley, ed., *When Race Becomes Real: Black and White Writers Confront Their Personal Histories* (Chicago: Lawrence Hill Books, 2002); Cooper Thompson, Emmett

Schaefer, and Harry Brod, *White Men Challenging Racism: 35 Personal Stories* (Durham, N.C.: Duke University Press, 2003).

140. For background on this topic, see Eileen O'Brien and Michael P. Armato, "Building Connections between Antiracism and Feminism: Antiracist Women and Profeminist Men," in France Winddance Twine and Kathleen M. Blee, eds., *Feminism and Antiracism: International Struggles for Justice* (New York: New York University Press, 2001), 277–291.

141. Messner, *Politics of Masculinities*, 49–62; Clatterbaugh, *Contemporary Perspectives on Masculinity*, 41–67; Alice Jardine and Paul Smith, eds., *Men in Feminism* (New York: Methuen, 1987); Tom Digby, ed., *Men Doing Feminism* (New York: Routledge, 1998); Steven P. Schacht and Doris Ewing, eds., *Feminism and Men: Reconstructing Gender Relations* (New York: New York University Press, 1998); Amanda Goldrick-Jones, *Men Who Believe in Feminism* (Westport, Conn.: Praeger, 2002).

142. Jess Bravin, "Members Only: How a Jewish Man Got into a Ritzy Club in Boca Raton, Fla.," *Wall Street Journal,* February 28, 2001, at A1; Ed Sherman and Greg Burns, "Fairways' Barriers Toppling," *Chicago Tribune,* February 2, 2003, Sec. 3, at p. 1.

143. Steve Reeves, "Shoal Creek Virtually All White a Decade After Controversy," *Scripps Howard News Service,* August 3, 2000. www.s-t.com/daily/08-00/08-03-00/b05sp099.htm.

144. Ann Blackman et al., "Putt for Dough," *Time* 152 (September 14, 1998): at 82H; Morgan Murphy and Katarzyna Moreno, "Grass Ceiling," *Forbes* 163 (May 31, 1999): 120; Tim Vanderpool, "Lawsuits Tee Off against Male Golf Clubs," *Christian Science Monitor,* October 16, 2001, 3; Alex Kuczynski, "It's Still a Man's, Man's, Man's World," *New York Times,* July 21, 2002, Sec. 9, at p. 1; Greg Burns, " 'Grass Ceiling' Impeding Women," *Chicago Tribune,* February 3, 2003, Sec. 3, at p. 1.

145. Sherman and Burns, "Fairways' Barriers Toppling"; Kuczynski, "It's Still a Man's, Man's, Man's World"; Marco R. della Cava, "Men Tee Up as Critics Tee Off; Members Explain Why All-Male Clubs Endure," *USA Today,* October 4, 2002, at A1.

146. Greg Burns and Ed Sherman, "Gender Gap Clear on Augusta Flap," *Chicago Tribune,* February 3, 2003, Sec. 3, at p. 1.

147. Daniel Golden, "Family Ties: Preferences for Alumni Children in College Admission Draws Fire," *Wall Street Journal,* January 15, 2003, at A1; Daniel Golden, "Extra Credit: At Many Colleges, The Rich Kids Get Affirmative Action," *Wall Street Journal,* February 20, 2003, at A1; Daniel Golden, " 'Buying' Your Way into College; So, Just How Much Do You Need to Donate to Get Your Kid In?" *Wall Street Journal,* March 12, 2003, at D1; Daniel Golden, "College Ties: For Groton Grads, Academics Aren't Only Keys to Ivies," *Wall Street Journal,* April 25, 2003, at A1; Daniel Golden, "For Supreme Court, Affirmative Action Isn't Just Academic," *Wall Street Journal,* May 14, 2003, at A1.

148. Julian Bond, "The Civil Rights Act: White Men's Hope," *New York Times,* June 24, 1990, Sec. 4, p. 21.

149. Foner, "Affirmative Action and History: Hiring Quotas for White Males Only," 926.

Chapter 4: Fair Play

1. Unless otherwise indicated, any information in this vignette that relates to Mr. Nadeau's biography comes from the following sources: Phil Nadeau, telephone conversation with author, July 29, 2002; Phil Nadeau, interview by author, Lewiston, Maine, August 28, 2002.

2. The Somalis-in-Lewiston story began to receive national media attention in June 2002, as a result of a lengthy article in the *Chicago Tribune* (Patrick T. Reardon, "A Yankee Mill Town Globalizes," *Chicago Tribune,* June 13, 2002, Sec. 5, at p. 1). Two events in particular resulted in considerable national news coverage of Lewiston's ethnic relations. The first event occurred in October 2002 when Lewiston Mayor Laurier Raymond issued a public letter asking potential Somali migrants to reconsider coming to Lewiston because he felt the city needed time to adjust, socially and economically, to the existing Somali population. The second event took place in January 2003; a white-supremacist group, the World Church of the Creator, held a sparsely attended rally in Lewiston. There were several thousand counter-demonstrators at a pro-diversity rally. Since then, the national media interest in the Somali presence in Lewiston seems to have subsided, for the most part.

3. In the 2000 census, 29.4% of Lewiston's residents indicated that they had French-Canadian heritage. The same year, 18.3% of them said they had French ancestry. Likewise, 10.2% of Lewistonians report they have Irish forebears, and 9.9% claim to be of English descent.

4. Charisse Jones, "Newcomers Give Old City a Look at Itself," *USA Today,* February 7, 2003, A13; Sara B. Miller, "A Lesson in Allaying Immigrant Tensions," *Christian Science Monitor,* August 11, 2003, 3; Maggie Jones, "The New Yankees," *Mother Jones* 29 (March/April 2004): 64–69.

5. As recently as 2000, Lewiston was 95.0% white, with a black population of 361 residents.

6. A wonderful source of information about the ethnic minority population of Lewiston is the monthly *Immigrant and Refugee/Multicultural Activity Report.* To view these reports, go to the Cultural Diversity section of the City of Lewiston's Web site (http://ci.lewiston.me.us/cultures/index.htm).

7. Somalis account for three percent of Lewiston's population — and nearly 50 percent of the recipients of General Assistance. Nadeau, interview.

8. Miller, "A Lesson in Allaying Immigrant Tensions."

9. Victoria Scott, telephone conversation with author, June 19, 2003; Kelley Bouchard, "Diversity Expert Takes Up Challenge in Lewiston," *Portland (Me.) Press Herald,* December 8, 2002, at 1A.

10. Jones, "The New Yankees"; Jones, "Newcomers Give Old City a Look at Itself"; Miller, "A Lesson in Allaying Immigrant Tensions."

11. Miller, "A Lesson in Allaying Immigrant Tensions."

12. Ibid.

13. Unless otherwise cited, all the information in this vignette comes from my lengthy telephone conversations with Professor Frederick R. Lynch on April 9, 2002 and April 29, 2003, as well as from my interviews with him in Claremont, California, on April 26, 2002 and May 12, 2003, and numerous e-mail communications.

14. The hardcover edition of Professor Lynch's first book came out in December 1989. In my reading of this book, I have relied on the paperback edition: Frederick R. Lynch, *Invisible Victims: White Males and the Crisis of Affirmative Action* (New York: Praeger, 1991).

15. Frederick R. Lynch, *The Diversity Machine: The Drive to Change the "White Male Workplace"* (New York: Free Press, 1997). The paperback edition, which includes a Preface by the author that updates the book, was published by Transaction in 2002.

16. For profiles of Lynch, see Peter Brimelow, "Spiral of Silence," *Forbes* 149 (May 25, 1992): 76–77; James Warren, "Diversity Dissonance; Fred Lynch a Leading Voice in Taking Affirmative Action to Task," *Chicago Tribune,* June 11, 1995, Sec. 5, p. 2.

17. Upland, California, is 54.8% white, 27.5% Latino, 7.3% black, and 7.1% Asian.

18. John David Skrentny, ed., *Color Lines: Affirmative Action, Immigration, and Civil Rights Options for America* (Chicago: University of Chicago Press, 2001); Hugh Davis Graham, *Collision Course: The Strange Convergence of Affirmative Action and Immigration Policy in America* (New York: Oxford University Press, 2002); John D. Skrentny, *The Minority Rights Revolution* (Cambridge, Mass.: Belknap Press of Harvard University Press, 2002).

19. Daniel C. Maguire, *A New American Justice: Ending the White Male Monopolies* (Garden City, N.Y.: Doubleday and Company, 1980), 3.

20. To learn more about these issues, go to the Web site of the American Society of Newspaper Editors (www.asne.org) and click on the "Diversity" icon. Then, on the next screen, click on the following icons: "ASNE's diversity mission" and "Newsroom employment census."

21. William McGowan, *Coloring the News: How Crusading for Diversity Has Corrupted American Journalism* (San Francisco: Encounter Books, 2001), passim.

22. Vernon Loeb, "For Deep Cover, CIA Seeks Deep Diversity; New Targets Reshape Agency's Hiring," *Washington Post,* May 31, 2000, at A1; Dana Priest, "The Slowly Changing Face of the CIA Spy; Recruits Eager to Fight Terror Are Flooding In, but Few Look the Part," *Washington Post,* August 9, 2002, at A1.

23. Matt Murray, "Corporate Goal: Ethnic Variety, No Quotas," *Wall Street Journal,* June 24, 2003, at B1.

24. Richard L. Zweigenhaft and G. William Domhoff, *Diversity in the Power Elite: Have Women and Minorities Reached the Top?* (New Haven, Conn.: Yale University Press, 1998), especially 178–181.

25. Ibid., 177.

26. See, e.g., Philip Moss and Chris Tilly, *Stories Employers Tell: Race, Skill, and Hiring in America* (New York: Russell Sage Foundation, 2001); Deirdre A. Royster, *Race and the Invisible Hand: How White Networks Exclude Black Men from Blue-Collar Jobs* (Berkeley: University of California Press, 2003).

27. Moss and Tilly, *Stories Employers Tell,* 158–162, 185–208.

28. Frederick R. Lynch, "Diversity and Preferences; Business Arguments Led the Way," *Washington Times,* July 14, 2003, A17. This opinion piece summarizes the themes of, and updates the coverage in, Lynch's second book, *The Diversity Machine.*

29. Ibid.

30. Ibid.

31. U.S. Census Bureau, *Statistical Abstract of the United States: 2003* (123rd ed.) (Washington, D.C.: U.S. Government Printing Office, 2003), Table 588.

32. Gillian Flynn, "White Males See Diversity's Other Side," *Workforce* 78 (February 1999): 52–55.

33. Lynne Duke, "Cultural Shifts Bring Anxiety for White Men; Growing Diversity Imposing New Dynamic in Workplace," *Washington Post,* January 1, 1991, at A1; Michele Galen et al., "White, Male, and Worried," *Business Week* (January 31, 1994): 50–55; Jonathan Kaufman, "Mood Swing: White Men Shake Off That Losing Feeling on Affirmative Action," *Wall Street Journal,* September 5, 1996, at A1.

34. Robin Wilson, "Among White Males, Jokes and Anecdotes," *Chronicle of Higher Education,* April 28, 1995, A20–A21.

35. For the most comprehensive study of reverse discrimination, see Lynch, *Invisible Victims.*

36. John P. Fernandez with Mary Barr, *The Diversity Advantage: How American Business Can Out-Perform Japanese and European Companies in the Global Marketplace* (New York: Lexington Books/Macmillan, 1993), 263.

37. Frederick R. Lynch, "Tales from an Oppressed Class," *Wall Street Journal,* November 11, 1991, A12.

38. Fred L. Pincus, *Reverse Discrimination: Dismantling the Myth* (Boulder, Colo.: Lynne Rienner Publishers, 2003).

39. U.S. Department of Education, *Title IX: 25 Years of Progress — June 1997* (Washington, D.C.: U.S. Department of Education, June 1997). For background on the history of Title IX, see Skrentny, *The Minority Rights Revolution,* 230–262.

40. National Center for Education Statistics, *Digest of Education Statistics, 2002* (Washington, D.C.: National Center for Education Statistics, 2003), 298 (Table 246).

41. Ibid., 201.

42. Ibid., 298 (Table 246).

43. Jacqueline E. King, *Gender Equity in Higher Education: Are Male Students at a Disadvantage?* (Washington, D.C.: American Council on Education, 2000).

44. Michelle Conlin, "The New Gender Gap," *BusinessWeek* (May 26, 2003): 74–80, 82.

45. National Center for Education Statistics, *Digest of Education Statistics, 2002,* 298 (Table 246).

46. Conlin, "The New Gender Gap," passim.

47. Ibid., 78–79, 82.

48. Ibid., 78.

49. Ibid.

50. There are few disparities related to gender overall in terms of the college-graduation rates of African Americans (16.4% for black men and 17.5% for black women) or Latinos (11.0% for Hispanic men and 11.2% for Hispanic women). However, there is a gender gap in this regard for Asian Americans: slightly more than one-half, or 50.9%, of Asian-American men have college degrees, compared to 43.8% of Asian-American women. U.S. Census Bureau, *Statistical Abstract of the United States: 2003,* Table 228.

51. U.S. Census Bureau, *Statistical Abstract of the United States: 2003,* Table 230.

52. Conlin, "The New Gender Gap," 82.

53. The biographical information in this vignette comes from three sources: Derek Korbe, interview by author, Montgomery, Alabama, March 16, 2001; Derek Korbe, telephone conversations with author, May 5, 2003 and June 7, 2004.

54. During the Fall 2001 Semester, the most recent period for which data are available, 8.4 percent (143 white males and 324 white females) of ASU's 5,590 students were white. "Fall 2001 Enrollment at HBCUs by Control, Level, Race, and Sex" (Silver Spring, Md.: National Association for Equal Opportunity in Higher Education, n.d.), Table 11.

55. A number of lawsuits in various states have challenged the historical disparities in funding formulas that handicapped HBCUs in relation to colleges and universities with predominantly white student bodies. In settling these cases, federal courts often ordered states to fund new programs and facilities at HBCUs and, in many cases, to take proactive steps to increase the nonblack student presence on campus. See, e.g., Tammerlin Drummond, "Black Schools Go White," *Time* 155 (March 20, 2000): 58; Patrik Jonsson, "A Delta Twist on Desegregation," *Christian Science Monitor,* March 27, 2001, at p. 1.

56. There are three types of scholarships at Alabama State University. The Incentive Scholarship, for students with a 2.7 G.P.A. in high school, covers tuition and books. The Academic Scholarship is awarded to students with a 3.0 high school G.P.A., and it covers tuition, books, and room and board. The Presidential Scholarship goes to those students with a 3.2 G.P.A. in high school; it includes the aforementioned benefits and a cash stipend of $450 per year. Dr. Steve Havron, interview by author, Montgomery, Alabama, March 15, 2001.

57. Michael Krikorian, "Need Seen for More Officers from Armenia," *Los Angeles Times,* July 15, 2001, B3; Sabrina Decker, "City Hall Less Diverse;

Burbank Bureaucracy Behind in Ethnic Mix," *Los Angeles Daily News,* August 23, 2001, N3.

58. Michele N-K Collison, "A Twist on Affirmative Action," *Chronicle of Higher Education,* November 24, 1993, A13–A14.

59. For example, Ohio Appalachian students, along with their peers of color, are served by Minority Student Programs and Services at Ohio State University. http://sfa.osu.edu/Programs/minority.asp. Moreover, Appalachian artists and arts organizations (and members of the four major ethnic/racial minority groups) are eligible for short-term and long-term artistic, financial, and programmatic assistance from the Minority Arts Program of the Ohio Arts Council. www.oac.state.oh.us/grantsprogs/MinorityArts.asp.

60. Phillip J. Obermiller and Michael E. Maloney, "Looking for Appalachians in Pittsburgh: Seeking Deliverance, Finding the Deer Hunter," in Kathryn M. Borman and Phillip J. Obermiller, eds., *From Mountain to Metropolis: Appalachian Migrants in American Cities* (Westport, Conn.: Bergin and Garvey, 1994), 20.

61. Lisa Cornwell, "Invisible Minority; Native Appalachians Fight Stereotypes as They Move to Urban Areas to Find a Better Life," *Charleston (W.Va.) Gazette,* February 15, 2003, 6A.

62. To learn more about the Urban Appalachian Council of Greater Cincinnati, go to www.uacvoice.org.

63. Thomas L. Friedman, "Clinton Swipes at Bush for Lack of Jewish Aides," *New York Times,* September 10, 1992, A20.

64. Zweigenhaft and Domhoff, *Diversity in the Power Elite,* 33–34.

65. David Hawkings and Brian Nutting, eds., *CQ's Politics in America 2004, The 108th Congress* (Washington, D.C.: CQ Press, 2003), 1050–1051; Michael Barone and Richard E. Cohen, *The Almanac of American Politics 2004* (Washington, D.C.: National Journal Group, 2003), 1656–1658.

66. Tom Brune, "Minority Status Not So Simple; Politics, Agency Quirks Often Shape Definition," *Seattle Times,* October 5, 1998, at A1.

67. Jake Rollow, "Latinos in Congress Still Split, But Future Holds Some Hope," *Weekly Report* (Hispanic Link), n.d. www.hispaniclink.org/weeklyreport/0309_rollow1.htm. See, too, Barone and Cohen, *The Almanac of American Politics 2004,* 194–196, 211–213, 218–219; Hawkings and Nutting, eds., *CQ's Politics in America 2004, The 108th Congress,* 88–89, 102, 107.

68. Hawkings and Nutting, eds., *CQ's Politics in America 2004, The 108th Congress,* 1029.

69. For more information about the Christopher Reeve Paralysis Foundation, go to www.crpf.org. See, too, Jerome Groopman, "The Reeve Effect," *New Yorker* (November 10, 2003): 82–88, 90–93.

70. Dale Russakoff, "A Public Airing of Private Ills; In Media Glare, Candidates Now Disclose Infirmities," *Washington Post,* September 24, 2002, at A1.

71. Mark Clayton, "Overview: The Gender Equation," *Christian Science Monitor,* May 22, 2001, at p. 11; Mark Clayton, "Admissions Officers Walk a Fine Line in Gender-Balancing Act," *Christian Science Monitor,* May 22, 2001, at p. 11; Mark Clayton, "Gender Gap Is Far from Academic for Colleges," *Christian*

Science Monitor, May 22, 2001, at p. 15; "Threats to College-Diversity Programs Pose Risks for Boys," *USA Today,* May 23, 2003, A14.

72. Clayton, "Overview: The Gender Equation"; Clayton, "Gender Gap Is Far from Academic for Colleges."

73. Clayton, "Overview: The Gender Equation"; "Threats to College-Diversity Programs Pose Risks for Boys."

74. For a recent study of this topic, see Robert L. Kaufman, "Assessing Alternative Perspectives on Race and Sex Employment Segregation," *American Sociological Review* 67 (August 2002): 547–572.

75. Helene M. Lawson, *Ladies on the Lot: Women, Car Sales, and the Pursuit of the American Dream* (Lanham, Md.: Rowman and Littlefield Publishers, 2000).

76. For recent discussions of these issues, see Patricia A. Roos, "Occupational Feminization, Occupational Decline? Sociology's Changing Sex Composition," *American Sociologist* 28 (Spring 1997): 75–88; Robin Wilson, "The 'Feminization' of Anthropology," *Chronicle of Higher Education,* April 18, 2003, A13.

77. "Where the Men Aren't," *Time* 161 (May 12, 2003): 53.

78. On these topics, see Christine L. Williams, *Gender Differences at Work: Women and Men in Nontraditional Occupations* (Berkeley: University of California Press, 1989); Christine L. Williams, ed., *Doing "Women's Work": Men in Nontraditional Occupations* (Newbury Park, Calif.: Sage Publications, 1993).

79. Christine L. Williams, *Still a Man's World: Men Who Do "Women's Work"* (Berkeley: University of California Press, 1995).

80. Ibid., 81.

81. Lisa Takeuchi Cullen, "I Want Your Job, Lady!" *Time* 161 (May 12, 2003): 52–54.

82. Ibid., 56.

83. Ibid., 54, 56.

84. Father Bernard E. Weir, interview by author, Columbus Junction, Iowa, February 3, 2002. I attended the Spanish-language Mass at St. Joseph's Church on February 3, 2002. For biographical information, I also relied on the following article: Gustav Niebuhr, "Across America, Immigration Is Changing the Face of Religion," *New York Times,* September 23, 1999, A18. Unless otherwise noted, all the biographical material in this vignette is based on my interview with Father Weir.

85. Columbus Junction had been a predominantly Anglo community until IBP opened a meat-packing plant there in 1985. By 1990, Latinos accounted for 14.5% of Columbus Junction's 1,616 people. The 2000 census found that the town of 1,900 was 59.9% Anglo and 39.0% Latino.

86. Albia, Iowa, a town of 3,706, is 97.4% white.

87. For the quotation, see Niebuhr, "Across America, Immigration Is Changing the Face of Religion."

88. Weir graduated from Briar Cliff College in Sioux City, Iowa, in 1978. He worked in religious education from 1978 to 1981, at which time he entered the seminary. Weir, interview.

89. Until he learned to speak Spanish, Weir had a young Mexican-American woman act as the translator for the Spanish-language Mass. Weir, interview.

90. Some Anglos attend the Spanish Mass in Columbus Junction. Weir, interview.

91. The Hispanic newcomers frequently turn to their parish priest for help in adjusting to life in southeastern Iowa. This type of assistance is traditionally beyond the purview of a priest with an exclusively Anglo parish. Weir, interview; Niebuhr, "Across America, Immigration Is Changing the Face of Religion."

92. Weir, interview.

93. Weir lives a bicultural, bilingual existence. He says, "I'm not sure what I am, but I'm not a white guy anymore. Part of it is I live biculturally and bilingually." Weir, interview.

94. For a useful overview of the Roman Catholic Church in the United States, see Chester Gillis, *Roman Catholicism in America* (New York: Columbia University Press, 1999). One can also find valuable information about the Catholic Church on the Internet, as in the U.S. Conference of Catholic Bishops' Web site (www.usccb.org) and the Vatican Web site (www.vatican.va).

95. William A. McGeveran Jr., ed., *The World Almanac and Book of Facts 2003* (New York: World Almanac Books, 2003), 638.

96. Philip Jenkins, *The Next Christendom: The Coming of Global Christianity* (New York: Oxford University Press, 2002), 58.

97. U.S. Census Bureau, *Statistical Abstract of the United States: 2003*, Table 80.

98. In India, for example, Catholics constitute a genuine minority. India, of course, is an overwhelmingly Hindu country. Christians account for two percent of the Indian population. Catholics make up the largest Christian denomination there, and the Catholic Church in India is well known for its efforts to help the poor and marginalized. Indian Catholics, to be sure, periodically come under attack from Hindu nationalists. Rev. Dr. Babu Joseph Karakombil, interview by author, New Delhi, India, September 25, 2003.

99. "Catholic America: The Trend Report," *Newsweek* 139 (March 4, 2002): 46.

100. European immigrants, particularly those who spoke a language other than English, usually chose between ethnic national parishes (those that appealed to a specific ethnic group) and territorial parishes (those that incorporated all the parishioners in a given geographical area). Gillis, *Roman Catholicism in America*, 59–64.

101. According to Leonard Dinnerstein and David M. Reimers, "In the 1990s the Irish constituted fewer than one fifth of the Catholics in the United States but about a third of the clergy and half of the hierarchy." Leonard Dinnerstein and David M. Reimers, *Ethnic Americans: A History of Immigration*, 4th ed. (New York: Columbia University Press, 1999), 153.

102. Father Edward Poettgen, telephone conversation with author, April 23, 2003; Father Edward Poettgen, interview by author, Stanton, California, May 13, 2003.

103. Associated Press, "Speaking Worshipers' Language; Catholic Church Seeks More Bilingual Priests," *Chicago Tribune,* January 5, 2001, Sec. 2, p. 6.

104. Ibid.

105. Ibid.

106. Catholic Masses are celebrated in at least 33 languages in the United States. For a listing of these Masses, go to www.masstimes.org and click on the icon for Non-English Services.

107. Gustav Niebuhr, "Vietnamese Immigrants Swell Catholic Clergy," *New York Times,* April 24, 2000, A17. For insights into Vietnamese-American Catholicism, I benefited enormously from my interviews with two experts on this topic (Father Michael Hoan and Rev. Dr. Anthony Dao): Father Michael Hoan, interview by author, Santa Ana, California, January 6, 2003; Rev. Dr. Anthony Dao, telephone conversation with author, March 1, 2003; Rev. Dr. Anthony Dao, interview by author, southeastern Wisconsin and northeastern Illinois, March 8, 2003.

108. Bishop Josu Iriondo, telephone conversation with author, April 30, 2002.

109. Bishop Josu Iriondo, e-mail to author, October 24, 2003.

110. Ibid.

111. Diana Jean Schemo with Laurie Goodstein, "O'Connor Successor Unclear, But the Challenges Are Not," *New York Times,* May 5, 2000, at A1.

112. Father Esequiel Sanchez, e-mail to author, September 24, 2003.

113. Father Esequiel Sanchez, interview by author, Chicago, Illinois, May 7, 2001.

114. Laurie Goering, "Mexico City Welcomes Cardinal George," *Chicago Tribune,* December 11, 2000, Sec. 1, p. 3.

115. Sanchez, interview.

116. Bishop John R. Manz, interview by author, Chicago, Illinois, April 3, 2003.

117. Ibid.

118. For more information about Saint Sabina, go to the parish's Web site: www.saintsabina.org. In addition, the Chicago daily newspapers — the *Chicago Tribune* and the *Chicago Sun-Times* — regularly cover Father Pfleger and events at Saint Sabina.

119. Father Michael Pfleger, interview by author, Chicago, Illinois, May 7, 2003.

120. Pfleger, interview.

121. In January 2003 Father Pfleger was the keynote speaker at the Dr. Martin Luther King Jr. Commemorative Service at Ebenezer Baptist Church in Atlanta. For the text of Father Pfleger's King Day speech, go to www.saintsabina.org/spotlight/kingdayspeech.htm.

122. The Latino Catholic population of the Archdiocese of Los Angeles is 74% Mexican, 14% Salvadoran, and 7% Guatemalan. Humberto Ramos, telephone conversation with author, September 10, 2001; Humberto Ramos, interview by author, Los Angeles, California, July 12, 2002.

123. In the 1930s Archbishop John Cantwell requested that seminarians learn Spanish if they aspired to be diocesan priests in Los Angeles. "Today," as Humberto Ramos points out, "all new priests being ordained for the Archdiocese of Los Angeles" speak another language besides English (e.g., Spanish, Tagalog, or Vietnamese). Humberto Ramos, e-mail to author, October 17, 2003.

124. Ramos, telephone conversation.

125. Ibid.

126. Ibid.

127. Father Colm Rafferty, interview by author, Los Angeles, California, January 5, 2003.

128. Cardinal Roger Mahony, interview by author, Los Angeles, California, May 13, 2003.

129. Ibid.

130. For example, Father Anthony Gonzalez, the pastor of Saint Frances Cabrini Church in South-Central Los Angeles, praises Cardinal Mahony for his inclusive style and outlook. Father Anthony Gonzalez, interviews by author, Los Angeles, California, July 13, 2002, and July 14, 2002.

131. Betsy Streisand, "The Cardinal's Highflyin' New Nest," *U.S. News and World Report* 133 (September 9, 2002): 10.

132. Mahony, interview.

133. Eighty-six percent of the scholarship recipients, many of whom are students of color, go on to college. Mahony, interview.

134. To learn more about the Cathedral of Our Lady of the Angels, go to www.olacathedral.org.

135. Cardinal Mahony says Los Angeles is presently 38% Catholic, and that it will be 50% Catholic in 2010. (He notes that these estimates do not count undocumented immigrants.) The Cardinal predicts that California itself will be 50% Catholic in 2020. Mahony, interview.

136. At present, the U.S. Latino population is 70% Catholic, 23% Protestant, 6% No Religious Preference/Other, and 1% World Religion. Hispanic Americans continue to be a heavily Catholic group, mainly because of the huge numbers of Latin American immigrants who come to the United States each year. The mostly Catholic waves of Latin American immigrants, particularly Mexicans, compensate for the inevitable attrition among native-born Latino Catholics. See Gastón Espinosa, Virgilio Elizondo, and Jesse Miranda, *Hispanic Churches in American Public Life: Summary of Findings* (Notre Dame, Ind.: Institute for Latino Studies, University of Notre Dame, January 2003), 14–16. www.hcapl.org/HCAPL_Summary_of_Findings_English.pdf.

137. Cathy Lynn Grossman, "A Changing Church; Immigrants, an Active Laity and Thriving Catholic Movements Will Lead the Way," *USA Today,* August 29, 2002, D5.

138. Bishop Ignatius Wang, interview by author, San Francisco, California, July 31, 2003.

139. Austin Flannery, ed., *Vatican Council II: The Conciliar and Post Conciliar Documents,* vol. 1, rev. ed. (Northport, N.Y.: Costello Publishing Company, 1992), 568.

140. For information about the 11 pontifical councils, go to www.vatican.va/roman_curia/pontifical_councils/index.htm.

141. Father Michael Blume, interview by author, Rome, Italy, May 17, 2003.

142. Monsignor Frank J. Dewane, interview by author, Vatican City, Vatican, May 19, 2003.

143. Dewane, interview. Dewane helped formulate the document, *The Church and Racism,* that was part of the Holy See's contribution to the dialogue at the World Conference. See Pontifical Council for Justice and Peace, *The Church and Racism: Towards a More Fraternal Society* (Vatican City: Pontifical Council for Justice and Peace, 2001).

144. Dewane, interview.

145. Jenkins, *The Next Christendom,* 194–198; John Carreyrou et al., "Spiritual Crossroads; Pope John Paul II's Legacy: Growing Flock, Widening Rifts," *Wall Street Journal,* October 17, 2003, at A1.

146. John L. Allen Jr., *Conclave: The Politics, Personalities, and Process of the Next Papal Election* (New York: Image/Doubleday, 2002). See, too, Alessandra Galloni, "Men Who Could Be Pope; Speculation Is Already Rife Over Which of the Cardinals Is Most 'Papabile,' or Popeable," *Wall Street Journal,* October 17, 2003, at B1.

147. Alton Ketchum, *Uncle Sam: The Man and the Legend* (New York: Hill and Wang, 1959), passim.

148. Ibid., 95–123.

149. Robert B. Costello, ed., *Random House Webster's College Dictionary* (New York: Random House, 1992), 1449–1450.

150. Ibid., 1190.

151. Dominic Pulera, *Visible Differences: Why Race Will Matter to Americans in the Twenty-First Century* (New York: Continuum, 2002), 164–166.

152. Elizabeth Llorente, "A Reunion of Heroes; Firemen in Powerful New Image," *(Bergen County, N.J.) Record,* September 2, 2002, at A1. For background on New York City firefighters, see Terry Golway, *So Others Might Live: A History of New York's Bravest: The FDNY from 1700 to the Present* (New York: Basic Books/Perseus Books Group, 2002).

153. Llorente, "A Reunion of Heroes."

154. Ibid.; Steve Strunsky, "One Year After – Photographer Says Life Has Changed since 9/11," *Providence (R.I.) Journal,* September 11, 2002, B9.

155. See, e.g., Clarence Page, "3 White Guys and a Flag: Symbols or Truth? In a Racial Stew over a 9–11 Statue," *Chicago Tribune,* January 16, 2002, Sec. 1, p. 17; Kathleen Parker, "3 White Guys and a Flag: Symbols or Truth? When Those Pesky Facts Get in the Way," *Chicago Tribune,* January 16, 2002, Sec. 1, p. 17; Lynne Duke, "Red, White, and Blue, for Starters; Firefighters Memorial Sparks a Diverse Debate," *Washington Post,* January 18, 2002, at

C1; John Leo, "Color Me Confounded," *U.S. News and World Report* 132 (January 28/February 4, 2002): 31.

156. Llorente, "A Reunion of Heroes"; "New Fundraising Stamp Honoring Heroes of 9/11 Issued Today in New York City," *PR Newswire,* June 7, 2002, at p. 1.

Chapter 5: The Power of Numbers

1. Mayor Scott L. King, interview by author, Gary, Indiana, January 11, 2001; Rich James, " 'Trash Ticket' Hinted," *Gary (Ind.) Post-Tribune,* July 7, 1990, B1, B2; Barry Saunders, "Mayor Race Gets White Candidate," *Gary (Ind.) Post-Tribune,* November 16, 1990, B1. This vignette was informed by my five visits to Gary, Indiana, between January 11, 2001, and September 11, 2002.

2. King, interview.

3. Rich James, "Gary Mayoral Candidate Scott King Outlines Plans," *Gary (Ind.) Post-Tribune,* April 4, 1991, B2; Barry Saunders, "Barnes' Strategy Paid Off; Incumbent's Ploy of Being Above Fray," *Gary (Ind.) Post-Tribune,* May 9, 1991, A1, A10; Robert A. Catlin, *Racial Politics and Urban Planning: Gary, Indiana, 1980–1989* (Lexington: University Press of Kentucky, 1993), 183, 185.

4. Catlin, *Racial Politics and Urban Planning;* Alex Poinsett, *Black Power Gary Style: The Making of Mayor Richard Gordon Hatcher* (Chicago: Johnson Publishing Company, 1970); James B. Lane, *"City of the Century": A History of Gary, Indiana* (Bloomington: Indiana University Press, 1978); Edward Greer, *Big Steel: Black Politics and Corporate Power in Gary, Indiana* (New York: Monthly Review Press, 1979); Raymond A. Mohl and Neil Betten, *Steel City: Urban and Ethnic Patterns in Gary, Indiana, 1906–1950* (New York: Holmes and Meier, 1986); Andrew Hurley, *Environmental Inequalities: Class, Race, and Industrial Pollution in Gary, Indiana, 1945–1980* (Chapel Hill: University of North Carolina Press, 1995); Wilbur C. Rich, *Black Mayors and School Politics: The Failure of Reform in Detroit, Gary, and Newark* (New York: Garland Publishing, 1996), especially 57–90; Peter Jennings and Todd Brewster, *In Search of America* (New York: Hyperion, 2002), 142–145, 148–152, 155–158, 163–167, 170–175, 178, 181–183.

5. King, interview; Don Terry, "In Mayoral Election, Race Is Real Issue," *New York Times,* November 5, 1995, Sec. 1, p. 28; James L. Tyson, "Gary Voters Refuse to Play Race Card in City Election," *Christian Science Monitor,* November 6, 1995, 3; Thomas Hardy, "Race Plays Role in Gary Mayor Bid; but Candidates Try to Downplay Its Part," *Chicago Tribune,* November 7, 1995, Sec. 2, at p. 1; Peter Kendall, "Gary's Black Citizens Appear Ready for a Change; Old Steel Town Willing to Trust a White Mayor," *Chicago Tribune,* November 9, 1995, Sec. 1, p. 3; Edward Walsh, "On Jan. 1, Gary Will Try Something Different — a White Mayor," *Washington Post,* December 17, 1995, A3; Warren Cohen, "It's Not Just Black and White," *U.S. News and World Report* 120 (January 22, 1996): 27; Karen L. Williams, "End of an Era in Gary, Ind.," *Emerge* 7 (March 1996): 44–46.

6. Mayor King's mother is one-half Swedish, one-quarter German, and one-quarter Austrian. His father's ancestors mainly trace their ancestry to the British Isles; it is possible that he has Native American blood as well. King, interview.

7. King, interview.

8. Ibid.

9. "Gary, Ind., Leads in Per Capita Homicides," *Associated Press,* January 2, 2004.

10. King, interview.

11. Gary received a considerable amount of favorable publicity when the city hosted the Miss USA pageant in 2001 and 2002. See, e.g., Mike Conklin, "Gary Hangs Its Hopes for a New Image on Miss USA," *Chicago Tribune,* January 4, 2001, Sec. 1, at p. 1.

12. Steve Patterson, "Stadium Flap Could Decide Race for Mayor; Cost Questioned," *(Gary, Ind.) Post-Tribune,* April 27, 2003, A7; Steve Patterson, "Welcome to the Steel Yard; King Says Clear from Start Who Should Have Stadium Naming Rights," *(Gary, Ind.) Post-Tribune,* May 15, 2003, at A1.

13. For information about the May 2003 primary campaign and results, see Patterson, "Stadium Flap Could Decide Race for Mayor"; Steve Patterson, "Harris Hailed for Role in Vote," *(Gary, Ind.) Post-Tribune,* May 8, 2003, at A1.

14. Steve Patterson, "Election Winners Look to Future," *(Gary, Ind.) Post-Tribune,* May 12, 2003, at A1.

15. Carole Carlson, "Board Approves City Building New School," *(Gary, Ind.) Post-Tribune,* June 25, 2003, A6.

16. Michael Butkovich, interview by author, Gallup, New Mexico, November 2, 2000. Much of the information in this vignette comes from my interview with Mr. Butkovich. For background information, I also relied on the *Gallup Independent,* which is an excellent source of information about Gallup, Butkovich, and Gallup High School.

17. Mark Yeoell, interview by author, Spokane, Washington, November 8, 2003.

18. Ibid.

19. Mark Yeoell, e-mail to author, April 12, 2004.

20. Yeoell, e-mail; Yeoell, interview.

21. Ibid.

22. Yeoell, e-mail.

23. Yeoell, interview.

24. Mark Yeoell, "Thoughts on the Nature of Prejudice" (Spokane, Wash.: Global Integrity Leadership Group, n.d.), 4.

25. Ibid.; Yeoell, e-mail.

26. Yeoell, "Thoughts on the Nature of Prejudice," 4.

27. Yeoell, e-mail.

28. Ibid.

29. Ibid.

30. Ibid.

31. Yeoell, "Thoughts on the Nature of Prejudice," 4.

32. A few minutes before I began presenting a public lecture at the University of Botswana in 2003, a young woman came into the auditorium for the talk and exclaimed, "He's white!" when she saw the speaker.

33. Hilary Kraus, "Speech on Race, Ethnic Relations Part of NIC Forum; Lessons on Difference Taught by Unlikeliest of Teachers," *(Spokane, Wash.) Spokesman Review,* November 3, 2003, A8.

34. *Essence* magazine, for example, recently compiled a list of "6 White Men We Love": Bono, Barry Charles Scheck, Steven Spielberg, Andrew Hacker, Jonathan Kozol, and Robert DeNiro. The magazine recognized these men because they contribute in positive ways to the African-American community. For the list, see Deborah Gregory, "6 White Men We Love," *Essence* 33 (November 2002): 172–173.

35. Dalton Conley grew up on the Lower East Side of New York. Conley lived, played, and studied in settings where whites were few and far between, but he documents how he still benefited from white privilege in those contexts. See Dalton Conley, *Honky* (Berkeley: University of California Press, 2000).

36. Eric Florence, interview by author, Liège, Belgium, October 8, 2003.

37. Abby Goodnough, "Race Declines in Importance in Board Search for Chancellor," *New York Times,* February 14, 2000, at B1.

38. Jodi Wilgoren, "After Diallo Shooting, New Focus on Hiring City Residents for Police," *New York Times,* February 28, 1999, Sec. 1, p. 25.

39. Most police chiefs are men. For information about their female peers, see Dorothy Moses Schulz, "Women Police Chiefs: A Statistical Profile," *Police Quarterly* 6 (September 2003): 330–345.

40. David Heinzmann and Gary Washburn, "Daley Picks Acting Chief as Top Cop; Black Chosen as Second in Command," *Chicago Tribune,* October 7, 2003, Sec. 1, at p. 1.

41. Patricia Callahan, "Uprising: Indians vs. Whites: The Politics of Race Roil a Quiet County," *Wall Street Journal,* October 31, 2002, at A1; Gwen Florio, "Indians Show Political Clout; Natives Throng Polls in 'White' S.D. County," *Denver Post,* January 8, 2003, at A1.

42. All the material in this vignette comes from my interviews with Mr. Patrick: Sherman Patrick, interview by author, Williamsburg, Virginia, October 22, 2003; Sherman Patrick, telephone conversation with author, March 16, 2004.

43. Cooper Thompson, Emmett Schaefer, and Harry Brod, *White Men Challenging Racism: 35 Personal Stories* (Durham, N.C.: Duke University Press, 2003). For historical background on this topic, see Herbert Aptheker, *Anti-Racism in U.S. History: The First Two Hundred Years* (New York: Greenwood Press, 1992).

44. Maria P. P. Root, *Love's Revolution: Interracial Marriage* (Philadelphia: Temple University Press, 2001), passim.

45. For a detailed overview of the social and legal issues surrounding trans-racial adoption, see Randall Kennedy, *Interracial Intimacies: Sex, Marriage, Identity, and Adoption* (New York: Pantheon Books, 2003), 386–518. For a

white male's personal reflections on this issue, see J. Douglas Bates, *Gift Children: A Story of Race, Family, and Adoption in a Divided America* (New York: Ticknor and Fields, 1993).

46. Joshua R. Goldstein, "Kinship Networks That Cross Racial Lines: The Exception or the Rule?" *Demography* 36 (August 1999): 399–407.

47. Professor Christopher Hewitt, interview by author, Bethesda, Maryland, October 20, 2003.

48. Matt Streadbeck, interview by author, Glendale, California, November 23, 2003.

49. Scott VanLoo, interview by author, Burbank, California, November 30, 2003.

50. Ibid.

51. Josh Buehner, interview by author, Bellevue, Washington, December 16, 2003; Josh Buehner, interview by author, Seattle, Washington, December 17, 2003; Josh Buehner, telephone conversations with author, August 14, 2003, September 4, 2003, October 24, 2003, November 19, 2003, January 6, 2004, and January 28, 2004.

52. Ibid.

53. One day in the fall of 1997 Buehner was accosted on NIC's campus by a white man who called him a "nigger lover," verbally attacked him for advocating on behalf of African Americans, and spat upon him. He also received a death threat on his answering machine. Buehner, interviews; Buehner, telephone conversations; Andrea Vogt, "Racial Insult Directed at NIC Club Leader; Equality Club President Targeted in Campus Incident," *(Spokane, Wash.) Spokesman Review,* October 11, 1997, at B1.

54. Buehner, interviews; Buehner, telephone conversations.

55. Mike McGavick, interview by author, Seattle, Washington, December 17, 2003. For biographical information about McGavick, see Bradley Meacham, "A Future in Politics for Safeco's CEO?; Mike McGavick's Resume: GOP Roots, Business Success," *Seattle Times,* May 19, 2003, at A1.

56. Safeco was No. 260 on the Fortune 500 in 2002, a year in which the company reported revenues of $7,065.1 million and profits of $301.1 million. "The 500: Top to Bottom," *Fortune* 147 (April 14, 2003): F11–F12, F-43, F-56. For more information about Safeco, go to the company's Web site (www.safeco.com).

57. Meacham, "A Future in Politics for Safeco's CEO?"; Todd Bishop, "Saving Safeco; CEO Made Tough Decisions That Put Company Back on Track," *Seattle Post-Intelligencer,* May 6, 2003, at C1; Bradley Meacham, "Safeco Says It Will Stop Selling Life Insurance; About 1,600 Workers May Be Affected," *Seattle Times,* September 30, 2003, at A1; Bradley Meacham, "Safeco Investors Tepid on Plan to Refocus by Spinning Off Unit," *Seattle Times,* October 3, 2003, at C1; Bradley Meacham, "Safeco's Employee Morale at Low Ebb; Layoffs, Selling of Unit Take Toll on Company," *Seattle Times,* November 1, 2003, C4.

58. Mike McGavick, telephone conversation with author, March 18, 2004.

59. McGavick, interview.

60. Kevin Carter, interview by author, Seattle, Washington, December 17, 2003.

61. Kevin Carter, e-mail to author, February 5, 2004.

62. Carter, interview.

63. McGavick, interview.

64. For this quotation, see Bishop, "Saving Safeco."

65. There are no affinity groups for employees at Safeco. Carter, interview.

66. Carter, e-mail.

67. Carter, interview.

68. Ibid.

69. Ibid.

70. Buehner, interviews; Buehner, telephone conversations.

71. At an early meeting of the Corporate Diversity Advisory Group, someone asked Buehner, "Why are you here?" The person evidently was surprised to see a young white man participating in the group. Buehner, interviews.

72. Buehner, interviews; Buehner, telephone conversations.

73. McGavick, interview.

74. Ibid.; Buehner, interviews; Buehner, telephone conversations.

75. Raphael Madison, interview by author, Seattle, Washington, December 17, 2003.

76. Madison's first boss was a good-old-boy Texan who disliked African Americans. He made his feelings on race clear to Madison from the first day he met him. Madison, interview.

77. Madison, interview.

78. Ibid.

79. Ibid.

80. Sometimes I ask diversity professionals the "John Smith question." First, I describe Smith. A thirtysomething white man of my acquaintance, John Smith appears to be unremarkable on every front. He is heavy-set and of average height, with average looks and a middle-income, public-sector job in a medium-sized Midwestern town. In all likelihood, he is Christian, heterosexual, and able-bodied. Then I query the diversity professionals as to where someone like Smith fits into their conception of diversity.

81. Carter, e-mail.

82. Carter, interview.

83. Ibid.

84. Buehner, interview, December 17, 2003.

85. Buehner, interviews; McGavick, interview.

86. "Biography/Biografie," Dirk Nowitzki Online Fan Resource. See www .dirknowitzkiofr.com/Bio.htm; Daniel Eisenberg, "The NBA's Global Game Plan," *Time* 161 (March 17, 2003): 63.

87. "Biography/Biografie"; Eisenberg, "The NBA's Global Game Plan," 59. For a wealth of statistics about Nowitzki, go to "NBA.com: Dirk Nowitzki Player Info." www.nba.com/playerfile/dirk_nowitzki/?nav=page.

88. Olivier Pheulpin, "The German Bird," *Basketball Digest* 28 (May 2001): at p. 56 (via EBSCO*host*); Jack McCallum, "Simply Marvelous," *Sports Illustrated* 96 (May 6, 2002): 36–41; Ian Thomsen, "Long Ranger," *Sports Illustrated* 98 (May 5, 2003): 48–51.

89. Pheulpin, "The German Bird."

90. Mark Starr and Allison Samuels, "Mixing It Up," *Newsweek* 139 (May 6, 2002): 50.

91. Eisenberg, "The NBA's Global Game Plan," 59–60, 63.

92. Ibid., 59.

93. For information about the Mavericks, go to the official Dallas Mavericks Web page (www.nba.com/mavericks/).

94. Arthur R. Ashe Jr., *A Hard Road to Glory: A History of the African-American Athlete, 1619–1918* (New York: Warner Books, 1988); Arthur R. Ashe Jr., *A Hard Road to Glory: A History of the African-American Athlete, 1919–1945* (New York: Warner Books, 1988); Arthur R. Ashe Jr., *A Hard Road to Glory: A History of the African-American Athlete Since 1946* (New York: Warner Books, 1988).

95. John Hoberman, *Darwin's Athletes: How Sport Has Damaged Black America and Preserved the Myth of Race* (Boston: Houghton Mifflin Company, 1997); Jon Entine, *Taboo: Why Black Athletes Dominate Sports and Why We Are Afraid to Talk About It* (New York: PublicAffairs, 2000).

96. Richard E. Lapchick, *2003 Racial and Gender Report Card* (Orlando: Institute for Diversity and Ethics in Sport with the DeVos Sport Business Management Program/University of Central Florida, 2003).

97. Ibid., 14.

98. Ibid., 15, 16.

99. S. L. Price and Grace Cornelius, "What Ever Happened to the White Athlete?" *Sports Illustrated* 87 (December 8, 1997): at p. 30 (via EBSCO*host*). For reflections on the themes of this article, see Kyle W. Kusz, " 'I Want to be the Minority': The Politics of Youthful White Masculinities in Sport and Popular Culture in 1990s America," *Journal of Sport and Social Issues* 25 (November 2001): 390–416.

100. Price and Cornelius, "Whatever Happened to the White Athlete?"

101. Ibid.

102. Lapchick, *2003 Racial and Gender Report Card*, 57–58.

103. Entine, *Taboo*, 273.

104. For more information about the National Hockey League, go to the NHL Web site (www.nhl.com).

105. Michael Farber, "Soul on Ice," *Sports Illustrated* 91 (October 4, 1999): at p. 62 (via EBSCO*host*).

106. Ibid.

107. Farber, "Soul on Ice"; Chuck O'Donnell, "Not Just a Black and White Issue," *Hockey Digest* 30 (January 2002): at p. 72 (via EBSCO*host*); "Black Hockey Players Look to More Blacks for Fan Support," *Jet* 104 (November 10, 2003): 46–50. For an overview of the challenges facing professional hockey, see

Jason La Canfora and Thomas Heath, "The Coming Ice Age; Mammoth Revenue Problems, Looming Lockout, Limited Fan Base Could Leave Game in the Cold," *Washington Post,* January 17, 2004, at D1.

108. For the NHL Diversity Web page, go to www.nhl.com/nhlhq/diversity.

109. Liz Clarke and Thomas Heath, "It's France's Way or the Highway; Chairman's Power Over the Ever-Expanding Sport Is Absolute," *Washington Post,* July 6, 2001, at A1; Liz Clarke, "Sport Is Governed with Absolute Power; Drivers Who Compete on the Circuit Understand It's a One-Way Street," *Washington Post,* July 7, 2001, at A1.

110. The NASCAR Web site (www.nascar.com) is a valuable source of information about NASCAR.

111. Liz Clarke, "NASCAR Is Shifting Gears; Younger, More Polished Drivers in Vogue as Sport Seeks to Remake Its Image and Satisfy Sponsors," *Washington Post,* June 9, 2001, at A1.

112. Robert Lipsyte, "NASCAR Reflects Americans' Lives," *USA Today,* October 29, 2003, A21. For an overview of NASCAR's present and future, see Tom Lowry, "The Prince of NASCAR," *BusinessWeek* (February 23, 2004): 90–94, 96, 98.

113. Chris Jenkins, "NASCAR Ends Donations to Jackson's Rainbow/PUSH," *USA Today,* July 29, 2003, C10.

114. Ibid.; Dustin Long, "Minorities Seek NASCAR Position; Drivers Say the Sport Can Do More to Appeal to Minorities," *Greensboro (N.C.) News Record,* October 9, 1999, at A1; Dianna Hunt, "Soaked Speedway; NASCAR Making Effort to Attract More Minorities," *Fort Worth (Tex.) Star-Telegram,* March 29, 2001, at p. 1; Sandra Pedicini, "As NASCAR Tries to Broaden Its Appeal, Racial Controversy Looms," *Knight Ridder Tribune News Service,* July 9, 2003, at p. 1; Viv Bernstein, "Nascar Looks Past White Male Robots," *New York Times,* January 7, 2004, at D1.

115. Lipsyte, "NASCAR reflects Americans' lives."

116. Lapchick, *2003 Racial and Gender Report Card,* 17–20, 22–23, 33–36, 37–46, 49–50, 51–53; Kenneth L. Shropshire, *In Black and White: Race and Sports in America* (New York: New York University Press, 1996), 36–102.

117. Randy Covitz, "Baseball Still Striving to Hire More Hispanic Executives," *Knight Ridder Tribune News Service,* September 11, 2003, at p. 1.

118. Shropshire, *In Black and White,* 128–141; Allison Samuels and Mark Starr, "The New Color Line," *Newsweek* 133 (May 3, 1999): 63.

119. Lapchick, *2003 Racial and Gender Report Card,* 54.

120. Ibid.

121. Lapchick, *2003 Racial and Gender Report Card,* 26–27.

122. Ibid., 24.

123. To learn more about the diversity issue as it relates to NFL head coaches, see Johnnie L. Cochran Jr. and Cyrus Mehri, *Black Coaches in the National Football League: Superior Performance, Inferior Opportunities* (Washington, D.C.: Mehri and Skalet, 2002). For more information about Cochran and Mehri's perspective on this topic, go to www.findjustice.com/ms/nfl/frameIndex.htm. See,

too, John Leo, "Playing Diversity Football," *U.S. News and World Report* 135 (August 11, 2003): 55; Jay Nordlinger, "Color in Coaching," *National Review* 55 (September 1, 2003): 25–26; Mark Maske and Leonard Shapiro, "Minority Hiring Is Lauded; NFL Makes 'Substantial Progress' in Coaching Ranks," *Washington Post,* January 22, 2004, at D1.

124. Andrew Hacker, *Mismatch: The Growing Gulf Between Women and Men* (New York: Scribner, 2003), 154, 155.

125. Daniel B. Wood and Mark Sappenfield, "Kobe Is Latest on NBA's Growing Rap Sheet," *Christian Science Monitor,* July 21, 2003, 3.

126. Robert W. Brown and R. Todd Jewell, "Is There Customer Discrimination in College Basketball? The Premium Fans Pay for White Players," *Social Science Quarterly* 75 (June 1994): 404.

127. Mark T. Kanazawa and Jonas P. Funk, "Racial Discrimination in Professional Basketball: Evidence from Nielsen Ratings," *Economic Inquiry* 39 (October 2001): 599–608.

128. Sean D. Johnson, "Wage Discrimination in the National Basketball Association: Is There Discrimination Based on Race?" *Villanova Sports and Entertainment Law Journal* 6:1 (1999): 27–48. http://vls.law.vill.edu/students/orgs/sports/back_issues/volume6/issue1/wage.html.

129. Brown and Jewell, "Is There Customer Discrimination in College Basketball?" 401–413.

130. Ibid., 402.

131. Hoberman, *Darwin's Athletes,* 3–27. See, too, John Simons, "Improbable Dreams," *U.S. News and World Report* 122 (March 24, 1997): 46–48, 50–52.

132. Rebecca Gardyn, "Putting the 'World' in the World Series," *American Demographics* 22 (April 2000): 28–30.

133. Stefan Fatsis and Suzanne Vranica, "Major League Baseball Agrees to $275 Million Deal in Japan; Dentsu Pays Hefty Increase on Renewal of TV Rights as Viewership Grows," *Wall Street Journal,* October 31, 2003, B4.

134. Eisenberg, "The NBA's Global Game Plan," 59–60, 63.

135. Eduardo Porter, "World Cup 2002: Si, Si! Zeal of Hispanic-Americans for Soccer Finals Benefits Spanish-Language Networks," *Wall Street Journal,* May 6, 2002, at B1; Matthew Benjamin, "Playing with the Big Boys," *U.S. News and World Report* 133 (July 1, 2002): 32–34.

136. For a study of how elite young white males react to certain multicultural issues, see Franklin T. Thompson, "The Affirmative Action and Social Policy Views of a Select Group of White Male Private High School Students," *Education and Urban Society* 36 (November 2003): 16–43.

137. Richard Nadeau and Richard G. Niemi, "Innumeracy about Minority Populations," *Public Opinion Quarterly* 57 (Fall 1993): 332–347; Lee Sigelman and Richard G. Niemi, "Innumeracy about Minority Populations," *Public Opinion Quarterly* 65 (Spring 2001): 86–94.

138. To learn more about this issue, see Dominic Pulera, *Visible Differences: Why Race Will Matter to Americans in the Twenty-First Century* (New York: Continuum, 2002), 282–285.

139. Professor Eric Newhall, interviews by author, Los Angeles, California, May 14, 2003, November 10, 2003, November 24, 2003, December 1, 2003, and March 23, 2004.

140. Newhall, interviews, November 10, 2003 and March 23, 2004. Newhall elaborates on this point: "When I read in the recent election for Governor of California that one candidate [Democrat Cruz Bustamante] was being attacked for being a member of MEChA, 'a hate group,' during his undergraduate days, I just shook my head in disbelief. The MEChA chapter at Occidental College in 1976 dealt with me as an individual, not a stereotype." Professor Eric Newhall, e-mail to author, April 14, 2004.

141. Newhall, interviews. According to *U.S. News and World Report,* Occidental ties DePauw University for being the 40th best national liberal arts college in the United States. "Best Liberal Arts Colleges–Bachelor's (national)," *U.S. News and World Report* 135 (September 1, 2003): 98–99.

142. Alice Y. Hom, interview by author, Los Angeles, California, November 24, 2003; Sriyanthi Gunewardena, interview by author, Los Angeles, California, March 26, 2004.

143. Dr. Frank Ayala, interview by author, Los Angeles, California, December 1, 2003; Rameen Talesh, interview by author, Los Angeles, California, December 1, 2003.

144. Oxy students choose their seminars; so it is not surprising that the demographic composition of each seminar does not necessarily reflect that of the first-year class as a whole. Newhall, interviews. See, too, Eric Newhall et al., "Institutionalizing Diversity: Learning and Living Communities at Occidental College," *Diversity Digest* 7:4 (2003). www.diversityweb.org/Digest/vol7no4/newhall.cfm.

145. Newhall, interviews; Professor Eric Newhall, e-mail to author, July 20, 2003.

146. Newhall, e-mail, July 20, 2003.

147. Ibid.

148. Ibid.

Chapter 6: The American Pantheon

1. Except where noted, all the information in these seven paragraphs about Sheldon Hall comes from my extensive interviews with Mr. Hall, both on the telephone and in El Paso. Mr. and Mrs. Hall graciously hosted me as their guest from January 12, 2002 to January 15, 2002.

2. Nancie L. Katz, "Some Fear Texans Trying to Gobble Up All the Glory," *Houston Chronicle,* November 24, 1991, A11; Sandra Sanchez, "Food for Thought: El Paso 'Origin' of Thanksgiving," *USA Today,* November 25, 1991, 8A; Associated Press, "Conquistadors, Pilgrims Battle over Holiday's Start;

Texans Lay Claim to Thanksgiving Rites," *Austin American Statesman,* November 26, 1991, A4; David Elliot, "Texans Claim 1st Thanksgiving and Brand Pilgrims as Turkeys," *Austin American Statesman,* November 25, 1993, at A1.

3. Elliot, "Texans Claim 1st Thanksgiving and Brand Pilgrims as Turkeys"; Suzanne Gamboa, "Pilgrims Crash El Paso's Thanksgiving Party," *Austin American Statesman,* April 26, 1992, B5.

4. See Gaspar Pérez de Villagrá, *History of New Mexico,* translated by Gilberto Espinosa and edited by F. W. Hodge (Los Angeles: Quivira Society, 1933).

5. Oñate's detractors usually cite the foot-chopping incident as the prime example of why they feel he should not be recognized, valorized, or venerated in any way. No other incident from Oñate's nine years as governor of New Mexico resonates more deeply with the anti-Oñate forces.

6. Sheldon Hall, letter to author, January 28, 2002.

7. In recent years, at least three respected historians have raised questions about the foot-chopping incident.

The historian Leon C. Metz posits that Oñate probably amputated only the toes, not the feet, of the Acoma slaves. According to Metz, this punishment would have been sufficiently severe to persuade the Indians not to rebel against Spanish rule, yet it would not have diminished the slaves' productivity. Leon Metz, "Like Him or Not, Oñate Is Part of Us," *El Paso Times,* May 1, 2000; Leon Metz, interview by author, San Elizario, Texas, January 13, 2002.

In addition, the historian John L. Kessell has this to say about the foot-chopping matter: "Only one brief mention in the record testifies that Oñate's punishment was carried out. Elsewhere in colonial Spanish America, on similar occasions, while the conqueror maintained his stern countenance, churchmen knelt at his feet to beg that he show paternal mercy and commute so harsh a sentence." Kessell concludes: "The absence of any subsequent reference to a one-footed Acoma slave, *un cojo,* raises doubts that Spaniards wielding axes or swords indeed followed through." See John L. Kessell, *Spain in the Southwest: A Narrative History of Colonial New Mexico, Arizona, Texas, and California* (Norman: University of Oklahoma Press, 2002), 84.

Marc Simmons, a biographer of Oñate, discusses Kessell's research on the topic. "Unless more Spanish documents come to light," concludes Simmons, "we will probably never know one way or the other." Marc Simmons, "Trail Dust: Horseplay with Juan de Oñate's Legacy," *Santa Fe (N.M.) New Mexican,* December 13, 2003, at B1.

8. Marc Simmons, *The Last Conquistador: Juan de Oñate and the Settling of the Far Southwest* (Norman: University of Oklahoma Press, 1991), 194–195.

9. For more information about the XII Travelers Memorial of the Southwest, go to www.twelve-travelers.com. The plans to honor Oñate with a statue in El Paso have been quite controversial. The El Paso City Council voted to install the statue at the El Paso International Airport, rather than in downtown El Paso, the original location. And, in accordance with the El Paso City Council's vote, the inscription on the statue will read "The Equestrian" instead of a

name that mentions the Spanish explorer. See Ginger Thompson, "As a Sculpture Takes Shape in Mexico, Opposition Takes Shape in the U.S." *New York Times,* January 17, 2002, A12; Ralph Blumenthal, "Still Many Months Away, El Paso's Giant Horseman Keeps Stirring Passions," *New York Times,* January 10, 2004, A7.

10. Frank Hall, telephone conversation with author, January 12–13, 2002.

11. For a list of the other "Thanksgivings," see "Alternative Claimants to the First American Thanksgiving," online at www.plimoth.org/Library/Thanksgiving/alternat.htm.

12. For a description of how Thanksgiving became a popular American holiday, see Janet Siskind, "The Invention of Thanksgiving: A Ritual of American Nationality," in Carole M. Counihan, ed., *Food in the USA: A Reader* (New York: Routledge, 2002), 41–58.

13. I toured the Franklin Delano Roosevelt Memorial in Washington, D.C., on July 28, 2001. See, too, the Web page of the Franklin Delano Roosevelt Memorial (www.nps.gov/fdrm/). For a valuable overview of the FDR Memorial by its designer, see Lawrence Halprin, *The Franklin Delano Roosevelt Memorial* (San Francisco: Chronicle Books, 1997).

14. Neely Tucker, "A Wheelchair Gains a Place at FDR Memorial," *Washington Post,* January 7, 2001, at C1; "President Clinton Dedicates FDR Wheelchair Statue Today; National Organization on Disability Led Campaign for and Funded Statue," *U.S. Newswire,* January 10, 2001, at p. 1; Jeffrey McMurray, "Statue of FDR in a Wheelchair to Be Dedicated; Showing President as He Really Lived Seen as Triumph for Disability Groups," *Seattle Times,* January 10, 2001, A2; Larry Lipman, "New Statue Shows FDR in Wheelchair," *Palm Beach (Fla.) Post,* January 10, 2001, 4A.

15. Lipman, "New Statue Shows FDR in Wheelchair"; McMurray, "Statue of FDR in a Wheelchair to Be Dedicated"; Tucker, "A Wheelchair Gains a Place at FDR Memorial"; "President Clinton Dedicates FDR Wheelchair Statue Today."

16. Hugh Gregory Gallagher, *FDR's Splendid Deception: The Moving Story of Roosevelt's Massive Disability and the Intense Efforts to Conceal It from the Public* (Arlington, Va.: Vandamere Press, 1999).

17. Ibid., xiii–xiv.

18. Lipman, "New Statue Shows FDR in Wheelchair"; McMurray, "Statue of FDR in a Wheelchair to be Dedicated"; Tucker, "A Wheelchair Gains a Place at FDR Memorial"; "President Clinton Dedicates FDR Wheelchair Statue Today."

19. John Updike, "Big Dead White Male," *New Yorker* 79 (August 4, 2003): 77–81.

20. Bernard Knox, *The Oldest Dead White European Males and Other Reflections on the Classics* (New York: W. W. Norton and Company, 1993), 25–26.

21. De Soto, Texas, and De Soto County, Florida, honor the Spanish explorer. Northwestern Mississippi is home to Hernando, the seat of De Soto County. There is also the De Soto National Forest there.

22. "Presidents' Day." www.patriotism.org/presidents_day/index.html.

23. Carol Morello, "Out of the Confederacy's Shadow; Va.'s New King Day a Symbolic Leap," *Washington Post,* January 15, 2001, at A1.

24. United States Postal Service, *The Postal Service Guide to U.S. Stamps,* 30th ed. (New York: HarperCollins, 2003).

25. For the etymology of these words, see William A. McGeveran Jr., ed., *The World Almanac and Book of Facts 2004* (New York: World Almanac Books, 2004), 620.

26. "The 100 Top Brands," *BusinessWeek* (August 4, 2003): 72, 74, 76, 78.

27. Sean O'Neal, *Elvis Inc: The Fall and Rise of the Presley Empire* (Rocklin, Calif.: Prima Publishing, 1996); Erika Doss, *Elvis Culture: Fans, Faith, and Image* (Lawrence: University Press of Kansas, 1999). Elvis Presley's official Web site (www.elvis.com) is a valuable source of information for his fans. For studies of Elvis impersonators, see Leslie Rubinkowski, *Impersonating Elvis* (Boston: Faber and Faber, 1997); William McCranor Henderson, *I, Elvis: Confessions of a Counterfeit King* (New York: Boulevard Books, 1997); Eric Lott, "All the King's Men: Elvis Impersonators and White Working-Class Masculinity," in Harry Stecopoulos and Michael Uebel, eds., *Race and the Subject of Masculinities* (Durham, N.C.: Duke University Press, 1997), 192–227.

28. Lisa DiCarlo, ed., "Top-Earning Dead Celebrities," Forbes.com, October 24, 2003. www.forbes.com/2003/10/24/cx_ld_1024deadcelebintro.html.

29. Jeffrey Zaslow, "Janis Who? Yesterday's Icons Don't Turn on Many Teens," *Wall Street Journal,* May 1, 2002, at B1.

30. Megan Rosenfeld, "Putting a Fresh Face on Jesus; Discovery, PBS Specials Explore Changing Images," *Washington Post,* April 15, 2001, at G1.

31. Craig MacGowan, dir., *The Face: Jesus in Art* (West Long Branch, N.J.: Kultur, 2001).

32. For two excellent books about Jesus, considered in the U.S. context, see Stephen Prothero, *American Jesus: How the Son of God Became a National Icon* (New York: Farrar, Straus, and Giroux, 2003); Richard Wightman Fox, *Jesus in America: Personal Savior, Cultural Hero, National Obsession* (New York: HarperSanFrancisco, 2004).

33. Prothero, *American Jesus,* 116–123.

34. Laurie Goodstein, "Religion's Changing Face; More Churches Depicting Christ as Black," *Washington Post,* March 28, 1994, at A1.

35. Ibid.

36. Ibid.; Prothero, *American Jesus,* 200–228; Laurie Goodstein, "Stallings Campaign Targets White Depictions of Jesus," *Washington Post,* April 10, 1993, at B1; Esther Iverem, "Seeing a Reflection in Stained Glass; Akili Ron Anderson Creates God in His Image," *Washington Post,* August 25, 1998, at C1.

37. *Jesus: The Complete Story* (No city: BBC Video/Warner Home Video, 2001). See, too, Rosenfeld, "Putting a Fresh Face on Jesus."

38. Rosenfeld, "Putting a Fresh Face on Jesus."

39. Mike Fillon, "The Real Face of Jesus," *Popular Mechanics* 179 (December 2002): at p. 68 (via EBSCO*host*).

40. It is acceptable to spell "Bighorn" as one word or two words ("Big Horn"). The one-word spelling is more common today.

41. I visited the Little Bighorn Battlefield National Monument on July 3, 2000. To learn more about the Battlefield National Monument, go to www.nps.gov/libi/. For sources about Custer and the battle, see, e.g., Louise Barnett, *Touched by Fire: The Life, Death, and Mythic Afterlife of George Armstrong Custer* (New York: Henry Holt and Company, 1996); Charles E. Rankin, ed., *Legacy: New Perspectives on the Battle of the Little Bighorn* (Helena: Montana Historical Society Press, 1996); Jeffry D. Wert, *Custer: The Controversial Life of George Armstrong Custer* (New York: Simon and Schuster, 1996); Herman J. Viola, ed., *Little Bighorn Remembered: The Untold Indian Story of Custer's Last Stand* (New York: Times Books, 1999); Larry Sklenar, *To Hell with Honor: Custer and the Little Bighorn* (Norman: University of Oklahoma Press, 2000).

42. Edward T. Linenthal, "From Shrine to Historic Site: The Little Bighorn Battlefield National Monument," in Charles E. Rankin, ed., *Legacy: New Perspectives on the Battle of the Little Bighorn* (Helena: Montana Historical Society Press, 1996), 306–319; C. Richard King, "Segregated Stories: The Colonial Contours of the Little Bighorn Battlefield National Monument," in S. Elizabeth Bird, ed., *Dressing in Feathers: The Construction of the Indian in American Popular Culture* (Boulder, Colo.: Westview Press, 1996), 167–180.

43. There are two reenactments of Custer's Last Stand every June in southeastern Montana. Custer's Last Stand Reenactment takes place in the Big Horn Valley, six miles west of Hardin, Montana. (A town with 3,384 residents, Hardin is 59.7% white, 30.5% American Indian, 5.5% Latino, and 3.9% multiracial.) This reenactment is part of Hardin's annual Little Big Horn Days. For more information, go to www.custerslaststand.org. And the Real Bird Reenactment of the Battle of the Little Bighorn occurs on the Real Bird ranch, near the Little Bighorn Battlefield National Monument. To learn more about the reenactments, see Brian Maffly, "Custer Loses Again," *Salt Lake (City, Utah) Tribune,* June 23, 2002, at A1.

44. "Indian Memorial–Little Bighorn Battlefield NM." www.nps.gov/libi/indmem.htm.

45. Barnett, *Touched by Fire,* 351–412; Shirley A. Leckie, *Elizabeth Bacon Custer and the Making of a Myth* (Norman: University of Oklahoma Press, 1993); Brian W. Dippie, "'What Valor Is': Artists and the Mythic Moment," in Charles E. Rankin, ed., *Legacy: New Perspectives on the Battle of the Little Bighorn* (Helena: Montana Historical Society Press, 1996), 209–230; Paul Andrew Hutton, "'Correct in Every Detail': General Custer in Hollywood," in Charles E. Rankin, ed., *Legacy: New Perspectives on the Battle of the Little Bighorn* (Helena: Montana Historical Society Press, 1996), 231–270; John P. Langellier, "Custer: The Making of a Myth," in Herman J. Viola, ed., *Little Bighorn Remembered: The Untold Indian Story of Custer's Last Stand* (New York: Times Books, 1999), 186–219.

46. For information about the Custer Battlefield Historical and Museum Association, go to www.cbhma.org. See, too, John J. Fialka, "Amid Victory

Cries at Little Bighorn, A Few Tears for Custer," *Wall Street Journal,* June 25, 2003, at A1.

47. " 'White Male Writers' Is the Title of English 112," *New York Times,* March 3, 1991, Sec. 1, p. 47.

48. Emily Wax, "Schools Are Seeking a Multicultural Holden," *Washington Post,* January 16, 2001, at A1.

49. See, e.g., Maria L. La Ganga, "S.F. Board OKs Reading of Works by Nonwhites," *Los Angeles Times,* March 21, 1998, at A1; Nanette Asimov, "S.F. High Schools to Get Diverse Authors List; Board OKs Key Mandate, but No Quota," *San Francisco Chronicle,* March 21, 1998, A15.

50. Dick Teresi, *Lost Discoveries: The Ancient Roots of Modern Science — from the Babylonians to the Maya* (New York: Simon and Schuster, 2002).

51. Jerry D. Stubben, "The Indigenous Influence Theory of American Democracy," *Social Science Quarterly* 81 (September 2000): 716–731.

52. Paul Matthews, interview by author, Milwaukee, Wisconsin, February 13, 2002; Paul Matthews, telephone conversation with author, January 9, 2004. For background on the Buffalo Soldiers, go to the Buffalo Soldiers National Museum's Web site (www.buffalosoldiermuseum.com).

53. Matthews, interview; Mathews, telephone conversation. I visited the Buffalo Soldiers National Museum in Houston, Texas, on January 28, 2002.

54. James N. Gregory, *American Exodus: The Dust Bowl Migration and Okie Culture in California* (New York: Oxford University Press, 1989); Charles J. Shindo, *Dust Bowl Migrants in the American Imagination* (Lawrence: University Press of Kansas, 1997).

55. Doris Weddell, interview by author, Kern County, California, April 25, 2002; Doris Weddell, interviews by author, Lamont, California, January 8, 2003 and January 22, 2004.

56. Earl Shelton, interviews by author, Lamont, California, January 8, 2003 and January 22, 2004. See, too, Earl Shelton, "Shelton's Scrapbook: Happy Memories of Life at the Camp," *Dust Bowl Journal,* October 2, 1996, 4, 16–19; Peter Jennings and Todd Brewster, *In Search of America* (New York: Hyperion, 2002), 243–244.

57. Ray Rush, interview by author, Lamont, California, January 22, 2004.

58. Ibid.; Shelton, interviews; Weddell, interviews. The Web site of the Dust Bowl Historical Foundation (www.weedpatchcamp.com) contains valuable information about the Foundation's efforts to preserve Weedpatch Camp. For national media coverage about these preservation efforts, see Jennings and Brewster, *In Search of America,* 243–244; Rene Sanchez, " 'Okie' Camp Memories Mellow; Storied Calif. Waystation May Host a New Wave of Migrants," *Washington Post,* August 12, 2001, A3; Patricia Leigh Brown, "Oklahomans Try to Save Their California Culture," *New York Times,* February 5, 2002, A22.

59. The three buildings from the 1930s are part of the National Register of Historic Places. Weedpatch Camp, which is now known as Sunset Camp, continues to host farm workers — mainly Mexicans — today.

60. Bill Farrell, "Beep Can't Tell Lie: Old Pix Gotta Go," *New York Daily News,* January 21, 2002, at p. 1; Brendan Miniter, "Battle of Brooklyn: Hang Some, Put Others Down," *Wall Street Journal,* January 25, 2002, W15.

61. There have been several examples of different changes over the years regarding the Columbus Day holiday.

In 2000, the Tarrant County Commission in Texas voted to have a paid César Chávez holiday for county employees, beginning in 2001. Due to budget constraints, the Chávez holiday replaced the paid holiday for county workers on Columbus Day. Bechetta Jackson, "Texas County Ditches Columbus for Chavez," *Seattle Times,* August 1, 2000, E8.

Seventeen states no longer celebrate Columbus Day as a paid holiday for state employees. South Dakota, for instance, substituted Native American Day for Columbus Day, beginning in 1990. Trent Seibert, "Hero? Monster? No Big Deal?" *Denver Post,* October 10, 2003, at B1.

62. Sharon Waxman, "For Directors, a Prize by Any Other Name; Racist Views of Film Pioneer Overshadow Art," *Washington Post,* March 16, 2000, at C1.

63. Kevin Sack, "Blacks Strip Slaveholders' Names Off Schools," *New York Times,* November 12, 1997, at A1; Steve Szkotak, "School Names Become Latest Civil War Skirmish," *(Memphis, Tenn.) Commercial Appeal,* December 21, 2003, A19; Patrik Jonsson, "New Doubts over the Old School Name," *Christian Science Monitor,* January 22, 2004, at p. 1.

64. Tom Wolfe, *A Man in Full: A Novel* (New York: Farrar, Straus, and Giroux, 1998), 580–581.

65. John Leo, "Color Me Confounded," *U.S. News and World Report* 132 (January 28, 2002): 31.

66. Allan Bloom, *The Closing of the American Mind: How Higher Education Has Failed Democracy and Impoverished the Souls of Today's Students* (New York: Simon and Schuster, 1987).

67. Lawrence W. Levine, *The Opening of the American Mind: Canons, Culture, and History* (Boston: Beacon Press, 1996).

68. Martin Green, *The Adventurous Male: Chapters in the History of the White Male Mind* (University Park: Pennsylvania State University Press, 1993); John F. Kasson, *Houdini, Tarzan, and the Perfect Man: The White Male Body and the Challenge of Modernity in America* (New York: Hill and Wang/Farrar, Straus and Giroux, 2001).

69. See, e.g., Warwick Anderson, "The Trespass Speaks: White Masculinity and Colonial Breakdown," *American Historical Review* 102 (December 1997): 1343–1370; Dana D. Nelson, *National Manhood: Capitalist Citizenship and the Imagined Fraternity of White Men* (Durham, N.C.: Duke University Press, 1998); Elizabeth Jameson, *All That Glitters: Class, Conflict, and Community in Cripple Creek* (Urbana: University of Illinois Press, 1998), 140–160.

70. Richard M. Sudhalter, *Lost Chords: White Musicians and Their Contribution to Jazz, 1915–1945* (New York: Oxford University Press, 1999).

71. I also used three U.S. dollars as a gratuity for the gentleman who showed us our rooms at the hotel.

72. For the figure about the cost of producing each U.S. banknote, see "United States dollar." *Wikipedia, The Free Encyclopedia.* http://en.wikipedia.org/wiki/United_States_dollar.

73. The United States Mint has a detailed Web site (www.usmint.gov) with much information about the nation's coins. For more information about America's paper currency, visit the U.S. Bureau of Engraving and Printing's Web site at www.moneyfactory.com. I toured the Bureau of Engraving and Printing in Washington, D.C., on October 23, 2003.

74. For an overview of U.S. numismatic history, see Richard Doty, *America's Money, America's Story: A Comprehensive Chronicle of American Numismatic History* (Iola, Wis.: Krause Publications, 1998). See, too, Arthur L. and Ira S. Friedberg, *Paper Money of the United States: A Complete Illustrated Guide with Valuations,* 17th ed. (Clifton, N.J.: Coin and Currency Institute, 2004); R. S. Yeoman, *A Guide Book of United States Coins 2004,* 57th ed., ed. Kenneth Bressett (Atlanta: Whitman Publishing, 2003).

75. Edward Epstein, "Reagan Image: New Deal for the Dime? Republicans in Congress Push to Honor 40th President at FDR's Expense," *San Francisco Chronicle,* December 6, 2003, at A1; Jim Geraghty, "House Tossup in Dime Design; Reagan Suggested to Replace FDR," *Washington Post,* December 8, 2003, A23; Sylvia Smith, "Souder's Coin Idea Flips on Controversy," *(Ft. Wayne, Ind.) Journal-Gazette,* December 14, 2003, 13A.

76. Yeoman, *A Guide Book of United States Coins 2004,* 94–96.

77. Ibid., 109–111.

78. Listed below are the four high-denomination Indian Head coins and the periods of time in which they were minted:

- Indian Head Gold Dollar: 1854 to 1889
- Indian Head Quarter Eagle ($2.50 gold piece): 1908 to 1929
- Indian Head Half Eagle ($5.00 gold piece): 1908 to 1929
- Indian Head Eagle ($10.00 gold piece): 1907 to 1933

For more information about these coins, see Yeoman, *A Guide Book of United States Coins 2004,* 197–198, 204, 216, 222–224.

79. The likeness of Booker T. Washington appeared on a commemorative half dollar from 1946 to 1951. And Booker T. Washington and George Washington Carver were depicted on a commemorative half dollar that was minted in 1951, 1952, 1953, 1954, and 1955. Yeoman, *A Guide Book of United States Coins 2004,* 236–237, 250.

80. Doty, *America's Money, America's Story,* 112–115.

81. Ibid., 113.

82. Ibid., 112–115.

83. Gretchen Barbatsis, ed., *Confederate Currency: The Color of Money, Images of Slavery in Confederate and Southern States Currency* (paintings by John W. Jones) (West Columbia, S.C.: Olive Press, 2002).

84. Yeoman, *A Guide Book of United States Coins 2004,* 96–103.

85. Ibid., 145–153.

86. Ibid., 111.

87. Ibid., 132–134.

88. Ibid., 171–175.

89. Ibid., 193.

90. Ibid.

91. Ibid., 194.

92. Bernard L. Ungar, "Marketing Campaign Raised Public Awareness But Not Widespread Use," *FDCH Government Account Reports,* September 13, 2002.

93. "Change May Be Ahead for U.S. Coins," CBSNews.com, September 9, 2002. www.cbsnews.com/stories/2002/09/09/national/main521271.shtml. See, too, Lynette Clemetson, "Penny in Their Thoughts: 2 Camps Debate New Look for Coins," *New York Times,* September 10, 2002, A22.

94. "New in 2004: Westward Journey Nickel Series." www.usmint.gov./mint _programs/index.cfm?action=nickel_series.

95. Friedberg, Friedberg, and Friedberg, eds., *Paper Money of the United States,* passim.

96. "As of May 31, 2003, of the $659,160,111,810 in total currency in worldwide circulation, $469,345,519,400 is in the $100 denomination." "$100 Note Fact Sheet." www.moneyfactory.com/document.cfm/18/94.

97. For this quotation, see "Selection of Portraits and Designs Appearing on Paper Currency." www.moneyfactory.com/document.cfm/18/118.

98. "Anti-Counterfeiting: Security Features." www.moneyfactory.com/section .cfm/7/35.

99. Ibid.

100. "More Secure, Colorful $20 Bill Makes Its Debut; Banks Begin Distributing Newly Redesigned Currency Today," Press Release, October 9, 2003. www.moneyfactory.com/newmoney/main.cfm/media/releases102003newyork.

101. Eduardo Levy Yeyati and Federico Sturzenegger, eds., *Dollarization* (Cambridge, Mass.: MIT Press, 2003); Dominick Salvatore, James W. Dean, and Thomas D. Willett, eds., *The Dollarization Debate* (New York: Oxford University Press, 2003).

102. "United States dollar." *Wikipedia, The Free Encyclopedia.*

103. The Australian dollar and Indonesian rupiah are commonly accepted in East Timor.

104. Charles Hutzler, "China Rethinks the Peg Tying Yuan and Dollar; Outside Pressure to Delink, Beijing's Fears of Losing Control Prod Possible Shift," *Wall Street Journal,* February 13, 2004, at A1.

105. "Secret Service: Iraqi Money Isn't Funny," CBSNews.com, April 23, 2003. www.cbsnews.com/stories/2003/04/24/iraq/main550988.shtml.

106. For the data on population and GDP, see McGeveran, ed., *The World Almanac and Book of Facts 2004,* 110, 759, 762, 783, 786, 788, 795, 797, 805, 821, 829, 838–839, 850.

107. To learn more about the euro, go to the Web site of the "Euro 2002 Information Campaign" (www.euro.ecb.int/).

108. Robert Block, "Some Muslims Advocate Dumping Dollar for the Euro," *Wall Street Journal,* April 15, 2003, at C1.

109. Robert J. McCartney, "Global Anxiety Propels Euro Above Dollar," *Washington Post,* January 31, 2003, at A1; Grainne McCarthy, "Central-Bank Meetings Promise Glimpse of Officials' Outlooks," *Wall Street Journal,* May 6, 2003, C14; G. Thomas Sims, "EU Officials Aim for Euro Stability, Instead of Strength," *Wall Street Journal,* January 20, 2004, at A2; Paul Blustein, "U.S. Will Not Intervene in Dollar's Slide Against Euro," *Washington Post,* February 3, 2004, at E1; Michael R. Sesit, "Dollar Climbs, Reversing Gains by Euro, Pound," *Wall Street Journal,* February 19, 2004, C4.

110. John Burgess, "Rising Euro Tests European Unity; Some Countries Complain of Falling Exports; Others Cite the Benefits of a Strong Currency," *Washington Post,* January 24, 2004, A13.

111. For background on the renaming controversy, see Ken Ellingwood, "Racial Issues Circle Around Atlanta's Airport and Mayors' Legacies," *Los Angeles Times,* August 12, 2003, A12; David M. Halbfinger, "Atlanta Is Divided Over Renaming Airport for Former Mayor," *New York Times,* August 13, 2003, A22; Patrik Jonsson, "What's in a Name? In Atlanta, a Whole Lot," *Christian Science Monitor,* August 15, 2003, 2–3; Dahleen Glanton, "Race Resurfaces to Split Atlanta," *Chicago Tribune,* September 2, 2003, Sec. 1, p. 8; Wes Smith, "Airport Name Battle Sparks Racial Friction," *Orlando Sentinel,* September 2, 2003, at A1; Larry Copeland, "Airport Renaming Splits Atlantans; Supporters of Two Former Mayors Debate Whose Name Is Most Worthy of Being on Facility," *USA Today,* October 3, 2003, A3; Doug Gross, "An Atlanta Institution May be Renamed; Airport Moniker Could Honor Former Mayor, If Council Majority Rules," *Washington Post,* October 12, 2003, A11. For the history of the Hartsfield-Jackson Atlanta International Airport, see "Hartsfield-Jackson Atlanta International Airport." *Wikipedia, The Free Encyclopedia.* http://en.wikipedia.org/wiki/Hartsfield-Jackson_Atlanta_International_Airport.

112. Ibid.

113. The Web site of Hartsfield-Jackson Atlanta International Airport (www .atlanta-airport.com) is a valuable source of information on the airport.

114. In San Francisco, the political pioneer's name is honored in many places, such as Harvey Milk Plaza, the Harvey Milk Center, the Harvey Milk Institute, the Harvey Milk Civil Rights Academy, and the Harvey Milk Lesbian, Gay, Bisexual and Transgender Democratic Club.

115. Susan Sinnott, *Extraordinary Hispanic Americans* (Chicago: Childrens Press, 1991).

116. Himilce Novas, *The Hispanic 100: A Ranking of the Latino Men and Women Who Have Most Influenced American Thought and Culture* (New York: Citadel Press/Carol Publishing Group, 1995), 22–26.

117. Nicolás Kanellos, *Hispanic Firsts: 500 Years of Extraordinary Achievement* (Detroit: Gale, 1997), 89. There also is an Internet site that makes this claim. See www.hispaniconline.com/hh/timeline/1930.html.

118. In 2000, for instance, the Central Library in Los Angeles was renamed the Richard J. Riordan Central Library in honor of then-Mayor Richard Riordan.

119. Jon Meacham, "Why We've Deified the Gipper," *Newsweek* 143 (December 29, 2003–January 5, 2004): 18.

120. The Web site of the Ronald Reagan Legacy Project, can be found at www.reaganlegacy.org.

121. See, e.g., Epstein, "Reagan Image: New Deal for the Dime?"; Geraghty, "House Tossup in Dime Design; Reagan Suggested to Replace FDR"; Smith, "Souder's Coin Idea Flips on Controversy"; Lisa Friedman, "Reagan Dime Makes Sense, Backers Say," *(Los Angeles) Daily News,* December 2, 2003, at N1; Erica Werner, "Reagan Fans in Congress Want Their Man on Coin; Republicans Put in Their Two Cents' Worth about Replacing FDR on Dime," *Oakland (Calif.) Tribune,* December 5, 2003, at p. 1; Jim Geraghty, "House Tossup in Dime Design; Reagan Suggested to Replace FDR," *Washington Post,* December 8, 2003, A23.

122. Jim Abrams, "Reagan Backers Want Hero on U.S. Currency," *Associated Press,* June 8, 2004.

Chapter 7: Big Mouths

1. "The First and Last Supper," *All in the Family,* VHS, directed by John Rich (1971; Culver City, Calif.: Columbia Tristar Home Video, 1998).

2. Ibid.

3. Ibid.

4. Ibid.

5. Donna McCrohan, *Archie and Edith, Mike and Gloria: The Tumultuous History of All in the Family* (New York: Workman Publishing, 1987), 38–40.

6. Ibid., 40–45.

7. Ibid., passim; Josh Ozersky, *Archie Bunker's America: TV in an Era of Change, 1968–1978* (Carbondale: Southern Illinois University Press, 2003), 63–65, 66–69, 70, 72, 75, 76, 77–78, 79, 81, 92, 97, 108, 109, 110, 112, 133. See, too, Carroll O'Connor, *I Think I'm Outta Here: A Memoir of All My Families* (New York: Pocket Books, 1998).

8. All the material in this vignette that relates to the film comes from the following source: *Falling Down,* VHS, directed by Joel Schumacher (1993; Burbank, Calif.: Warner Home Video, 1996).

9. David Gates, "White Male Paranoia," *Newsweek* 121 (March 29, 1993): 48–53.

10. *Disclosure,* VHS, directed by Barry Levinson (1994; Burbank, Calif.: Warner Home Video, 1995).

11. J. Hoberman, "Victim Victorious: Well-Fed Yuppie Michael Douglas Leads the Charge for Resentful White Men," *Village Voice,* March 7, 1995, 31–33.

12. Anthony Bozza, *Whatever You Say I Am: The Life and Times of Eminem* (New York: Crown Publishers, 2003), 236–237.

13. To learn more about Jeff Foxworthy, go to www.jefffoxworthy.com.

14. For more about Jeff Wayne, go to his Web site (www.jeffwayne.com). See, too, Scott Harris, "Making a Living as a White Male," *Los Angeles Times,* January 5, 1995, 3; Glenn Doggrell, "A Right-Wing Act? That's White," *Los Angeles Times,* March 30, 1995, 6; Glenn Doggrell, "Feminists, Militant Gays Get Roasted in 'Barbecue,'" *Los Angeles Times,* April 3, 1995, 2.

15. Doggrell, "Feminists, Militant Gays Get Roasted in 'Barbecue.' "

16. Doggrell, "A Right-Wing Act?"

17. Ibid.

18. Jeff Wayne, *It's O.K. to Be a White Male* (Westlake Village, Calif.: Uproar Entertainment, 1995).

19. Larissa MacFarquhar, "The Populist," *New Yorker* 80 (February 16 and 23, 2004): 132–145. Michael Moore's official Web site can be found online at www.MichaelMoore.com.

20. MacFarquhar, "The Populist," 132.

21. Ibid., passim.

22. Richard Corliss, "The World According to Michael," *Time* 164 (July 12, 2004): 62–66, 69–70.

23. Professor Eric Newhall, interview by author, Los Angeles, California, March 23, 2004.

24. Matthew Rothschild, "Jim Hightower," *Progressive* 67 (November 2003): 32. See, too, "Shall We Chautauqua?" www.jimhightower.com/tour/index.asp.

25. For information about Hightower, go to his Web site (www.jimhightower .com).

26. Hightower's recent books provide considerable details about his populist perspective. See Jim Hightower, *There's Nothing in the Middle of the Road but Yellow Stripes and Dead Armadillos* (New York: HarperCollins, 1997); Jim Hightower, *If the Gods Had Meant Us to Vote They Would Have Given Us Candidates* (New York: HarperCollins, 2000); Jim Hightower, *Thieves in High Places: They've Stolen Our Country — and It's Time to Take It Back* (New York: Viking, 2003).

27. "Meet Jim." www.jimhightower.com/jim.

28. Ibid.

29. Ibid.

30. Ibid.

31. Ibid.

32. Rothschild, "Jim Hightower," 31.

33. Jason Zengerle, "Talking Back," *New Republic* 230 (February 16, 2004): 23.

34. Ibid.

35. Ibid.

36. Mark de la Viña, "Air Partisan," *American Demographics* 26 (February 2004): 22.

37. William McGowan, *Coloring the News: How Crusading for Diversity Has Corrupted American Journalism* (San Francisco: Encounter Books, 2001), 246.

38. Mark de la Viña, "Air Partisan," *American Demographics* 26 (February 2004): 21.

39. Ibid.

40. Ibid., 21, 22.

41. Zengerle, "Talking Back," 19, 22.

42. To learn more about *The Rush Limbaugh Show,* go to www.rushlimbaugh .com. For biographical information about Limbaugh, see Evan Thomas, " 'I Am Addicted to Prescription Pain Medication,' " *Newsweek* 142 (October 20, 2003): 42–47.

43. Zengerle, "Talking Back," 22.

44. Ibid.

45. de la Viña, "Air Partisan," 21; Zengerle, "Talking Back," 19, 22–25; Jacques Steinberg, "Limbaugh Is Back on the Air, With Fans and Foes All Ears," *New York Times,* November 17, 2003, at E1; Pamela McClintock, "Rush Back on Airwaves," *Daily Variety* (November 18, 2003), 3, 33.

46. Visit the Sean Hannity Web site (www.hannity.com) for more information about this multimedia personality. To learn more about *Hannity & Colmes,* go to www.foxnews.com/hannityandcolmes. See, too, Michael A. Lipton and Jennifer Frey, "The (Far) Right Stuff," *People* 57 (February 11, 2002): at p. 117 (via EBSCO*host*); Robin Finn, "Run the Country? No. He Just Wants to Rouse It." *New York Times,* October 25, 2002, B2; Valerie Block, "Homegrown Host Creates a Rush," *Crain's New York Business* 19 (February 17, 2003): at p. 1 (via EBSCO*host*).

47. Block, "Homegrown Host Creates a Rush"; Finn, "Run the Country?"; Lipton and Frey, "The (Far) Right Stuff."

48. James Poniewozik, "Sean Hannity," *Time* 160 (November 11, 2002): 8.

49. Scott Collins, *Crazy Like a Fox: The Inside Story of How Fox News Beat CNN* (New York: Portfolio, 2004); Daniel M. Kimmel, *The Fourth Network: How Fox Broke the Rules and Reinvented Television* (Chicago: Ivan R. Dee, 2004). See, too, the Fox News Channel's Web site (www.foxnews.com).

50. To learn more about Bill O'Reilly, go to www.billoreilly.com. *The O'Reilly Factor* Web site (www.foxnews/oreilly) is an excellent source of information about this program.

51. Tom Lowry, "The O'Reilly Factory," *Business Week* (March 8, 2004): 74.

52. Ibid., 73–74.

53. Zengerle, "Talking Back," 23–24.

54. To learn more about Air America Radio, go to www.airamericaradio.com. See, too, de la Viña, "Air Partisan," 20–22; Shorto, "Al Franken, Seriously," 43, 82–83; Richard Corliss, "Enter Talking, Stage Left," *Time* 163 (April 12, 2004): 66; Elizabeth Jensen, "Air America's Co-Founder, Programming Chief Leave," *Los Angeles Times,* April 28, 2004, C5; Jacques Steinberg, "2 Senior Executives Leave Air America Radio," *New York Times,* April 28, 2004, C6; Teresa Wiltz,

"Air America Radio Hits Turbulence on Takeoff," *Washington Post,* April 28, 2004, at C1.

55. Russell Shorto, "Al Franken, Seriously," *New York Times Magazine* 153 (March 21, 2004): 38–43, 82–84.

56. For biographical information about Rose, see Del James, "The Rolling Stone Interview: Axl Rose," *Rolling Stone* (August 10, 1989); Danny Sugerman, *Appetite for Destruction: The Days of Guns n' Roses* (New York: St. Martin's Press, 1991), 58–59. I visited Lafayette, Indiana, on April 16, 2002, to learn more about Axl Rose's hometown. People of color now account for about 15 percent of Lafayette's population.

57. Sugerman, *Appetite for Destruction,* 22, 28, 60–78, 100–101, 119–120, 157, 160.

58. Guns n' Roses, "One in a Million," *GN'R Lies* (Los Angeles: Geffen Records, 1988). For background on the song, see Sugerman, *Appetite for Destruction,* 228–229; James, "The Rolling Stone Interview: Axl Rose."

59. See, e.g., Patrick Goldstein, "Behind the Guns N' Roses Racism Furor; the Continuing Debate over Whether the Band's Song "One in a Million" promotes bigotry," *Los Angeles Times,* October 15, 1989, 68; Jon Pareles, "Ugly Tone of Bigotry Has Hit the Charts," *San Francisco Chronicle,* October 15, 1989, 37; Juan Williams, "Fighting Words; Speaking Out Against Racism, Sexism and Gay-Bashing in Pop," *Washington Post,* October 15, 1989, at G1.

60. Williams, "Fighting Words"; James, "The Rolling Stone Interview: Axl Rose"; Goldstein, "Behind the Guns N' Roses Racism Furor"; Pareles, "Ugly Tone of Bigotry Has Hit the Charts"; Sugerman, *Appetite for Destruction,* 3–4, 10–11, 13, 15–16; Richard Cromelin, "Guns N' Roses Shows Some Mettle," *Los Angeles Times,* October 21, 1989, at p. 1.

In 2000 Rose chose to delete two songs — "One in a Million" and "Look at Your Game Girl" — from subsequent pressings of G n' R albums. He said that the two tracks were "too easily misinterpreted." David Wild, "Axl Speaks," *Rolling Stone* (February 3, 2000): 24.

61. For Daniels's perspective on these songs, see Charlie Daniels, *Ain't No Rag: Freedom, Family, and the Flag* (Washington, D.C.: Regnery Publishing, 2003), 3–5, 7–9.

62. "Only a Pawn in Their Game," written by Bob Dylan. Copyright © 1963 by Warner Bros. Inc. Renewed 1991 Special Rider Music. International copyright secured. Reprinted by permission.

63. Ibid.

64. "Southern Man," by Neil Young. © 1975 Broken Arrow Music (BMI). All Rights Reserved. Used by Permission. Warner Bros. Publications U.S. Inc., Miami, FL 33014.

65. Marley Brant, *Freebirds: The Lynyrd Skynyrd Story* (New York: Billboard Books, 2002), 82–84, 97–98.

66. Jimmy McDonough, *Shakey: Neil Young's Biography* (New York: Random House, 2002), 336.

67. Everlast, *Eat at Whitey's* (New York: Tommy Boy Music, 2000).

68. Bozza, *Whatever You Say I Am*, 234–258.

69. Eminem, "White America," *The Eminem Show* (Santa Monica, Calif.: Aftermath Records, 2002).

70. Bruce Feiler, "Gone Country," *New Republic* 214 (February 5, 1996): at p. 19 (via EBSCO*host*); Bruce Feiler, "Has Country Music Become a Soundtrack for White Flight?" *New York Times,* October 20, 1996, Sec. 2, pp. 38, 40; John Marks, "Breaking a Color Line, Song by Song," *U.S. News and World Report* 126 (April 12, 1999): 46–47.

71. "Okie from Muskogee," written by Merle Haggard and Roy Burris. Copyright © 1969 Sony Tree Publishing Company. All rights reserved.

72. James N. Gregory, *American Exodus: The Dust Bowl Migration and Okie Culture in California* (New York: Oxford University Press, 1989), 238–245.

73. For a wealth of information about Hank Williams Jr., see his official Web site: www.hankjr.com.

74. Hank Williams Jr., *America (The Way I See It): Original Classic Hits, Vol. 18* (Nashville: Curb Records, 1998).

75. "If the South Woulda Won," written by: Hank Williams Jr. Published: Bocephus Music, Inc. BMI. Copyright: 1988. Admin: Dave Burgess Enterprises. All Rights Reserved. Used by permission.

76. Ibid.

77. Toby Keith, *Unleashed* (Nashville: DreamWorks Records Nashville, 2002).

78. Toby Keith, *Shock'N Y'all* (Nashville: DreamWorks Records Nashville, 2003).

79. Josh Tyrangiel, "America's Ruffian," *Time* 163 (March 1, 2004): 75.

80. Darryl Worley, *Have You Forgotten?* (Nashville: DreamWorks Records Nashville, 2003).

81. "Have You Forgotten?" by Wynn Varble and Darryl Wade Worley. © 2003 Warner-Tamerlane Publishing Corp., EMI April Music Inc. and Pittsburgh Landing Songs. All Rights for Pittsburgh Landing Songs Administered by EMI April Music Inc. All Rights Reserved. Used by Permission. Warner Bros. Publications U.S. Inc., Miami, FL 33014.

82. Peggy McIntosh, "Afterword: The Growing Influence of Right-Wing Thought," in Abby L. Ferber, ed., *Home-Grown Hate: Gender and Organized Racism* (New York: Routledge, 2004), 230.

83. Norman Mailer, "The White Man Unburdened," *New York Review of Books* 50 (July 17, 2003): at p. 4. www.nybooks.com/articles/16470.

84. Ed Leibowitz, "Charlton Heston's Last Stand," *Los Angeles Magazine* 46 (February 2001): at p. 60 (via EBSCO*host*).

85. Charlton Heston, *In the Arena: An Autobiography* (New York: Simon and Schuster, 1995); Charlton Heston, *To Be a Man: Letters to My Grandson* (New York: Simon and Schuster, 1997); Charlton Heston and Jean-Pierre Isbouts, *Charlton Heston's Hollywood: 50 Years in American Film* (New York: GT Publishing, 1998). See, too, Leibowitz, "Charlton Heston's Last Stand"; Margot Hornblower, "Have Gun, Will Travel," *Time* 151 (July 6, 1998): 44–46.

86. Heston, *To Be a Man,* passim; Hornblower, "Have Gun, Will Travel"; Leibowitz, "Charlton Heston's Last Stand"; Charlton Heston, *The Courage to Be Free* (Kansas City, Kan.: Saudade Press, 2000).

87. Hornblower, "Have Gun, Will Travel"; Leibowitz, "Charlton Heston's Last Stand."

88. Heston, *The Courage to Be Free,* 9.

89. Patrick J. Buchanan, *Right from the Beginning* (Boston: Little, Brown, and Company, 1988).

90. Jeremy D. Mayer, *Running on Race: Racial Politics in Presidential Campaigns, 1960–2000* (New York: Random House, 2002), 247.

91. Patrick J. Buchanan, *The Death of the West: How Dying Populations and Immigrant Invasions Imperil Our Country and Civilization* (New York: Thomas Dunne Books/St. Martin's Press, 2002), 7.

92. For the Web site of *Buchanan and Press,* go to www.buchananandpress .msnbc.com.

93. The American Cause Web site (www.theamericancause.org) is an excellent source of information about this organization.

94. Buchanan, *The Death of the West,* 222.

Chapter 8: Changing America

1. Harris Wofford, *Of Kennedys and Kings: Making Sense of the Sixties* (New York: Farrar, Straus, Giroux, 1980), 11–22.

2. Wofford, *Of Kennedys and Kings,* 23–28. For background on the significance of race in the 1960 presidential campaign, see Jeremy D. Mayer, *Running on Race: Racial Politics in Presidential Campaigns, 1960–2000* (New York: Random House, 2002), 9–39.

3. Wofford, *Of Kennedys and Kings,* passim; Senator Harris Wofford, interview by author, Washington, D.C., October 21, 2003.

4. Wofford, interview.

5. Harris Wofford Jr., *It's Up to Us: Federal World Government in Our Time* (New York: Harcourt, Brace, and Company, 1946). The quotation is found on page ix.

6. Wofford, interview; Clare and Harris Wofford Jr., *India Afire* (New York: John Day, 1951).

7. Wofford, interview; Wofford, *Of Kennedys and Kings,* 110.

8. Wofford, *On Kennedys and Kings,* 110.

9. Wofford, interview; Wofford, *Of Kennedys and Kings,* 11–123, 461–483.

10. Wofford, *Of Kennedys and Kings,* 124–167.

11. Ibid., 165.

12. Wofford, interview; Wofford, *Of Kennedys and Kings,* passim.

13. Wofford, *Of Kennedys and Kings.*

14. Jack W. Germond and Jules Witcover, *Mad as Hell: Revolt at the Ballot Box, 1992* (New York: Warner Books, 1993), 62–77; Phil Duncan, ed., *CQ's Politics in America 1994: The 103rd Congress* (Washington, D.C.: CQ Press, 1993), 1286–1288.

15. Germond and Witcover, *Mad as Hell,* 328, 329; Peter Goldman et al., *Quest for the Presidency, 1992* (College Station: Texas A and M University Press, 1994), 279, 280, 282.

16. To learn more about America's Promise, go to www.americaspromise.org.

17. The material in this account draws upon the popular press and my interviews with Professors Hood and Rudebusch: Professor Edward Hood, telephone conversations with author, September 13, 2003 and November 26, 2003; Professor Edward Hood, interview by author, Garden Grove, California, March 19, 2004; and Professor George Rudebusch, interview by author, Pasadena, California, March 26, 2004.

18. Hood, telephone conversation, November 26, 2003.

19. Ibid.

20. Two hundred fifty NAU faculty members were eligible to participate in the class-action lawsuit. Only five males and five females declined to join the suit.

21. Professor George Rudebusch, e-mail to author, June 8, 2004.

22. Ibid.

23. Ibid.

24. *Rudebusch v. Hughes,* 313 F.3d 506 (9th Cir. 2002).

25. Hood, telephone conversation, November 26, 2003.

26. For information about Bakke, see Susan Welch and John Gruhl, *Affirmative Action and Minority Enrollments in Medical and Law Schools* (Ann Arbor: University of Michigan Press, 1998).

27. *Johnson v. Transportation Agency,* 480 U.S. 616 (1987).

28. Fred L. Pincus, *Reverse Discrimination: Dismantling the Myth* (Boulder, Colo.: Lynne Rienner Publishers, 2003), 107–109.

29. Ibid., 109.

30. Ibid., 109–110.

31. Ibid., 117–119.

32. Ibid., 129.

33. Ibid.

34. Ibid., 129, 137.

35. Ibid., 137–138.

36. Ibid., 138.

37. For the different ways in which white males react to reverse discrimination, see Frederick R. Lynch, *Invisible Victims: White Males and the Crisis of Affirmative Action* (New York: Praeger, 1991), 56–70.

38. Paul W. Valentine, "Md. State Police Settle Suit by White Troopers; 99 Officers Said They Were Victims of Bias," *Washington Post,* April 6, 1995, D3; Earle Eldridge, "Ford Settles 2 Lawsuits by White Male Workers," *USA Today,* December 19, 2001, B3.

39. Jim Carlton, "Award in Reverse-Discrimination Case to Further Stir Academic-Hiring Debate," *Wall Street Journal,* April 1, 1999, at p. 1.

40. Thomas Stewart, telephone conversation with author, September 20, 2003; Thomas Stewart, interview by author, Spokane, Washington, November 8, 2003.

41. Ibid.

42. Ibid.

43. Committee on the Judiciary, "Testimony of Tom Stewart," Subcommittee on the Constitution with the U.S. Senate Committee on the Judiciary Subcommittee on the Constitution, Federalism, and Property Rights, U.S. House of Representatives, October 19, 1995. www.house.gov/judiciary/2117.htm.

44. Stewart, interview; Stewart, telephone conversation.

45. Andrea Stone, "The Other Side of 'Quotas,'" *USA Today,* July 19, 1995, 2A.

46. Committee on the Judiciary, "Testimony of Tom Stewart."

47. Stewart, interview; Stewart, telephone conversation.

48. Vice President Walter Mondale, interview by author, Minneapolis, Minnesota, April 6, 2004; Walter Mondale, "The Path to Equality: The 1984 Mondale/Ferraro Ticket," Mondale Lectures on Public Service, March 10, 2004. See, too, Mayer, *Running on Race,* 190–191; Steven M. Gillon, *The Democrats' Dilemma: Walter F. Mondale and the Liberal Legacy* (New York: Columbia University Press, 1992), 353–357.

49. Gillon, *The Democrats' Dilemma,* 1–52.

50. Mondale, interview.

51. Mayer, *Running on Race,* 178.

52. Mondale, interview; Mayer, *Running on Race,* 178–179; Gillon, *The Democrats' Dilemma,* 52–162, 391.

53. Mayer, *Running on Race,* 179–180; Gillon, *The Democrats' Dilemma,* 163–317.

54. Mayer, *Running on Race,* 180–190; Gillon, *The Democrats' Dilemma,* 317–358.

55. Mondale, interview.

56. Mayer, *Running on Race,* 188–192.

57. Mondale, interview; Mayer, *Running on Race,* 192–200; Gillon, *The Democrats' Dilemma,* 357–390.

58. Marjorie Connelly, "Who Voted: A Portrait of American Politics, 1976–2000," *New York Times,* November 12, 2000, Sec. 4, p. 4.

59. Mondale, interview; Gillon, *The Democrats' Dilemma,* 391–402.

60. Mondale, interview.

61. Mondale, "The Path to Equality," 10.

62. Mayer, *Running on Race,* passim; Thomas Byrne Edsall with Mary D. Edsall, *Chain Reaction: The Impact of Race, Rights, and Taxes on American Politics* (New York: W. W. Norton and Company, 1992); John D. Skrentny, *The Minority Rights Revolution* (Cambridge, Mass.: Belknap Press of Harvard University Press, 2002), passim.

63. Connelly, "Who Voted: A Portrait of American Politics, 1976–2000."

64. Ibid.

65. Susan Page, "'Til Politics Do Us Part: Gender Gap Widens; Highly Educated Couples Often Split on Candidates," *USA Today,* December 18, 2003, at A1.

66. Alexandra Marks, "Real Gender Gap in Politics: Men," *Christian Science Monitor,* April 21, 2000, at p. 1.

67. Karen M. Kaufmann and John R. Petrocik, "The Changing Politics of American Men: Understanding the Sources of the Gender Gap," *American Journal of Political Science* 43 (July 1999): 864–887.

68. Page, " 'Til Politics Do Us Part."

69. Patricia Edmonds and Richard Benedetto, "Angry White Men; Their Votes Turn the Tide for GOP; 'Men Want to Torch' Washington," *USA Today,* November 11, 1994, at 1A.

70. Charles Krauthammer, "Myth of the Angry White Male," *Washington Post,* May 26, 1995, A27.

71. Ibid.

72. Jim Drinkard, "Most Political Donors Are White Males; New Law Expected to Swell Their Clout," *USA Today,* August 26, 2003, at A1.

73. Ibid.

74. See, e.g., Lee Hockstader, "Surprise Front-Runner in La. Governor's Race; Son of Indian Immigrants Seeks 'Bubba' Vote," *Washington Post,* October 4, 2003, A6; Kris Axtman, "A New Face Rises in Bayou Politics," *Christian Science Monitor,* October 15, 2003, at p. 1.

75. Derrick Z. Jackson, "Dean's Appeal to South Cuts Across Race," *Boston Globe,* November 7, 2003, A19; Charles Krauthammer, "The Perfect Liberal Storm," *Washington Post,* November 7, 2003, A31.

76. Jackson, "Dean's Appeal to South Cuts Across Race."

77. Page, " 'Til Politics Do Us Part: Gender Gap Widens."

78. David E. Sanger, "At Speedway, Bush Courts Race Fans, Dads Included," *New York Times,* February 16, 2004, A17; Mike Allen and Liz Clarke, "Gentlemen, Start Your Campaigns; President Takes the Race for 'NASCAR Dads' to the Daytona 500," *Washington Post,* February 16, 2004, at A1.

79. Ibid.

80. Jim VandeHei, "Democratic Hopefuls Play Down Gun Control," *Washington Post,* October 26, 2003, at A1.

81. Ibid.

82. Except for the specifically cited material, this vignette draws upon material in the public record and my interview with Senator Watts (Senator Eugene Watts, interview by author, Dublin, Ohio, March 25, 2002).

83. Senator Eugene Watts, e-mail to author, November 22, 2002.

84. For a detailed profile of Watts, see Greg Davies, "The Junkyard Dog of the Ohio Senate," *Columbus Monthly* (November 1997). The article begins on page 108.

85. During the 1980s, the 16th District took in the southern part of Franklin County, Ohio, including much of Columbus. In the 1990s, the 16th District was made up of the western part of Franklin County. It was whiter, more upscale, and more Republican than its predecessor. Watts, interview.

86. As a legislator, Senator Watts periodically encountered accusations of insensitivity from African Americans and others for his blunt, no-nonsense

approach to politics. However, even his political foes generally say that this out-spoken politico is charming and affable in his interpersonal interactions. See Davies, "The Junkyard Dog of the Ohio Senate."

87. Senator Eugene Watts, e-mail to author, June 3, 2004.

88. "Getting Athletes Back on Track; Ohio's Schools Haven't Raised Academic Standards, So the Legislature Gets the Job by Default," *Cleveland Plain Dealer,* March 26, 1999, 10B.

89. Watts, e-mail, November 22, 2002.

90. National Conference of State Legislatures, *Initiative and Referendum in the 21st Century: Final Report and Recommendations of the NCSL I&R Task Force* (Denver, Colo., and Washington, D.C.: National Conference of State Legislatures, July 2002).

91. Nomenclature is a matter of hot debate here. I use the words "preferences" and "affirmative action" interchangeably, as do most journalists in the mainstream media. By doing so, I am not in any way expressing opposition to affirmative action, diversity programs, or multicultural initiatives.

92. Ward Connerly, *Creating Equal: My Fight Against Race Preferences* (San Francisco: Encounter Books, 2000). See, too, "ACRI People: Ward Connerly." www.acri.org.

93. Connerly, *Creating Equal,* 137–158; Ward Connerly, telephone conversation with author, March 10, 2004.

94. Connerly, *Creating Equal,* passim.

95. Ward Connerly, interview by author, Long Beach, California, March 13, 2004.

96. "Ward Connerly," *American Enterprise* 14 (April/May 2003): at p. 18 (via EBSCO*host*).

97. Ibid.; Connerly, *Creating Equal,* passim.

98. A liberal white man of my acquaintance describes Connerly as an "opportunist." This is one of the tamer epithets that Connerly's detractors have used to disparage him.

99. Connerly, telephone conversation.

100. "Ward Connerly."

101. The ACRI Web site (www.acri.org) includes much information about the Institute.

102. To learn more about the American Civil Rights Coalition, go online to www.acrc1.org.

103. Justin Jones, interview by author, Sacramento, California, March 12, 2004.

104. Diane Schachterle, interview by author, Sacramento, California, March 12, 2004.

105. Connerly, telephone conversation.

106. Here is the operative language in Proposition 209: "The state shall not discriminate against, or grant preferential treatment to, any individual or group on the basis of race, sex, color, ethnicity, or national origin in the operation of public employment, public education, or public contracting."

107. Connerly, telephone conversation; Connerly, *Creating Equal,* 159–180; Lydia Chávez, *The Color Bind: California's Battle to End Affirmative Action* (Berkeley: University of California Press, 1998), 1–162.

108. Chávez, *The Color Bind,* 163–254; Connerly, *Creating Equal,* 181–202.

109. Chávez, *The Color Bind,* 211–241.

110. Connerly, *Creating Equal,* 213–215; Jesse Katz, "Houston Thinks Globally in OK of Preferences," *Los Angeles Times,* November 6, 1997, at A1; Sam Howe Verhovek, "Referendum in Houston Shows Complexity of Preferences Issue," *New York Times,* November 6, 1997, at A1.

111. Connerly, *Creating Equal,* 215–217; Katz, "Houston Thinks Globally in OK of Preferences"; Verhovek, "Referendum in Houston Shows Complexity of Preferences Issue"; R. A. Dyer, "Race Preference Foes across U.S. Face Uphill Fight; Houston Vote Illustrates Power of Affirmative Action's Support," *Houston Chronicle,* November 9, 1997, at p. 1.

112. Verhovek, "Referendum in Houston Shows Complexity of Preferences Issue."

113. Connerly, *Creating Equal,* 215–217; Katz, "Houston Thinks Globally in OK of Preferences"; Dyer, "Race Preference Foes across U.S. Face Uphill Fight"; Verhovek, "Referendum in Houston Shows Complexity of Preferences Issue."

114. Connerly, *Creating Equal,* 219–231; Heath Foster, "Affirmative Action Rules Tossed Out by State Voters," *Seattle Post-Intelligencer,* November 4, 1998, at A1.

115. Connerly, *Creating Equal,* 234–245; Foster, "Affirmative Action Rules Tossed Out by State Voters"; Tom Brune, "Poll: I-200 Passage Was Call for Reform," *Seattle Times,* November 4, 1998, at A1.

116. Connerly, *Creating Equal,* 247–261; Terry M. Neal and David S. Broder, "Affirmative Action Tears at Fla. GOP; Gov. Bush Moves to Block Divisive Ballot Initiative," *Washington Post,* May 15, 1999, at A1; Rick Bragg, "Affirmative Action Ban Meets a Wall in Florida," *New York Times,* June 7, 1999, A16; Heath Foster, "Battleground Moves to Florida; Opponents of Affirmative Action Programs Are Taking Their Cause South in an Effort to Force a National Debate," *Seattle Post-Intelligencer,* July 8, 1999, at A1; Steve Bousquet, "Preference Campaign Shifts to Florida; After California and Washington Successes, Ward Connerly Seeks to Dismantle Affirmative Action Again," *(Portland, Or.) Oregonian,* December 5, 1999, A20; Joe Follick, "Affirmative Action Foe Suspends Battle," *Tampa (Fla.) Tribune,* May 9, 2000, at p. 1.

117. For information about this initiative, go to the "Prop. 54: Racial Privacy Initiative" Web site (www.racialprivacy.org).

118. Connerly, interview; Jones, interview; Schachterle, interview. See, too, Haya El Nasser, "Voters Shoot Down Proposition on Collecting Racial Information," *USA Today,* October 9, 2003, A9; Ward Connerly, "Not a Chance; The Electoral Journey of Proposition 54," *National Review Online,* October 15, 2003. www.nationalreview.com/comment/connerly200310150818.asp.

119. Robert E. Pierre, "Affirmative Action Foes Seek Mich. Referendum; Initiative Would Amend State's Constitution," *Washington Post,* March 5, 2004, A3.

120. Betsy DeVos, "Affirmative Action Brawl in Michigan Would Be Divisive, Neglect True Reform," *Grand Rapids (Mich.) Press,* July 22, 2003, A7; Steven Harmon, "Local GOP Sidesteps Anti–Affirmative Action Bid," *Grand Rapids (Mich.) Press,* July 24, 2003, A17.

121. Connerly, interview.

122. Ibid.; Pierre, "Affirmative Action Foes Seek Mich. Referendum." The Michigan Civil Rights Initiative Web site (www.michigancivilrights.org) provides useful information on this proposed ballot initiative.

123. "Ward Connerly."

124. *Hopwood v. State of Texas,* 84 F.3d 720 (5th Cir. 1996).

125. *Gratz v. Bollinger,* No. 02–516, 2003 WL 21434002 (U.S. June 23, 2003).

126. *Grutter v. Bollinger,* No. 02–241, 2003 WL 21433492 (U.S. June 23, 2003).

127. David Hawkings and Brian Nutting, eds., *CQ's Politics in America 2004: The 108th Congress* (Washington, D.C.: CQ Press, 2003), 66.

128. Thomas B. Edsall, "Census a Clarion Call for Democrats, GOP; As Nation Changes, Parties Are Warned They Need New Tactics to Woo Voters," *Washington Post,* July 8, 2001, A5.

129. Ibid.

130. Peter Schrag, "In California, White Men Are the Silent Plurality," *New York Times,* September 14, 2003, Sec. 4, p. 3; John Micklethwait and Adrian Wooldridge, "California's New Trend: Big-Tent Republicans," *New York Times,* October 5, 2003, Sec. 4, at p. 1. To learn more about Schwarzenegger's cultural significance, see Michael Blitz and Louise Krasniewicz, *Why Arnold Matters: The Rise of a Cultural Icon* (New York: Basic Books, 2004).

Chapter 9: The Perils of Prejudice

1. For an excellent overview of Butler and Aryan Nations, see Raphael S. Ezekiel, *The Racist Mind: Portraits of American Neo-Nazis and Klansmen* (New York: Viking, 1995), 122–142; Kevin Flynn and Gary Gerhardt, *The Silent Brotherhood: The Chilling Inside Story of America's Violent Anti-Government Militia Movement* (1989; reprint, New York: Signet, 1995), especially 64–94. In addition, the Web site of the Aryan Nations World Headquarters (www.twelvearyannations.com) contains much information about this hate group. See, too, "Aryan Nations Creed," in Jeffrey Kaplan, ed., *Encyclopedia of White Power: A Sourcebook on the Radical Racist Right* (Walnut Creek, Calif.: AltaMira Press, 2000), 468–470.

2. Gretchen Albrecht-Hellar, interview by author, Sandpoint, Idaho, November 8, 2003.

3. For information about the Kootenai County Task Force on Human Relations, go to its Web site (www.idahohumanrights.org).

˙ 4. Unless otherwise cited, all the material in this vignette derives from my observations, the public record, and my extensive interviews with the following individuals (listed in alphabetical order):

- Norman Gissel. Norman Gissel, interviews by author, Kootenai County, Idaho, August 3, 2003, August 4, 2003, and November 6, 2003; Norman Gissel, telephone conversation with author, September 11, 2003;

- Marshall Mend. Marshall Mend, interview by author, Hayden, Idaho, August 3, 2003; Marshall Mend, interview by author, Los Angeles, California, October 19, 2003; Marshall Mend, telephone conversations with author, January 29, 2004, April 4, 2004, and May 29, 2004;

- Tony Stewart. Professor Tony Stewart, telephone conversations with author, July 1, 2003, September 11, 2003, October 26, 2003, and May 30, 2004; Professor Tony Stewart, interviews by author, Kootenai County, Idaho, August 3, 2003, August 4, 2003, August 5, 2003, November 6, 2003, and November 7, 2003; Professor Tony Stewart, interviews by author, Kootenai County, Idaho, and Bonner County, Idaho, November 8, 2003.

5. Before his death in 2002, Bill Wassmuth, who was once a Catholic priest in Coeur d'Alene, played an important role in the Task Force and the human rights movement in the Northwest and elsewhere. See Andrea Vogt, *Common Courage: Bill Wassmuth, Human Rights, and Small-Town Activism* (Moscow: University of Idaho Press, 2003).

6. For recent developments regarding Richard Butler and the Aryan Nations, see Nia Hightower, "The Company He Keeps," *Intelligence Report* (Winter 2003): 49.

7. Mend, telephone conversation, April 4, 2004.

8. *Choosing Democracy: Strategic Plan for the Proposed Human Rights Center* (Coeur d'Alene, Idaho: Human Rights Education Institute, June 20, 2003). The material about the Human Rights Education Institute and the Human Rights Center also draws upon the following sources: Stewart, interviews; Stewart, telephone conversations; Senator Mary Lou Reed, interview by author, Coeur d'Alene, Idaho, November 7, 2003.

9. Unless otherwise cited, all the material in this vignette comes from the definitive source on the Kirk shooting, the 607-page report prepared by Judge Samuel Van Pelt. See Samuel Van Pelt, ed., *Report of the Special Investigator to the Governor and to the Chairman of the Judiciary Committee of the Nebraska Legislature* (December 1, 1984). I went to Cairo, Nebraska, on August 13, 2001.

10. Joel Dyer, *Harvest of Rage: Why Oklahoma City Is Only the Beginning* (Boulder, Colo.: Westview Press, 1997), 40–42.

11. On Gordon Kahl, see James Corcoran, *Bitter Harvest: Gordon Kahl and the Posse Comitatus: Murder in the Heartland* (New York: Viking, 1990).

12. Daniel Levitas, *The Terrorist Next Door: The Militia Movement and the Radical Right* (New York: Thomas Dunne Books/St. Martin's Press, 2002), 230–231.

13. Carol M. Swain and Russ Nieli, eds., *Contemporary Voices of White Nationalism in America* (New York: Cambridge University Press, 2003), 164–165.

14. William L. Pierce [Andrew Macdonald, pseud.], *The Turner Diaries,* 2d ed. (1980; reprint, Hillsboro, W.Va.: National Vanguard Books, 1999); William L. Pierce [Andrew Macdonald, pseud.], *Hunter* (Hillsboro, W.Va.: National Vanguard Books, 1989).

15. Carol M. Swain, *The New White Nationalism in America: Its Challenge to Integration* (New York: Cambridge University Press, 2002), 6–7.

16. Kathleen M. Blee, *Inside Organized Racism: Women in the Hate Movement* (Berkeley: University of California Press, 2002), 3.

17. Christopher Hewitt, *Understanding Terrorism in America: From the Klan to al Qaeda* (London: Routledge, 2003), 42.

18. "Active Hate Groups in the United States in the Year 2002," *Intelligence Report* (Spring 2003): 36–41.

19. *Dangerous Convictions: An Introduction to Extremist Activities in Prisons* (New York: Anti-Defamation League, 2002).

20. Swain, *The New White Nationalism in America;* Swain and Nieli, eds., *Contemporary Voices of White Nationalism in America;* James Ridgeway, *Blood in the Face: The Ku Klux Klan, Aryan Nations, Nazi Skinheads, and the Rise of a New White Culture,* 2d ed. (New York: Thunder's Mouth Press, 1995); Betty A. Dobratz and Stephanie L. Shanks-Meile, *"White Power, White Pride!" The White Separatist Movement in the United States* (New York: Twayne Publishers, 1997); Jeffrey Kaplan, ed., *Encyclopedia of White Power: A Sourcebook on the Radical Racist Right* (Walnut Creek, Calif.: AltaMira Press, 2000); Carol M. Swain, *The New White Nationalism in America: Its Challenge to Integration* (New York: Cambridge University Press, 2002).

21. David H. Bennett, *The Party of Fear: From Nativist Movements to the New Right in American History,* 2d ed. (New York: Vintage Books/Random House, 1995); Mark Potok, "The American Radical Right: The 1990s and Beyond," in Roger Eatwell and Cas Mudde, eds., *Western Democracies and the New Extreme Right Challenge* (London: Routledge, 2004), 41–61.

22. Swain, *The New White Nationalism in America,* 326–346.

23. Abby L. Ferber, "Introduction," in Abby L. Ferber, ed., *Home-Grown Hate: Gender and Organized Racism* (New York: Routledge, 2004), 6.

24. Jeffrey Kaplan, " 'Leaderless Resistance,' " *Terrorism and Political Violence* 9 (Autumn 1997): 80–95; Louis R. Beam, "Leaderless Resistance," in Jeffrey Kaplan, ed., *Encyclopedia of White Power: A Sourcebook on the Radical Racist Right* (Walnut Creek, Calif.: AltaMira Press, 2000), 503–511.

25. Hewitt, *Understanding Terrorism in America,* 78–80; Roberto Suro, "Terrorism's New Profile: The Lone Wolf," *Washington Post,* July 22, 1998, at A1; Jo Thomas, "New Face of Terror Crimes: 'Lone Wolf' Weaned on Hate," *New York Times,* August 16, 1999, at A1.

26. Professor Brian Levin, interview by author, Southern California, November 27, 2003.

27. Professor Brian Levin, e-mail to author, March 3, 2004.

28. Blee, *Inside Organized Racism*; Abby L. Ferber, *White Man Falling: Race, Gender, and White Supremacy* (Lanham, Md.: Rowman and Littlefield Publishers, 1998); Abby L. Ferber, ed., *Home-Grown Hate: Gender and Organized Racism* (New York: Routledge, 2004).

29. Ibid.

30. Abby L. Ferber, "Constructing Whiteness: The Intersections of Race and Gender in U.S. White Supremacist Discourse," *Ethnic and Racial Studies* 21:1 (1998): 51.

31. Mark Potok, "Into the Mainstream," *Intelligence Report* (Spring 2003): no page.

32. Heidi Beirich and Mark Potok, "Keeping America White," *Intelligence Report* (Winter 2003): 31–33. To learn more about the Center for American Unity, go to www.cfau.org. The URL for VDARE is www.vdare.com.

33. Mark Potok, "Looking Forward," *Intelligence Report* (Fall 2003): no page. See, too, Heidi Beirich and Mark Potok, "40 to Watch," *Intelligence Report* (Fall 2003): 15–48.

34. The source of this quotation is the "Stormfront.org White Pride World Wide: White Nationalist Resource Page" (www.stormfront.org).

35. Swain and Nieli, eds., *Contemporary Voices of White Nationalism in America*, 153–165.

36. Ibid., 153–154; Jeffrey Kaplan, "Don Black," in Jeffrey Kaplan, ed., *Encyclopedia of White Power: A Sourcebook on the Radical Racist Right* (Walnut Creek, Calif.: AltaMira Press, 2000), 23–24. See, too, Steve Dunne, "New Media: Where the Hate Is: Steve Dunne Explores White Supremacy on the Web," *(Manchester, U.K.) Guardian,* June 25, 2001, 50; Tara McKelvey, "Father and Son Target Kids in a Confederacy of Hate," *USA Today,* July 16, 2001, D3.

37. "Stormfront.org for Kids" (http://kids.stormfront.org).

38. Ibid.; McKelvey, "Father and Son Target Kids in a Confederacy of Hate."

39. Kaplan, "Don Black," 24.

40. "The Gossip," *Intelligence Report* (Fall 2003): 46.

41. "The Ties That Bind," *Intelligence Report* (Fall 2001): 10.

42. Dunne, "New Media: Where the Hate Is."

43. For information about this topic, consult the entire Fall 2001 issue of the *Intelligence Report*. See, too, Jeffrey Kaplan and Leonard Weinberg, *The Emergence of a Euro-American Radical Right* (New Brunswick, N.J.: Rutgers University Press, 1998); Jeffrey Kaplan and Tore Bjørgo, eds., *Nation and Race: The Developing Euro-American Racist Subculture* (Boston: Northeastern University Press, 1998).

44. Martin A. Lee, *The Beast Reawakens* (Boston: Little, Brown, and Company, 1997), 343–344.

45. Kenneth S. Stern, "Lying About the Holocaust," *Intelligence Report* (Fall 2001): 50–55.

46. Kaplan and Weinberg, *The Emergence of a Euro-American Radical Right,* 4.

47. Steven L. Jacobs and Mark Weitzman, *Dismantling the Big Lie:* The Protocols of the Elders of Zion (Los Angeles: Simon Wiesenthal Center in association with KTAV Publishing House, 2003).

48. Friedrich Kubler, "How Much Freedom for Racist Speech? Transnational Aspects of a Conflict of Human Rights," *Hofstra Law Review* 27 (1998): at p. 335; Karen L. Bird, "Racist Speech or Free Speech? A Comparison of the Law in France and the United States," *Comparative Politics* 32 (July 2000): 399–418.

49. "When Laws Conflict," *Intelligence Report* (Fall 2001): 61.

50. Brian Levin, "Cyberhate: A Legal and Historical Analysis of Extremists' Use of Computer Networks in America," *American Behavioral Scientist* 45 (February 2002): 958–988.

51. Ibid., 960–964.

52. Ibid., 965–985.

53. Ibid.

54. "Active Hate Web Sites in the United States in the Year 2002," *Intelligence Report* (Spring 2003): 42–47.

55. Brian Levin, "Hate International," *Intelligence Report* (Winter 2003): 45.

56. James Latham, "From America, with Hate," *Intelligence Report* (Fall 2003): 56–58.

57. "White Pride World Wide," *Intelligence Report* (Fall 2001): 26–27.

58. Ibid., 27–30.

59. Ibid., 24–26.

60. "White Power Bands," *Intelligence Report* (Fall 2001): 31.

61. For more information about these purveyors of white power music, go to the Web sites of the following companies: Resistance Records (www.resistance.com), Panzerfaust Records (www.panzerfaust.com), and Micetrap Records (www.micetrap.net).

62. Martin A. Lee, "Reawakening the Beast," *Intelligence Report* (Fall 2001): 38–49.

63. For an excellent biography of Duke, see Tyler Bridges, *The Rise of David Duke* (Jackson: University Press of Mississippi, 1994). Duke self-published his autobiography: David Duke, *My Awakening: A Path to Racial Understanding* (Mandeville, La.: Free Speech Press, 1999). See, too, John McQuaid, "Duke's Decline," *(New Orleans, La.) Times-Picayune*, April 13, 2003, at p. 1.

64. McQuaid, "Duke's Decline"; Martin A. Lee, "Insatiable," *Intelligence Report* (Spring 2003): 52–58, 60.

65. For the Web site of the European-American Unity and Rights Organization, or EURO, go to www.whitecivilrights.com.

66. McQuaid, "Duke's Decline"; Martin A. Lee, "The Wandering Jew-Hater," *Intelligence Report* (Spring 2003): 58–59.

67. Lee, "The Wandering Jew-Hater," 59; Lee, "Insatiable," 60; McQuaid, "Duke's Decline"; "Freed from Prison, David Duke Mounts a Comeback," *Intelligence Report* (Summer 2004): 2.

68. Most of the information in this vignette comes from my extensive interviews with Mr. Berlet (Chip Berlet, interviews by author, Middlesex County,

Massachusetts, December 8, 2003, December 9, 2003, and December 10, 2003). Chip Berlet and his wife, Karen Moyer, were gracious hosts during my visit to the Boston area in December 2003. For autobiographical information about Berlet, see "Chip Berlet," in Cooper Thompson, Emmett Schaefer, and Harry Brod, *White Men Challenging Racism: 35 Personal Stories* (Durham, N.C.: Duke University Press, 2003), 90–98. See, too, "Chip Berlet: Biographical Information." www.publiceye.org/berlet/Berlet_Bio.htm; "Chip Berlet: Selected Published Work." www.publiceye.org/berlet/Berlet_Articles.htm. Unless I note otherwise, all the material in the paragraphs about Berlet comes from the aforementioned sources. The opening paragraph also draws upon my interview with Walter Gill (Walter Gill, telephone conversation with author, January 21, 2004).

69. Dean John W. Rice's course, "The Black Experience in America," at the University of Denver played an important role in shaping Berlet's mindset on civil rights issues. Rice was the most influential professor in Berlet's academic development. Berlet, interviews.

70. The Political Research Associates Web site (www.publiceye.org) provides much information about this watchdog group. I thank the staff and leadership of PRA for allowing me to conduct research at their office on December 8, 2003, December 9, 2003, and December 10, 2003.

71. Berlet's publications include two books: Chip Berlet, ed., *Eyes Right! Challenging the Right Wing Backlash* (Boston: Political Research Associates/ South End Press, 1995); Chip Berlet and Matthew N. Lyons, *Right-Wing Populism in America: Too Close for Comfort* (New York: Guilford Press, 2000).

72. Professor Jeffrey Kaplan, interview by author, Oshkosh, Wisconsin, March 4, 2004.

73. I interviewed Professor Eatwell (Professor Roger Eatwell, interview by author, Bath, Avon, United Kingdom, October 6, 2003) to learn more about his expertise on such topics as Fascism and the British National Party (BNP). For more information about Dr. Eatwell, go to "Roger Eatwell – Research Profile." www.bath.ac.uk/ adsexp/People/mlsre.html.

74. See Tolerance.org's "U.S. Map of Human Rights Groups" online at www.tolerance.org/maps/human_rights/state.jsp?state_id=39.

75. One can find information about the Center for New Community at its Web site (www.newcomm.org). Similarly, to learn more about the Center for Democratic Renewal, go to www.thecdr.org. The URL for Political Research Associates is www.publiceye.org.

76. Go to the American Jewish Committee Web site (www.ajc.org) to learn more about this organization.

77. www.ajc.org/WhoWeAre/MissionAndHistory.asp.

78. Kenneth Stern, interview by author, New York, December 11, 2003.

79. For information about the Anti-Defamation League, visit its Web site: www.adl.org.

80. Brian Marcus, interview by author, New York, December 11, 2003.

81. Ibid.; *Racist Groups Using Computer Gaming to Promote Violence Against Blacks, Latinos, and Jews* (New York: Anti-Defamation League, 2002). www.adl.org/videogames/videogames_print.asp.

82. Marcus, interview.

83. For the main Web site of the Southern Poverty Law Center, go to www.splcenter.org.

84. To learn more about the Intelligence Project, see www.splcenter.org/intel/intpro.jsp.

85. For more information about Teaching Tolerance, see www.splcenter.org/center/tt/teach.jsp.

86. The Tolerance.org Web site (www.tolerance.org) is an excellent source of information about this initiative.

87. To learn about the Civil Rights Memorial, go to www.splcenter.org/center/crmc/civil.jsp.

88. Morris Dees with Steve Fiffer, *A Lawyer's Journey: The Morris Dees Story* (Chicago: American Bar Association, 2001), passim.

89. "SPLCenter.org: Center History." See www.splcenter.org/center/history/history.jsp.

90. Mark Potok, interview by author, Montgomery, Alabama, September 16, 2003.

91. Ibid.

92. For more information about the Simon Wiesenthal Center, go online to www.wiesenthal.com.

93. "Simon Wiesenthal Center Worldwide Offices." www.wiesenthal.com/about/office_index.cfm.

94. For more information about the Task Force Against Hate, go to the Web page of the Simon Wiesenthal Center's Eastern Office (www.wiesenthal.com/taskforce/index.cfm).

95. Richard Eaton, interviews by author, Los Angeles, California, November 3, 2003 and July 2, 2004.

96. Gloria McMillan, telephone conversation with author, October 27, 2003; Gloria McMillan, interviews by author, Los Angeles County, California, October 27, 2003, November 3, 2003, and November 25, 2003.

97. To learn more about the Museum of Tolerance, go to www.wiesenthal.com/mot or www.museumoftolerance.com. These Web sites also include information about the New York Tolerance Center.

98. See "Simon Wiesenthal Center Worldwide Offices." (www.wiesenthal.com/about/office_index.cfm). To learn more about the Wiesenthal Center's global reach, I interviewed Leo Adler, Director of National Affairs for the Friends of Simon Wiesenthal Center for Holocaust Studies in Canada (Leo Adler, telephone conversation with author, September 9, 2003) and Sergio Widder, the representative of the Simon Wiesenthal Center Latin America in Argentina (Sergio Widder, telephone conversation with author, January 8, 2004).

99. "Rabbi Marvin Hier — *Dean and Founder.*" www.wiesenthal.com/about/hier.cfm. "Rabbi Abraham Cooper — *Associate Dean.*" www.wiesenthal.com/

about/cooper.cfm. "Rabbi Meyer H. May, Executive Director Simon Wiesenthal Center and Museum of Tolerance." www.wiesenthal.com/about/may.cfm.

100. "Rabbi Abraham Cooper — *Associate Dean*"; Rabbi Abraham Cooper, interview by author, Los Angeles, California, November 25, 2003.

101. Ibid.

102. Ibid.

103. Stern, interview.

104. To learn more about the Gonzaga University Institute for Action Against Hate, go to www.gonzaga.edu/againsthate. My account about the Institute also draws upon the following sources: Stern, interview; Professor George A. Critchlow, interview by author, Spokane, Washington, November 7, 2003; Professor Jerri Shepard, interview by author, Spokane, Washington, November 8, 2003.

105. Kenneth S. Stern, "Getting to the Root of Hate in a Challenging World," *Seattle Times,* March 16, 2004.

106. Ibid.; Stern, interview.

107. Stern, "Getting to the Root of Hate in a Challenging World."

108. Ibid.

109. "The Founder – James Cameron." See www.blackholocaustmuseum.org/cameron.html.

110. Ibid.; James Cameron, *A Time of Terror* (1982; reprint, Baltimore: Black Classic Press, 1994); James H. Madison, *A Lynching in the Heartland: Race and Memory in America* (New York: Palgrave, 2001).

111. Cameron, *A Time of Terror,* 195–201; Madison, *A Lynching in the Heartland,* 123–125.

112. "The Founder – James Cameron."

113. Madison, *A Lynching in the Heartland,* passim. See, too, the Web site of America's Black Holocaust Museum (www.blackholocaustmuseum.org).

114. Dr. James Cameron, interview by author, Milwaukee, Wisconsin, October 14, 2003.

115. Unless otherwise noted, the four paragraphs about Stetson Kennedy in this chapter draw upon my interviews with Mr. Kennedy: Stetson Kennedy, interviews by author, Duval County, Florida, and St. Johns County, Florida, January 14, 2004; Stetson Kennedy, interview by author, Jacksonville, Florida, January 15, 2004.

116. Stetson Kennedy, letter to author, January 28, 2004.

117. For biographical accounts about Stetson Kennedy, see "Stetson Kennedy," in Studs Terkel, *Coming of Age: The Story of Our Century by Those Who've Lived It* (New York: New Press, 1995), 391–400; "Stetson Kennedy," in Cooper Thompson, Emmett Schaefer, and Harry Brod, *White Men Challenging Racism: 35 Personal Stories* (Durham, N.C.: Duke University Press, 2003), 27–36. See, too, Louis J. Salome, "Stetson Kennedy; He Infiltrated the Klan and Lived to Tell About It; The Original 'Angry Young Man' Still Finding Wrongs to Right," *Palm Beach (Fla.) Post,* August 19, 2001, at 1A; Alliniece T. Andino, "White Voice for Blacks Tells of Lonely Struggle; Rights Icon Joined Klan to

Expose It," *(Jacksonville, Fla.) Florida Times Union,* January 10, 2002, at A1; Diane Roberts, "The Ballad of Stetson Kennedy," *St. Petersburg (Fla.) Times,* March 7, 2004, at 1P.

118. To learn more about Kennedy's pioneering anti-Klan undercover work, see Stetson Kennedy, *The Klan Unmasked* (1954; reprint, Boca Raton: Florida Atlantic University Press, 1990). The quotation cited in this Note comes from the following source: Stetson Kennedy, letter to author, February 11, 2004.

119. See Kennedy, *The Klan Unmasked*; Stetson Kennedy, *Palmetto Country* (1942; reprint, Tallahassee: Florida A & M University Press, 1989); Stetson Kennedy, *Southern Exposure* (1946; reprint, Boca Raton: Florida Atlantic University Press, 1991); Stetson Kennedy, *Jim Crow Guide: The Way It Was* (1955; reprint, Boca Raton: Florida Atlantic University Press, 1990); Stetson Kennedy, *After Appomattox: How the South Won the War* (Gainesville: University Press of Florida, 1995).

120. Kennedy, interview, St. Johns County, Florida, January 14, 2004; Kennedy, letter to author, January 28, 2004.

121. Kennedy, letter to author, January 28, 2004.

122. Kennedy intends to turn his two-story cottage into a retreat, workshop, and resource for writers, activists, and thinkers. For more information about the Stetson Kennedy Foundation, go to www.stetsonkennedy.com.

123. Kennedy, interviews; Kennedy, letter to author, January 28, 2004.

Epilogue: Promises to Keep

1. Dink Gentry, interview by author, De Queen, Arkansas, June 4, 2001. For an excellent article that provides background information about the demographic transformation of De Queen, see Anne Hull, "Ascent and Eclipse in a Small Town; Hispanics' Climb Leaves Some Ark. Locals Behind," *Washington Post,* October 8, 2000, at A1.

2. Dink Gentry, interview; DeLois Gentry, interview by author, De Queen, Arkansas, June 4, 2001.

3. Ibid.

4. Ibid.

5. Alejandro Camarillo, interview by author, De Queen, Arkansas, June 4, 2001.

6. Scott VanLoo, telephone conversation with author, September 6, 2002; Scott VanLoo, interview by author, Burbank, California, November 30, 2003. Eaton, Colorado, is 85.4% white and 12.6% Latino. The town has ten American Indian residents. I visited Eaton, Colorado, and Greeley, Colorado, on July 12, 2002.

7. VanLoo, telephone conversation; Solomon Little Owl, telephone conversations with author, July 16, 2002, July 24, 2002, and May 5, 2003; Jeff Van Iwarden, telephone conversation with author, January 31, 2003. For more information about The Fighting Whites, go to the team's Web site (www.cafepress.com/fightinwhite).

8. Little Owl, telephone conversations.

9. "National Radio Variety Show to Honor THE FIGHTING WHITES," Press release, May 13, 2003.

10. Ibid.; Little Owl, telephone conversations; Van Iwarden, telephone conversation; VanLoo, telephone conversation.

11. Fran Spielman, "Alderman: Extend City Rules to Gays; Tunney Seeks Same Limits on Contracts, Rights on Health Care," *Chicago Sun-Times,* July 9, 2003, 14; Fran Spielman, "Daley Holds Out Hope of Gay Set-Asides If Past Bias Can Be Proven," *Chicago Sun-Times,* July 10, 2003, 3.

12. Mary Williams Walsh, "Where G.E. Falls Short: Diversity at the Top," *New York Times,* September 3, 2000, Sec. 3, at p. 1; Diane Brady, "Crashing GE's Class Ceiling," *BusinessWeek* (July 28, 2003): 76–77.

13. Jim Rutenberg, "News Anchors and the Cathode-Ray Ceiling," *New York Times,* June 3, 2002, at C1; Eric Deggans, "Diversity Takes a Step Back; World Shrugs," *St. Petersburg Times,* June 13, 2002, at 1D.

14. Jim Rutenberg and Bill Carter, "Generational Shift: Brokaw Announces He'll Retire in '04," *New York Times,* May 29, 2002, at A1; Lisa de Moraes, "NBC's Tom Brokaw to Bow Out with 2004 Elections," *Washington Post,* May 29, 2002, at C1.

15. Jim VandeHei, "Two Years After White House Exit, Clintons Shaping Democratic Party," *Washington Post,* June 21, 2003, at A1.

16. For background on Jordan, see his autobiography: Vernon E. Jordan Jr., with Annette Gordon-Reed, *Vernon Can Read! A Memoir* (New York: PublicAffairs, 2001).

17. In 2003 this issue arose three times during my speaking engagements in various countries. At a public lecture at the University of Botswana in Botswana, one man cited the leadership of Secretary of State Colin Powell and National Security Adviser Condoleezza Rice as indications that the United States offered many opportunities for African Americans. Another person brought up the African-American role in the U.S. military at the University of Leeds in the United Kingdom, where a young man also asked me when I thought a woman or minority would be elected President of the United States. A young lady raised a similar question at the Università della Calabria in Italy, whereupon I told her that we have never had a female or minority President — or a chief executive who traced his or her ancestry to Southern or Eastern Europe.

18. *CIA – The World Factbook – Iceland.* See www.cia.gov/cia/publications/factbook/geos/ic.html.

19. Nicolas Pelham, "Arab Women Demand Quotas," *Christian Science Monitor,* November 6, 2002, 7.

20. Certain groups predominate among Canada's visible minority population: Canada is 3.4% Chinese, 3.0% South Asian, 2.2% black, 1.0% Filipino, 1.0% Arab/West Asian, and 0.7% Latin American. Descendants of the first residents of Canada also encompass several different groups — North American Indians make up 2.1% of the Canadian population, while the Métis account for

1.0% and the Inuit are 0.2% (the percentages exceed 3.2% because of rounding). For Canadian census data, see the Web site of Statistics Canada (www.statcan.ca).

21. "New Immigrants," *Monitor* (Spring 2003). See www.cic.gc.ca/english/ monitor/issue01/02-immigrants.html. For more information about immigration to Canada, visit the Web site of Citizenship and Immigration Canada (www.cic.gc.ca).

22. www.chrc-ccdp.ca/ee/Acts/act-ee.asp?/=e.

23. This transformation is most evident in Toronto, Montréal, and Vancouver, the destinations for 49 percent, 14 percent, and 13 percent, respectively, of new immigrants to Canada in 2002. "New Immigrants."

24. *CIA – The World Factbook 2002 – Australia.* Online see www.cia.gov/cia/ publications/factbook/geos/as.html#People.

25. According to one source, designated groups are "namely members of the Aboriginal race of Australia or persons who are descendants of indigenous inhabitants of the Torres Strait Islands, persons who have migrated to Australia and whose first language is not English, and the children of such persons, and persons with a physical and mental disability." "Obligations Under the Equal Employment Opportunity," July 5, 2001. www.workplace.gov.au.

26. To learn more about gender-equality efforts in Australia, go to the Web site of the Equal Opportunity for Women in the Workplace Agency (www.eowa.gov.au/).

27. *CIA – The World Factbook 2002 – New Zealand.* See www.cia.gov/cia/ publications/factbook/geos/nz.html#People.

28. According to Section 19(2) of the New Zealand Bill of Rights Act 1990, as amended by the Human Rights Act 1993, "Measures taken in good faith for the purpose of assisting or advancing persons or groups of persons disadvantaged because of discrimination that is unlawful by virtue of Part II of the Human Rights Act 1993 do not constitute discrimination." www.oefre.unibe.ch/law/icl/nz01000_.html/#S019_.

29. For background on this and related topics, see, e.g., David Dunkerley et al., *Changing Europe: Identities, Nations, and Citizens* (London: Routledge, 2002).

30. Dr. Marco Martiniello, interview by author, Liège, Belgium, and Brussels, Belgium, October 8, 2003. For information about the Centre d'études de l'ethnicité et des migrations (CEDEM) at the University of Liège, go to www.ulg.ac.be/cedem.

31. See, e.g., Marco Martiniello and Andrea Rea, eds., *Affirmative Action: Des discours, des politiques et des pratiques en débat* (Brussels, Belgium: Academia Bruylant, 2004).

32. Dr. Daniel Sabbagh, interview by author, Paris, France, February 23, 2004.

33. Daniel Sabbagh, *L'Egalité par le droit: les paradoxes de la discrimination positive aux États-Unis* (Paris: Economica, 2003). Sabbagh draws upon the material in his book in the following English-language article: Daniel Sabbagh,

"Judicial Uses of Subterfuge: Affirmative Action Reconsidered," *Political Science Quarterly* 118 (Fall 2003): 411–436.

34. Sabbagh, interview.

35. Dr. Marco Martiniello, e-mail to author, April 18, 2004.

36. Michèle Lamont, *The Dignity of Working Men: Morality and the Boundaries of Race, Class, and Immigration* (New York: Russell Sage Foundation, 2000), passim; Erik Bleich, "The French Model: Color-Blind Integration," in John David Skrentny, ed., *Color Lines: Affirmative Action, Immigration, and Civil Rights Options for America* (Chicago: University of Chicago Press, 2001), 270–296; William Safran, "Pluralism and Multiculturalism in France: Post-Jacobin Transformations," *Political Science Quarterly* 118 (Fall 2003): 437–465. See, too, Charles Fleming and John Carreyrou, "Religious Scrap; In France, Policy on Muslims Comes to Head on Scarves," *Wall Street Journal*, June 26, 2003, at A1.

37. For reflections on these issues in the United Kingdom, see Steven M. Teles, "Positive Action or Affirmative Action? The Persistence of Britain's Antidiscrimination Regime," in John David Skrentny, ed., *Color Lines: Affirmative Action, Immigration, and Civil Rights Options for America* (Chicago: University of Chicago Press, 2001), 241–269; Bob Rowthorn, "Migration Limits," *Prospect* (February 2003): 24–31.

38. According to the 2001 Census, Indians are the largest ethnic minority group in the United Kingdom; they account for 1.8% of the population. Other numerically significant ethnic minority groups include: Pakistanis (1.3%), people of mixed ethnic origins (1.2%), black Caribbeans (1.0%), black Africans (0.8%), Bangladeshis (0.5%), and the Chinese (0.4%). For U.K. Census data, go to National Statistics Online (www.statistics.gov.uk/).

39. Dr. Ian G. Law, interview by author, Leeds, West Yorkshire, United Kingdom, March 26, 2003. See, too, Teles, "Positive Action or Affirmative Action?" 241–269; Ian Law and Malcolm Harrison, "Positive Action, Particularism, and Practice," *Policy Studies* 22:1 (2001): 35–50; Ian Law, *Race in the News* (Houndmills, United Kingdom: Palgrave, 2002), 138–156.

40. Teles, "Positive Action or Affirmative Action? The Persistence of Britain's Antidiscrimination Regime," 241–269.

41. In the Scandinavian countries that do not have separate Ministries of Gender Equality, the Ministry of Social Affairs (Iceland), the Ministry of Children and Family Affairs (Norway), and the Ministry of Social Affairs and Health (Finland) handle this issue.

42. Knut Oftung, "Men and Gender Equality in the Nordic Countries," in Ingeborg Breines, Robert Connell, and Ingrid Eide, eds., *Male Roles, Masculinities, and Violence: A Culture of Peace Perspective* (Paris: UNESCO Publishing, 2000), 143–162.

43. Professor Dag Blanck, telephone conversation with author, March 11, 2003.

44. Dirk Hermann, interview by author, Centurion, Gauteng, South Africa, February 11, 2003; Dirk Hermann, interview by author, Cape Town, Western

Cape, South Africa, July 13, 2004. See, too, Ferial Haffajee, "Discrimination in Reverse," *Financial Mail (South Africa)*, December 20, 2002, 14.

45. The membership of Solidarity, meanwhile, is becoming more diverse: Ten percent of its members are Coloured, mainly from the Western Cape. Women now account for 25 percent of Solidarity's members, a percentage that increases each year. Hermann, interview. The information regarding the types of workers who belong to Solidarity comes from Haffajee, "Discrimination in Reverse."

46. For information about Solidarity, go to the trade union's Web site (www.solidariteit.co.za).

47. These findings draw upon Hermann's research on the effects of affirmative action on the attitudes and life chances of white males who worked in a large parastatal (Eskom). Hermann conducted this research while writing a master's thesis for a degree in industrial sociology. Hermann, interview; "White Workers Need Inspiring Goals: Solidarity," *Global News Wire/SAPA (South African Press Association)*, November 8, 2002.

48. Hermann, interview.

49. Thomas Mabasa, "Union to Tackle Affirmative Action," *Citizen*, December 10, 2002, 1, 2.

50. "Union Aims at 'Balanced' Affirmative Action Law," *Global News Wire/SAPA (South African Press Association)*, August 2, 2001.

51. Hermann, interview; Haffajee, "Discrimination in Reverse"; Dirk Hermann, e-mail to author, May 14, 2004.

52. Hermann, interview. See, too, the Web site of the Come Home Campaign (www.comehome.co.za). The Come Home Campaign is co-sponsored by Solidarity.

53. For a general overview of race relations in South Africa, I benefited from my interviews with three experts on the country: Dr. Anthea Jeffery, Special Research Consultant at the South African Institute of Race Relations in Johannesburg (Dr. Anthea Jeffery, interview by author, Braamfontein, Gauteng, South Africa, February 11, 2003); Professor Adrian Guelke, director of the Centre for the Study of Ethnic Conflict at Queen's University in Belfast (Professor Adrian Guelke, interview by author, Belfast, County Antrim, United Kingdom, March 27, 2003); and Dr. Robert Mattes, Associate Professor of Political Studies at the University of Cape Town (Dr. Robert Mattes, telephone conversation with author, April 24, 2003; Dr. Robert Mattes, interview by author, Rondebosch, Western Cape, South Africa, July 15, 2004). These scholars, of course, are not responsible for any of the conclusions that I make in this section.

54. *CIA – The World Factbook 2002 – South Africa*. Online at www.cia.gov/cia/publications/factbook/geos/sf.html#People.

55. The term "black" in South Africa often refers to Africans, Coloureds, and Indians. One can view the text of Employment Equity Act No. 55 of 1998 at www.labour.gov.za/docs/legislation/eea/act98-055.html.

56. For the text of the Equality Act, see Shadrack B. O. Gutto, *Equality and Non-Discrimination in South Africa: The Political Economy of Law and Law Making* (Claremont, South Africa: New Africa Education, 2001), 328–341.

The Equality Act became mostly operational on June 16, 2003. This milestone received little attention in South Africa. Anthea Jeffery writes, "The Chapter on promoting equality is still not in operation, but all the provisions barring unfair discrimination are in effect. The equality courts are functioning but, as yet, have heard few cases — and the few that have come have involved instances of direct discrimination (e.g., a coloured man being refused access to a bar, but not his white companion)." Dr. Anthea Jeffery, e-mail to author, June 7, 2004.

57. Wilmot James and Jeffrey Lever, "The Second Republic: Race, Inequality, and Democracy in South Africa," in Charles V. Hamilton et al., eds., *Beyond Racism: Race and Inequality in Brazil, South Africa, and the United States* (Boulder, Colo.: Lynne Rienner Publishers, 2001), 29–61.

58. Rachel L. Swarns, "Rarity of Black-Run Businesses Worries South Africa's Leaders," *New York Times,* November 13, 2002, at A1.

59. Gutto, *Equality and Non-Discrimination in South Africa,* 192.

60. James Lamont, "Blacks Still on the Bench," *Financial Times,* January 26, 2002, 24.

61. Mattes, telephone conversation.

62. Rachel L. Swarns, "South Africa's New Poor: White and Bewildered," *New York Times,* September 12, 2000, A4; Danna Harman, "In South Africa, Poverty Tinged with a New Color," *Christian Science Monitor,* July 12, 2001, at p. 1; Ann M. Simmons, "South African Whites Say Deck Is Stacked against Them," *Los Angeles Times,* June 19, 2002, at A1.

63. Some South African expatriates, of course, left the country during the apartheid era. For information about emigration from South Africa, see "Statistics on Emigration," Come Home Campaign. www.comehome.co.za/asp/statistics .asp; Robert Mattes, "White Man's Burden Redux: Tales from the New South Africa," *Common Review* 1 (n.d.). www.greatbooks.org/tcr/mattes12.shtml.

64. Jeffery, interview; Danna Harman, "S. Africa's Island of Whites," *Christian Science Monitor,* December 4, 2002, at p. 1; Anne-Marie O'Connor, "Nonwhites Need Not Apply Here," *Los Angeles Times,* March 30, 2003, A24; Laurie Goering, "Afrikaners Finding Themselves Adrift in New South Africa," *Knight Ridder Tribune News Service,* April 30, 2004, at p. 1; Alexandra Zavis, "Afrikaners Embittered; Decade of Changes," *Washington Post,* May 2, 2004, A28.

65. Goering, "Afrikaners Finding Themselves Adrift in New South Africa"; Harman, "S. Africa's Island of Whites"; O'Connor, "Nonwhites Need Not Apply Here"; Zavis, "Afrikaners Embittered; Decade of Changes"; Rachel L. Swarns, "In a New South Africa, an Old Tune Lingers," *New York Times,* October 7, 2002, at A1.

66. Mattes, telephone conversation.

67. Ibid.

68. Mattes, "White Man's Burden Redux."

69. Lawrence Schlemmer, "Race Relations and Racism in Everyday Life," *Fast Facts* (September 2001): 2–12.

70. Mattes, telephone conversation; Mattes, "White Man's Burden Redux."

71. For an interesting study of white reactions to life in post-apartheid South Africa, see Melissa E. Steyn, *"Whiteness Just Isn't What It Used to Be": White Identity in a Changing South Africa* (Albany: State University of New York Press, 2001).

72. Robert Mattes et al., *Democratic Governance in South Africa: The People's View,* Afrobarometer Working Paper No. 24 (Cape Town, South Africa/ Accra, Ghana/East Lansing, Mich.: Afrobarometer, 2003), 26–27.

73. Ibid., 24–27.

74. Danna Harman, "South Africans Try to 'Beat' a Segregated Past," *Christian Science Monitor,* September 26, 2002, at p. 1; Rachel L. Swarns, "Mingling Despite Mistrust in South Africa," *New York Times,* December 9, 2002, at A1.

75. Lawrence Schlemmer, "Between a Rainbow and a Hard Place: Threats and Opportunities in Racial Reconciliation in South Africa," *Fast Facts* (December 2001): 2–12.

76. Ferial Haffajee, "Mbeki Adjusts His Aim," *Financial Mail (South Africa),* January 10, 2003, 19.

77. Robert Mattes, "Uniquely African?" in Steven M. Burgess, *SA Tribes: Who We Are, How We Live, and What We Want from Life in the New South Africa* (Claremont, South Africa: David Philip Publishers, 2002), 91–93.

78. Ralph Ellison, "What America Would Be Like without Blacks," in David R. Roediger, ed., *Black on White: Black Writers on What It Means to Be White* (New York: Schocken Books, 1998), 160–167.

79. Professor Eric Newhall, interview by author, Los Angeles, California, November 24, 2003.

Acknowledgments

Many wonderful people shared their insights with me, or contributed in some other way to this book. During the years that I worked on *Sharing the Dream*, I discussed matters related to race, gender, and ethnicity with hundreds of Americans and people in other countries, in airports, on airplanes, after public lectures, and in many other venues and contexts.

In particular I wish to thank the following individuals: Professor Nabeel Abraham, Leo Adler, Gretchen Albrecht-Hellar, John L. Allen Jr., Governor Victor G. Atiyeh, Dr. Frank Ayala, Peter Baylies, Chip Berlet and Karen Moyer, Professor Dag Blanck, Father Michael Blume, Tova Brandt, Josh Buehner, Michael Butkovitch, Alejandro Camarillo, Dr. James Cameron, Paul Cameron, Caroline Carter, Kevin Carter, Angelique Chambliss, Patricia Churray, Vince Clark, Colbert Coldwell, Ward Connerly, Rabbi Abraham Cooper, Professor George A. Critchlow, Rev. Dr. Anthony Dao, Monsignor Frank J. Dewane, Dr. Michael Downey, Richard Eaton, Professor Roger Eatwell, Ann Enriquez, Eric Florence, Dink and DeLois Gentry, Walter Gill, Norman and Diana Gissel, Father Anthony Gonzalez, Professor Adrian Guelke, Sriyanthi Gunewardena, Frank Hall, Sheldon and Jane Hall, Eugene and Dorothy Harter, Jennifer Hatges, Dr. Steve Havron, Dirk Hermann, Professor Christopher Hewitt, Hogan Hilling, Father Michael Hoan, Alice Y. Hom, Professor Edward Hood, Dorothy Pitman Hughes, Bishop Josu Iriondo, Dr. Anthea Jeffery, Allison and Eloisa Jones and family, Justin Jones, Professor Jeffrey Kaplan, Rev. Dr. Babu Joseph Karakombil, Sean Kennedy, Stetson Kennedy, Professor John L. Kessell, Mayor Scott L. King, Derek Korbe, Jim and Debbie Kurtti, Dr. Ian G. Law, Professor Brian Levin and Dr. Sara-Ellen Amster, Helen Lind, Solomon Little Owl, Dr. Guy Logsdon, Anna Marie Lux, Professor Frederick R. Lynch, Melinda MacCall, William and Eleanor Macfarlane, Raphael Madison, Donna Magnuson, Cardinal Roger Mahony, Bishop John R. Manz, Brian Marcus, Dianne Markley, Dr. Marco Martiniello, Jay Massey, Professor Robert Mattes, Paul Matthews, Bobbi Matthews, and Arnold Matthews, Dick and Gracie Mayo, Mike McGavick, Gloria McMillan, Marshall and Dolly Mend, Leon C. Metz, Vice President Walter Mondale, Cathy Myers, Phil Nadeau, Coke Newell, Professor Eric Newhall, Professor Francis B.

Nyamnjoh, Professor Eileen O'Brien, Sandra Parks, Sherman Patrick, Dr. Erlend D. Peterson, Father Michael Pfleger, Father Edward Poettgen, Dena Porter, Mark Potok, Father Colm Rafferty, Humberto Ramos, Scott Reed and Senator Mary Lou Reed, Professor Deirdre Royster, Professor George Rudebusch, Ray Rush, Dr. Daniel Sabbagh, Father Esequiel Sanchez, Diane Schachterle, Victoria Scott, Earl Shelton, Professor Jerri Shepard, Eunice Smith, Maureen Socha, Professor Frank F. Sousa, Maija Stadius, Kenneth Stern, Thomas Stewart, Professor Tony Stewart, Matt Streadbeck, Rameen Talesh, Dr. Andrew Thompson, Jeff Van Iwarden, Scott VanLoo, Alicia Vargas, Charles Wallace, Bishop Ignatius Wang, Senator Eugene Watts, Doris Weddell, Father Bernard Weir, Christine West, Sergio Widder, Jim Wilmot, Reverend Douglas Wilson, Senator Harris Wofford, and Mark Yeoell.

The vignette about Jim Kurtti appeared in a slightly different form in the *Daily Mining Gazette.* I thank John Elchert, the newspaper's publisher, for allowing me to use this material in *Sharing the Dream.*

I am very fortunate to be represented by Ron and Mary Lee Laitsch of Authentic Creations Literary Agency. Their counsel, support, and encouragement make it a pleasure to work with them.

At Continuum, it was great to work with Frank Oveis and his colleagues again. Frank has taught me much about the literary world. I value his candid advice and feedback.

Members of my immediate family deserve recognition for their consistent backing of my literary efforts. My aunt, Martha Cone, has helpfully clipped numerous newspaper articles and tracked the placement of my first book, *Visible Differences,* in various libraries. I also thank my great-uncle, Hans Weiter, for spending hours discussing our family history with me.

My parents, Dr. Margaret Pulera and Mr. Eugene Pulera, made this book possible by creating a nurturing environment for me to research and write *Sharing the Dream.* I am very grateful to them for their love, encouragement, and significant financial support.

My sister, Maria, is my best friend and closest confidant. She has helped me in countless ways, from shooting the photo for the dust jacket to tracking down permissions for song lyrics. I appreciate her love, loyalty, and extraordinary helpfulness very much.

All errors of fact or interpretation are mine alone.

Index